Society for Arabian Studies Monographs No. 10

Series editors D. Kennet & St J. Simpson

Death and Burial in Arabia and Beyond

Multidisciplinary perspectives

Edited by

Lloyd Weeks

BAR International Series 2107
2010

Published by

Archaeopress
Publishers of British Archaeological Reports
Gordon House
276 Banbury Road
Oxford OX2 7ED
England
bar@archaeopress.com
www.archaeopress.com

BAR S2107
Society for Arabian Studies Monographs 10

Death and Burial in Arabia and Beyond: Multidisciplinary perspectives

© Archaeopress and the individual authors 2010

ISBN 978 1 4073 0648 3

Printed in England by CMP (UK) Ltd

All BAR titles are available from:

Hadrian Books Ltd
122 Banbury Road
Oxford
OX2 7BP
England
bar@hadrianbooks.co.uk

The current BAR catalogue with details of all titles in print, prices and means of payment is available free from Hadrian Books or may be downloaded from www.archaeopress.com

Society for Arabian Studies Monograph Series

Series editors: D. Kennet & St J. Simpson

The *Society for Arabian Studies Monograph Series* was launched in 2004 with the intention of encouraging the publication of peer-reviewed monographs on the archaeology, early history, ethnography, epigraphy and numismatics of the Arabian Peninsula and related matters. Creating a specific monograph series within the *British Archaeological Reports International Series* is intended to allow libraries, institutions and individuals to keep abreast of work that is specifically related to their areas of research. Whilst research and conference volumes in the series will all be peer-reviewed according to normal academic procedures, the decision was taken to allow the publication of doctoral theses, field reports, catalogues and other data-rich work without peer review where this will permit the publication of information that, for one reason or another, might not otherwise be made available.

Already published:

BAR –S1248, 2004 Sasanian and Islamic Pottery from Ras al-Khaimah *Classification, chronology and analysis of trade in the Western Indian Ocean* by Derek Kennet with a contribution by Regina Krahl. Society for Arabian Studies Monographs No. 1. ISBN 1 84171 608 1.

BAR –S1269, 2004 Trade and Travel in the Red Sea Region *Proceedings of Red Sea Project I held in the British Museum October 2002* edited by Paul Lunde and Alexandra Porter. Society for Arabian Studies Monographs No. 2. ISBN 1 84171 622 7.

BAR –S1395, 2005 People of the Red Sea *Proceedings of Red Sea Project II held in the British Museum October 2004* edited by Janet C.M. Starkey. Society for Arabian Studies Monographs No. 3. ISBN 1 84171 833 5.

BAR –S1456, 2005 The Tihamah Coastal Plain of South-West Arabia in its Regional Context c. 6000 BC – AD 600 by Nadia Durrani. Society for Arabian Studies Monographs No. 4. ISBN 1 84171 894 7.

BAR –S1661, 2007 Natural Resources and Cultural Connections of the Red Sea *Proceedings of Red Sea Project III held in the British Museum October 2006* edited by Janet Starkey, Paul Starkey and Tony Wilkinson. Society for Arabian Studies Monographs No. 5. ISBN 9781407300979

BAR –S1776, 2008 La Péninsule d'Oman de la fin de l'Age du Fer au début de la période sassanide (250 av. – 350 ap. JC) by Michel Mouton. Society for Arabian Studies Monographs No. 6. ISBN 978 1 4073 0264 5

BAR –S1826, 2008 Intercultural Relations between South and Southwest Asia *Studies in commemoration of E.C.L. During Caspers (1934-1996)* edited by Eric Olijdam and Richard H. Spoor. Society for Arabian Studies Monograph No. 7. ISBN 978 1 4073 0312 3

BAR –S2052, 2009 Connected Hinterlands *Proceedings of Red Sea Project IV held at the University of Southampton September 2008* edited by Lucy Blue, John Cooper, Ross Thomas and Julian Whitewright. Society for Arabian Studies Monographs No. 8. ISBN 978 1 4073 0631

BAR –S2102, 2010 Ports and Political Power in the *Periplus Complex societies and maritime trade on the Indian Ocean in the first century AD* by Eivind Heldaas Seland. Society for Arabian Studies Monographs 9. ISBN 978 1 4073 0578 3. £29.00.

Potential contributors

Please contact the editors in the first instance:

Dr Derek Kennet: Department of Archaeology, Durham University, South Road, Durham, England DH1 3LE
Derek.Kennet@durham.ac.uk
Dr St John Simpson: Department of the Middle East, The British Museum, London, England WC1B 3DG
ssimpson@thebritishmuseum.ac.uk

Contents

Preface and Acknowledgements iv

Introduction to the contributions on burial archaeology v
Lloyd Weeks

Remarks on Neolithic burial customs in south-east Arabia 1
Adelina U. Kutterer

Ornamental objects as a source of information on Neolithic burial practices at al-Buhais 18, UAE and neighbouring sites 11
Roland de Beauclair

On Neolithic funerary practices: were there "necrophobic" manipulations in 5th-4th millennium BC Arabia? 17
Vincent Charpentier and Sophie Méry

The burials of the middle Holocene settlement of KHB-1 (Ra's al-Khabbah, Sultanate of Oman) 25
Olivia Munoz, Simona Scaruffi and Fabio Cavulli

Results, limits and potential: burial practices and Early Bronze Age societies in the Oman Peninsula 33
S. Méry

Life and Death in an Early Bronze Age community from Hili, Al Ain, UAE 45
Kathleen McSweeney, Sophie Méry and Walid Yasin al Tikriti

Patterns of mortality in a Bronze Age Tomb from Tell Abraq 55
Kathryn Baustian and Debra L. Martin

Discerning health, disease and activity patterns in a Bronze Age population from Tell Abraq, United Arab Emirates 61
Janet M. Cope

Early Bronze Age graves and graveyards in the eastern Ja'alan (Sultanate of Oman): an assessment of the social rules working in the evolution of a funerary landscape. 71
J. Giraud

An inventory of the objects in a collective burial at Dadna (Emirate of Fujairah) 85
Anne Benoist and Salah Ali Hassan

Collective burials and status differentiation in Iron Age II Southeastern Arabia 101
Crystal Fritz

Camelid and equid burials in pre-Islamic Southeastern Arabia 109
Aurelie Daems and An De Waele

The emergence of mound cemeteries in Early Dilmun: new evidence of a proto-cemetery and its genesis c. 2050-2000 BC 115
Steffen Terp Laursen

Probing the early Dilmun funerary landscape: a tentative analysis of grave goods from non-elite adult burials from City IIa-c 141
Eric Olijdam

The Bahrain bead project: introduction and illustration 153
Waleed M. Al-Sadeqi

The burial mounds of the Middle Euphrates (2100-1800 B.C.) and their links with Arabia: the subtle dialectic between tribal and state practices 165
Christine Kepinski

Reuse of tombs or cultural continuity? The case of tower-tombs in Shabwa governorate (Yemen) 173
Rémy Crassard, Hervé Guy, Jérémie Schiettecatte and Holger Hitgen

A reverence for stone reflected in various Late Bronze Age interments at al-Midamman, a Red Sea coastal site in Yemen 179
Edward J. Keall

The Arabian Iron Age funerary stelae and the issue of cross-cultural contacts 191
Jérémie Schiettecatte

Sabaean stone and metal miniature grave goods 205
D'arne O'Neill

Excavations of the Italian Archaeological Mission in Yemen: a Minaean necropolis at Barāqish (Wadi Jawf) and the Qatabanian necropolis of Ḥayd bin ʿAqīl (Wadi Bayḥān) 215
Sabina Antonini and Alessio Agostini

Funerary monuments of Southern Arabia: the Iron Age – early Islamic traditions 225
Juris Zarins

Burial contexts at Tayma, NW Arabia: archaeological and anthropological data 237
Sebastiano Lora, Emmanuele Petiti and Arnulf Hausleiter

Feasting with the dead: funerary Marzeaḥ in Petra 249
Isabelle Sachet

Biomolecular archaeology and analysis of artefacts found in Nabataean tombs in Petra 263
Nicolas Garnier, Isabelle Sachet, Anna Zymla, Caroline Tokarski, Christian Rolando

The monolithic *djin blocks* at Petra: a funerary practice of pre-Islamic Arabia 275
Michel Mouton

Colouring the dead: new investigations on the history and the polychrome appearance of the Tomb of Darius I at Naqsh-e Rostam, Fars 289
Alexander Nagel and Hassan Rahsaz

Introduction to the contributions on Arabia and the wider Islamic world 299
Janet Starkey

The intercessor status of the dead in Maliki Islam and in Mauritania 303
Corinne Fortier

Cairo's City of the Dead: the cohabitation between the living and the dead from an anthropological perspective 311
Anna Tozzi Di Marco

Observations on death, burial, graves and graveyards at various locations in Ra's al-Khaimah Emirate, UAE, and Musandam *wilayat*, Oman, using local concerns 319
William and Fidelity Lancaster

Shrines in Dhofar 329
Lynne S. Newton

Wādī Ḥaḍramawt as a Landscape of Death and Burial 347
Mikhail Rodionov

Attitudes, themes and images: an introduction to death and burial as mirrored in early Arabic poetry 353
James E. Taylor

Jewish burial customs in Yemen 361
Dina Dahbany-Miraglia

In anima vili: Islamic constructions on life autopsies and cannibalism 365
José Mª Bellido-Morillas and Pablo García-Piñar

Instituting the Palestinian dead body 369
Suhad Daher-Nashif

Papers read at the Conference..383

Preface and Acknowledgements

This volume represents the proceedings of the conference entitled "Death, Burial and the Transition to the Afterlife in Arabia and Adjacent Regions" that was held at the British Museum from November 27th to 29th, 2008. The conference was organised by the editor on behalf of the Society for Arabian Studies as one of its series of biennial conferences which had previously focused on the Red Sea region.[1] Many thanks are due to the Society and to the British Museum for their continued support of academic research into the history and culture of Arabia and its neighbours.

The conference organising committee comprised Dr. Lloyd Weeks (organiser and instigator, University of Nottingham), Dr. Harriet Crawford (Institute of Archaeology, UCL), Dr. St John Simpson (British Museum), Dr. Janet Starkey (Durham University) and Dr. Shelagh Weir (School of Oriental and African Studies, University of London). All organising committee members deserve thanks for their considerable input into developing themes, recruiting speakers, chairing sessions, running workshops, averting disasters and the many other components of running a successful conference. Further thanks are due to the Treasurer of the Society for Arabian studies, Col. Douglas Stobie, for his sound financial advice during planning and, most importantly, for his general unflappability. Administrative assistance during the conference was also provided by Dr. Ardle MacMahon.

The conference could not have taken place without considerable direct financial support from a number of institutions. Thus, we gratefully acknowledge contributions from the University of Nottingham, the British Institute for the Study of Iraq, the Leigh Douglas Memorial Fund and the British-Yemeni Society and the waiving of facility costs by the British Museum. The publication of these proceedings is possible due to the support of the Society for Arabian Studies, and thanks are due to its President, Miss Beatrice de Cardi OBE, its Chair, Ms. Sarah Searight, and to the editors of the Society's Monograph Series, Dr. Derek Kennet (Durham University) and Dr. St John Simpson. A substantial contribution to the editing of the volume was made by Dr. Alexandra Porter (British Museum), for which she is warmly thanked.

Finally, thanks must go to those who attended and presented their work at the conference itself, in the main sessions, in the workshops, and in the poster sessions. The breadth and quality of this research, and the gathering of such a large and engaging group of scholars with shared interests, provided for a very memorable and enjoyable conference.

Lloyd Weeks

The Editor

---

[1] Previous Society for Arabian Studies Red Sea conference publications include:
Lunde P. and Porter, A. (eds). 2004. *Trade and Travel in the Red Sea Region: Proceedings of the Red Sea Project I held in the British Museum October 2002*. Oxford: Archaeopress. BAR International Series 1269, Society for Arabian Studies Monographs No. 2.
Starkey J.C.M. (ed.) 2005. *People of the Red Sea: Proceedings of Red Sea Project II held in the British Museum October 2004*. Oxford: Archaeopress. BAR international Series 1395, Society for Arabian Studies Monographs No. 3.
Starkey J.C.M., Starkey P. and Wilkinson T. (eds) 2007. *Natural Resources and Cultural Connections of the Red Sea: Proceedings of Red Sea Project III held in the British Museum October 2006*. Oxford: Archaeopress. BAR International Series 1661, Society for Arabian Studies Monographs No. 5.

Introduction to the Contributions on Burial Archaeology

Lloyd Weeks

This volume represents the proceedings of the conference entitled "Death, Burial and the Transition to the Afterlife in Arabia and Adjacent Regions" that was held at the British Museum from November 27th to 29th, 2008. The conference promoted a broad consideration of the cultural traditions related to death and burial across the Arabian Peninsula, from prehistory to modern times, and was the first to attempt a cross-disciplinary study of burial archaeology in Arabia. The major themes of the conference included:

- specific local/regional burial traditions of ancient Arabia and adjacent regions
- implications of burial data for aspects of contemporaneous living societies
- beliefs surrounding death and the transition to the afterlife
- landscapes of death and burial
- burial and pilgrimage
- recent and contemporary ideas and practices relating to death and burial.

The conference included 38 papers in the plenary sessions, nine papers in two additional workshops (on Bronze Age Southern Arabia and on the Islamic world) and 14 poster presentations: of these, 36 are presented in this volume. The full conference programme is provided at the end of this volume, in addition to abstracts of the presentations that are not published here.

The conference subject and themes were developed in response to a number of personal and scholarly perceptions. Of initial (if not primary) importance were my own first experiences of Arabia as an archaeology student, working with the Sydney University team in the United Arab Emirates (U.A.E.). Not only was our project focused upon recording and excavating Bronze Age collective burials, our weekend field excursions into the mountains or to Al Ain revealed to us literally hundreds of ancient burial cairns often sited in prominent locations near modern oasis settlements. In contrast to other areas of the Near East, where large settlement mounds dominate the landscape and provide a tangible indication of the great time-depth of human occupation, the Emirates and Oman provided a very different picture. In south-eastern Arabia early settlement remains were often ephemeral, tells all but absent, and only burial cairns provided testament to the enduring human presence in the region. It was a landscape, in some important respects, structured by death and burial.

Many archaeologists who have worked in the region have investigated these cairns, and discussed their significance for our understanding of the prehistoric societies of south-eastern Arabia. In their recent monograph, Serge Cleuziou and Maurizio Tosi (2007) have gone as far as to suggest that the first complex societies of south-eastern Arabia grew "in the shadow of the ancestors". Similar things might very well be said of the burial traditions of Bahrain – ancient Dilmun – where approximately 75,000 burial mounds provide overwhelming evidence for the significance of death and burial for the Bronze Age societies of this region (Højlund 2008).

Thus, one of the main motivations for this conference was to highlight the incredibly rich burial archaeology of Arabia, and to draw together, compare, and contextualise field research from across the Arabian Peninsula. This is possible now due to the relatively recent development of reliable archaeological and chronological frameworks for prehistoric Arabia, reflecting the youth of Arabian archaeology as a discipline. For example, aside from sporadic investigations by earlier scholars and political residents (such as E.L Durand, F.B. Prideaux, E.J.H. Marshall and P.B. Cornwall), archaeology in eastern Arabia was not firmly established until the mid-20th century with the work of the Danish missions to Bahrain and Abu Dhabi/Al Ain (Bibby 1970), and expanded only from the late 1970s with the work of numerous local and international teams. Similarly, despite earlier archaeological, epigraphical, and historical research on remains of the Sabaean period, most prehistoric components of south-western Arabia's archaeological heritage were not clearly identified until the 1980s (Edens and Wilkinson 1998: 56) and an understanding of the Bronze Age burial archaeology of south-western Arabia developed only from the late 1990s (e.g. Steimer-Herbet et al. 2007, 2006; Steimer-Herbet 2004; Braemer et al. 2001). These recently discovered south-western Arabian Bronze Age burial traditions represent but one facet of a peninsula-wide Bronze Age practice of monumentalising burials. Although their significance and interpretation remains uncertain, contributions in these proceedings demonstrate that such pan-Arabian parallels are by no means limited to the Bronze Age. Given the increasingly specialised, isolated, and fragmented nature of archaeological research communities, each possessing independent research traditions and methodologies, it is hoped that these proceedings will promote a broader regional perspective on burial traditions across Arabia.

The fragmentation of research no doubt also plays a role in the fact that Arabia's striking prehistoric mortuary evidence has rarely been introduced into the wider discourse on burial archaeology in the ancient Near East, as an examination of relevant conference sessions and proceedings will attest (e.g. BANEA 2008; Campbell and Green 1992; Laneri 2007). This is partly an issue of geographical terminology, whereby Arabia is perceived as peripheral to a tightly defined Near Eastern "heartland" focused upon the Fertile Crescent. We might also consider the influence of post-processual approaches to archaeology that have developed since the 1980s, emphasising, as they do, close contextual interpretation of archaeological remains and cultural specificity over broader intercultural comparisons (e.g. Barrett 1988). Whilst not wishing to promote cross-cultural archaeological comparisons in search of "laws" of human behaviour as a model of archaeological research, a number of contributions to these proceedings demonstrate that there *are* insights to be gained from placing the many regional burial traditions of ancient Arabia into their broader archaeological context on both a pan-Arabian and a Near Eastern scale.

The present volume is divided into two major sections; one on the burial archaeology of pre-Islamic Arabia and adjacent regions, and one covering multidisciplinary approaches to death and burial in Arabia and the Islamic world. The Islamic section is the subject of a separate introduction by Janet Starkey (p. 313). Here, I review the contributions to this volume from burial archaeology, which are presented in geographical and chronological groups reflecting (with some changes) the order of papers and sessions at the original conference.

South-Eastern Arabia

The sections on the burial archaeology of Arabia begin with south-eastern Arabia – the modern day United Arab Emirates and Oman – with a total of 12 papers presenting evidence from the Neolithic period in the 6th millennium BC to the late Pre-Islamic period. Four contributions cover the Neolithic period in south-eastern Arabia. The papers by **Kutterer** and by **de Beauclair** focus predominantly on northern sites; most importantly the 5th millennium BC site of Jabal Buheis 18 (BHS18) in Sharjah, U.A.E., with more than 500 interred individuals, but also recently discovered contemporary and earlier sites nearby at Jebel Faya. Research at these sites has dramatically expanded our understanding of Neolithic burial practices in south-eastern Arabia, and Kutterer's review paper places the material in its regional context as well as discussing the complexity of BHS18 burial practices and the difficulty of their archaeological reconstruction using the familiar and canonical terms of "primary" and "secondary" burials.

De Beauclair's research on the jewellery and personal adornments associated with the BHS18 burials raises further questions regarding the presence or absence of jewellery in primary burials and those with redeposited material, highlighting the possible role of jewellery in the burial ritual as a marker of the transition from the living to the dead. As with most of the burial archaeology studies presented at this conference, analysis of the burial remains also had much to say about the life of the group: in the case of BHS18 particularly seasonal mobility and subsistence. Although analysis of the astounding BHS18 assemblage is only preliminary, the reviews highlight the presence of a range of burial types, some common and some "atypical". It is clear that both adherence to and divergence from "normal" modes of burial will be critical factors in explaining the role of burial to the Neolithic societies that inhabited the region, and more specifically for interpreting individual burials.

The evidence of Neolithic burials from south-eastern Arabia is also reviewed by **Charpentier and Méry**, who address not only the complexity of primary, secondary and multiple burials but also the cultural beliefs and identity that are revealed by materials interred the burials alongside human remains, most spectacularly the deposition of turtle skulls, bones and shells in the burials at Ra's al-Hamra 5 and 10 in eastern Oman. They also discuss the possible evidence for "necrophobia" in the burials at the Suwayh 1 necropolis. Widely represented in the ethnographic literature, such fears that the dead may continue to act on/in the living world represent an interesting component of the "agency" of the dead. The study of contemporary burials from the site of Ra's al-Khabbah KHB-1 by **Munoz, Cavulli and Scaruffi** provides additional evidence on the variability of Neolithic burial practices, most interestingly on the partial natural "mummification" of primary burials prior to secondary interment that is also recorded at BHS18 (Kutterer, this volume).

The Early Bronze Age (Hafit and Umm an-Nar period) burial traditions of south-eastern Arabia are presented and discussed in a series of five papers that take varying approaches to the archaeological record. **Méry** provides an initial overview of the evidence from the Umm an-Nar period (c. 27/2600-2000 BC), particularly that recovered from the Al Ain oasis in the U.A.E. This focuses upon the development of elaborate, stone-built, monumental tomb architecture that is a feature of the 3rd millennium BC across south-eastern Arabia, the appearance of alternative burial types represented by external collective pit-graves associated with the monumental tombs, and the cultural connections and craft specialization that can be documented through study of ceramic assemblages found in tombs and contemporary settlements.

Méry's conclusions on chronology are particularly important for the understanding of Umm an-Nar burial practices, and are supplemented by the detailed studies of Umm an-Nar period skeletal remains presented by **McSweeney, Méry and al Tikriti** (for the Hili N collective pit-grave), **Baustian and Martin**, and **Cope** (for the Tell Abraq collective Umm an-Nar tomb). The numbers of burials are enormous – c. 700 at Hili N, c. 360 at Tell Abraq – and they represent a fundamental source for information on past populations, including demography, mortality profiles, diet, health, and daily activities. Whilst similarities in osteological activity markers in each assemblage point to a life of hard physical exertion in the Early Bronze Age, there are interesting contrasts in overall health and stature between the coastal and interior populations.

In the final paper dealing with the Early Bronze Age, **Giraud** applies GIS analyses to the investigation of the distribution of thousands of Hafit and Umm an-Nar period tombs in the Ja'alan region of eastern Oman. Her assessment of changing tomb positioning through time provides insights into not only the "landscape of identity" created by these burial monuments, but also hints at the dramatic reorientation of physical and social space that accompanied the rise of oasis-based agricultural communities in the 3rd millennium BC. Her studies serve as an important predictive baseline for examining funerary landscapes other areas of south-eastern Arabia.

A further three papers appear in the section on south-eastern Arabia. **Benoist and Hassan** present and discuss the artefactual evidence obtained from a relatively rich – if disturbed – Middle Bronze Age (Wadi Suq) tomb at Dadna in Fujairah, U.A.E., that was re-used in the Late Bronze and Iron Ages. The tomb's finds are contextualised chronologically on a region-wide basis, and the study provides further evidence in support of continuity in burial locations (and traditions?) from the early 2nd to the mid-1st millennium BC, a period which otherwise witnessed dramatic changes in material culture and society. The following paper by **Fritz** examines Iron Age material, particularly ceramics, from collective graves in the Wadi al-Qawr (Ra's al-Khaimah, U.A.E.) in the search for evidence of social hierarchies. In this case, ceramic grave goods provide little evidence for status differentiation in Iron Age burial contexts, contrasting strongly with evidence from contemporary settlements where possible "elite" structures, particularly columned halls, are associated with the paraphernalia of feasting and drinking that suggest active displays of status and "competitive generosity" (e.g. Magee 2007: 90-91; cf. Clark and Blake 1994).

The final paper in this section, by **Daems and De Waele**, moves partially away from the issue of human burial to focus upon animals, especially large animals such as equids and camelids, whose skeletal remains are important if uncommon finds in Bronze Age and later burial deposits from eastern Arabia. Daems and De Waele argue, from a wide review of the literature, that fundamental and pervasive human-animal interrelationships in the living world underpinned the appearance of such animal burials, and their ability to symbolise the wealth, power and status of the humans that they were buried with.

The Central Persian Gulf and Mesopotamia

Following the section on south-eastern Arabia, there are four papers related to the Bronze Age communities of the central Persian Gulf region, particularly the island of Bahrain or ancient Dilmun, and its neighbouring regions. The first paper, by **Laursen**, represents the continued effort of the Bahrain Burial Mounds Project (Højlund 2008; Højlund et al. 2008) to map, describe, and interpret the Bronze Age burial mounds on the island. Following a series of important publications (Laursen 2008, 2009), in this volume Laursen uses the results of digitized tomb distributions (extracted from aerial photography) to investigate the growth of specific burial types and "mound cemeteries" that both reflected and reinforced increased social complexity in the region at the very end of the 3rd millennium BC. Chronological precision gained from the examination of a range of artefact classes, especially exotic pottery and indigenous administrative devices ("Arabian Gulf seals"), allows Laursen to tightly link the developing burial traditions of the island with changes in Dilmun's participation in the Persian Gulf exchange network. The Bahrain Burial Mounds Project offers the unique and highly admirable prospect of rediscovering what were, prior to their decimation in the Petroleum Age, unparalleled "fossilised landscapes from prehistory" (Laursenand Johansen 2008: 137).

The subsequent paper by **Olijdam** builds upon the work of the Bahrain Burial Mounds Project, by analysing various material components of assemblages from City II period Dilmun burial mounds. In a very broad review of the evidence, Olijdam is able to demonstrate how a study of artefactual evidence from the tombs offers a different perspective than the study of their architecture alone. Rather than challenging the interpretations of social status developed by predominantly architectural studies, this study provides a clear indication of the complexity of factors that governed the selection of materials for the grave. These included not only the status of the individual interred there, but perhaps also that of the organisers of the funeral and, amongst "non-elite" tombs, the possible membership of a range of politically, ritually and/or economically-configured social groups.

The contribution by **Al-Sadeqi** provides a further instance of the importance of detailed studies of artefacts recovered from these Bahraini burials. Although preliminary, Al-Sadeqi's study of the beads from Dilmun and Tylos period tombs and initial steps towards the creation of an analytical typology highlight the range of intercultural exchange contacts that underpinned Dilmun's growth in both the Bronze Age and the Hellenistic period.

The final paper in this section, by **Kepinski**, puts the Bronze Age burial practices of Bahrain into a much broader geographical and cultural context. In comparing the rare burial mounds of the middle Euphrates region with their parallels in eastern Arabia – especially Dilmun – Kepinski suggests that these structures are the product of contested social and economic interactions between sedentary and nomadic (or recently sedentarised) Amorite groups. In her conception, burial mounds not only indicate "the interconnection of local, tribal and state practices", but also persistent and pervasive cultural connections between nomadic Amorite groups in eastern Arabia and those on the arid margins of Mesopotamia.

South-Western Arabia

In total, six papers deal with the archaeological record of death and burial in south-western Arabia, i.e. modern-day Yemen. The earliest material, dated to the South Arabian Bronze Age, is discussed by **Crassard et al.**, and is interesting for its demonstration of periods of later Iron Age re-use of the tombs. Many parallels for this situation can be drawn with south-eastern Arabian burial traditions (as documented in this volume by Benoist and Hassan and Fritz), and such re-use is a testament not only to continuity in subsistence and lifestyles across millennia as highlighted by Crassard et al., but also to the continued visibility of these tombs and their creation of a long-lived, active, burial landscape.

The other paper on Bronze Age material is by **Keall**, who focuses on the site of al-Midamman on the Tihamah coast of Yemen. Here, excavation of a monumental construction incorporating massive stone uprights, first recorded by archaeologists in the late 1990s, revealed evidence of "commemorative acts of interment" characterised by the presence of buried artefacts and of human burials. Keall's research reveals the multiple stages of development of the site's monumental structures (including associated settlement areas), emphasises the unusual "reverence" for stone indicated by the prevailing use a resource completely foreign to the region, and highlights the unique nature of al-Midamman within prehistoric Arabia.

Moving into the 1st millennium BC, the paper by **Schiettecatte** discusses the evidence of Iron Age funerary stelae from the region. From an analysis of their chronology and onomastics, Schiettecatte challenges existing iconographical studies claiming diffusion (or even migration) from north Arabia, instead offering the hypothesis of endogenous development from a common western Arabian cultural background. His paper represents an important new perspective on this fundamental issue in Arabian prehistory.

Another paper on the 1st millennium BC burial traditions of south-western Arabia is provided by **O'Neill**, who discusses miniature artefacts from the Awām cemetery in the Mārib oasis. Miniatures of clay, stone and metal are abundant in the graves at Awām, and have parallels in contemporary non-burial contexts. Although their specific cultural meaning remains obscure, O'Neill suggests that the ritualisation of everyday artefacts through miniaturisation was an important aspect of miniature deposition in the highly symbolic context of Sabaean mortuary practices.

The contribution by **Antonini and Agostini** presents the results of excavations at the Minaean necropolis of Barāqish and the Qatabanian necropolis at Ḥayd bin ʿAqīl, in Yemen. Although contemporary, these sites show dramatically variant burial practice that is related by the authors to the fact that they contained the burials of different elements of society. The tombs at Ḥayd bin ʿAqīl are those of the Qatabanian families residing in the adjacent town of Tamnaʿ, whereas those at Barāqish – often empty of human remains – are suggested to belong to members of nomadic groups who resided seasonally outside the city walls.

The final paper on south-western Arabia, by **Zarins**, investigates one specific burial type – the so-called "boat-shaped" tomb – that occurs over a large part of southern Arabia, including Dhofar (Oman), the Mahra Governorate in Yemen, and the island of Soqotra. A broad review of the dating evidence allows Zarins to bracket the construction of these monuments to the period from c. 400-1000 AD, and he links the evidence with the burials of "powerful clan or lineage individuals" from various MSAL-speaking groups.

North-Western Arabia

The last section on the burial archaeology of Arabia focuses upon NW Arabia, specifically the sites of Tayma (Saudi Arabia) and Petra (Jordan). The first paper, by **Lora, Petiti and Hausleiter** examines the burials and skeletal remains from the 1st millennium BC cemetery of Tal'a, just to the south-eastern of the contemporary town of Tayma. Archaeological and osteological analyses allow the authors to suggest that the cemetery contains collective family burials. The authors also present material evidence for specific funerary rituals and artefacts associated with family members, especially juveniles. Although the tombs were robbed or otherwise disturbed in antiquity – a situation that characterises the vast majority of burials known from ancient Arabia – these detailed analyses are able to provide important information to reconstruct burial practices at Tayma.

The second paper in this section, by **Mouton**, examines burial practices of the late pre-Islamic period across the Arabian Peninsula, with a particular focus on Nabataean Petra and the contemporary sites of Mleiha (Sharjah, U.A.E.) and Qaryat al-Fau (Saudi Arabia). Mouton's recent fieldwork at Petra dramatically changes our perspective on these widely separated sites, and demonstrates the undeniable "morphological and conceptual parallels" in their burial rituals. Mouton relates these parallels to a common nomadic heritage and to economic interrelationships developed through the trans-Arabian exchange system.

Nabataean funerary rituals are the focus of the paper by **Sachet**, specifically the "funerary banquets" of Petra at which family and companions commemorated the deceased. The banquets reflect a mixture of influences from both local nomadic traditions and the wider Mediterranean world, and Sachet's historical, archaeological, and architectural study allows her to examine chronological changes in the nature and scale of the funerary banquet, and to correlate these with the wider socio-economic development of Petra from the 1st century BC to the early centuries AD.

The related paper by **Garnier et al.** takes a very different approach, using a battery of scientific techniques to examine the archaeological residues of funerary rituals in Nabataean tombs. Analyses of residues extracted from libation holes in a number of tombs provide information on the components of libations and fumigations undertaken as part of Nabataean funerary rituals – generally dairy products, vegetal oils, and coniferous resins. More surprisingly, archaeological residues from the "Incense Tomb" represent metallurgical activities including the working of iron and brass. The study demonstrates the power of well designed and implemented programmes of scientific analysis to contribute to our understanding of otherwise "lost" aspects of the distant past.

Beyond Arabia

The final paper in the burial archaeology section takes us further afield – outside the confines of Arabia proper – to consider Achaemenid Persian tomb façades in Fars province, Iran. The contribution by **Nagel & Rahsaz** uses detailed conservation work to demonstrate the original vivid colouring of the tomb of Darius I at Naqsh-e Rostam. Their research indicates that this polychromy was as clear an attestation of the wealth and power of the ruler for whom it was built as its architectural design and construction. Such studies, moreover, have implications for our understanding of the original appearance of many of the carved stone monuments and statues of ancient Arabia and the wider Near East.

Preservation of the Archaeological Record

As a final note, I hope that this volume can take us some way towards addressing the fundamental challenges of describing and interpreting the burial archaeology record of Arabia. The papers presented here provide an up-to-date overview of the state of the evidence and of current approaches to research that can inspire and facilitate further programmes of field, laboratory, and archival research.

More importantly, I hope that these proceedings will also highlight to a wide audience the importance of Arabia's archaeological heritage, an irreplaceable cultural resource that is under tremendous threat in many areas. The recent destruction of Arabia's burial archaeology heritage has been commented upon by a number of reviewers (Højlund 2008; De Cardi 2003) and is part of a very long term trend in the destruction of sites by later human activities resulting in many instances from the very nature of human occupation in arid Arabian environments (Edens and Wilkinson 1998: 61; al-Jahwari and Kennet 2008). The global significance of aspects of Arabia's archaeological record is clear. Laursen and Johansen (2008: 137), for example, have fairly described the massive burial mound fields of Bahrain as representing "a cultural heritage without parallel elsewhere in the world", yet less than one-third of the original c. 75,000 Bronze Age mounds on the island have survived the massive development of the last century (Højlund 2008). In at least one instance, such significance *has* been recognised by the granting of World Heritage status – to the 3rd Millennium BC necropolis and settlement site of Bat in Oman – but many sites of equal or greater significance remain poorly protected. As the contributions to this volume indicate, these archaeological remains are not just monuments to death, but keys to understanding the ancient living societies that created them. Aspects of ancient religion, gender, kinship, social complexity, inter-cultural contact, demography, and health, amongst many other factors, are accessible to well-planned and executed archaeological research at these monuments. Their continued preservation and study is a matter of greatest importance for Arabia in the present day.

Note on Transliteration

Arabic words and names are transliterated using either the common form in which they have entered English usage (e.g. Umm an-Nar, Wadi Suq) or following the scheme set out in the *Proceedings of the Seminar for Arabian Studies*, vol. 39 (2009: vii).

References

BANEA 2008. Session on "Theorising Death and Discard in the Ancient Near East". Accessed 9/2/2010 at http://www.liv.ac.uk/sace/events/confer/banea/FinalProgram.doc.

Barrett J.C. 1988. The living, the dead and the ancestors: Neolithic and Early Bronze Age mortuary practices. Pages 30-41 in J.C. Barrett and I.A. Kinnes (eds), *The Archaeology of Context in the Neolithic and Bronze Age: Recent Trends*. Sheffield: Department of Archaeology and Prehistory, University of Sheffield.

Bibby T.G. 1970. *Looking for Dilmun*. New York: Knopf.

Braemer F., Steimer-Herbet T., Buchet L., Saliège J.-F. and Guy H. 2001. Le bronze ancien du Ramlat as-Sabatayn (Yémen). Deux nécropoles de la première moitié du IIIe millénaire à la bordure du désert: Jabal Jidran et Jabal Ruwaiq. *Paléorient* 27/1: 21-44.

Campbell S. and Green A. 1992. *The Archaeology of Death in the Ancient Near East*. Oxford: Oxbow.

Clark J.E. and Blake M. 1994. The Power of Prestige: Competitive Generosity and the Emergence of Rank Societies in Lowland Mesoamerica. Pages 17-30 in E.M. Brumfiel and J.W. Fox (eds.), *Factional Competition and Political Development in the New World*. Cambridge: Cambridge University Press.

Cleuziou S. and Tosi M. 2007. *In the Shadow of the Ancestors: The Prehistoric Foundations of the early Arabian Civilization in Oman*. Muscat: Ministry of Heritage and Culture, Sultanate of Oman.

De Cardi B. 2003. Is there a future for the Emirates' past? Pages 133-150 in D.T. Potts, H. Al Naboodah and P. Hellyer (eds), *Archaeology of the United Arab Emirates: Proceedings of the First International Conference on the Archaeology of the U.A.E.* London: Trident Press.

Edens C. and Wilkinson T.J. 1998. Southwest Arabia During the Holocene: Recent Archaeological Developments. *Journal of World Prehistory* 12: 55-119.

Højlund F. 2008. *The Burial Mounds of Bahrain: Social Complexity in Early Dilmun*. Moesgaard: Jutland Archaeological society Publications.

Højlund F., Hilton A.S., Juel C., Kirkeby N., Laursen S.T. and Nielsen L.E. 2008. Late third-millennium elite burials in Bahrain *Arabian Archaeology and Epigraphy* 19/2: 144-155.

Al-Jahwari N.S and Kennet D. 2008. A field methodology for the quantification of ancient settlement in an Arabian context. *Proceedings of the Seminar for Arabian Studies* 38: 203-214.

Laneri N. (ed.) 2007. *Performing Death: Social analyses of Funerary Traditions in the Ancient Near East and Mediterranean.* Chicago: The Oriental Institute of the University of Chicago.

Laursen S.T. 2008. Early Dilmun and its rulers: new evidence of the burial mounds of the elite and the development of social complexity, c. 2200–1750 BC. *Arabian Archaeology and Epigraphy* 19/2: 156-167.

Laursen S.T. 2009. The decline of Magan and the rise of Dilmun: Umm an-Nar ceramics from the burial mounds of Bahrain, c.2250–2000 BC. *Arabian Archaeology and Epigraphy* 20/2: 134-155.

Laursen S.T. and Johansen K.L. 2008. Appendix 1. The potential of aerial photographs in future studies of mound cemeteries. Pages 137-148 in F. Højlund (ed.) *The Burial Mounds of Bahrain: Social Complexity in Early Dilmun.* Moesgaard: Jutland Archaeological society Publications.

Magee P. 2007. Beyond the Desert and the Sown: Settlement Intensification in Late Prehistoric Southeastern Arabia. *BASOR* 347: 83-105.

Steimer-Herbet T. 2004. *Classification des sépultures à superstructure lithique dans le Levant et l'Arabie Occidentale (IVe Et IIIe millénaires Avant J.-C).* Oxford: Archaeopress. BAR International Series 1246.

Steimer-Herbet T., Saliège J.-F., Sagory T., Lavigne O. and as-Saqqaf A. 2007. Rites and funerary practices at Rawk during the fourth millennium BC (Wadi 'Idim, Yemen). *Proceedings of the Seminar for Arabian Studies* 37: 281-294.

Steimer-Herbet T., Davtian G. and Braemer F. 2006. Pastoralists' tombs and settlement patterns in Wādī Washʿah during the Bronze Age (Ḥaḍramawt, Yemen). *Proceedings of the Seminar for Arabian Studies* 36: 257-265.

Author's Address:

Dr. Lloyd Weeks
Dept. of Archaeology
University of Nottingham
University Park NG7 2RD
Nottingham, UK
lloyd.weeks@nottingham.ac.uk

Remarks on Neolithic burial customs in south-east Arabia

Adelina U. Kutterer

Summary

This paper deals with Neolithic burial customs in SE-Arabia and focuses especially on al-Buhais 18 (Sharjah, UAE), a cemetery dating to the 5th millennium BC. At this site the remains of more than 500 individuals were excavated. Some of these were buried in primary graves, which means that the deceased were interred in their flesh. The others were found in secondary graves, as their skeletal remains were brought to BHS18 after decomposition at another place. Some special interments are highlighted in detail. The complexity of burial practises, especially in terms of addressing them unambiguously as either "primary" or "secondary" burials, is demonstrated. In a wider context, these burial customs do not indicate large differences in comparison to contemporary sites like Fay-NE15. Later Neolithic sites along the Omani coast – like RH5 – also follow these traditions of burial practises. However, a new window on early burial customs in SE-Arabia is opened by recent discoveries at the older site Fay-NE10, dating to the 6th millennium BC: according to histological analyses of charred bone fragments, human ashes were deposited in this small cave over a long period of time.

Keywords: Neolithic burial customs, al-Buhais 18, primary burials, secondary burials, cremation

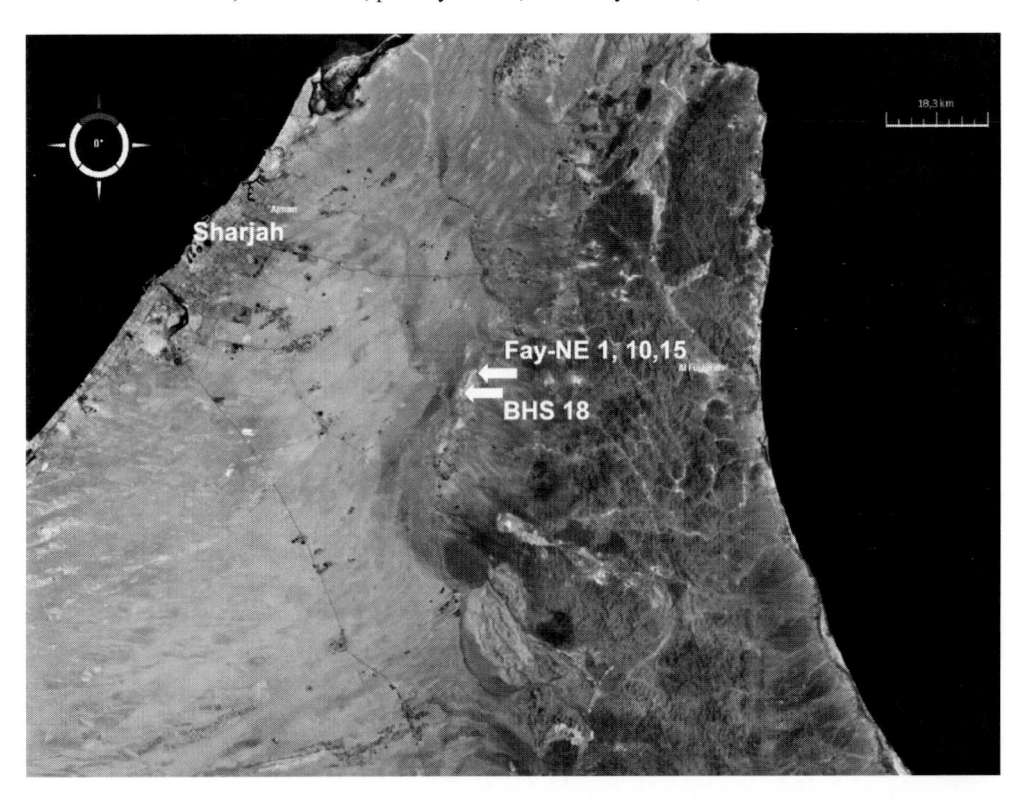

Figure 1. Location of the mentioned sites BHS18, Fay-NE1, Fay-NE10 and Fay-NE15 in the central region of Sharjah, UAE (Satellite image World Wind, NASA).

Burial customs at al-Buhais during the 5th millennium BC

The discovery of al-Buhais 18 in 1995 marked a milestone in gaining a better view on Neolithic life and death in south-east Arabia. Excavations at the site, which is situated in the desert mid-way between the Arabian Gulf and the Gulf of Oman in the Central Region of the Emirate of Sharjah (Fig. 1), took place until the year 2005. They yielded insight not only into burial practises but also into population structure, the economy and many other aspects of life in the 5th millennium BC (Uerpmann M *et al.* 2006; Kiesewetter 2006; Uerpmann M & Uerpmann H-P 2008). Analyses of animal bones from the site show that the people were nomadic herders. They kept sheep and goats, of which they used milk and meat, and also some cattle, which apparently were only used for meat. Hunting provided only about 10% of the meat consumed while the group stayed at BHS18. Obviously the site was regularly visited during a yearly cycle of nomadic movements leading from the coast to the *Hajar* Mountains – presumably in summer – and back to the coast for the winter.

Many fireplaces are scattered in the plain surrounding the burial ground of BHS18, indicating camp sites of the respective groups during their stays in the Buhais area. Eight radiocarbon dates from these fireplaces are contemporaneous with the same amount of radiocarbon dates for ashes and human bones from the graveyard

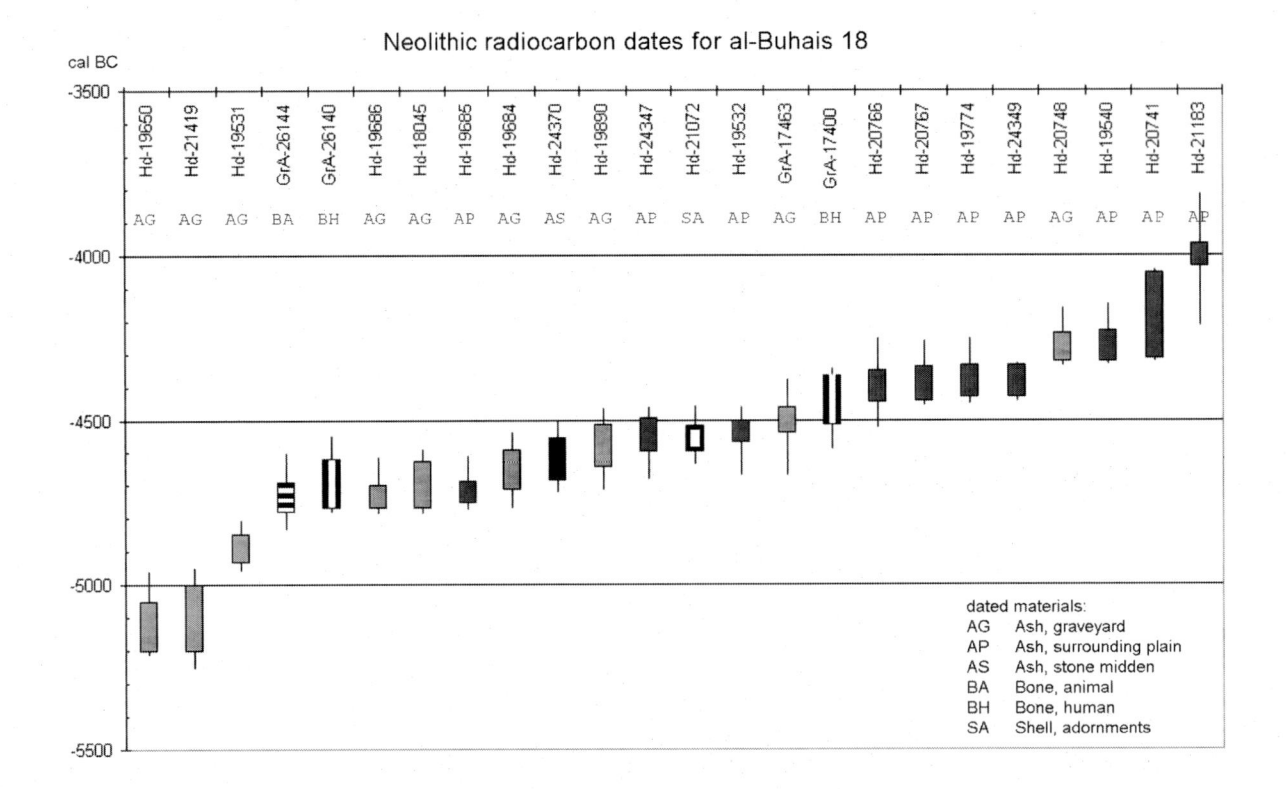

Figure 2. Calibrated radiocarbon dates for al-Buhais 18 (box indicating the 1σ-range and whiskers the 2σ-range of dates calibrated with CALIB 5).

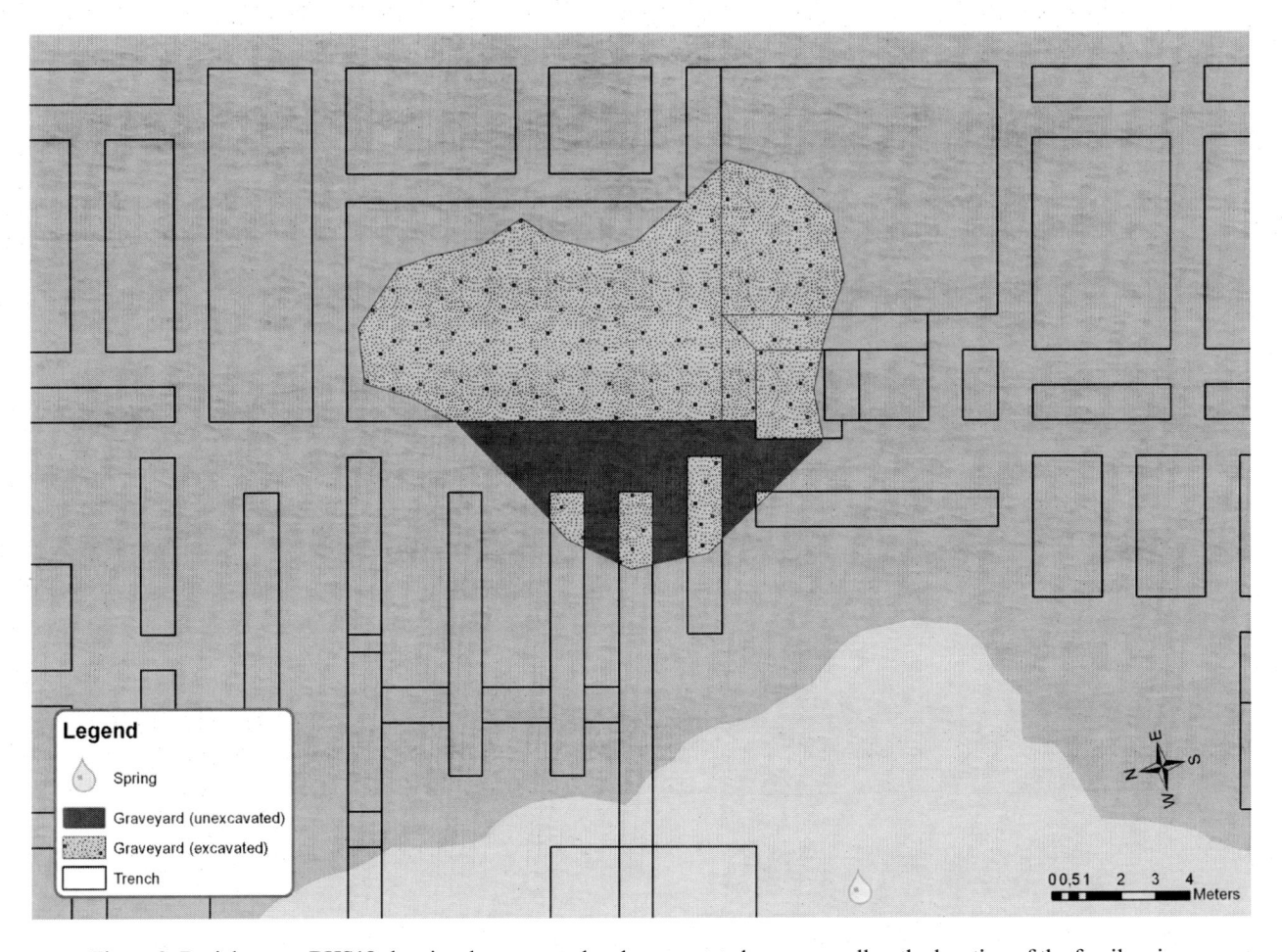

Figure 3. Burial area at BHS18 showing the excavated and unexcavated areas as well as the location of the fossil spring.

itself (Fig. 2). Dates on an ass bone and on ashes from the stone midden close to the graveyard are in the same time range, spanning the third and second quarter of the 5th millennium BC. Three dates on ashes from the deepest strata of the graveyard indicate earlier visits to the site itself. Two potentially later dates from fireplaces in the plain give evidence for later presence before the onset of the 4th millennium dry period, which marks the end of the Neolithic in this area. According to the distribution of radiocarbon dates the graveyard of BHS18 seems to have been used for about 500 years, around the middle of the 5th millennium BC. The Neolithic population was attracted to the site by a – nowadays fossil – spring at the slope, just above the graveyard. It can be assumed that the spot just below the spring was used as a graveyard in order to mark this important resource as some sort of possession of the respective group.

The human remains excavated at al-Buhais 18 until the year 2000 were studied by Henrike Kiesewetter (2006). The present author excavated and analysed the skeletons found during the following campaigns until 2005.[1] As visible in Figure 3, about 20% of the graveyard was left unexcavated in order to leave archaeological and anthropological remains *in situ* for possible future research with advanced methods of excavation and analysis. Nevertheless, the area used for burials can quite exactly be delimited, because exploration trenches were excavated in all directions around the grave field. They clearly show the borders of the graveyard and indicate that it was a well confined, more or less heart-shaped area. With an extension over a little more than 100 m² it was surprisingly small. The total number of interments at al-Buhais 18 can be estimated to about 660 by adding 20% to the minimum number of 549 actually excavated individuals. Obviously the burial ground was densely packed with c. 6.6 individuals per square meter, although there is no conceivable physical barrier against using a larger area of the immediate surroundings of the site.

One of the most important features of the site is the co-existence of primary and secondary burials. In a primary burial the body of the deceased is buried shortly after death, before decomposition of the soft tissues. The skeleton is then found in an articulated state, unless the remains were disturbed later by natural or human effects. Secondary burials are interments of more or less disarticulated skeletal remains of corpses that had decomposed somewhere else and were then (re)-buried. In al-Buhais 18 both types of burials occur as singular or less frequently as multiple interments which were found in unmarked grave pits. As later graves often disturbed earlier ones, the graves do not seem to have had durable markers in the Neolithic period as well.

The primary burials are always in a flexed position, and are more often placed on their right side than on their left side. In 113 skeletons out of 118 primary burials the side of the body on which they were laid could clearly be identified. Of these 84 are right-sided and 29 left-sided.

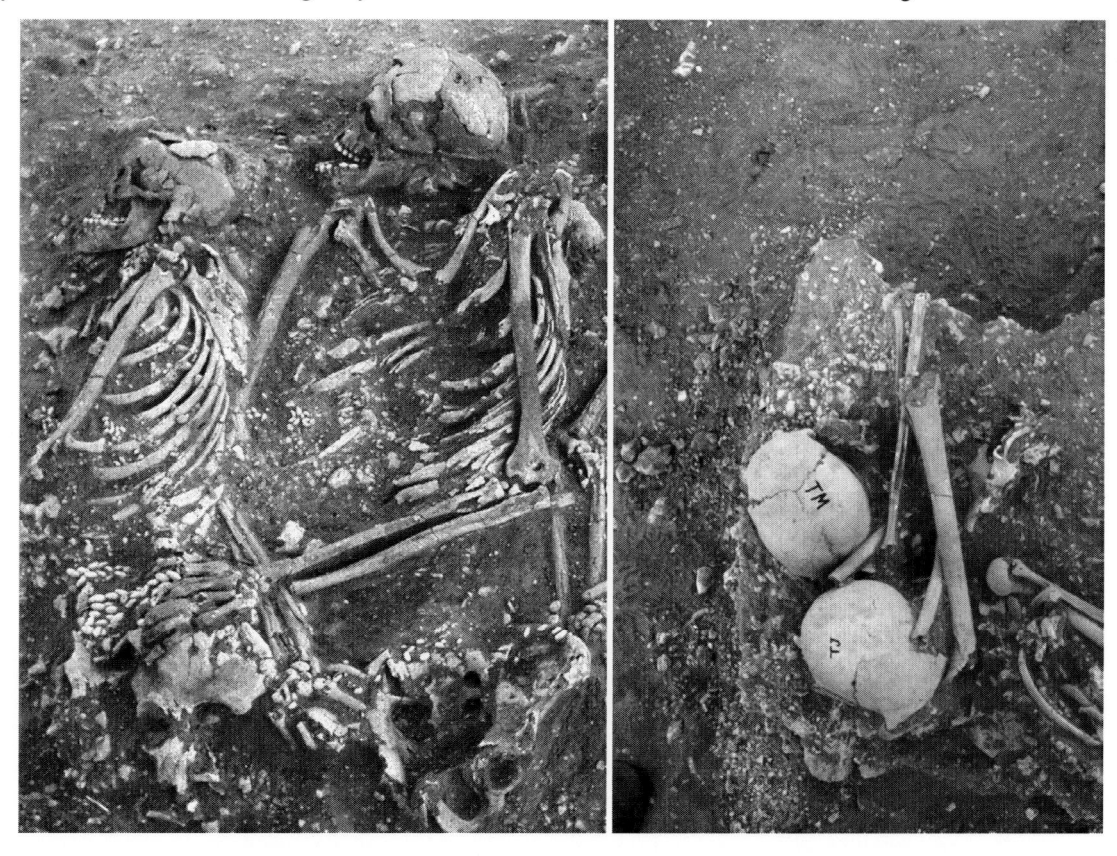

Figure 4. Examples of primary (left) and secondary (right) burials at BHS18.

---

[1] Thanks are due to M. Binder and N. Nicklisch who helped with recording the skeletons in 2003 and 2004.

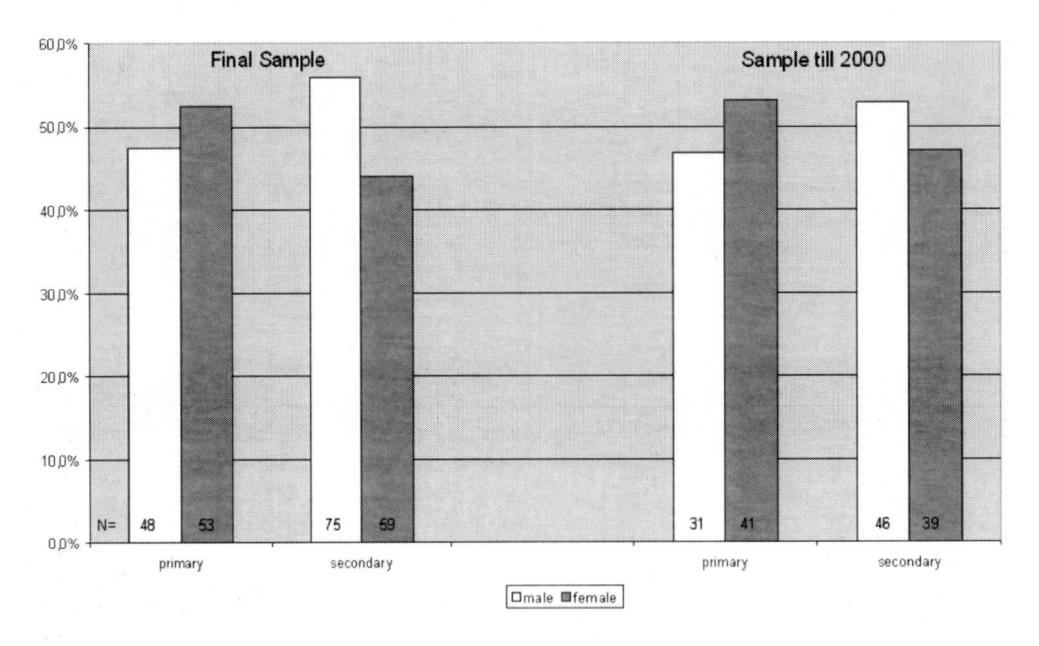

Figure 5: Ratio of males to females in primary and secondary burials at BHS18.

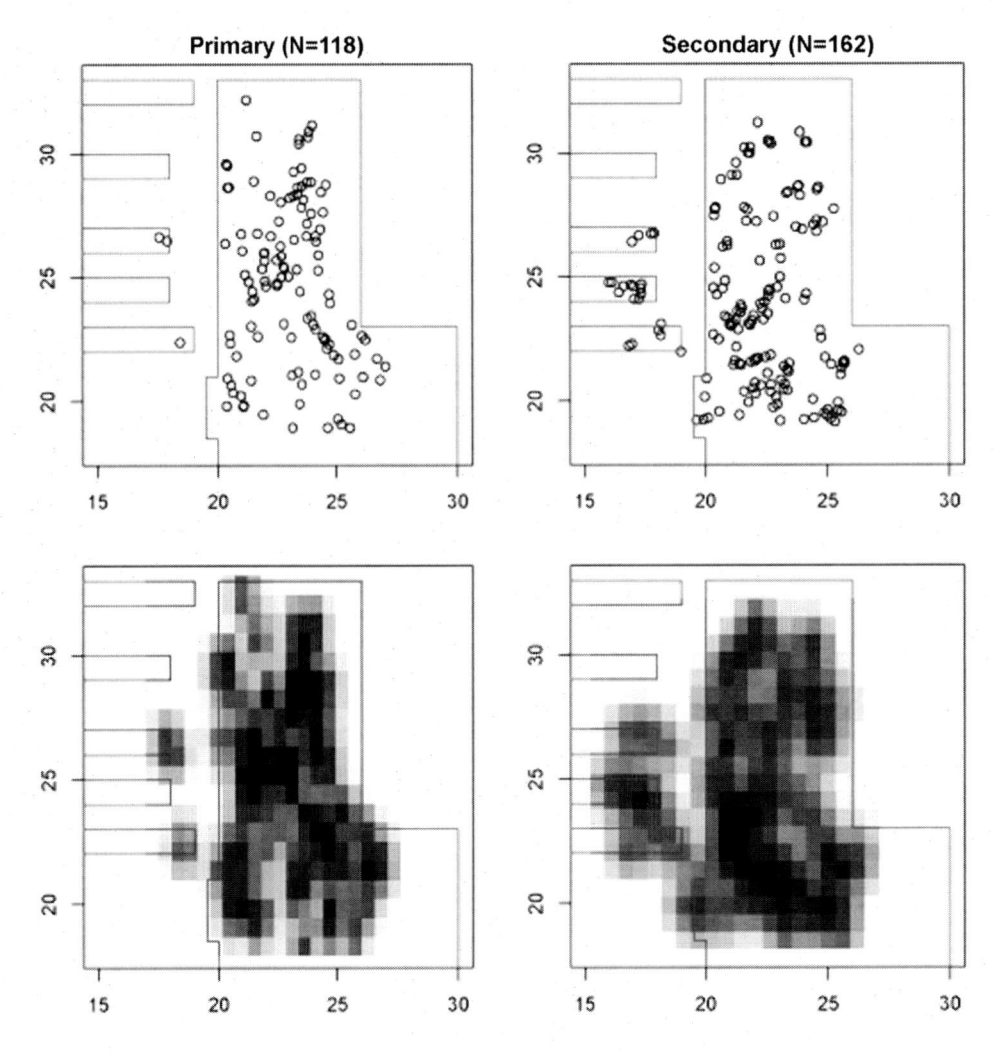

Figure 6: Density map of primary and secondary burials at BHS18 showing a higher density of secondary burials in the peripheral parts of the graveyard.

The head of a primary burial in al-Buhais 18 is normally oriented to the east. The arms are usually bent, sometimes with both hands in front of the face and sometimes with one hand in front of the face and the other near the knees. There are also some cases of multiple burials, where one arm is placed on the body of another individual (Fig. 4, left side) in an embrace. Up to five individuals were interred together in primary burials.

Secondary burials usually consist of a bundle of long bones with the skull placed on top, besides or in front of it (Fig. 4, right side). The small bones of hands and feet etc. are usually missing. In secondary burials the long bones and the skull are generally oriented east-west as well, with the face looking to the east. Here also up to five individuals could be found together in one grave-pit. In contrast to the primary burials, usually no grave goods were observed in the secondary ones.

There is an interesting demographic difference between primary and secondary burials, already indicated in the sample published by Kiesewetter (2006). Her results are altered to a certain degree when including the newly excavated skeletons. While the relation between slightly fewer males and some more females remains unchanged for the primary burials, the surplus of males in secondary burials increases remarkably in the total sample (Fig. 5). This is due to a higher density of secondary burials in the peripheral parts of the graveyard (Fig. 6) excavated after 2000. Thus, the change in the male-female relation is – at least partially – caused by the increased percentage of secondary burials in the total sample. Generally speaking, males seem to have had a better chance to be re-buried from a primary into a secondary burial.

It seems plausible that the primary burials represent individuals who died locally in the al-Buhais area. The interpretation of the secondary burials is, however, more difficult. Obviously the respective individuals had been buried somewhere in the first place, but it is largely unknown where this was. There are two general possibilities: On the one hand, they could have been brought to al-Buhais 18 from another site, but they might also have been re-excavated from another grave at the same graveyard. The latter assumption cannot totally be ruled out for BHS18, as there are indications for the re-excavation of burials in a particular corner of the site. This is an area at the southern edge of the graveyard, west of x=24m and north of y=16m. The natural sediments in this area are disturbed by irregular digging down to a depth of around 1m. Occasional splinters of human bone and dispersed finds of beads indicate that adorned primary burials were dug up and removed from this area. It is, however, not clear if these individuals were re-buried at al-Buhais or whether they were taken to other places.

One argument for secondary burials that were brought from elsewhere to Buhais is the sex-ratio mentioned before. As men were more often re-buried than females, a larger deficit of males should be expected among the primary burials at the site. Further evidence for an outside origin of the skeletal remains buried in secondary graves is given by the fact that non-local stones were found in the sediments associated to several of the secondary burials.

Figure 7: Secondary burial TG with some misplaced skeletal elements (e.g. the vertebral column and *Os sacrum*).

Figure 8: Hand of secondary burial of individual TG, holding a seashell.

One particular secondary burial is of major interest in this context. It does not look like a "typical" secondary burial, but rather like a primary burial at first sight. In fact, those who re-buried this and six neighbouring individuals apparently tried to make them look like primary burials by placing the skeletal elements more or less in anatomical order. All of them appear to be lying on their right side and one of them still has an intact ribcage. A closer view of the male individual TG shows the lower part of the vertebral column in anatomical order – but, as can be seen from the position of the *Os sacrum* – deposited upside down (Fig. 7). The long bones of arms and legs are also put more or less in the places were they would be found in a primary burial, but also often in reverse position. Obviously the corpse was in a state of partial decomposition when it was excavated from its primary interment. Therefore some skeletal parts were still connected by soft tissues while others were already disconnected.

The skeletal hand of individual TG held a seashell which he apparently already had in his hand when he was buried for the first time (Fig. 8). The sediment inside the shell still contains the small blue wadi-pebbles from its primary burial site. These bluish pebbles are also found in other parts of this burial, as well as in a number of other secondary burial pits. They indicate an origin from a primary grave somewhere in the *Hajar* Mountains, where ophiolite pebbles are the main components of wadi sediments. In addition, a small snail shell was found near the body. As there is no perforation or use-wear, this is not an adornment. Rather it is also part of the sediment in which the corpse was buried first, because it is from a freshwater snail, *Melanoides tuberculata*, still common in streams and ponds throughout the *Hajar* Mountains. The nearest mountain wadis with permanent streams are about 25 km away from al-Buhais as the crow flies. Thus, the skeletal remains of this individual – probably together with those of 6 others – were carried to al-Buhais from at least that distance. And they were not laid down there as typical secondary burials but in a way which mimics primary burials. What the people wanted to achieve by doing this is an interesting, but still open question.

These exceptional burials highlight the complexity of burial rites at that time and also indicate the advanced anatomical knowledge of the al-Buhais population. They also clearly show that these people had no fear of physical contact with the remains of their deceased. In this respect they are part of a long tradition in the Middle East starting in the Natufian of the Levant, where it was already common to re-bury skeletons in secondary burials (Bar-Yosef & Belfer-Cohen 1989: 164)

While the majority of secondary burials at al-Buhais can immediately be identified as such, there are also a few interments which cannot easily be called either primary or secondary. At least two skeletons were found in an extremely crouched position. A corpse in its flesh could not be bent and folded in that way. It rather seems that these corpses were buried as dry mummies after complete desiccation. Although anatomically intact, these skeletons do not wear personal adornments – reminding of the lack of such grave-gifts in secondary burials.

In conclusion the terms "primary" and "secondary" do not necessarily reflect the categories meant by the people who buried their deceased at al-Buhais. We are still far from understanding the meaning of the differences in burial rites which are behind the different forms of the observed interments.

Apart from cultural reasons there might also be more practical explanations for some of the complexity seen in secondary burials at al-Buhais: some of it might result from the variability of the landscapes used by the Neolithic herders during their seasonal cycles. While being in the higher parts of the mountains, it may have been difficult to find a place where a proper primary burial pit could have been dug. A rock crevice blocked with some boulders might have served as primary grave chamber there. Under the local climatic conditions a corpse left in such a cavity would become mummified, because its soft tissues would desiccate rather than decay. A dry wadi bed may also have retarded the decay of a corpse, so that its condition at re-excavation might have been as it was described for the man with the shell in his hand. Contrary to all other burials at al-Buhais 18, this particular grave (TG) contains objects other than adornments which have to be considered grave-goods. Not only the shell in his hand but also a ground adze-blade and a bone implement were found with this individual.

Comparable sites in SE-Arabia

In spite of the wealth of new information gathered at al-Buhais there remain many question marks around burial customs of the 5th millennium in SE-Arabia. Contemporary shell middens on the Gulf coast – like Jazirat al-Hamra in Ra's al-Khaimah or al-Madar (the former 'site 69') and RA 6 in Umm al-Qaiwain (Boucharlat et al. 1991: 68; Uerpmann M & Uerpmann H-P 1996: 127; for RA6 pers. comm. with Uerpmann H-P & Uerpmann M) – yielded some human remains from disturbed burials. They indicate a situation as in the small graveyard found at UAQ2 (Phillips 2002). This last site, also in Umm al-Qaiwain, has similarities with al-Buhais, but also with the 4th millennium graveyards on shell middens along the Omani coast – like those at Ra's al-Hamra (Salvatori 2007). We do not know if the lack of large graveyards at coastal sites of the 5th millennium in the Emirates only indicates insufficient research in this area, or if the regular burial grounds belonging to these sites were in the interior. There is some evidence that the nomadic inhabitants of al-Buhais may have lived at the coast for part of the year. One cannot rule out the possibility that at least some of the secondary burials represent people who died at coastal sites. But even if this is the case, al-Buhais 18 cannot have been the only large 5th millennium graveyard in the Emirates.

A site similar to al-Buhais 18 seems to have been found – less than 20 km away – at the northern end of Jebel Faya near the mouth of a wadi. At this site, called FAY- NE15, a triple primary burial was excavated in 2006. The way of interment has similarities with al-Buhais 18 insofar as the corpses lie on their left side with the heads oriented towards the east (Fig. 9). At least two of them seem to be placed in each other's arms as could be observed in several multiple primary graves at al-Buhais. The adornments found with this burial also closely resemble those from al-Buhais. Other analogies are a radiocarbon date of the adjacent settlement area, which is in the range of the al-Buhais dates, as well as the fact that both sites are situated close to a fossil spring and in an area at the interface between mountain and plain close to important sources of flint raw material (Kutterer & de Beauclair 2008).

Figure 9: Detail of the burial at Fay-NE15, showing two of the skulls with associated adornments.

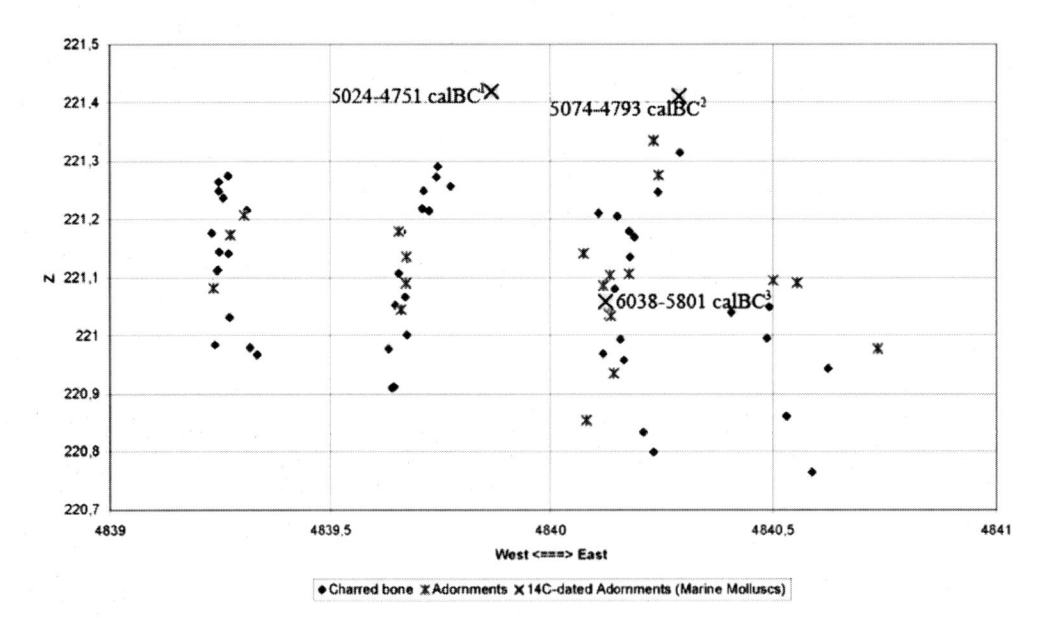

Figure 10: Distribution of charred bone, adornments and ^{14}C-dates in Fay-NE10 (1: 6665±45; 2: 6710±45; 3: 7714±59 bp)

A general similarity of burial customs with what was described for al-Buhais is seen at the later sites of the 4th millennium BC along the mountainous coast of north-eastern Oman. The co-existence of primary and secondary burials is repeated there, as well as their fairly strict orientation to easterly directions. Differences consist in more elaborate grave constructions and in the existence of obvious grave-gifts apart from personal adornments. In the graves at Ra's al-Hamra 5 (RH 5), the best studied site in this respect, special molluscs as well as skulls and carapaces of turtles are mentioned. "Trophies" from exceptional animals obtained by hunting and fishing also seem to have been deposited in some graves (Uerpmann H-P & Uerpmann M 2003: 187, 209, 260). These differences may be due to increased sedentism based on the predominant exploitation of marine resources (Uerpmann H-P & Uerpmann M 2003: 163-251). The mountainous coast of north-eastern Oman provided natural conditions where Neolithic economy could survive the dryness of the fourth millennium BC and where the basic burial customs of this period seem to have persisted into the 4th and – at the site Wadi Shab GAS1 – apparently into the beginning of the 3rd millennium BC (Gaultier et al. 2005; Usai & Cavallari 2008).

Considerations about earlier burial customs

While the aforementioned archaeological activities along the Omani coast provide insight into burial customs of the final Neolithic in SE-Arabia, comparable knowledge on the periods preceding al-Buhais 18 is not available. Even the chronological structure of these earlier parts of the Neolithic is still less clear (Charpentier 2008; Uerpmann M forthcoming; Uerpmann H-P & Uerpmann M forthcoming), because stratigraphic observations have only been made very recently. Sites at Jebel Faya in the central region of the Sharjah Emirate are again of crucial importance. At the site called FAY-NE 1, less than 1 km south of FAY-NE15 (Figure 1), a stratigraphic sequence through Palaeolithic and into Neolithic layers was discovered – unfortunately without preservation of human or animal bones. At the site FAY-NE10, situated between NE 1 and NE15, a small flint workshop of the Middle Neolithic was discovered underneath early historic and late prehistoric layers (Uerpmann M et al. 2008). A deep sounding, made at FAY-NE10 in 2007, was dug on two m^2 with 8 subsquares of 50x50 cm and spits of a depth of about 2.5cm in the northern part of the cave. Numerous fragments of charred or calcinated bone were found in all 8 subsquares of the deep sounding, distributed over a depth of more than 50 cm (Fig. 10). Apart from the bone fragments there are only flints and a number of small perforated marine snail-shell-beads from these layers (comp. de Beauclair, this volume). Two samples of the burned bones from different depths and separate squares were thin-sectioned and examined microscopically in the bone lab at Tübingen and identified as human by the author in collaboration with J. Wahl.[2] This identification was cross-checked and confirmed by G. Grupe and S. Doppler at the Bio-Centrum in Munich. All in all, there seems to be a thick deposit of sediments in the small cave, which is rich in small burnt bone fragments – apparently all from humans.[3]

Although not much can be said at the present state of research, the deposit of cremated human remains at FAY-NE10 is certainly not from an accidental incineration of a single human corpse. It rather indicates a prolonged use of this little cave for the deposition of human "ashes". Up

---

[2] Thanks are due to J. Kutterer and B. Ligouis for the preparation of thin sections and digital images.

[3] Further lab research on these finds has been agreed upon by Profs. H.-P Uerpmann (Tübingen) and G. Grupe (Munich).

to now there is only one radiocarbon date from the middle of the respective layers measured on one of the perforated marine snail shells (Fig. 10). It yielded a date of 7714 ± 59bp (Hd-26062). Calibrated cautiously with a reservoir correction of 300±100 years, this date comes to 6038-5801 years cal BC, thus falling into the end of the 7th or the beginning of the 6th millennium BC. Radiocarbon dates from the top of the Middle Neolithic layer are much younger and contemporary with the beginning of human presence at al-Buhais. The vertical distance of less than 40cm between these dates indicates a fairly low rate of sedimentation at FAY-NE10. Therefore it seems possible that the layers with incinerated human bones accumulated during quite a long period beginning before 6000 BC and ending after 5500 BC. The cremations reported for Tell el-Kerkh in Syria (Arosio & Meozzi 2008) are later and not comparable to the cremations seen at FAY-NE10 because there larger skeletal parts are still preserved. Such observations were also made in Neolithic burials in Qatar (Hublin et al. 1988), RH5 (Santini 2002) and to a lesser degree also at al-Buhais 18 (Kiesewetter 2006: 120). The highly burned and dispersed bone fragments from Fay-NE10 have up to now no parallels in the region. With regard to the topic of this paper one could say that these fragments of microscopically identified human bones from Jebel Faya have opened a completely new window on early burial customs in SE-Arabia.

References

Arosio P. & Meozzi D. 2008. Stone Pages Archaeo News: Cremation site unearthed in Syria. Available at: http://www.stonepages.com/news/archives/002971.html [Accessed January 27, 2009].

Bar-Yosef O. & Belfer-Cohen A. 1989. The origins of sedentism and farming communities in the Levant. *Journal of World Prehistory* 3/4: 447-498.

Boucharlat R., Haerinck E., Phillips C.S. & Potts D.T. 1991. Note on an Ubaid-pottery site in the Emirate of Umm al-Qaiwain. *Arabian Archaeology and Epigraphy* 2/2: 65-71.

Charpentier V. 2008. Hunter-gatherers of the "empty quarter of the early Holocene" to the last Neolithic societies: chronology of the late prehistory of south-eastern Arabia (8000–3100 BC). *Proceedings of the Seminar for Arabian Studies* 38: 93-116.

Gaultier M., Guy H., Munoz O., Tosi M. & Usai D. 2005. Settlement structures and cemetery at Wadi Shab-GAS1, Sultanate of Oman: Report on the 2002 and 2003 field seasons. *Arabian Archaeology and Epigraphy* 16/1: 1-20.

Hublin J.J., Tillier A.M. & Vandermeersch, B. 1988. Etude du squelette humain découvert a Khor (Qatar). Pages 185-194 in M. L. Inizan (ed.), *Mission archéologique française à Qatar tome 2*. Paris: Éditions Recherche sur les Civilisations.

Kiesewetter H. 2006. Funeral monuments and human remains from Jebel Al-Buhais. Pages 103-380 in H.-P. Uerpmann, M. Uerpmann, & S. A. Jasim (eds.), *Funeral Monuments and Human Remains from Jebel Al-Buhais. The Archaeology of Jebel al-Buhais, Volume 1*. Tübingen: Department of Culture and Information Government of Sharjah United Arab Emirates/Kerns Verlag.

Kutterer A. & de Beauclair R. 2008. FAY-NE15 – another Neolithic graveyard in the central region of the Sharjah Emirate? *Arabian Archaeology and Epigraphy* 19/2: 134-143.

Phillips C. 2002. Prehistoric middens and a cemetery from the southern Arabian Gulf. Pages 169-186 in S. Cleuziou, M. Tosi, & J. Zarins (eds), *Essays on the Late Prehistory of the Arabian Peninsula*. Rome: Instituto Italiano per L'Africa e L'Oriente. Serie Orientale Roma XCIII.

Salvatori S. 2007. The prehistoric necropolis at Ra's al Hamra 5 (Muscat - Oman). *Journal of Oman Studies* 14.

Santini G. 2002. Burial Complex 43 in the RH-5 prehistoric graveyard at Ra's al-Hamra, northern Oman. Pages 147-168 in S. Cleuziou, M. Tosi, & J. Zarins (eds), *Essays on the Late Prehistory of the Arabian Peninsula*. Rome: Instituto Italiano per L'Africa e L'Oriente. Serie Orientale Roma XCIII.

Uerpmann H.-P. & Uerpmann M. 2003. *The Capital Area of Northern Oman: Stone Age Sites and their Natural Environment*. Part 3. Beihefte zum Tübinger Atlas des Vorderen Orients. Reihe A (Naturwissenschaften), Nr. 31/3. Wiesbaden: Dr. Ludwig Reichert.

Uerpmann H.-P. & Uerpmann M. 2009. Early Fishers and Herders: The Neolithic Period in the UAE. In P. Jayanti (ed.), *New Perspectives on Recording UAE History*. Abu Dhabi: National Center for Documentation and Research.

Uerpmann M. Forthcoming. The Holocene Stone Age in southeast Arabia – a reconsideration. In Conard, N. J., Meadow, R.H. & Morales, A. (eds), *Archaeology and Human Ecology in Southwestern Asia. Contributions in Honour of Hans-Peter Uerpmann*. Tübingen.

Uerpmann M. & Uerpmann H.-P. 1996. 'Ubaid pottery in the eastern Gulf - new evidence from Umm al-Qaiwain (U.A.E.). *Arabian Archaeology and Epigraphy* 7/2: 125-139.

Uerpmann M. & Uerpmann H.-P. 2008. Neolithic faunal remains from al-Buhais 18 (Sharjah, UAE). Pages 97-132 in H.-P. Uerpmann, M. Uerpmann, & S. A. Jasim (eds), *The Natural Environment of Jebel Al-Buhais: Past and present. The Archaeology of Jebel al-Buhais, Volume 2*. Tübingen: Department of Culture and Information Government of Sharjah United Arab Emirates/Kerns Verlag.

Uerpmann M., Uerpmann H.-P. & Händel M. 2008. Lithic resources and their procurement at and around Jebel al-Buhais and Jebel al-Faya. Pages 53-70 in H.-P. Uerpmann, M. Uerpmann, & S. A. Jasim (eds), *The Natural Environment of Jebel Al-Buhais: Past and present The Archaeology of Jebel al-Buhais, Volume 2*. Tübingen: Department of Culture and Information Government of Sharjah United Arab Emirates/Kerns Verlag.

Uerpmann M., Uerpmann H.-P. & Jasim S.A. 2006. Früher Wüstennomadismus auf der Arabischen

Halbinsel. Pages 87-103 in S. R. Hauser (ed.), *Die Sichtbarkeit von Nomaden und saisonaler Besiedlung in der Archäologie, multidisziplinäre Annäherungen an ein methodisches Problem*. Halle: Mitteilungen des SFB 9, Orientwissenschaftliche Hefte.

Usai D. & Cavallari A. 2008. The lithic industry of Wadi Shab, a Middle Holocene site on the coast of Oman. *Arabian Archaeology and Epigraphy* 19/2: 121-133.

Author's Address
Adelina U. Kutterer
Zentrum für Naturwissenschaftliche Archäologie
Institut für Ur- und Frühgeschichte und Archäologie des Mittelalters
Rümelinstraße 23
72070 Tübingen
Germany
adelina.kutterer@uni-tuebingen.de

Ornamental objects as a source of information on Neolithic burial practices at al-Buhais 18, UAE and neighbouring sites

Roland de Beauclair

Summary

The Neolithic site of al-Buhais 18 (Sharjah, United Arab Emirates) has yielded a large number of ornamental objects (pierced molluscs, stone and shell beads). Many of these have been found in a secure funerary context, thus offering a starting point for the investigation of burial practices through the analysis of jewellery use. An important result of this analysis is the observation that the frequency and style of decoration depended on the age of the deceased. The data are also used to investigate jewellery use in burials in relation to its use by living members of the Neolithic community. Based on these results, some hypotheses are developed on the intentions and beliefs structuring mortuary practices and the role of jewellery as one element in the passage from the living to the dead. Additionally, recent findings of ornamental objects from two other Neolithic sites in the same area are presented and discussed: FAY-NE15, which is thought to be contemporary to al-Buhais 18, and FAY-NE10, which predates it.

Keywords: Neolithic; al-Buhais 18; funerary practices; personal adornments; marine shells

Introduction

From its discovery in 1995, the site of al-Buhais 18 (BHS18, Emirate of Sharjah, UAE) with its cemetery, campsites and ancient spring and with its ample evidence for a mobile pastoralist system in the 5th millennium BC has profoundly changed our understanding of the Neolithic of south-eastern Arabia. Final publication of the project is in progress, with two volumes already available (Uerpmann, Uerpmann & Jasim 2006; Uerpmann, Uerpmann & Jasim 2008). Results of the excavations are also summarized by A. Kutterer (this volume).

In this paper, I would like to focus on results coming from the analysis of ornamental objects from BHS18. I also intend to show some approaches to better understand the significance of jewellery in burial practices. The recent discovery of several other Neolithic sites in the same area, which also yielded some ornamental objects, opens up the possibility to study additional aspects of jewellery use. In the last part of this paper, preliminary findings from the contemporary site of FAY-NE15 and the older site of FAY-NE10 are presented and discussed.

On Costume and Customs

The excavation of more than 500 buried individuals at al-Buhais 18 has brought to light large quantities of ornamental objects. They were found mainly in the context of primary burials, whereas secondary burials contained very few such objects. This association of ornamental objects with primary burials offers a starting point for the investigation of burial practices through the analysis of jewellery use.

Altogether, more than 24,000 ornamental objects were recovered. Among them are pierced molluscs of different species and pearls, but also beads with artificial shapes, e.g. disc beads, tubular beads or barrel shaped beads. Many of these beads are also made of shell, others of dark soft stone and, less frequently, of other stones including calcite and carnelian.

In many cases, it was possible to reconstruct how these objects were combined and worn as pieces of jewellery or 'ornamental ensembles'. Popular ensembles include head decorations, earrings, facial decorations, necklaces, pendants, hip decorations, and bracelets.

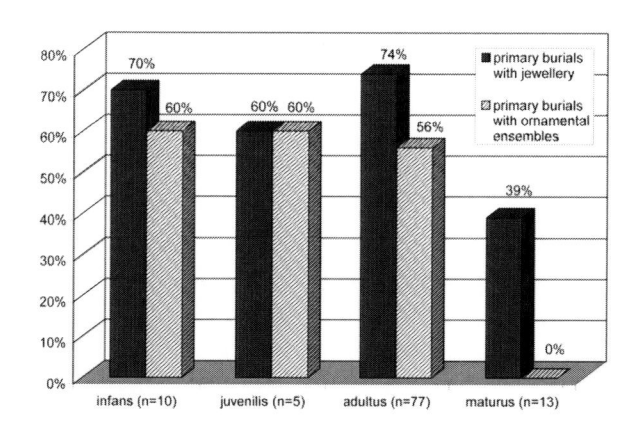

Figure 1. Jewellery frequency relative to age at BHS18.

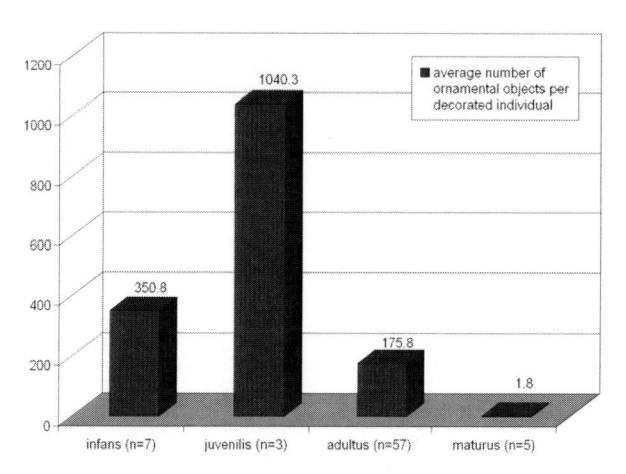

Figure 2. Jewellery quantity relative to age at BHS18.

Detailed presentations of the material and an analysis of the patterns and rules related to jewellery use have been given previously (de Beauclair 2005, de Beauclair 2005-2008 [2009], de Beauclair 2008, de Beauclair, Jasim, and

Uerpmann 2006). An important result was the discovery that jewellery use depended on the age of the deceased, whereas gender distinctions were only minor. Age data was available for 105 individuals from primary burials. They were grouped into four age classes: *infans* (0-14 years), *juvenilis* (15-19y.); *adultus* (20-40y.), and *maturus* (>40y). The proportions of decorated individuals (Fig. 1) are relatively stable for children, adolescents and adults, but markedly lower for mature individuals. This pattern appears even more clearly when looking at individuals with recognizable ornamental ensembles, which have not been reported from a single mature individual. Similarly, those mature individuals which were decorated only had a minimal number of beads (Fig. 2). From this perspective, the opulent decoration of children and adolescents becomes evident, even though the high average value for adolescents must be attributed to one extremely rich burial and the fact that this class only consists of three individuals.

Differences between age classes were also observed regarding preferred bead types: disc and tubular beads were very popular for children and also adolescents. For adults and especially mature individuals, pierced molluscs were preferred to the expense of beads types with an artificial shape. Finally, the age of the deceased also influenced shell size: small varieties were often chosen for children and youths. Small and big shells are balanced in adults between 20 and 40 years, and big specimens were preferred for older people.

Adorning the Dead and the Living

For an understanding of the meaning of jewellery in funerary practices, it is essential to know whether it played a similar role during the life of the al-Buhais people. It is possible that personal adornments were not important at all in daily life, or that they were used for different means according to different rules. This question arises regularly in the study of burial contexts, and it is not easy to answer. Four lines of reasoning are presented here, in the form of hypotheses, which are considered helpful for this problem.

"Typical burials"

This hypothesis is based on the observation that there were cultural rules governing the deposition of bodies. One of these rules is the placing of the primary burials on their right side. Another is the cranial orientation towards the east. However, these rules were not absolute, and in both cases there is a certain percentage of differing burials (about 25 percent). They are referred to as 'atypical burials' in this context. We cannot know for sure whether these atypical burials are evidence of a certain *laissez-faire* concerning burial rites, or whether in fact different rules were applied, but rules nonetheless. The following analysis is based on the first assumption.

Furthermore, if this neglect of burial rites could be linked to a relative scarcity of ornamental objects, this would be seen as an indication that the presence of jewellery was determined more by burial rites than by secular use. On the other hand, if jewellery was predominantly relevant during life, e.g. as a social or ethnic marker, both typical and atypical burials should be equipped with jewellery in a similar way.

The percentage of burials with jewellery is slightly higher in right-sided burials, but this is by no means statistically significant. The same is true for the frequency of ornamental ensembles. However, the mean number of beads per decorated individual varies markedly, being higher (227 pieces) in right-sided burials than in left-sided ones (144). This could indicate a preferred use of jewellery in 'typical burials', but the case is weak since the high number of beads is mainly due to two exceptionally rich individuals.

In the analysis of body orientation, neither the percentage of decorated individuals nor the number of beads per decorated individual indicate a special status of the eastern orientation. Only the proportion of individuals with ornamental ensembles indicates a preference of 'typical burials', but again, the values are not statistically significant.

Therefore, no clear preferential treatment of typical burials and vice versa no discrimination against atypical burials can be noted. According to the premises stated above this could mean two things: either the 'atypical' burials are in fact not atypical but rather the result of specific rules implying the same degree of care and importance for these burials as for the ones lying on their right side or oriented to the east. Or alternatively, the amount and frequency of jewellery in the grave is not determined by the burial rites but rather by some other, independent, cause, presumably lying in the realm of the living population.

Anatomical positions of adornments

The second hypothesis builds on the assumption that if jewellery is used only in burial rites, the objects could be placed anywhere on the body of the deceased. In other words: if the objects are all placed in ways which would also make sense for living people, it is very likely that, in fact, the objects were used in life and not exclusive and reserved for use in funerary rites.

The vast majority of ornamental objects or ensembles are positioned on the bodies of the deceased in such a way that the objects could be worn in life. There are only very few possible exceptions. Semi-perforated beads, 41 of which have been recovered, don't fall into this category, as they seemingly were worn on the upper lip and at the ears. The dominance of life-like positions of jewellery is strong evidence that ornamental objects were not used solely in burial rites. However, this does not tell us whether jewellery was worn in everyday life or reserved for special occasions, like initiations, marriages or other ceremonies.

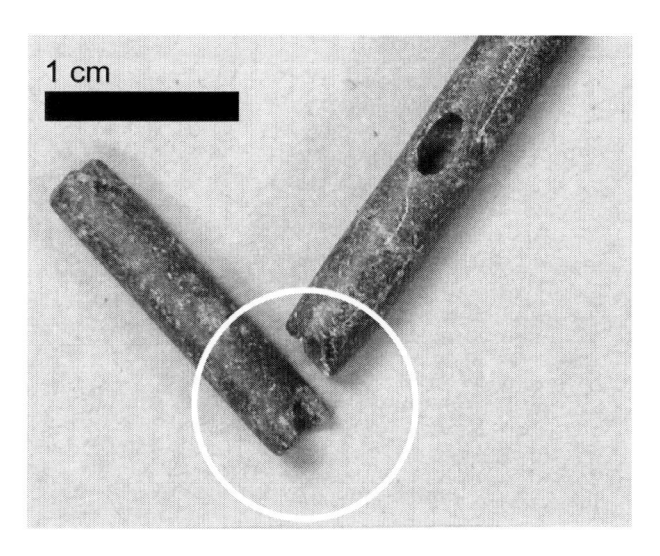

Figure 3. Tubular beads with damaged ends (Find no. 53767).

Signs of use

This hypothesis states very simply that if the ornamental objects were worn in daily life, signs of use wear should be visible. Lacking a microwear analysis, only a few macroscopic observations can be noted. First, some tubular beads made of serpentinite are damaged at their ends in a way that reminds of them being worn on a string for some time (Fig. 3).

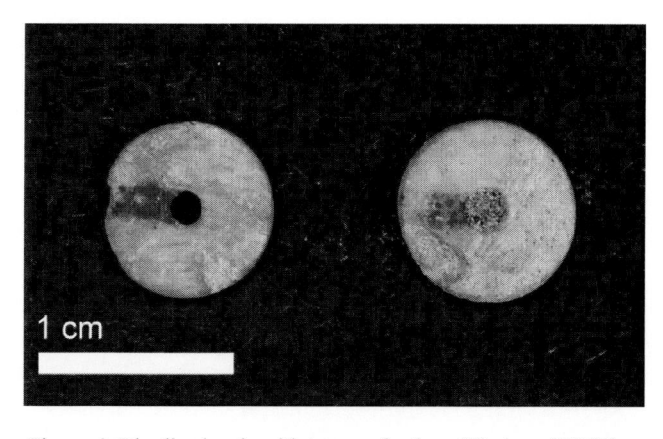

Figure 4. Big disc beads with traces of colour (Find no. 75167).

Another indication for the use of ornamental objects over a longer period of time may be seen in 18 disc beads with colour residues (Fig. 4). The regular pattern of red streaks must be the result of continuous friction between a coloured string and the bead. The colour would not have been transferred onto the beads if the garment was never worn by a living person.

These two observations only concern very few objects, but nonetheless they can serve as an indication for an everyday use of at least some types of beads. On the other hand, if jewellery was used widely in the daily life of the prehistoric nomads, more signs of use wear would have to be expected.

Beads in the living area

It is fortunate that the site of al-Buhais 18 consists not only of the graveyard but also of other functional zones, including areas with fireplaces which are interpreted as remnants of camps. Radiocarbon dates (see Kutterer, this volume) show that this living area and the graveyard are contemporary, although occupation of the living area may have started earlier.

The last hypothesis makes use of ornamental objects from this area. As there are no workshops or other concentrations of ornamental objects, the pieces found there are considered lost objects. If beads were only used in funerary contexts, there should be the same bead types both in burials and in the living area. If, however, the latter area produces a different picture, this must be the result of a different use of jewellery there.

A total of 1,152 stray finds, hardly 5 percent of all ornamental objects, have been found outside the graveyard boundary. In relation to the assumed period of site use of several centuries, these are surprisingly few objects. If jewellery was worn regularly, it is very likely that more beads would have been lost in the sand, as a result of broken beads or strings. This is a strong indication that personal ornament was not used widely in everyday life. On the other hand, the frequency of bead types shows remarkable differences between the two functional zones. Pierced molluscs, namely *Polinices* and *Veneridae* are much more important in the living area than in the graveyard. Disc beads give an ambiguous picture: while small disc beads are rare, the big subtype is relatively frequent in the living area. Finally, none of the 114 barrel-shaped beads comes from this part of the site.

All this shows that jewellery was not reserved for the dead. But apparently, jewellery use in life was limited and followed different styles or rules. One possible explanation might be that jewellery was worn by living members of the community, but not in everyday life. Instead, personal ornaments may have been reserved for use on certain important occasions, maybe in the course of ceremonies or *rites de passage* like coming of age, marriage or, obviously, death. Or, jewellery was used in everyday life, but in a more simple style with a predominance of pierced molluscs and disc beads.

On the role of jewellery in burial rites

This brings us to the question of the function and importance of jewellery in the course of the funerary rites or beyond. In the preceding section, it has been demonstrated that the use of jewellery for the dead does not mirror its use in the living community. The observation that burials of children and adolescents were provided with at least as much jewellery as those of adults shows that the main function of jewellery probably was not the display of acquired status or wealth, because in this case, the amount of jewellery should augment with the age of the deceased. The almost complete absence of jewellery in secondary burials also points in the same direction. If the aim was to document wealth, jewellery could have been added to the bone piles of the secondary burials as well.

Adornments in burials cannot be interpreted as a personal possession either. If people accumulated their personal sets of jewellery in the course of their lives, older individuals would wear the same adornments as younger ones, perhaps complemented by additional objects. This is in contrast to the actual observations at BHS18, where different styles of jewellery can be observed in relation to age, and burials of mature individuals are characterised by their poorness in adornment.

All these observations lead me to think of jewellery as having its place in the process of burial, in some sort of *rite de passage* (Van Gennep 1986: 142-159). Community members would decorate the dead for the passage. After completion of the burial process, jewellery may have lost its importance. This would explain the absence of jewellery in secondary burials. However, the concept of rites of passage does not explain why the dead at al-Buhais 18 were decorated so differently depending on their age. An observation noted by the ethnographer Robert Hertz (Hertz 1907: 134) could give an idea on this subject: possibly the untimely death of a child or adolescent would have caused greater anxiety in the community and required a more lavish burial than the death of an old person whose life had been accomplished.

Beyond al-Buhais 18: FAY-NE15

While the wealth of material of BHS18 remains unchallenged, ornamental objects have also come to light recently in two Neolithic sites around Jebel Faya, just 20 km north of BHS18 in a similar topographic setting. At Jebel Faya NE-15 (FAY-NE15), which seems to be contemporaneous to BHS18, three individuals buried together in a multiple burial were found during a limited exploration excavation (Kutterer & de Beauclair 2008). They were adorned with an important number of ornamental objects. In total, 949 pieces were recovered, which show a remarkable similarity to the finds from BHS18 and fit perfectly into the classificatory system developed for the latter site.

Ancilla, disc beads and tubular beads are the most important types at both sites. No new types appear that have not been recorded at BHS18. Some types are missing, but these are rare types even at al-Buhais with a much bigger assemblage. Tubular beads occur in almost equal numbers in the white and the dark variety. This balance is known again from the BHS18 material, and their use in a similar alternating pattern is attested, too. Even the mean diameter of the beads is almost identical with BHS18, and lies at 4.4 mm.

But there are also some differences. For example, while at BHS18 two size classes of *Ancilla* are present, only the small variety occurs at FAY-NE15. And in tubular beads, long specimens are more frequent. With the diameter being the same, this leads to a more slender appearance of the tubular beads from FAY-NE15. It can be concluded that the type set of ornamental objects is identical at FAY-NE15 and BHS18. It is only within these types that different preferences can sometimes be observed concerning the size of objects.

What are the implications of these observations for the relationship between both sites? Given a radiocarbon date of a fireplace close to the graves at FAY-NE15 in the early fifth millennium B.C., simultaneous to the main occupation of al-Buhais 18, the similarity in ornamental objects could be seen as an indication that we are dealing with only one group which frequented both sites. This could be seen as part of the pattern of mobility of this nomadic population. However, our interpretation of BHS18 as a central burial place does not fit well with this scenario. Bodies were brought to al-Buhais from as far away as the Hajar Mountains, therefore it seems unlikely that the same group would have maintained a second burial place so close to the central graveyard.

Another possibility, which can also only be tested with the help of direct radiocarbon dates of the graves to be obtained in the future, is that the slight deviations of the Faya beads from those of BHS18 in fact indicate a difference in chronology. The sites may have been occupied successively, the second one being used after the first one had to be given up. However, the fact that both sites are in very similar ecological settings would make it unlikely that in a situation of environmental deterioration, one site would offer markedly better conditions than the other thus leading to a small-scale shift in mobility patterns.

Finally, the differences between the beads – slight as they are – could be an indication for differing habits between related, but nevertheless different groups. Two groups with the same cultural background could have been present in this area to exploit the natural resources such as flint outcrops and watering places for their animals. They may have been in contact, and skeletal evidence from BHS18 seems to show that this contact was not always friendly (Kiesewetter 2006: 190-193), maybe as a result of competition over limited resources. Ornamental objects in this context could have been used as a marker of identity – and the slight differences noted could have to do with this message.

Type	n FAY-NE10
Ancilla cf. *farsiana*	8
Engina mendicaria	1
Polinices mammilla	11
Dentalium	3
Disc beads	1
Total	**24**

Table 1. Ornamental objects from FAY-NE10.

Before al-Buhais 18: FAY-NE10

Yet another site, FAY-NE10, a rockshelter on the eastern slope of Jebel Faya, puts us in the position to learn more about the temporal depth of south-east Arabian jewellery tradition. Neolithic layers predating the occupation of BHS18 have been found (Kutterer, this volume). From these layers, 24 dispersed ornamental objects were recovered in the 2007 field season (Table 1).

Obviously, the very high proportion of molluscs is remarkable. With *Ancilla* cf. *farsiana*, *Engina mendicaria* and *Polinices mammilla*, three gastropod species are present which also constitute the three main species in the BHS18 material. Apart from these, three pieces of *Dentalium* were found, two fragments and one complete shell (17.9 mm long). This is especially noteworthy because *Dentalium*, although a popular ornamental object throughout prehistory, is totally absent from both BHS18 and FAY-NE15.

Another interesting observation is the very small size of most gastropods: *Polinices* from FAY-NE10 have a length of 3.0 to 7.4 mm, with a mean value of 5.3 mm, whereas the mean at BHS18 lies at 14.4mm. Similarly, *Ancilla* measures 5.2 to 6.9mm with a mean value of 6.2mm, which corresponds to the smallest specimens from BHS18 (size distribution with two peaks at 9.5mm and 15.5mm). Only the single *Engina* shell is relatively big (length 11.9mm). Despite their small size, all gastropod shells were pierced, with only one exception. Apart from these molluscs, only one disc bead (diameter 5.6mm) made of light green stone has been found.

Thus, many bead types known from BHS18 are missing at FAY-NE10. Even though the very small sample from FAY-NE10 does not permit secure interpretations yet, it seems likely that bead types like shell disc beads, tubular beads or barrel shaped beads were either not yet current in the times preceding the occupation of al-Buhais 18 or they were not yet used in burial contexts. Whether this reflects cultural choices, advances in production technique, or a widening of trade networks, must remain an open question for now.

The same is true when it comes to the use of these ornamental objects on the site. With the identification of burnt human bones, cremations are attested for the first time in this period in south-eastern Arabia (Kutterer, this volume). At present, we cannot tell whether the ornamental objects were also exposed to fire. The analysis of this question would allow to differentiate between the possible use of ornamental objects in funerary practices and a more secular use in the life of the people who frequented FAY-NE10 in the Early Neolithic.

References

de Beauclair R. 2005. *Seashells in the Desert. A Study of Personal Adornments from the Neolithic Graveyard of al-Buhais 18, Sharjah, U.A.E.* Unpublished MA Thesis, Eberhard Karls Universität Tübingen.

de Beauclair R. 2005-2008 [2009]. La parure funéraire de la nécropole néolithique de Jebel al-Buhais 18 (Émirats Arabes Unis). *Préhistoire Anthropologie Méditerranéennes* 14: 39-52.

de Beauclair R. 2008. Funerary rites in a Neolithic nomad community in Southeastern Arabia: the case of al-Buhais 18. *Documenta Praehistorica* 35: 143-152.

de Beauclair R., Jasim S.A. & Uerpmann H.-P. 2006. New results on the Neolithic jewellery from al-Buhais 18, UAE. *Proceedings of the Seminar for Arabian Studies* 36: 175-187.

Hertz R. 1907. Contribution à une étude sur la représentation collective de la mort. *L'année sociologique* 10: 48-137.

Kiesewetter H. 2006. Analyses of the Human Remains from the Neolithic Cemetery at al-Buhais 18 (Excavations 1996-2000). Pages 103-380 in H.-P. Uerpmann, M. Uerpmann & S.A. Jasim (eds), *Funeral Monuments and Human Remains from Jebel al-Buhais. Vol. 1. The Archaeology of Jebel al-Buhais, Sharjah, United Arab Emirates.* Tübingen: Kerns Verlag/Sharjah: Department of Culture and Information, Government of Sharjah, U.A.E.

Kutterer A.U. & de Beauclair R. 2008. FAY-NE15 – another Neolithic graveyard in the central region of Sharjah Emirate? *Arabian Archaeology and Epigraphy* 19: 133-142.

Uerpmann H.-P., Uerpmann M. & Jasim S.A. (eds). 2006. *Funeral Monuments and Human Remains from Jebel al-Buhais. Vol. 1. The Archaeology of Jebel al-Buhais, Sharjah, United Arab Emirates.* Tübingen: Kerns Verlag/Sharjah: Department of Culture and Information, Government of Sharjah, U.A.E.

Uerpmann H.-P., Uerpmann M. & Jasim S.A. (eds). 2008. *The Natural Environment of Jebel al-Buhais: Past and Present. Vol. 2. The Archaeology of Jebel al-Buhais, Sharjah, United Arab Emirates.* Tübingen: Kerns Verlag/Sharjah: Department of Culture and Information, Government of Sharjah, U.A.E.

Van Gennep A. 1986. *Übergangsriten (Les rites de passage).* Frankfurt/New York: Campus.

Authors' Address

Roland de Beauclair
Zentrum für Naturwissenschaftliche Archäologie
Universität Tübingen
Rümelinstr. 23
D-72070 Tübingen
Germany
roland.de-beauclair@uni-tuebingen.de

On Neolithic funerary practices: were there "necrophobic" manipulations in 5th-4th millennium BC Arabia?

Vincent Charpentier and Sophie Méry

Summary
This paper reviews the evidence for Neolithic burial practices in SE Arabia, focusing in particular on sites in the Ja'alan region of eastern Oman. Attention is given to the nature of material buried with human remains, including jewellery and, most interestingly, the bones and shells of green turtles in the burials of Ra's al-Hamra 5 and 10. The paper concludes with a discussion of the possible evidence for "necrophobia" at the 5th millennium BC Neolithic necropolis of Suwayh 1.

Keywords: South-eastern Arabia, Neolithic, burials, necrophobia

Introduction

In the Persian Gulf, archaeological research of the past fifty years has concentrated on the Bronze Age, on the Dilmun and Magan cultures, and their relations with the regions located between Mesopotamia and the Indus Valley. Archaeologists have paid less attention to the late prehistory of the Gulf, except in relation to exchange between this region and the Ubaid culture of lower Mesopotamia.

Excavations concerning the Neolithic period in Arabia are rare; twenty sites at most have been excavated between Kuwait and the Sultanate of Oman. Most of these are coastal occupations, in the form of large shell-middens. Only a dozen Neolithic necropolises have been identified in the Oman peninsula, as unlike the monumental collective tombs of the early Bronze Age, the necropolises of the 5th-4th millennia are located within the settlements themselves and are particularly discreet, thus difficult for the archaeologist to detect. In the province of Ja'alan (Sultanate of Oman) only three are known, in spite of more than twenty years of intense research. They are Suwayh SWY-1, Ruways RWY-3, Ra's al-Khabbah KHB-1 and perhaps Ra's al-Wuddaya WD-58.

It is in this context that we present a funerary practice so far not identified in the Neolithic of Arabia, and we propose to relate it to an ideology of "necrophobia". At this point it is only a working hypothesis, and rests upon the data from the excavation of tombs in three necropolises of the 5th-4th millennia, particularly that of Suwayh 1, which is the earliest known necropolis in the Sultanate of Oman. Its excavation is quite recent and was carried out during a program begun in 1996 on a series of shell-middens on the shores of the Indian Ocean (Charpentier 2008; Charpentier, Marquis & Pellé 2003).

Why collect the dead together?

In Arabia, well before the advent of our modern GIS and teams of funerary archaeologists, Joseph Halévi in Yemen, as well as Bertram Thomas in Oman, St. John Philby and Reverand Zemmer in Saudi Arabia, noticed that the protohistoric funerary monuments occupied outstanding points on the land (Halévi 1873; Philby 1939; Thomas 1931; Zwemmer 1900). Following Colin Renfrew in Great Britain or Claude Masset in France, work in Arabia today tends to demonstrate that beyond their sepulchral role, these tombs are above all the affirmation of the living and the marker of a new social order (Cleuziou 2006). We know less whether the preferred location of necropolises on high points predates the early Bronze Age. However, beginning in the 5th millennium, they occupy knolls or promontories, as at Ra's al-Khabbah, Ruwayz, Suwayh, Ra's al-Hamra and Wadi Shab in Oman and UAQ-2 in the United Arab Emirates. They are also sometimes found at the foot of jebels and near springs, as at Buhais-18 or Faye NE-15, two necropolises which are, with that of Suwayh 1, the oldest in the Oman peninsula. On the other hand, we know nothing yet of the funerary practices of the hunter groups of the early Holocene (11th-8th millennia BC), nor of the possible continuation of their tradition during the Neolithic. In any case, and for the same reasons as the creation of trade over long distances, grouping of the deceased and the necropolis are characteristic of the Neolithic and are indicative of new social relations.

Primary, multiple, secondary but never collective

In the Neolithic, funerary structures are always graves dug in the substratum. Except for a few partly burned skeletons at al-Buhais (Kiesewetter 2006) and Ruwayz, incineration was unusual and the only funerary practice was inhumation. The graves were filled after deposit of the body (laid on the right or left side, legs folded or in a constrained position, sometimes an arm bent, hand near the face). The burials are often simple (Fig. 1:1) but can also be multiple (Fig. 1:3), and groups of 2 to 5 individuals, adults and children, are in evidence at al-Buhais-18 and at Ra's al-Hamra-5, for example. Successive primary burials are also attested at Buhais-18 and at Umm al-Quwain-2 (Kiesewetter 2003, 2006; Phillips 2002), while empty spaces were reserved in certain tombs of Wadi Shab 1 (Gauthier et al. 2005).

Other types of burial existed in parallel, as indicated by the succession of some forty primary deposits on a large sandy hillock in Umm al-Quwain-2, while complex primary and secondary deposits have recently been recognized at Buhais-18 (Kieswetter 2006; Kutterer, this volume and pers. comm.). It has been suggested that

Figure 1. 1: Simple burial G 93 at Ra's al-Hamra (after Salvatori 2007); 2: secondary burial; 3: multiple burial at Jebel Buhais (after Kiesewetter 2006).

these are collective burials (Cleuziou 2005; Cleuziou and Tosi 2007), but we do not agree, as a collective burial is by definition a closed and empty space which is accessed many times (Leclerc 2003). As voluminous as it is, structure 43 of Ra's al-Hamra 5 (Salvatori 2007) is not a collective burial either but a group of successive deposits dug into the earth, for which the interpretation remains to be made. And we think that it is in these particular types of deposits that one of the origins for collective burials at the beginning of the early Bronze Age (Hafit period) should be looked for.

In the Neolithic, manipulations after deposit of the body or bodies were also practised within burials in eastern Arabia. This is the case for tomb 68 inf. of Ra's al-Hamra 5, which contained the bones of 5 individuals, and structure 6 of Wadi Shab 1, with an incomplete skeleton in connection; these are interpreted by the excavators as decarnation pits (Salvatori 1996, 2007; Gauthier et al. 2005). The process of de-fleshing appears to have been "passive" as no traces of voluntary stripping of the bones (traces of cutting, etc.) have been identified.

Secondary burials are definitely present, but generally in the minority in the necropolises (less than 10% at Ra's al-Hamra RH-5). They are the result of a process over a particular period of time, and imply several funerary manipulations and temporary locations. Buried in its definitive grave, the deceased then no longer possesses funerary objects, except in rare cases, as at Jebel al-Buhais 18 (Fig. 1:2) (Uerpmann, forthcoming).

Funerary objects and deposits in the primary burials of the 5th-4th millennia BC

The objects discovered in the Neolithic burials are individual, not collective as in the case especially of the Jemdet Nasr vessels in the Hafit period tombs (Méry 1995). As in other regions in the same periods, individual ornaments played an important role in eastern Arabia in the funerary context, with various compositions of

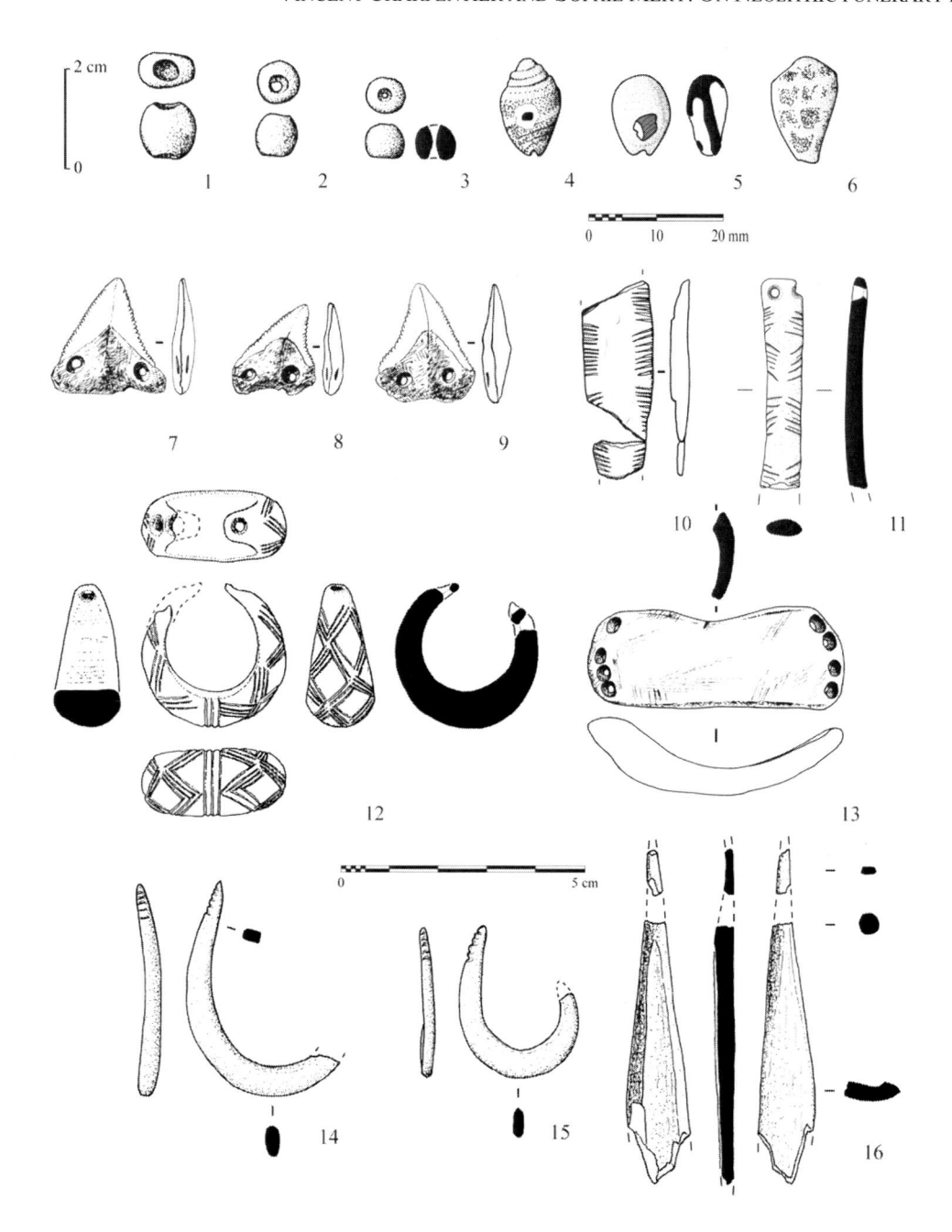

Figure 2. 1-3: pearls, Suwayh 1 (1, tomb 4; 2-3, sect. 6); 4-6: shells beads, al-Haddah BJD-1: 4. *Engina mendicaria*, 5. *Prunum terverianum*, 6. *Conus* sp; 7-9: shark tooth arrowheads, Suwayh 1; 10: laurel leaf shaped pendant, Suwayh 2; 11: shell pendant, Suwayh 10; 12: chlorite earring, Suwayh 2; 13: element of composite bracelet, *Conus* Sp, Ruwayz 1; 14-15: shell fishhooks, Suwayh 2; 16: bone awl, Suwayh 2. (Drawings G. Devilder; H. David).

necklaces, bracelets and anklets, as well as belts, headdresses and hairnets (de Beauclair, Jasim & Uerpmann 2006; Kiesewetter, Uerpmann & Jasim 2000; Salvatori 2007). In these assemblages, the chlorite and shell beads are by far the most numerous, assembled in ornaments of black and white. In the 5th millennium, *Ancilla farsiana* is the most numerous shell in the burials of al-Buhais 18, while *Engina mendicaria* appears to be more frequent in the assemblages of the 4th millennium on the Omani shores of the Indian Ocean (Fig. 2:4). Also present are composite bracelets in *Conus* sp. (Fig. 2:13), laurel leaves in mother-of-pearl of *Pinctada margaritifera* (Fig. 2:10) at Buhais 18 and Ra's al-Hamra 5 and 10, for example. At the end of the 5th millennium, long tubular beads appear to become more frequent, and decorated chlorite earrings appear in the assemblages (Fig. 2:12).

The presence of remarkable, even exceptional pieces also characterises the assemblages dated to the 5th-4th millennia, which leads us to believe that these Neolithic societies were more "inegalitarian" than some have suggested in the past, that is, they were organised on hierarchical lines other than just those of age and sex. Fine beads in the necropolises of Suwayh 1 (Fig. 2:1-3), Buhais 18, Jebel Faya NE-15 and Ra's al-Hamra 5, but also cornelians found in those of al-Buhais and Faya may be included among these prestigious objects (de

Beauclair, Jasim & Uerpmann 2006; Charpentier, Marquis & Pellé 2003; Kiesewetter, Uerpmann & Jasim 2000; Kutterer & de Beauclair 2008). A very large laurel leaf made from the distal part of a *P. margaritifera*, discovered at the foot of a tomb of Ruwayz 3, and a chloritite bracelet of exceptional size from Suwayh 1 are part of this category of objects and are also finely worked. Among the weapons, the axes of al-Buhais 18 are also included in this group (Jasim, Uerpmann & Uerpmann 2005; Kutterer this volume), as well as projectile points made from the teeth of very large sharks (*Carcharhinus leucas*) (Fig. 2:7-9) (Charpentier *et al.* 2009), which come from the necropolises of Ra's al-Khabbah and Ra's al-Hamra 5 and 10 (Salvatori 1996, 2007; Santoni 1987, 2002. Cavulli, Munoz & Scaruffi 2008).

Other instruments and tools, more ordinary or more finely worked, accompanied the deceased in the hereafter and constituted, we believe, strong marks of identity for the Neolithic groups of eastern Arabia. These are mother-of-pearl fishhooks in roughout form or as finished pieces (Fig. 2:14-15), at Buhais 18, Ra's al-Hamra 5, 10 Wadi Shab 1, and flint or schist blades at Ra's al-Khabbah 1, Wadi Shab 1 and Ra's al Hamra 5 (Gauthier *et al.* 2005; Kiesewetter, Uerpmann & Jasim 2000; Salvatori 2007; Santoni 1987). Finally, needles, punches etc. are present in most of the necropolises (Fig. 2.16) (Buhais, UAQ-2, Ra's al-Hamra, Wadi Shab) (Gauthier *et al.* 2005; Jasim, Uerpmann & Uerpmann 2005; Phillips 2002; Salvatori 2007).

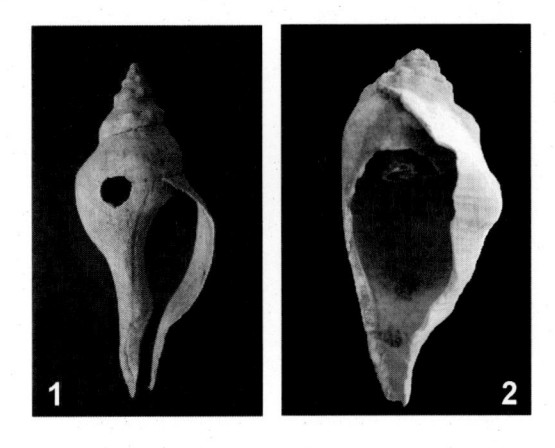

Figure 3. Conch shells. 1: *Fasciolaria trapezium* (grave deposit), Suwayh 1; 2: *Lambis truncata sabae*, Suwayh 20.

Several types of shell were deposited beside the deceased, sometimes in front of them. These are the valves of *P. margaritifera*, *Callista* sp., shells of *Thonna* sp. and large conches of *Fasciolaria trapezium* (Fig. 3:1) *Lambis truncata sabae* (Fig. 3:2) and *Tutufa tutua bardeyi*. The deceased may hold a discoid or oval pebble in one hand (Ra's al-Hamra 5, Wadi Shab 1) (Gauthier *et al.* 2005; Salvatori 1996, 2007).

The deposit of skulls of green turtles (*Chelonia midas*) near the face of the deceased is probably one of the most spectacular discoveries made at Ra's al-Hamra 5 and 10 (Biagi & Salvatori 1986; Salvatori 1996; Santoni 1987) (Fig. 4:1-3). Another reference to the turtle, little white pebbles similar to turtle eggs cover the remains of certain individuals in these two necropolises, and bone elements of *Chelonia mydas* or even entire turtle shells were integrated with the covering slabs. The importance of this marine reptile in the *idéel* world (Godelier 1998) of the Omani coastal societies of the 5th and 4th millennia is thus a remarkable fact, which we believe has to do with identity. The skulls of turtles and of *F. trapezium, T. tutufa bardeyi,* and *L. truncata sabae* were deposited on the top of several tombs of Ra's al-Hamra and Suwayh 1; these deposits were certainly related to the funeral ceremonies. A grave at Ra's al-Hamra 5 contained twelve turtle skulls (Salvatori 2007, Frazier 2005).

Finally, although the presence of ashy levels in the tombs or in the hearths situated nearby was often reported, that of deposits of exceptionally large fish (*Tuna*, etc.) on the top of the tombs is rarer but attested at Ra's al-Hamra 5 and at UAQ-2. These different deposits are interpreted as possible "funerary banquets" (Salvatori 2007; Gauthier *et al.* 2005; Uerpmann & Uerpmann 2003).

What do we learn from the necropolis of Suwayh?

Suwayh 1, the only 5th millennium necropolis identified in the Sultanate of Oman, was destroyed during the construction of the coastal road in 2003. A second necropolis, dated to the 4th millennium, which we also identified at Ruwayz 3, suffered the same fate during the construction of a house in 2005-2006.

Dated to 4400-4200 BC, the four tombs of Suwayh 1 were dug in the 5th millennium levels and sealed by an occupation dated to 4200 BC (Charpentier, Marquis & Pellé 2003). These individual burials dug directly into the earth contained two adults and two children. Except for a partially faced large grave, burial 3 was covered with stones in its central part, upon which a hearth was installed. Another particularity of burial 2 lies in the covering slabs indicating its location. The installation of this covering was certainly associated with the burial, as a piece of slab refits with another, the latter found placed directly on the individual.

A necrophobic practice in the Omani Neolithic?

The tombs of Suwayh 1 are especially distinguished by the slabs deposited directly on the bodies of the deceased. Thus, a heavy stone covered the mandible and the top of the thorax of the individual of tomb 2 (Fig. 5:1-2), which was laid on the left side in a slightly flexed position. Tomb 1 contained an adult in a constrained position, lying on the right side, the right hand near the face and the left hand crushed by a stone slab (Fig. 5:3-5). The very young child of burial 3 had a slab on the hand. The blocks laid on the individuals are of hard limestone or calcarenites of local origin, but they do not come directly from the site, where only eolianites are present.

Figure 4. 1-3: skulls of turtle (*Chelonia mydas*) deposited in graves at Ra's al-Hamra 5. After Salvatori (2007).

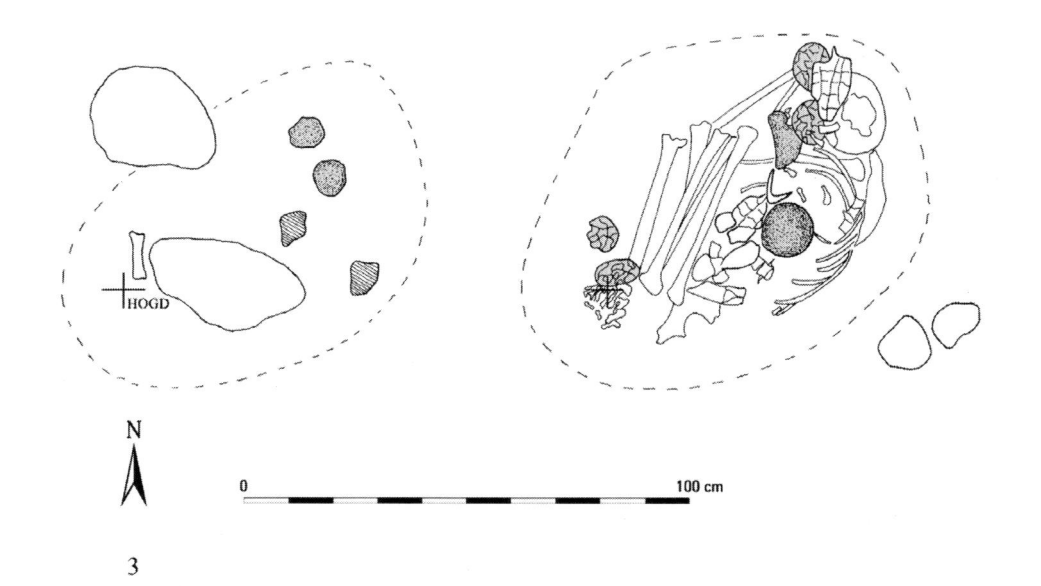

Rubbed smooth, the block of tomb 1 probably comes from an ancient shore, while the blocks of tombs 2 and 3 could have come from the only nearby limestone massif, Suwayh 5, which is 900 m distant as the crow flies. Moreover, the decomposition of individuals 1, 2 and 3 took place in filled-in space and no body was disturbed – except for that of tomb 1, the skull of which was accidentally moved during the digging of the grave of tomb 2.

The deposit of a stone directly on the deceased is thus not fortuitous in these burials; on the contrary it is an intentional act intended to hold the deceased in place. This practice has already been recognized in the 4th millennium necropolises of Ra's al-Hamra 5 and 10 (Salvatori 1996, 2007, Santini 1987), and perhaps Wadi Shab 1 (Gauthier *et al.* 2005). On the other hand it has not been identified in the necropolis of Jebel al-Buhais (pers. comm. H.-P. & M. Uerpmann 2002, 2008).

We pointed out this practice in 2003 (Charpentier, Marquis & Pellé) and return to this subject today, to propose the possibility of necrophobic practices in the Omani Neolithic.

Figure 5. Suwayh 1 necropolis (around 4400-4200 BC). 1-2: grave no. 2; 3-5: grave no. 1. (Photos Vincent Charpentier).

To understand the possible relation between pinning the deceased to the ground and a practice of necrophobic type, it must be remembered what necrophobia is and what its manifestations are in an archaeological context. Necrophobia is the fear held by the living that the dead will interfere in their space, and necrophobic practices cover all the procedures intended to prevent this supposed return of the dead. These procedures, widely described in popular literature, are varied, and can affect not only the burial but also the dwelling and the objects belonging to the deceased. We will mention for example the cremation of shoes, intended to prevent the possible walking about of the dead (pers. comm. Charlier 2007). The deposit of a stone in the burial is another act, but it is not always related to necrophobia. In medieval and modern Europe, a stone is sometimes placed under the mandible of the deceased to prevent what is called "the sardonic smile", due to the post-mortem slipping of the jaw (pers. comm. V. Delattre, F. Gentili 2008).

For the early periods, necrophobic practices have been pointed out by various authors – Iron Age Italy, even the Levant in the Neolithic – although diagnostic elements remain rare. Khirokitia, a Neolithic Cypriot site, is the case that is the closest to Suwayh, as many skeletons were found covered with natural blocks or more rarely, seed querns, on the thorax or the skull. Although Alain Lebrun, director of this excavation, only mentions an "anchoring to the ground" (Lebrun 1989), Saponetti et al. (2007) have recently interpreted these manipulations as necrophobic. Does this practice of the Cypriot Neolithic find an echo in the Omani Neolithic of Suwayh and Ra's al-Hamra?

In any case, a single additional element could reinforce the necrophobia hypothesis in eastern Arabia. At Ra's al-Hamra, Alfredo Coppa reports a very particular manipulation on this site: the voluntary breaking of human mandibles, whose fragments are then turned around in some secondary burials of the necropolis (Salvatori 2007).[1] This act is intentional according to A. Coppa, but it is to be noted that certain specialists in funerary archaeology doubt the anthropic nature of this breakage (pers. comm. O. Munoz 2008), proposing rather natural breaking under the weight of the burial coverings.

By way of a conclusion

In the Oman peninsula, during the Neolithic, a variety of manipulations were practised during the primary burial but also afterward, and up to the secondary burial, which appears to complete, at least for certain individuals, the funerary process (Munoz, this volume). In a coastal environment, funerary practices reflect beliefs strongly related to the sea, in which the turtle *Chelonia mydas* held an important place, and covers both a symbolic and a social dimension, by contributing to the cohesion of certain groups.

Could other beliefs, in this case necrophobic, have existed in the local Neolithic? The hypothesis deserves to be put forth, but remains to be demonstrated as the confirmation of necrophobic manipulations is delicate, as in the case of the Cypriot Neolithic. Other reasons could explain such deposits associated with the deceased.

References

de Beauclair R., Jasim S.A. & Uerpmann H-P. 2006. New results on the Neolithic jewellery from al-Buhais 18, UAE. *Proceedings of the Seminar for Arabian Studies* 36: 175-187.

Charpentier V. 2002. Archéologie de la côte des Ichtyophages : coquilles, squales et cétacés du site IVe-IIIe millénaires de Ra's al-Jinz. Pages 73-99 in S. Cleuziou, M. Tosi & J. Zarins (eds), *Essays on the late Prehistory of the Arabian Peninsula.* Rome: Serie Orientale XCIII.

Charpentier V. 2008. Hunter-gatherers of the "empty quarter of the early Holocene" to the last Neolithic societies: chronology of the late prehistory of south-eastern Arabia (8000–3100 BC). *Proceedings of the Seminar for Arabian Studies* 38: 93-116

Charpentier V., Marquis P. & Pellé E. 2003. La nécropole et les derniers horizons Vème millénaire du site de Gorbat al-Mahar (Suwayh SWY-1, Sultanat d'Oman): premiers résultats. *Proceedings of the Seminar for Arabian Studies* 33: 11-19.

Charpentier V., Méry S., Fortini E., & Pellé E. 2009. « Un chef est un requin qui voyage par terre ». Fonctions et statuts des armatures de projectile en dent de *Carcharhinus leucas* et aiguillon caudal de raie dans l'Arabie des VIe-IIIe millénaires av. notre ère. *Arabian Archaeology and Epigraphy* 20: 9-17.

Cleuziou S. 2005. Pourquoi si tard ? Nous avons pris un autre chemin. L'Arabie des chasseurs-cueilleurs de l'Holocène au début de l'Age du Bronze. Pages 123-148 in G. Guilaine (ed.), *Au marges des grands foyers du Néolithique. Périphéries débitrices ou créatrices ?* Paris: Errance.

Cleuziou S. 2006. La société de Magan à l'Age du Bronze : Entre tribu et État. Pages 43-66 in P. Charvát, B. Lafont, J. Mynářová & P Lukáš (eds), *L'État, le pouvoir, les prestations et leurs formes en Mésopotamie ancienne. Actes du Colloque assyriologique franco-tchèque.* Univerzita Karlova v Praze: Filozofická fakulta.

Cleuziou S. & Tosi M. 2007. *In the Shadow of the Ancestors: the prehistoric foundation of the early Arabian civilisation in Oman.* Muscat: Ministry of Heritage and Culture.

Frazier F. 2005. Marine turtles – the ultimate tool kit: A review of worked bones of marine turtles. Pages 359-382 in H. Luik, A.-M. Choyke, C. Batey & L. Lõugas (eds), *From Hooves to Horns, from Mollusc to Mammoth, Manufacture and Use of Bone Artefacts from Prehistoric Times to the Present. Proceedings of*

---

[1] Let us remember that the lower jaw in humans was long considered to be the joining of two bones and that its single character was not discovered until 1535 by Andreas Vasalius (Vésale) (1543), thus putting an end to the dogma of Galenism.

the 4th Meeting of the ICAZ Worked Bone Research Group. Tallinn.

Godelier M. 1998. *L'idéel et le Matériel, pensée, économies, sociétés*. Paris: Fayard.

Halévi J. 1873. Voyage au Nedjran. *Bulletin de la Société de Géographie*, série 6.6: 5-31; 249-273; 581-606.

Kiesewetter H. 2003. The Neolithic population at Jebel al-Buhais 18: Remarks on the funerary practices, paleodemography and paleopathology. Pages 36-43 in D. Potts, H. Al-Naboodah & P. Hellyer (eds), *Archaeology of the United Arab Emirates, Proceedings of the first International Conference on the Archaeology of the U.A.E*. London: Trident.

Kiesewetter H. 2006. Analyses of the human remains from the Neolithic cemetery at al-Buhais 18 (excavations 1996-2000). Pages 103-259 in H.-P. Uerpman, M. Uerpman and S.A. Jasim (eds), *Funeral monuments and human remains from Jebel al-Buhais. The Archaeology of Jebel al-Buhais*, 1. Sharjah: Dept. of Culture and Information, Government of Sharjah, United Arab Emirates.

Kiesewetter H., Uerpmann H.-P. & Jasim S.A. 2000. Neolithic jewellery from Jebel-al Buhais 18. *Proceedings of the Seminar for Arabian Studies* 30: 137-146.

Kutterer A. & de Beauclair R. 2008. FAY-NE15 – another Neolithic graveyard in the central region of the Sharjah Emirate? *Arabian Archaeology and Epigraphy* 19: 133-142.

Le Brun A. 1989. Le Néolithique de Chypre et sa relation avec le PPNB du Levant. *Paléorient* 15/1: 161-167.

Leclerc J. 2003. Sépulture collective, espace sépulcral collectif. Pages 321-322 in P. Chambon & J. Leclerc (eds), *Les pratiques funéraires néolithiques avant 3500 av. J.-C. en France et dans les régions limitrophes*. Paris: Mémoire de la Société préhistorique française XXXIII.

Méry S. 1995. Archaeology of the borderlands: 4th millenium BC Mesopotamian pottery at Ra's al-Hamra RH-5 (Sultanate of Oman). *Annali* 55: 193-206.

Méry S. & Charpentier V. 2002. Around Suwayh (Ja'alan): a summary of some recent discoveries from coastal shell-middens of Eastern Arabia. *Journal of Oman Studies* 12: 181-195

Philby H. St. J.-B. 1939. *Sheba's daughters*. London: Methuen.

Phillips C. S. 2002. Prehistoric middens and a cemetery from the southern Arabian Gulf. Pages 169-186 in Cleuziou, S., Tosi, M. & Zarins, J. (eds), *Essays on the Late Prehistory of the Arabian Peninsula*. Rome: Serie Orientale XCIII.

Salvatori S. 1996. Death and ritual in a population of coastal food foragers in Oman. Pages 205-222 in G. Afanas'ev, S. Cleuziou, R. Lukacs & M. Tosi (eds) *The Prehistory of Asia and Oceania, Colloquium XXXII, Trade as a Subsistence Strategy. Post-Pleistocene Adaptations in Arabia and Early Maritime Trade in Indian Ocean*. XIII International Congress of Prehistoric and Protohistoric Sciences: Forli Abaco.

Salvatori S. 2007. The Prehistoric graveyard of Ra's al-Hamra 5, Muscat, Sultanate of Oman. *Journal of Oman Studies* 14: 5-202.

Santini G. 1987. Site RH-10 at Qurum and a preliminary analysis of its cemetery: an essay in stratigraphic discontinuity. *Proceedings of the Seminar for Arabian Studies* 17: 179-198.

Santini G. 2002. Burial Complex 43 at the prehistoric graveyard of Ra's al-Hamra in the northern Oman. Pages 147-167 in Cleuziou, S. Tosi, M. & Zarins, J. (eds), *Essays on the Late Prehistory of the Arabian Peninsula*. Rome: Serie Orientale XCIII.

Saponetti S., Scattarella F., De Lucia A. & Scattarella V. 2007. Paleobiology, palaeopathology and necrophobic practices in Early Iron Age burials (IX–VII Century BC) in Capo Colonna, Trani, Apulia, Southern Italy – the state of health of a small sample from Iron Age. *Coll. Antropol.* 31/1: 339-344.

Thomas B. 1931. *Alarms and excursions in Arabia*. London: G Allen & Unwin.

Uerpmann M. Forthcoming. *The Holocene Stone Age in Southeast Arabia – A Reconsideration*.

Uerpmann H.-P. & Uerpmann M. 2003. *Stone Age Sites and their Natural Environment, the Capital Area of Northern Oman*, Part III. Beihefte zum Tübinger Atlas des vorderen Orients, Reihe A (Naturwissenschaften) Nr. 31/3.

Vésale A. 1543. *De humani corporis fabrica Libri septem*. Bâle: Johannes Oporinus.

Zwemmer S.M. 1900 [1986]. *Arabia, the cradle of the Islam*. London: Darfd.

Authors' addresses

Vincent Charpentier
Inrap, ArScAn UMR 7041 du CNRS
Maison René Ginouvès de l'Archéologie et de l'Ethnologie
21, allée de l'Université
92023 Nanterre cedex, France
emails: vincent.charpentier@mae.u-paris10.fr / vincent.charpentier@inrap.fr

Sophie Méry
ArScAn UMR 7041 du CNRS
Maison René Ginouvès de l'Archéologie et de l'Ethnologie
21, allée de l'Université
92023 Nanterre cedex, France
email: sophie.mery@mae.u-paris10.fr

The burials of the middle Holocene settlement of KHB-1 (Ra's al-Khabbah, Sultanate of Oman)

Olivia Munoz, Simona Scaruffi and Fabio Cavulli[1]

Summary
During the Joint Hadd Project excavations at the Middle Holocene coastal site of KHB-1 in the Ja'alān region (Sultanate of Oman), a number of human remains were discovered in the settlement dating from the 5th-4th millennia BC. Two burials were situated in the stratigraphic sequence: one is related to an abandonment span between the first and the second occupational phases while the second is associated with the most recent occupation of the settlement. Through a detailed analysis of these burials, it was possible to determine the different aspects of the biology (age, sex, pathologies) of the two individuals. The first grave contains the well preserved skeletal remains of a young woman buried in a crouched position, lying on her left side, with bent arms and hands placed in front of the head and feet lying outside of the pit. All the bones were found in strict anatomical connection, attesting a primary burial. Four stones were placed above the burial. The second grave contains the semi-articulated remains of a mature adult. Several bones are missing (skull, mandible, bones of the arms) and whereas some anatomical connections are preserved others are disturbed, suggesting a primary deposition affected by later disturbances. Examination of the accurate documentation collected during excavation of the graves permitted a precise taphonomic study of the depositions, allowing considerations to be made relating to different yet important aspects of the funerary practices of the Middle Holocene Arabian coastal community.

Keywords: Burials, Funerary practices, Middle Holocene, Oman, Arabia

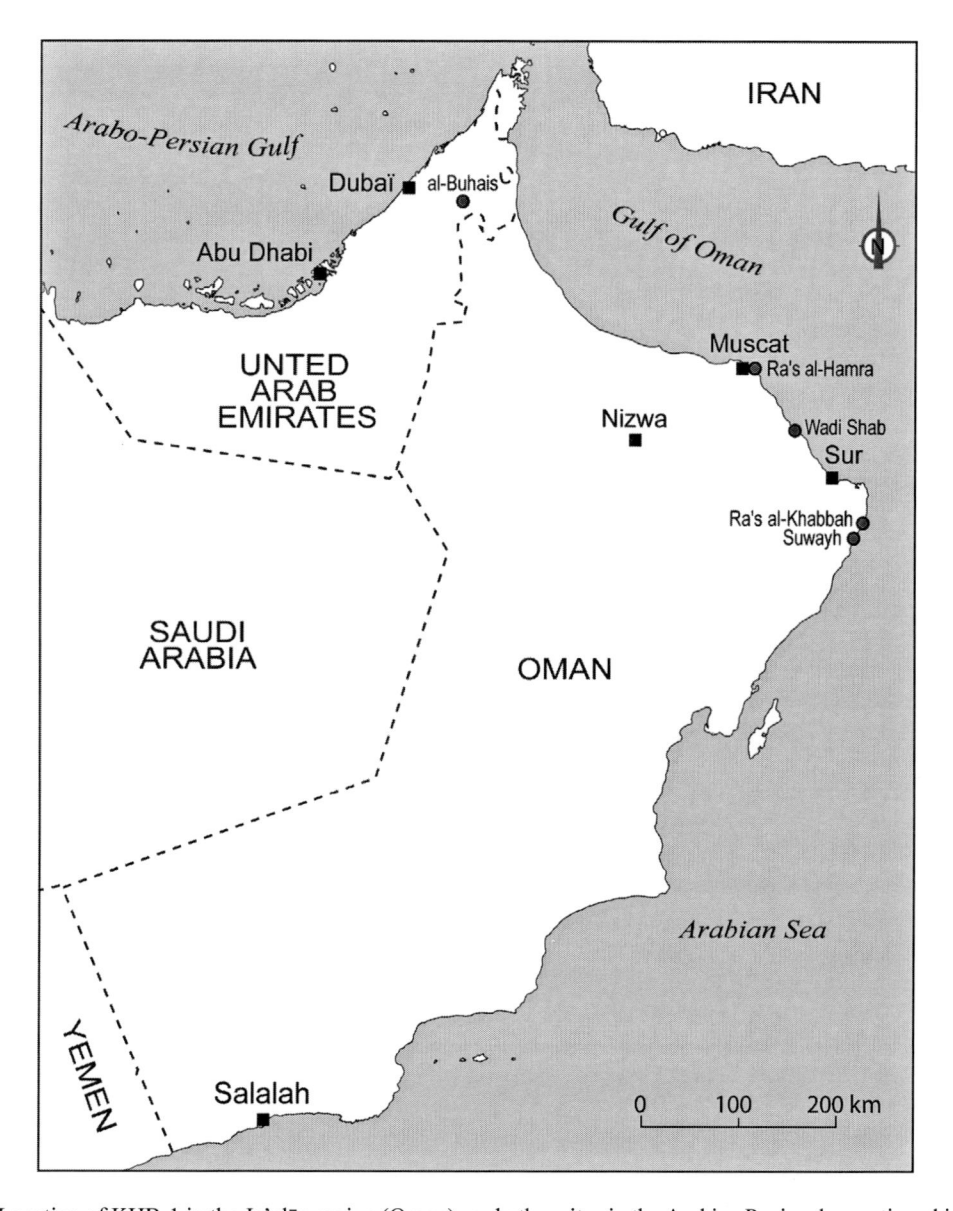

Figure 1. Location of KHB-1 in the Ja'alān region (Oman), and other sites in the Arabian Peninsula mentioned in the text.

Figure 2. Aerial view of KHB-1 settlement located on a rocky terrace 34 m above the sea level.

Introduction

The site of KHB-1 (Ra's al-Khabbah) is one of the few 5th-4th millennia BC settlements of the Ja'alān coast (Sultanate of Oman) (Magnani *et al.* 2007) (Fig. 1). The site is located above a rocky erosion terrace 34 metres above sea level (Fig. 2) and is characterised by a pluristratified anthropic deposit with evidence of structural elements like hearths, wind screens and small circular huts (Cavulli 2004a, b, c). Economic activities were principally based on the exploitation of coastal resources (marine and lagoon) as demonstrated by the faunal data (principally fish bones and shells) and by the material culture (net sinkers and shell hooks; Cavulli & Scaruffi 2008; Cavulli *et al.* 2009). The scarcity of mammal bones (wild and domesticated) has led to the consideration of the moderate impact of hunting and pastoralism in subsistence, although the role of domesticated animals is still a debated topic. Six phases of occupation have been recognised from the stratigraphic excavation of the deposit, alternating with periods of abandonment.

Human remains were discovered in the central area of the settlement (Figs. 3 and 4): some bones belonging to a foot and hands were collected in Area E and two graves were excavated in the stratigraphic sequence in Area F. The older burial is immediately subsequent to the earliest occupation of the site, while the latter is associated with the most recent occupational phase. Through a detailed analysis of these remains it has been possible to determine the different biological traits (age, sex, pathologies) of both individuals, providing interesting data on burial practices of the Arabian Middle Holocene.

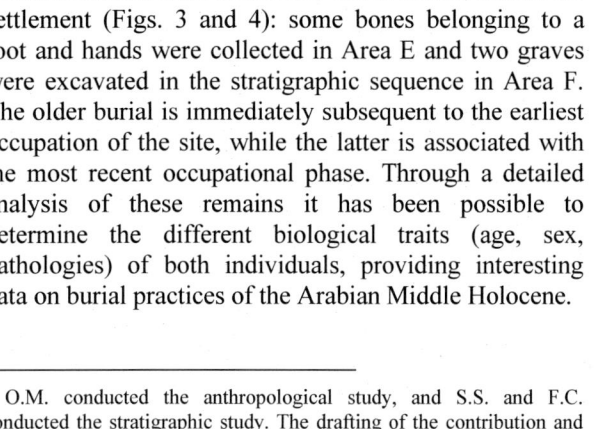

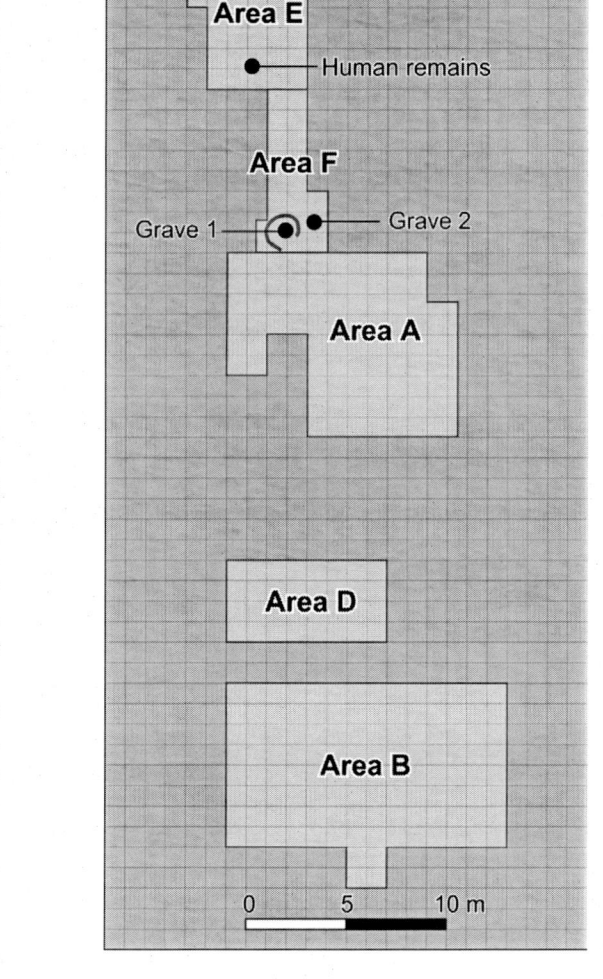

Figure 3. Map showing the distribution of human remains at KHB-1.

---

[1] O.M. conducted the anthropological study, and S.S. and F.C. conducted the stratigraphic study. The drafting of the contribution and the conclusions are the result of collective work by the authors.

Grave 1

Grave 1 contains the remains of an individual laid in a shallow pit which is situated exactly in the centre of an earlier circular hut of phase I. The grave pit cut the occupation level of the structure, indicating that the burial was subsequent to the abandonment of the hut itself.

The individual was buried in a crouched position and laid on his left side, with arms bent and hands placed in front of the head, tucked under a stone, while the feet lie outside of the pit (Fig. 5). The orientation of the body is SW-NE, with the face gazing northward. The skeleton is almost complete, including the ossicles of the inner ear. The majority of the bones were found in strict articulation suggesting a primary burial with the body placed directly into the shallow pit (Duday & Guillon 2006).

A number of *Anadara* clamshells were found in front of the individual's face but the placement is probably casual. A large bivalve shell (*Pecten* sp.) deposited close to the body but outside of the pit may be interpreted as a burial good or offering for the deceased (Fig. 5, top right). Four large stones were placed along the four edges of the pit, corresponding to head, shoulders and feet (Fig. 5, bottom right).

Sex and Age at death: The morphology of the hip bones has allowed the determination of the sex of the individual as a woman (Bruzek 2002). Furthermore, the presence of a marked *sulcus praeauricularis* could indicate that the

Figure 4. View of the two burials (top: grave 1; bottom: grave 2).

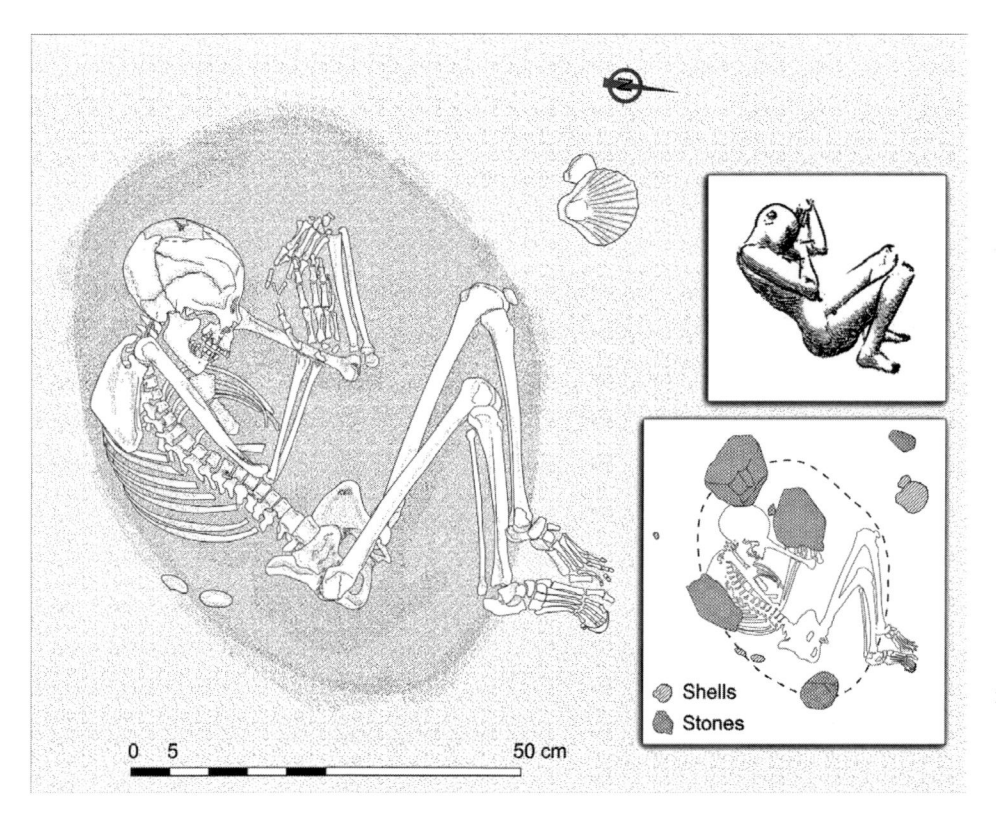

Figure 5. Layout made after rectified photography (left) and reconstruction of grave 1 (top right). Four stones were placed on the body, and a *Pecten* sp. laid outside the pit (bottom right).

woman was parous.[2] The juvenile aspect of the pubic symphysis, the clavicle sternal epiphysis and the iliac crest still in the process of fusion, as well as the low wear on the third molar, indicate that the woman was around 20-25 years old when she died.

Stature: The stature estimated from the ulna length is 158.1 ± 4.3 cm (Trotter 1970).

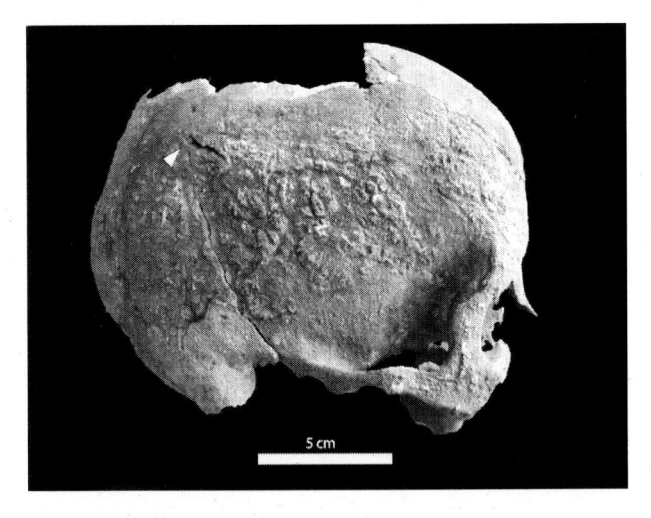

Figure 6. Traumatic lesion, stamp-shaped, and associated fractures on the right parietal of the woman buried in grave 1.

Pathologies: Two lines of fracture coming from a supero-lateral trauma, stamp-shaped and about 2 cm long, have been observed on the right parietal bone (Fig. 6). Considering that the covering stone was not lying exactly on this part of the skull, and that the skull and the fractures were covered by a saline crust, the hypothesis of a recent trauma is excluded. Moreover, this suggests that the trauma was *peri-mortem,* but given the bad preservation of the internal table it is impossible to determine if it happened *ante-mortem* and thus could have caused the death.

Additionally, some indications of joint disease have been observed on the lower thoracic vertebrae. Concerning dental pathologies, we have noticed several examples of enamel hypoplasia, attesting stresses during childhood. The degree of attrition is moderate and calculus is present but slight. Neither carious lesions nor abscesses were recorded.

Morphological variations: The right humerus shows a septal aperture. Both tibias present strongly marked squatting facets.[3]

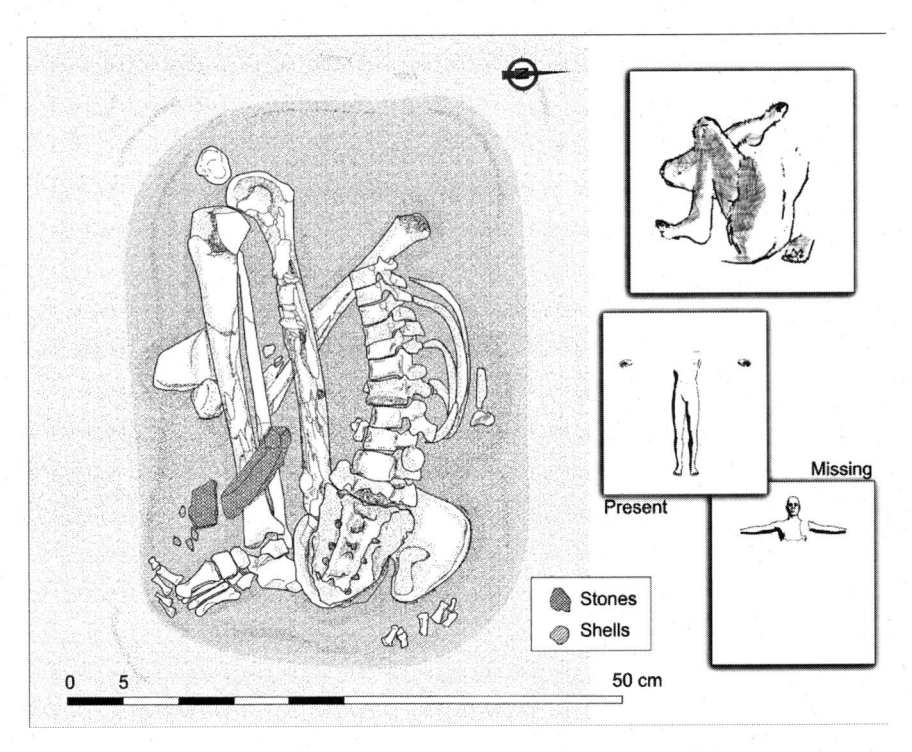

Figure 7. Layout made after rectified photography and reconstruction of grave 2 (top right). Sketch indicating present and missing parts of the body in grave 2 (bottom right).

---

[2] This formation may result from obstetrical trauma during the course of delivery, or correspond to an increased stress at the site of ligamentous insertion. Formerly, anthropologists used the preauricular sulcus in estimating the parity of skeletal remains as a deep, pitted groove was believed to indicate previous pregnancy. Recently the validity of this relationship has been questioned. In their study on the paraglenoid sulcus, Schemmer *et al.* (1995) tested the relationship to parity in 70 adult female subjects; a statistically significant relationship was found, with deep grooves occurring only in parous women.

[3] These morphological variations, are known to have a familial inheritance, and are thus included in non-metric variation trait lists, scored in biological distance studies (Buikstra & Ubelaker 1994; Finnegan 1978; Saunders 1978). Nevertheless, some of these traits are also considered as occupational stress indicators (e.g. the vastus notch of the patella, related to the insertion of the *vastus lateralis* muscle, associated with chronic knee flexion, as in squatting (Capasso *et al.* 1998:121), or the squatting facets of the distal tibia, related to repeated squatting posture (Boule 2001; Capasso *et al.* 1998: 127).

Grave 2

In the second grave, the semi-articulated remains of an adult were situated in an oval pit, just below the surface of the deposit, cutting the uppermost levels of occupation phase V.

Many bones of the skeleton are totally absent: skull and mandible, clavicles, right scapula, long bones from the upper limbs, upper part of the rachis (from first cervical vertebra to seventh thoracic vertebra), sternum and upper ribs (Fig. 7, bottom right). The bones recovered are very fragmented, eroded and friable. Some labile articulations are preserved (distal part of the feet) whereas others are dislocated (hands, scapula-thorax), suggesting a primary deposition *in situ* affected by later disturbances (Fig. 7, left). This hypothesis is also confirmed by the presence of several small bones. However, a similar condition could also be the result of the dislocation of the body in a perishable container from a different place, thus preserving some anatomical connections and small bones. Although the evidence is not able to clearly support one hypothesis or the other, it is evident that the burial has been massively perturbed by removing some bones when the body was still presenting some anatomical connections. Partial mummification of some parts of the body could have been involved, as such evidence has been found in other arid environments (Maureille & Sellier 1996).

The general orientation of the flexed body is west-east, with the upper part towards the west. Of particular interest is the considerable flexion of the right lower limb, that indicates a very contracted position of the entire body, artificially constrained. This particular position has already been noted in several graves from the Wadi Shab GAS-1 cemetery, dating from the same period (Gaultier *et al.* 2005).

Two flint artefacts (one long blade and one broken flake) were deposited with the body close to the ankle. One perforated shark tooth from the sieving was associated with the burial (Fig. 8, left).

In the absence of preserved collagen, the inorganic (bioapatite) fraction of a long bone sample from grave 2 (US 176) was dated using AMS technique. The powdered bone was pretreated and CO_2 was extracted following previously published protocols (see e.g. Sereno *et al.* 2008) at by J. F. Saliège LOCEAN (UPMC, Paris, France). Radiometric dating was carried out at LMC14 (Saclay, France) and indicates that the individual died during the 4th millennium BC (SacA11382: 5015 ±30 BP; $\delta^{13}C$ = -10.10). As it is likely that the diet of this individual included a significant portion of marine resources, it is not possible to translate directly this ^{14}C age into an exact date (Munoz *et al.* 2008). Depending on the proportion of marine resources ingested and taking into account the local marine reservoir effect (DR= 210 ± 15, Saliège *et al.* 2005) the calibrated 1σ age ranges vary between 3245-3075 cal. BC (for a 100% marine diet) and 3929-

Figure 8. Flint artefacts deposited on the ankle of the adult in grave 2; perforated shark tooth associated with grave 2.

3715 cal. BC (for a 100% continental diet; see e.g. Munoz *et al.* 2008).[4]

Sex and age at death: The hip bones are too fragmentary to allow a reliable sexual diagnosis. However the robustness of the post-cranial skeleton of this individual is remarkable.
Several signs of degenerative pathologies associated with the strong wear of teeth could indicate that the deceased was rather mature at the time of the death.

Stature: No complete long bone has been found, preventing any stature estimation.

Pathologies: Degenerative joint diseases were recorded on both patellae and on the right hallux, as well as on the lower thoracic vertebrae. A small consolidated trauma was recognised on the lateral face of the 5th right metatarsal. Concerning the dental pathologies, we have observed a severe degree of attrition on the disarticulated teeth present associated with significant tartar accumulation; no carious lesions were observed. Finally, some *calculi* were recovered in the abdominal region (Fig. 9). Their biological analysis, in progress, will be presented in a future publication.

---

[4] Calibration was undertaken using the Calib Rev 5.0.1, marine04.14c Calibration data set (Hughen *et al.* 2004) and Calib Rev 5.0.1, intcal04.14c Calibration data set (Reimer *et al.* 2004).

Figure 9. Calcifications found in the abdominal region of the adult buried in grave 2.

Human remains from Area E

Several human small bones associated with the right patella were recovered in Area E (Figure 3). The remains, chronologically contemporaneous to Grave 2, were covered by three slabs which were already visible from the surface of the deposit. Bones of a right foot and both right and left hands are believed to belong to at least one single adult individual. The first metatarsal and phalanges show important degenerative joint diseases. On the patella, a supra lateral notch was observed (see footnote 3, p. 28).

Conclusions

The two graves discovered at KHB-1 have improved our knowledge of burial practices during the Middle Holocene in the Ja'alān region and in the Arabian context. The more recent grave (Grave 2) and the scattered bones collected close to the surface can be related to a more recent use of the area, whereas the earliest grave (Grave 1) demonstrates an enduring interconnection between the living area and the graveyard since the earliest phases of occupation of the site. The uniqueness of this burial in relation to earlier occupations should be linked to the hypothesis of a seasonal occupation of the site (followed by semi-sterile layers) by a group which possibly buried their dead in a different area, far from KHB-1. This could support the seasonal character of the site itself, possibly occupied during the winter months (when fish are abundant along the coast; Cavulli 2004a, b). The particular location of Grave 1 at the centre of a hut suggests that the choice was not casual but indicates a precise desire to link a living space to a burial ritual.

Despite the fact that few individuals have been recovered, we can suggest that two distinct types of burial practices are represented in the site: a) primary intact burials, Grave 1; and b) burials incorporating post-depositional body treatment, Grave 2. The isolated bones of a foot and hands might also belong to a secondary deposition, because of the combination of anatomical parts deposited together. The secondary treatment of the body in these two graves may probably be linked to particular ritual practices still unknown. Both primary and secondary burial practices are known in other burial sites across the Arabian peninsula such as al-Buhais 18 (Kiesewetter 2006), Wadi Shab GAS-1 (Gaultier *et al.* 2005), and Ra's al-Hamra RH-5 (Salvatori 2007).

Individuals from Grave 1 and 2 were both buried in a flexed lateral *decubitus* position, showing strict similarities with graves from the contemporaneous burial site at GAS-1, the older graves discovered at Suwayh SWY-1 (Charpentier *et al.* 2003) and BHS-18, or the more recent ones excavated at RH-5 and RH-10 (Santini 1987). The presence of covering stones, as attested in Grave 1, is also recorded in the sites of GAS-1, SWY-1, Ra's al-Wuddayah WD-58, a site close to Ra's al-Jinz (Charpentier *et al.* 2003:18) and Ra's al-Hamra RH-5 and RH-10. Such covering stones are not known in the graves from BHS-18 (Kiesewetter 2006: 116). The scarcity of grave goods is again comparable to the GAS-1 and SWY-1 sites, highlighting a great difference with the wealthier deposits from BHS-18 (Kiesewetter *et al.* 2000), RH-5 and RH-10.

The recognized pathologies, stress and activity indicators, such as degenerative joint diseases, dental enamel hypoplasia and squatting facets, should be compared to other skeletal remains from the region by further studies.

Acknowledgements

We sincerely wish to thank the Ministry of Heritage and Culture of Oman, and especially Ms Byubwa Ali Al-Sabri, director of the Department of Excavations and Archaeological Research. We are grateful to Maurizio Tosi and Serge Cleuziou, directors of the Joint Hadd Project. We thank Anne-Marie Lézine (LSCE, UMR 1572 CNRS-CEA Gif-sur-Yvette) and Jean-François Saliège (LOCEAN, UMR 7159 CNRS/IRD/Université Pierre et Marie Curie, Paris) for the dating, and Christophe Moreau and Jean-Pascal Dumoulin (LMC14, Saclay) for the very efficient handling of the radiocarbon measurements. We would like to thank Hervé Guy, Matthieu Gaultier, Michel Signoli, Estelle Herrscher for their contribution to the anthropological study, carried out in Ra's al-Jinz in 2004, and Mark Tomasi for the English revision.

References

Boule E.-L. 2001. Osteological features associated with ankle hyperdorsiflexion. *International Journal of Osteoarchaeology* 11/5: 345-349.

Buikstra J. E. & Ubelaker D. (eds.) 1994. *Standards for data collection from human skeletal remains*. Fayetteville: Arkansas Archaeological Survey Research Series 44.

Bruzek J. 2002. A method for visual determination of sex, using the human hip bone. *American Journal of Physical Anthropology* 117: 157-168.

Capasso L., Kennedy K.A.R. & Wilczack C.A. 1999. *Atlas of occupational markers on human remains*. Teramo: Edigrafital S.p.A.

Cavulli F. 2004a. L'insediamento di KHB-1 (Ra's al-Khabbah, Sultanato dell'Oman): lo scavo, i resti strutturali e i confronti etnografici. *Ocnus* 12: 37-48.

Cavulli F. 2004b. Problemi stratigrafici relativi allo scavo di sedimenti sciolti in ambiente arido. *Ocnus* 12: 49-62.

Cavulli F. 2004c. Khabbah 1: un villaggio di pescatori raccoglitori del V millennio a.C. *Scoprire. Scavi del Dipartimento di Archeologia*, Ante Quem, Bologna: 225-229.

Cavulli F. & Scaruffi S. 2008. Stone vessels from KHB-1, Ja'lān region, Sultanate of Oman. *Proceedings of the Seminar for Arabian Studies* 38: 89-92.

Cavulli F., Cristiani E. & Scaruffi S. 2009. Techno-functional analysis at the fishing settlement of KHB-1 (Ra's al-Khabbah, Ja'lān, Sultanate of Oman). *Proceedings of the Seminars of Arabian Studies* 39: 73-80.

Charpentier V., Marquis P. & Pellé E. 2003. La nécropole et les derniers horizons V^e millénaire du site de Gorbat al-Mahar (Suwayh, SWY-1, Sultanat d'Oman): premiers résultats. *Proceedings of the Seminar for Arabian Studies* 33: 11-19.

Duday H. & Guillon M. 2006. Understanding the circumstances of decomposition when the body is skeletonized. Pages 117-157 in A. Schmitt, E. Cunha & J. Pinheiro (eds.) *Forensic Anthropology and Medicine*. Totowa: Humana Press.

Finnegan M. 1978. Non-metric variation of the infracranial skeleton. *Journal of Anatomy* 125/l: 23-37.

Gaultier M., Guy H., Munoz O., Tosi M. & Usai D. 2005. Settlement structures and cemetery at Wadi Shab-GAS1, Sultanate of Oman: Report on the 2002 and 2003 field seasons. *Arabian Archaeology and Epigraphy* 16: 1-20.

Hughen K.A, Baillie M.G.L., Bard E., Beck J.W., Bertrand Chanda J.H., *et al.* 2004. Marine04 marine radiocarbon age calibration, 0-26 cal kyr BP. *Radiocarbon* 46: 1059-1086.

Kiesewetter H., Uerpmann H.-P. & Jasim S.A. 2000. Neolithic jewellery from Jebel al-Buhais 18. *Proceedings of the Seminar for Arabian Studies* 30: 137-146.

Kiesewetter H. 2006. Analysis of the Human Remains from the Neolithic Cemetery at al-Buhais 18 (Excavations 1996-2000). Pages 106-380 in H.-P. Uerpmann, Uerpmann M. & Jasim S.A. (eds.) *Funeral Monuments and Human Remains from Jebel al-Buhais*. The archaeology of Jebel al-Buhais, Sharjah, UAE, vol.1, Tübingen.

Magnani G., Bartolomei G., Cavulli F., Esposito M., Marino E.C., Neri M., Rizzo A., Scaruffi S., & Tosi M. 2007. U-series and radiocarbon dates on mollusc shell from the uppermost layer of the archaeological site of KHB-1, Ra's al Khabbah, Oman. *Journal of Archaeological Science* 34: 749-755.

Maureille B. & Sellier P. 1996. Dislocation en ordre paradoxal, momification et décomposition: observations et hypothèses. *Bulletins et Mémoires de la Société d'Anthropologie de Paris* 8 : 313-327.

Munoz O., Zazzo A., Saliège J.-F. & Cleuziou S. 2008. *Reconstructing the diet of ancient fishermen of Ra's al-Hadd and Ra's al-Jinz (Sultanate of Oman) using radiocarbon dates*. Poster presented at the "Désert d'Afrique et d'Arabie: Environnement, climat et impact sur les populations" conference held at the Académie des Sciences, Paris, September 8th-9th 2008.

Reimer P.J., Baillie M.G.L., Bard E., Bayliss A., Beck J.W., *et al.* 2004. Intcal04 terrestrial radiocarbon age calibration, 0-26 cal kyr BP. *Radiocarbon* 46:1029-1058.

Saliège J.-F., Lézine A.-M. & Cleuziou S. 2005. Estimation de l'effet réservoir ^{14}C marin en mer d'Arabie. *Paleorient* 31/1 : 64-69.

Salvatori S. 2007. The Prehistoric Graveyard of Ra's al-Hamra 5, Muscat, Sultanate of Oman. *The Journal of Oman Studies* 14.

Santini G. 1987. Site RH-10 at Qurum and a preliminary analysis of its cemetery: an essay in stratigraphic discontinuity. *Proceedings of the Seminar for Arabian Studies* 17: 179-198.

Saunders S. R. 1978. *The Development and Distribution of Discontinuous Morphological Variation of the Human Infracranial Skeleton*. National Museum of Man Mercury Series No. 81. Ottawa.

Schemmer D., White P.G. & Friedman L. 1995. Radiology of the paraglenoid sulcus. *Skeletal Radiology* 25: 204-209.

Sereno P.C., Garcea E.A.A., Jousse H., Stojanowski C.M., Saliège J-F, *et al.* 2008. Lakeside Cemeteries in the Sahara: 5000 Years of Holocene Population and Environmental Change. *PLoS ONE* 3/8: e2995. Available from: http://dx.doi.org/10.1371/journal.pone.0002995.

Trotter M. 1970. Estimation of stature from intact long limb bones. Pages 71-83 in T. D. Steward (ed.), *Personal Identification in Mass Disasters*. Washington, D.C: Smithsonian Institution.

Authors' addresses
Olivia Munoz
Université de Paris 1/CNRS UMR 7041
Maison de l'Archéologie et de l'Ethnologie
21 allée de l'Université
F-92023 Nanterre Cedex (France)
e-mail: oliviamunoz@free.fr

Simona Scaruffi
Dipartimento di Archeologia
University of Bologna
Department of Archaeology
Piazza San Giovanni in Monte, 2
I-40124 Bologna (Italy)
e-mail: simonascaruffi@yahoo.it

Fabio Cavulli
Laboratorio di Preistoria "B. Bagolini"
Dipartimento di Filosofia
Storia e Beni Culturali
University of Trento
Corso 3 Novembre 132
I-38100 Trento (Italy)
e-mail: Fabio.Cavulli@unitn.it

Results, limits and potential: burial practices and Early Bronze Age societies in the Oman Peninsula

S. Méry

Summary

This paper presents the results of research carried out between 1998 and 2008 at Hili (eastern region of Abu Dhabi, United Arab Emirates), by a multidisciplinary team consisting of archaeologists, archaeological scientists, anthropologists, geologists, potters and stonecutters. The research incorporated the excavation of a collective pit-grave from the end of the Umm an-Nar Period, the study of the extraction, cutting, and setting up of the stone used to construct EBA tombs at Jebel Aqlah and Hili, and the study of local techniques of pottery fabrication at the end of the 3rd millennium BC.

Keywords: Arabia, Bronze Age, collective grave, architecture, pottery

Introduction

Without texts, iconography or specific finds in context, we know nothing today of funeral rites and their development in the Oman Peninsula during the Neolithic and Bronze Age, although we are able to identify certain funerary practices and activities based on data from excavations and studies of material. In the present article I will concentrate on the Early Bonze Age, especially its second phase the Umm an-Nar Period between 2700/2600 and 2000 BC, as data are more numerous and accurate for this time period.

Our knowledge of funerary practices is dependent upon the state of preservation of the remains, and the funerary monuments in the Oman Peninsula are usually ruined and incomplete. The bone material is not always preserved, and when it is, it usually consists of poorly preserved fragments. Another limitation is that our knowledge depends very directly upon the standards of excavation, study and publication. Finally, our hypotheses and classifications are conditioned by certain methodological or theoretical presuppositions: this is the case for the palaeo-demographic reconstructions, whose principles and procedures differ widely among researchers of different schools. This is not without effect on the mortality curves as well as on the hypotheses concerning the possible causes of death, and thus on the comparisons which can be made between sites. I will not enter into this debate, which more directly concerns the physical anthropologists who study the skeletal remains. Despite these reservations, it is clear that the data from funerary archaeology available today in the Oman Peninsula throw important light on ancient societies – their population, their social organisation – which is discussed here for the Umm an-Nar period.

The most frequent funerary structure in the Umm an-Nar period is the monumental circular stone tomb (Figs. 1 and 2), whose dimensions and number of compartments doubled over time (e.g. Vogt 1985, Frifelt 1991, Gagnaison et al. 2004). These are collective tombs, in which burials took place as deaths occurred, the deaths appearing to have been natural for the most part, over a period of time which is very difficult, even impossible, to estimate based on published data, but which was probably not more than one to two centuries according to the pottery assemblages. Correspondingly, the individuals buried in each tomb number from several dozen to nearly 400 (Fig. 3), although the calculation of MNI (Minimum Number of Individuals) is such a complex procedure for such deposits that it would be more correct to speak of "estimates", especially as almost all of the tombs of this type have been plundered.

In the Oman Peninsula during the Umm an-Nar period, two other types of burial exist, but they are much more rarely found, due to lack of efficient research. These are pit-graves, dug near the older monumental tombs (Figs. 1 and 4), which exhibit two types:

(1) collective graves, dating to the very end of the Umm an-Nar period and prefiguring the underground tombs of the Wadi Suq period (Al Hadouh 1989; Al Tikriti 1989; al Tikriti and Méry 2000). The pit-graves are large in size and were discovered in an undisturbed state, which is *never* the case for the circular tombs. The grave at Hili contains the remains of 700 individuals (MNI), without any selection by age or sex, according to the work of K. McSweeney (this volume), and whose natural deaths occurred over a time period of 100 to 200 years at the most, according to the radiocarbon dating on bones and charcoal and to the analysis of the artefacts. Everyone in the community had access to the collective burial.

(2) graves filled with bone material and artefacts, dated to about 2400 BC for the few tombs we know; these are secondary burials, with adaptations (Benton 1996, Montchablon et al. 2003).

Aims of the recent research conducted at Hili and methods of study

We know that profound transformations occurred in the societies of the Oman Peninsula at the end of the Neolithic, leading to the emergence of new societal configurations in the Bronze Age, but the mechanisms in play are still largely to be documented and clarified. Whatever the mechanisms and their relation to climatic developments, it is in the 3rd millennium that an agricultural system appeared which was to last to the

Monumental Circular Tombs, collective graves

◄ c. 3100-2700 BC - Hafit Period: truncated cone, single chamber

◄ c. 2700-2100 BC - Umm an-Nar Period: truncated semi-sphere, several chambers

Pit-tombs, associated with monumental circular tombs

◄ c. 2200-2000 BC - end of Umm an-Nar Period collective graves

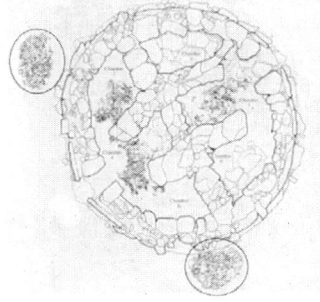

◄ c. 2400 BC - secondary burials

Figure 1. The three types of funerary structures in the Early Bronze Age of the Oman Peninsula.
After Benton 1996. Photos S. Méry, W.Y. Al Tikriti, P. Yole

Figure 2. Main architectural features of the monumental circular tombs during the Umm an-Nar period.
Photos S. Jassim, C. Velde. Drawing H. David.

Figure 3. The Umm an-Nar period monumental circular tombs are collective tombs, in which burials took place as deaths occurred. After Potts 2000 (right), photo S. Cleuziou (left)

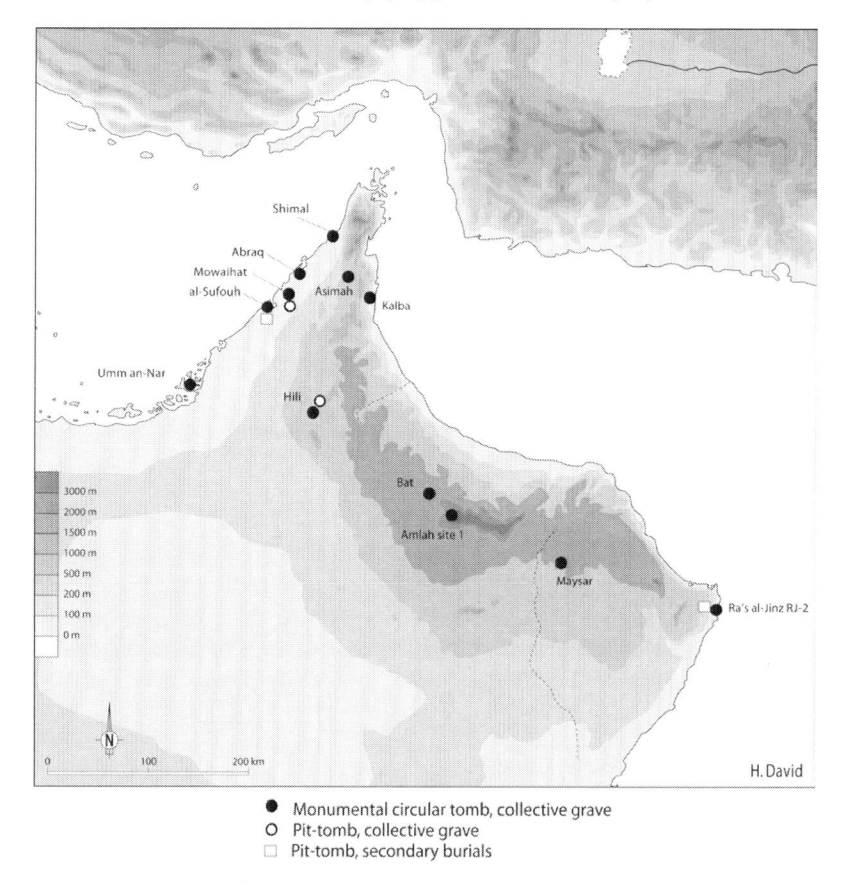

Figure 4. Distribution of the three types of Umm an-Nar period funerary structures.

present day: the oasis, based on the irrigated cultivation of the date palm, and which concentrates the sedentary occupations in the piedmont areas and in the mountain valleys, in contact with the wadis and the water tables (Tengberg 2003).

It does not appear that there was a local seat of invention for pottery (unlike Khuzistan and Baluchistan beginning in the 7th millennium); the pottery production established in the Oman peninsula in the 3rd millennium appears to have been a well-developed craft, with its origin in the Kech-Makran region and south-eastern Iran (Méry 2000, Potts 2005). However, this initial phase of production corresponds to the ferment of a technical and stylistic technique peculiar to the Oman peninsula, which grew during the 3rd millennium, along with other arts related to

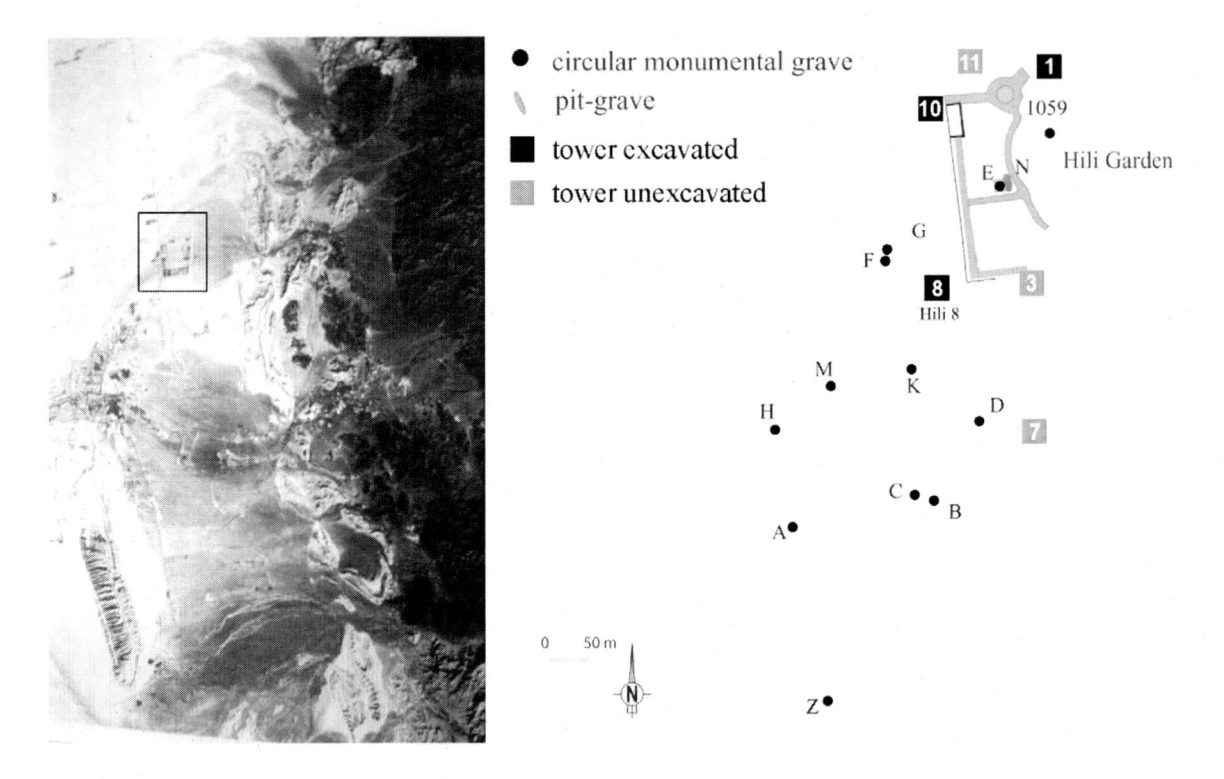

Figure 5. Distribution of the Umm an-Nar tombs at Hili. Drawing P. Dubeuf.
The architecture of the tombs was studied in order to better establish the relative chronology.

fire (such as copper metallurgy and possibly ornaments in faience). Other specialised craftwork developed in the same period, in particular finely worked stone, mud brick construction and vessels in soft stone. All this contributes to forming the image of a "coherent" cultural entity, in any case one that shares an ensemble of rules and representations, first of all in the funerary domain.

The most recent advances in funerary archaeology enable us today to record these processes more precisely, and it is this which I will attempt to show in presenting the results of research carried out between 1998 and 2008 at Hili, by a multidisciplinary team consisting of archaeologists, archaeological scientists, anthropologists, geologists, potters and stonecutters. Our research concerned three aspects:

1) Excavation was resumed at one of the rare collective pit-graves mentioned earlier, firstly excavated in by M. Al Haddu (1989) (Fig. 4). At Hili N, the funerary deposits of this grave were intact, with a complex but readable stratigraphy, covering the last two centuries of the 3rd millennium. The relative chronology of the different funerary deposits and the succession of funerary manipulations were reconstructed with field anthropologists specially trained in the excavation of complex collective burials (Gatto et al. 2003; McSweeney et al. 2008; Méry et al. 2001; Méry et al. 2004; Méry et al. 2008).

2) The study of the extraction, cutting, and setting up of the stone used to construct EBA tombs at Jebel Aqlah and Hili. This facilitated a better understanding of ancient techniques and craft specialisation, and clarified the relative chronology of the Umm an-Nar tombs (Gagnaison et al 2006). The core of that study was constituted by the tombs at Hili Garden and Hili Fun city (Fig. 5). Numerous tombs of the Umm an-Nar circular monumental type were excavated at Hili in the period from the early 1960s to the early 80s, and the study aimed to establish the relative chronology of these Umm an-Nar tombs based mainly on a study of their finely worked stone. This was necessary as two-thirds of the tombs lacked the artefacts and pottery necessary for relative dating.

3) Finally, the techniques of pottery fabrication were studied, in particular the techniques of shaping, in order to work on the question of the ancient techniques and craft specialisation. Such issues are central to debates surrounding the EBA in the Oman Peninsula.

Main results of the research conducted at Hili

Tomb Numbers and Chronology

The first result of our research was a re-evaluation of the number of monumental tombs at Hili and the duration of the period during which they were constructed was possible. It was previously considered that 14 circular tombs were constructed at Hili over a time period of 600 or 700 years, from about 2700/2600 to 2000 BC. But our studies have shown that this time span is shorter, as there was probably no construction of Umm an-Nar circular tombs after 2300-2200 BC at Hili. Moreover the total

Figure 6. The facing-stones of three Umm an-Nar monumental circular tombs, whose location at Hili is still not known, were reused in Hili 8 settlement. Photos S. Méry.

Figure 7. Top: Diorite percussion tools used for the cutting and picking of the calcarenite blocks. Bottom: in the Umm an-Nar period, cutting and dressing of the facing blocks was completed at the place where the tombs were to be constructed and the search for the 'perfect join' was growing through time. Photos P. Dubeuf and S. Méry.

number of tombs is not 14 but 17, in addition to the pit-grave, because there were three more circular tombs at Hili Garden (still not located), indicated by facing stones that were reused at the beginning of Period II at the Hili 8 settlement (Fig. 6). Moreover a tomb was discovered, or better, re-discovered by ADACH south of the enclosure of the archaeological park, and designated tomb Z. It was excavated in the early 1970s but forgotten thereafter.

Tomb Construction Techniques

The second result of our research was an improved understanding of the processes of construction of the tombs and the architectural sequence at Hili. C. Gagnaison (2006) has researched the origin of the construction stones and identified many traces of extraction in the layers of a limestone range, the Jebel Aqlah, located 1.5 km from Hili. The zones which were preferentially exploited in the different phases of the Umm an-Nar period were able to be defined. The local limestone, hard and difficult to work, breaks easily when cut: the blocks were thus summarily prepared on the Jebel Aqlah, which limited problems of transport and loss. During the Umm an-Nar period, cutting and dressing of the facing blocks was completed at the place where the tombs were to be constructed, in order to adjust the joins. The search for the 'perfect join' was growing through time, as documented by J.-C. Bessac and P. Dubeuf (Fig.

Figure 8. The oldest Umm an-Nar circular tombs include small facing stones only, worked on the edge and superficially dressed. Photos J.-C. Bessac, S. Méry.

Figure 9. Tomb H is the most recently constructed monument among of the oldest group of monumental Umm an-Nar circular tombs at Hili. Photo S. Méry

Figure 10. Tomb A, one of the most elaborate Umm an-Nar circular tombs at Hili is characterized by large facing stones, worked parallel to the edge and carefully dressed on the 5 sides. Photo P. Dubeuf.

Figure 11. As for Tomb M, Tomb J is classified in the intermediate chronological group of Umm an-Nar tombs at Hili. Photo S. Méry.

7). Only stone tools were used by the stonecutters; dozens of fragments of these diorite percussion tools, whose efficiency has been proven by experimentation, were found around the Hili tombs and on Jebel Aqlah.

Except for these two very early Umm an-Nar tombs at Hili, constructed at the same time, it is now clear that the tombs were built one after the other and that there was a continuous and almost *linear* development in the quality of construction during the Umm an-Nar period (Gagnaison et al. 2006). Tomb Z, south of the cemetery, is the earliest tomb (Fig. 8); Tomb 1059, located in the heart of the Umm an-Nar settlement, is the latest one.

The oldest tombs are the simplest, with small facing stones, worked on the edge and superficially dressed

(Figs. 8 and 9). This work may have been carried out by individuals who cut stone only occasionally. The youngest tombs are the most elaborated ones, with much bigger facing stones, worked parallel to the edge and carefully dressed on the 5 sides (Fig. 10). According to J.-C. Bessac, these later stonemasons were experienced craftsmen, no longer limited by size to the thickness of the natural stone layer, which enabled reduction of the number of courses. The tombs with underground chambers belong to this group.

Other tombs at Hili are classified in an intermediate group (Fig. 11), including the tombs identified from the reused facing stones at Hili 8 (Fig. 6). This indicates that Tomb M is not the oldest Umm an-Nar tomb as was previously thought (Cleuziou 1989). It also shows that the beginning of the Umm an-Nar period precedes Period IIa at Hili 8.

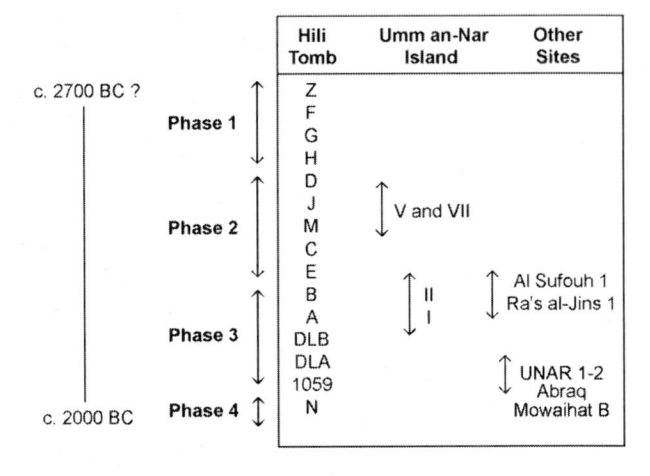

Figure 12. The relative chronology of the Umm an-Nar tombs at Hili and their correspondence with other Umm an-Nar tombs (monumental circular tombs and pit-graves) from the Oman peninsula.

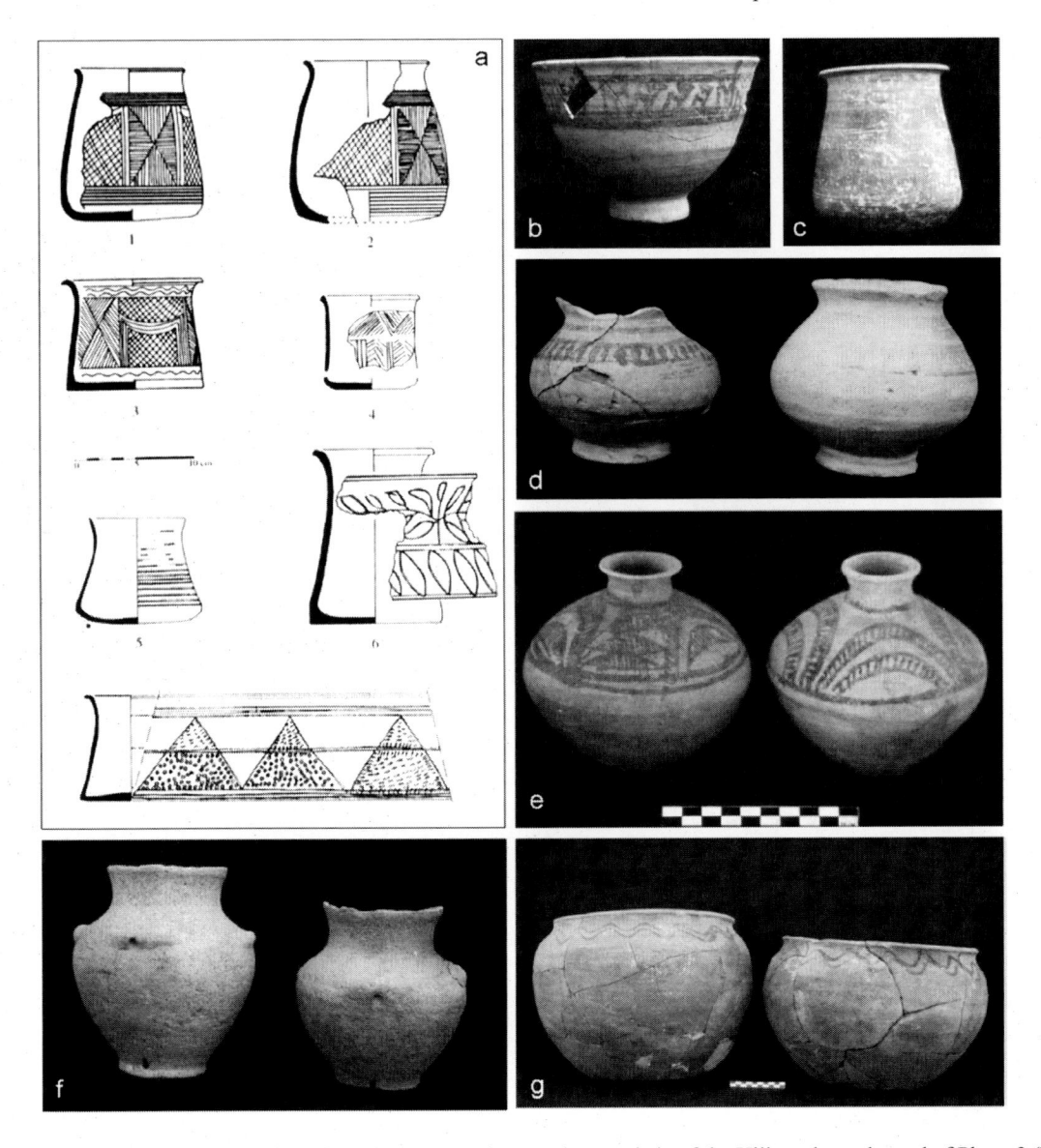

Figure 13. Some examples of imported and local pottery wares and types characteristic of the Hili tombs at the end of Phase 3 (Tomb A at Hili North). Many of the same types are associated with the first use of pit-grave N. Examples a-d: Dasht (Kech Makran, Pakistan); e: south-eastern Iran; f: Oman Peninsula; g: Hili. Not to scale. Drawing P. Gouin, photos S. Méry.

Chronological Phases at Bronze Age Hili

A third result of our research is the fact that four chronological phases are now reconstructed for Hili in the Umm an-Nar period (McSweeney et al. 2008). Our phases are primarily based on architectural analysis. Phases 1 to 3 correspond to the period of construction of the circular monumental tombs, Phase 4 to the pit-grave at Hili. The correspondence between Hili tombs and other Umm an-Nar tombs in the U.A.E. is illustrated in Fig. 12. We know very little about **Phase 1**, c. 2700-2600 BC, as the tombs (Z, F, G, H) were in a ruined state when discovered. Material was rare, but also remains unpublished.

Phase 2 corresponds to the construction of the *intermediate circular tombs*, from about 2600-2500 BC. Little is known about the grave goods, except for Tomb M – in the middle of the sequence. Its pottery has good parallels with Period I, IIa-c1 and IIc2 at Hili 8 settlement, and we also know that Phase IIa corresponds to the construction of a building at Hili 8 which incorporates facing stones from Umm an-Nar tombs that are similar, but not identical, to those of Tomb M.

Phase 3 corresponds to the elaborate tombs, constructed from about 2400 BC. The most elaborate are the later ones. They date to a late but not final phase of the Umm an-Nar period, characterised by the importance of imported prestige artefacts from the Dasht valley in Kech-Makran, the Indus valley and possibly south-east Iran, but local and regionally-produced thrown pottery vessels are also characteristic (Fig. 13).

In **Phase 4**, no further monumental circular tombs were constructed at Hili, but the pit-grave was dug ca. 2200/2100 BC. Grave goods from the first period of use of the pit-grave indicate that the population and the social structure did not change as the local pottery is the same (in wares and types), and the proportion and composition of personal ornaments, including imported or rare items, are the same or similar (Fig. 13). During the second period of use of the pit-grave, the population did not change, although some important changes did occur. Exchange networks, such as with the Indus peoples, became less frequent and types of imported goods differed. Even more significant is the development of local pottery production.

Craft Specialisation

As a final result of our research, the excavation of these tombs and the analysis of the pottery they contained provide information on pottery production and craft specialisation within an EBA oasis such as Hili. The excavations carried out since the end of the 1960s have produced evidence for the existence of an agricultural and village population at Hili, but also of craftsmen whose degree of specialisation increased in the 3rd millennium – stonecutters as we have seen, but also potters. Small-scale metallurgy was also practised at the site, and possibly the cutting of soft stone, indicated by the discovery of a block of chlorite near Tomb H.

The technological analyses and the experiments which we have carried out together with S. Van der Leeuw and A. Dupont-Delaleuf during the study of the material from several tombs at Hili (tomb M, tomb A of Hili North and the pit-grave tomb N) have provided evidence for the use of thrown bases for the shaping of domestic pottery (Fig. 14). This is certain at Hili from at least 2600 BC, but throwing in the strict sense of the complete pot – that is, of a centred ball of clay, hollowed and raised – was probably not yet mastered.

This technique is not even certain 500 years later, as indicated by the extensive technological study which we have made of the material from the pit-grave. If so, it would have been exceptional, concerning only small or medium-sized vessels. Most of the domestic pottery was made from coils which were finished or shaped on the wheel, or from turned coils on a pinched, round flat ball of clay. But some were shaped on a thrown base.

The variety of technical styles and the degree of technical skill necessary indicates that knowledge of pottery fabrication at Hili continued in differentiated traditions. As indicated by the material discovered in the pit-grave, several "units" of production would have functioned at the same time at the end of the 3rd millennium, and produced groups of vessels which the technological and typological study is able to distinguish. I believe that this is the expression of an important phase of technological innovation in the region in this period, a phase of innovation that is perceptible in other domains, as shown for the funerary architecture.

Were the makers of domestic pottery specialists? Probably, in the sense that they mastered techniques not shared by everyone. Did they produce their pottery within the home or in specialised workshops? We have too few elements to judge this. However, a minimum of four "units" of production have been defined for each main phase of funerary deposit in the pit-grave of Hili, and these "units" of production were contemporary in their operation. We may thus suppose that production was probably organised within households. The fact that technical differences were observed between each unit supports this hypothesis, especially as these gaps persisted over time, through several generations. Were these full-time specialists? Probably not, as the techno-economic system existing at Hili in this period was founded on exploitation of the resources of an agricultural oasis, and it is reasonable to suppose that these potters were also farmers.

Conclusion

The excavation of Tomb N and the re-examination of the large circular tombs of Hili have provided new information on the chronology and the development of craft techniques and trade in the Umm an-Nar period. The monumental circular tombs do not represent the only model in use in the Oman Peninsula at the end of the

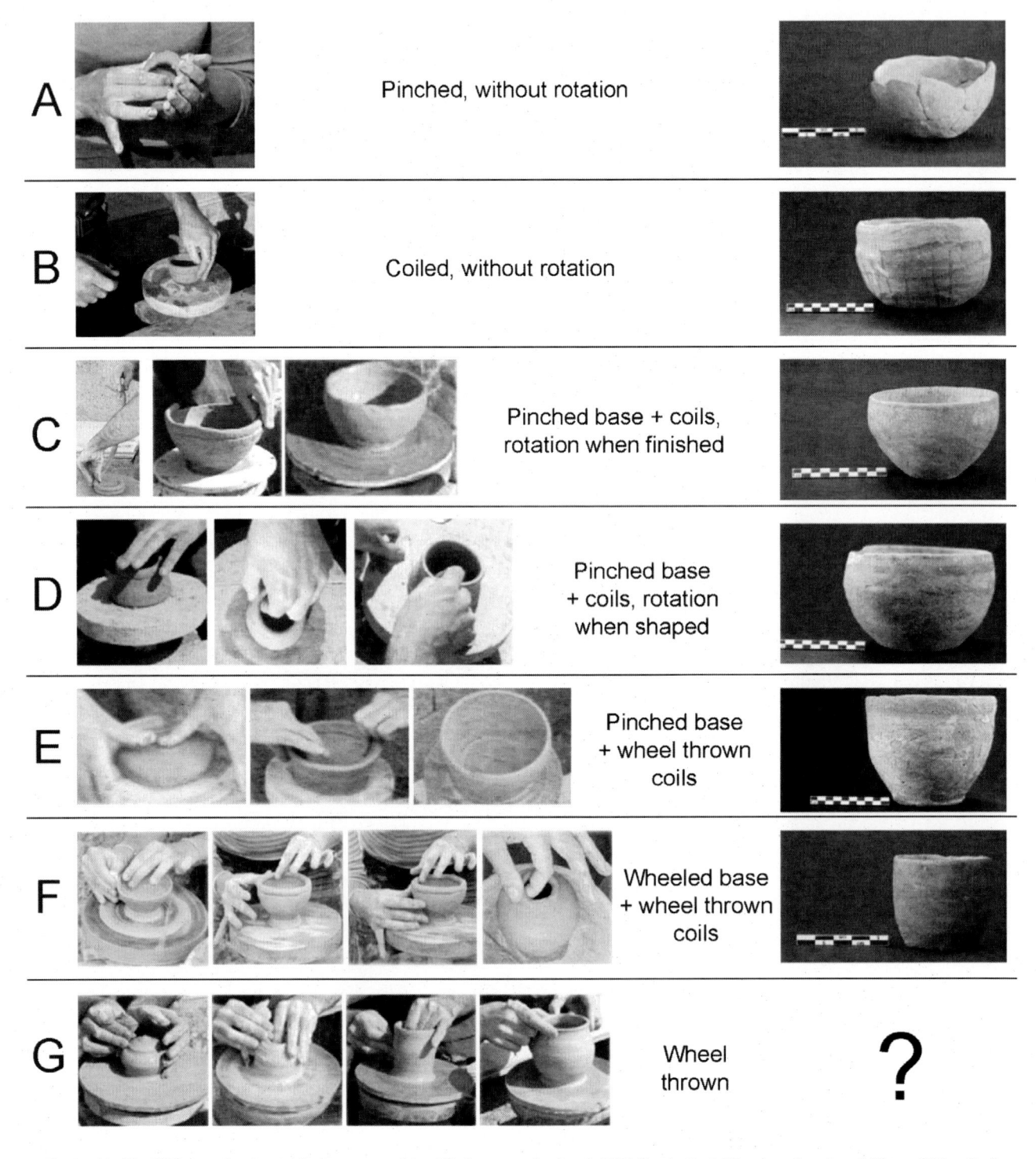

A		Pinched, without rotation
B		Coiled, without rotation
C		Pinched base + coils, rotation when finished
D		Pinched base + coils, rotation when shaped
E		Pinched base + wheel thrown coils
F		Wheeled base + wheel thrown coils
G		Wheel thrown ?

Figure 14. Six different shaping techniques were identified among the local (Hili Sandy Red Ware) and regional (Omani Fine Red ware) pottery wares at Hili, but wheel throwing of complete vessels (technique G) is not certain at the end of 3rd millennium BC. Photos J.-P. Bérubé, A. Dupont-Delaleuf, S. Méry.

Early Bronze Age, and the collective pit-graves of the end of the Umm an-Nar period do represent a new type of tomb, which appeared about 2200 BC and disappeared at the turn of the 2nd millennium. These changes correspond to the end of the Umm an-Nar period and herald the enormous subterranean tombs of "Wadi Suq" type. At about 2000 BC, this new "Wadi Suq" culture was to emerge throughout the Oman Peninsula, and all aspects of the material culture were to change or be re-arranged again. This was to be the Middle Bronze Age.

Acknowledgements

The French archaeological mission in the UAE is sponsored by the Ministry of Foreign Affairs-Paris; we thank Mr Lanapats and Dr J.-F. Jarrige of the

Commission des Fouilles. In Al Ain, Emirate of Abu Dhabi, our work was sponsored by the Department of Antiquities and Tourism in Al Ain thanks to the support of its formal Director, Saif bin Ali al Darmaki, and from 2006, by ADACH. We thank M. Mohamad Khalaf al Mazrui, Dr Samiasri and Dr al-Tikriti. Thanks to the kind authorisation the Ministry of Heritage and Culture, Sultanate of Oman, and the Director of Excavations and Archaeological Studies, Ms Biubwa Ali Al-Sabri, we could extend our studies to the Jebel Aqlah, Sultanate of Oman, 1 km east of Hili.

References

Benton J. n.d. *Excavations at Al Sufouh. A third millennium site in the Emirate of Dubai. Abiel I.* Leiden: Brepols.

Cleuziou S. 1989. The chronology of protohistoric Oman as seen from Hili. Pages 47-78 in P.M. Costa & M. Tosi (eds), *Oman Studies*. Rome: Serie Orientale Roma LXIII, IsMEO.

Gagnaison C., Barrier P., Méry S., & Al Tikriti W.Y. 2004. Extractions de calcaires éocènes à l'Age du Bronze et architecture funéraire à Hili (Emirat d'Abou Dhabi). *Revue d'Archéométrie* 28 : 97-108.

Gatto E., Basset G., Méry S., & McSweeney K. 2003. Etude paléodémographique et utilisation du feu à Hili N, une sépulture collective en fosse de la fin de l'âge du Bronze ancien aux Emirats Arabes Unis. *Bulletins et Mémoires de la Société d'Anthropologie de Paris* n.s. t. 15: 1-2, 25-47.

Haddu (Al) M.M. 1989. Preliminary report on the excavation of Tomb N, Hili Gardens. *Archaeology in the United Arab Emirates* V: 55-71 (in Arabic).

McSweeney K., Méry S., & Macchiarelli R. 2008. Rewriting the end of Early Bronze Age in the United Arab Emirates, through the anthropological and artefactual evaluation of two collective Umm an-Nar graves at Hili (Eastern region of Abu Dhabi). *Arabian Archaeology and Epigraphy* 19: 1-14.

Méry S. 2000. *Les céramiques d'Oman et l'Asie moyenne, une archéologie des échanges à l'Âge du Bronze*. Paris: CNRS Editions.

Méry S., McSweeney K., Rouquet J., Basset G. & Al-Tikriti W.Y. 2008. New evidence of funerary practices at the end of the Early Bronze Age at Hili, United Arab Emirates. Pages 200-208 in E. Olijdam & R.H. Spoor (eds.), *Intercultural Relations Between South and Southwest Asia. Studies in Commemoration of E.C.L. During Caspers (1934-1996)*. Archaeopress BAR International Series, Oxford.

Méry S., McSweeney K., Van der Leeuw S. & Tikriti (Al) W.Y. 2004. New approaches to a collective grave from the Umm An-Nar period at Hili (UAE). *Paléorient* 2: 163-178.

Méry S., Rouquet J., McSweeney K., Basset G., Saliège J.-F. & Tikriti (Al) W.Y. 2001. Re-excavation of the Early Bronze Age collective Hili N pit-grave (Emirate of Abu Dhabi, UAE): results of the first two campaigns of the Emirati-French Project. *Proceedings of the Seminar for Arabian Studies* 31: 161-178.

Montchablon C., Crassard R., Munoz O., Guy H., Bruley-Chabot G. & Cleuziou S. 2003. Excavations at Ra's al-Jinz RJ-1: stratigraphy without tells. *Proceedings of the Seminar for Arabian Studies* 33: 31-47.

Potts D. T. 2000. *Ancient Magan. The secrets of Tell Abraq*. London: Trident Press.

Tengberg M. 2003. Archaeobotany in the Oman Peninsula and the role of Eastern Arabia in the spread of African Crops. Pages 229-237 in K. Neumann, A. Butler & S. Kahlheber (eds) *Food, Fuel and Fields. Progress in African Archaeobotany*. Köln: Heinrich-Barth-Institut. Africa Praehistorica. Monographien zur Archäologie und Umwelt Afrikas.

Tikriti (Al) W.Y. 1989. Umm an-Nar culture in the Northern Emirates: third millennium BC tombs at Ajman. *Archaeology in the United Arab Emirates* 5: 89-99.

Tikriti (Al) W.Y. & Méry S. 2000. Tomb N at Hili and the question of the subterranean graves during the Umm an-Nar period. *Proceedings of the Seminar for Arabian Studies* 30: 205-219.

Vogt B. 1985. *Zur Chronologie und Entwicklung der Gräber des späten 4. -2. Jt. v. Chr. auf der Halbinsel Oman : Zusammenfassung, Analyse und Würdigung publizierter wie auch unveröffentlichter Grabungsergebnisse*. Unpublished doctoral thesis, Georg-August Universität, Göttingen.

Author's Address

Dr Sophie Méry
CNRS, UM7041 ArScAn, MAE R. Ginouvès
21 allée de l'université
92023 Nanterre cedex
France
sophie.mery@mae.u-paris10.fr

Life and death in an Early Bronze Age community from Hili, Al Ain, UAE

Kathleen McSweeney, Sophie Méry and Walid Yasin al Tikriti

Summary

The Early Bronze Age collective pit-grave, Hili N produced the largely undisturbed and well-preserved, though disarticulated, fragmented and commingled, remains of over 700 individuals. Such a large number of individuals provides a useful basis for compiling a biological profile of the community served by the tomb. While the condition of the remains made the osteological analysis challenging, some interesting indications of health in an Early Bronze Age community at the end of the Umm an-Nar period have emerged. In this paper the evidence for dental disease, anaemia and other diseases, trauma, mortality profiles, stature, and other non-specific indicators of skeletal stress are considered. These results provide a basis to observe and compare the evidence from other sites and periods in prehistoric Arabia, so that a picture of health and disease among early populations in the area can be developed.

Keywords: anthropology, palaeopathology, Bronze Age, Arabia, collective grave

Introduction

The Early Bronze Age, pit-grave, Tomb N, from Hili, Al Ain, United Arab Emirates (UAE), dating to the end of the Umm an-Nar period, has been described elsewhere in detail (see, for example, Méry *et al.* 2001, 2004, 2008). A further account will not be repeated here other than briefly. Hili N is unusual in that it was a pit grave, rather than, more typical for the period, an upstanding circular tomb. The grave, 2.5m deep, 6.6m long and 2m wide, had approximately 1.75 metres depth of human remains and artefacts (Haddu 1989; Méry *et al.* 2001) and dates to the very end of the Umm an-Nar period (Méry *et al.* 2008).

The site was excavated in two phases: the first series of excavations took place from 1984 to 1989, and were carried out by a team from the Department of Antiquities and Tourism (DAAT), Al Ain, directed by one of the authors (W.Y.T.) (Haddu 1989). A second series of annual campaigns occurred from 1998 to 2006. The purpose of the second phase was to excavate a section left *in situ* following the initial excavations (Fig. 1) (Méry *et al.* 2001, 2008). The second campaign was a joint project undertaken by the French Mission in the UAE and DAAT and was co-directed by two of the authors (S.M. and W.Y.T.). The human remains were examined by one of the authors (K.M.), also in two phases: 1) those remains

Figure 1. Hili N in the 1980s. Note the unexcavated section (arrows). This is the area excavated in the Phase 2 excavations.

Figure 2. Hili N in 1984, prior to excavation. Note the covering slabs.

retrieved from the phase 1 excavations; and 2) those from the most recent joint campaign. The phase 1 anthropological analysis formed part of the research for a PhD thesis presented to the University of Edinburgh (McSweeney 2003). This brief paper incorporates the anthropological findings from both campaigns.

Condition of the Remains

The aim of most human skeletal analyses is to create, as accurately as possible, a biological profile of the individual or group of individuals being examined. Any interpretation of skeletal analysis will inevitably have inherent inaccuracies and one of the greatest impediments to proper interpretation is bias in the sample. It is never possible to be certain that a whole community is present in a skeletal assemblage. However, a collective grave such as Hili N provides an opportunity to capture a greater proportion of the dead in a population than burial in spatially distributed individual graves, where parts of the cemetery may have been destroyed, or left unexcavated. Furthermore, a subterranean as opposed to an upstanding monument, depending on the environmental conditions, may also help to optimise preservation; graves that are invisible in the landscape are less likely to have been disturbed, an unfortunate fate of many of the upstanding Umm an-Nar tombs. In addition, as can be seen from the presence of roofing slabs in the photograph in Fig. 2, Hili N was undisturbed and, apart from some damage to the deposits in the upper layer (Haddu 1989), the contents were intact; an intact grave further helps to maximise the potential information that can be extracted. It is quite likely therefore, and this has been borne out by the results of the anthropological analysis, that the skeletal contents of Hili N accurately represent the local community that used the grave.

Furthermore, as was shown by the Phase 2 excavations that revealed hundreds of articulated body parts, Hili N was a place of primary deposition, and not, as may have been otherwise assumed from the apparent state of disarticulation, an ossuary for the secondary deposition of remains initially buried elsewhere (Méry *et al.* 2004). Skeletal remains from primary burials are more likely to be complete than those that have been redeposited; in the latter, smaller bones often become lost and under-represented in the skeletal assemblage (Mays 1998). The risk of sample bias was therefore minimal; however, the

Figure 3. Hili N remains: (a) *in situ* commingled skeletal material; (b) fragmentary remains; (c) articulated spine and thorax; (d) complete foot bones in the process of being sorted.

extracted data was constrained by the nature of the Hili N skeletal material, which was extremely fragmented and commingled (Fig. 3a and 3b). While bone tissue was generally well preserved thanks to a favourable environment, unfortunately, many bones, especially the larger skeletal elements, had been reduced to small fragments, probably as a result of rearrangement of the remains within the internal space of the tomb. Consequently, there were only a small number of complete long bones and very few intact skulls. Dental remains were also in poor condition. While mandibular, and to a lesser extent, maxillary fragments had survived fairly well, most of the teeth that had been *in situ* at the time of death, had been lost *post mortem*, and the crowns of the few teeth that were still *in situ* in the socket had largely become damaged.

On the contrary, many smaller bones, such as those of the hand and foot (Fig. 3d), patellae and vertebrae, as well as immature bones, had survived mostly intact. The fact that the sub-adult population amounted to 43% of the total is testimony to the good survival of immature bone (see below). It appears that smaller bones were protected from fragmentation because their size and shape allowed them to slip into spaces between larger bones.

Methodology

Huge volumes of commingled and fragmentary remains (hundreds of thousands of complete and incomplete bones) that could not be reassembled into individual skeletons necessitated an entirely different methodology to that normally applied to the osteological analysis of discrete inhumations. Ideally, when assessing age at death, sex or the presence of disease, the full skeleton should be examined and a consensus arrived at from various strands of evidence. Although the improved retrieval methods used in the Phase 2 excavations optimised the recovery and collation of articulating bones (Méry *et al.* 2001), in most cases, each bone from the Hili N skeletal assemblage had to be viewed in isolation. This means that estimations of demographic details will be less informative than that obtained from complete skeletons. Notwithstanding this constraint, a vast amount of anthropological data have been extracted that can help build a picture of the Hili N community.

Biological Profile of the Hili N Community

Based on counts of the most commonly occurring bone element, the petrous part of the temporal bone, it has been estimated that a minimum of 700 individuals were buried in the Hili N pit-grave.

High sub-adult mortality is indicated (43%), and of this proportion 58% had died before the age of 5 years. According to Lewis (2007), the period that a child is most at risk is 6 months to 3 years and this concurs with the Hili N results. The assessment of adult age at death was disappointing; only about 13% could be placed into a specific age category: young, middle, or old adulthood. Most that could be said of the majority of adults was that they had reached adulthood, so the extent of adult longevity could not be precisely explored. However, as the evidence for skeletal degeneration appears low, this may indicate that, in general, most adults did not live into advanced adulthood.

Sex was assessed (albeit tentatively in the absence of intact skulls and pelvic bones, the most sexually diagnostic areas of the skeleton) largely on the basis of secondary sexual morphological traits. Females and probable females accounted for 44% of the total; males and probable males for 40%, and 16% of adults were sexually non-dimorphic, i.e., their dimensions fell between the ranges for modern males and females. Although limited, these results does not suggest that there was any bias towards either sex in the grave.

Stature, calculated on the basis of metatarsal lengths, less reliable than that based on complete limb bones (the most common method of assessing height), indicated an average female height of 157.7 cm, with a range of 147.8 cm to 163.5 cm, and an average of 171.1 cm, with a range of 164.6 cm to 183.4 cm for males. These, relatively small, average heights are very similar to that of other contemporaneous populations in the Arabian Peninsula, suggesting the methods used may not have had too detrimental an effect on the accuracy of the results (McSweeney 2003; McSweeney forthcoming).

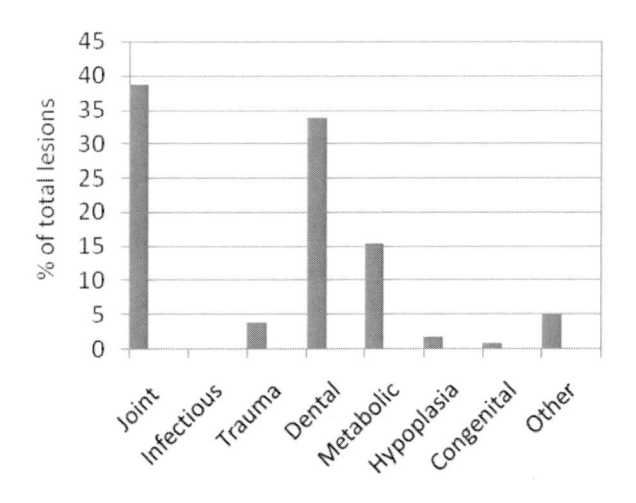

Figure 4. Hili N pathological lesions according to type as a percentage of total.

Pathology

Identified pathological lesions have been collated and roughly grouped according to the classification of disease, i.e., trauma, joint disease, metabolic disease, dental disease, dental hypoplasia (not a disease as such, but a manifestation of non-specific skeletal stress), congenital anomalies and a miscellaneous category that includes conditions of unclear aetiology (Fig. 4). The use of these categories of disease is not intended to convey a firm diagnosis of the lesions; they are simply a means by which similar types of lesions, of *possibly* the same aetiology, can be analysed.

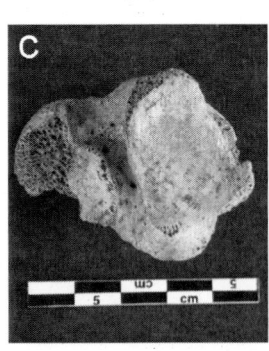

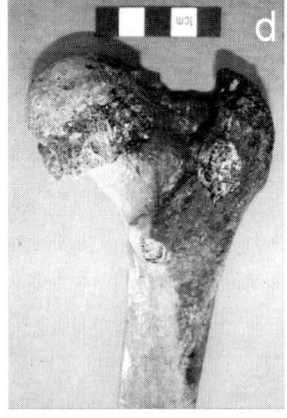

Figure 5. Hili N Joint disease: (a) right scapula showing osteoarthritis of the shoulder; (b) arthritis of the neck; (c) talus with lipping around the talocalcaneal joint of the foot; (d) mushroom-shaped femoral head and marginal lipping is indicative of osteoarthritis of the hip.

Joint Disease

The most frequently occurring lesions (38.6%) were recorded at the joints (Fig. 5). While this may seem high, it should be remembered that: 1) frequencies are based on affected bones and do not represent individuals; (2) vertebral osteophytosis (lipping), a normal development in the ageing process are included; and (3) there are 24 vertebrae in the spine and it is normal for individuals to have more than one spinal joint affected. Other diseased joints, according to percentage frequency, were the feet and ankles (36%), knees (23%), mandible (10%), hands (10%), elbows (7%) and hips (3%).

While there are many different types of diseases that can affect the joints, the most common in modern clinical medicine is osteoarthritis, a degenerative condition, closely associated with activity and ageing, and it is osteoarthritis that has been most commonly found on skeletal remains (Roberts and Manchester 2005: 105). Diagnosing a specific joint disease from disarticulated remains is difficult, especially as the pattern of distribution of joints affected is crucial to diagnosis (Rogers & Waldron 1995), but osteoarthritis is the most likely cause. Its presence may be significant; in modern medicine the disease is uncommon in individuals below the age of 40 years (Waldron 2009). Although we can never be sure that this pattern would have been the same in the past, it does give some insight into the longevity of some of the individuals.

Recent clinical evidence has shown that the most common joints for osteoarthritis to develop are the main weight bearing joints, the hip and the knee, and those of the hands (Waldron 2009: 31). The relative frequencies indicated above are likely to at least partly to reflect the condition of the skeletal material and not just clinical significance. For example, the low level of lesions at the hip (3%) is probably due to the relatively poor survival of pelvic bones and femurs. Of note, ankle and foot bones were more commonly affected than hand bones and had the commonest skeletal area involvement other than the spine. This is particularly interesting in view of the fact that osteoarthritis of the feet and ankles occurs relatively infrequently in modern medicine (Waldron 2009). The aetiology of osteoarthritis although multifactorial, is strongly associated with activity, and in the case of foot bones is probably associated with mobility.

Infectious Disease

There was very little evidence for infectious disease. Most types of infectious disease are short-lived and leave no trace on the skeleton, although some chronic infectious diseases, such as tuberculosis and leprosy, may do. In the absence of articulated skeletons, no chronic infectious diseases were identified. Two examples of middle ear disease, one case of osteomyelitis, and several occurrences of non-specific inflammation of bone (periostitis) were noted.

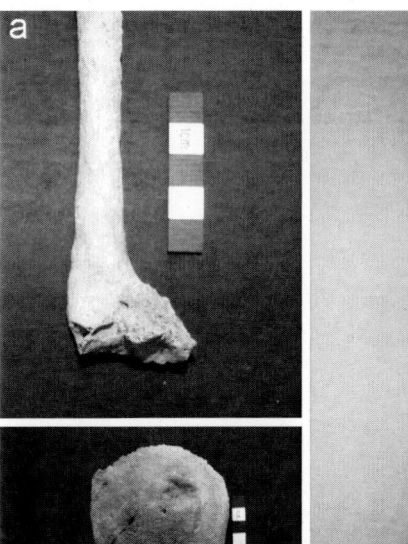

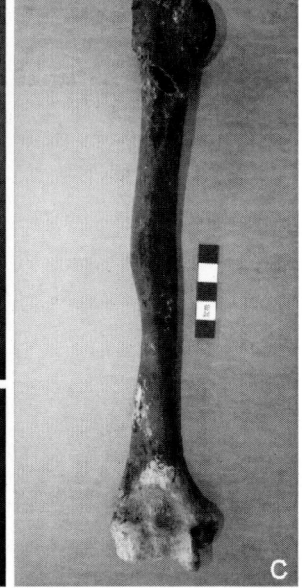

Figure 6. Hili N: sample of traumatic lesions: (a) healed Colles fracture of the distal radius; (b) healed skull fracture; (c) healed mid-shaft fracture of the humerus.

Trauma

Some examples of trauma can be seen in Fig. 6. Healed fractures were most commonly found on the smaller bones, such as those of the hand and foot, ribs, vertebrae and clavicles. The infrequency of fractures on other bones, such as the limbs or skulls, is very likely to be reflective of the *post mortem* fragmentation of these bones.

It is very likely that most of the healed fractures had occurred as a result of everyday accidents. While, fractures of the cranium, face, ribs, and forearm, often associated with interpersonal violence, were noted, these were largely of low frequencies, and while some violent incidents no doubt occurred in Bronze Age Hili, as in any community, there is no reason to suppose that this was widespread.

Dental Disease

The condition of jaw bones varied from small fragments, consisting of one or two tooth places, to complete mandibles. As indicated above most of the jaw fragments were edentulous, either because the teeth had fallen out of their sockets *post mortem*, or had been lost during life, or both. A large number of loose teeth were also present, although these were far less in number than empty tooth sockets. Many of these loose teeth had become damaged and were also in poor condition.

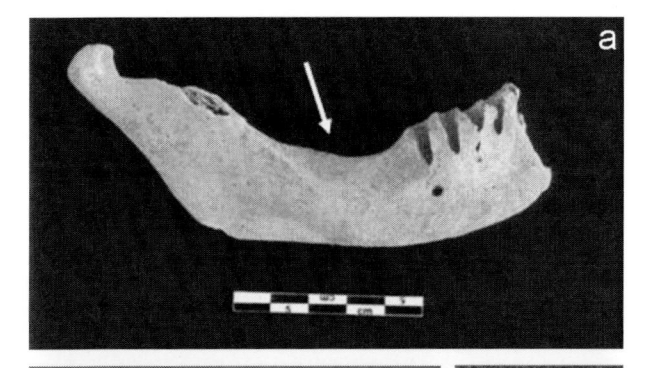

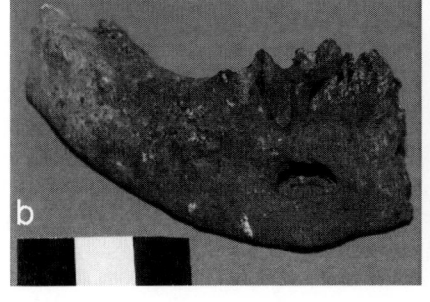

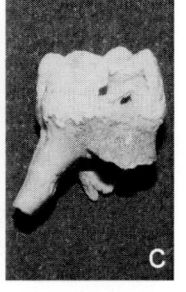

Figure 7. Hili N: Dental disease: (a) typical mandible from Hili N. The right hemi-mandible has sockets for both incisors, the canine and first premolar, indicating that these teeth had been *in situ* at the time of death, but had subsequently fallen out of their sockets *post mortem*. Healed bone at the sites for the second premolar and all three molars (arrow), point to these teeth being lost some time before death; (b) mandible fragment with dental abscess; (c) deciduous molar with carious lesion.

Despite the poor condition of the dentition, a high frequency of dental disease was evident. The most striking factor was the prevalence of *ante mortem* tooth loss; 64% of all adult jaw fragments had missing teeth. A typical mandible had anterior teeth present at the time of death (although lost *post mortem*) and the posterior teeth missing *ante mortem* (Fig 7a). The cause of the high level of tooth loss in the Hili N individuals is not entirely clear from the surviving evidence. The aetiology of tooth loss might normally be deduced from an examination of surviving teeth and jaws. For example, if the caries rate of the surviving dentition is high, then it may be deduced that the *in vivo* loss is probably as a result of dental decay. However, with the Hili N remains, not only are those teeth lost during life not available for examination, but, with some rare exceptions, the dentition that had been present at death had mostly been lost *post mortem* (Fig. 7a).

Similar patterns of tooth loss have been reported from other prehistoric Gulf populations. It has been assumed by many that such loss is a consequence of the development of caries as a result of eating dates (for example, Bondioli, Coppa & Macchiarelli 1998; Nelson *et al*. 1999; Hojgaard, 1984).

There is no unequivocal direct evidence to show that caries was the main cause of tooth loss at Hili N. As indicated above, one method of assessing the contribution of caries to tooth loss is to examine the frequency of caries in the surviving teeth. If there was a high prevalence of caries, it would be reasonable to assume that tooth decay was a major contributory factor. Unfortunately, those teeth that had not been lost during life have not survived very well. Of the surviving teeth belonging to both adults and children, 6% were carious (Fig. 7c). This overall caries rate appears to be quite moderate. In a survey of caries frequency from ten sites in Arabia from different periods ranging from the Mesolithic to the Islamic, Littlejohn & Frolich (1993) found caries rates to range from 0% to 25%. Of Bronze Age sites examined, Umm an-Nar Island had a caries rate of 2.4%. The highest frequency, 25%, was based on only 28 teeth from 'Site 5', Ras al Khaimah, in the northern Emirates, dating to 100 BC - 100 AD. In Iron Age Oman, Nelson *et al*. (1999), who claimed that high levels of caries and *ante mortem* tooth loss were due to the consumption of dates, observed a caries rate per tooth of 18.4% for 141 teeth; a corrected rate of 32.4% of 182 teeth was calculated to take account of missing teeth. This assumes that the missing teeth were lost as a result of decay.

A caries rate of 6.0% for all teeth from Hili N, although higher than the 2.4% observed on Umm an-Nar Island, is therefore quite moderate when compared with other Gulf sites. In general, the rates given in the publications mentioned above are based on much smaller populations than Hili N and relative tooth survival appears to be much better. Therefore, although clearly a factor, the relative importance of the caries rate at Hili N, based on such proportionally few teeth, is less than conclusive. Dental disease is accepted as being highly complex with a number of interlinked causes and manifestations. Lukacs (1989) suggested that the various causal factors in dental disease should be thought of in terms of whether they are primary or secondary. The primary causes of *ante mortem* tooth loss are caries, calculus and attrition, while other conditions, ultimately leading to tooth loss, are secondary. Thus, the pathway of eventual tooth loss from the three primary causes and subsequent secondary causes was said to be (Lukacs 1989: 265):

1) Caries → pulp exposure → abscess → resorption → tooth loss
2) Calculus accumulation → periodontal disease → abscess → resorption → tooth loss
3) Attrition → pulp exposure → abscess → resorption → tooth loss.

The modest Hili N caries rate does not provide *prima facie* evidence for caries being the main cause of tooth loss. Besides caries, dental abscesses (Fig. 7b), calculus, periodontal disease and advanced attrition were also frequent occurrences at Hili N. Therefore, as there was evidence for all three primary causes in the Hili dental remains, *in vivo* tooth loss at Hili is most likely to be multifactorial and not simply the result of tooth decay. Regardless of the cause, it is clear that most individuals suffered from very poor dental health that must have reflected on everyday life. The high levels of dental infection that were clearly present, whether the result of caries, advanced attrition, or periodontal disease, must have had a detrimental effect on the general well-being of the population and in some cases may even have been fatal.

Anaemia

Secondary effects of haemolytic anaemia, in the form of expansion and pitting of the cranial vault (porotic hyperostosis) and in the orbital roofs (cribra orbitalia), were found on many hundreds of fragments. These manifestations can occur alone or together. It has been claimed that the development of porotic hyperostosis indicates a more severe expression of the condition (Blom *et al.* 2005). The preponderance of these lesions indicates that the condition was common in the community. Unfortunately because of the disarticulated and fragmented condition of the Hili N crania, it is not possible to estimate an accurate number of individuals affected. Assessments of other Umm an-Nar period skeletal assemblages have indicated frequencies of cribra orbitalia of 37.2%, 33.3 % and 18% of individuals affected at Al Sufouh, Mowaihat and Unar 2, respectively (Blau 2001) and a prevalence within this range in the Hili N population is not unreasonable.

Anaemia is a general term for a variety of conditions that result in a reduction in the number of red blood cells. Bony changes occur as a result of the need for expansion of the spaces occupied by red marrow to allow for the compensatory production of red blood cells. It is accepted that such changes only occur during childhood because of the greater need for red blood cell production during growth (e.g. Stuart-Macadam 1985; Mays 1998: 143), i.e., the lesions, regardless of whether they are visible in

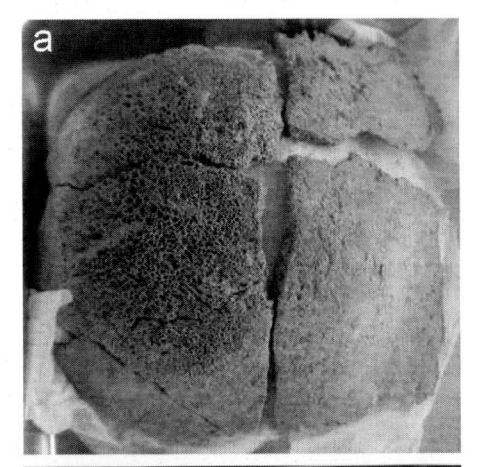

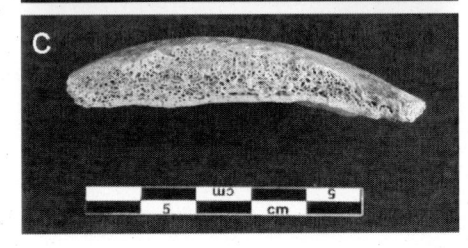

Figure 8. Examples of porotic hyperostosis at Hili N: (a) complete but fragmentary parietal with active changes; (b) fragment of parietal showing healing lesions; (c) profile view of a fragment of parietal showing expansion of vault thickness.

sub-adults or adults are expressions of childhood anaemia. It was clear that a large proportion of the affected fragments belonged to children, although the nature of the Hili N material meant that the true age of these individuals at the time of death could not be accurately assessed. In very young children the lesions were mostly active, indicating that the period of stress was ongoing at death (Fig. 8a); while in older children and adults the lesions had healed (Fig. 8b) and in some cases the bone had partly remodelled. Blom *et al.* (2005), in a study of pre-Columbian Peruvian skeletal assemblages, found a direct relationship between death in childhood and porotic hyperostosis and this appears to be true of the Hili N children.

Anaemia has been attributed to a number of causes such as genetic abnormalities, weaning, insufficient iron in the diet, gastrointestinal parasitizes and bacterial infection. It is also claimed to be an adaptive response to malaria. Genetic anaemias such as thalassaemia and sickle cell anaemia, which are prevalent in the United Arab Emirates today, were considered but ruled out on the basis that the post-cranial skeletal changes that are normally found in these diseases were not present.

Dental Hypoplasia

Dental hypoplasia is a caused by an interruption in the development of dental enamel during childhood while the teeth are forming. They occur following periods of malnutrition or illness and commonly manifest as a horizontal ridge on the enamel. Such linear lesions, if not removed by advanced attrition or decay, can remain on the teeth for life. By assessing the position of the lesions, the age of the child when the period of stress occurred can be calculated. The presence of several hypoplastic lesions in the same dentition, as was frequently found on the Hili N teeth, indicate recurrent periods of stress.

Hypoplastic lesions were noted on about 10% of teeth available for examination. More than half of these were from immature individuals. Dental hypoplasia has been linked with decreases in longevity (Goodman & Armelagos 1989) and as the majority of the affected individuals did not survive into adulthood, the presence of these stress markers do appear to be reflective of the poor health during childhood suffered by some members of the population. A direct link with poor nutrition or disease during childhood, however, cannot be established, as hypoplasia may be a consequence of either.

Figure 9. Examples of congenital anomalies from Hili N: (a) fragment of sacrum with open sacral crest indicating the presence of spina bifida occulta; (b) congenital fusion of the middle and distal phalanges of the toe.

Congenital Conditions

Congenital conditions include a number of diseases and anomalies that range from the very minor to those that are not viable with life. As is the case with most archaeological skeletal assemblages very little congenital disease was identified at Hili N. It is unlikely that children born with severe conditions would have survived. Some minor developmental anomalies were identified and two examples are shown in Fig. 9. Fig. 9a shows an example of spina bifida occulta, a neural arch defect that can be developmental or genetically determined and occurs in most populations (e.g. 2.7% in early British skeletal material; Brothwell & Powers 1968). Another frequently occurring skeletal anomaly was congenital fusion of the middle and distal phalanges of the toe (Fig. 9b). This is considered to be a fairly common skeletal variant (George 2001).

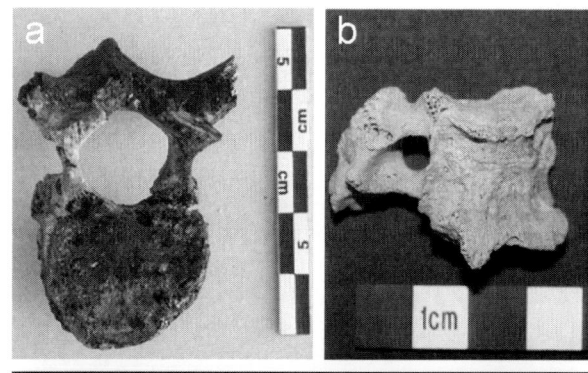

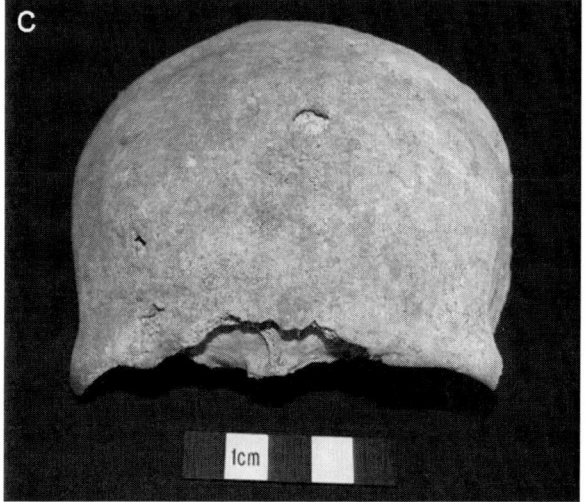

Figure 10. Some diseases of unknown aetiology from Hili N: (a) asymmetrical lumbar vertebra indicating the presence of scoliosis of unknown cause; (b) additional bony growth resulting in fused vertebrae – possibly ankylosing spondylitis; (c) perforations on the external surface of the skull, a possible case of multiple myeloma (a type of cancer of plasma cells).

Miscellaneous Diseases

Any assessment of disease based on skeletal analysis will be limited by a number of factors. It is often not possible to arrive at a conclusive diagnosis, largely because of the non-specific nature of bony lesions. As the anatomical distribution of lesions can aid diagnosis the inherent difficulties were compounded by the absence of articulated skeletons in the Hili N assemblage. Some conditions that must remain unknown or implied are shown in Fig. 10.

Conclusions

Despite the high degree of fragmentation, the large volume and relatively undisturbed nature of the human bone assemblage of the Hili N pit-grave suggests that it is probably representative of the community that used the tomb and this has enabled the building of a picture of life and death of a community that lived at the end of the Umm an-Nar period.

The pit-grave contained the remains of more than 700 individuals. A large percentage (43%) of the individuals was sub-adult; a rate of child mortality to be expected in a prehistoric society. Among the adults there was no evidence of bias towards either sex. These factors indicate that there was no selectivity among the Hili N remains and that the grave was a burial place for the whole community. Radiocarbon dating has indicated that the tomb was in use for around 100 to 200 years (Méry et al. 2008), which would indicate a mortality rate of between 3.5 to 7 individuals per year. Assuming that the majority of the dead in the community were indeed buried in the pit grave, the community at any one time would have been quite small, probably around 100 individuals or less.

A relatively high level of disease was noted. Several individuals, the actual number difficult to assess, suffered from some form of metabolic disease, indicated by porotic hyperostosis and cribra orbitalia. The absence of characteristic post-cranial lesions means that it is unlikely that diseases such as scurvy, rickets or one of the genetic anaemias was the cause. The skeletal changes may be manifestations of iron deficiency anaemia, although, if so, it should not be assumed that this was the result of the dietary insufficiency of iron; such deficiencies may also be due to disease processes. According to Stuart-Macadam (1991), however, the presence of porotic hyperostosis may also be indicative of a natural protective response to pathogens, common in tropical and sub-tropical regions, and may not necessarily be indicative of disease *per se*.

Dental health was extremely poor; sixty-four per cent of adult jaw fragments had teeth missing *ante mortem*. The rate was similar to that of some other prehistoric populations in the Gulf, where caries was related to the consumption of dates. The poor survival of teeth that had been *in situ* at the time of death and widespread tooth loss during life meant that the cause of tooth loss in the Hili N population could not be clearly established. An overall caries prevalence rate of 6%, especially in the light of the widespread *in vivo* molar loss, does, however, indicate that dental decay was a factor. Tooth loss was often accompanied by a high frequency of periodontal disease and dental abscesses, both of which can ultimately result in tooth loss; this implies a multifactorial origin.

The impression gained from the analysis of the Hili N group is of a population of fairly small stature, with some evidence for stress. This is clear from the high rate of child mortality, indications of young adult age at death, a fairly high frequency of hypoplasia, evidence for widespread anaemia, and very poor dental health. The highest mortality rate was in children between the ages of three months and 4 years. High mortality in this age group is normally taken as a key indicator of poor nutrition in under-developed countries today. However, poor nutrition and disease are often inextricably interlinked and it is not possible to relate the findings from Hili N to poor nutrition alone, although this may have played a part.

Acknowledgements

The Phase 1 excavations were conducted by the Department of Antiquities and Tourism, Al Ain. The Phase 2 excavations were jointly financed by the then Department of Antiquities and Tourism, Al Ain (subsequently the Abu Dhabi Authority for Culture and Heritage) and the *Sous-direction des sciences sociales, humaines et de l'archéologie* (Ministère des Affaires étrangères, France). The authors would like to give special thanks to M. Mohammad Amir al Neyiadi of ADACH, Al Ain, for his continued support over the years.

References

Blom D.E., Buikstra J.E., Keng L., Tomczak P.D., Shoreman E. & Stevens-Tuttle D. 2005. Anemia and childhood mortality: Latitudinal patterning along the coast of pre-Columbian Peru. *American Journal of Physical Anthropology* 127/2: 152-169.

Bondioli L., Coppa A., & Macchiarelli R. 1998. From the coast to the oasis in prehistoric Arabia: what the skeletal remains tell us about the transition from a foraging to the exchange economy? Evidence from Ra's al-Hamra (Oman) and Hili North (UAE). *International Union of Prehistoric and Protohistoric Sciences: Proceedings of the XIII Congress* 5. Forli': 229-234.

Brothwell D. & Powers R. 1968. Congenital malformationsof the skeleton in earlier man. In D.R. Brothwell (ed.) *Skeletal biology of earlier human populations*. Symposia of the Society for the study of Human Biology 8. London: Pergamon Press.

Cole A.E. 1935. Inheritance of a fused joint in the index finger: Ankylosis of the distal interphalangeal joint of the index finger. *Journal of Heredity* 26: 225-228.

Frifelt K. 1991. *The island of Umm an-Nar, vol. 1. Third millennium graves*. Aarhus: Jutland Archaeology Society Publications XXVI: 1.

George M. 2001. Biphalangeal fifth toe: an increasingly common variant. *Journal of Anatomy* 198: 251.

Goodman A.H. & Armelagos G.J. 1989. Infant and childhood morbidity and mortality risks in archaeological populations. *World Archaeology* 21/2: 225-243.

Haddu M.M. 1989. Preliminary report on the excavation of Tomb N, Hili Gardens. (In Arabic). *Archaeology in the United Arab Emirates* V.

Hojgaard K. 1984. Dentitions from Janussan (Bahrain). Pages 63-71 in P. Lombard, & J.-F. Salles (eds), *La Necropole de Janussan (Bahrain)*. Travaux de la Mission de l'Orient 6.

Lewis M. 2007. *The Bioarchaeology of Children. Perspectives from Biological and Forensic Anthropology*. Cambridge University Press.

Littlejohn J. & Frolich B. 1993. Fish-eaters and farmers; dental pathology in the Arabian Gulf. *American Journal of Physical Anthropology* 92: 427-447.

Lukacs J.R. 1989. Dental pathology: methods for reconstructing dietary patterns. In, Iscan, M.Y. &

K.A.R. Kennedy (eds.), *Reconstruction of Life From the Skeleton*: 261-286. New York: Alan R. Liss, Inc.

McSweeney K. 2003. *The Connections Between Health and Diet in Prehistoric Populations*. Unpublished PhD Thesis, University of Edinburgh.

McSweeney K. Forthcoming. *Hili N, Al Ain, United Arab Emirates: The Human Remains*.

Mays S. 1998. *The Archaeology of Human Bones*. London: Routledge.

Méry S., McSweeney K., Van der Leeuw S. & al Tikriti W.Y. 2004. New approaches to a collective grave from the Umm an-Nar Period at Hili (UAE). *Palaeorient* 30/1: 163-178.

Méry S., McSweeney K., Rouquet J., Basset G. & al Tikriti W.Y. 2008. New evidence of funerary practices at the end of the Early Bronze Age at Hili, United Arab Emirates. Pages 200-208 in E. Olijdam & R.H. Spoor (eds), *Intercultural Relations Between South and Southwest Asia. Studies in Commemoration of E.C.L. During Caspers (1934-1996)*. Oxford: Archaeopress (BAR International Series) 1826.

Méry S., Rouquet J., McSweeney K., Basset G., Saliège J.-F. & al Tikriti W.Y. 2001. Re-excavation of the Early Bronze Age collective Hili N pit-grave (Emirate of Abu Dhabi, UAE): results of the first two campaigns of the Emirati-French Project. *Proceedings of the Seminar for Arabian Studies* 31: 161-178.

Nelson G.C., Lukacs J.R. & Yule P. 1999. Dates, caries and early tooth loss during the iron age of Oman. *American Journal of Physical Anthropology* 108: 333-343.

Roberts C. & Manchester K. 2005. *The Archaeology of Disease, Third Edition*. Stroud: Alan Sutton Publishing.

Rogers J. & Waldron T. 1995. *A Field Guide to Joint Disease in Archaeology*. Chichester: Wiley.

al Tikriti W.Y. & Méry S. 2000. Tomb N at Hili and the question of the subterranean graves during the Umm an-Nar period. *Proceedings of the Seminar for Arabian Studies* 30: 205-219.

Waldron T. 2009. *Palaeopathology*. Cambridge Manuals in Archaeology. Cambridge University Press.

Authors' Addresses

Dr Kathleen McSweeney
Archaeology, School of History, Classics and Archaeology
University of Edinburgh
Old High School, Infirmary Street
Edinburgh EH1 1LT
UK
Email: kath.mcsweeney@ed.ac.uk

Dr Sophie Méry
UMR7041, CNRS, Maison de l'Archaeologie et de l'Ethnologie, R. Ginouvés,
21 allée de l'Université
F-92023, Nanterre cedex
France
Email: sophie.mery@mae.u-paris10.fr.

Dr Walid Yasin al Tikriti
Abu Dhabi Authority for Culture and Heritage,
Al Ain National Museum
PO Box 15715, Al Ain
Abu Dhabi
United Arab Emirates.
Email: wyasin@emirates.net.ae

Patterns of mortality in a Bronze Age tomb from Tell Abraq

Kathryn Baustian and Debra L. Martin

Summary

The tomb at Tell Abraq was used for a 200 year period (c. 2200BC to 2000BC) and at least 362 individuals are represented in this mortuary collection. The bones are highly commingled and individuals (except for one) could not be ascertained. Analysis of individual bones has revealed a largely robust and healthy population, however the high frequency of premature infants (last trimester) and newborns suggest some level of stress for this vulnerable age segment of the population. One articulated individual, unique for the tomb, has been diagnosed with some form of neuromuscular disease (such as poliomyelitis). This 18-year old female's body was somehow protected from the processes that disarticulated and commingled the other individuals in the tomb. These preliminary analyses of the human remains suggest that the community was practicing a variety of mortuary activities that included the interment of miscarried or aborted fetuses.

Key Words; Tell Abraq, bioarchaeology, paleopathology, mortuary

Introduction

The archaeological site of Tell Abraq is located in the United Arab Emirates. It is a multi-period Bronze Age site near the Arabian Gulf coast on the Oman Peninsula. It lies on the border between the emirates of Sharjah and Umm al-Quwain. Excavation of Tell Abraq took place during five field seasons between 1989 and 1998 by an international team of archaeologists led by Dr. Dan Potts of the University of Sydney. The primary feature excavated at the site was a raised fortification constructed in several phases throughout the three millennia of occupation (Potts 1993b:423, 2001:40-49). The massive tower, approximately 40m in diameter and 8m high, was built of a combination of mud bricks and stone (Potts 1989:270, 2001: 40).

Tell Abraq was occupied from approximately c.2200BC to c.400BC by a mostly sedentary population (Potts 1993a:591). The 1991 field season resulted in the discovery of a large stone mortuary tomb 10 meters to the west of the fortress where it served as the repository for deceased individuals for a period of 200 years (c.2200BC to c.2000BC) in the late third millennium BC (Potts 1993a:591, 2000:44).

The Tomb in a Larger Perspective

A comprehensive review of mortuary practices in the eastern Arabian Peninsula during this time period supports both similar and different preferences for interment structures of the deceased. Four styles of graves are known to have been utilized in this region from approximately 3100 to 1300BC. These styles include Hafit-type (Frifelt 1975:59-61), Umm an-Nar (Potts 2001:39), Wadi Suq (Potts 1993b:428), and that of the early Dilmun period (Soweileh 1995:196-198). The Umm an-Nar burials share similar characteristics including circular design, above-ground stone construction, interior chambers formed by crosswalls, and a size ranging from 4 to 14 meters in diameter (Frifelt 1975:59-61). Wadi Suq and Dilmun period burials have different characteristics including variations in shape, partially subterranean chambers, and smaller size (Soweileh 1995:196-198).

Figure 1. The Tell Abraq tomb after excavation, looking north.

The tomb at Tell Abraq, utilized during the late 3rd millennium BC, is Umm an-Nar in style. It was constructed of worked limestone blocks and beach rock in a circular shape measuring 6 meters across (Potts 1993a:591, 2000:45). A flat stone floor was laid down prior to the construction of an interior dividing wall that forms the barrier of the two internal chambers. A doorway was formed using a keystone that could be removed as additional deceased individuals were interred in the tomb. A portion of the ossuary, the western chamber, was discovered to have been disturbed at some point following its use; however it does not appear to have been looted (Potts 2000:44) (Figure 1).

Taphonomy

The tomb at Tell Abraq was used continually for approximately a 200 year period. As individuals throughout this period became deceased, their remains were placed within the eastern or western chamber above the already-interred remains. The nature of the bone bed suggests several mortuary practices for placing the dead in the tomb. There were some articulated parts of bodies, especially towards the lower part of the tomb (Figure 2). Yet the complete disarticulation and commingled nature of the majority of the bones suggests the possibility of secondary burial of skeletal remains only (Figure 3). Decomposition over time may have permitted bone elements to settle and commingle, leaving virtually no articulated individuals except for one in the whole of the tomb, and this unique individual is discussed below.

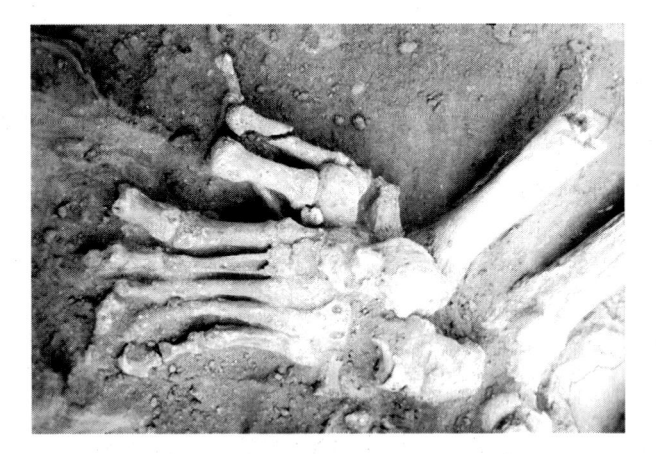

Figure 2. An example of articulated remains found within the generally disarticulated and commingled skeletal remains from Tell Abraq.

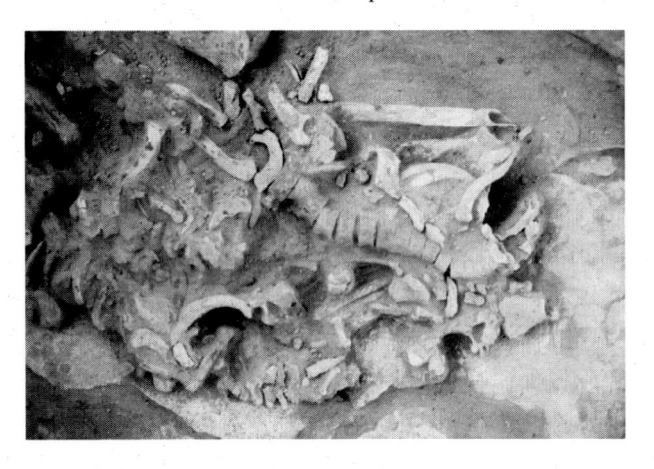

Figure 3. A second example of articulated remains found within the generally disarticulated and commingled skeletal remains from Tell Abraq.

Contributing to the taphonomy of the tomb and human remains are environmental factors such as the arid environment and sandy soil. While the dry air could provide good conditions for preservation of the bone, it also can allow for easier fracturing as moisture is lost from the tissue. Most of the long bones in the tomb are broken, but many of the hand and foot bones, along with smaller bones such as the patella, were completely preserved. There was virtually no carnivore damage on any of the bones, suggesting that it was fairly tightly sealed in ancient times. A small percentage of the bones showed burning on the outer surface, and this could have been from sources of light such as candles being placed in the tomb during interment.

Tomb Excavation

Excavation of the tomb took place over four field seasons under the direction of Debra Martin of the University of Nevada, Las Vegas, and Alan Goodman of Hampshire College. Excavation was a challenge due to the dense bone bed. Items found with the human skeletal remains include grave offerings such as ceramic and stone vessels, copper and bronze rings, spearheads, ostrich eggshell fragments, beads, and infant "feeding" shells (Potts 1993a:591). Trade goods from the Indus Valley and other nearby locations include Harappan weights, pottery, and gold pendants (Potts 2000:46-47). Although linking individuals with grave goods was often difficult, sometimes proximity, such as an ivory hair comb still adhering to a cranium, helped associate items to specific individuals.

Paleodemography

Recently the human skeletal remains have been transported to the University of Nevada, Las Vegas, for analysis. The minimum number of individuals (MNI) was established at 362 for the collection. There are minimally 280 adults and 82 subadults. MNI for adults was determined using the right talus (an ankle bone) and MNI for subadults was ascertained using the right femur (thigh bone). All age categories are well represented suggesting that all individuals were interred in the tomb.

Preliminary analysis of the adults in this population suggests that they were largely afflicted by nonspecific infections (periosteal reactions) and osteoarthritis. Most notably, however, are the overall large and robust sizes of bones and the high degree of ossified ligaments. Adult remains show a range of muscle enthesopathies and degenerative joint diseases at the articular surfaces indicating strenuous or repetitive activity. Specifically, stress markers of the feet, knees, and shoulder regions suggest activity perhaps related to grinding or pounding grains in kneeling positions (Blau 1996:167). Additionally, the site of Tell Abraq was positioned close to the sea so maritime activities may also have been responsible for some of the adult pathologies (Blau 1996:168).

The tomb and collection at Tell Abraq are particularly important because it is one of the very few known sites not to have been looted in antiquity (Potts 2000:44). The context of the site has therefore been preserved for present-day interpretation. The portion of the tomb that was disturbed however likely resulted in a loss of up to 25% of the skeletal material from the western chamber. Even with this in consideration, the collection is still vital to bioarchaeological research in this region and time period. Contemporaneous collections are not nearly as large and may not be able to offer as much information as this collection from Tell Abraq.

Premature Infants and Newborns: Trying to Come of Age at Tell Abraq

A focused analysis of the children's long bones has revealed an unusual pattern of premature infants (6-9 lunar months) and newborns in the tomb. This finding is unique among Bronze Age burial populations as many of these children potentially represent miscarriages or spontaneous abortions, typically a population not given full mortuary treatments. It is therefore assumed that these individuals held some recognition as members of the community.

Age distribution of subadult femora revealed the following distribution: 29% 8 lunar months to neonate; 41% neonate to 2 years; 18% 2 years to 5 years; and 11% over 5 years of age. The high prevalence of very young children is intriguing particularly for the fact that many of them exhibit active periosteal reactions. This suggests that newborn mortality was at least in part due to nonspecific systemic infections. The pathologies do not appear to be nutritionally-related and the local environment and ecology featured a wide variety of resources for a sufficient diet.

Examination of the left tibiae and right femora has shown that approximately half of the specimens show at least a minimal infectious reaction, if not an extensive one. Nearly all of these are bones of children under 2 years of age. The local environment likely represented a number of health challenges to both mothers and infants including a variety of endemic diseases (leishmaniasis, acute diarrheal disease, upper respiratory disease, and brucellosis) and high fluoride levels. These are suggested biological factors that may be responsible for high infant mortality.

Cultural Impacts on Biology

Cultural factors have also been considered as having a role in the health of this community. For example, the long tradition of child marriages and marriage to first cousins (which both act to increase infant mortality) in this region of the world may have contributed significantly to infant mortality and maternal morbidity. This practice is still common in the region today among many Arab countries and serves as a tool of economic stabilization among families. Research has indicated that consanguinity results in higher prevalence of birth defects and autosomal recessive diseases such as cystic fibrosis, thalassemia, sickle-cell anemia, osteochondrodysplasias, and deafness (Al-Gazali, Alwash, & Abdulrazzaq 2005: 189-192). Our high frequency of very young infants in the collection has prompted a consideration of this cultural practice as a factor in the high infant mortality at Tell Abraq. In searching for factors that might explain the premature infants and neonates, we also consider the effect of young mothers in the survival of their offspring. A long tradition of marriage of females around the age of 16 and pregnancy promptly after is relevant to our research as skeletally immature mothers have a higher risk of preterm birth. Finally, our research considers the breastfeeding and weaning practices that may have occurred in this population. Cultural beliefs in early cessation of breastfeeding may have had an effect on the health and illness susceptibility of infants and young children in this skeletal collection.

One Articulated Skeleton: Unusual Burial Treatment, Unusual Individual

Excavation of the 362 commingled individuals in the tomb was a complicated task. Working in small units (1 x 1 m squares, subdivided further into four 50 x 50 cm sectors), layer by layer, bones of every age and sex were distributed in a jumbled and random way. On rare occasions, several vertebrae or articulated long bones were found, but the vast majority of the individuals interred there were commingled.

The only exception to this was a complete, articulated and fairly well-preserved skeleton that was found in the passageway linking the eastern and western chambers, directly opposite the presumed entrance to the tomb. Based on dental eruption, epiphyseal union and morphology of the pelvis, the burial is likely that of an 18 year old female. Her body was found lying in a flexed position in the passageway, with disarticulated and jumbled bones both below and above her (Figure 4).

It is difficult to understand how and why this one burial was placed in such a way that there was virtually no disarticulation of the skeleton. This individual is obviously a primary interment in a tomb that contained a varied mortuary program. One hypothesis is that her unusual medical condition marked her as different and perhaps dangerous, and her body was put in some very durable bag that eroded more slowly than the body. By the time the leather, wood, or fibrous body bag or box eroded, the body was already well positioned above and below other disarticulated bodies and bones in the tomb.

The burial is represented by a nearly complete, very gracile skeleton that is relatively normal except for the following: She has the forward molding of the sacrum and coccyx and lateral splaying of the ischia that is consistent with chronic sedentism. She has early osteoarthritic changes in the right knee and ankle consistent with habitual overuse of the right leg. She has mild cavo-valgus deformity of the left foot diagnostic of some kind of neuromuscular disorder. There is mild inflammation (periosteal pitting) in almost all of the joint systems of the appendages inferring some level of pain and discomfort. Her dentition is in an advanced state of loss and decay, as noted by antemortem tooth loss, caries, and abscessing.

Based on the observations of the skeleton, it appears fairly certain that this young adult woman was suffering from some form of progressive neural muscular atrophy contracted in her mid-teens that made her weakened enough to leave her chronically sedentary. Because some muscles of the arm show development and use, and because of the osteoarthritis on right side, she likely was

Figure 4. The complete, articulated and fairly well-preserved skeleton located near the entrance of the Tell Abraq tomb.

using her body in ways that compensated for the more pronounced muscular atrophy on the left side.

The pelvic changes are adaptive, rather than developmental. The right leg was used more when compared to the left. The extreme atrophy of both fibulae suggests that towards the end of her life, she used her legs less. The proximal anterior fibula is the attachment site of two major muscles involved in movement of the ankle (peroneus longus and brevis) and there is virtually no hint that these muscles were used. The right ankle and knee show signs of developed traumatic osteoarthritic changes as a result. Taken together, these developments suggest some movement and weight-bearing but not of the kind normal for a young adult.

In contrast to these observations from the hip and leg, the wear on the proximal ulnae and the tuberosities on the proximal radius suggest movement and use in the arms. Perhaps tasks or work was done habitually from a sitting position. Alternatively, she may have used her arms to move her body around since she may not have been able to coordinate and use her legs for normal ambulation.

The antemortem loss of teeth (presumably due to caries and abscesses) and the poor dental health are curious. Dates were certainly a staple of the diet and could have been the source of the caries and abscessing (Potts 2000:45).

Was this woman considered special and taken care of, or ostracized and marginal to the life of the community? Her placement in the tomb dramatically sets her apart from all others buried there. Because there was so much disarticulation and commingling of the other 361 individuals, this person's completely articulated skeleton suggests that her body was protected from the actions of individuals responsible for inserting new individuals into the tomb. It is possible that many of the individuals in the tomb represent secondary burials of the gathered-up remains of bodies buried or curated elsewhere (Martin & Baustian 2008). The presence of some burned bone, and a small number of cutmarks support that at least some individuals in the tomb were culturally modified prior to interment. Some of the disarticulation and commingling is likely due to those responsible for putting individuals in the tomb. With one small entrance into the tomb, it would have been expedient to keep shoving bones towards the back as new burials were put in. This young woman would have had to have been bundled up tightly in a very durable material, such as cloth, twine, or wood. Because she has commingled individuals under her and on top of her (see Figure 4), the material would have had to resist decay until the last of the individuals were placed in the tomb.

The unusual extra step of wrapping the body in the mortuary behavior of her kinsmen suggests that this young woman's social persona during life was also unusual. Was she a revered member of the community, or was she considered to be dangerous to the group because of her increasing disability and deformities? The amount of dental disease suggests a diet very high in carbohydrates, almost as if she was fed a steady diet of dates. The curved sacrum suggests increased sedentism. The beginnings of calcaneo-cavo-valgus deformity in the one foot suggests that walking would have been increasingly difficult.

Summary

The 362 individuals identified in the tomb at Tell Abraq offer a valuable insight to daily life at this and other Bronze Age Arabian communities. Through a bioarchaeological approach, we have tried to understand broad patterns of demography, pathology, and lifestyle by integrating osteological analysis within the archaeological context of the site. Our observations have shown a highly robust and muscular population at the center of a bustling trade and migration economy.

There are still a number of questions regarding the role of children within the community however it is clear that the mortuary tomb may provide some explanation. Subadults over the age of 5 seem greatly under-represented in the tomb yet there are a great number of premature infants so initial findings suggest that younger children could have been highly susceptible to illness while older children had resistance and survived to adulthood. In examining health in Bronze Age Arabia, analysis utilizing a consideration of biological, environmental, and cultural factors may provide a better understanding of all the processes that can affect mortality and morbidity in a community. Furthermore, unique findings like those provided by the nearly complete articulated individual can offer additional interpretations for life among a particular community like Tell Abraq. Ultimately, however, the site and skeletal collection of Tell Abraq present worthwhile research that highlights the complementary nature of biological anthropology and archaeology while providing important contributions to Arabian prehistory.

Acknowledgements

We are grateful to the Society for Arabian Studies for inviting us to participate in the 2008 seminar at the British Museum. Dr. Daniel Potts continues to be a source of support and information in the analysis of the human remains.

References

Blau S. 1996. Attempting to Identify Activities in the Past: Preliminary Investigations of the Third Millennium BC Population at Tell Abraq. *Arabian Archaeology and Epigraphy* 7: 143-176.

Frifelt K. 1975. A Possible Link Between the Jemdet Nasr and Umm an-Nar Graves of Oman. *Journal of Oman Studies* 1: 57-80.

Al-Gazali L.I., Alwash R. & Abdulrazzaq Y.M. 2005. United Arab Emirates: Communities and Community Genetics. *Community Genetics* 8:186-196.

Martin D.L. & Baustian K. 2008. Invited Presentation, Patterns of Mortality and Morbidity in the Commingled Tomb from Tell Abraq. Society for Arabian Studies, Death Burial and the Transition to the Afterlife in Arabia. British Museum, London 27-29 November.

Potts D.T. 2001. Before the Emirates: an Archaeological and Historical Account of Developments in the Region c. 5000 BC to 676 AD. Pages 28-69 in E. Ghareeb & I. Al Abed (eds), *Perspectives on the United Arab Emirates*. London: Trident.

Potts D.T. 2000. Arabian Time Capsule. *Archaeology* 53: 44-48.

Potts D.T. 1993a. A New Bactrian Find from Southeastern Arabia. *Antiquity* 76: 591-596.

Potts D.T. 1993b. Rethinking Some Aspects of Trade in the Arabian Gulf. *World Archaeology* 24: 423-440.

Soweileh A. 1995. Typology of Dilmun Burial Mounds. Pages 196-198 in S. Campbell & A. Green (eds) *The Archaeology of Death in the Ancient Near East*. Oxford: Oxbow.

Authors' Addresses

Kathryn Baustian
University of Nevada, Las Vegas
Department of Anthropology
4505 Maryland Parkway 455003
Las Vegas, NV 89154
Baustian@unlv.nevada.edu

Debra L. Martin
University of Nevada, Las Vegas
Department of Anthropology
4505 Maryland Parkway 455003
Las Vegas, NV 89154
Debra.Martin@unlv.edu

Discerning Health, Disease and Activity Patterns in a Bronze Age Population from Tell Abraq, United Arab Emirates

Janet M. Cope

Summary

An unusual elevated transverse ridge was documented at the midtrochlear notch of the ulna in 58% of an adult sample from the Umm an-Nar tomb (c. 2200-2000 BC) at Tell Abraq, United Arab Emirates. In this investigation the ulna (n=164), radius (n=201), scaphoid (n=274) and lunate (n=226) bones were assessed for morphological variations and pathology. Eighty-five percent of assessed radii had a depressed attachment site for the volar carpal ligament and 34% of the scaphoid bones had an exaggerated dorsal ridge for attachment of the dorsal carpal ligament of the wrist. There was a strong positive correlation found between the presence of the transverse midtrochlear ridge (TTR), proximal elbow joint OA (r_s=0.330, p<0.01) and size (r_s=0.263, p<0.01). There was no relationship observed between side and distal radioulnar joint OA or side and the presence of the TTR. The transverse midtrochlear ridge as observed on these specimens is a newly described morphological variation. This finding in conjunction with those found on the radii and scaphoid bones supports previous research suggesting that the inhabitants of Tell Abraq lived physically arduous lives.

Keywords: paleopathology, radiocarpal ligament, osteoarthritis

Introduction

Bronze Age skeletal populations are relatively rare, so the remains from the Tell Abraq tomb are of particular interest for what can be learned about health and behavior. Tell Abraq, a large prehistoric settlement on the southern coast of the Persian Gulf, within the Oman peninsula is likely to have been active in trade during the Bronze Age, particularly during the period to which the tomb dates, c. 2200-2000 BC (Potts 1990a, 1993a). Skeletal analysis is frequently used to determine health and disease status as well as to support theories of activity patterns in prehistoric populations. Evaluation of the morphology and pathology of the Tell Abraq skeletal remains within the cultural context can provide a more complete assessment of life and health in this rare population.

Tell Abraq is the only multi-period site in southeastern Arabia with a continuous sequence of occupation extending from the late Umm an-Nar period (ca. 2200 - 2000 BC) through the Wadi Suq period (2000-1200 BC) and Iron Age (ca. 1200 – 400 BC) (Potts 1989, 1990a, 1993a, b, c). A well-preserved collective tomb dating to the earliest period of occupation was discovered on the site during the 1989 season and excavated during the fourth and fifth seasons (1993, 1998). Potts (2000) tells us that this was a population of coastal Arabians with a mixed economy consisting of fishing and shellfish gathering, horticulture (date palm, wheat and barley), animal husbandry (herding of domesticated sheep, goat and cattle) and hunting (dugong, wild camel, oryx, gazelle, etc).

Objects deposited in the tomb (as well as in the settlement layers) demonstrate clearly that this coastal population had ties to populations in neighboring regions, including Mesopotamia, Iran, Bahrain, the interior of Oman, Central Asia (Bactria) and the Indo-Pakistan area. Although many of the larger skeletal components were damaged, some of the smaller bones from both the upper and lower extremities were complete and in good condition (Blau 1996; Cope et al. 2005: 393). Preliminary paleopathological and paleodemographic studies of the skeletal remains from the tomb reveal that the Tell Abraq adults were well-nourished, robust and physically active, with an estimated life span of fifty years of age (Potts 1993a, b; Blau 1996; Martin et al. 1999:199; Turner et al. 2002; Cope et al. 2005). The origins of the individuals from this population remain as yet undetermined but the site's far-flung relations make it at least plausible to suggest that not all of the individuals interred in the tomb were indigenous to southeastern Arabia. Some may have come from any of the neighboring regions listed above.

The Tell Abraq tomb was used over a 200 year period (circa 2200-2000 B.C.) and the skeletal remains are disarticulated and commingled due to the mortuary practices of this population during this period (Blau 2001:174-175). Upon death an individual would be placed in the tomb and then later moved aside to make room for newly deceased. As a result many of the larger components are mostly indiscernible due to secondary taphonomic influences (Blau 1996; Martin et al. 1999: 191; Turner et al. 2002). While this presents a challenge in reconstructing demographic parameters of the population, preliminary assessment by Martin and colleagues (1999:191; Baustian & Martin, this volume) suggests that the minimal number of individuals in the tomb was well over 200 adults and 150 sub-adults, representing all age categories and both sexes.

In this study the ulna, radius, lunate and scaphoid bones from the Tell Abraq tomb, United Arab Emirates (UAE) are examined for evidence of pathology and morphological variations. The ulnae were of specific interest because of an elevation noted at the deepest portion of the trochlear notch (Fig. 1) that has not previously been discussed in the anthropological, medical or kinesiological literature. Although anthropologists report the existence of this transverse midtrochlear ridge (TTR) on other skeletal assemblages, it has not been documented in the literature (pers. Comm. April 9, 2008, AAPA). This variation on the ulna poses interesting

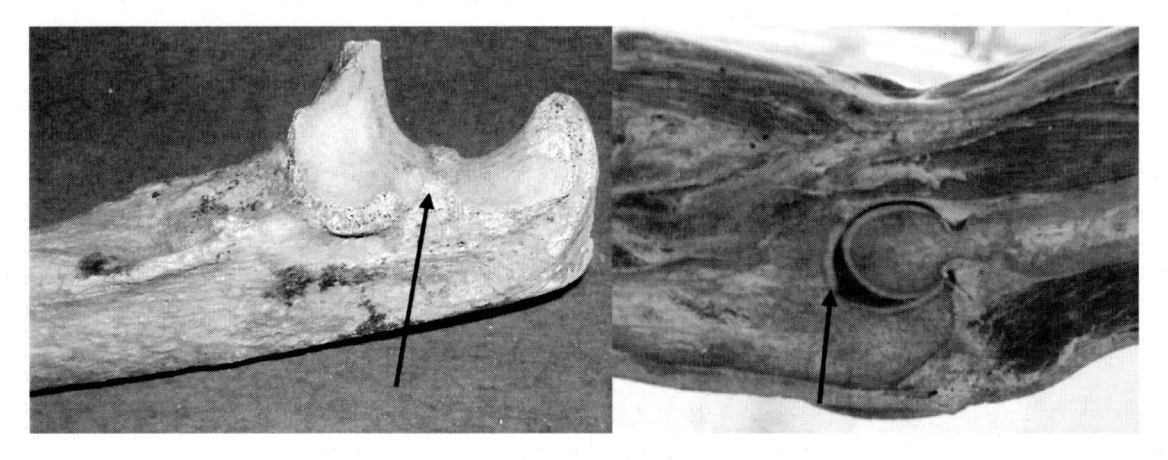

Figure 1. Left: Tell Abraq specimen. Arrow indicates the anatomical variation at the trochlear notch, as named by Cope, the transverse midtrochlear ridge. Right: longitudinal section of a modern day specimen with normal humeroulnar joint. No hyaline cartilage, no TTR and no contact between the humerus and ulna are observed on this specimen.

Bone	Total	Right	% Right	Left	% Left
Ulna	164	135	82.3%	29	17.7%
Radius	201	101	49.8%	100	49.3%
Scaphoid	274	MNI: 140	51.1%	134	48.8%
Lunate	226	96	42.5%	130	57.5%
TOTALS	**865**	**472**	**51.3%**	**393**	**48.7%**

* MNI of 140 is based upon number of right scaphoid bones

Table 1. Siding of ulna, radius, scaphoid and lunate.

questions as related to this population. Was this a familial trait, normal for the indigenous people in this collection, a pathological condition, or an adaptation that developed over the course of a lifetime?

Methods and Materials

Upper extremity skeletal remains from the Tell Abraq tomb in the UAE, currently housed in the Department of Anthropology and Ethnic Studies at the University of Nevada, Las Vegas, were used for this analysis. Specifically the ulna (n=166), radius (n=201), scaphoid (n=274) and lunate (n=226) bones were assessed for morphological variations and osteoarthritis. Indicators of infection or trauma were also recorded. All bones were sided using the guidelines of White and Folkens (2000: 187-198) and Bass (2003: 162-176) (Table 1) and then evaluated for variations and osteoarthritis. The radius and ulna were measured at the mid-shaft in both sagittal and coronal planes and the area at this region calculated. Bone specific anomalies and pathologies are described below.

Ulna: The humeroulnar joint is an incongruent uniaxial synovial joint that affords flexion and extension at the elbow joint. The hook or C-shaped trochlear notch of the ulna has a central crest running superoinferiorly that articulates with a midline groove on the distal spool-shaped trochlea of the humerus. This central crest acts to increase the stability of the humeroulnar joint (Levangie & Norkin 2005: 275-277; Oatis 2004: 187-206; Steele & Bramblett 1988: 158-172). The proximal and distal portions of the trochlear notch articulate with the humerus while the horizontal midline section, with no hyaline cartilage, does not articulate with the humerus when the elbow joint is at rest (Fig. 1) (Eckstein et al. 1994: 647-651; Eckstein et al. 1995a:, 1995b:327, 1999; Jacobs & Eckstein 1997: 317-319; Levangie & Norkin 2005: 274-276; Neumann 2002:137-144 ; Oatis 2004: 193-195). Specimens that had a visible, palpable elevation in the midtrochlear region were deemed as having the TTR.

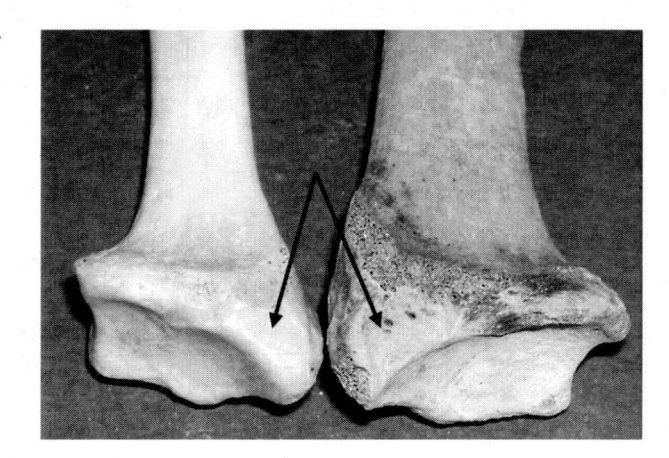

Figure 2. Left: modern day specimen of a left distal volar radius with arrow indicating convex surface for attachment of the radiocarpal ligament. Right: Tell Abraq specimen with arrow indicating a concave surface for attachment of the radiocarpal ligament on right distal radius.

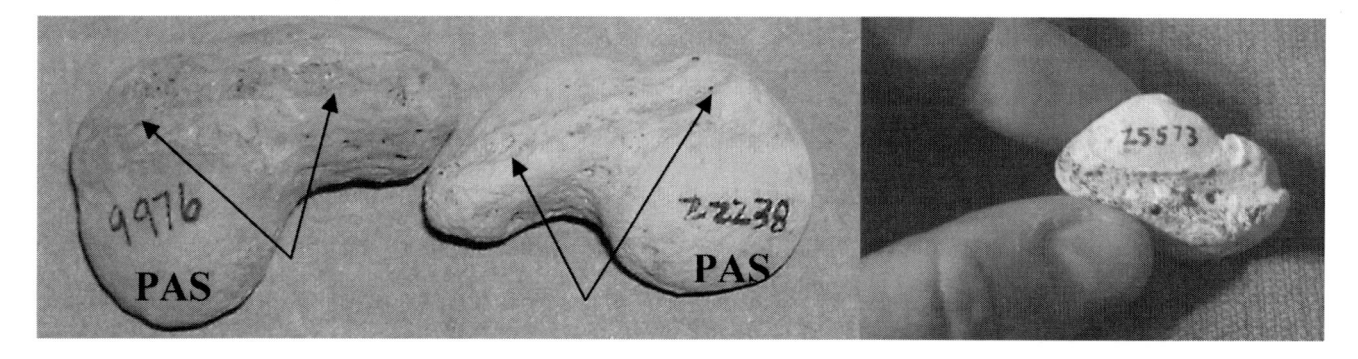

Figure 3. Left: arrows indicate dorsal ridge on scaphoid bones from Tell Abraq. PAS = Proximal Articular Surface or radiocarpal surface which was relatively free of arthritic deterioration in this population. Right: exaggerated dorsal ridge.

The medial collateral ligament of the elbow is stressed by most activities of daily living, while the radial collateral ligament is not (Amis et al. 1979). Osteoarthritis at the humeroulnar joint is frequently observed in individuals known to engage in repetitive elbow flexion, extension and/or rotational activities with their forearms (Dutton 2008: 667-716; Oatis 2004: 201-239; Neumann 2002: 142-144).

Radius: Radiocarpal ligament facet morphology (Fig. 2) was assessed. The distal radius articulates with the scaphoid and lunate to form the radiocarpal joint. The volar carpal ligament has multiple attachments on the anterolateral surface of the radius to various carpal bones. This strong ligament attaches to a facet on the radius that is anteromedial to the distal attachment site of the brachioradialis muscle. From this facet the radiocarpal ligament has oblique attachments to the lunate, scaphoid and capitate and longitudinal attachments to the scaphoid and trapezium (radial collateral ligament segments). This volar radiocarpal ligament network provides stability at the wrist (Levangie & Norkin 2005: 310-311).

Scaphoid: The dorsal radiocarpal ligament attachment site was examined for the presence or absence of an exaggerated ridge (Fig. 3). The scaphoid has a poor vascular supply to the northern pole which impedes healing (Neumann 2002: 174) and, thus, if damaged, has a tendency to displace palmarly during extension of the wrist at the midcarpal row. The dorsal carpal ligament has broad oblique attachments from the dorsal lateral surface of the distal radius to the dorsal surfaces of the scaphoid, lunate and triquetral bones. This ligament provides stability during motions at the wrist, especially supporting the scaphoid that tends to collapse into flexion during wrist extension (Oatis 2004: 246-249; Levangie & Norkin 2005: 312-315).

Lunate: The lunate was assessed for side and degree of OA as is consistent with Kienböck disease, a form of osteochondrosis. Kienböck's disease occurs when there is devascularization and ultimately destruction of the lunate bone. Negative ulnar variance (shortened ulna) and mechanical stress are both reported as causes of Kienböck's disease (Levangie & Norkin 2005: 309; Neumann 2002: 176). Although the etiology continues to be debated (Salter, 1999: 353-354; Saidoff & McDonough, 2002: 711; Brukner & Khan 2007: 324-325), the resulting wrist pain and carpal instability of patients with Kienböck's is not. Patients often have difficulty gripping objects and have severely limited range of motion at the wrist (Dutton 2008: 315; Neumann 2002: 176; Salter 1999: 353-354).

Code	Name	Description
0	CLEAR	no signs of porosity, lipping, eburnation, articular surface intact
1	MINOR DETERIORATION	less than 1/3 articular surface porosity, minimal osteophyte formation, no lipping, no eburnation.
2	MILD LIPPING OR DETERIORATION	less than 1/3 articular surface porosity, lipping of less than 1/3 of the circumference of joint edge.
3	MODERATE LIPPING AND ROUGH FACET	1/3 or greater articular surface porosity, lipping around 1/3 or greater of the joint circumference; no greater than 2/3 porosity or lipping.
4	SEVERE FACET DAMAGE AND EBURNATION	2/3 or greater of articular surface porosity, lipping of 2/3 of the joint circumference, eburnation present (Fig. 2).

Table 2. Osteoarthritis coding system (Cope et al. 2005).

Bone	n	Sagittal Range mm	Sagittal mean mm	Coronal Range mm	Coronal mean mm	Pearson Product Correlation	Area Mean mm	Area Range SDev
ULNA	103	9.3-16.76	12.52	11.43-21.13	17.08	r = .664*	169.8	92-226.63 s = 38.98
RADIUS	118	9.24-16.74	12.57	12.48-22.10	16.90	r = .728*	166.4	99.5-267.3 s = 42.23

* Correlation is significant at the .01 level (1-tailed)

Table 3. Descriptive analysis of midshaft measurements of radius and ulna bones.

Osteoarthritis coding: Osteoarthritis was categorized by the degree and extent of deterioration observed on articular surfaces. A coding system developed by Cope et al. (2005: 393) of 0 representing no evidence of OA to 4 representing the presence of eburnation or severe facet damage was used (Table 2). Osteoarthritis is characterized by the progressive deterioration of articular cartilage and hypertrophy and remodeling of subchondral bone. Assessment for articular surface porosity, marginal lipping and the presence of osteophytes and/or eburnation was conducted to determine the degree of OA.

Reliability: A Pearson product-moment correlation coefficient method was computed to validate intra-observer reliability for siding, OA coding and size six months from initial data collection. Thirty or more bones were selected for each category and evaluated with significant reliability ranging from (r=0.920, p<0.01) for siding; (r=0.942, p<0.01) for OA coding; to (r=0.962, p<0.01) for size assignment.

Data Analysis: Frequency analyses were calculated on the total number of each bone, side, and OA assessment results. As seen in Table 3, descriptive statistics and Pearson Product Correlations are provided for the mid-shaft diameters (sagittal and coronal) of the ulna and radius bones. The area of an ellipse was calculated (π x radius of sagittal x radius of coronal) for both the ulna and radius bones. Spearman rho correlations were used to assess relationships between degree of OA on the wrist bones and to assess size and degree of OA on the radius and ulna bones. In addition Spearman rho correlations were computed for side and size and for the presence/absence of the TTR on the ulna and radiocarpal ligament attachment site assessment on the radius.

Results

As seen in Table 1, a total of 865 bones, were evaluated, and the minimum number of individuals was determined to be 140 based on the number of right scaphoid bones in this sample. There were 365 forearm and 500 carpal bones; 472 right and 393 left.

Ulna: One hundred sixty four ulnae were assessed, 135 right and 29 left bones. One hundred and forty three of the specimens were assessed for the presence of the trochlear ridge. Findings show that 58% (n=83) of them had this elevation, while 42% (n=60) did not have the ridge. One hundred fifty one ulnae were assessed for OA. As seen in Table 4, there were signs of OA on 75% of the proximal right and 61% of the proximal left ulnae. Overall, the proximal ulna had signs of OA on 73% (n=93) of the specimens, while the distal head of the ulna had OA on 35% (n=8) of the specimens.

Spearman rho correlation was used to assess for relationships between the presence of the TTR and various characteristics (side, size, extent of OA) of these ulnae (Table 5). Significant (p<0.01) positive linear relationships were found among an elevated TTR and the presence of proximal OA (r_s=0.370), size (r_s=0.347) and distal OA (r_s=0.375). There was no relationship found between an elevated TTR and side (r_s=0.060).

Ulna (103) and radius (118) bones were measured in both the sagittal and coronal planes (Table 3). The area means for each bone are large as compared to modern populations; up to 1.45 times larger in some cases (Sakaue 2004: 76-79).

Radius: There were 201 radii assessed for side, 101 right and 100 left bones. One hundred eighty radii were assessed for OA. The proximal head of the radius had evidence of OA on only 9% of the specimens, while the distal radius had OA on 40% of the specimens. Neither proximal nor distal OA on the radius covaried with any other variables (side, size, volar radiocarpal facet).

Fifty nine radii were assessed for the volar radiocarpal ligament facet. Fifteen percent (n=9) of the radii had a convex attachment site whereas 85% (n= 50) had a concave attachment site. Of those that had a concave facet, 68% (n=34) had a slightly concave facet, while 32% (n=16) had a depressed concave facet.

Scaphoid: There were 274 scaphoid bones assessed for side, 140 right and 134 left bones. The scaphocapitate, radioscaphoid and dorsal radiocarpal joint capsule surfaces of the scaphoid bones were assessed for OA and found to be in good condition (Table 6). Osteoarthritis was nearly absent on the radiocarpal surface, with no OA on 97% of the bones. There were arthritic changes on the capitate surface on 44% of the total specimens. It was moderate to severe on 14% of these scaphoid bones.

	Total Bones Assessed	No OA	Some OA Code 1-4	Moderate to Severe OA Code 2-4
Ulna	Total Bones Assessed			
Proximal **Right**	n = 105	25% n = 26	75% n = 79	50% n = 52
Proximal Left	n = 23	39% n = 9	61% n = 14	39% n = 9
Distal **Right**	n = 17	59% n = 10	41% n = 7	30% n = 5
Distal Left	n = 6	83% n = 5	17% n = 1	16% n = 1
Radius	Total Bones			
Proximal **Right**	n = 56	95% n = 53	5% n = 3	2% n = 1
Proximal Left	n = 52	87% n = 45	13% n = 7	10% n = 6
Distal **Right**	n = 35	60% n = 21	40% n = 14	4% n = 5
Distal Left	n = 37	60% n = 22	40% n = 15	21% n = 8

Table 4. Osteoarthritis at the Ulna and Radius.

	Side	Size	OA Proximal	OA Distal
Correlation to Ridge	.060*	.263*	.330*	.375*
N	142	116	126	9

* Correlation is significant at the .01 level (1-tailed).

Table 5. Transverse midtrochlear ridge and other variables on the ulna.

Scaphoid Surface	No OA	Minimal OA Code 1-4	Moderate to Severe OA Code 2-4
Capitate	56%	44%	14%
Radial	97%	3%	2%

Table 6. OA present on the articular surfaces of the scaphoid.

The dorsal ridge was severely elevated on 16% of the specimens assessed, with an equal distribution of both left and right scaphoid bones. The status of the capitate articular surface and the dorsal ridge (distal radiocarpal joint capsule attachment) were strongly associated. If the capitate surface demonstrated OA, then the dorsal ridge was likely to be elevated (r_s=0.585, p<0.01). In addition, the absence of OA at any one of the surfaces was a good indicator that there would be no OA on any of the other surfaces.

Lunate: There were 96 right and 130 left lunate bones assessed. Eleven percent of the lunate bones (n=25) had signs of OA. When present, OA was observed 96% of the time on the left side (n=24).

Discussion

Arthritic destruction was quite specific on these carpal bones. Forty four percent of the scaphoid bones had arthritic changes on the capitate surface (14% moderate to severe) indicating that the scaphocapitate joint was distressed in this population. The attachment of the dorsal carpal ligament on the scaphoid was exaggerated on 16% of individuals and strongly correlated with arthritic changes. This ligament is particularly active in stabilization of the scaphoid in wrist flexion (Levangie & Norkin, 2005: 310-315).

Eleven percent of individuals had lunate arthritic deterioration that might indicate onset of Kienböck's disease. The concave surfaces of both the lunate and scaphoid bones articulate with the proximal convex surface of the capitate bone; a pivotal bone in all wrist motions (Neumann 2002: 176). When moving the hand into an extended position, the scaphoid is locked against the capitates, tightening the volar carpal ligament and increasing the stability at the wrist (Levangie & Norkin 2005: 313). With flexion and extension at the wrist, the dorsal carpal ligament and volar carpal ligament tighten, respectively. When distraction forces are applied all ligaments must work to stabilize the surrounding structures. In radial and ulnar deviation, the scaphoid and lunate slide as the capitate rolls, tightening the lateral portion of the palmar intercarpal and ulnar carpal ligaments, followed by the medial portion of the palmar intercarpal and radiocarpal ligaments, respectively (Neumann 2002: 174-185).

Side did not correlate with any variables on the radius, ulna or scaphoid bones, but it did correlate strongly with OA on the lunate bone in 11% of the population (96% left). Thus far, this is the only variable that is correlated with side in the upper extremities in this population.

The distal radius had signs of OA on 40% of the bones. These data indicate that the distal radius was the site of the most wear at the radiocarpal joint. Thirty-five percent of specimens assessed had signs of OA distally, while 73% of them had signs of OA proximally.

Blau (1996) assessed several foot bones from this same population, reporting morphological variations indicative of persistent squatting, kneeling and walking. When in the quadrupedal position or when kneeling and leaning on the upper extremities, the kinematic forces are at first transmitted through the radiocarpal joint. The interosseous membrane transmits this superiorly directed force from the radius to the ulna and then redirects it towards the larger, more stable humeroulnar joint (Neumann 2002: 143-145; Levangie & Norkin 2005: 273-295). As a result of this pattern of force transmission, the distal radius and proximal ulna are more susceptible to mechanical wear and tear (Neumann 2002: 143-145).

In this study there were higher levels of arthritic destruction at the distal radius and proximal ulna bones consistent with the kinematics of force transmission as stated above. This may have resulted from individuals leaning on their hands to: perform agricultural tasks, process plant foods, lay bricks or perhaps knead clay in the fabrication of bricks.

As in previous research of the thumb with this population, side was not found to be related to OA (Cope et al. 2005: 396). These data lend support to the existing hypothesis that the individuals from the Tell Abraq tomb regularly participated in heavy bimanual activities.

Is the aging process itself the cause of OA? Or does a longer life provide the opportunity for musculoskeletal trauma to create a cumulative effect? Advancing age (Lawrence et al. 1990) and excessive body mass have both been directly linked to the presence of OA and must be controlled for (Weiss 2005). As the individuals from Tell Abraq are disarticulated and commingled it makes aging the upper extremity bones improbable if not impossible. In this research only adult specimens were utilized and thus we are provided with a sample population with an age range spanning approximately 30 years (20s to 50s). Fusion of the forearm bones occurs between 14 and 24 years of age (Klepinger 2006: p.51; Scheurer and Black 2000: 289-307) and death typically occurred in the sixth decade (Potts 1993a). Upper extremity skeletal components are non-weight bearing, thus eliminating body mass as a variable related to the onset of OA as is often seen in the spine, hips and knees. The results of this research are consistent with findings for OA in individuals of this age range with arthritic deterioration on approximately 35% of the distal radii, but higher than expected for this age range at the humeroulnar joint with OA on 73% of individuals (Lawrence 1990; Weiss 2005).

Although age is a strong contributing factor to the development of OA, there are additional variables to consider: acute trauma, systemic issues, repeated mechanical stress and body mass. Shieh and Athanasiuo (2003:1-3) report that repeated mechanical loading on the chondrocytes and cartilage at joints results in deterioration of these structures leading to OA. Kennedy (1989) and other researchers who study the impact of occupational stress on the skeleton (Larsen et al. 1995: 147-156, Rogers and Waldron 1995; Brandt 1996; Larson 1997: 161-194) agree that OA can develop at specific joints as a result of an individual's occupation or daily routines. People who are physically challenged by their work are more likely to develop OA at joints than their more sedentary counterparts (Larsen 1997: 163, 194). They are also more likely to develop more robust musculature and bones (Knusel 2000). The American Academy of Orthopaedic Surgeons report that in the years 1991-2004 the most commonly replaced joints in the human body due to destruction by OA are the knee, hip, shoulder and various joints of the hand (Center for Disease Control 2004). These joints are either weight bearing or, as in the trapeziometacarpal joint (TMC), subject to considerable repetitive stress.

Archaeological analysis of material culture suggests that the individuals from Tell Abraq traveled both across the sea and on foot to nearby communities (Potts 1993b). They lived in mud huts, used brick extensively and fabricated towers and tombs of limestone ashlar blocks that were carefully finished. This population harvested a diet rich in seafood as evidenced by the tens of thousands of mollusc shells, shark and other bony fish skeletal remains found in and around the tomb (Potts 2003). Skeletal remains of sheep, goats and zebu cattle suggest that domesticated animals were also used as a food source (Potts 1990b, 1993a).

Ground and grinding stones, that are used to increase the digestibility of grains, were plentiful at Tell Abraq (Potts 2000: 25, 70-71). These stones can be used to smooth and soften hides, crack or pry open molluscs, or fabricate other stone tools (Aston et al. 2000). The actions of grinding, prying or even rubbing with stone on stone requires repetitive flexion and extension at the wrist and elbow, and is often paired with rotation at the forearm.

Osteoarthritis at the proximal elbow joint was common and positively correlated with the presence of the TTR (r_s=0.330, p<0.01). Repeated resisted flexion and extension in a shortened range of motion can generate the wear and tear necessary to develop OA at the proximal ulna. Further research is warranted into the etiology and prevalence of the TTR. Assessing both living and historical populations may assist us in understanding the existence of this interesting anatomical variation at the elbow joint.

Individuals from Tell Abraq harvested food from the nearby ocean that may have involved the use of nets and small fishing vessels. The force required to drag a heavily loaded net against concurrent tidal flow would create significant and repeated stress on the humeroulnar joint. Paddling is a well known stressor to the joints of the upper extremities including causing OA at the sternoclavicular (Hawkey & Merbs 1995) as well as the humeroulnar joints (Lai & Lovell 1992) in various seafaring populations. Weaving nets and fabricating small watercraft would cause repeated stress to the joints of the digits, wrists and elbows.

In this research there was a positive linear relationship observed between the presence of the TTR, proximal ulna OA and size. Cope and colleagues (2005: 396-398) formerly established a positive linear relationship between robusticity and TMC joint OA. This could point to a division of labor by size in this population. These tasks were likely to have been bimanual, mechanically stressful and repetitive in nature.

The presence of exaggerated ligamentous attachment sites on both the scaphoid and distal radius suggests high levels of mechanical stress at the wrist. These ligaments provide support to the wrist in flexion and extension as well as ulnar and radial deviation.

Analysis of the material culture from excavations at Tell Abraq has revealed that rowing, fishing, farming and building with bricks and ashlar limestone are all potentially to blame for the pathologies observed on the upper extremity skeletal remains. Rowing, dragging nets, kneading clay to make bricks and lifting heavy stones all require bimanual use of the upper extremities, where the humeroulnar joint would be heavily loaded or subject to overuse through repetitive activity. Weaving with palm fronds, rowing canoes, participating in agricultural tasks and processing plant foods could all have contributed to the OA observed on these skeletal remains.

Conclusions

There is much to be gleaned from the upper extremity skeletal remains from the Tell Abraq tomb. Although disarticulated and commingled, the specimens on whole were in excellent condition with little taphonomic damage. The physical expression on the skeleton within the context of the material culture and the archaeological evidence can suggest activity patterns during life.

The arthritic changes are minimal but very specific on the carpal bones, and moderate OA was observed at both the distal radius and proximal ulna. Side was found to correlate only to OA at the lunate bone, suggesting that typically physical labor placed bilateral stress on the upper extremities. Pathology patterns, in combination with the common existence of the TTR (58%) at the elbow, are suggestive of weight bearing through the

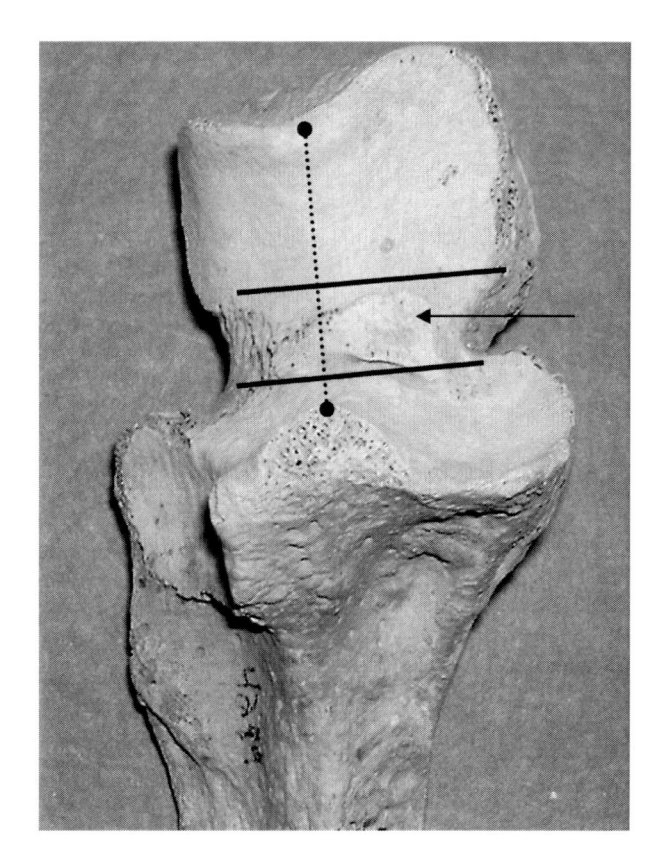

Figure 4. Central crest on the trochlear notch running longitudinally (dashed line) and trochlear ridge running medial to lateral (arrow). The area between the solid lines is the midtrochlear region.

upper extremities and repetitive and resisted flexion and extension at the elbow and wrist. The Transverse Midtrochlear Ridge warrants further investigation to assess kinesiological etiology as well as biocultural prevalence (Fig 4).

Patterns on pottery and the presence of other artifacts (ivory, ceramics, metals, stone vessels, beads) found at the Tell Abraq tomb offer significant evidence of trade. As this was a sea front port, it is possible that the people buried in this tomb may have been mariners that stopped here, settled, and later died. More likely, they may have been indigenous to this region and engaged in trade across or along the Arabian Gulf. Regardless, the condition and markers on the upper extremity skeletal remains suggest that they participated in activities such as fishing, rowing, casting and retrieving nets, agricultural tasks, brick-making and/or carrying heavy objects. It is likely that participation in these often repetitive and heavy bimanual tasks contributed to the trauma observed on these individuals.

References

Amis A.A., Dowson D., Wright V. & Miller J.H. 1979. The derivation of elbow joint forces, and their relation to prosthesis design. *Journal of Medical Engineering & Technology* 3: 229-234.

Aston B.G., Harrell J.A. & Shaw I. Stones. 2000. In Nicholson PT & Shaw I, (eds), *Ancient Egyptian Materials and Technology*. Cambridge: Cambridge University Press.

Bass W.M. 2003. *Human osteology: a laboratory and field manual of the human skeleton*. 4th ed. Columbia: Missouri Archaeological Soc.

Blau S. 2001. Limited yet informative: pathological alterations observed on human skeletal remains from third and second millennia BC collective burials in the United Arab Emirates. *International Journal of Osteoarchaeology* 11: 173–205.

Blau S. 1996. Attempting to identify activities in the past: preliminary investigations of the third millennium BC population at Tell Abraq. *Arabian Archaeology and Epigraphy* 7/2: 143-177.

Brandt K. 1996. *Diagnosis and nonsurgical management of osteoarthritis*. Professional Communications Inc.

Bridges P.A. 1993. The effect of variation in methodology on the outcome of osteoathritic studies. *International Journal of Osteoarchaeology* 3: 289-295.

Brukner P. & Khan K. 2007. *Clinical sports medicine*. 3rd ed. New York: McGraw Hill. Centers for Disease Control and Prevention, National Center for Health Statistics. 2004. *National hospital discharge summary. Joint replacements from head to toe*. American Academy of Orthpeadic Surgeons.

Cope J.M., Berryman A.C., Martin D.L. & Potts D.T. 2005. Robusticity and osteoarthritis at the trapezoimetacarpal joint in a bronze age population from Tell Abraq, UAE. *American Journal of Physical Anthropology* 126/4: 391-400.

Dutton M. 2008. *Othropaedic Examination, Evaluation, and Intervention*. 2nd ed. New York: McGraw Hill.

Eckstein F., Merz B., Schön M., Jacobs C.R. & Putz R. 1999. Tension and bending, but no compression alone determine the functional adaptation of subchondral bone in incongruous joints. *Anatomy and Embryology* 199/1: 85-97.

Eckstein F., Merz B., Muller-Gerbl M., Hokzknecht N., Pleier M. & Putz R. 1995a. Morphomechanics of the humero-ulnar joint: joint space width and contact area as a function of load and angle. *Anatomical Record* 243: 318-326.

Eckstein F., Merz B., Muller-Gerbl M., Hokzknecht N., Pleier M. & Putz R. 1995b. Morphomechanics of the humero-ulnar joint: II. Concave incongruity determines the distribution of load and subchondral mineralization. *Anatomical Record B* 243: 318-326.

Eckstein F., Lohe F., Muller-Gerbl M., Steinlechner M. & Putz R. 1994. Stress distribution in the trochlear notch. *Journal of Bone & Joint Surgery (BR)* 76: 647-53.

Hawkey D.E. & Merbs C.F. 1995. Activity-induced musculoskeletal stress markers (MSM) and subsistence strategy changes among ancient Hudson Bay Eskimos. *International Journal of Osteoarchaeology* 5/4: 324-338.

Jacobs C.R. & Eckstein F. 1997. Computer simulation of subchondral bone adaptation to mechanical loading in an incongruous joint. *Anatomical Record* 249: 317-326.

Kennedy K.A.R. 1989. Skeletal markers of occupational stress. In Iscan MY & Kennedy KA (eds), *Reconstruction of life from the skeleton*. New York: AR Liss.

Klepinger L.L. 2006. *Fundamentals of Forensic Anthropology*. New York: Wiley & Sons.

Knusel C.J. 2000. Bone adaptation and its relationship to physical activity in the past. In Cox M & Mays S (eds), *Human osteology in archaeology and forensic science*. Cambridge, UK: Cambridge University Press.

Lai P. & Lovell N.C. 1992. Skeletal markers of occupational stress in the Fur Trade: A case study from a Hudson's Bay Company Fur Trade post, *International Journal of Osteoarchaeology* 2/3: 221-234.

Larsen C.S. 1997. *Bioarchaeology: Interpreting behavior from the human skeleton*. New York: Cambridge University Press.

Larsen C.S., Craig J., Sering L.E., Schoeninger M.J., Russell K.F., Hutchinson D.L. & Williamson M.A. 1995. Cross homestead: life and death on the Midwestern frontier. In Grauer AL (ed.), *Bodies of evidence: reconstructing history through skeletal analysis*. New York: Wiley Liss.

Lawrence R.C., Everett D.F. & Hochberg M.C. 1990. Arthritis. In *Health status and well-being of the elderly: national health and nutrition examination I epidemiologic follow-up survey*. Oxford University Press.

Levangie P.K. & Norkin C.C. 2005. *Joint structure and function: a comprehensive analysis*, 4th Edition. Philadelphia: FA Davis.

Martin D.L., P.K. Stone, N. Parker, M.M. Margolis, F. Harris & V.R. Perez. 1999. Paleodemography and paleopathology of a Bronze Age skeletal population from Tell Abraq, United Arab Emirates. *American Journal of Physical Anthropology* 108/S28: 199.

McKern T.W., & Steward T.D. 1957. *Skeletal age changes in young American males*. Natick, Massachusetts: quartermaster research and development command technical report EP-45.

Neumann D.A. 2002. *Kinesiology of the musculoskeletal system: foundations for physical rehabilitation*. St. Louis: Mosby.

Oatis C.A. 2004. *Kinesiology: the mechanics and pathomechanics of human movement*. New York: Lippincott, Williams & Wilkins.

Portney L.G. & Watkins M.P. 2000. *Foundations of clinical research: applications to practice*. 2nd ed. New Jersey, Prentice Hall Health.

Potts D.T. 1989. Excavations at Tell Abraq, 1989. *Paleorient* 15/1: 269-271.

Potts D.T. 1990a. *A prehistoric mound in the Emirate of Umm al-Quaiwain, UAE: excavations at Tell Abraq in 1989*. Copenhagen: Munksgaard.

Potts D.T. 1990b. *The Arabian Gulf in Antiquity*. Oxford: Clarendon.

Potts D.T. 1993a. Four seasons of excavation at Tell Abraq (1989-1993). *Proceedings of the Seminar for Arabian Studies* 23: 117-126.

Potts D.T. 1993b. The late prehistoric, protohistoric, and early historic periods in Eastern Arabia (ca. 5000-1200 B.C.). *Journal of World Prehistory* 7/2: 163-212.

Potts D.T. 1993c. Rethinking some aspects of trade in the Arabian Gulf. *World Archaeology,* 24/3: 423-440.

Potts D.T. 2000. *Ancient Magan: the Secrets of Tell Abraq.* London: Trident Press.

Potts D.T., Naboodah H.A. & Hellyer P. 2003. *Archaeology of the United Arab Emirates. Proceedings of the first international Conference on the Archaeology of the UAE.* London: Trident Press.

Rogers J. & Waldron T. 1995. *A field guide to joint disease in archaeology.* New York: J Wiley.

Saidoff D.C. & McDonough A.L. 2002. *Critical pathways in therapeutic intervention: extremities and spine.* St. Louis: Mosby.

Sakaue K. 2004. Sexual determination of long bones in recent Japanese. *Anthropological Science* 112: 75-81.

Salter R. 1999. *Textbook of disorders and injuries of the musculoskeletal system.* 3rd ed. Philadelphia: Williams and Wilkins.

Scheuer L. & Black S. 2000. *Developmental juvenile osteology.* Boston: Academic Press.

Shieh A.C. & Athanasiuo K.A. 2003. Principles of cell mechanics for cartilage tissue engineering. *Annals of Biomedical Engineering* 3: 1-11.

Steele D.G. & Bramblett C.A. 1988. *The anatomy and biology of the human skeleton.* College Station, TX: Texas A&M Univ Pr.

Turner B., Goodman A., Martin D. & Potts D.T. 2002. From heels to height: estimating stature based on the talus at Tell Abraq, UAE. *American Journal of Physical Anthropology* 34 Supplement: 157.

Weiss E. 2005. Understanding osteoarthritis patterns: an examination of aggregate osteoarthritis. *Journal of Paleopathology* 16/2: 87-98.

White T.D. & Folkens P.A. 2000. *Human osteology.* San Diego: Academic Pr.

Author's Address
Janet M. Cope, PhD, OTR/L
Clinical Anatomist, Anthropologist
Dept of Physical Therapy Education
100 Campus Drive, Campus Box 2085
Elon University
Elon, NC 27244-2010
jcope2@elon.edu

Early Bronze Age graves and graveyards in the eastern Ja'alan (Sultanate of Oman): an assessment of the social rules working in the evolution of a funerary landscape

J. Giraud

Summary

The last five years of surveys carried out by the Joint Hadd Project from 2002 to 2007 in the eastern Ja'alan (Sultanate of Oman) have recorded a considerable number of funerary structures: 3000 dating from the very end of the 4th to the beginning of the 2nd millennium BC. These graves still mark the landscape of the province in a remarkable way. The survey data were explored and interpreted through a GIS, confirming previous hypotheses ("Hafit" type tombs are located on various high points while "Umm an-Nar" tombs are located on low and medium terraces near the settlements), and providing a clearer and more detailed interpretation of their position in the geographical and cultural landscape. In total, 54 "Hafit" and 10 "Umm an-Nar" graveyards of varying size in a range of settings were defined and analyzed with the help of various methods of spatial analysis, uncovering changing spatial and social rules for the placement of the ancestors in the landscape. The role of both sets of factors is assessed from available data, forming part of a predictive model that can be tested on other areas of the Oman Peninsula.

Keywords: Sultanate of Oman, 3rd millennium B.C., landscape archaeology, graves, location

Introduction

The present landscape of the Arabian peninsula is lined with thousands of stone funerary towers dating from the Bronze Age (Figs. 1 and 2). They can be found on crests, hills, near trails or villages and have always puzzled travellers. Very early on, archaeologists became interested in these ancient tombs, especially in their location and distribution. Different hypotheses were put forward in an attempt to explain their distribution: these tombs might mark resources such as wells, fishing areas, ancient roads, paths, and perhaps territories (Cleuziou 2002). In these hypotheses, the act of marking resources or territories is significant. It means that these tombs indicate to foreigners that people live here; they warn the foreigner that they are about to cross a territory with precise boundaries and exploitable resources.

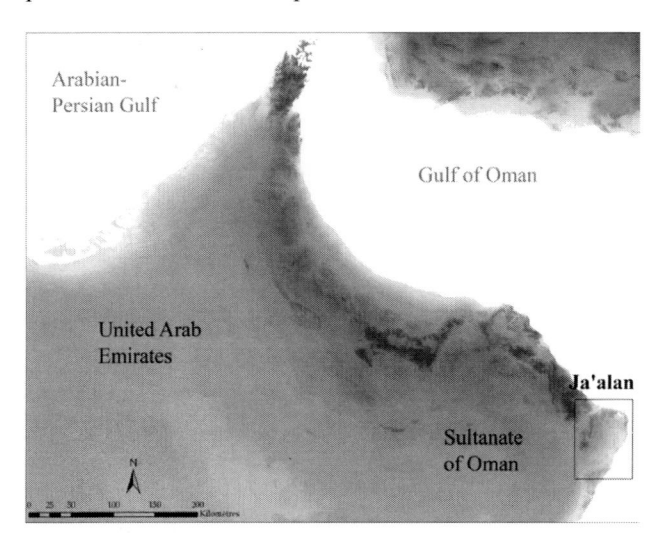

Figure 1. Location of the Ja'alan in the Oman peninsula (J. Giraud).

The study of the spatial organisation of the 3000 tombs (Giraud 2007; Giraud & Cleuziou 2009) situated in the Ja'alan, in the Sultanate of Oman, allows us to put forward another hypothesis concerning this funerary landscape (Fig. 1). It may be that these tombs were implanted in the landscape not so much for the foreigner's benefit, but rather as part of agricultural settlements (Giraud 2009). We seem to be in the presence of a polar spatial organisation with a simple pattern of centre and periphery. This polar spatial organisation was established through excavations (Blin 2007).

The study of the evolution of this funerary space, based upon the analysis of about a hundred tombs dating from the Umm an-Nar period (c. 2500-2000 BC), as well as the thousands of tombs from the Hafit period (c. 3100-2700 BC), reinforces this impression of a centre. In fact, all of the identified centres are closely related to the environment of the time. This raises questions regarding the changes in economic orientation that may have happened in the region.

The funerary landscape of Hafit Period (c. 3100-2700 B.C.)

New Data

Between 2002 and 2007, systematic surveys were done in the Ja'alan, following earlier prospection by the Joint Hadd Project directed by S. Cleuziou and M. Tosi (Giraud & Gernez 2007). About a thousand archaeological structures were identified, mainly on the coast. The various survey teams had only made a few inland incursions, from which they had obtained a general map of the large ensemble of tombs in the region. During the period from 2002-2007, we focused more particularly on the inland region, with only a few coastal investigations. As a result, we have been able to survey and precisely locate over 4000 structures of various eras, 2661 of which date from the Hafit Period.

Since the beginning of the Joint Hadd Project, numerous paleo-environmental studies have been undertaken. These studies have allowed us to develop a clearer impression

Figure 2. Photograph of a Bronze Age funerary landscape at Shiya'; Hafit period tombs are on the top of coastal terrace, and Umm an-Nar period tombs are in the plain near the modern village (J. Giraud).

of the Bronze Age environment of the region, from climatological, geographical, botanical and faunal perspectives. The palynological data (Lézine *et al.* 2002: 229) indicate that the climate was semi-arid but slightly more humid than today. According to the sedimentary data (Berger *et al.* 2005: 58-59), the sea level was higher by 5 to 6 metres and there were open lagoons. These data allowed us to reconstruct the Bronze Age coastline, which was more indented than it is now (Berger *et al.* 2005; Giraud 2007: 278-281). Carpological and anthracological data (Tengberg 2005: 43-44) point to a richer flora of mainly acacia tree steppe.

Study of the tombs of the Hafit period and their location

Unfortunately, Hafit tombs were only dated morphologically, as it was in impossible to dig or sound them all. They are tronconic tombs (Fig. 3a), which consist of a single circular funerary chamber. They have double separated by an interior space filled with small stones and gravel. Some cases of single and triple walls were also found. The walls were all built from local material, which explains the diversity in their morphology; tombs made from river pebbles cannot look like tombs made from large limestone slabs. This is one of the reasons why we avoided making a typology based on the general form of the tombs. As a group, the tombs were rather well preserved; more than half are at least 1 m high, with 25% being between 1 and 2.5 m high.

The location (Fig. 3b and 4a and 4b) of the Hafit tombs seemed a good starting point for the study of this funerary landscape. It soon came out that they were built on very precisely defined orographic, geologic and topographic places. Sandy areas such as sabkhas, beaches or dunes were less popular than rocky areas such as limestone hills, alluvial terraces, pediments and jebels. In sandy areas, the average density of tombs is $0.05/km^2$, whereas in rocky areas, it is 18 tombs/km^2 (Fig. 4c). This preference for the rocky areas could come from a will to construct tombs in areas where building material is readily available. However, if we look more closely at the topographic location of the tombs, it turns out that most of them are also found on the high points of the rocky areas, at the summit of jebels for instance, or at the top of hills, terraces, glacis and pediments. We thus have a tomb density ten times greater in the high ground than in the plains, from 0.17 tombs/km^2 in the plains to 1.7 tombs/km^2 in the high ground (Fig. 4d).

The fact that the tombs were established on the high points shows a conscious social effort was made when building them. In fact, abundance of building material was not the only criteria for building tombs, otherwise, they would have been built in the plains or at the bottom of these orographic elements, not at the top. The decision to build on a summit indicates that they wanted their tombs to be seen from afar.

General distribution of tombs: the notion of necropolises

The location of tombs thus seems to spring from precise social choices. But what about their distribution? Are the tombs isolated or grouped? On the ground, they appear grouped into necropolises but their funerary space has rather blurred boundaries.

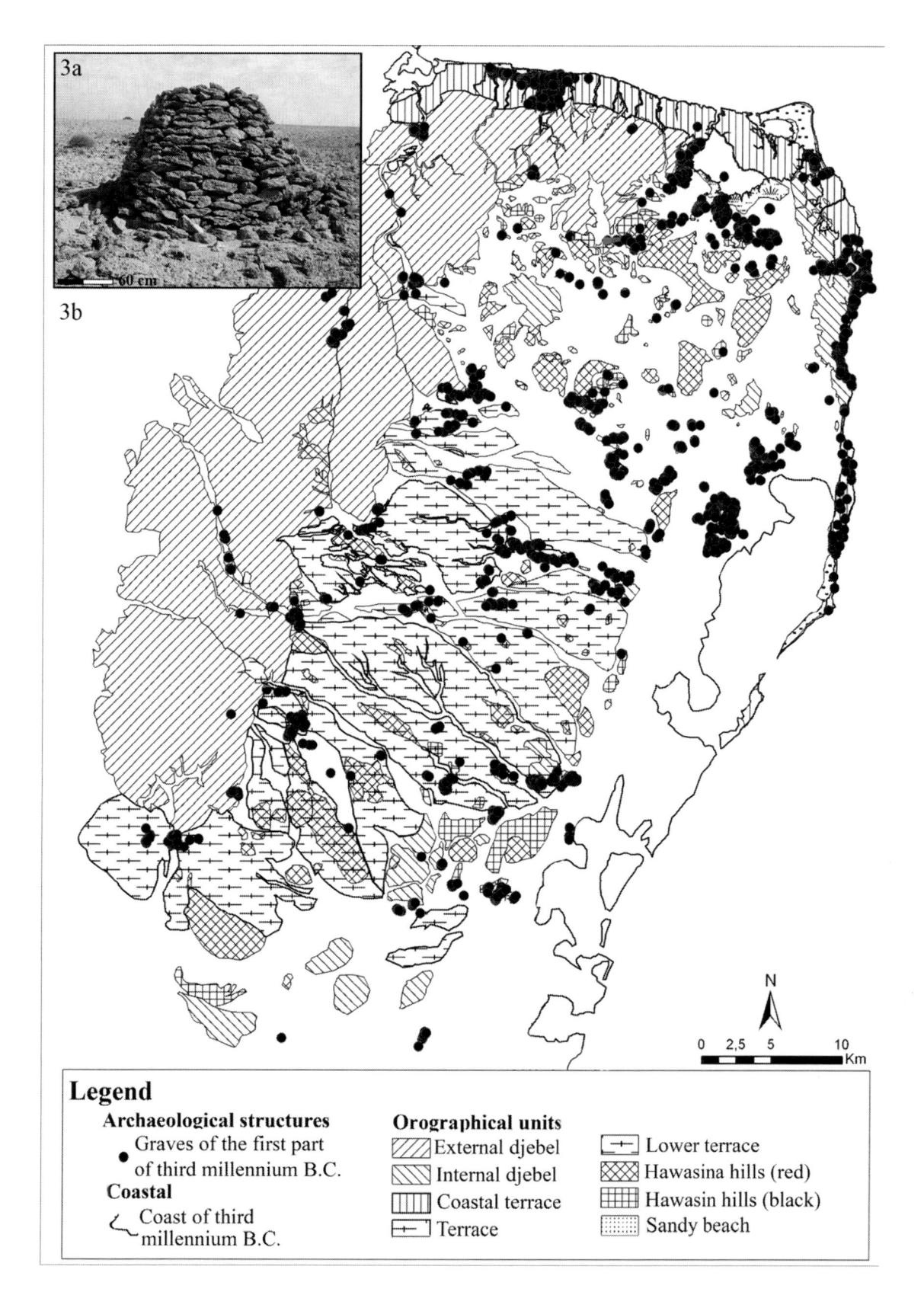

Figure 3. (a) Photograph of a typical tomb of the Hafit period, and (b) a map of the locations of Hafit tombs in the Ja'alan (J. Giraud).

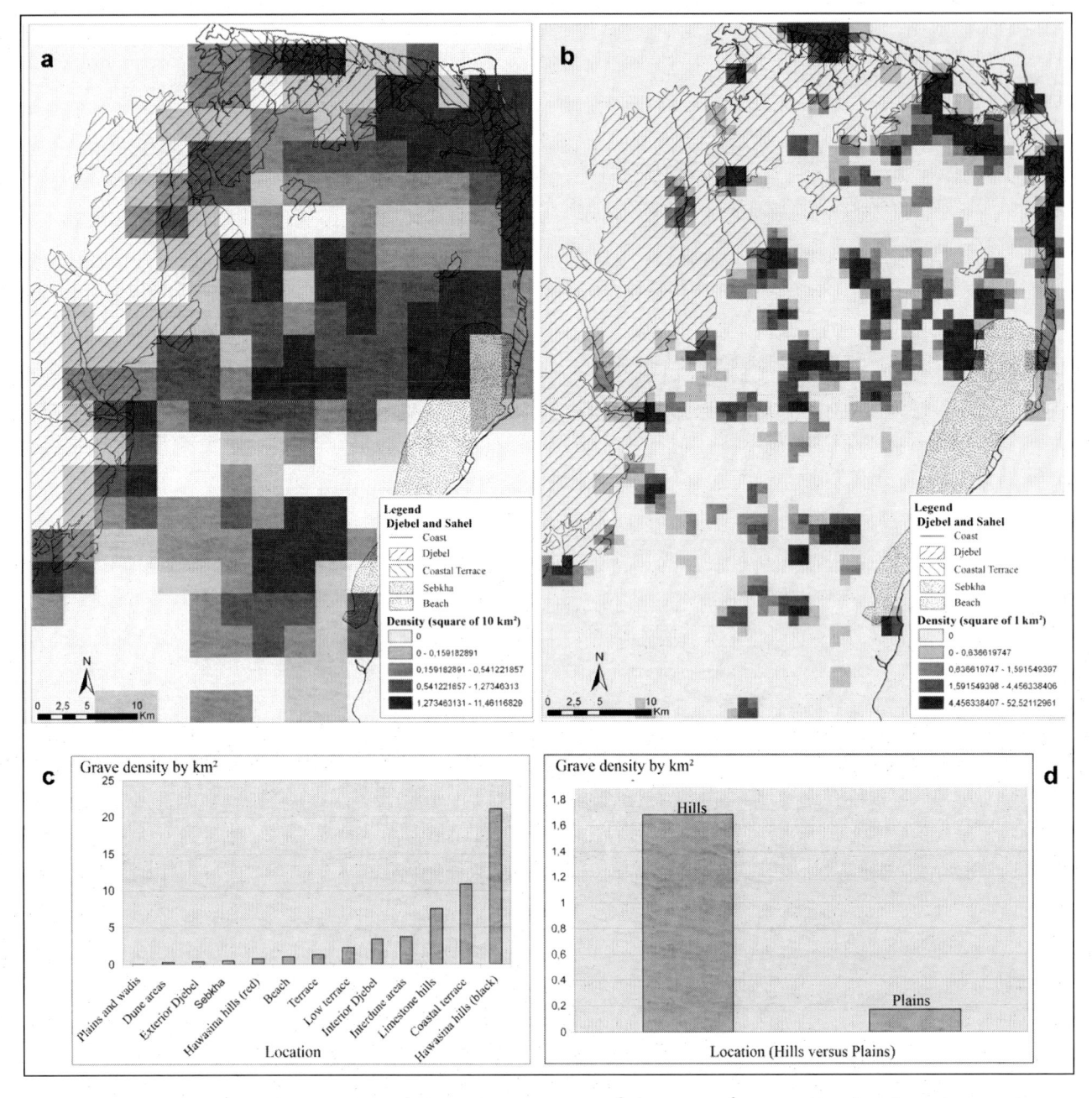

Figure 4. Maps of tomb density with different scales: (a) square of 10km² and (b) 1 km². The density of Hafit tombs on various topographical elements (c and d) (J. Giraud).

Density maps (Fig. 4a and 4b) using several scales of analysis have revealed a significant distribution of Hafit tombs, with a real space structuration. The lower resolution density map produced using grid squares of 10 km² (Fig. 4a) shows that there are both empty areas and areas where the tomb concentration reaches 52 per 10 km². The higher resolution density map produced using grid squares of 1 km² (Fig. 4b) is much more precise and confirms this phenomenon. Three types of areas were identified: areas of around 2 to 5 km² where the tomb density is considerable, intermediate areas with an average tomb density, and areas where tombs are totally absent. It is notable that the intermediate areas surround the denser areas. The further we get from the dense areas, the fewer tombs we find by km². Geographers call this a centre-periphery phenomenon, with tombs arranged in distinct clusters. They could in fact be necropolises with a dense centre, a less dense periphery and empty areas in between.

Several phenomena converge here. Firstly, a spatial discontinuity shows that it is possible to establish necropolis boundaries. Secondly, the centre-periphery phenomenon indicates that necropolis centres can also be located.

Necropolis delimitations

A necropolis is characterized by the spatial proximity and strict synchrony of structures. Space is therefore defined. Several methods of spatial analysis were tested, but the one that gave useful results is the method of the buffer

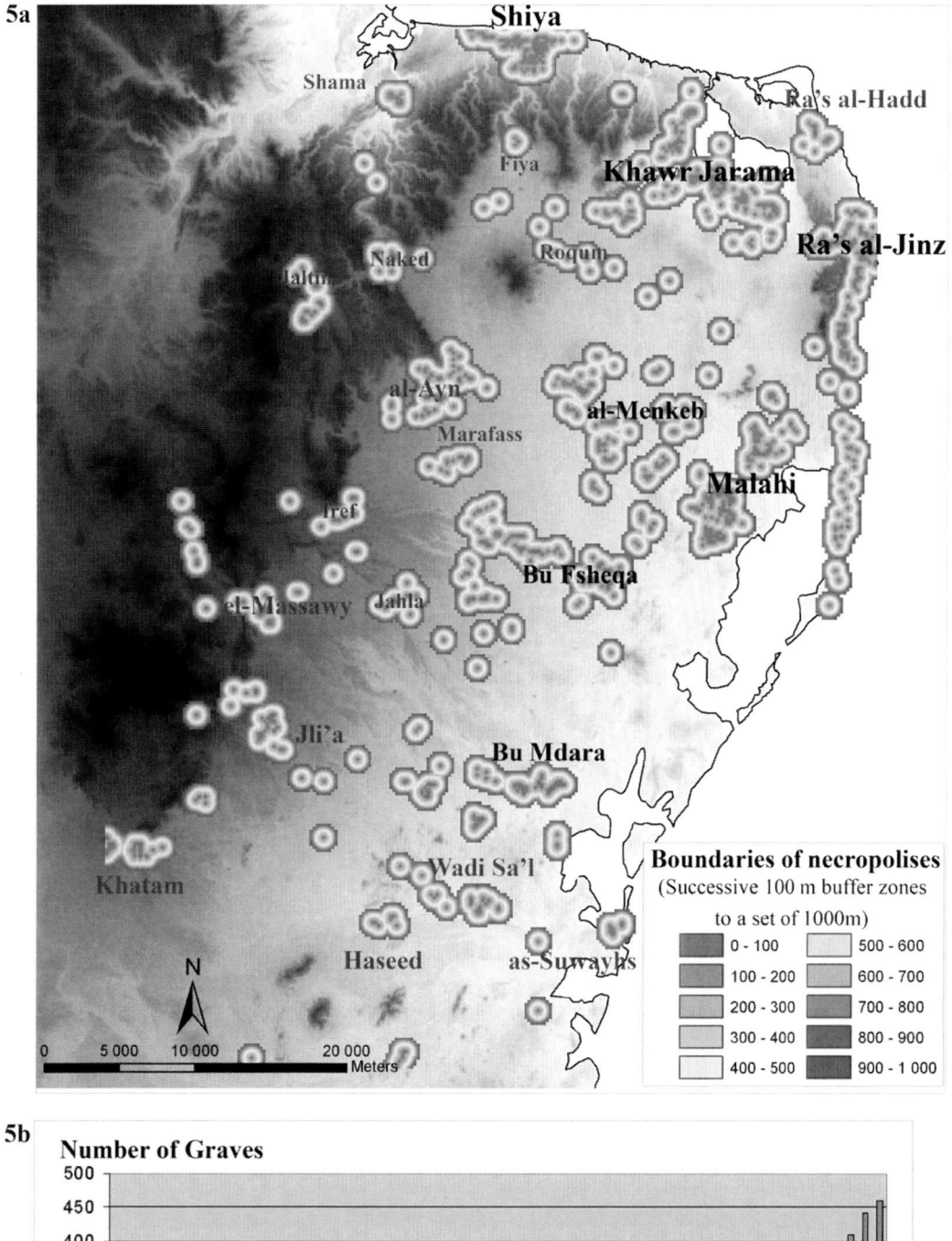

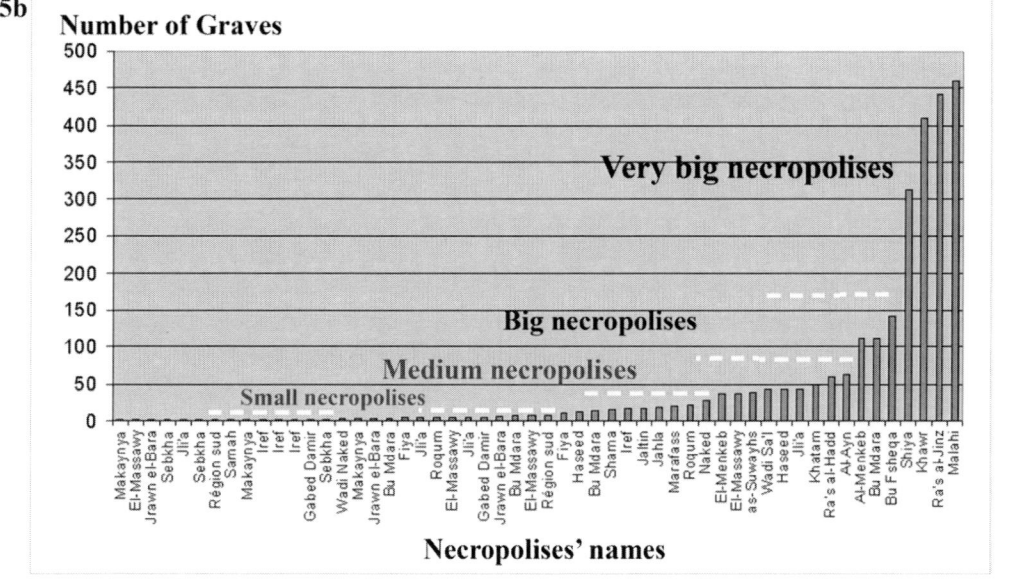

Figure 5. (a) Map of necropolis boundaries and (b) of the five categories of necropolises of the Hafit period (J. Giraud).

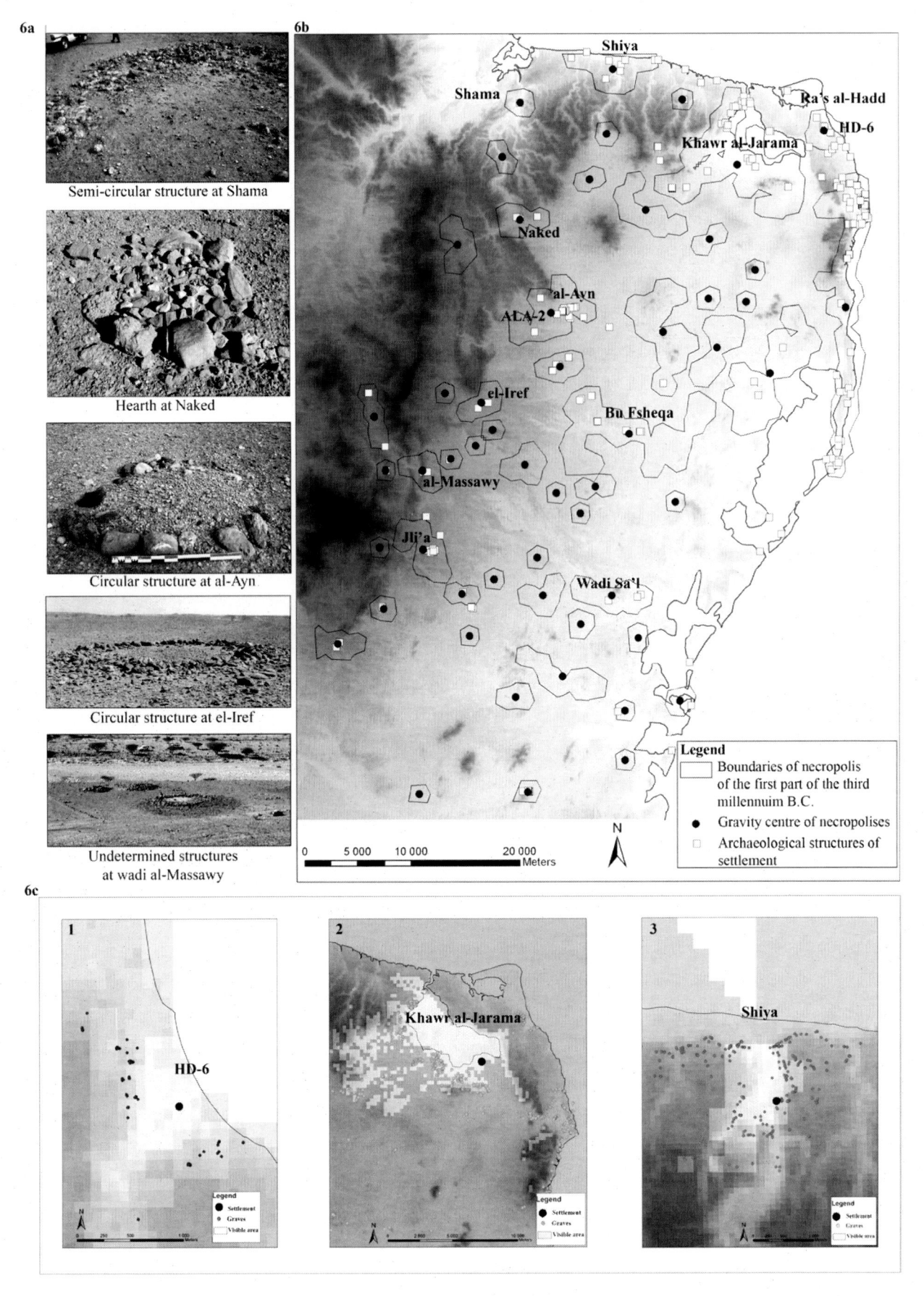

Figure 6. (a) Photograph of different types of archaeological structures found in the centre of necropolises; (b) the map of the gravity centers of Hafit necropolis in relation to the undetermined archaeological structures recorded; and (c) three examples of viewshed maps of different sites – HD-6, Khawr al-Jarama and Shiya (J. Giraud).

area. It is used by creating, around each tomb, a buffer area that is determined using a radius corresponding to a Euclidian distance. The radius of the area then allows us to measure the grouping of tombs. The inclusion of tombs in a group is made according to a given radius. We tested several radii, including 500 m, 1000 m, 1500 m, 2000 m, etc.

The analysis with a 500 m radius shows small necropolises related to isolated tombs but not related to bigger ensembles. They occupy very distinct geographical groups. The analyses made with radii of 1500 and 2000 m indicate that all the tombs are linked together, with no discrete groups really springing up, yet, as we saw before, empty zones exist between different density areas. One radius only (1000 m) allowed us to create a map where tombs appear in small, separated groups with defined boundaries, as this Euclidian distance seems to precisely reflect the ancient boundaries of necropolises of the Hafit period (Fig. 5a).

If we take a closer look at the distances that unite tombs over a 1000 m radius, we can see that the majority of tombs are only separated from each other by a distance ranging from several metres to about a hundred metres, which make them appear as small clusters within the necropolis. These clusters are then linked together with an average distance of 200-300 m and then form necropolises with well-defined boundaries.

Several methods (Giraud 2007: 426) were tested but it is interesting to note that the most relevant results come from a method that doesn't take into account the irregularities on the ground. Yet, societies in the Hafit period made good use of the high ground. Then how can we explain that the Euclidian distance better transcribes these groups of tombs? If the tombs are found in the high points, it is so that they are seen from afar individually, but perhaps also, as an ensemble. Following this logic, the tombs would have been built close to each other so as to be seen from one to the other. This placement therefore does not rely on a spatial practice based on real distances but on a will to visually spatialize the structures and to make them exist as an ensemble. As visually, we tend to treat space following a horizontal pattern, this could explain our results. The fact that visual distances are straight lines "as the crow flies" could explain our results.

54 necropolises

This type of analysis allowed us to define 54 Hafit period necropolises over the 3000 km^2 of the region. They come in different sizes, and four to five categories were determined (Fig. 5b):

- The very large necropolises: Malahi, Ra's al-Jinz, Kwar Jarama-Jsays, and Shiya. They all contain between 300 and 450 tombs. It is interesting to note that they are all located on the coast and near the lagoons.
- The large necropolises: Bu Fsheqa, Bu Mdara, and al-Menkeb. These contain between 100 and 150 tombs. They are located inland, between the coast and the large Jebel Khamis.
- The medium necropolises: al-Ayn, Ra's al-Hadd, Khatam, Jli'a, Haseed, Wadi Sa'l, as-Suwayh, el-Massawy, and al-Menkeb north. They are more numerous and contain less than a hundred tombs, usually around 50. They are found everywhere across the region.
- The small necropolises: Naked, Roqum, Marafass, Jaltin, Iref, Shama, etc. They are the most important category in terms of numbers. The count of tombs falls between a dozen to about 30 tombs. They are usually located near the large or very large necropolises. In some cases they may be grouped together.
- The last category corresponds to isolated or coupled tombs. This category forms a relatively small proportion of the corpus, but still comprises 14 cases. Sometimes, we are in the presence of tombs not included in the necropolis using the buffer area method but found near it, and sometimes, the tomb really is totally isolated.

Necropolis centres

As mentioned earlier, these necropolises have a notable characteristic. The density analysis showed that in their centre, funerary structures were more or less densely distributed. This is due to the centre-periphery phenomenon. The further we get from the centre, the fewer tombs we find, but what could explain this spatial process? I would like to add two more facts that we observed on the ground. Very dense tomb areas are very often linked with actual Bedouin dwellings, which are more or less permanent. Moreover, these structures are also associated with stone structures difficult to interpret but that we couldn't date without excavating, such as hearths, rectangles or circles of stones (Fig. 6a).

In order to explain these findings and answer to the question of the density gradation, we had to be able to define more clearly the centres of the necropolises. Several methods (Giraud 2007: 429-431) were used, but the most effective means was through calculation of the gravity centre by GIS. We took the centre of gravity of the area of the necropolises as defined by the buffer method.

We then compared the location of the necropolis centres with that of the undetermined structures found on the plain (Fig. 6b). It is obvious that a spatial correlation exists between the two. Across the assemblage of the 54 necropolises, 20 have their centre precisely located where the undetermined structures are, which means a 37% positive correlation. This percentage may not seem much but if we only count necropolises where we have found varied undetermined structures, it increases to 83%. In fact, only 24 necropolises also showed other structures in the plain, and 20 of them have their centre on or very near these structures. This percentage now appears much more significant and leads us to ask about dwellings.

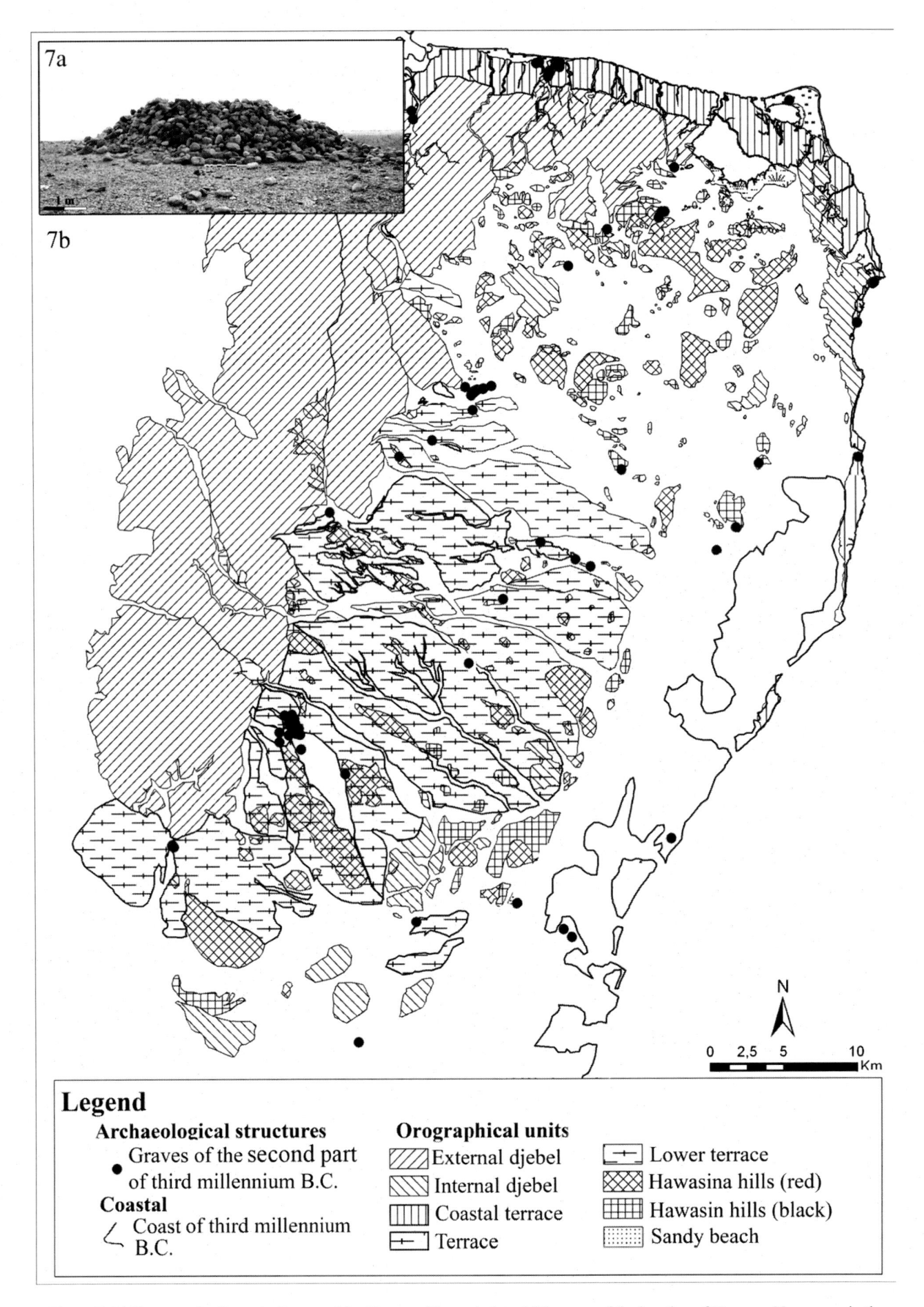

Figure 7. (a) Photograph of a typical grave of the Umm an-Nar period, and (b) a map of the location of Umm an-Nar graves in the Ja'alan (J. Giraud).

Only three settlements from the Hafit period have been excavated: Hili 8, HD-6 and ALA-2, the last two located in the Ja'alan region (Fig. 6b). They raise a lot of questions about the nature of dwellings, their location and their form. This method, which calculates the positive correlation between centre of the necropolis and the location of undetermined structures, allowed us to find the location of the sites despite taphonomic problems. The site ALA-2 (Blin 2007) was found like this, as well as others, not yet excavated at Shama and Khawr-Jarama, where evidence of a typical 3rd millennium B.C. *Conus* sp. shell-working industry was found (Charpentier 1994). Other as-yet-undated structures that can only have been dwellings were also found across the Ja'alan, for instance at al-Massawy, Jli'a, Wadi Sa'l, Khatam, Bu Fsheqa and Shiya (Fig. 6b). According to our model, the dwellings stood at the centre of the necropolis, in the area most occupied by the tombs.

If this method gives us a clearer idea of the location of the dwellings, it still appears that in some cases the gravity centre is a substantial distance, up to several hundred metres, from the dwellings. For instance, the site HD-6 is 1 km away from the gravity centre of its necropolis. Therefore, we attempted to establish if another model could be put forward using the 'viewshed' function of the GIS. This function determines the areas visible from a particular point in space. In other words, it takes topography into account. We noticed that the HD-6 site appears to be at the visual centre of its necropolis (Fig. 6c.1). Similarly, in the other cases (Fig. 6c.2 and 3) where we found archaeological structures that did not correspond to the gravity centre of the necropolis, viewshed analysis indicated that the structures corresponded with the visual centre, i.e. Khawr Jarama (Fig. 6c.2), Wadi Sa'al, Shiya (Fig. 6c.3), Shama, etc.

From these models, it seems that the placement of Hafit tombs is to be understood not from the exterior, but from the interior. The tombs' purpose is not to define a territory for potential foreigners but to create a centre that would correspond to dwellings. It is from the dwellings, or centre, that the placement of tombs in the necropolis was organised. It has to be visible in whole from each of the dwellings. The criteria that better explains the spatial implantation of each tomb is therefore visual. The necropolis thus functions to define a living space: that of the village.

The funerary landscape of the Umm an-Nar period (2700-2000 B.C.)

The funerary landscape of the middle and later 3rd millennium BC sees the development of a parallel funerary landscape (Cleuziou 2002). Very often, successive funerary spaces try to differ from the previous ones in order to 'outdo' them. However, in this case, we are in the presence of a new funerary space that, far from erasing the first, reinforces and completes it (Fig. 2). It incorporates tombs with a very different architecture and distribution. However these Umm an-Nar tombs seem to share the same cultural values as the previous ones and are built in a parallel way and with the same methods as that of the earlier tombs. We were able to record and precisely locate 93 tombs dating from the Umm an-Nar period over the area of study. A brief discussion of their spatial organisation follows.

Study of the tombs and their location

As for the Hafit tombs, Umm an-Nar tombs were defined through their morphology (Fig. 7a). They have a circular plan but with a significant diameter (7-15 m). The funerary chamber is circular and divided into internal chambers. During surveys, we determined that the tombs of the region could have between 2 and 8 chambers. The walls of the tombs are composed of double walls: two exterior walls with internal filling consisting of small stones and gravel. Some of them have kept their exterior walls, composed of worked stones. These stones are mostly exogenous to the region. Unfortunately, these tombs are not well-preserved. Principally located in the plain, they have been partly destroyed in order to use their stones again.

The placement of the Umm an-Nar tombs (Figs. 7b and 8) is substantially different from earlier tombs. This time, the high points are neglected and the tombs are on plains and alluvial terraces. No tombs were located on jebels, high hills, sabkha or beaches. We recorded a few on the alluvial plains but most of the time they were found on alluvial terraces, coastal terraces and hillocks a few meters high (Fig 8c and 8d). A small proportion was situated on high terraces, but they are actually on the terrace and not along the edges, as seen previously. These tombs therefore occupy different spaces and don't seem to have been built to be seen. The logic behind their implantation is thus different to those discussed earlier.

General distribution of tombs: the notion of necropolises

The placement of Umm an-Nar tombs reinforces the view of a landscape produced through precise social choices. The question of tomb distribution remains essential: are they grouped or isolated?

On the ground, it is obvious that these tombs are grouped in small necropolises. The high and low resolution density maps with grid squares of 10 km^2 and 1 km^2 indicate that the phenomenon is even more local than was the case for the earlier tombs. The average density on the whole of the region is 0.026 tombs/km^2. The low resolution density map (Fig. 8a) shows small regions with a density 30 to 50 times higher (1.54 tombs/10 km^2) than the average density on the whole area, which is 0.087 tombs/10 km^2. There is a majority of empty areas of tombs. The high resolution density map (Fig. 8b) reinforces this idea of very small areas of 1 to 4 km^2 with a large concentration of tombs. These centres are surrounded by a small periphery, less dense, but of only 1 to 2 km radius. We can therefore reconstruct a very local process defined by small necropolises, without a centre-periphery phenomenon as before. These necropolises have boundaries that can be easily reproduced on a map.

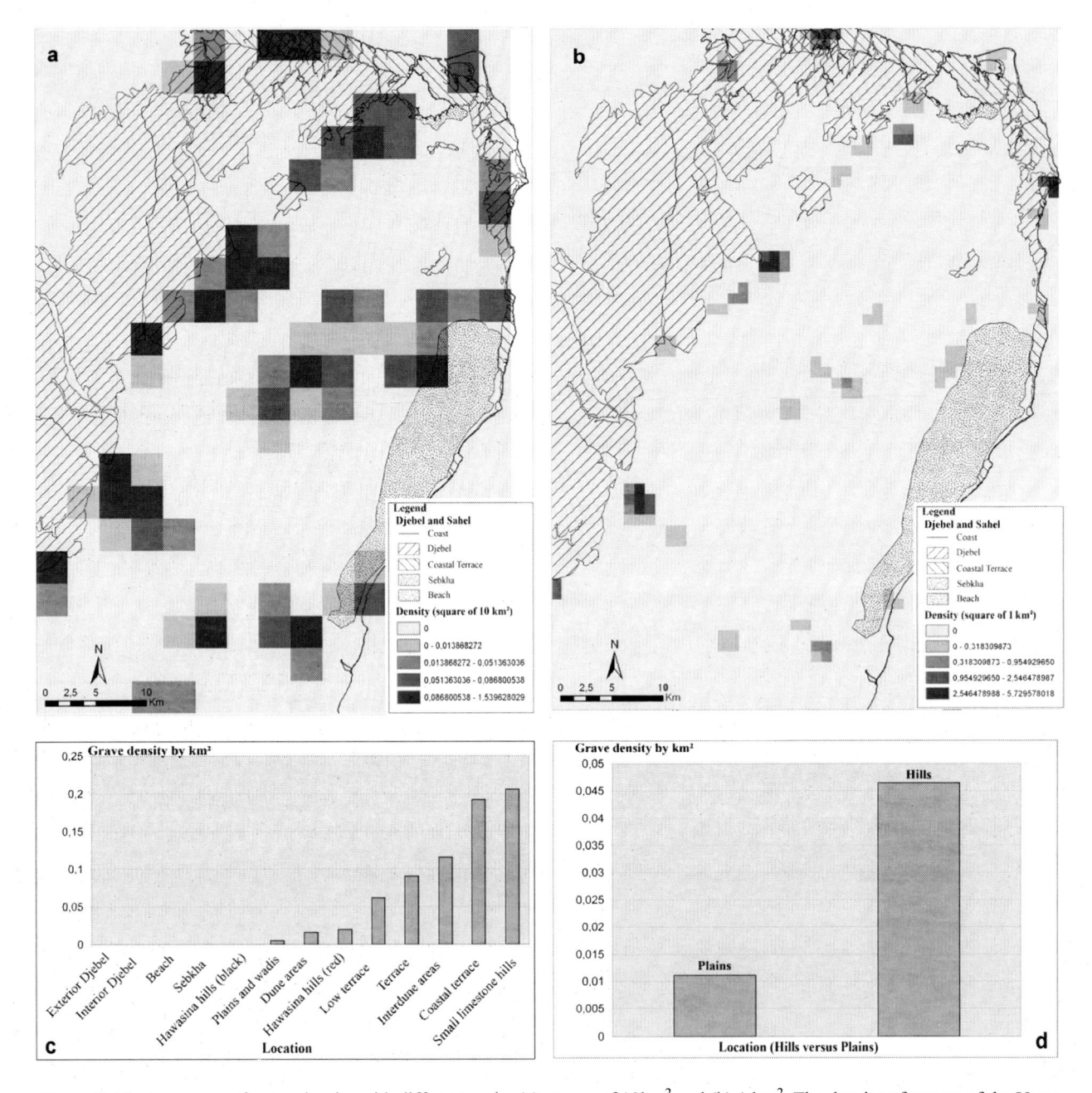

Figure 8. The two maps of grave density with different scale: (a) square of 10km² and (b) 1 km². The density of graves of the Umm an-Nar period on various topographical elements (c and d) (J. Giraud).

Necropolis delimitation

According to the buffer area method, we managed to isolate a number of Umm an-Nar necropolises. The most appropriate Euclidian distance is that of 500 m. This distance allows us a more precise regrouping of the tombs in necropolises (Fig. 9a). However, we can make two observations: within the set of necropolises, some of the tombs remain isolated. These isolated tombs are not exceptions but rather to be considered as necropolises in themselves, as they share with necropolises the same status and occupy a defined area. The second observation is that all the necropolises, except HD-1 and as-Suwayh, are located within a space defined by the necropolises from the first half of the 3rd millennium B.C. (Fig. 9a).

We therefore have a continuity of the funerary space: one within another.

It would seem logical that the implantation of the necropolises of this period was not made with a view to being seen, but rather with a desire to gather in a delimited space at the heart of the first funerary space.

28 necropolises

The analysis of the buffer areas allowed us to find the boundaries of 28 Umm an-Nar period necropolises over the 3000 km² region. They have different sizes and three categories can be determined (Fig. 9b and 9a):

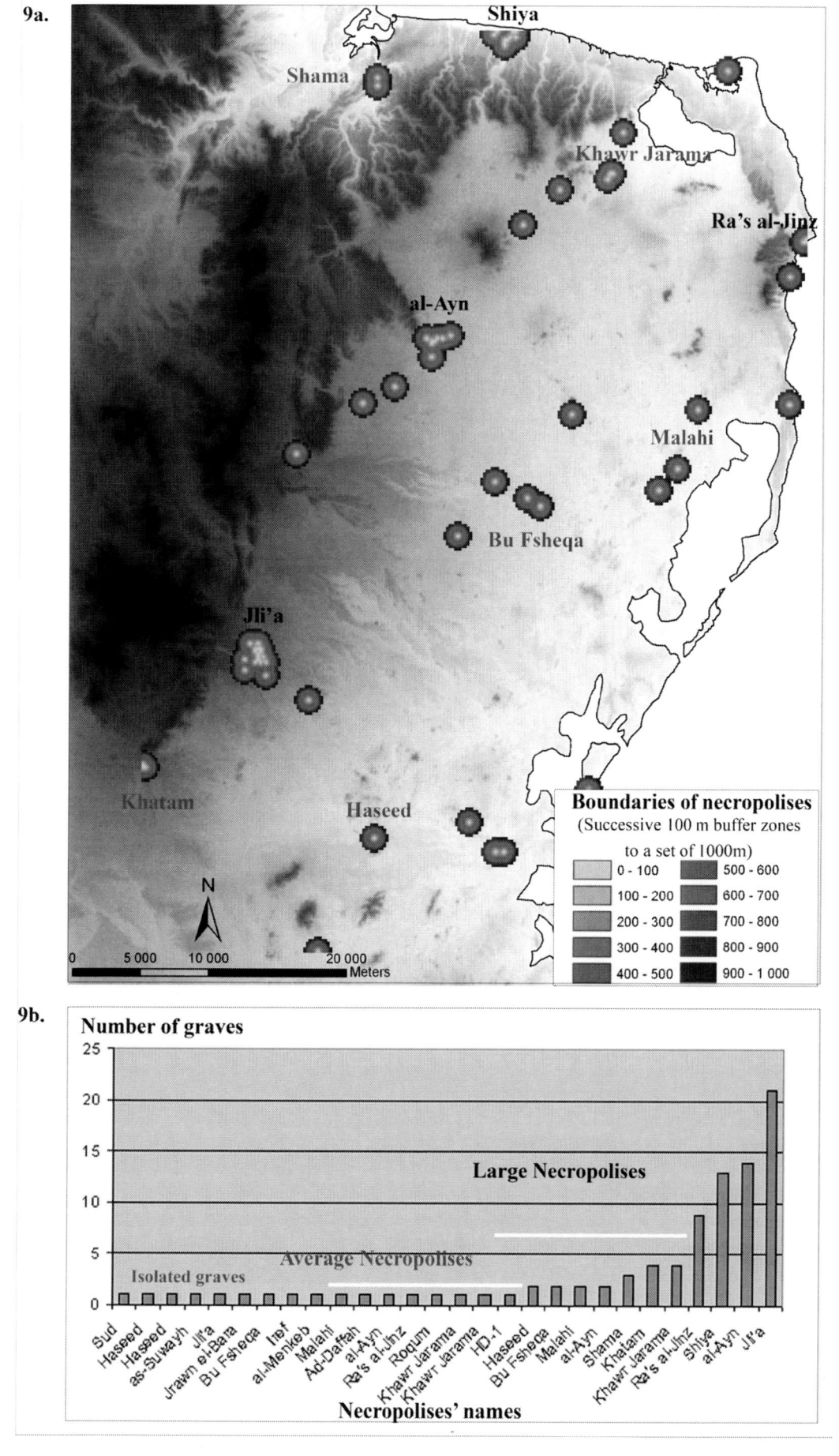

Figure 9. (a) Map of Umm an-Nar necropolis boundaries, and (b) of the three categories of Umm an-Nar necropolis (J. Giraud).

DEATH AND BURIAL IN ARABIA AND BEYOND: MULTIDISCIPLINARY PERSPECTIVES

- Large necropolises: Jli'a, al-Ayn, Shiya, and Ra's al-Jinz. They feature up to 20 tombs but generally contain about 15. These necropolises are comparable to the first class of necropolises of the earliest period, which are the largest ones.
- Medium necropolises: Khawr-Jarama, Khatam, Shama, Malahi, Bu Fsheqa, and Haseed. They are more numerous and contain 2 to 4 tombs. They can be compared to the second and third categories of the previous period.
- Isolated tombs. They are quite numerous and are distributed throughout the area of study, but are mainly found closer to medium and smaller necropolises.

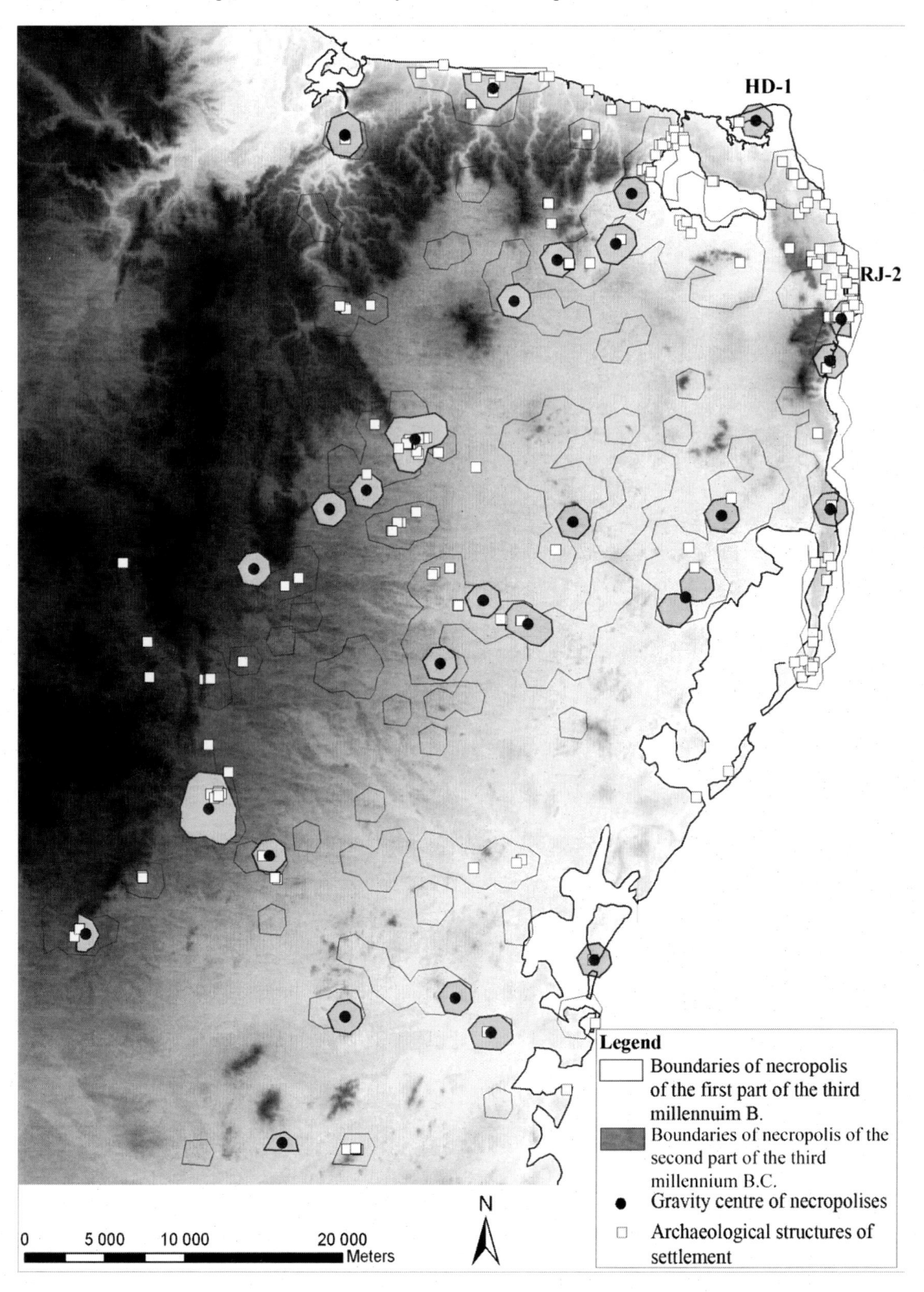

Figure 10. Map of the gravity center of Umm an-Nar necropolises and their relation to undetermined archaeological structures recorded (J. Giraud).

- Large necropolises: Jli'a, al-Ayn, Shiya, and Ra's al-Jinz. They feature up to 20 tombs but generally contain about 15. These necropolises are comparable to the first class of necropolises of the earliest period, which are the largest ones.
- Medium necropolises: Khawr-Jarama, Khatam, Shama, Malahi, Bu Fsheqa, and Haseed. They are more numerous and contain 2 to 4 tombs. They can be compared to the second and third categories of the previous period.
- Isolated tombs. They are quite numerous and are distributed throughout the area of study, but are mainly found closer to medium and smaller necropolises.

Necropolis centres

We also tried to determine where the gravity centres of these Umm an-Nar period necropolises were so as to be able to link them with undetermined structures, as we did previously (Fig. 10). Overall, 50% of the assemblage of necropolises have a gravity centre spatially associated with undetermined archaeological structures. Out of 18 necropolises displaying this type of structure, 14 gravity centers are associated to them, which represents a 77% positive correlation. This positive correlation was observed for the RJ-2 site (Cleuziou & Tosi 2000), which is a large site of this period, and the HD-1 site, excavated by J. Reade (Reade 1990).

The results are quite close to previous results, which may be explained through several phenomena. Throughout SE Arabia, we find tombs located very close to dwellings, e.g. at Umm an-Nar Island (Frifelt 1991; Frifelt 1995), Bat (Gentelle & Frifelt 1989), Hili 8 (Cleuziou 1979, Cleuziou 1989), RJ-2 (Cleuziou & Tosi 2000), etc. It is therefore quite logical to find possible dwelling structures at the heart of these necropolises. The connection between these structures and the gravity centre of the necropolises of the two periods is not surprising: only the choice of tomb location is changing, the dwellings remain in the same place. As the necropolises of the second period are found within the first necropolises, they only re-invest in already built dwellings.

We are therefore here in a new space that completes the previous one. It is clear that the first funerary space had been established for 500 years with the foundation and development of the first Hafit period necropolises. As a result, there was no need to reinforce the funerary landscape, nor the funerary identity of the area. The dead thus were appropriated by the living through the integration of the funerary space within the living space.

Conclusions

The study and analysis of the distribution of thousands of tombs from the early 3rd millennium B.C. and of scores of tombs from the second half of the 3rd millennium B.C. allowed us to set up a spatial organisation model that integrated necropolises and dwellings. Gradually, the inhabitants of the dwellings produced a visible funerary space. This process may be attributed to spatial appropriation, something that all sedentary societies do. The societies that we are speaking of had different ways of occupying their space, and in this case, the spatial staging of the ancestors allowed people to identify and bond with their surroundings. It is not so much a territorial appropriation as the setting of a landscape that places the group within the staging of its genealogical history.

Once this "landscape of identity" was established during the Hafit period, it was no longer necessary to carry on specifying it for the second period. The necropolises from this second period are located at the heart of the dwellings. This evolution indicates a change in spatial perception. Let us not forget that dwellings also go hand in hand with a significant agricultural space. It is interesting to note that places where it would be physically possible to implant date-palm trees are also located in these dwelling areas (Giraud 2007).

We may be observing the first occupation of oases, that is to say village centres coupled with little gardens based upon domesticated date palms and surrounded by their funerary spaces. If we consider all of the Ja'alan region, the large sites of the Hafit period are situated near the lagoons and the coast, whereas in the Umm an-Nar period, when the funerary change occurs, the influential towns are situated inland and in the north. This important change may be due to the progressive disappearance of the lagoons, but also to the reinforcement of the oasis areas in the piedmont zone, although more research is necessary in order to validate this hypothesis.

This study allowed us not only to develop new methods that can be applied during surveys, but also allowed the identification of a complex geographical space – developed through a process of spatial appropriation by local communities – that may well indicate the birth of the oases.

Aknowledgements

I thank Serge Cleuziou and Maurizio Tosi for accepting me into the Joint Hadd Project team, and for allowing me to survey for 5 years throughout the Ja'alan. I would also like to thank everyone who helped me during the survey (G. Gernez, J.-F Berger, G. Davtian, N. Bernigaud, C. Sevin-Allouet, E. Portat, J. Delmotte, S. Righetti and others), and Sheikh Khamis Nasser al-Amri for his friendship and his willingness to help me in the field. I would also like to thank the Ministry of Heritage and Culture for their help, in particular Mrs. Biwba al-Sabri, without whom this study would not have been possible.

References

Berger J.-F., Cleuziou S., Davtian G., Cremashi M., Cattani M., Cavulli F., Charpentier V., Giraud J., Marquis P., Martin C., Méry S., Plaziat J.-C. & Saliège, J.-F. 2005. Évolution paléogéographique du Ja'alan (Oman) à l'Holocène moyen: impact sur l'évolution des paléomilieux littoraux et les stratégies d'adaptation des communautés humaines. *Paléorient* 31: 46-63.

Blin O. 2007. Al-Ayn: a Small Settlement and Palm Tree Garden in Eastern Oman. Pages 248-250 in S. Cleuziou & M. Tosi (eds), *In the Shadow of the Ancestors: The Prehistoric Foundations of the Early Arabian Civilization in Oman.* Muscat: Ministry of Heritage and Culture.

Cartwright C. R. 1998. Seasonal Aspects of Bronze and Iron Age Communities at Ra's al-Hadd, Oman. *Journal of Environmental Archaeology* 3: 97-103.

Charpentier V. 1994. A specialized production at regional scale in Bronze Age Arabia: shell rings from Ra's al-Junayz area (Sultanate Oman). Pages 157-170 in K. Koskemienni & A. Parpola (eds), *South Asian Archaeology 1993.* Helsinki: Suomalainen Tiedeakatenia.

Cleuziou S. 1979. Les deuxième et troisième campagnes de fouilles a Hili 8. *Archaeology in The United Arab Emirates* II-III: 19-29.

Cleuziou S. 1989. Excavation at Hili 8: a preliminary report on the 4th to 7th campaigns. *Archaeology in the United Arab Emirates* V: 61-85.

Cleuziou S. 2002. Présence et mise en scène des morts à l'usage des vivants dans les communautés protohistoriques : L'exemple de la péninsule d'Oman à l'âge du bronze ancien. Pages 17-31 in M. Molinos & A. Zifferero (eds), *I primi popoli d'Europa.* Florence: All insegna del Giglio.

Cleuziou S. & Tosi M. 2000. Ra's al-Jinz and the prehistoric coastal cultures of the Ja'alan. *Journal of Oman Studies* 11: 19-74.

Cleuziou S. & Tosi M. 2007. *In the Shadow of the Ancestors: The Prehistoric foundations of the Early Arabian Civilization in Oman.* Muscat: Ministry of Heritage and Culture.

Frifelt K. 1991. *The Island of Umm an-Nar Volume I: Third Millennium Graves.* Aarhus: Aarhus University Press.

Frifelt K. 1995. *The Island of Umm an-Nar Volume II: The Third Millennium Settlement.* Aarhus: Aarhus University Press.

Gentelle P. & Frifelt K. 1989. About the distribution of the third millennium graves and settlements in the Ibri area of Oman. Pages 119-126 in P.M. Costa & M. Tosi (eds), *Oman Studies: Papers on the Archaeology and History of Oman.* Rome: Is.M.E.O.

Giraud J. 2007. *Restitution d'un espace géographique ancien: la province du Ja'alan à l'Âge du Bronze (Sultanat d'Oman).* Unpublished PhD dissertation, Université de Paris 1 Panthèon-Sorbonne.

Giraud J. & Cleuziou S. 2009. Funerary landscape as part of the social landscape and its perceptions: three thousand early Bronze Age burials in the eastern Ja'alan (Sultanate of Oman). *Proceedings of Seminar for Arabian Studies* 39: 163-180.

Giraud J. & Gernez G. 2006. Les prospections dans la province du Ja'alan (Sultanat d'Oman): D'un terrain désertique à l'analyse du système d'habitat au IIIe millénaire av. J.-C. *Table ronde - Prospection archéologique en milieux désertiques et tropicaux.* Nanterre: Cahier des thèmes transversaux.

Lézine A.-M., Saliège J.-F., Mathieu R., Tagliatella T. L., Méry S., Charpentier V. & Cleuziou S. 2002. Mangroves of Oman during the late Holocene: climatic implications and impact on human settlements. *Vegetation History and Archaeobotany* 11: 221-232.

Reade J. 1990. Excavations at HD-1. Pages 34-35 in S. Cleuziou, J. Reade & M. Tosi (eds), The *Joint Hadd Project. Summary Report on the third Season (October 1987-February 1988).* Rome: Mimeo, ERA 30 CNRS IUON.

Tengberg M. 2005. Les forêts de la mer. Exploitation et évolution des mangroves en Arabie orientale du Néolithique à l'époque Islamique. *Paléorient* 31: 39-45.

Authors' address
Dr. Jessica Giraud
UMR 7041, Maison de l'archéologie et de l'ethnologie
Équipe du Village à l'état au Proche et Moyen-Orient
Boite 14, 21 allée de l'Université
92023 Nanterre Cedex
France
e-mail: giraud.jessica@gmail.com

An inventory of the objects in a collective burial at Dadna (Emirate of Fujairah)

Anne Benoist and Salah Ali Hassan

Summary

In 1994, S. Ali Hassan (Dept. of Antiquities, Fujairah) carried out a rescue excavation on a collective burial accidentally discovered at Dadna, in Fujairah Emirate. It produced a huge quantity of material which was studied in 2000 by A. Benoist (French Archaeological Mission in the U.A.E.). This material indicates periodical re-use of the grave from the second millennium BC until the middle Iron Age (6th century BC), and is presented and discussed in this article.

Introduction

The aim of this article is to present the material collected inside the grave of Dadna during a rescue excavation carried out by the Department of Antiquities of Fujairah. Dadna is located in the northern part of the Emirate of Fujairah, c. 7 km to the south-east of Dibba along the eastern coast. The grave is located in the southern part of the village, approximately 100 m to the east of the road in a small passage surrounded by recent houses. It was accidentally discovered in 1995 during the installation of an electrical cable. At that occasion the department of Antiquities from Fujairah was alerted and decided to undertake a rescue excavation.

This excavation took place in December 1995 under the supervision of Salah Ali Hassan. It lasted one month during which the chamber of the grave was emptied to its floor, reached at a depth of 80 cm. Material and bones were collected and stored in the Museum of Fujairah. The grave was re-filled after the excavation in order to allow the installation of the new cable.

In 2000, A. Benoist accepted to study the material collected inside the grave. S. Eliès drew a map of the architectural remains still visible on the surface (Fig. 1). Dadna grave is a long subterranean burial including two elongated and parallel spaces, broadly oriented east-west, which might have been parts of a single U-shaped chamber. Subterranean graves with a U-shaped chamber are represented in the region at Qidfa (two U-shaped tombs were excavated at Qidfa by the Department of Antiquities of al Aïn in 1986 under the supervision of W. Yasin al Tikriti but remain unpublished) and Mereshid (Benoist *et al.* 2000 Fig. 28).

The walls of the grave were built in large unshaped local stones disposed in two lines with their long side perpendicular to the face of the wall. The central part of the walls was filled with small stones, gravel and yellowish sand. Nothing remains from the covering of the grave, which may have been made of large slabs, as it was the case in other subterranean graves from the region.

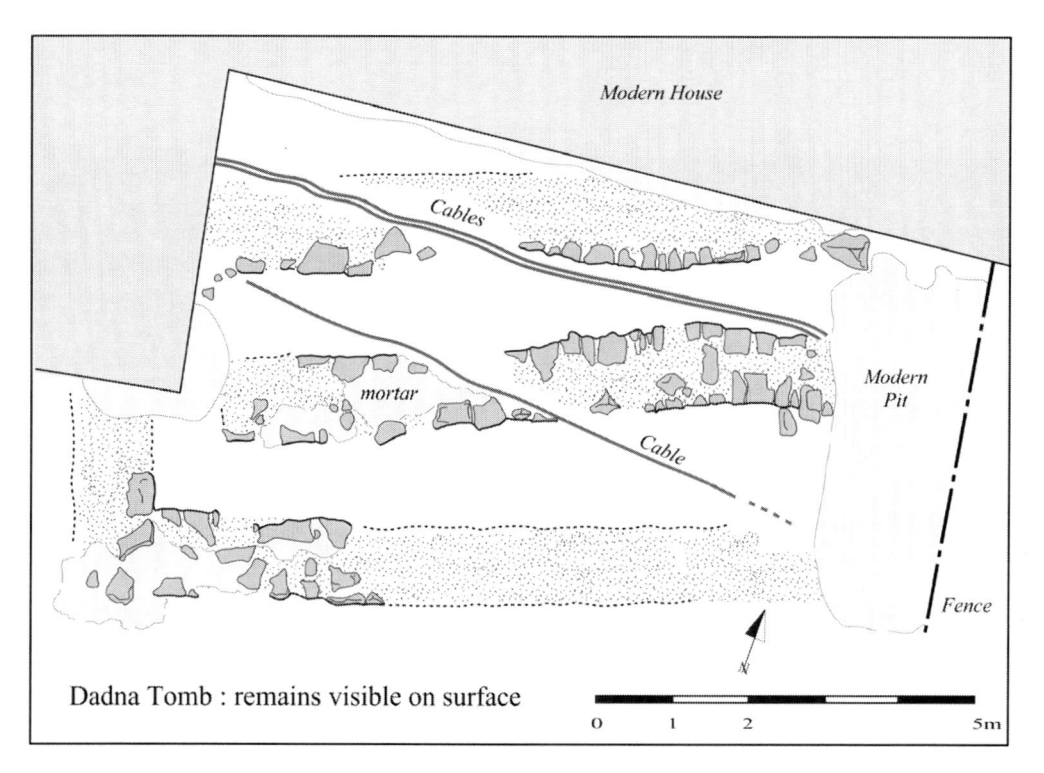

Fig. 1. Dadna grave: remains visible on surface.

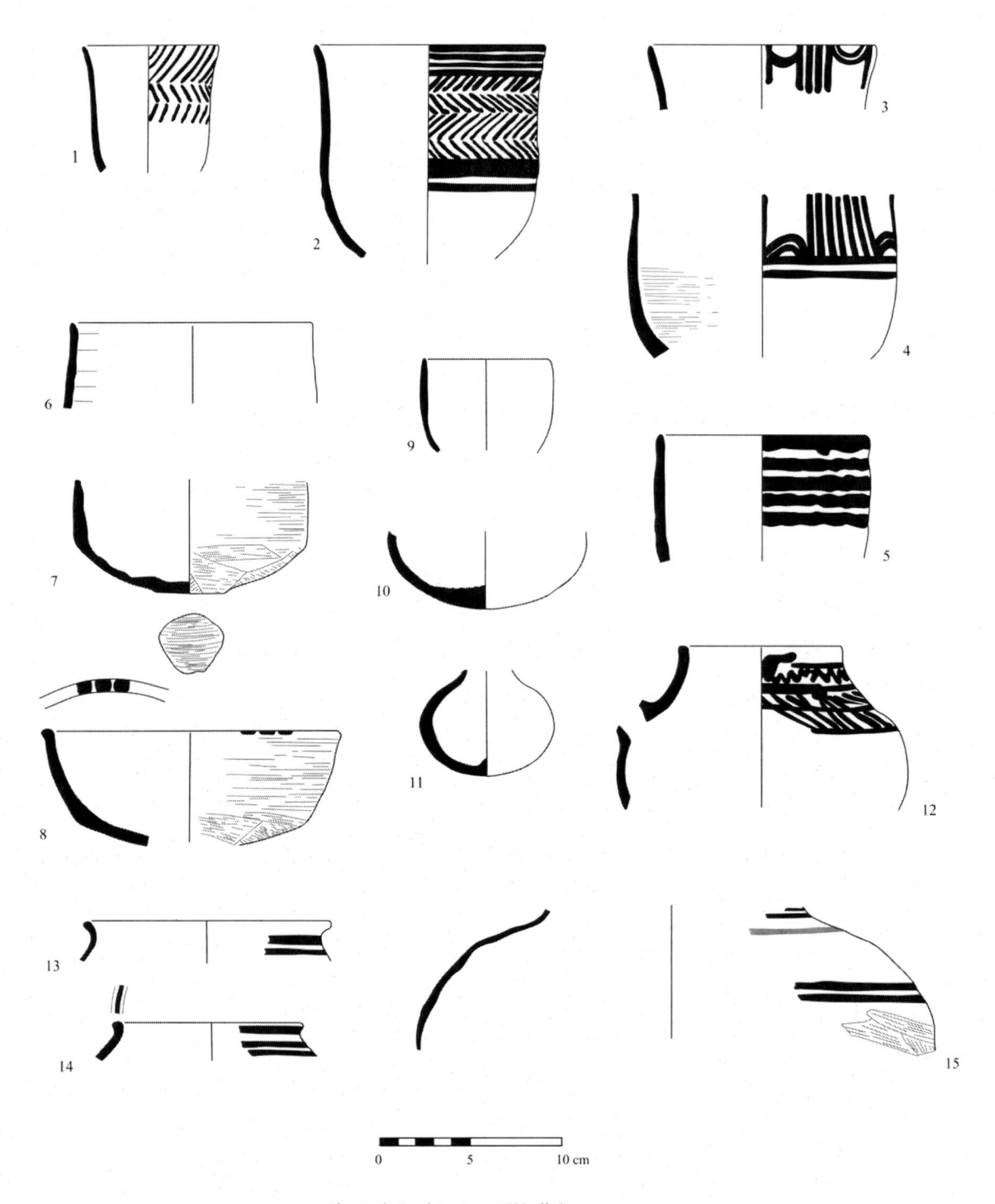

Figure 2. Dadna grave: Wadi-Suq pottery.

A huge quantity of bones was found and the grave was certainly a collective burial. But the study of the bones by an anthropologist would be necessary for proposing a first estimation of the number of individuals buried inside. As no detailed map was made during the excavation showing the position of the bones, our idea of the organisation of the deposits in the grave is not precise. The deposits were heavily disturbed in antiquity and during more recent times.

The grave produced a high quantity of material including pottery, softstone vessels, bronze arrowheads, one bronze bowl, elements of jewellery in metal (bronze, electrum), shell and stone buttons and beads of various types. This material includes elements of different dates, from the Wadi Suq period (2000-1600 BC) until the Iron Age II/III Period (around 600 BC) and speaks for a long period of use.

Pottery

Among the 855 potsherds collected, 210 are fragments of rims and allow an identification of the shape of the vessel which they belong to. Our study of the pottery is based on

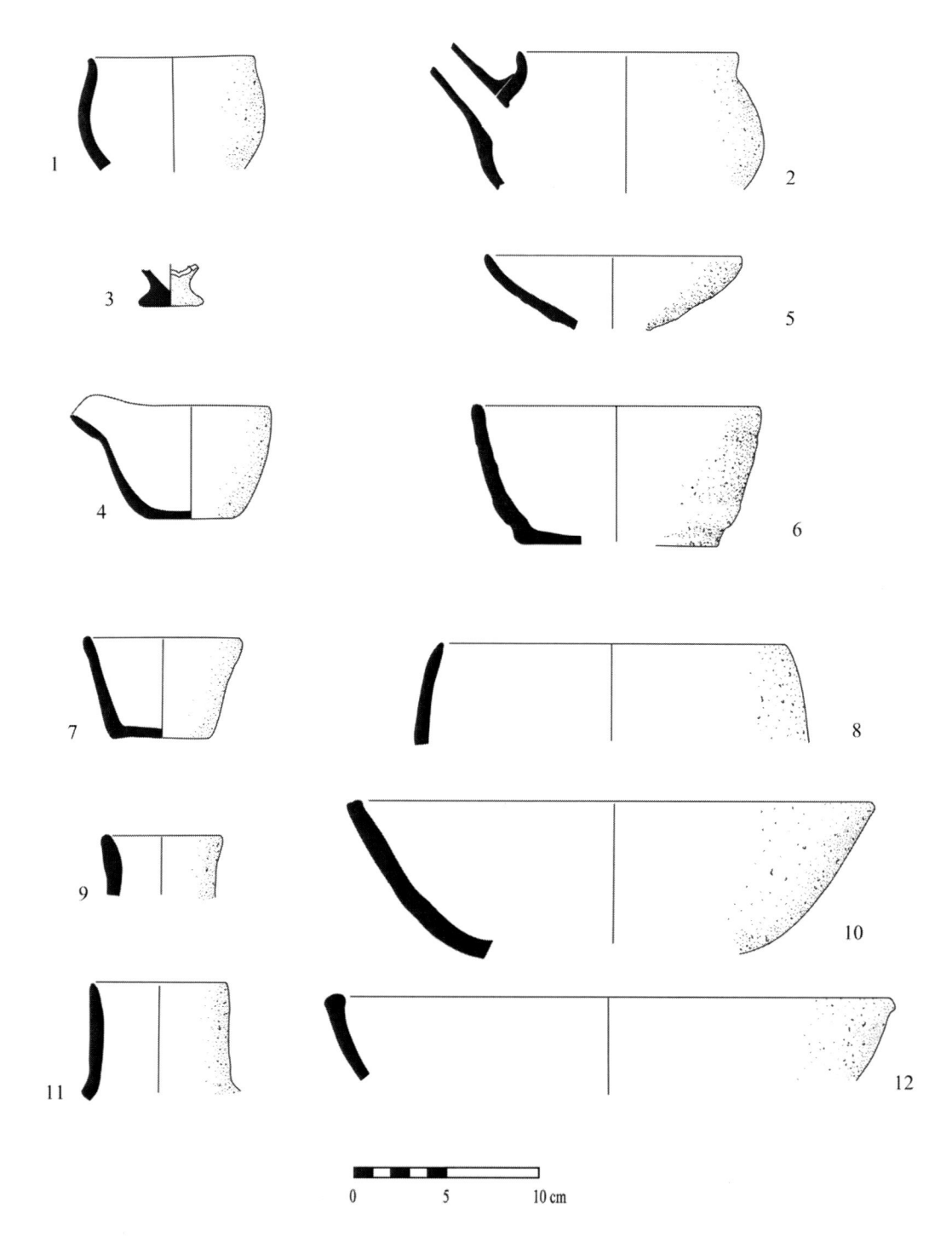

Figure 3. Dadna grave: Late Bronze Age (1-3) and Early Iron Age (5-12) pottery.

these 210 pieces. These include 27 vessels characteristic of the Wadi Suq Period, 3 pieces recalling Late Bronze Age potteries and 175 Iron Age vessels, including mainly Iron Age II examples, but also few which may be dated from Iron Age I.

Wadi Suq Pottery (2000-1600 BC)

The 27 Wadi Suq vases collected in the grave are all in the *"céramique semi fine"* defined by S. Méry (Méry 2000: 249-271). They have a thin wall and a fine temper. Thin horizontal lines on the surface of the potsherds suggest that vessels were put in shape on a rotating base. Traces of scraping and string cutting appear outside on the base of several vases. Most vessels have a thin slip or wash, brown or white in colour. Nineteen are painted in black or dark brown. Shapes include goblets, pots, jugs, miniature flask, and shallow bowls.

Goblets include examples with a straight vertical upper part decorated outside with painted wavy lines (Fig. 2:5). These are also represented at Hili in Tomb B (Méry 2000: Fig. 160:1) and might be dated from the beginning of Wadi Suq period, around 2000 BC. Goblets with a concave upper part also appear. Some, decorated with chevrons (Fig. 2:1, 2), recall examples from level III at Hili-8 (Méry 2000: Fig. 160:8), and or from grave SH103 at Shimal (Vogt and Franke-Vogt 1987: Fig. 23:10). Others, decorated with small opposite half-circles separated by vertical parallel lines (Fig. 2:3, 4) can be compared to goblets from graves 1, 6, and SH102 at Shimal (Méry 2000: 160 and Fig. 266:4-6), or from the Wadi Suq itself (Frifelt 1975: Fig. 22b).

Pots include three pieces with thickened rim and painted decoration of large horizontal bands (Fig. 2:13, 14, 15) which find some parallels at Hili-8 in Level III, and two spouted vessels decorated with horizontal bands and wavy lines (one example Fig. 2:12). All can be compared to examples collected in level III at Hili-8 (Méry 2000: Fig. 161:9-10; Fig.162:8), spouted jars recall examples from SH103 at Shimal (Vogt and Franke Vogt 1987: Fig. 24:2, 4, 5). A miniature flask with a globular body and a concave neck (Fig. 2:11) find good parallels at Shimal (De Cardi 1988: Fig. 7:50-54). A bowl with a thickened rim decorated with groups of small squares disposed on the top of the rim was also collected (Fig. 2:8). According to C. Velde (pers.comm) two similar bowls were found in Wadi Suq contexts in Shimal.

Late Bronze Age Pottery (1600-1250 BC)

A few fragments may be dated from the Late Bronze Age. The most typical is a fragment of footed goblet made in a coarse brown fabric (Fig. 3:3), which finds good parallels at Shimal SX in the levels of period III (Vogt and Franke Vogt 1987: Fig. 43:3-8). Footed goblets were also found in large quantity in the tomb of Sharm (Barker 2002: Fig. 4). According to C. Velde to whom they were shown, two other vessels may be dated from this period: one is a deep globular bowl (Fig. 3:1), the second is a globular and short-necked pot with a tubular spout (Fig. 3:2). Similar shapes were found on the settlement SX at Shimal (Vogt and Franke Vogt 1987: Fig. 42:6).

Iron Age I pottery (1250-1000 BC)

From Iron Age I may be dated a small group of vessels made in a coarse fabric, handmade and heavily tempered with mineral and vegetal inclusions. These vessels are neither slipped nor decorated. They include straight-sided or slightly convex bowls and cups (Fig. 3:5, 6, 7, 8, 10, 12) which all find parallels at Tell Abraq (Potts 1990: Fig. 133:1-4; Fig. 134:1-7; Fig. 135:1-4, 11; Fig. 137:2), Shimal (Vogt and Franke Vogt 1987: Fig. 41:1-6; Velde 1992 Pl. 73:Eso01, Eso03) or Kalba (Carter and Magee 1999: Fig. 9:1, 2, 3, 6). Two necked jars (Fig. 3:9, 11) can be linked to similar examples from Tell Abraq (Potts 1990: Fig. 131:1-11), Shimal (Velde 1992: Pl. 72:Efl06), Kalba (Carter and Magee 1999: Fig. 9:11-12) and from the collective burial in Bithnah (Corboud et al 1994: Fig. 8:1, 3, 7). A spouted bowl in the same fabric (Fig. 3:4) finds its best parallels among the common slipped wares from Iron Age II period at Rumeilah I (Boucharlat and Lombard 1985: Pl. 45:2-4) and al Madam (necropolis AM-32: Boucharlat and Pécontal-Lambert 1990: Fig. 7:11) and might be of slightly later date.

Iron Age II Pottery (1100-600 BC)

Iron Age II pottery includes common ware slipped or painted, fine painted ware, grey ware imitating softstone vessels, and fine grey ware. Common slipped and painted wares and grey ware imitating softstone vessels include different fabrics. The most frequent is reddish or brown with a mineral temper including red and white grits. It appears on all eastern coastal sites. Slips are mainly red, dark red-brown or black. Vessels are handmade, and probably finished on a slow rotating base.

Common slipped ware and painted ware include convex bowls (Fig. 4:2, 3, 4, 5; Fig. 5:2, 10), carinated bowls (Fig. 4:1, 7, 8, 9, 12; Fig. 5:1, 3, 5, 6, 7, 8), undulated bowls (Fig. 4:10, 11, 13; Fig. 5:4), and small jars with perforated lugs (Fig. 4:6). All find good parallels in other Iron Age graves, such as Fashgha-1[1] in Wadi al Qawr area, Bithnah-4,[2] al Qusais (Taha 1982: Fig. 14) and also appear on several Iron Age II settlements such as Husn Madhab (Benoist 2000: Fig. 197:5), al Madam,[3] Muweilah (Magee 1996: Fig. 15), Rumeilah[4] and Hili-2 (Rahman, 1980: Fig. 4, Fig. 5). Some of these also appear in Oman at Raki-2 (Weisgerber and Yule 1999: Fig. 13:21), at Lizq (Kroll 1991: Fig. 1:16, 17, 20) and in the Honeycomb cemetery of Bawshar (Costa et al. 1999: Fig. 49, 52, 55, 58).

Common Painted wares (61 vessels collected) represent 35 % of the identified Iron Age shapes, a proportion comparable to other funeral contexts in Eastern Emirates (Bithnah: 22 %) but generally higher than on settlements in this region (Husn Madhab, Bithnah-24, Husn Awhalah: less than 15 %). Decoration patterns include:

- criss cross patterns placed outside below the rim eventually associated with pendant squares on the inside, below the rim (Fig. 5:1, 2). This motif is particularly well represented in the western part of the Emirates, at Rumeilah I (Boucharlat and Lombard 1985: PL. 49:15-21, 23, 24), Muweilah (Magee 1996: Fig. 15), and al Madam (Benoist & Mouton 1994:

---

[1] Phillips 1987: Fig. 11:35; Fig. 13:48 (carinated bowls); Fig. 7:2, 8; Fig. 9:19, 22; Fig. 10:26-30 (bowls with marked shoulder); Fig. 7:1, 5, 7; Fig. 8:12, 17; Fig. 9:18, 20; Fig. 11:33-34 (convex bowls); Fig. 7:6; Fig. 8:16; Fig. 9:21, 24; Fig. 11:37, 39, 40 (undulated bowls); Fig. 18:1 (Jars with pierced lugs).
[2] Corboud et al. 1996: Pl. 1:1-4. (convex bowls); Pl. 2:5-6 (bowls with marked shoulder); Pl. 5:11-14 (carinated bowls); Pl. 3:1 (undulated bowl).
[3] Benoist & Mouton 1994: Fig. 5:1-2 (convex bowls); Benoist, Cordoba & Mouton 1997, Fig. 6:3, 8, 9 (bowls with marked shoulder); Benoist 2000, Fig. 124:10, 11, 17; Fig. 143:19; Fig. 144:12 (carinated bowls); Benoist & Mouton 1994, Fig. 5:9, 12 (undulated bowls); Benoist, Cordoba & Mouton 1997, Fig. 6:7 (jar with pierced lugs).
[4] Boucharlat and Lombard 1985: Pl. 45:1, 3 (convex bowls); Pl. 45:6, 14; Pl. 49:17; Pl. 51:1 (bowls with marked shoulder); Pl. 45:8; Pl. 49:1, 18, 20-22, Pl. 56:2, 4 (carinated bowls); Pl. 43:2, 4, 5, 7, 10, 15, Pl. 57:15 (undulated bowls); Pl. 47:1, Pl. 52:1, Pl. 59:8, Pl. 77:13 (jars with pierced lugs).

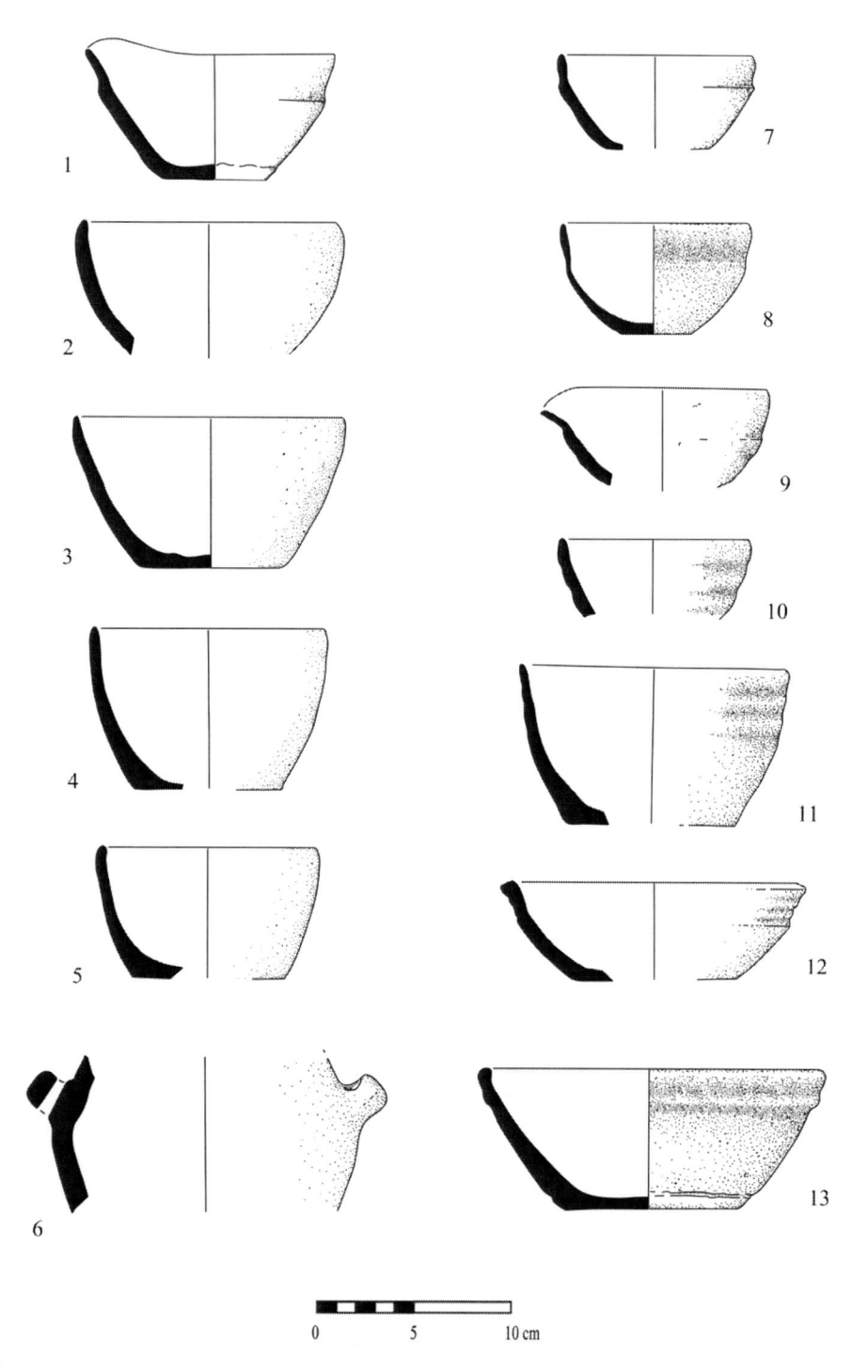

Figure 4. Dadna grave: Iron Age II common slipped ware.

- Fig. 5:13) and was also recorded in Saudi Arabia (Gazdar, Potts, Livingstone 1984:81-82 and Pl. 79-B; Zarins, Ibrahim, Potts, Edens 1978, Pl. 25:181). On the Eastern coast it is represented in the Sharm tomb (Barker 2002: Fig. 22.4, 8).
- oblique or vertical short lines and wavy lines placed outside, inside, or on both sides, below the rim (Fig. 5:4-10). These are very frequent in central Oman at Lizq (Kroll 1991: Fig. 1:18, 19; Kroll 1998: Fig. 1:1, 3, 4, 13, 14), Maysar (Weisgerber & Yule 1999: Fig. 10:4) and in the Honeycomb cemetery at Bawshar[5] but also appear on the Eastern Coast (Husn Madhab: Benoist & Corboud 1998: Fig. 1:1), in the mountains (Bithnah-4: Corboud et al 1996: Pl.2:3-8; Pl. 5:4-7, 13, 14, 17, Wadi al Qawr: Phillips 1987: Fig. 17:1, 2, 6, 9; Fig. 18:13, 14) and in the western foothills (Rumeilah: Boucharlat & Lombard 1985: Pl. 49:3 – 7, 10; Pl. 56:4.; al Madam: Benoist, Cordoba, Mouton

---

[5] Costa et al. 1999: Fig. 8:1, Fig. 9:17, 19, Fig. 10:22, Fig. 11:32-34, Fig. 12:49.

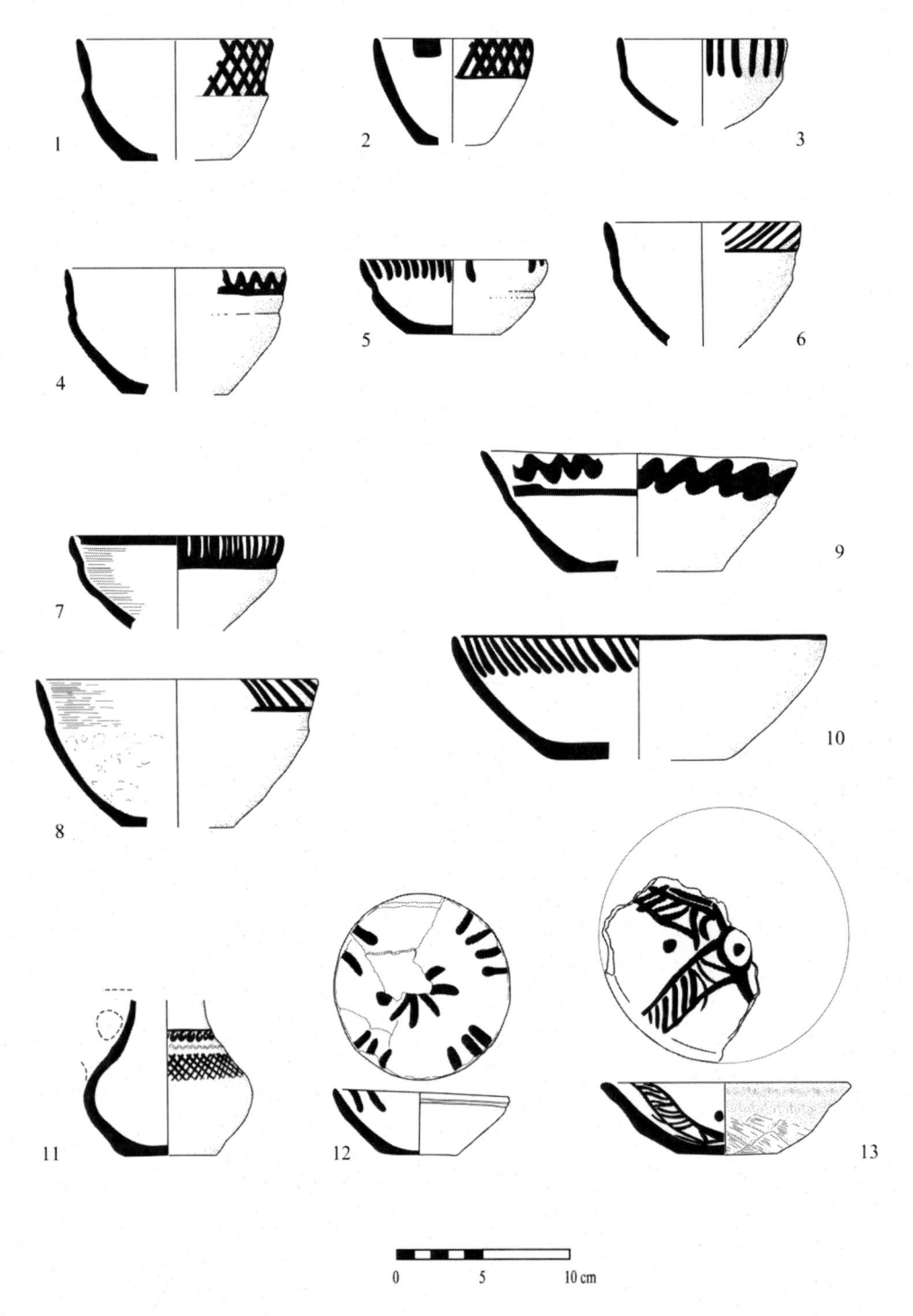

Figure 5. Dadna grave: common and fine painted ware.

1997: Fig. 6:1, 2, 4.; Tell Abraq: Potts 1991: Fig. 112:5, 7).
- Vertical lines and star designs appear on the inside of three bowls (e.g. Fig. 5:12); which find exact parallels at Bithnah-4 (Corboud *et al.* 1996: PL. 5:12, 15)
- Hatched triangles appear on the inside of three other examples (e.g. Fig. 5:13). It can be compared with examples from Hili-2 (Rahman 1980: Fig. 6), Sharm (Barker 2002: Fig. 25.9) and the al Hajjar cemetery in Bahrain (Lombard & Kervran 1989: Fig. 8:15). The example illustrated in Fig. 5:13 shows traces of scraping on the base recalling a technique more common among Wadi Suq productions.

A small jug from Dadna, probably a bridge spouted vessel in **fine red painted ware**, is decorated with criss-cross patterns, wavy lines and spirals (Fig. 5:11). Fine Painted ware is a specific macroscopic group encountered on many Iron Age sites which seems to have been exchanged throughout eastern Arabia (Magee *et al.* 1998). Bridge spouted vessels are present at Rumeilah (Boucharlat & Lombard 1985: PL. 48:9, 19; PL. 49:12), Muweilah (Magee 1997: Fig; 17), Husn Madhab (Benoist

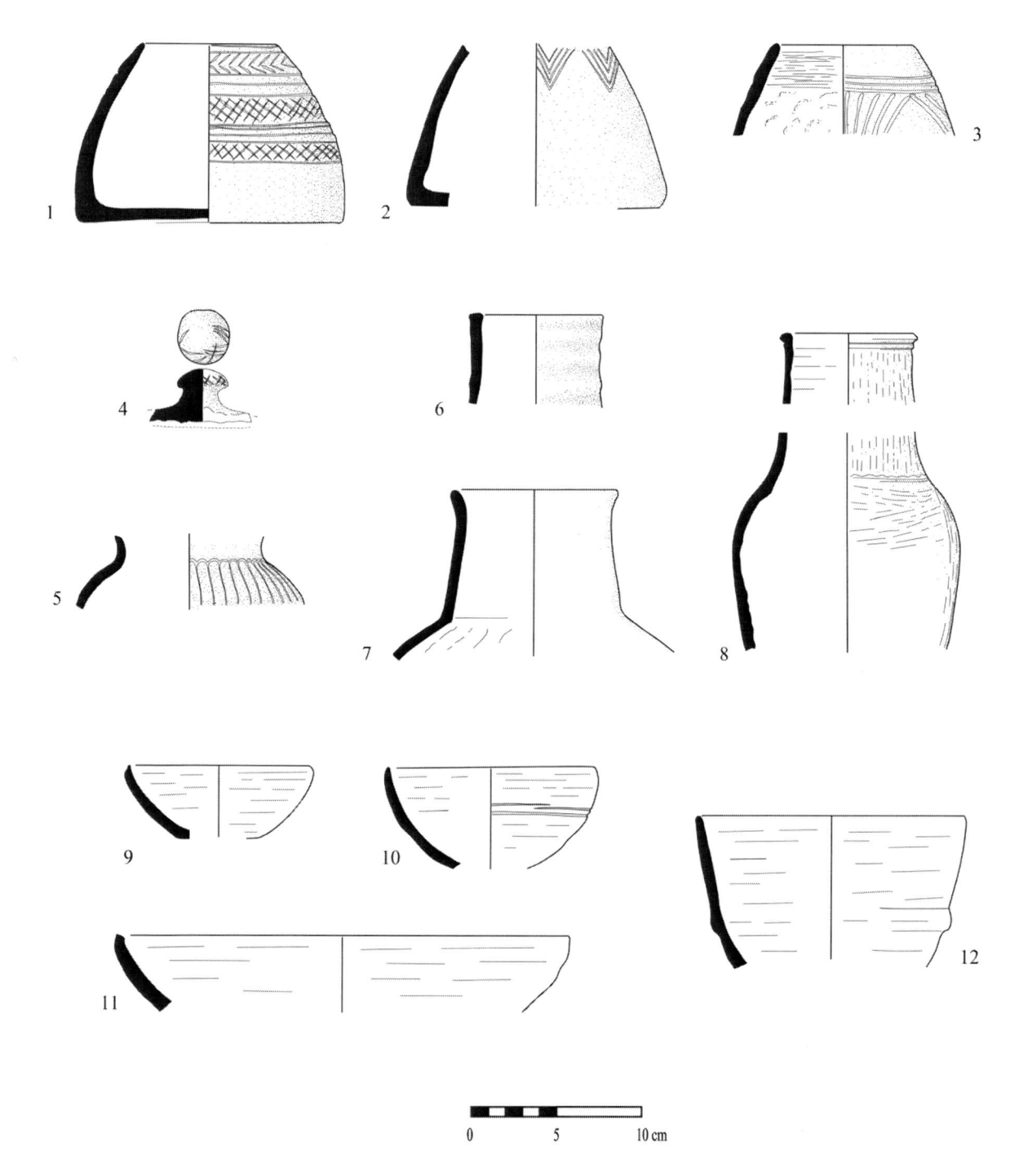

Figure 6. Dadna grave: grey ware "softstone imitation" (1-5), fine grey ware (6-8), burnished slipped ware (9-12).

& Corboud 1998: Fig. 1:3), and Lizq (Kroll 1991: Fig. 1:3, 14, 15). They are obviously of Iranian inspiration (Magee 1996:246-247; Magee 1997). Spiral motifs occasionally appear on these vessels, e.g. at Bithnah-24 (Benoist *et al.* 2004: Fig. 4:8).

Grey ware "softstone imitation" represents 9 % of the Iron Age identified shapes collected in Dadna grave. These ceramics are known in the Oman peninsula during Iron Age II Period and seem to disappear at the beginning of Iron Age III, although their models in softstone remain in use until the end of Iron Age. This category is often present in small quantity on Iron Age sites in different regions of the U.A.E. (al Ain, al Madam, Wadi al Qawr, Husn Madhab, Dibba) and in Oman (Maysar, Ra's al Hadd). It might have been exported in other regions as is suggested by two fragments collected at Kidmat Tarub (Rougeulle 2001: Fig. 3:1, 2) on the eastern coast of Yemen.

Shapes include tronconical pots (Fig. 6:1-3) decorated with incisions of large triangles a decoration pattern also well attested at Fashgha-1 (Phillips 1987: Fig. 20:6), Sharm (Barker, 2002: Fig. 31.2, 3) and Bithnah-4 (Corboud *et al.* 1994: Pl. 19:1-3) on the vessels in grey ware as well as on the ones in softstone. A piece is

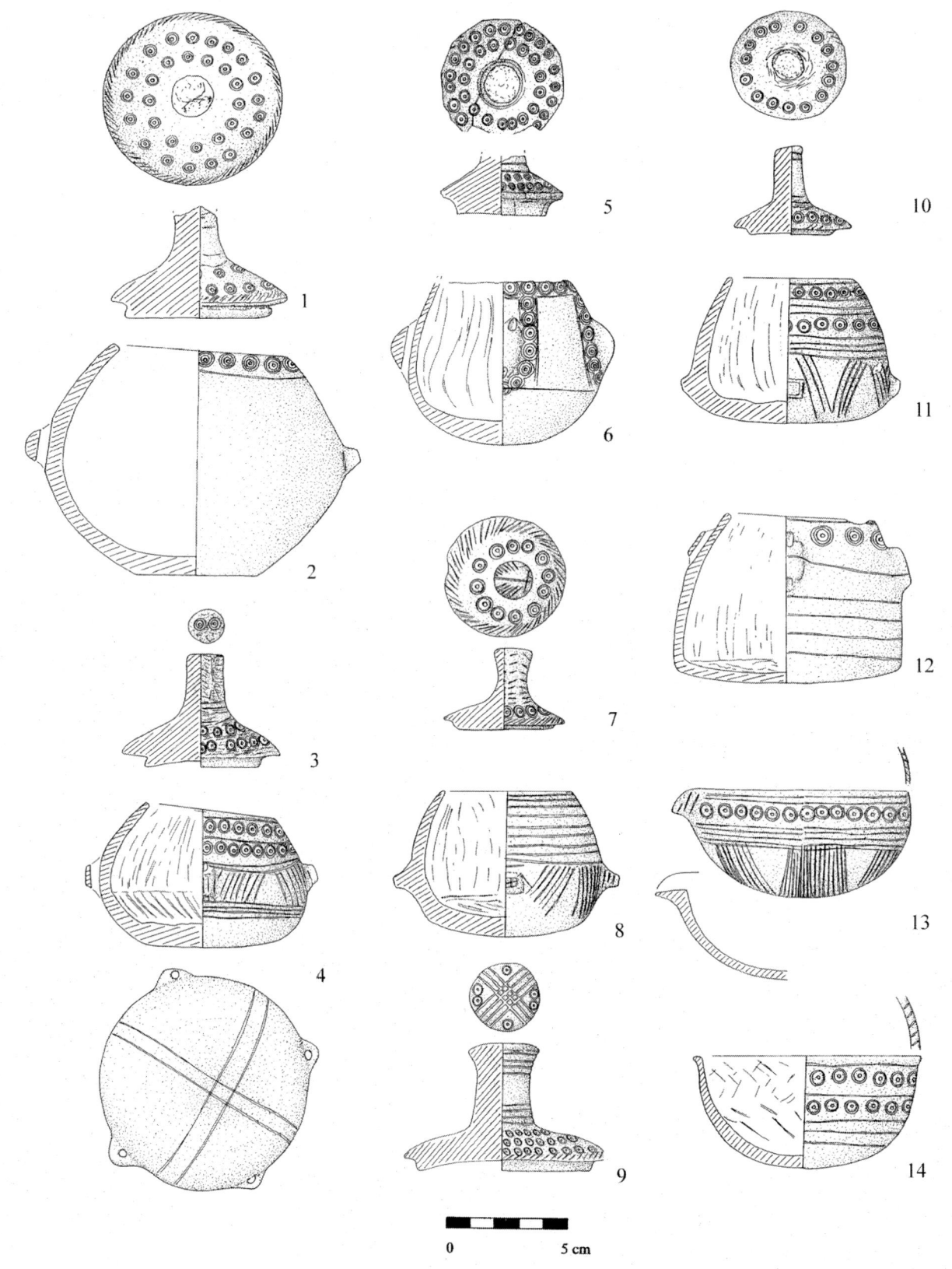

Figure 7. Dadna grave: Wadi-Suq steatite vessels.

decorated with horizontal bands of chevrons and criss-cross patterns (Fig. 6:1), a decoration pattern also recorded at Fashgha-1 (Phillips 1987: Fig. 29:22). There was only one lid in pottery associated with these vessels (Fig. 6:4): it seems to us probable that some lids in softstone were used to cover pots in grey ware "softstone imitation". Small necked jars decorated with lintels (Fig. 6:5) – a design also present on some softstone vessels – find parallels in Fashgha-1 (Phillips 1987: Fig. 19:1) and in House G at Rumeilah (Benoist 2000: Fig. 49:12.).

Dadna grave also produced 6 necked jars in a **fine grey ware** characterised by a grey paste, fine, wheelmade, with traces of smoothing, of burnishing or of polishing on the surface (Fig. 6:6-8). On some pieces, the burnishing of the surface has a decorative effect, being horizontal on the body and vertical on the neck of the jars. In the United Arab Emirates, such a fine grey ware was only identified at Rumeilah I (Benoist 2000: Fig. 49:13), at Bithnah (Corboud et al 1996: Pl. 10:3-6) and in the Wadi al Qawr graves (Fashgha-1: Phillips 1987: Fig. 20:5, 10). This pottery might have been imported from another region.

Potteries from end of Iron Age II/beginning of Iron Age III Period

Six vessels from Dadna grave present a dark red slip showing clear traces of **horizontal burnishing** and can be related to ceramics from al-Thuqaibah settlement in al Madam plain, dated from the first part of Iron Age III. They include:

- Shallow bowls with a thinnered rim (Fig. 6:9-10). One of them presents an horizontal incision and finds an exact parallel at Thuqaibah (Benoist 2000: Fig. 136:6).
- One deep bowl with a raised rib on the lower part (Fig. 6:12), which recalls strongly a bowl found at Thuqaibah (Benoist 2000: Fig. 136:1).
- One shallow bowl with a flattened rim (Fig. 6:11), which finds numerous equivalents among the burnished maroon slipped wares from Thuqaibah (Benoist 2000: Fig. 135:3-5, 7-9), and also appears in layers from the late pre-Islamic A period at Mleiha (Mouton 1992, Fig. 13:10).

Thuqaibah burnished slipped ware also includes some shapes which find close parallels in Iran and along the Persian Gulf in Achaemenid contexts.[6] In Dadna burnished slipped wares do not include any of these shapes. This element is interesting as it suggests that in this region the appearance of horizontal burnishing might have been a little bit earlier than the appearance of the interregional set of shapes usually related to Iron Age III period.

Softstone vessels

A total of 49 vessels in softstone were recorded in the grave. Most are classical Wadi Suq and classical Iron Age II vessels, but a few examples might be dated from Late Bronze Age or early Iron Age.

Wadi Suq softstone vessels (2000-1600 BC)

Most of the softstone vessels discovered in the grave can be dated from Wadi Suq Period (33 examples of the 49 in total). They include lids and suspension vessels.

Lids are circular in shape with a high cylindrical button, a slight conical upper part and a flat or slightly concave base (Fig. 7:1, 3, 5, 7, 9, 10). All lids are finely polished, but traces of cutting occasionally appear under the polishing. Lids are incised on top, with simple or double dotted circles often combined with a range of fine short oblique lines around the border. Similar pieces were collected in great number in the collective burials of Shimal[7] and in the grave AS.20 in Asimah region (Vogt B 1994: Fig. 28:2, 3).

Suspension vessels are numerous. One large globular vessel, with four lugs placed in the upper part (Fig. 7:1), decorated with a line of double dotted circles underlined by a horizontal line appears as relatively archaic in style, recalling Umm an Nar traditions. But the base of the vase is flat and the stone in which it is made is light grey in colour, two elements which are more typical of the Wadi Suq Period. Thus it might be dated from the beginning of Wadi Suq Period.

Several vessels of oval shape, with a slightly convex wall and a slightly flattened base, with four lugs placed in the lower part of the vase (Fig. 7:8, 11) decorated with motifs organised in two superimposed horizontal sequences, the upper sequence including dotted circles and/or horizontal lines and the lower one including oblique lines organised in chevrons appear as classical Wadi Suq productions and find good parallels in Shimal,[8] Sharm (Ziolkowski 2001: Fig. 24) and in Asimah (grave 100: Vogt 1994: Fig. 42:1, 2). Very close to these classical Wadi Suq examples is a pot bearing four lugs at mid height, on which a classical Wadi Suq decoration is completed by two vertical double lines crossing each other on the base of the vessel (Fig. 7:4).

One beehive-shaped pot appears to be a little bit more original (Fig. 7:12). It has a slightly convex incurving wall and an almost flat base, with four lugs placed in the upper part. Its decoration consists of a single line of double dotted circles in the upper part and some horizontal lines in the lower part. With the exception of the lugs, the shape of this last example is not without parallels from Shimal, described by C. Velde as representative of the end of Wadi Suq Period (Velde 2003: Fig. 5:6-10).

An original decoration appears on an oval-shaped vessel, with a convex base, bearing four lugs at mid height (Fig.7:6). It consists of a line of double dotted circles in the upper part, with which are associated four curving lines of dotted circles surrounding the four lugs. This decoration might be an example of what C. Velde describes as "the disappearance of the strict order of decoration" beginning at the end of the Wadi Suq Period (Velde 2003:108). As our vessel does not include typical Late Bronze Age motifs (net motifs, leaves, etc), and as

---

[6] The latter are shallow cups with incurving rim, carinated bowls, and globular pots with everted rim. These shapes have been linked by P. Magee (1996b) with Iranian shapes from the Achaemenid Period.

[7] Vogt and Franke-Vogt 1987: Fig. 34:1-2, 7-9 (SH 99); Fig. 26:6-10, Fig. 27:2-5 (SH 103); Fig. 28:1 (SH.103).
[8] Vogt and Franke-Vogt 1987: Fig. 33:5, 6 (SH 99); Fig. 5:3 (SH 101); Fig. 15:3, 4 (SH 102); Fig. 25:5-8 (SH. 103).

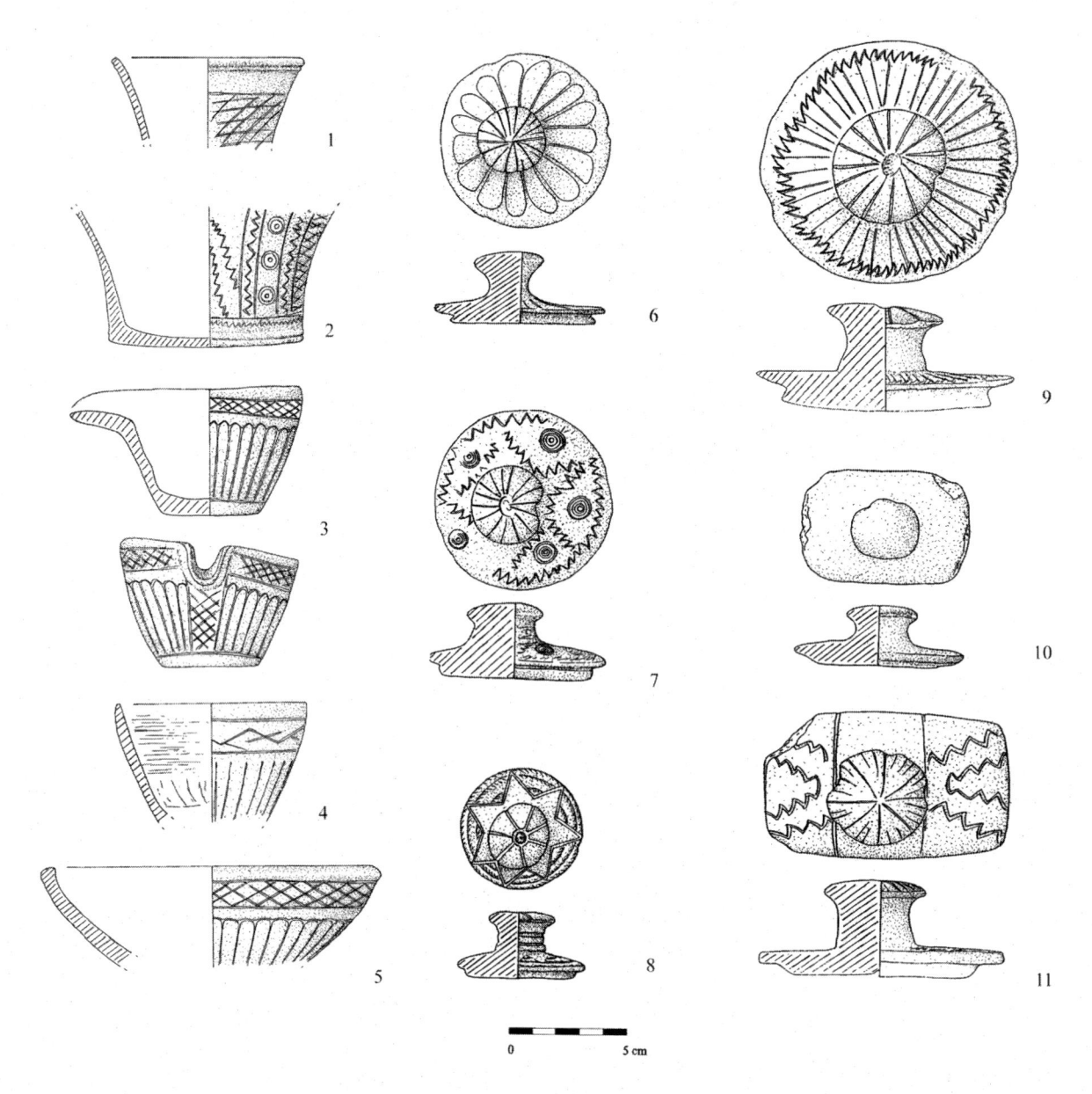

Figure 8. Dadna Grave: Late Bronze Age/Early Iron Age (1-2, 7) and Iron Age (3-6, 8-11) steatite vessels.

its shape remains in the tradition of Wadi Suq shapes we propose to place it at the very beginning of this movement of diversification of decoration (i.e. the end of Wadi Suq period), rather than in a later period.

Two shallow bowls (Fig. 7:13, 14) incised outside with dotted circles and horizontal lines disposed in the upper part were also collected. One has groups of vertical parallel lines incised on the base. These decoration patterns are typical of the Wadi Suq Period. One piece has a small pitched spout. Exact parallels can be found at Shimal in graves SH 102 and SH 103 (Vogt B and Franke-Vogt U 1987: Figs. 14:2, 25:2).

Late Bronze Age-Early Iron Age vessels (1600-1000 BC?)

Dadna grave did not produce any examples of what could be considered as "classical" Late Bronze Age softstone vessels, as described by C. Velde (2003). However, two fragments of bowls or goblets with a slightly concave wall (Fig. 8:1, 2) could be related to examples recorded at other sites by different authors who called them "intermediate" between Wadi Suq and Iron Age Periods (Potts 1991, Phillips 1997) and who proposed a date at the end of the Bronze Age or beginning of the Iron Age.

One piece is decorated with one horizontal line in the upper part and oblique incisions organised in net pattern in the lower part. Net motifs are mentioned among late Wadi Suq and Late Bronze Age Vessels by C. Velde (2003: Fig. 6). On the second example, a design of dotted circles is associated to a design of small zig-zags, a motif which is considered as more characteristic of the Iron Age. Such an association also appears on concave goblets recorded in grave SH 102 at Shimal, in a Late Bronze Age context (Vogt and Franke-Vogt 1987: Fig. 14:3, 4). A similar piece showing the same association was

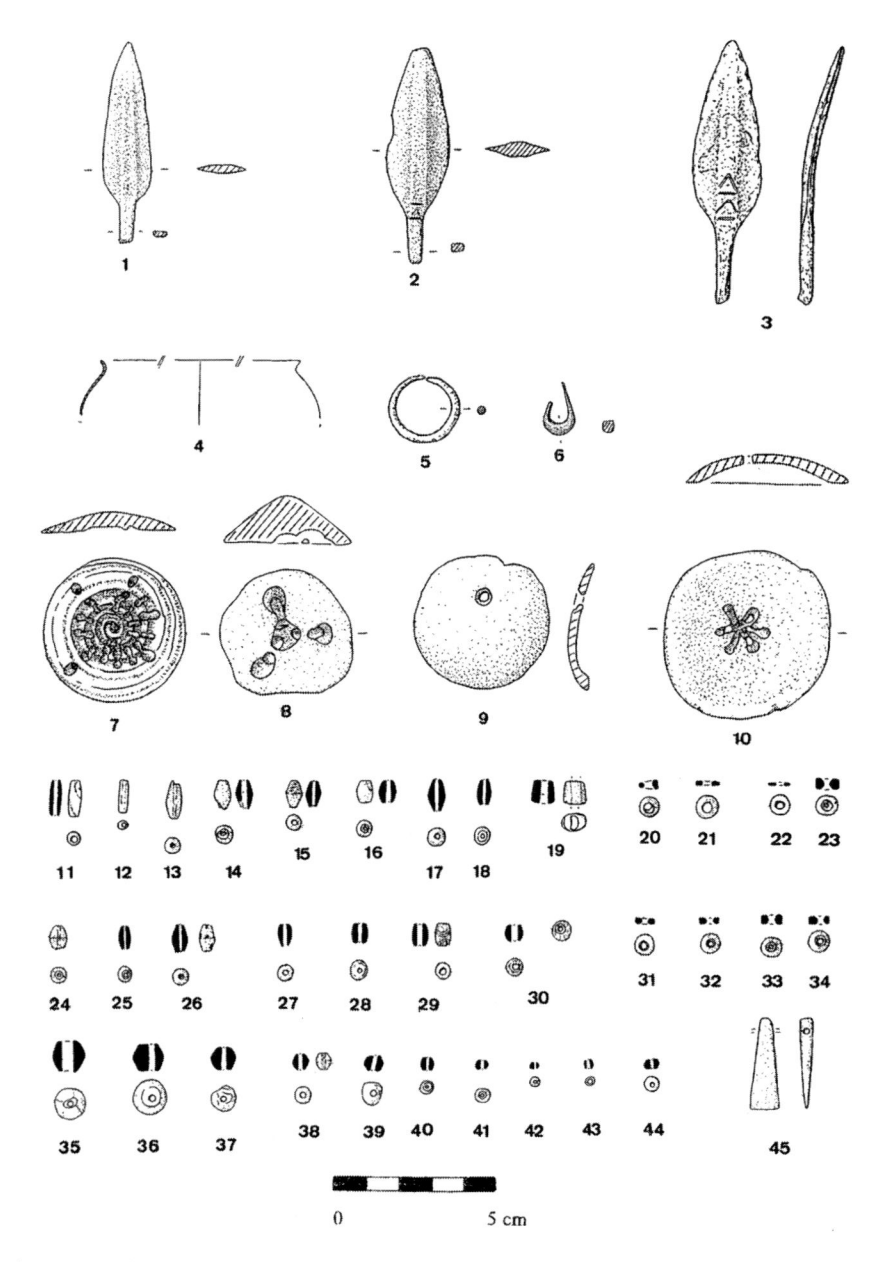

Figure 9. Dadna grave: metal items (1-6), stone or shell buttons (7-10) and beads (11-45).

collected in the tomb at Sharm (Ziolkowski 2001: Fig. 26) and examples also appear in the grave Fashgha-1 in the Wadi al Qawr (Phillips 1987: Fig. 25:11), dated from Iron Age Period.[9] Thus if these vessels might have appeared during Late Bronze Age Period, they might also have continued to be sporadically produced or used during Iron Age Period.

Association between double dotted circles and zigzag lines also appears in Dadna on a lid which should be placed in Iron Age Period owing to its shape, very similar to usual Iron Age II ones (Fig. 8:7). D.T. Potts proposed to date two similar lids found in Tell Abraq to the beginning of the Iron Age (Potts 1991: Fig. 131-132).

Iron Age II softstone vessels (1100-600 BC)

In total, 14 Iron Age softstone vessels were collected, mostly rectangular or rounded lids with a characteristic mushroom-profiled button, often coarsely polished, with traces of scraping still visible on the base (Fig. 8:6-11). These display incisions of lintels and straight lines disposed in star around the central button, associated with a line of small zigzag around the border. These motifs are paralleled on several Iron Age sites such as Rumeilah (Boucharlat and Lombard 1985: Pl. 61:1, 11), Fashgha-1 (Phillips 1987: Fig. 31:28, 29, 30; Fig. 32:31 Fig. 33:34, 35, 36), the Sharm tomb (Ziolkowski 2001: Figs. 41, 69) and Bawshar (Costa *et al.* 1999: Fig. 22:124-126), and appear also in Bahrain (Lombard 1985: Fig. 40:115). A single piece shows a design of triangles combined with

---

[9] In this grave absolutely no material which could be dated from Wadi Suq or Late Bronze Age Period was collected, although the architecture of the grave is comparable to the typical architecture of Wadi Suq graves. The absence of any material dated from the second millennium BC first convinced C. Phillips to date the building of the grave to the Iron Age Period (Phillips 1997).

thin hatched lines (Fig. 8:8). A similar design appears at Rumeilah (Boucharlat and Lombard 1985: Pl. 61:4), Qarn Bint Sa'ud (Lombard 1985: Fig. 103:346), Bawshar (Costa et al 1999: Fig. 21:123) and Hili-15 (Benoist 2000:193). Only one small fragment of the base of an Iron Age tronconical vase was recorded. Bowls handmade and finely polished on both sides are incised with lintel motifs and criss-cross patterns (Fig. 8:3, 5). They find parallels at Fashgha-1(Phillips 1987: Fig. 28:17-19; Fig. 29:20-21; Fig. 30:25, 27; Fig. 24:26), Qarn Bint Sa'ud (Lombard 1985: Fig. 97:312), Maysar-36 (Lombard 1985: Fig. 97:311) and Bawshar (Costa et al 1999: Fig. 17:91, 93; Fig. 20:111).

Metal

Only 6 metal objects were collected, including 3 arrowheads in bronze of lanceolate shape with a quadrangular tang (Fig. 9:1-3), recalling examples from Rumeilah (Boucharlat and Lombard 1985: Pl. 62:1, 2.), Fasghgha-1(Phillips 1987: Fig. 37:2-6; Fig. 38:10), Tell Abraq (Potts 1991: Fig. 121-122), Bawshar (Costa et al. 1999: Fig. 23:153) and Maysar-36 (Lombard 1985: Fig. 105:363). Two are decorated with incisions placed on the central part. These incisions replace them in a long tradition attested in the region from the Late Bronze Age up until Iron Age II. Incised arrowheads appear for example in Shimal (Vogt and Franke-Vogt 1987: Fig. 19:2-7, 9, 10; Fig. 20:1-7), Galilah (Donaldson 1984: Fig. 26) and al Qusais (Lombard 1985: Fig. 105:364). Signs identical to those found in Dadna grave are attested at Bithnah (Corboud et al. 1996: Pl. 24:10-12) and Fashgha-1 (Phillips 1987: Fig. 38:12, 13) and in the Sharm tomb (Weeks 2000: Fig. 3). Other metal items include one earring in bronze (Fig. 9:5) similar to examples from in grave SH 102 at Shimal (Vogt and Franke-Vogt 1987: Fig. 18:9-11), 1 small ear pendant in electrum (Fig. 9:6), and a bronze vessel rim (Fig. 9:4) similar to a bronze vessel from Qarn Bint Sa'ud (Lombard 1985: Fig. 110:391).

Stone or Shell buttons

Four buttons were collected (Fig. 9:7-10). Two are made in the apex of large *conus* shell, the other two in a white calcareous stone. All present a convex or pointed top and a flat base in which are pierced one or several holes of fixation located in the centre. Similar shell buttons have been recorded at Dibba (Bibby 1970: 351-354), in cairn 20 on the Jebel Hafit (Friflet 1968: 170), in Shimal (Vogt and Franke-Vogt 1987: Fig. 18:1, 4), Fashgha-1 (Phillips 1987: Fig. 39:1) and Bithnah (Corboud et al. 1996: Pl. 27), some with incisions, others undecorated, but all with a shape and a system of fixation similar to the ones attested in Dadna.

Beads

In total, 75 beads in stone, shell or bone were collected in the grave (Fig. 26:11-35). They include:
- 31 whitish flat cylindrical beads, in shell or bone, generally fishbone, with a conical perforation (Fig. 9:20-23; 31-34), comparable to examples from Sharm (Barker 2001: Fig. 3: 1-4), Shimal (Vogt and Franke-Vogt 1987: Fig. 16:14-19), Fashgha-1 (Phillips 1987: Fig. 39:8), Bawshar (Costa et al. 1999: Fig. 22:138), and grave As 100 and As 24 at Asimah (Vogt 1994: Fig. 44:9, 11, 12; Fig. 37:17-20).
- one cylindrical bead in bone, as long as it is large, entirely polished with an axial perforation slightly conical in section (Fig. 9:19) recalling pieces from grave SH 102 at Shimal (Vogt and Franke-Vogt 1987: Fig. 16:4; Fig. 17:4) .
- two long cylindrical beads in bone or shell pierced with an axial perforation (Fig. 9:11-12) paralleled at Shimal (Vogt and Franke-Vogt 1987: Fig. 16:1-3; Fig. 36:8; Fig. 48:12-13), Sharm (Barker 2001: Fig. 3: 5) and Rumeilah (Boucharlat and Lombard 1985: Pl. 66:13-14).
- one triangular pendant in bone with a transversal perforation near the summit of the triangle (Fig. 9:45) recalling examples from Rumeilah (Boucharlat and Lombard 1985: Pl. 66:15), Sharm (Barker 2001: Fig. 3: 16), Fashgha-1 (Phillips 1987: Fig. 39:1) and Bawshar (Costa et al. 1999: Fig. 22:140-143).
- 25 long and short biconical beads of various stones (often carnelian) with an axial perforation, cylindrical or conical in profile (Fig. 9:13-18, 24-30, 35-38) similar to examples from Sharm (Barker 2001: Fig. 3: 6, 7), Shimal (Vogt and Franke-Vogt 1987: Fig. 16:8; Fig. 17:14; Fig. 28:4, 10; Fig. 36:11), Rumeilah (Boucharlat and Lombard 1985: Pl. 66:10, 11, 21-23, 26), Fashgha-1 (Phillips 1987: Fig. 39:3), Bawshar (Costa et al. 1999: Fig. 22:136, 145, 146) and in grave As 100 at Asimah (Vogt 1994: Fig. 44:14).
- Seven spherical beads in various stones including carnelian (Fig. 9:39-44) recalling examples from Shimal (Vogt and Franke-Vogt 1987: Fig. 16:12, 13), Asimah (Vogt 1994: Fig. 44:13), Sharm (Barker 2001: Fig. 3: 17), Rumeilah (Boucharlat and Lombard 1985, Pl. 66:12), Fashgha-1 (Phillips 1987: Fig. 39:2) and Bawshar (Costa et al. 1999: Fig. 22:139).

Conclusion

The material collected inside the grave includes objects from Wadi Suq, Late Bronze Age, Iron Age I and Iron Age II Periods. Although there are some inequalities in the quantity of material collected from a period to another (Late Bronze Age and Iron Age I being little represented), this situation suggests a continuity of funeral customs from second to first millennium BC. Such a continuity has been observed in other regions of the U.A.E. notably in Wadi al Qawr, where according to Phillips (1997), collective graves reflecting a typical Wadi Suq architecture might have been still built during Iron Age.

A cultural continuity in funeral customs from Middle Bronze until Iron Age seems also to have prevailed in all Fujairah region, if we consider the material associated with different collective burials which all could be classified owing to their architecture as "second millennium graves" (Mereshid, Bidyah, Qidfa, Dibba,

Sharm, Bithnah), where different collections of objects dating from the second and first Millennia BC are represented, in different proportions from one grave to another[10] and from which no important break can be underlined from one period to another. Dadna is an example of the funeral monuments that developed in this region from the Middle Bronze to the Iron Age III Period, and which represent the dominant mode of burial over a long period. The exclusive use of this burial type is attested by the absence in the region of large-scale graveyards of individual graves,[11] such as appeared during Iron Age Period in other regions in eastern Arabia, e.g. at al-Qusais and al-Madam.

Objects from Dadna find several parallels on other sites in the region, which shows the full integration of Dadna area in the regional exchange pattern. Most of the materials represented in the grave can be compared to similar material recorded on other sites, and it is likely that a proportion of funeral goods were obtained from regional trade.

A few vessels in pottery or in softstone combine techniques or decoration patterns from the Wadi Suq and Iron Age Periods. These associations suggest a slow and progressive change of craft traditions in the region, some of which have been underlined elsewhere (e.g. at Tell Abraq and in the Wadi al Qawr), whilst others are presented here for the first time (e.g. traces of scraping on an Iron Age painted bowl). Our present data are still too limited to allow a full understanding of cultural changes from the Bronze Age to the Iron Age, but observations of such resurgences tend to multiply. Their precise and exhaustive recording in different regions of eastern Arabia might help to define better the way heritage and innovations have interacted on handicraft traditions in each area before they finally developed into a standardised Iron Age II culture. In this, the few examples from Dadna might contribute to a precise understanding of regional evolution.

Dadna grave has also produced a small assemblage of pottery which appears to contradict the chronological boundary that has been defined between Iron Age II and III in the region. The six vessels in dark red burnished ware only find parallels in Iron Age III contexts, but the assemblage does not include the most typical *leitfossils* from this period. This point is promising, as it suggests that some distinction might be made between the introduction and development of a technique of decoration and the one of an interregional set of shapes usually considered as of Iranian origin.

Finally the main lack of information regarding Dadna grave remains funeral practices which might have been put on light if the excavation could have been made in better conditions. This situation points to one of the main problems encountered by local Departments in the region: they have to face an extremely quick development leading to the disappearance of many archaeological sites, and do not yet consist of groups of specialists large enough to face all circumstances. This situation exemplifies the need for a larger investment by the international community to provide scientific help for research and for the training of local specialists – not only in archaeology but also in other associated disciplines such as physical anthropology.

References

Barker D. 2001. Stone, paste, shell and metal beads from Sharm. *Arabian Archaeology and Epigraphy* 12/2: 202-222.

Barker D. 2002. Wadi Suq and Iron Age Period ceramics from Sharm, Fujairah (U.A.E.). *Arabian Archaeology and Epigraphy* 13/1: 1-94.

Benoist A. 2000. *La céramique de l'Age du Fer en péninsule d'Oman: 1350-300 av. J.C.* Unpublished PhD Thesis, University of Paris I, Paris.

Benoist A. 2002. Quelques réflexions à propos de l'utilisation des céramiques dans la péninsule d'Oman au cours de l'Age du Fer (1350-300 av J.C). *Paléorient* 27/1: 45-67.

Benoist A., Colson M., Dalongeville R., and Eliès S. 2002. *Archaeological Investigations in Fujairah 2000: a first preliminary report.* CNRS. Lyons and Nanterre, January 2002. Report submitted by the French Archaeological Mission to the Department of Antiquities of Fujairah.

Benoist A., Corboud P. 1998. Husn Madhab, Fujairah. In Mouton M. (ed.), *Assemblages céramiques des sites de l'Age du Fer en péninsule d'Oman. Documents d'Archéologie de l'Arabie n° 1*. Maison de l'Orient, CNRS, Lyon (CD-Rom).

Benoist A. & Mouton, M. 1994. L'Age du Fer dans la plaine d'al Madam (Sharjah, U.A.E): Prospections et fouilles récentes. *Proceedings of the Seminar for Arabian Studies* 24: 1-12.

Benoist A. & Reade J. 1998. Ra's al Hadd, Sultanat d'Oman. In Mouton M. (ed.), *Assemblages céramiques des sites de l'Age du Fer en péninsule d'Oman. Documents d'Archéologie de l'Arabie n° 1*. Maison de l'Orient, CNRS, Lyon (CD-Rom).

Benoist A., Cordoba J, Mouton M. 1997. The Iron Age in al Madam (Sharjah, U.A.E): some notes on three seasons of work. *Proceedings of the Seminar for Arabian Studies* 27: 59-74.

Bibby G. 1970. *Looking for Dilmun*. Pelican. Hammondsworth.

Boucharlat R. & Lombard P. 1985. The oasis of Al Aïn in the Iron Age: excavations at Rumeilah, survey at Hili-14. *Archaeology in the U.A.E.* 5: 44-65.

Boucharlat R., & Pécontal-Lambert A. 1990. The excavations at Jabal Buhais. Boucharlat R. Ed.

---

[10] The Wadi Suq period and Late Bronze Age are predominant in the Mereshid assemblage, whereas Iron Age material is rare – 6 pots (as observed by the author during a study of grave goods of Mereshid). I contrast, in a grave like Bithnah, Wadi Suq objects are absent whereas Iron Age items are numerous (Corboud *et al.* 1996).

[11] With the exception of two individual graves excavated in Bithnah area, which produced one potsherd each that might be dated from Iron Age, although without any certainty (Corboud *et al.* 1996:10).

Archaeological Survey in the Sharjah Emirate 1990 and 1992. A Sixth interim report. Maison de l'Orient, Lyon.

Carter R., & Magee P. 1999. Agglomeration and regionalism: south-eastern Arabia between 1400 and 1100 BC. *Arabian Archaeology and Epigraphy* 10:161-179.

Corboud P., Castella A.C., Hapka R., & Im Obersteg P. 1994. *Archaeological Survey of Fujairah 3 (1993). Preliminary report on the 1993 campaign.* Swiss-Liechtenstein Foundation for Archaeological Research Abroad, Bern, Vaduz, Geneva and Neuchatel.

Corboud P., Castella A.C., Hapka R., & Im Obersteg P. 1996. *Les tombes protohistoriques de Bithnah.* Terra Archaeologica 1. Monographies de la fondation Suisse-Liechtenstein pour les recherches archéologiques à l'étranger, Mainz.

Costa P.M., Graziosi Costa G., Yule P., Kunter M., Phillips C. & Bin Ahmad bin Bakhit al Shanfari A. 1999. Archaeological research in the area of Muscat. Pages 1-90 in Yule P. (ed.), *Studies in the Archaeology of the Sultanate of Oman.* Orient Archäologie Band 2.

David H. 1996. Style and evolution: softstone vessels during the Bronze Age in the Oman Peninsula. *Proceedings of the Seminar for Arabian Studies* 36: 31-46.

De Cardi B. 1988. The grave good from Shimal tomb B in Ras al Khaimah. Pages 45-71 in D.T. Potts (ed.), *Araby the Blest.* Copenhagen: Carsten Niebuhr Institute.

Donaldson P. 1984. Archaeological investigations in the Oman Peninsula. *Oriens Antiquus* 23: 191-312.

Frifelt K. 1968. Archaeological investigations in the Oman Peninsula. *Kuml* 1968:159-176.

Frifelt K. 1975. On prehistoric settlement and chronology of the Oman Peninsula. *East and West* 25: 359-425.

Garzdar M.S., Potts D.T. & Livingstone A. 1984. Excavations at Thaj. *Atlal* 8/1:55-108.

Kroll S. 1991. Zu den Beziehungen eisentzeitlicher bemalter Keramikkomplexe in Oman und Iran. Pages 315-320 in Schippman, K., Herding A. & Salles J.F (eds), *Golf Archäologie: Mesopotamien, Iran, Kuwait, Vereinigte Arabische Emirate und Oman.* Göttingen.

Kroll S. 1998. Lizq. In Mouton M. (ed.), *Assemblages céramiques des sites de l'Age du Fer en péninsule d'Oman. Documents d'Archéologie de l'Arabie n° 1.* Maison de l'Orient, CNRS, Lyon (CD-Rom).

Lombard P. 1985. *L'Arabie orientale à l'Age du Fer.* Unpublished PhD Thesis, University of Paris I, Paris.

Lombard P. & Kervran M. 1989. *Bahrain National Museum Archaeological collections: a selection of pre-islamic Antiquities from excavations 1954-1975.* Bahrain.

Magee P. 1996a. Excavations at Muweilah. Preliminary report on the first two seasons. *Arabian Archaeology and Epigraphy* 7/2: 195-213.

Magee P. 1996b. The chronology of the south-eastern Arabian Iron Age. *Arabian Archaeology and Epigraphy* 7/2: 240-252.

Magee P. 1997. The Iranian Iron Age and the chronology of settlement in south-east Arabia *Iranica Antiqua* XXXII: 91-108.

Magee P., Grave P., Yasin al Tikriti W., Barbetti M., Yu Z. & Bailey G. 1998. New evidence for specialized ceramic production and exchanges in the Southeast Arabian Iron Age. *Arabian Archaeology and Epigraphy* 9/2: 236-245.

Méry S. 2000. *Les céramiques d'Oman et l'Asie Moyenne:une archéologie des échanges à l'Age du Bronze.* Paris: Editions du CNRS.

Mouton M. 1992. *La péninsule d'Oman de la fin de l'Age du Fer au début de la période Sassanide (250 av. J-C. – 250 ap. J-C).* PhD Thesis, University of Paris I, Paris. (Published as BAR International Series 1776. Oxford: Archaeopress.)

Phillips C.S. 1987. *Wadi al Qawr, Fashgha-1. The excavation of a prehistoric burial structure, ras al Khaimah, U.A.E., 1986.* Department of Arachaeology, University of Edinburgh, project paper n° 7.

Phillips C.S. 1997. The pattern of settlement in the Wadi al Qawr. *Proceedings of the Seminar for Arabian Studies* 27:205-218.

Potts D. 1990. *A prehistoric mound in the Emirate of Umm al Qaiwain, U.A.E. Excavations at Tell Abraq in 1989.* Copenhagen: Munksgaard.

Potts D. 1991. *Further excavations at Tell Abraq.* Copenhagen: Munksgaard.

Rahman S.U. 1980. Report on Hili-2 settlement: 1976-1979. *Archaeology in the United Arab Emirates* II-III: 8-18.

Rougeulle A. 2001. Notes on pre and early Islamic Harbours of Hadramawt (Yemen) *Proceedings of the Seminar for Arabian Studies* 31: 203-214.

Taha M. Y. 1983. The archaeology of the Arabian Gulf during the first millennium BC. *Al Rafidan* III-IV: 75-87.

Velde C. 2003. Wadi Suq and Late Bronze Age in the Oman Peninsula. Pages 102-114 in Potts D., al Naboodah H. & Hellyer P. (eds), *Archaeology of the United Arab Emirates.* London: Trident Press.

Vogt B. 1994. *Asimah: an account of two month rescue excavations in the mountains of Ra's al Khaimah U.A.E.* Dubai: Department of Antiquities and Museums, Ra's al Khaimah.

Vogt B. & Franke Vogt U. 1987. *Shimal 1985/1986. Excavations of the German Archaeological Mission in Ras al Khaimah, U.A.E.* Berlin: Berliner Beitrage zum vorderen Orient 8.

Weeks L. 2000. Metal Artefacts from the Sharm Tomb. *Arabian Archaeology and Epigraphy* 11: 180-198.

Weisgerber G. & Yule P. 1999. Preliminary Report of the 1996 season of Excavation in the Sultanate of Oman. Pages 97-118 in Yule P. (ed.), *Studies in the Archaeology of the Sultanate of Oman.* Orient Archäologie Band 2.

Zarins J., Ibrahim M. Potts D. & Edens C. 1978. Comprehensive archaeological survey program: preliminary report on the survey of the central province. *Atlal* 3: 9-43.

Ziolkowski M. 2001. The soft stone Vessels from Sharm, Fujairah, United Arab Emirates. *Arabian Archaeology and Epigraphy* 12/1: 10-86.

Authors' Address
Anne Benoist
UMR 5133 - Archéorient
Maison de l'Orient et de la Méditerrannée - Jean Pouilloux
7 rue Raulin, 69365 Lyon Cedex
France
email: anne.benoist@mom.fr

Salah Ali Hassan
Head Archaeologist
Fujairah Tourism & Antiquities Authority
PO Box 500
Fujairah, UAE
cute_sos@hotmail.com

Collective Burials and Status Differentiation in Iron Age II Southeastern Arabia

Crystal Fritz

Summary
This paper re-examines the ceramic remains from the Iron Age II (1100-600) burials in the Wadi al Qawr, United Arab Emirates, in order to identify burial practices and investigate status differentiation. These burials are stone-built, multi-chambered and house multiple individuals. They offer an opportunity for examining both funerary ritual and the archaeological correlates of it. In addition, because of the number of burials and the amount of artifacts recovered from them, it was possible to address questions of status differentiation among the living. Burial remains are among the most useful archaeological indices of status differentiation. Despite the clear evidence for emergent elites from a number of settlements in the region, the burial evidence suggests that status differentiation was not pervasive. There is little evidence of status differentiation either among or within the burials. The lack of status differentiation in burials helps us to understand various problematic aspects of the political economy during this period.

Keywords: Wadi al Qawr, collective burial, status differentiation, pottery, archaeology.

Introduction

Burial practices during the Iron Age II period in southeastern Arabia are not well understood. Relatively few burials have been excavated and even fewer published. Analyses of the contents of burials and their significance are extremely rare. This paper investigates the archaeological remains from three Iron Age burials in the Wadi al Qawr, Ras al Khaimah, U.A.E. The archaeological evidence from the tombs serves as a basis for an attempt to use mortuary-theory-based analysis of these remains to inform our understanding of the political economy and social organization of the larger society.

Iron Age Burials

Iron Age burials in southeastern Arabia take two forms, single interment cairns and stone-built communal tombs. Single burial cairns are found individually or in small groups at many sites including in the Hili region (Cleuziou 1989: 72), Jebel Buhais (Boucharlat and Pecontal-Lambert 1997:16) and the Wadi al Qawr (Doe and de Cardi 1983, Phillips 1987, 1997). This simple burial type generally consists of a shallow (ca. 1 m in depth) pit covered by irregular stones. Contents usually consist of one to three vessels and the occasional bronze arrowhead. A number of pit burials of this type were also discovered at Al-Qusais in Dubai (Taha 2009: 78-87, 95-103) as well as examples of communal burials.

Communal burials are primarily found in mountainous contexts including at Bithnah (Corbud et al. 1996: 103-6), Sharm (Barker 2002, Blau 1999, Weeks 2000, Ziolkowski 2001) and in the Wadi al Qawr. Several communal tombs were excavated in the Wadi al Qawr in the emirate of Ras al Khaimah, U.A.E., where Beatrice de Cardi and Brian Doe conducted archaeological survey and Carl Phillips undertook excavations of several sites (Doe and de Cardi 1983, Phillips 1997). Phillips published an overview of his findings in the wadi in 1987 as part of the *Proceedings of the Seminar for Arabian Studies* and a detailed description of one of the most notable tombs, Fashgha 1, in 1997.

The archaeological remains from three of the communal tombs in the Wadi al Qawr, Wa'ab 4, Fashgha 2 and

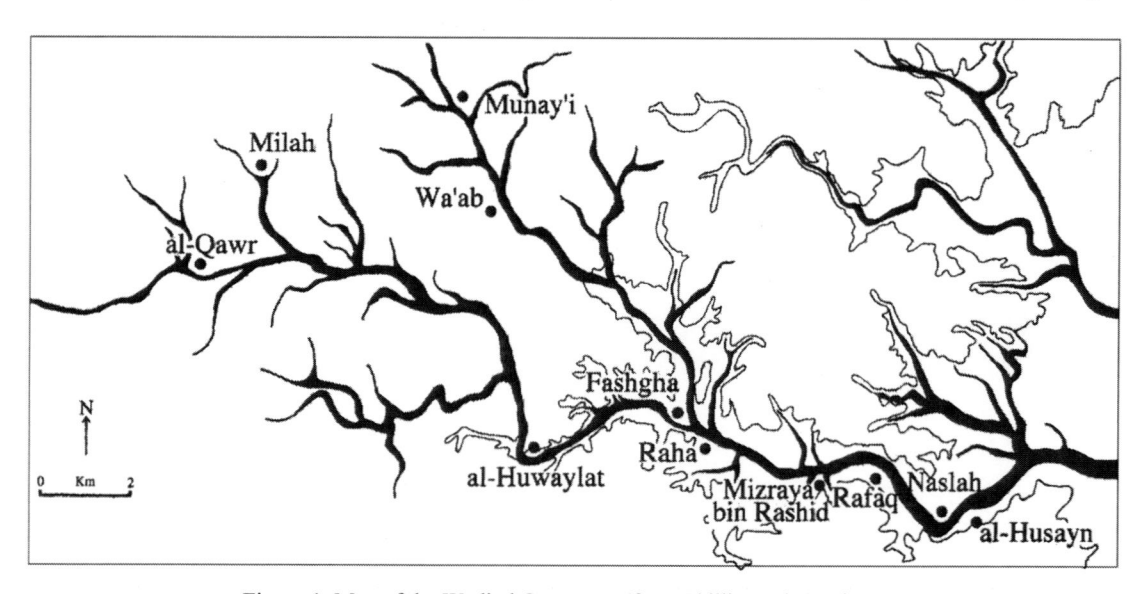

Figure 1. Map of the Wadi al Qawr area (from Phillips n.d. 4. Fig 1.3)

Naslah 1, are the foundation of this study. These tombs are among the best preserved of those excavated and contained a significant amount of Iron Age material. Although Phillips briefly mentions each of these in his 1987 article, they have not been fully assessed. This analysis is based upon the ceramic remains from the tombs, which have not previously received more than a cursory mention.

Wadi al Qawr

The Wadi al-Qawr (Figure 1) in the emirate of Ras al-Khaimah is an important route through the al-Hajjar mountains connecting the Batinah coast to the inland al-Madam plain. It is home to a number of different archaeological sites from a broad range of time periods.

Wa'ab 4

The site of Wa'ab is located on the track between the modern villages of al-Huwaylat and Munay'i (Phillips n.d.: 12-18). Fifteen small mounds were identified on either side of the track, three of which were excavated. Wa'ab 1, 2 and 3 are robbed tombs that probably date to the Wadi Suq period or second millennium BCE whereas Wa'ab 4 dates primarily to the Iron Age (Phillips 1997: 210).

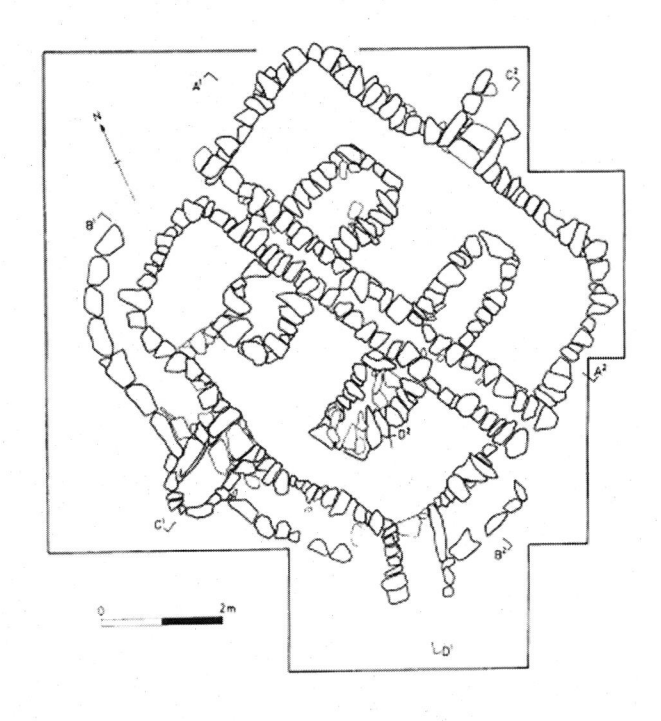

Figure 2. Plan of tomb Wa'ab 4 (from Phillips n.d. 42. Fig. 5.2)

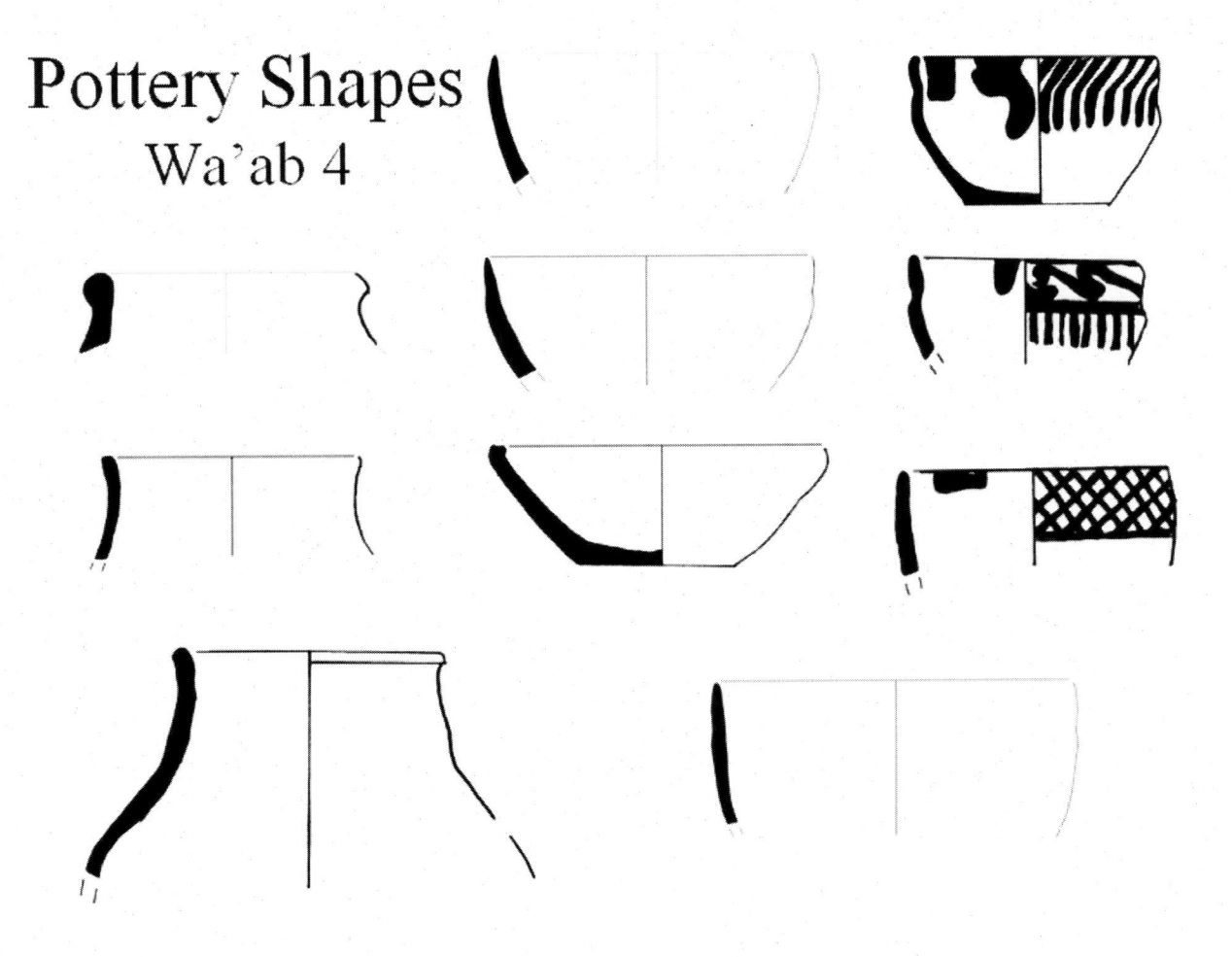

Figure 3. Sample of pottery forms from Wa'ab 4.

102

Wa'ab 4 is a stone-lined, roughly rectangular tomb with two chambers (Figure 2). Each chamber is approximately 8 m N/S by 2-3 m E/W and is separated by a 0.5-m space running N/S producing an inner area of ca. 6 x 6 m divided into two halves. Each chamber has a stone-lined entrance in the center of its longer wall, one opening to the east and the other to the west. The western chamber also has a smaller entrance near the southern corner. Two pillars constructed of rough stones, presumably to support a roof that does not survive, were found in each chamber.

The deposits within the tomb consisted of sand, gravel and infrequent larger stones. The density of finds was greater in the lowest 20 cm of the deposit. Finds included pottery, soft-stone vessels, metal and shell objects and fragmentary human remains (Phillips n.d.: 45-46). The vast majority of finds within the tomb date to the Iron Age. The presence of a limited amount of Wadi Suq period material, however, suggests that the tomb was constructed prior to the Iron Age and reused.

The ceramic assemblage (Figure 3) consisted of 54 vessels, including 10 jars and 44 bowls. Of these, 39 were small, thinned rim bowls. The small jars have flaring necks and simple rims. Most of the bowls are plain and 10-15 cm diameter. Eleven of the bowls had painted decoration. The painted bowls have motifs comparable to those found at Rumeilah, Muweilah and other Iron Age settlement sites in the region.

Naslah 1

Naslah is also home to a cluster of sites, including three stone-built tombs (Naslah 1, 2 and 4) and the remains of a settlement (Naslah 3). Naslah 2 and 4 were small tombs built during the Wadi Suq period and re-used during the Iron Age, but few artifacts were recovered from them and it is unlikely they held more than a few individuals (Phillips n.d.: 200-216). Naslah 1, however, was larger and its contents better preserved.

Naslah 1 is cut into bedrock and is 1 m in depth (Figure 4). The central part of the tomb is approximately eight meters in diameter and the burial chamber itself is approximately 1 m wide and ring-shaped. The interior of the external chamber is also about 1 m wide and the entire structure is about 3 m wide and forms a u-shape around the southern half of the central chamber. There is an entrance to the outer chamber on the southern side and the central chamber is connected to the outer by a second opening that is not aligned with the external entrance. Both entrances were lined with cut stone slabs. The internal entrance was blocked at an unknown stage with a large vertical slab. Although the excavators do not note any stratigraphic or other evidence for multiple construction phases, the closing of the internal entrance suggests that the outer chamber was a later addition (Phillips n.d.: 140). Both chambers were originally roofed with large stone slabs.

The walls of the tomb were preserved to approximately 40 cm in height and in some places the roofing slabs were

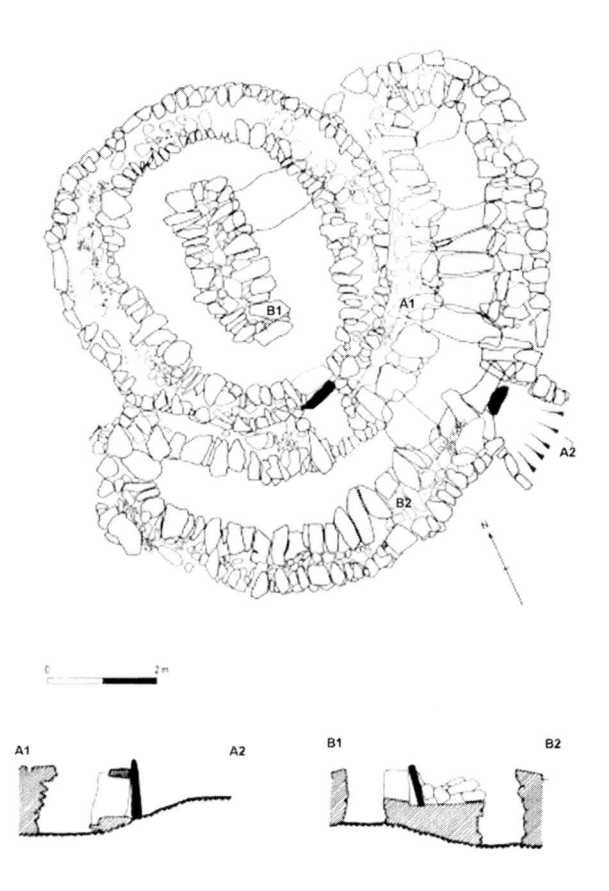

Figure 4. Plan of Naslah 1 (from Phillips n.d. 139. Fig. 7.2)

in-situ at the time of excavation. The deposits within the tomb filled the entire chamber and appeared to be disturbed, more so in the external chamber. Finds were distributed throughout the deposits.

Examination of the fragmentary skeletal remains yielded a minimum number of thirty individuals (Phillips n.d.: 140). Some animal bones were also identified. The burial goods consisted mostly of pottery and softstone vessels. As with Wa'ab 4, the comparative ceramic chronology indicates that this tomb was constructed during the Wadi Suq period and reused during the Iron Age.

The ceramic assemblage (Figure 5) consists of 85 vessels, including 16 jars and 72 bowls, of which 52 were small, thinned-rim bowls. Twenty-three examples had painted motifs. The one example of a large storage vessel was not complete and is unique within the assemblages. The incised decoration on the exterior is typical of large cordoned storage vessels found elsewhere. Again small bowls dominate the assemblage and a minority has painted motifs familiar from Iron Age settlements.

Fashgha 2

Fashgha 2 is among a cluster of sites located at the junction of the Wadi al-Qawr and the Wadi Munay'i, including three tombs and the remains of a settlement (de Cardi 1984: 204, Doe and de Cardi 1983: 31). Only the ceramics from Fashgha 2 are included in this study. Fashgha tomb 1 has been published and Fashgha tomb 3 contained very few finds.

Pottery Shapes
Naslah 1

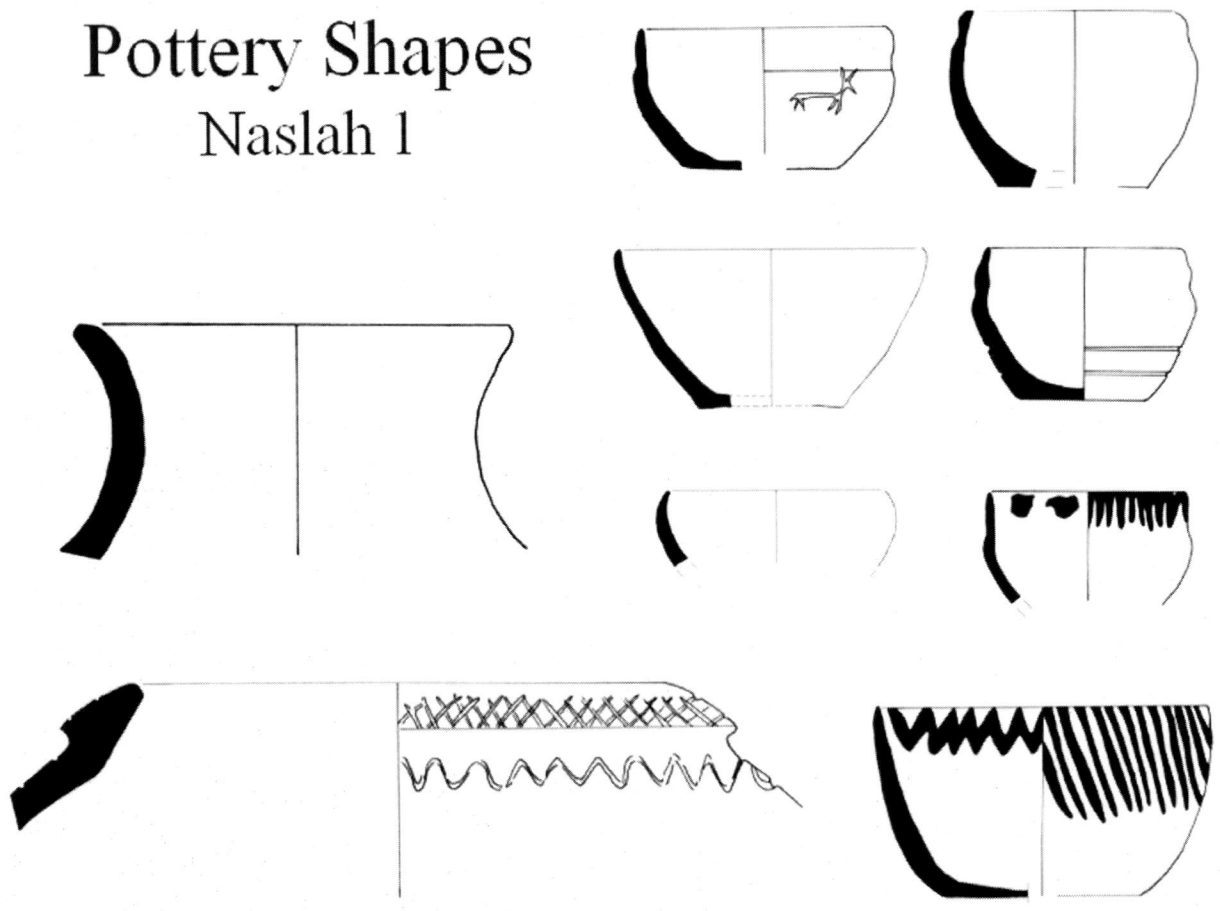

Figure 5. Sample of pottery forms from Naslah 1.

Tomb Fashgha 2 (Figure 6) is located at the eastern end of the terrace area. It is cut into the bedrock and lined with unworked stone. Both the main tomb chamber and secondary chamber are ca. 1m deep and 1 m wide. The tomb is round with a central pillar. It was accessed through an opening on its southern side and an additional chamber that hugs the western side of the tomb was accessed via the main tomb chamber (Phillips n.d.: 97-98).

As was the case with the other tombs, the majority of the material found in the tomb dates to the Iron Age period, but a small amount of earlier material indicates a Wadi Suq construction date. The ceramics (Figure 7) consist of nine jars and 42 bowls, of which 21 were painted. Again, the jars were mostly simple necked types and the bowls mostly of thinned rim types, some with decorative motifs characteristic to the region.

Overview of the tombs

The examined tombs from the Wadi al Qawr are each communal tombs. They were constructed during the Wadi Suq period and reused extensively in the Iron Age II period. For this reason, it is difficult to assign cultural significance to the architectural form. The relationship between the Iron Age II society and the preceding Iron Age I populations is unclear. The architectural form does not include any indication that the various chambers were designated for different segments of society. There is no

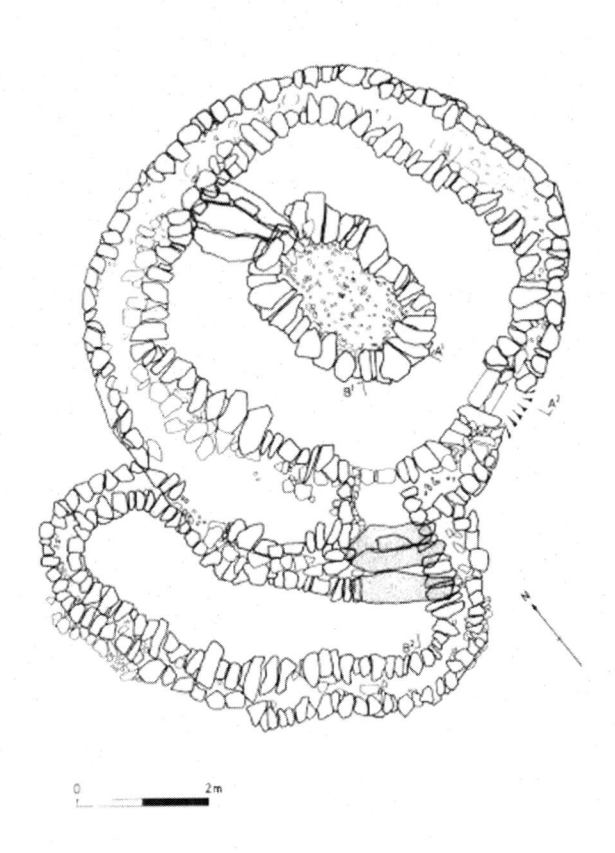

Figure 6. Plan of Fashgha 2 (from Phillips n.d. 98. Fig. 6.20)

Pottery Shapes
Fashgha 2

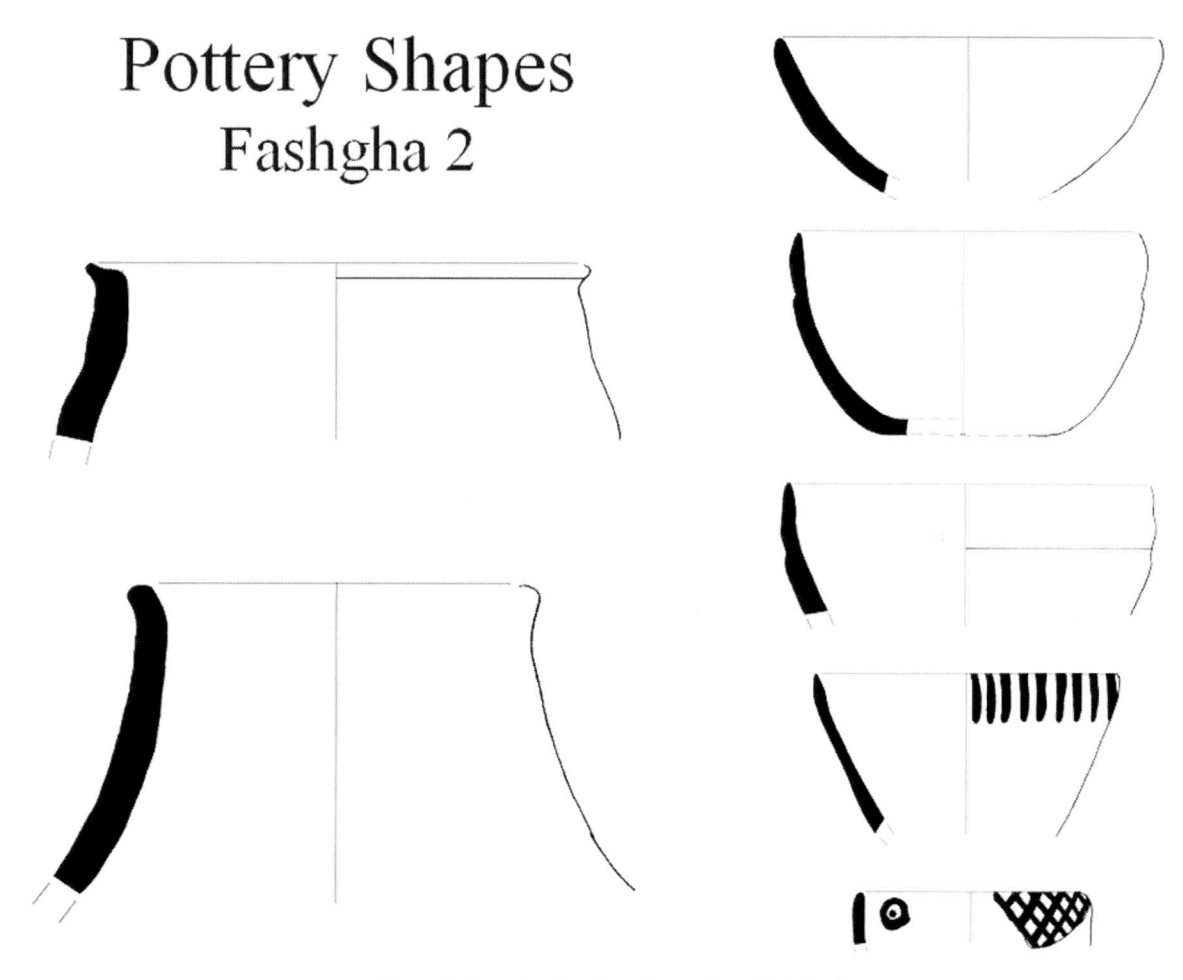

Figure 7. Sample of pottery forms from Fashgha 2

evidence that different sections of the burials varied in either construction or decorative elements. Because the deposits within the tombs are very disturbed it is not possible to identify burial goods associated with individuals.

The Ceramics

An analysis of the ceramic assemblage as a whole was employed to investigate socio-economic differentiation among the interred. Although a statistical analysis of the data might produce quantifiable results, the level of preservation in these tombs is probably too poor to make such an analysis reliable. Instead only general interpretations of the data are possible.

The same forms are characteristic of each of the tombs. Small bowls, sometimes carinated, are the most common type. The few jars recovered are almost all of the flaring-rim type. These same forms are found at sites throughout the region. The groups using these tombs had a shared material culture that was common to the whole region of southeastern Arabia during the Iron Age.

In each tomb context, however, more than half of the vessels are made in what is probably a locally made ware. In each case, the most common fabric is unique to that tomb. The presence of unique locally made wares at each of the three tomb sites suggests that the groups using the tombs each had independent ceramic production. This trait, importantly, supports the hypothesis that each tomb was used by a closed group of people (as opposed to one group using all of the tombs, etc.).

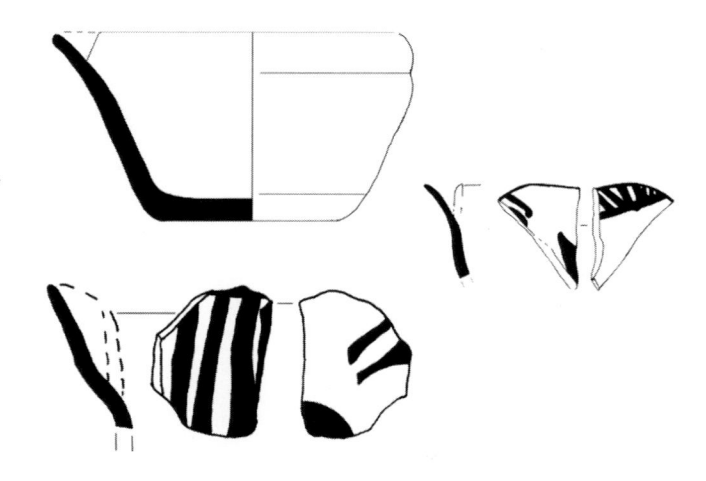

Figure 8. Examples of spouted bowls.

Only the fine painted ware is comparable to fabrics found at the other sites. It is not entirely clear that these painted wares are not local products as well, as fabrics in this study were primarily differentiated on the basis of inclusions, of which fine wares had none. The motifs depicted on the painted examples, however, are directly comparable to examples found at other sites in southeastern Arabia, including Muweilah, Rumeilah, Tell Abraq and Hamriyah. In particular, the motifs are almost identical to those found on vessels produced in Al Ain.

In fact, these similarities among the burial pottery and that found at other types of sites means that it is unlikely that any pottery form or decorative motif was specific to mortuary practice. One possible exception is the spouted bowl (Figure 8), which appears a few times in the burials and is not attested elsewhere.

Overview

It is possible to identify several characteristics typical of the large communal tombs in the Wadi al Qawr. The primary type of ceramic grave good is a small bowl, usually with thinned carinated or incurving walls. There is little difference among the bowls within the tombs in terms of size or elaboration, the only distinction of note being between painted and unpainted types. The bowl forms are the same as those found at settlements across the region. There is, however, much less variation in the types and particularly the sizes of bowls in the burial contexts.

Very little is known about the burial rituals. Interestingly, there is no evidence of either the snake iconography or bridge spouted vessels that are often associated with other types of "ceremonial" sites in the region.

The remains from these tombs provide useful body of material for this type of study, as each seems to be associated with a local settlement area and a local ceramic fabric. To date, the burial areas associated with the major settlements elsewhere in the region, such as Rumeilah, Muweilah and Tell Abraq, have not been identified. Thus, these burials represent the best examples of bounded burial areas associated with smaller groups within the regional cultural milieu.

It is clear that the burial groups using these tombs were part of the regional political economy, as represented by shared material culture. The contents of these tombs can therefore be analyzed as an index of political economy and social structure in the Iron Age II period overall.

During the Iron Age II period, southeastern Arabia witnesses a boom in the number and size of settlements across the region. The presence of elites as a corollary of intensification has been proposed on the basis of the appearance of "columned halls" at several sites. The mortuary remains, however, are evidence against the existence of an entrenched hierarchy or centralized political control of the larger region as a primary component of the intensification of the period.

Theoretical Background

Burials are one of the primary contexts in which differences of status are manifest archaeologically. The pioneering work of Binford and Saxe established the foundations of burial remains as proxies for social and economic differentiation (Saxe 1970, Binford 1971: 6-29). Binford used cross-cultural ethnographic studies to propose that elements of the "social persona" of the deceased could be recognized in archaeological remains of funerary practice and that these characteristics varied according to the rank and social position of the person in life (Binford 1971: 6-29).

In another study fundamental to mortuary archaeology, Saxe proposed that elements of social identity, which are often tied up with economic status, are reflected in practices associated with the disposal of the dead (Saxe 1970). Among his hypotheses is the suggestion that more complex societies represent elements such as rank and social status, in addition to age, sex and personal achievement through burial attributes (Parker Pearson 1999: 29-31).

Tainter expanded upon these ideas, suggesting that greater energy expenditure in individual graves, in such forms as architectural elaboration and luxury grave goods, is linked to status differentiation. Those who have greater status are "worth" more in terms of time and money to those still living.

Essentially, it is possible to see the structure of status differences in a society based upon the distribution of different types of burial practices. As Chris Peebles has suggested, the existence of multiple repeatedly used types is indicative of specific status roles that are represented formally in them (Peebles and Kus 1977: 421-448). If the frequency of the various types is pyramidal in nature one can hypothesize a hierarchical social structure among the living.

Conclusions

The hypothesis of this paper is that substantial socio-economic stratification reflected in varying status distinctions would be visible in the relative distribution of ceramic types. There is no identifiable differentiation among the tombs in different areas or among the various sections of individual tombs. The only variation of note is between painted and unpainted bowls. It is possible that the finer fabric painted examples, which form a minority of the ceramic assemblage, represent the grave goods of a higher status group among the living. This is, however, very limited evidence of stratification. The potential for two status groups only indicates that social and economic differentiation was quite limited.

Nor is there evidence that separate bounded burial areas existed for high status individuals, such as rulers and/or their families. We must assume that even small groups such as those inhabiting the Wadi al Qawr had some sort of local leader. The burial evidence suggests that local leaders were not expressing their power over the community in conspicuous burial practices in the Wadi al Qawr, and indeed there is little evidence elsewhere in the region for such displays.

This paper represents what can only be called a first attempt at second level mortuary analysis for the Iron Age II period. An analysis of the abundant softstone vessels from these tombs is currently underway and surely will shed more light on the burial practices of the Iron Age II. It is my hope that by beginning to tease out the burial practices, we may be better able to recognize differences among them throughout the region in the future.

Acknowledgements

Many thanks to The National Museum of Ras al Khaimah, U.A.E., Christian Velde, Imke Mollering and Ahmad Hilal for all of their accommodating assistance and for providing access to the materials and documentation presented here. Thanks also go to Peter Magee.

References

Barker D. 2002. Wadi Suq and Iron Age period ceramics from Sharm, Fujairah (U.A.E.). *Arabian Archaeology and Epigraphy* 13: 1-94.

Binford L. 1971. Mortuary practices: their study and their potential. Pages 6-29 in J.A. Brown (ed.), *Approaches to the Social Dimensions of Mortuary Practice*. Washington DC: The Society for American Archaeology.

Blau S. 1999. The people at Sharm: an analysis of the archaeological human skeletal remains. *Arabian Archaeology and Epigraphy* 10/2: 190-204.

Boucharlat R. & Pecontal-Lambert A. 1997. The 1990 excavations at Jabal Buhais: an Iron Age cemetery. Pages 11-14 in R. Boucharlat (ed.), *Archaeological Surveys and Excavations in the Sharjah Emirate, 1990 and 1992. A Sixth Interim Report*. Lyon: Maison de l'Orient.

Cleuziou S. 1989. Excavations at Hili 8: A Preliminary Report on the 4th to the 7th Campaigns. *Archaeology in the United Arab Emirates* 5: 61-87.

Corboud P., Castella A.C., Hapka R. & Im-Obersteg P. 1996. *Les tombes protohistoriques de Bithnah, Fujairah, Émirates Arabes Unis*. Mainz: von Zabern.

de Cardi B. 1984. Survey in Ras al-Khaimah, U.A.E. Pages 210-216 in R. Boucharlat & J.-F. Salles (eds), *Arabie orientale, Mesopotamie et Iran méridional de l'Age du Fer au début de la période islamique*. Paris: ADPF.

Doe B. & de Cardi B. 1983. Archaeological survey in southern Ras al-Khaimah, 1982 - Preliminary Report. *Proceedings of the Seminar for Arabian Studies* 13: 31-35.

Parker Pearson M. 1999. *The Archaeology of Death and Burial*. College Station: Texas A&M University Press.

Peebles C. & Kus S. 1977. Some archaeological correlates of ranked societies. *American Antiquity* 42: 421-48.

Phillips C. 1996. *Wadi al-Qawr, Fashgha 1. The Excavation of a Prehistoric Burial Structure in Ras al-Khaimah, UAE 1996*. Vol. 7, University of Edinburgh Project Paper. Edinburgh: University of Edinburgh.

Phillips C. 1997. The pattern of settlement in the Wadi al-Qawr. *Proceedings of the Seminar for Arabian Studies* 27: 205-18.

Phillips C. 1998. Wadi al-Qawr. In M. Mouton (ed.), *Assemblages céramiques des sites de l'Age du Fer de la péninsule d'Oman*. CD-ROM. Lyon: GREMMO/Maison de l'Orient, 1998.

Phillips C. n.d. Unpublished preliminary report on excavations in the Wadi al-Qawr, held in the Ras al-Khaimah Museum.

Saxe A. 1970. *Social Dimensions of Mortuary Practices*. Michigan: University of Michigan.

Taha M. 2009. *The Discovery of the Iron Age in the United Arab Emirates*. Abu Dhabi: Ministry of Culture, Youth and Community Development.

Weeks L. 2000. Metal artefacts from the Sharm tomb. *Arabian Archaeology and Epigraphy* 11: 180-98.

Ziolkowski M.C. 2001. The soft stone vessels from Sharm, Fujairah, United Arab Emirates. *Arabian Archaeology and Epigraphy* 12/1: 10-86.

Author's Address

Crystal Fritz
608 S Randolph 4W
Philadelphia, PA 19147
USA
Crystal.fritz@gmail.com

Camelid and equid burials in pre-Islamic southeastern Arabia

Aurelie Daems and An De Waele

Death is a black camel that lies down at every door.
Sooner or later you must ride the camel.
(Saudi proverb)

Abstract
The burial of small and large animals in connection with the burial of one or more human beings is a phenomenon that has been largely attested in the Arabian Peninsula and adjacent regions. From the earliest Bronze Age through to the advent of Islam, there is substantial evidence for this type of human-animal interaction taking place beyond life, in or next to the grave. Both small (sheep/goat/chicken) and large animals (camelids/equids) occasionally supplement the burial assemblage or form the pinnacle of some seemingly special burials. This paper explores some theoretical aspects of human-animal interdependency in pre-Islamic southeastern Arabia, from a theoretically informed perspective and by drawing on the evidence that is at hand.

Keywords: Southeastern Arabia, camelid, equid, burial, pre-Islamic

Introduction

The following paper offers some preliminary thoughts on the intentional burial of camelids and equids, of which most are connected to the burial of one or more humans. The area of interest is Southeastern Arabia from the Bronze Age to the advent of Islam. This paper was triggered by Ghent University excavations of an equid that was lying in direct association with a large Tylos period tomb at Shakhoura, Bahrain (Figure 1). Several archaeologists have been confronted with similar forms of burials throughout Southeastern Arabia, and authors such as Mashkour (1997), Vogt (1994), the Uerpmanns (Uerpmann & Uerpmann 1997, 1999, 2002) and Jasim (1999) have previously addressed this topic. Their works form the essential foundation for the discussion of issues related to motivation, impact and meaning of the practice. In this paper we summarize and explore the evidence currently at hand and reflect on the possible reasons behind this human-animal relationship that extends beyond the mortal lifetime of the protagonists.

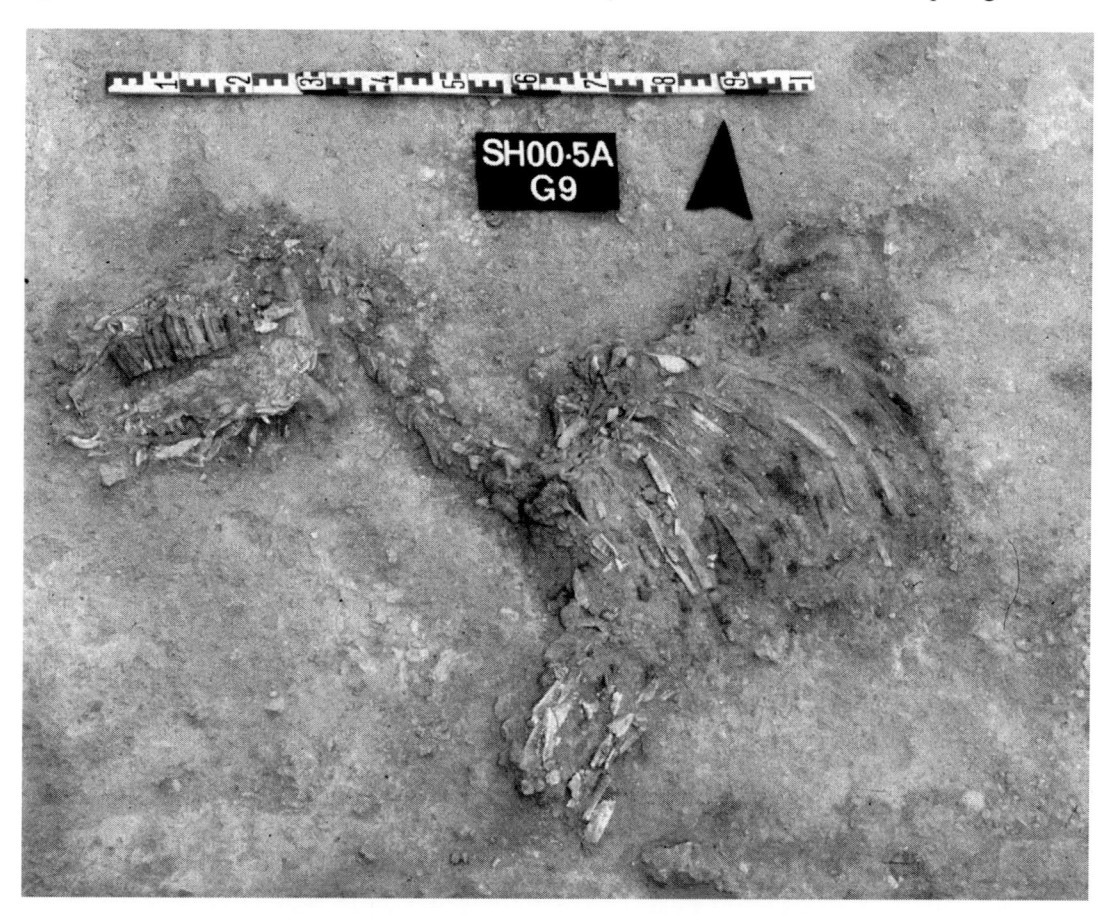

Figure 1. Equid burial unearthed at Shakhoura mound 5A, Bahrain (© Ghent University).

Camelid and Equid Domestication

Literally hundreds of human tombs dated from the Bronze Age to the advent of Islam have been unearthed throughout Southeastern Arabia. In contrast, only 36 examples of intentional burial of large animals – in this case camelids and equids – are so far known or published. The majority of these buried animals belong to the domesticated sort. And a note on what this means is apposite here. Indeed, 'domestication' should be viewed as beneficial for both humans and animals. It is a relationship based on mutual interaction, in which success and failure depend on the degree of benefit for both parties (O'Connor 1997: 151). This relationship begins with the thorough and lengthy behavioral observation. In the first stage, hunting revolves around meat, hair and skin procurement. Subsequently, this results in herding and taming in which the collection of dung for fuel and milk are envisaged. In the final stage, burdens are loaded on the animal's back and attempts are made at riding (Retsö 1991: 188). This lengthy trial and error process culminates in the animal being fully tamed and controlled by humans. The relationship resulting from this is then one of undeniable inter-dependency.

The exact date for the onset of camelid and equid domestication in Southeastern Arabia is still partly a matter of debate. Suffice it to say that camelid bones are reported from the 6th millennium BC in Abu Dhabi, south of the Baynunah plantation (Beech et al. 2009) and in al-Buhais 18 during the 5th millennium BC (Uerpmann & Uerpmann 2002: 237). Increasing quantities of camel remains appear during the 3rd and 2nd millennia BC at Saar and Qalat al Bahrain, both in Bahrain (Uerpmann & Uerpmann 2002: 238) and in the U.A.E. at the sites of Umm an-Nar Island, Hili 8, Rhas Ghanada (Wapnish 1997: 407) and especially at Al Sufouh 2, a unique slaughtering place for wild camels (von den Driesch & Obermaier 2007: 133).

The first clear cut evidence for the domestication of camelids in Southeastern Arabia comes from Qalat al-Bahrain excavation 519, during the City III period (Uerpmann & Uerpmann 1997: 243) and from Iron Age II levels at Tell Abraq in the U.A.E. (Uerpmann M. 2001: 232; Uerpmann & Uerpmann 1999: 460; von den Driesch & Obermaier 2007: 149). As the Uerpmanns (Uerpmann & Uerpmann 2002) have convincingly demonstrated, the impetus for domestication of camelids in Southeastern Arabia could have been triggered by close cultural and economic ties with Mesopotamia, Egypt and the Levant during the 3rd millennium BC.

Distinguishing wild equids from their domesticated counterparts is more problematic for Southeastern Arabia. Domesticated donkeys seem to be present from the Bronze Age in Mesopotamia and Oman (Uerpmann H.-P. 1991: 30). The appearance of domesticated horses in Southeastern Arabia is even harder to asses (Uerpmann & Uerpmann 1997: 248). In fact one of the earliest evidences of the presence of this animal in Arabia comes from the graveyard of Mleiha, dated to the first two centuries AD (Uerpmann & Uerpmann 1997: 248). In Mesopotamia, Egypt and the Levant, the horse started to be used as a means for transport from the first half of the 2nd millennium BC onwards (Uerpmann & Uerpmann 2002: 251). By analogy, using camels as mounts for exploring hitherto vast and undiscovered patches of desert land must surely have stimulated the experimentation with camelids for that means.

Camelid and Equid Burials in Southeastern Arabia: The Evidence

The first reported intentional burials of camels on the Arabian Peninsula come from Oman at Bronze Age Maysar 22 (Uerpmann & Uerpmann 2002: 248). After this period up to the 1st millennium BC, evidence for this practice is either too scattered or not explicit enough to label them as intentional. The situation changes from the first half of the 1st millennium BC and onwards to the turning of the millennium, corresponding well with the more intensive use of these animals in daily life. Examples of 1st millennium BC camelid burials are found at Mezruah in Qatar (Lecomte, Boucharlat & Culas 1989: 33; Frifelt 1985: 102), at Raybun XVII (Vogt 1994: 287) and Beles in Yemen (Vogt 1994: 279), in Oman at al-Hammariyat, Bat and Samad (Frifelt 1985: 103; Vogt 1994: 289-290), on Bahrain at Jidd Hafs (Herling & Salles 1993: 164) and Shakhoura (Daems & Haerinck 2001: 92), and in the Emirates at Jebel Hafit (Uerpmann 1999: 97) and ed-Dur, with discoveries of camelid burials by the French, British and Belgian teams (Lecomte, Boucharlat & Culas 1989; Ward 1990: 31; Haerinck 2001: 44). The most spectacular camelid burials however were found at the extended site of Mleiha, where a local team directed by Sabah Jasim uncovered at least 12 camelid and 2 horse burials in close connection to 14 possible human burials (Mashkour 1997; Uerpmann 1999: 103; Jasim 1999). Additionally, a French team found 6 camelid burials close to looted human tombs at the same site (Mashkour 1997: 727). The most recent of these intentional large animal burials in pre-Islamic Southeastern Arabia are the ones unearthed at Jebel al Buhais 12 and Jebel al-Emalah; dated to the 7th century AD (Uerpmann & Uerpmann 1999: 455).

The intentional burial of equids in connection with humans is, unsurprisingly, far less well represented in the archaeological record of Southeastern Arabia. The only examples are the two animals from Mleiha mentioned above and one from Shakhoura, Bahrain. At Mleiha, two equid skeletons were buried with two camelids (Jasim 1999: 70). At Shakhoura, the skeleton of presumably a donkey (Gautier, pers. comm.) was unearthed, of which the fore and hind legs were partly missing and of which the back seems to have been deliberately burned (Daems & Haerinck 2001: 94, fig. 7). The animal was lying underneath the impressive burial mound 5A, flanking one of the sides of the main Tylos tomb.

In Southeastern Arabia, this intentional burial of large animals thus generally occurs in connection with a human tomb, although some examples are known of seemingly isolated burials. In the former case the animals are buried inside or in the immediate vicinity of a larger human tomb such as at Shakhoura (Daems & Haerinck 2001), ed-Dur area AV (Haerinck 2001: 44) and Jebel al Buhais 12 (Uerpmann & Uerpmann 1999: 455) for example. In the latter case, animals can be buried inside larger living quarters or living spaces such as at ed-Dur area F (Lecomte, Boucharlat & Culas 1989). The human burials with which some of the large animal tombs are associated are generally rather impressive. They are rectangular (Mashkour 1997: 727), cut neatly in the bedrock, and have a North-South orientation (Haerinck 2001: 44). They are often made of limestone blocks with the walls and floors at times plastered with gypsum (Jasim 1999: 76) or covered with mud-bricks. In several of these human burials, refined burial gifts were also found.

Several of the camelids unearthed at the sites just mentioned assumed a kneeling position. Their neck was often tilted backwards, implying that these beasts were slaughtered on the spot by cutting their throat and were buried inside a pit in which they were first forced to kneel. In ed-Dur area F, the unearthed camelid was recovered in a building considered as the residence of a sheikh (Ward 1990: 6). The animal was interred together with a broken iron dagger and an iron ring, the latter items reinforcing the belief that the animal was brought alive to its last resting place and then slaughtered on the spot (Lecomte, Boucharlat & Culas 1989: 34).

Beside this iron dagger and iron ring recovered with the ed-Dur camelid, other gifts were also sometimes interred with intentionally-buried camelids. In ed-Dur area K for instance, a shell neck pendant and a green glazed pilgrim's flask were found. At Mleiha, which was partially looted, gifts accompanying the camelid burials included, but were possibly not restricted to, glass vessels, gold and ivory beads and plaques, metal rods and iron arrowheads (Jasim 1999: 74). One horse at Mleiha even received a full harness made of gold components and with the bit still in its mouth (Jasim 1999: 79). Aside from this single example, we do not know if full riding gear and attire was standard for every intentional camelid or equid burial.

Apart from the gifts with which they were or were not buried, it is important to stress some extra factors concerning age, species and gender of these animals; that is, in those cases in which these characteristics have been reported. At the site of Mleiha, the buried camelids were either dromedaries (n=9) or camel hybrids (n= 3), which were crossbreeds between the Bactrian and the Arabian camel (Uerpmann 1999: 102). Camel hybrids are believed to have been status animals as they are stronger, faster and larger than both their parents (Uerpmann 1999: 111; Potts 2004). These hybrids were furthermore the ones found close to the central grave at Mleiha. These were thus the ones that were selected to accompany or be buried close to the deceased. None of the camel hybrid bones showed indisputable traces of consumption. They seem thus to have been slaughtered not to be eaten, but in order to accompany one or more human burials, when they were at their highest economical value as beasts of burden. The nine other dromedaries found at Mleiha were predominantly female and at the pinnacle of their breeding capacities (Uerpmann 1999: 108, 116). At much later Jebel al-Buhais, the buried camel was also a female dromedary, buried together with a supposed warrior (based on the different iron arrowheads found in the tomb; Uerpmann & Uerpmann 1999: 455). This may suggest that the status and importance that the camelids had in life for the people to which they belonged or with which they were connected, needed to be reflected in the afterlife.

It is difficult to determine the gender of the people with whom these large animals were buried. At ed-Dur in area AV, tomb 5156, two ungendered camelids accompanied a large tomb containing multiple burials of various periods, in which both men and women of different ages were interred (Haerinck 2001: 49). A group of iron arrowheads located inside the human tomb, such as at one tomb at Mleiha, at Shakhoura 5A and Jebel al Buhais 12, might be indirect evidence for the interred person being male. Since the connection between gender and age of the buried animal in connection with gender and age of the deceased has not been a primary focus in the past, it is hard to draw reliable conclusions on this matter at this point.

The Meaning and Significance of Camelid and Equid burials

Sparse though the evidence may be, some reflections concerning this practice of *intentionally* burying large animals in pre-Islamic Southeastern Arabian society can already be put forward. As there are examples of these animals being buried with members of society, at least some members of those societies must have cared about what it meant to own or to be connected to these animals in life and beyond. Whether these animals were life-long property of the deceased, prize beasts, or gifts sent by individuals of equal esteem from rival or neighboring tribes for the death of a fellow 'chief', is harder to assess.

Although we know the importance of owning large animals in Southeastern Arabian society today, there are simply not enough written accounts that inform us of the social importance of these animals in the past. The burial of camelids and equids is not restricted to the Arabian Peninsula. In Mesopotamia, for example, the kings of Ebla offered horses upon the death of a tribesman as a token of esteem and respect. The most telling evidence for equid burials in Mesopotamia comes from the late 3rd millennium BC tombs 1 and 4 at Umm el-Marra in Syria (Schwartz et al. 2006: 604) where several equid hybrids were ritually sacrificed and buried with small infants and sumptuous gifts such as gold and silver artefacts. Other slightly less luxurious equid burials are known from Abu Salabikh (Postgate 1982: 56), Tell Razuk (Gibson 1981: 73), Tell Madhur (Roaf 1984: 113), Tell Sabi Abyad (www.sabi-abyad.nl.), Ur, Kish and Susa (Postgate 1982: 56).

Written evidence does inform us of multiple contacts between the Arabian Peninsula and regions further to the North, particularly involving the dealing of camels. But it is still unclear whether this specific burial practice is indigenous to Southeastern Arabia, or if it was adopted from Mesopotamia, seeing the various examples we have there for equids.

It is not unreasonable to suggest that in Southeastern Arabia – as in many other societies – large animals were viewed as important economic partners of some members of the tribe; inextricably intertwined with their master or mistress through failure and success. Camelids played a prominent role in Southeastern Arabian society from the onset of their taming onwards. They were used in the transport of many valuable items, from the Southern part in Oman and Yemen through to Mesopotamia and the Levant, and even as far as Greece and Rome in later times (Retsö 1991: 190). They mainly carried Arabian frankincense, myrrh, and copper ore, but also spices and stones coming as far away as India (Hoch 1995: 252; Saud al Saud 1996: 130). The importance of camels in daily life is also reflected in their breeding and lactating capacities. In Iron Age Muweilah, camels appear to have been kept for breeding purposes (Magee in Benoist 2007: 50, footnote 59), securing lactation. Indeed, lactating camels can produce up to 10 litres of milk a day (Hoch 1995: 252), making them more favorable for food resources than donkeys or horses would be in the same environment. Camel skin was used for storage to make water containers and tents. In later Islamic Arabia, offering camel meat to guests was at times seen as an act of faith (Vogt 1994: 280, footnote 8).

In the Arabian past and up to very recently, men and women alike must thus have been well aware that in order to survive and to keep their kin and their tribes prosperous, they had to rely on good, healthy, strong and fast beasts of burden that equally provided meat, milk, skin and hair. It is thus not unreasonable to suggest that owning these animals was a constant source of pride and status, as well as of competition and rivalry. People may have felt the need to display this status, in life and in death.

The practice of burying only the best and the strongest animals of the herd – as the evidence that is currently at hand suggests – must surely have been reserved for special occasions and/or for special persons within the community. Had this not been the case, then we would have expected this practice to be much more widespread. Indeed, a survey of contemporary pre-Islamic burial grounds in Southeastern Arabia shows us that this specific burial practice is rather uncommon. This implies that the phenomenon was reserved for special purposes, and for people of some esteem, be they elders, wise men, tribesmen or the herdsmen receiving these animals after death. Based on the size of the burials, their orientation and the burial of often clearly valuable gifts, it is possible – as H.-P Uerpmann (1999: 116) has suggested for Mleiha – that these burials are related to the funeral of a noble family. Or, as Jasim (1999: 100) has suggested, they belonged to soldiers, warriors or other aids of a master with which they were buried. Vogt and Mashkour situated the killing of these animals in the sphere of ritual sacrifice, where mounts are to be used by their master upon resurrection after death in order to travel to eternal life.

Vogt (1994: 287) sees these large animals only as "grave goods", reserved for high status warriors in pre-Islamic Arabia. According to him (Vogt 1994: 286), the gifts accompanying these animals are all associated with their slaughter and thus only have a practical function. However, the evidence from Mleiha and ed-Dur clearly attests otherwise and seems to indicate the social importance of these buried animals. The burial of these camelids and equids cannot have been arbitrary since they seem to be connected with the most important human burials on the site.

In conclusion, we suggest that these animals may have been the 'social equals' and the pride of their owner. Indeed, a tribe's wealth in great part depended on the strength, power and capacities of its herd. If these animals had the capacity to partly symbolize the power that a tribe's head could acquire, wield and secure in life, they could also symbolize the ending of this power once the tribe's head or the importance of the tribe altogether, dies. The sacrifice of camels by Bedouins close to their ancestor's tombs took place up until the mid 20th century AD (Henninger 1981: 191), but what this sacrifice really meant for the persons carrying out the practice remains unclear. What is certain, however, is that people living in close connection with animals and depending on them for their survival and the survival of their kin *do* have the profound capacity to interact and empathize with these animals by seeing and treating them as equals, and by making sure they walk together in life and, as may be the case for our burials, far beyond in death.

References

Beech M., Mashkour M., Huels M. & Zazzo A. 2009. Prehistoric camels in south-eastern Arabia: the discovery of a new site in Abu Dhabi's Western Region, United Arab Emirates. *Proceedings of the Seminar for Arabian Studies* 39: 17-30.

Benoist A. 2007. An Iron Age II snake cult in the Oman peninsula: evidence from Bithnah (Emirate of Fujarah). *Arabian Archaeology and Epigraphy* 18/1: 34-54.

Daems A. & Haerinck E. 2001. Excavations at Shakhoura (Bahrain). *Arabian Archaeology and Epigraphy* 12/1: 90-95.

Frifelt K. 1985. Further Evidence of the Third Millennium BC Town at Bat in Oman. *Journal of Oman Studies* 7: 89-105.

Gibson M. (ed.) 1981. *Uch Tepe I. Tell Razuk, Tell Ahmed al-Mughir, Tell Ajamat*. Chicago: Oriental Institute.

Haerinck E. 2001. *The University of Ghent South-East Arabian Archaeological Project. Excavations at ed-*

Dur (Umm al-Qaiwain, United Arab Emirates). Vol. II. The Tombs. Leuven: Peeters.

Henninger J. 1981. Le sacrifice chez les Arabes, Pages 189-203 in Henninger J. (ed.), *Arabica Sacra. Aufsätze zur Religionsgeschichte Arabiens und seiner Randgebiete*. Göttingen: Vandenhoeck & Ruprecht.

Herling A. & Salles J.-F. 1993. Hellenistic Cemetries in Bahrain. Pages 161-182 in Finkbeiner U. (ed.), *Materialien zur Archäologie der Seleukiden- und Partherzeit in südlichen Babylonien und im Golfgebiet. Ergebnisse der Symposien 1987 und 1989 in Blaubeuren (Deutsches Archäologisches Institut, Abteilung Baghdad)*. Tübingen: Ernst Wasmuth Verlag.

Hoch E. 1995. Animal bones from the Umm an-Nar Settlement. Pages 249-256 in Frifelt K. (ed.), *The Island of Umm an-Nar. Volume 2: The Third-Millennium Settlement*. Jutland Archaeological Society Publications 26/2.

Jasim S.A. 1999. The Excavation of a Camel Cemetery at Mleiha, Sharjah, U.A.E. *Arabian Archaeology and Epigraphy* 10/1: 69-101.

Lecomte O., Boucharlat R., and Culas J.M. 1989. Les fouilles françaises. *Mesopotamia* XXIV: 29-56.

Mashkour M. 1997. The Funeral Rites at Mleiha (Sharja-U.A.E.), the Camelid Graves. *Anthropozooligica* 25-26: 725-736.

O'Connor T.P. 1997. Working at relationships: another look at animal domestication. *Antiquity* 71/271: 149-156.

Postgate J.N. 1982. Abu Salabikh. Pages 48-61 in Curtis J. (ed.), *Fifty Years of Mesopotamian Discovery: the work of the British School of Archaeology in Iraq: 1932-1982*. Hertford: Stephen Austin & Sons.

Potts D.T. 2004. Camel hybridization and the role of *Camelus Bactrianus* in the ancient Near East. *Journal of the Economic and Social History of the Orient* 47: 143-165.

Retsö J. 1991. The domestication of the camel and the establishment of the frankinsence road from South Arabia. *Orientalia Suecana* 40: 187-219.

Roaf M. 1984. 'Tell Madhur. A summary report on the excavations. *Sumer* 43: 109-161.

Saud al Saud A. 1996. The domestication of camels and inland trading routes in Arabia. *Atlal: The Journal of Saudi Arabian Archaeology* 14: 129-136.

Schwartz G.M., Curvers H.H., Dunham S.S., Stuart B. & Weber J.A. 2006. A third-millennium B.C. elite burial complex at Umm al-Marra, Syria: 2002 and 2004 excavations. *American Journal of Archaeology* 110/4: 603-641.

Uerpmann H.P. 1991. Equus africanus in Arabia. Pages 12-33 in Meadow R. & Uerpmann H.-P. (eds.), *Equids in the Ancient World. Volume II*. Wiesbaden: Dr Ludwig Reichert Verlag. Beihefte zum TAVO Reihe A 19/1.

Uerpmann H.-P. 1999. Camel and horse skeletons from protohistoric graves At Mleiha In the Emirate of Sharjah (U.A.E.). *Arabian Archaeology and Epigraphy* 10/1: 102-118.

Uerpmann M. 2001. Remarks on the animal economy at Tell Abraq. *Proceedings of the Seminar for Arabian Studies* 31: 227-233.

Uerpmann M. & Uerpmann H.-P. 1997. Animal bones from Excavation 519 at Qala'at al-Bahrain. Pages 235-262 in Høylund F. and Andersen H.H. (eds.), *Qala'at al-Bahrain. Volume 2. The Central Monumental Buildings*. Moesgaard: Jutland Archaeological Society Publications 30/2.

Uerpmann H.-P., & Uerpmann M. 1999. The camel burial of al-Buhais 12 (Sharjah, U.A.E.). Pages 455-462 in Dobiat C. and Leidorf K. (eds.), *Historia Animalum Ex Ossibus. Festschrift für Angela Von den Driesch*. Rahden.

Uerpmann H.-P. & Uerpmann M. 2002. The appearance of the domestic camel in South-East Arabia. *Journal of Oman Studies* 12: 235-260.

Vogt B. 1994. Death, resurrection and the camel. Pages 279-290 in Nebes N. (ed.), *Arabia Felix. Beiträge zur Sprache und Kultur des vorislamischen Arabien. Festschrift Walter W. Müller zum 60. Geburtstag*. Wiesbaden: Harrassowitz Verlag.

von den Driesch A. & Obermaier H. 2007. The hunt for wild dromedaries during the 3rd and 2nd millennia BC on the United Arab Emirates Coast. Camel bone finds from the excavations at Al Sufouh 2, Dubai, UAE. Pages 133-167 in Grupe G. and Peters J. (eds.), *Skeletal Series and their socio-economic context*. Rahden: Verlag Marie Leidorf GmbH. Documenta Archaeobiologiae 5.

Wapnish P. 1997. Camels. Pages 407-408 in Meyers E.M. (ed.), *The Oxford Encyclopedia of Archaeology in the Near East, Volume I*. New York.

Ward F. 1990. *The first-second century AD graves at Ed-Dur, UAE*. Unpublished MA dissertation, University of Edinburgh.

The emergence of mound cemeteries in Early Dilmun: new evidence of a proto-cemetery and its genesis c. 2050-2000 BC[1]

Steffen Terp Laursen

Summary

This paper focuses on the major transformation in the social organization of Early Dilmun society which led to the emergence of the vast mound cemeteries in Bahrain. The paper examines this transformation on the basis of developments within the transitional mounds of a "proto-cemetery" dated to c. 2050-2000 BC, which has been identified within the greater Karzakkan Cemetery. It is argued that the emergence of the compact Dilmun cemeteries is a product of new, larger and more permanent rural settlements. Further; it is demonstrated that the earliest parts of the cemetery were associated with a characteristic *Radial Wall Type* of mound that can be set in relation to individuals of prominent rank within a low-level village hierarchy. It is demonstrated that seals of Persian/Arabian Gulf Type (henceforth: Arabian Gulf Type) emerge simultaneously with the cemetery and that this type is distinct from the later Dilmun seals. Together with the introduction of a broad variety of imported vessels from Mesopotamia, SW Iran and the Indus, the evolution in local pottery is taken to reflect a fundamental restructuration of Dilmun's network of exchange at the time of the emerging cemeteries. The proto-cemetery is seen as a reflection of a social system which pre-dates the Dilmun state proper that apparently developed after the fall of the Ur III state.

Keywords: Burial mounds, Early Dilmun, social complexity, networks

Introduction

In spite of the paucity of data on social organization in late third millennium Dilmun (c.2200-2050 BC), it remains fairly clear that society was somewhat nascently developed, in terms of social inequality and institutional complexity. Notwithstanding the exceptional evidence of specialization found in the appearance of a sizeable copper workshop on the beach by Qala'at al-Bahrain (per. Ib) (Højlund & Andersen 1994: 467), the general picture is that of modest organizational complexity.

It has recently been proposed that a small number of burial mounds, encircled by outer ring walls, reflect the tombs of the paramount social elite throughout the Early Dilmun period (Laursen 2008: 164). These *ring mounds* appear in two types, which are chronologically successive, and an excavated mound of the earliest type has been dated too c.2200-2100 BC by means of C-14 (Højlund et al. 2008: 152).[2] The spatial distribution and homogeneous size of the earliest ring mounds suggest that the incipient social hierarchy with which they were supposedly associated was composed of fairly small polities organized in a system of relative mutual autonomy (Laursen 2008).

In the last century of the third millennium BC, a virtual revolution unfolds in the organization of Early Dilmun society, as witnessed by expressions of sudden great social complexity in the archaeological record. Some of the most tangible evidence of this transition is the fortification of the settlement at Qala'at al-Bahrain in per. IIa by means of a city wall enclosing an area of 15 ha (Højlund & Andersen 1994: 469; Højlund 1999: 74) and the traces of a large building in the city centre (Højlund & Andersen 1997:15). These new public undertakings are seen as contemporary with the first use of seals, testified by the stamp seals of Arabian Gulf Type (Kjærum 1994: 341). This, moreover, implies that official measures are now taken towards an institutionalization of the advancing trade economy (Højlund 1989:50). From this time (c. 2050-2000 BC) onwards, the paramount social elite are entombed in the much larger ring mounds which now appear exclusively within the Aali Cemetery (Højlund 2007: 25-31; Laursen 2008: 160-165). Together, the evidence suggests the dawn of a new and far more potent political authority, in all likelihood based at Qala'at al-Bahrain, which was ultimately to establish a "dynastic lineage" and exercise its dominion across the lands of Dilmun. Accordingly, the initial late third millennium signs of organizational change are met by evidence of continued ascent in social complexity during the first two centuries of the second millennium (Højlund 2007). This is, for example, manifested at Qala'at in the form of a 12 m wide avenue, flanked by large public buildings, running north-south through the city centre (Højlund 1999: 75; Højlund & Andersen 1997: 16), in new and larger temple complexes at Barbar (Andersen & Højlund 2003: 233-241), in the introduction of the Dilmun seal proper (Kjærum 1994: 345), and in the founding of a trade colony on Failaka, Kuwait (c. 2000 BC). After 1800 BC, Early Dilmun society seemingly witnessed an organizational collapse, but regrettably the events which surround the sudden demise are clouded by a general dearth of evidence in the region.

One of the interesting aspects of the major transformation of Early Dilmun society is that it also left abundant traces in the burial praxis of the common population. Traditionally, the Dilmunites were inhumed in cairn-like

---
[1] This study falls under the umbrella of the Bahrain Burial Mound Project established in 2006 by the Directorate of Culture & National Heritage in Bahrain and Moesgaard Museum in Denmark. The author has a PhD-scholarship at the section of Prehistoric Archaeology, University of Aarhus and this study is intended in the future to form a part of a dissertation.
[2] Mound BBM 20907 has been radiocarbon dated by the AMS Dating Centre at the University of Aarhus (AAR-12218). The probability distributions are as follows: 68.2% probability: 2205 BC (52.0%) 2131 BC, 2086 BC (16.2%) 2051 BC and 95.4% probability: 2284 BC (9.5%) 2248 BC, 2234 BC (62.0%) 2110 BC, 2104 BC (23.9%) 2036 BC (IntCal04) (Højlund et al. 2007:152)

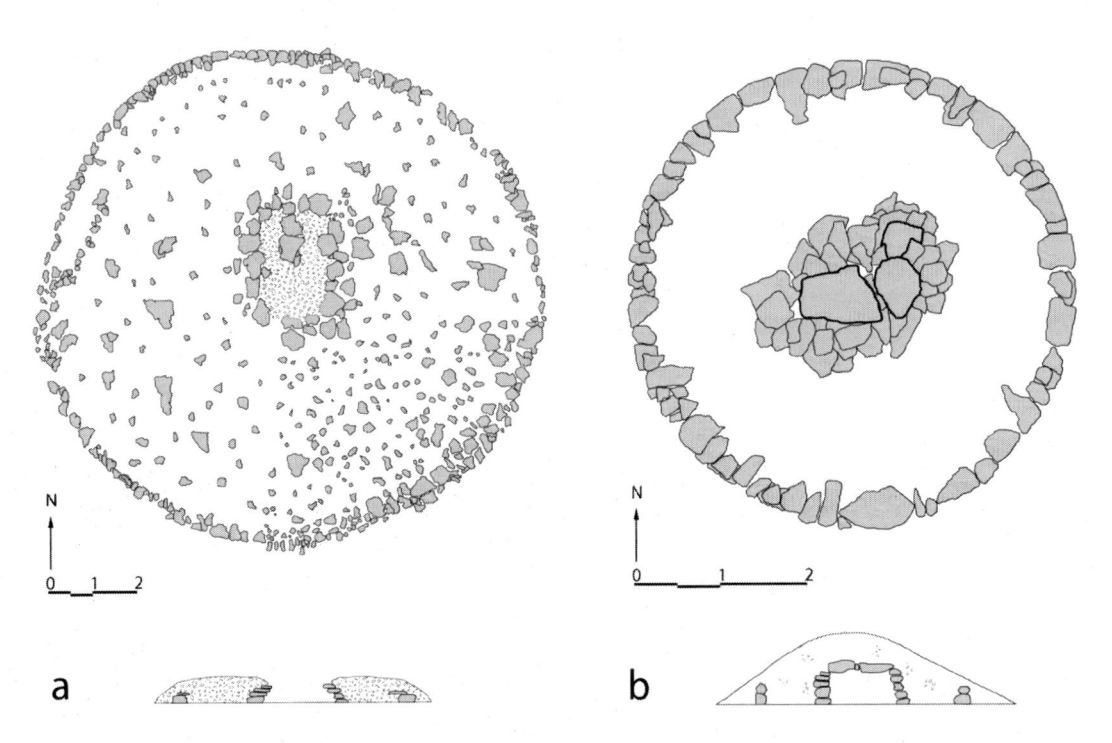

Figure 1. The two major types of mounds in Early Dilmun: mound *a* is an example of the low and rocky so-called Early Type while *b* is an example of the conical and sandy mound of the succeeding Late Type.

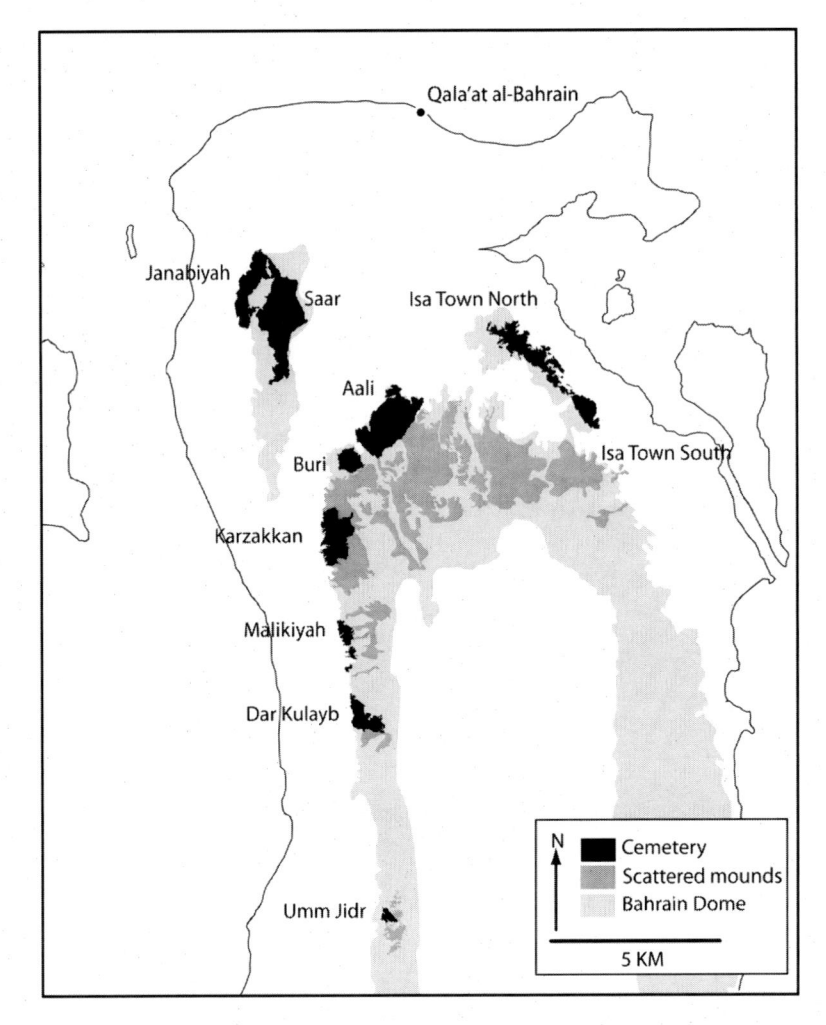

Figure 2. The distribution of Early Dilmun burial mounds on the limestone formations of the northern half of Bahrain Island. The ten compact cemeteries are shown in black whereas the areas with thin scatters of Early Type mounds are shown in dark grey shading.

burial mounds scattered along wadies but simultaneously with (and no doubt as a consequence of) changes in socio-political organization, vast mound cemeteries suddenly begin to emerge.

Starting from the perspective of the emerging cemeteries, this paper focuses on the major transformation of Dilmun society and aims to improve our understanding of the background and character of these developments. In this connection, focus is aimed at chronological studies of selected grave goods in the burial mounds based on the idea that they are particularly well suited for the study of change. The use of exotic pottery in the tombs is highly sensitive to alterations in the networks of trade and thus exposes the establishment of new trade relations in addition to the decline or termination of existing ones. Furthermore, by examining the spatial distribution of the first indigenous stamp seals, which are considered a hallmark of the appearance of public trade institutions, it is possible to correlate their introduction with changes in burial praxis. In this regard, the present contribution on the development of burial customs may also be seen as a contribution to the internal chronology of some of the different archaeological components which are taken as expressions of the emerging Early Dilmun state proper.

Early Dilmun burial mounds in Bahrain

The Early Dilmun burial mounds have, in general terms, been assigned to an early and a late type, which in addition to differences in their construction, are found in contrasting parts of the landscape (Lowe 1986; Cornwall 1943: 231; Frohlich 1986: 49). The Early Type (Fig. 1.a) is normally low and the central chamber is small and crudely built. The mounds, which generally display moderate variation in terms of size and chamber layout, are physically distinguished from the succeeding Late Type by having a flattened top and a characteristic fill consisting of a mixture of large rocks and gravel. Mounds of the Early Type have been recorded on the northern and western slopes of the limestone dome in the centre of Bahrain Island (Fig. 2) in numbers which approximately 28,000 (contra the 17,000 stated in Laursen 2008: 160) and their distribution is generally scattered and governed by the meandering course of minor wadis, the banks of which they seem to follow (Laursen 2008: Fig. 4-5). Occasionally the graves are furnished with imported ceramics such as either a single Black-on-red vessel of Oman peninsula origin or a particular Mesopotamian-type vessel with a characteristic pointed base and ridged rim (Lowe 1986: Figs. 6 and 9; Lombard 1999: Figs. 7-8). Collectively, the imported vessels suggest that the bulk of Early Type mounds should be dated to c. 2200-2050 BC.

The mounds of Late Type (Fig. 1.b) are distinctly different from the Early Type. They are characterized by a conical shape and a better-fashioned central chamber with large tabular capstones, covered with mound fill consisting of gravel mixed with soil. Generally, there is far more differentiation with regard to mound and chamber size than was the case with the former type and this ads credence to the impression of emerging social hierarchies. The Late Type mounds are exclusively found in ten large and compact cemeteries (Fig. 2), each of which occupies a sloping stretch of the limestone dome typically with a western aspect.

Figure 3. Map of the 9,290 burial mounds recorded in Karzakkan cemetery. The mounds "belonging" to the cemetery are shown in black and are mostly of the Late Type, while the scattered mounds in its periphery all belong the Early Type. The two larger wadis which subdivide the cemetery into three sections are distinguishable as wide "empty" trails though the dense distribution of mounds. The three question marks along the western edge of the site denote the hypothetical location of polities each of which occupied a section of the cemetery. The dashed-line square represents the area of investigation while the circular area inside it illustrates the suggested extent of the proto-cemetery. Contours are at c. 20 ft. vertical intervals.

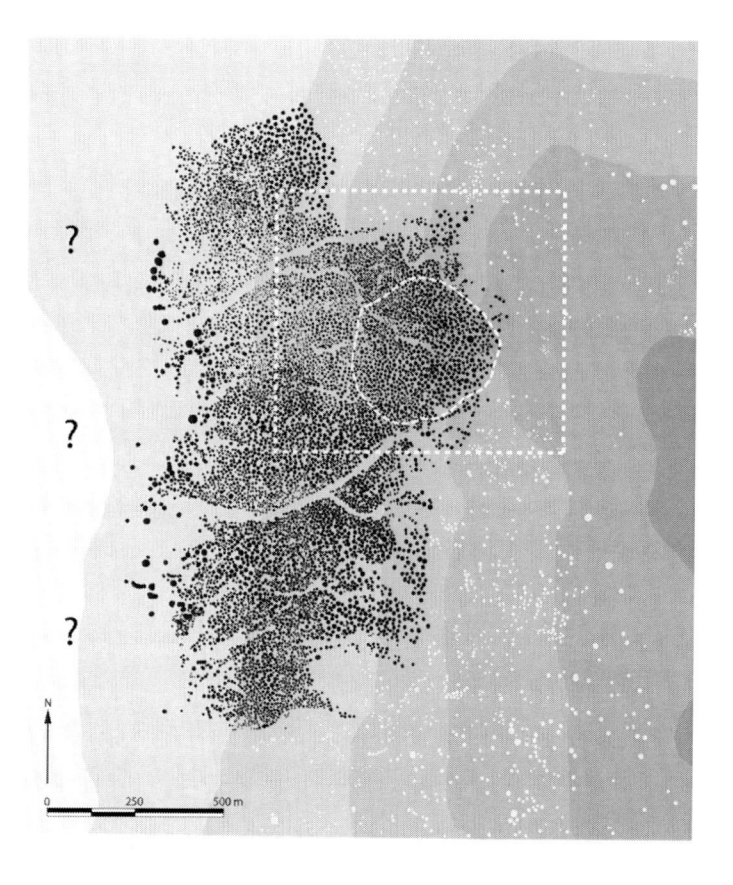

The importance of the genesis of these mound cemeteries for our understanding of the earliest days of the rising Dilmun state proper is emphasised when the abrupt nature of the transition in burial praxis is examined closely. The Karzakkan cemetery is of particular interest in this connection because the site has yielded substantial evidence of where the mounds first clustered (Fig. 3), providing a unique opportunity to monitor the crucial period of change from the micro-level perspective of individual interments.

The Karzakkan cemetery

The Karzakkan cemetery is located in a long strip of cemeteries that runs down the western side of the Bahrain Dome (Fig. 2) and is, with its 9,290 recorded burial mounds, the second largest cemetery in Bahrain, surpassed only by the cemetery of the "royal" elite near Aali. Contrary to the Aali cemetery, and regardless of its imposing size, the evidence suggests that the Karzakkan cemetery should be considered a cemetery of the "commoners" (Fig. 3). Hence, tombs of the paramount elite, such as the previously mentioned ring mounds, are absent and although larger mounds with shaft entrance (a later development), which testify to some social stratification, are abundant along the cemetery's western edge, all excavated examples without exception lack the double-storied chamber construction which characterizes the aristocratic tombs from Aali (Mackey 1929: 9), Janabiyah (Højlund 2007: 42) and possibly Umm Jidr (Cornwall 1943: 232). Given our present insights, it seems reasonable to infer that Karzakkan represents a cemetery for the entombment of a broad spectrum of the ordinary early Dilmun population. It is generally believed that the population entombed in the cemetery originated in a number of associated villages located in the fertile areas with palm gardens west of the cemetery (Højlund 1989:48; Højlund 2007: Fig. 265). The Early Dilmun settlement excavated near Saar (Killick & Moon 2005) undoubtedly provides a useful example of the size and organization of the villages flanking the Karzakkan cemetery.

Two relatively large wadis cut their way down the limestone slope and, in this way, subdivided the landscape of the cemetery into three sections, with the largest one located in the middle. It is highly likely that the wadis, as spatial borders and as potential suppliers of water for irrigation, had considerable structural influence on both the location of the settlements, as well as where their respective subsections of the cemetery were "founded".

In the early 1980s, after the first couple of excavation seasons, Australian archaeologist A. Lowe had become aware of the presence of an area in Karzakkan with burial mounds which were of a transitional character (Lowe 1986: Fig. 2). The area which Lowe treated, under the name B-South, is located in the western parts of our investigation area (Fig. 3). Today, a much larger number of mounds have been excavated in this part of the cemetery and a clearer picture of its development has consequently emerged. On the basis of mound typology and artefact patterning, it is now possible to isolate a fairly limited cluster of mounds which formed what is here labelled a *proto-cemetery* (Fig. 3).

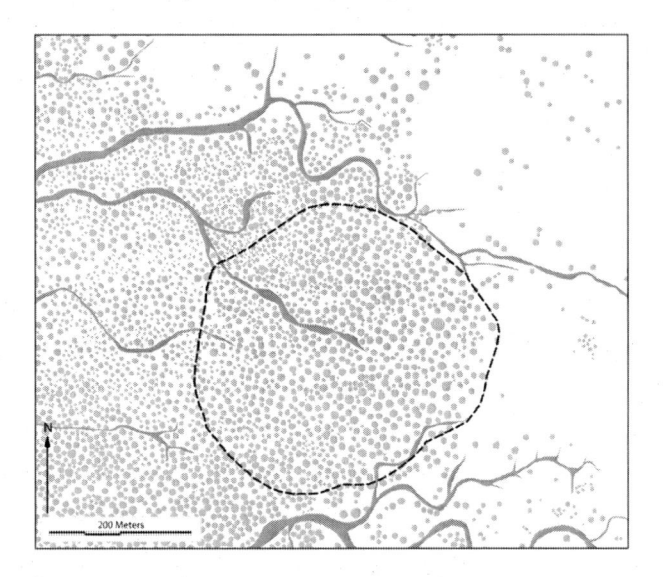

Figure 4. The investigated area showing the proto-cemetery (dashed-line circle), burial mounds and wadis (grey shading).

The Investigation Area

The investigation area is located approximately midway down the eastern edge of the Karzakkan cemetery (Fig. 3). The terrain falls gradually, from the top of the slopes around 30 masl in the eastern part of the area to c. 17 masl along its western edge (Fig. 4). As the inclination eases off, in the eastern end of the area near the high ridge of the dome, the above mentioned wadis that divide the entire cemetery fan-out in the northern and southern ends respectively. The scatters of burial mounds found to the east of the crowded cemetery consist exclusively of Early Type mounds but these also appear as a thin backdrop within the actual cemetery.

In 1980, excavations began to the north of the Karzakkan cemetery in areas dominated by the scatters of Early Type burial mounds,[3] while the first investigations of the cemetery itself did not commence until 1982. Generally, the excavation campaigns were governed by the stages in which roads and housing plots were gradually laid out and incorporated in the new city (Fig. 5). In the investigation area, excavations continued with varying intensity throughout the 1980s and into the early 1990s, moving through the burial mounds in an east-west motion. Concurrent with innumerable other mound excavations in Bahrain, more than 1,100 burial mounds were excavated in the investigation area alone.

The rescue excavations were carried out by the staff of the Bahrain Museum, often in collaboration with teams of foreign archaeologists, the majority of which came from

---
[3] Of these, the major sites are: New City seasons 1980-82; B1-B9 seasons 1981-83; and B-East seasons 1982-83

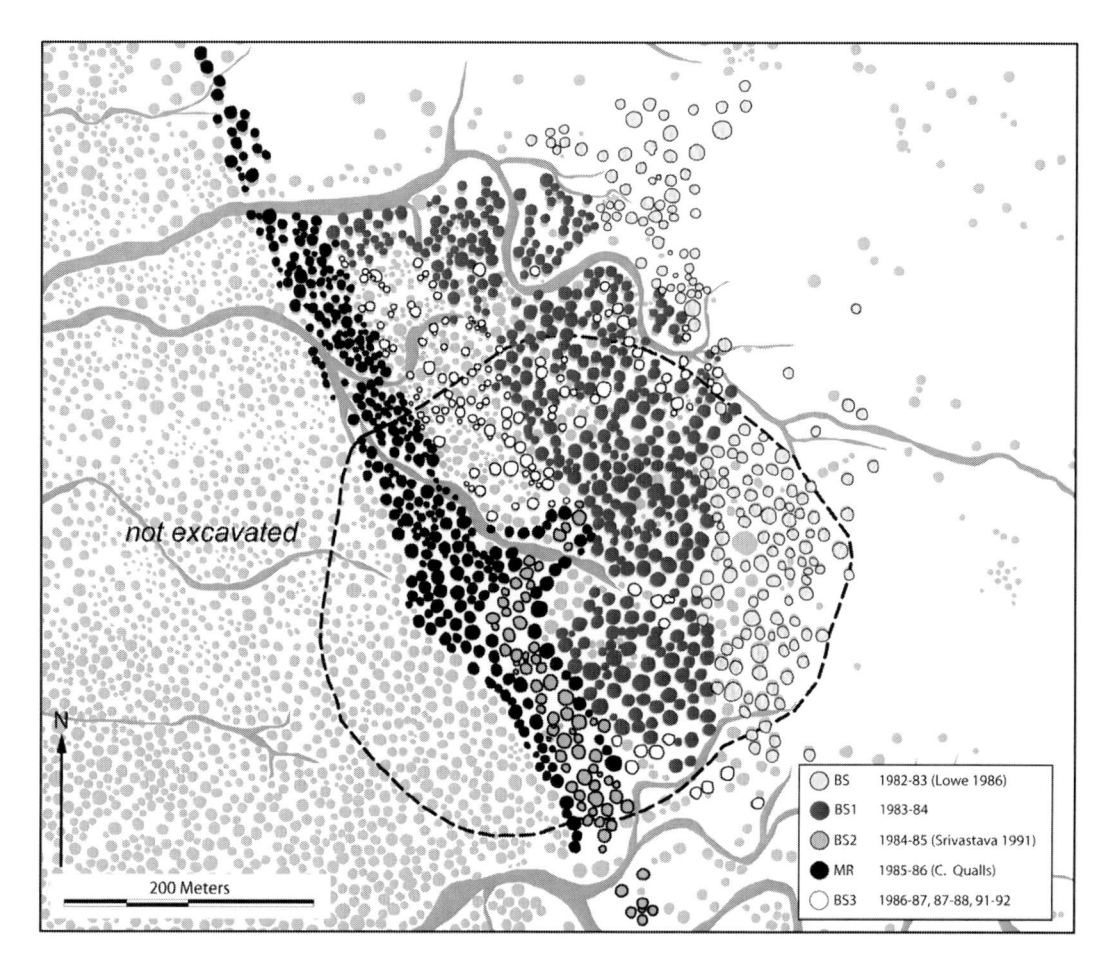

Figure 5. The investigation area. The legend shows the area codes and excavation season of the campaigns which the present author has been able to relocate in the area of investigation. The individual mound number is recorded in a database, where all mounds additionally have been provided with a unique "Bahrain Burial Mound number" (BBM). The proto-cemetery is shown as a dashed-line.

Australia. An Indian expedition to Bahrain undertook the excavations of 70 burial mounds in parts of area BS2 in 1984-85 (Srivastava 1991). This site was located in the transect of *Sheikh Hamad Road* which, still un-named at the time, was commonly referred to as the "Main Road" or MR. In the 1985-86 seasons which followed the Indian expedition the remaining 320 burial mounds in the main road transect were excavated by the staff of the Bahrain Nation Museum under the direction of Dr. C. Qualls.

It now turns out that these two western most campaigns coincidentally ran straight though the oldest parts of the cemetery and that, in this way, they fortuitously provided a 776 meter long and approximately 5-10 burial mounds wide "sample trench" though what in this paper is considered the foundation or proto-cemetery of Karzakkan (Fig. 5).

In the formative years of the Bahrain Museum, proper systems for the recording and storing of archaeological data had not been fully incorporated. As a result, the documentation and artefacts from the extensive rescue excavations in Hamad Town were archived in a less than optimal fashion. At present, it is practically impossible to look up information on a particular burial mound and see what was found in its chambers. Consequently, any distribution plot of artefacts, presented in this paper, should not be regarded as representative of the amount originally recovered. However, in respect to pottery, this problem is less pronounced in our sample trench, in part because of the selected material published by Srivastava (1991) but also because, fortunately, the staff of the Bahrain Museum made drawings of pottery shortly after its recovery in 1985-86. Finally, the present author had the opportunity to document large amounts of pottery, together with all the stamp seals from Hamad Town, during two visits at the Bahrain Museum in 2007 and 2008.[4]

The emergence of the Karzakkan cemetery

Previously it has been proposed that the construction of the Early Dilmun burial mounds and the organization of the cemeteries was pre-planned, well-regulated and

---

[4] I take this opportunity to warmly thank Shaikha Mai bint Muhammad Al Khalifa, Minister of Culture & Information, for generously supporting the Bahrain Burial Mound Project and for allowing me to study the collection at Bahrain Museum. Curator Mustafa Salman and Superintendent Khalid Al Sindi are also thanked for their assistance and guidance during both my visits.

undertaken by a class of specialists within Early Dilmun society (Srivastava 1991: 17). This conclusion is entirely unsupported by the archaeological record. Conversely, the process in which the cemeteries emerged must have been highly dynamic, and as "monumental end-products", the cemeteries cannot be considered pre-planned. Consequently, whatever chronological phases we isolate will inherently constitute partly subjective divisions of little actual meaning to the prehistoric population that generated them in the first place. With this in mind, one should logically not expect that the analytical or interpretive boundaries which we introduce to the final and static burial mound distribution were consciously perceived or respected in prehistory. The growth of the cemeteries was probably governed indirectly by complex social rules in which the near-universal "proximity to entombed ancestors", together with considerations of social rank and class, undoubtedly played a substantial structuring role.

It is important to reflect on these distinctions because when we introduce something like a spatially bounded proto-cemetery, we are on the one hand constructing something which is almost entirely removed from the reality of the past society, while on the other hand we are isolating components of something which potentially was of great symbolic significance to the identity of the prehistoric population. In respect to the former, I argue that no one discrete phase in the formation of the cemetery was ever consciously perceived by the population and that in absolute terms it is thus rather arbitrary. With regard to the latter, one must alternatively expect that when the burial mounds, as demonstrated here, began to form a compact cluster during the "proto-cemetery phase", the mound builders must have become consciously aware of the fact that they had now become distinctly differentiated from the traditional burial custom of the ancestors; with whatever revolution/change in social values this may have entailed. Simultaneously, this conscious notion of a major change must have found support in the changing appearance of new burials, as the flat and rocky Early Type mound was abandoned in favour of the sandy and conical construction of the Late Type mound.

Burial mounds with radial walls

The mounds in the investigation area are predominantly of the Late Type (Fig. 1.a) but Lowe points to the fact that many of these "Barbar mounds" deviated from the normal conical shape by having an unusually flattened top. The area additionally holds a smaller number of Early Type mounds (Fig. 1.b), the majority of which, as pointed out by Lowe (1986: 74), must have encroached on the land prior to the emergence of the compact cemetery.

However, of primary interest, to the identification of the proto-cemetery, is a special variant of the Late Type mound which is recorded almost exclusively in the investigation area (Fig. 6). The defining feature of this *Radial Wall Type* is the presence of stone walls which radiated from the central chamber to the ring wall.

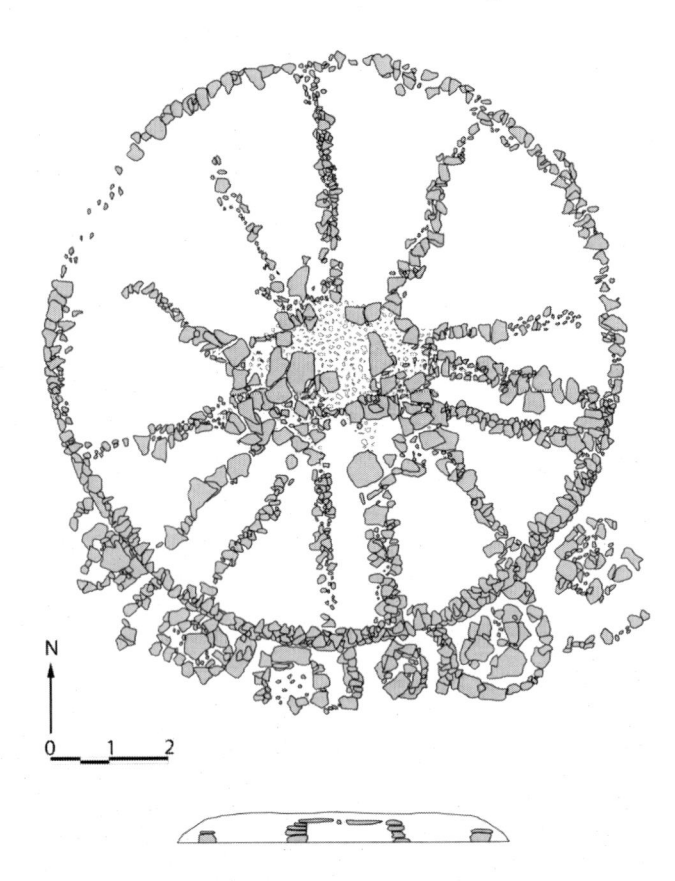

Figure 6. Mound of Radial Wall Type with six subsidiary chambers attached to the southern side of the ring wall. Although the central chamber originally had a cover of capstones it has clearly been disturbed by grave robbers.

The radial walls consist of un-worked stones which were laid in a varying number of courses, forming a low partition wall that, in finished condition, would seem to have stood freely exposed only for a short time before the mound fill eventually covered the central chamber. The radial walls are typically dispersed at regular intervals around the central chamber from which they radiate at more or less the same angle and, while obviously this symmetry was consciously intended, irregular constellations are still rather frequent. The recorded number of radial walls varies from 1 to 13 and the better preserved and fully excavated burial mounds thus outline sun- or star-like patterns, which probably reflect parts of their underlying symbolic connotation. Judging from the available documentation, it would seem that the mound fill covered the radial walls entirely and that, in this way, they were visible only in the process of construction and, in all likelihood, during the actual ritual of interment. A number of excavations further document that both Late Type mounds and mounds of the Radial Wall Type had up to four concentric rings of stones carefully placed on the surface of the burial mound.

The mounds of Radial Wall Type are almost always flattened and, hence, they both resemble the flattened

respectively.[6] Conversely, with minor exceptions, the 5-6 meter interval actually constitutes the minimum diameter of mounds of Radial Wall Type. Statistically, the diameters of the Radial Wall Type mounds are significantly different from those of both the Early and Late mounds and it is thus clear that this type, which peaks with 32% in the 7-8 meter interval, can also be differentiated by its modestly larger diameter.

Spatial distribution of the mound types

The archival problems mentioned above, have affected access to excavation drawings such as top plans and sections. Since all typological re-classifications of burial mounds in this study are based on examination of those very drawings, this has had significant influence on the representativeness of mound types on the distribution map presented below.

However, top plans from the two excavation campaigns in our sample trench could be accessed and this has made it possible to classify all burial mounds in this section.[7] With respect to the excavated mounds east of the "sample trench", however, it has only proven possible to locate documentation on a minority of mounds and, consequently, in this "eastern area" it has only been possible to assign mounds to a specific type in a minority of cases.[8] The burial mounds in the investigation area have been classified according to their respective mound types (Fig. 8), but in spite of the smaller sample from excavations east of the road transect it is still possible to obtain a reasonable impression of the original distribution from the present picture.

It is evident that mounds of Early and Radial Wall Type cluster in the southern half of the road transect, whereas the Late Type mounds are omnipresent but completely monopolize its northern half. It is also clear that the distribution of Early and Radial Wall Type mounds roughly respects the course of the wadis and this provides a clue as to how this early part of the cemetery emerged. One can imagine that before new land was occupied, the mounds were carefully located adjacent to existing mounds in order to fill out the vacant spaces between the wadis, and that the proto-cemetery thus emanated from a more or less commonly shared nucleus. The distribution of mound types in the unsystematically sampled area east

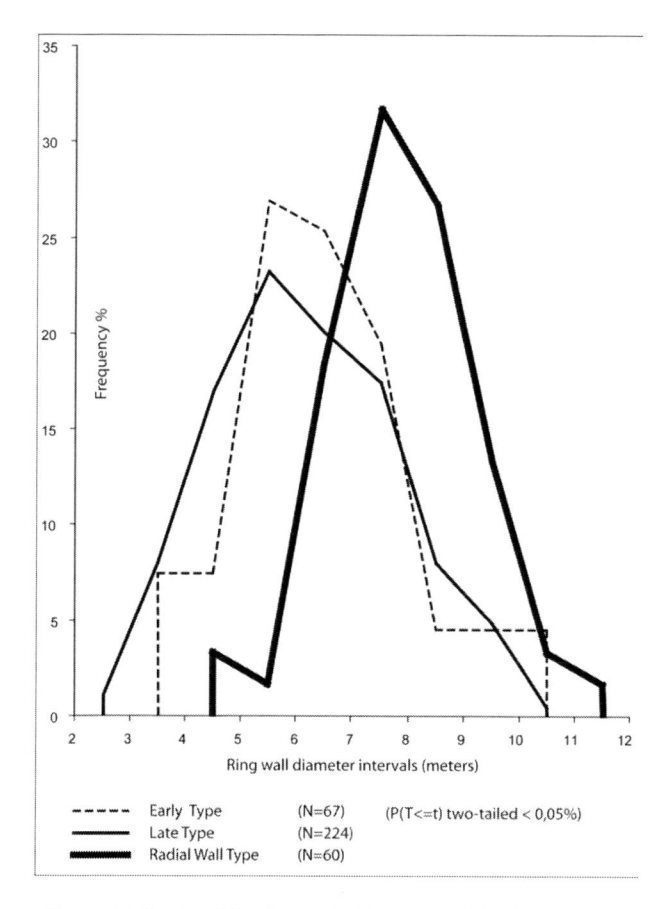

Figure 7. Graph of the ring wall diameters of the three mound types in the investigation area.

Late Type variant which is known from the area *and* the mounds of Early Type. In this way, the low and tabular profile of the mounds with radial walls indicates that they take up an intermediary chronological position between the always flattened Early Type and the proper Late Type mounds of conical shape (Lowe 1986). Mounds of Radial Wall Type are discernible from mounds of Early Type amongst other reasons because the central chamber is covered by a number of cap-stones, as is the case with the conventional burial mounds of Late Type. Furthermore according to Lowe (1986: 74), the central chambers encountered in mounds with radial walls were typically more than 2 meters in length and thus exceeded the normal chamber length in mounds of Late Type found in area BS.[5] In combination with the astral symbolism of the radial walls, the larger chambers indicate that this special type was reserved for individuals of some rank in the village communities – an impression which finds further support in the consistently large diameters of these burial mounds. The ring wall diameters of the three mound types from the area have been plotted in Fig. 7. The Early and Late Type mounds display a very similar frequency in the different intervals and the frequency of both types peaks in the 5-6 m interval with 27% and 23%

---

[5] It has unfortunately not been possible to pursue the question of chamber length variation relative to mound type further in this study because the relevant data were inaccessible.

[6] The variation in diameter observed between Early and Late Type mounds is statistically insignificant at the 0.05% confidence level.
[7] Dr. Sivastava (1991) originally proposes a division of the 70 mounds excavated by Indian expedition into 4 types and 21 subtypes. I have examined the original documentation and reclassified the mounds according to the three simple type definitions presented in this paper. The burial mounds from the Main Road excavation had already been classified according to types corresponding to the three presented in this paper (database held on floppy discs at Bahrain Museum). All plans were, however, inspected by the author and a considerable number were reclassified.
[8] Since only inked copies of the original pencil drawings were used in this study another bias has seemingly been introduced. In this selection process most mounds of Early Type seem to either not have been drawn in the field or at least not to have been inked. Thus when an Early Type mound has been recorded anyway it is typically because it appeared on a top plan together with a Late Type mound.

of the road transect fully supports the observations from the road transect and, consequently, the theoretical borders of the proto-cemetery used in this paper have been defined on the basis of the well structured distribution of Radial Wall Type mounds. Spatially, this cluster corresponds to an undulating local plateau which, in absolute terms, constitutes some of the highest ground in the Karzakkan cemetery. In terms of visibility/exposure from the hypothetical settlement in the low-lying areas in the west, the location of the proto-cemetery constitutes an obvious first choice, which again supports its interpretation as primary to the formation of the Karzakkan Cemetery. The chronological arrangement of the proto-cemetery and the surrounding mounds of Late Type is, however, also clearly expressed in the morphological variation of locally produced pottery found in the tombs.

The development of local pottery in the investigation area

The tombs of the cemetery have yielded a vast range of locally manufactured pottery types; some of which stem from the domestic kitchen inventory, while others undoubtedly represent a selection of more "ritually related" fine wares. A small collection of the vessels from our "sample trench" has been selected in order to illustrate local ceramic evolution and to verify the suggested chronological development of the mound cemetery. This pottery has been assigned to early and late groups respectively (Fig. 9).

To the earliest pottery group belongs a characteristic handmade vessel type that has a very distinctive, painted red-tan decoration on the upper shoulder and neck that usually consists of two horizontal bands which encase one or more horizontal wavy lines (Fig. 9.1-5). Remains of plum slip are frequently preserved and the high unmarked shoulders terminate in a slightly curved neck with an out-turned rim. On a general level it is feasible to assign local vessels with high shoulders to the earliest pottery tradition of the cemetery, e.g. in Fig. 9.6-7. A number of quite diverse vessels with ridging on the entire body is also associated with the proto-cemetery (Fig. 9.8-11) and these are clearly reminiscent of Qala'at al-Bahrain per. IIa pottery (Højlund & Andersen 1994: Fig. 580). An apple-shaped miniature type with a characteristic plum-red slip is also clearly associated with the early pottery group (Srivastava 1991: Fig. 5-10) and it must be noted here that the heterogeneous group of pear-shaped vessels with plum-red slip appear for the first time in the mounds of the proto-cemetery (cf. Lowe 1986: Fig.8). Finally, hole-mouth cooking vessels of types which are well attested from the settlement contexts of

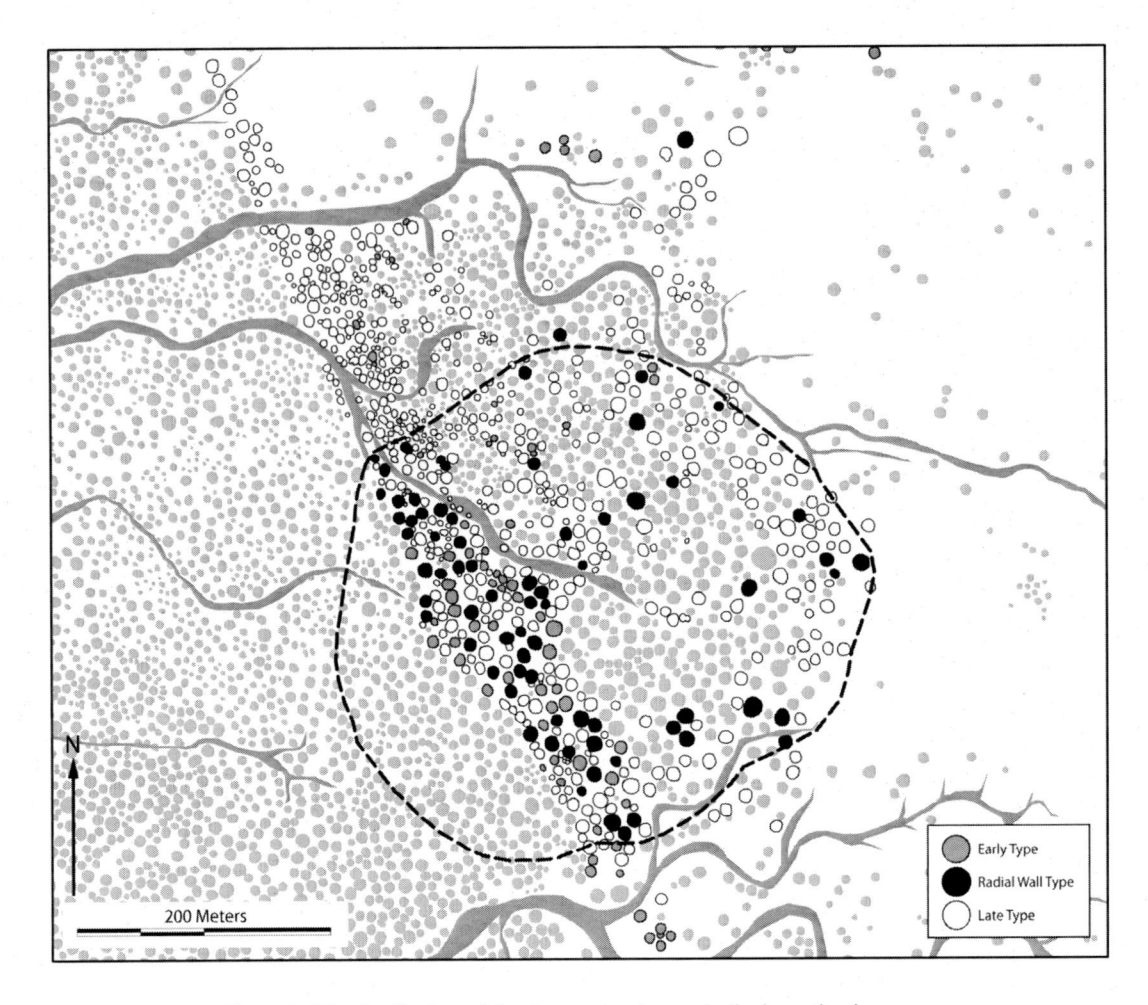

Figure 8. The distribution of the three mound types in the investigation area.

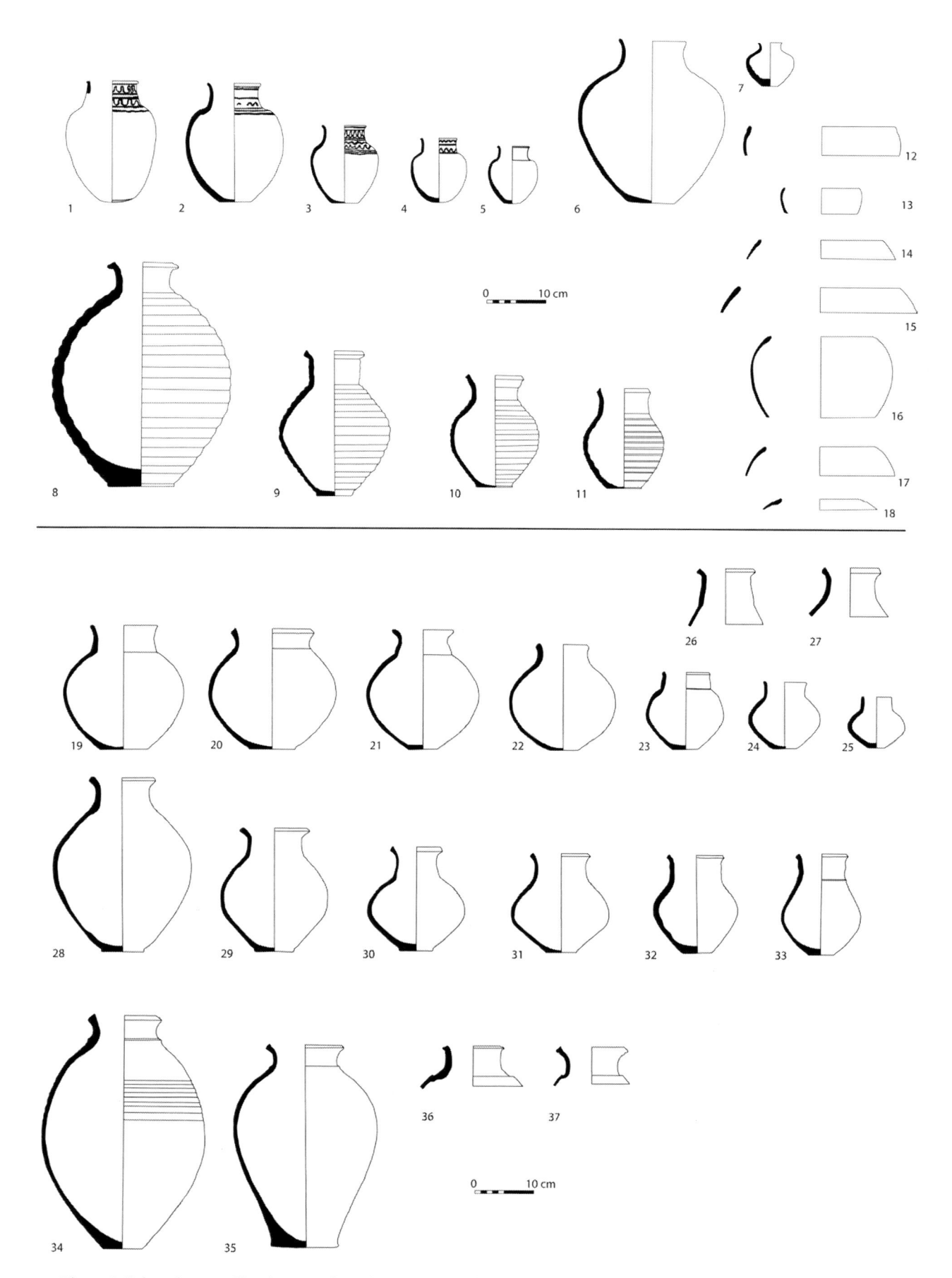

Figure 9. Selected types of local pottery from the campaigns of the *Main Road 1985-86* (C. Qualls) and *BS2 1984-85* (Indian expedition to Bahrain) which constitute the "sample trench" of the survey. Nos. 1-18 in the upper part of the figure are representative of the early ceramic group while nos. 19-37 represent the later ceramic group. Information on the individual vessels and drawings is listed in Appendix 1.

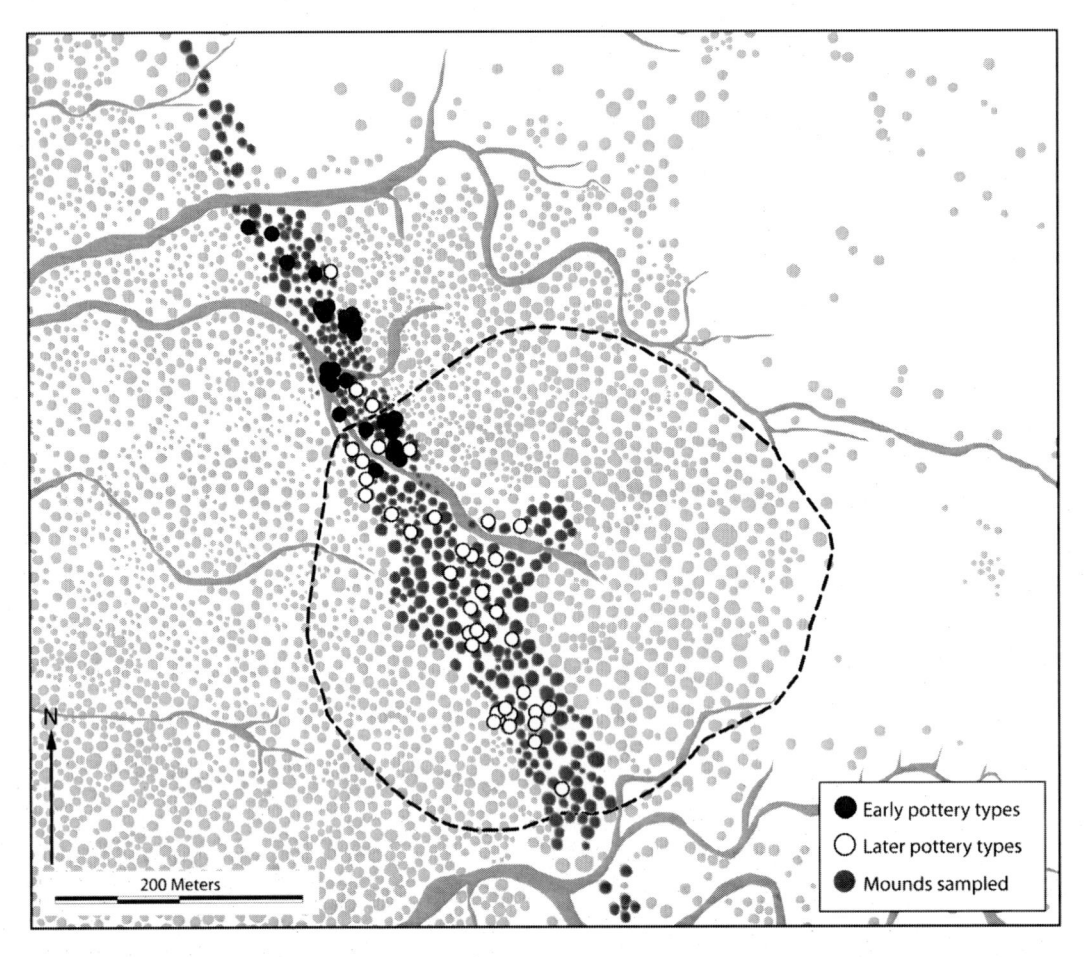

Figure 10. The distribution of the early and later ceramic groups in the investigation area. The *Main Road* and *BS2* mounds which constitute the sample trench have been emphasised with dark grey shading to illustrate the sample area.

both Qala'at al-Bahrain and Saar (Højlund & Andersen 1994: type B13-15; Carter 2005: S1-2) are exclusively found in the proto-cemetery (Fig. 9.12-18) and are not a component of the later funerary inventory. Here, they were habitually deposited near the ring wall or in the upper mound fill; conceivably as containers of food offerings or as parts the ritual kit used in the funerary feast suggested by the frequent discovery of charred bones of butchered and roasted caprids in the tombs (Kveiborg 2007: 149). The vessels were most likely broken deliberately and thus were taken out of circulation because religious taboos prevented the feast participants from removing them from (the liminal space of) the cemetery.

Three very broad types illustrate the variation in the late pottery group which represents local ceramic types that succeeded the proto-cemetery phase and which display an unambiguous development in the pottery tradition. The first type consists of a group of relatively similar jars characterized by a globular body, small base, and short neck (Fig. 9.19-25). Vessels of the second type have a biconical body and a rim that is generally more flaring than on former type (Fig. 9.26-33). Finally, larger vessels with a noticeably marked neck/shoulder transition should be noted (Fig. 9.34-37). As a general impression, it should

be noted that triangular rims seem to become more frequent in burials outside the proto-cemetery.

The distribution of the early and late pottery in the sample trench is depicted in Fig. 10 and, as expected, there is only a small overlap around the wadi tributaries that branch out near the north western edge of the proto-cemetery. The chronological separation of the proto-cemetery mounds finds strong support in the contrasting distribution of the early and late ceramic types. But attention must be paid to the fact that other chronologically less sensitive types, which for reasons of clarity were excluded here, appear throughout the excavated parts of the investigation area.

The Dilmun burial jar with scored rim

One of the icons of the early Dilmun funerary assemblage is the so-called *burial jar with scored rim*. The type displays considerable morphological variation. It is primarily found in association with burials and only to a lesser extent in settlement and temple deposits. At Qala'at al-Bahrain, the type (B73) appears infrequently from per. IIa but gains modest popularity in per. IIb-c. (Højlund & Andersen 1994: Fig. 388). It is also associated with Barbar temple phase IIb (Andersen & Højlund 2003: Fig. 519-525) and Failaka per. 1 and 2 (Højlund 1987: 111).

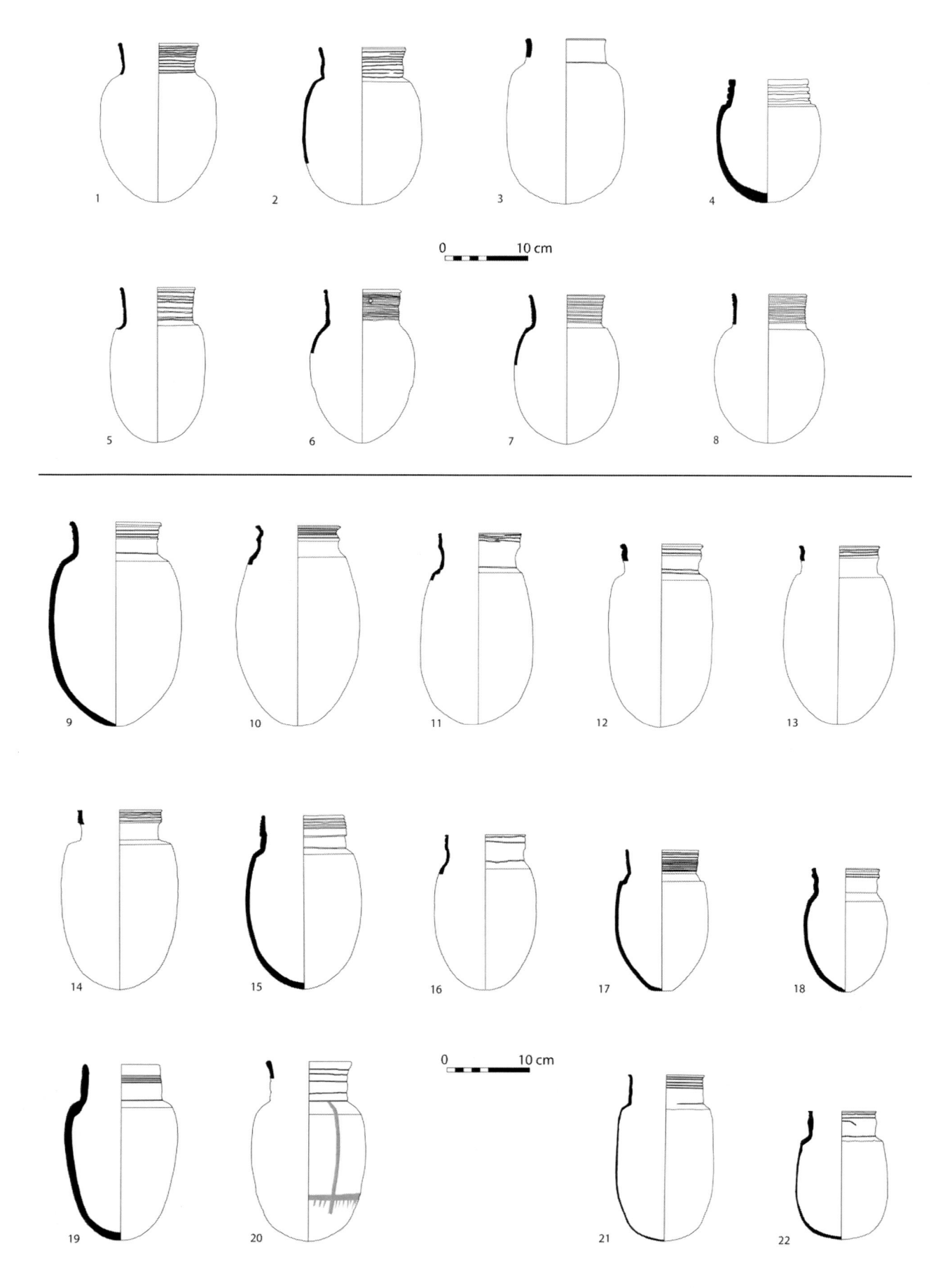

Figure 11. Complete examples of the Dilmun burial jar with scored rim. Nos. 1-8 belong to the first subtype while nos. 9-22 belong too the later subtype. Information on the individual vessels and drawings is listed in Appendix 1.

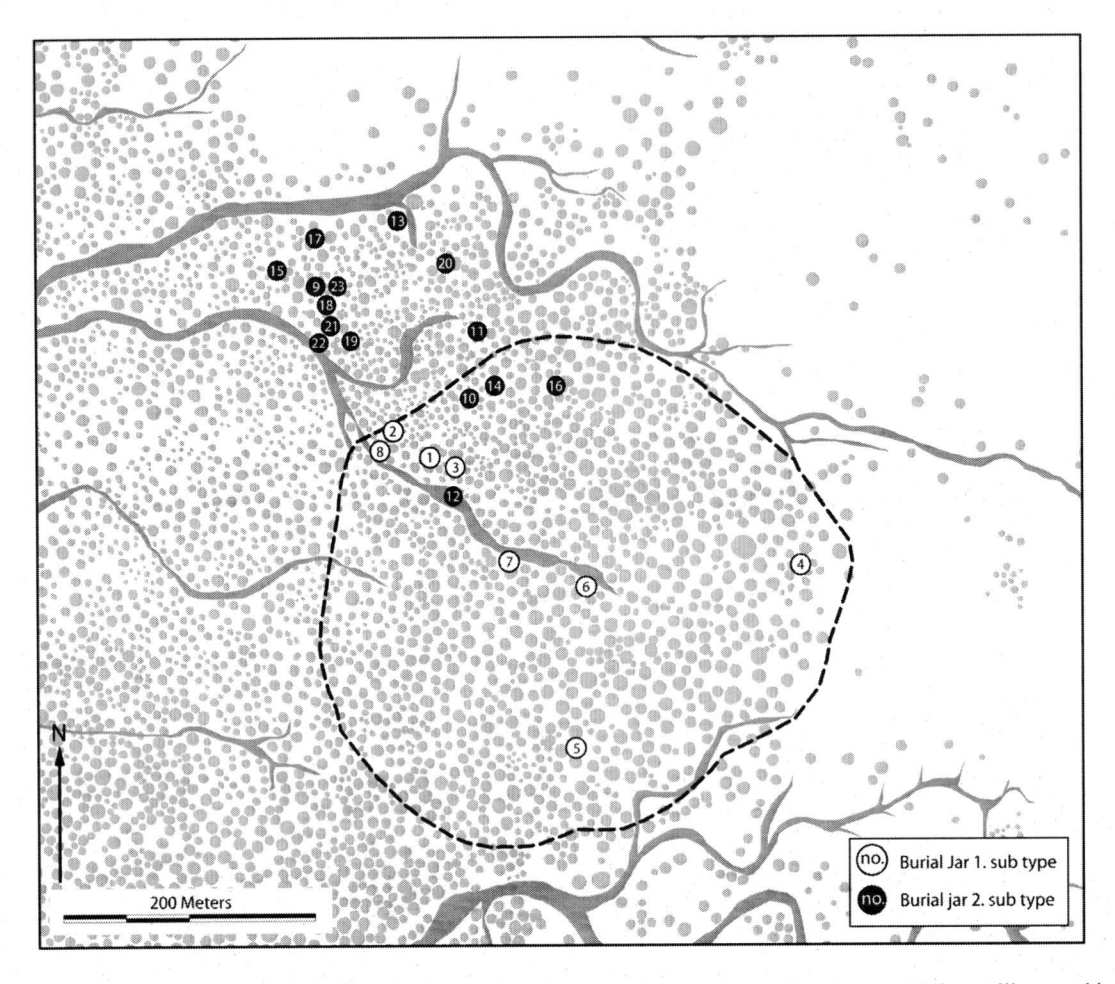

Figure 12. The distribution of Dilmun burial jars with scored rim in the investigation area. Note that no. 23 is not illustrated in Fig. 11 but has been classified to the second subtype on the basis of a photo taken by the author.

C. Velde has, identified the terminal development of the type in the subterranean burials of the Karranah 1 cemetery (Velde 1998: Fig. 3.1-4), in association with collective graves that belong to a post Qala'at al-Bahrain per. IIc phase (cf. Højlund 2007: 13). In connection with the transition to compact cemeteries, it is of great interest that "burial jars" are a novel introduction to the ceramic assemblage and that they are entirely absent in the mounds of Early Type.

The areas inside and outside the proto-cemetery have been used to explore new chronologically sensitive subtypes of the earliest Dilmun burial jars. Twenty three complete burial jars have been uncovered in the investigation area and they have been divided into an early and a later subtype which must account for the morphological evolution of the earliest burial jars (Fig. 11). The first subtype has a short squat body and horizontal scorings along the full length of the neck (Fig. 11.1-8), whereas vessels of the second subtype generally are taller and distinguished from the former by a far more elongated body and by horizontal scorings restricted to a characteristic thickened panel below the rim informally referred to as the "screw-top" (Fig. 11.9-22).

The spatial distribution of the two burial jar subtypes is highly structured and, although the first subtype appears exclusively within the proto-cemetery, it is clear that the type concentrates along its northern perimeter (Fig. 12). The second type is also found along the edge of the proto-cemetery but it clusters north thereof. Among the jars of the second subtype, there are a few examples that have somewhat transitional features (Fig. 11.21-22). This includes the more rounded bases and squat bodies of the former type in combination with the partial neck scoring of the second type which is, however, without the expected thickening of the scored "screw-top" section under the rim. Significantly, all burial jars come from mounds of Late Type and on the basis of their distribution the tentative conclusion may be suggested that burial jars were first introduced to the funerary assemblage after the proto-cemetery had existed for some time and, further, that the first subtype was short-lived and by all appearance, rapidly replaced by a more the "classic" Dilmun burial jar conforming to our second subtype.

The seals

The stamp seals of Arabian Gulf and Mature Dilmun Type, for which the archaeology of Bahrain is so renowned (Crawford 2001: 15), have primarily been linked to the chronology of Early Dilmun on the basis of the stratigraphic excavations at Qala'at al-Bahrain

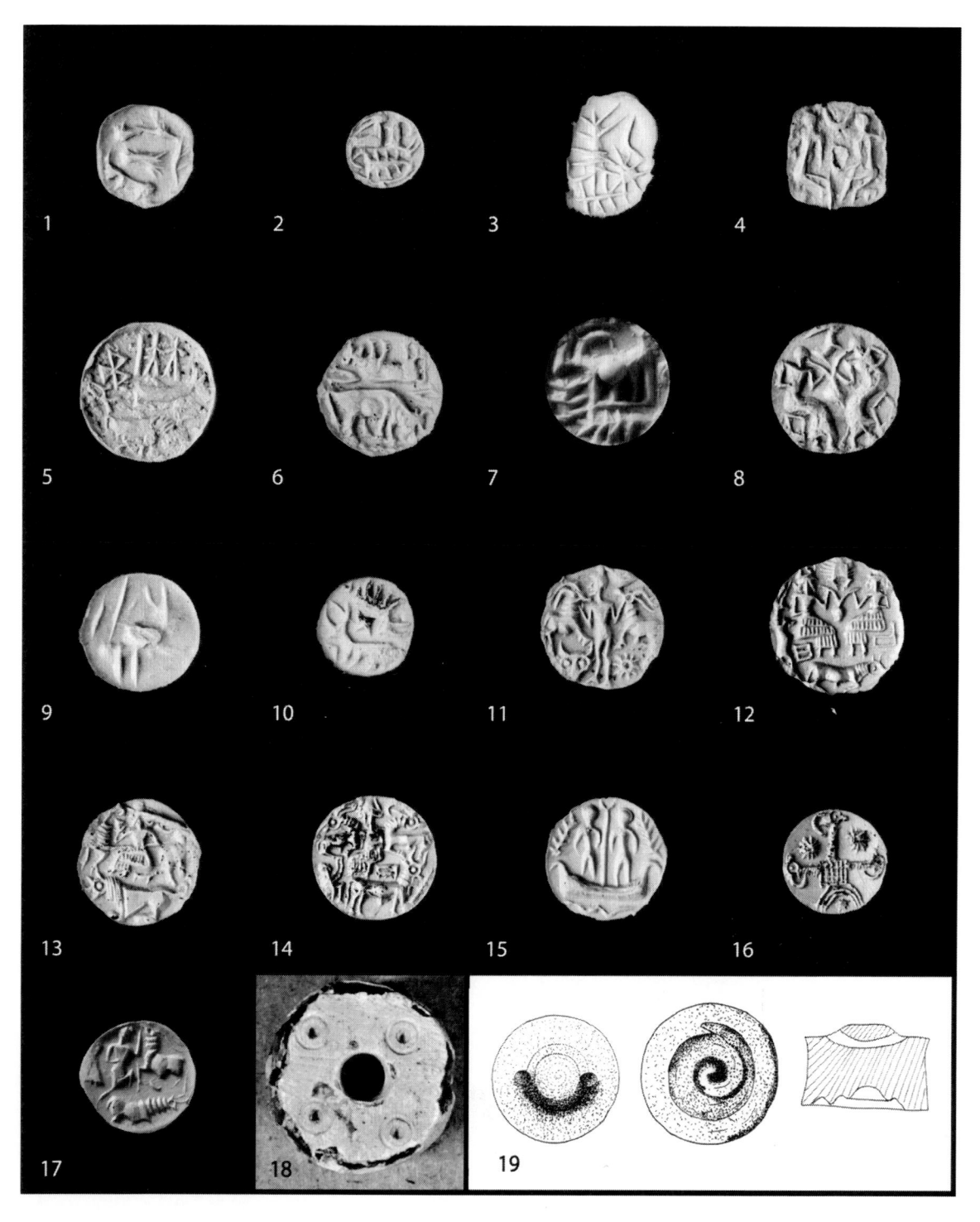

Figure 13. The seals found in the investigation area. Note that seals no. 20 and 21 are not illustrated. Not to scale. Information on the individual seals and drawings is listed in Appendix 1.

(Kjærum 1994: 319-350) and Saar (Crawford 2001: 39), and only to a lesser extent through stylistic analyses of seals from Failaka (Kjærum 1980). The Arabian Gulf Type is, together with the seals of Proto Dilmun Type, dated to per. IIa while the later seals of mature Dilmun Type are seen as emerging at the transition to per. IIb (Kjærum 1994: Fig. 1758). Generally, the present archaeological evidence from the Gulf favours the "Middle Chronology" (cf. Crawford 2001: 20) and P. Kjærum's earliest glyptic style (IA), which is associated with seals of mature Dilmun Type, is securely fixed to the year 1923 BC in the "Middle Chronology" on the basis of a seal impression on a tablet which is dated to the tenth year of Gungunnum of Larsa (1932-1906 BC) (Hallo & Buchanan 1965). An impression of a Dilmun type seal also appears on a tablet from Susa which can be dated to the earliest Isin-Larsa period (Amiet 1974: 109). Twenty stamp seals and one cylinder seal have been uncovered in our investigation area (Fig. 13). Of these, two stamp seals (Fig. 13.5, 8) and the single cylinder seal (Fig. 13.18) have been published previously (Srivastava 1991: Fig. 53; Denton & Al-Sindi 1996).

Seen from an evolutionary perspective, a group of four

heterogeneous stamp seals appear to pre-date the seals of proper Arabian Gulf Type (Fig. 13.1-4). Of these, the first three seals are circular and, though they have a glyptic style similar to that of the Arabian Gulf style, they lack the distinct reverse boss. Rather they are hemispherical with a single perforation. The fourth seal is of square shape with a small perforated square boss on the reverse and thus vaguely resembles the classic Indus Valley seals. However, the depiction on this seal has parallels to the north-west, where "men drinking often from tubes" is an enduring theme in Mesopotamia (e.g. Woolley 1934: Pl.200:101-105). As exemplified in Fig. 13 (nos. 8, 12 and 13), the drinking theme is continuously employed in both the Arabian Gulf and Dilmun seals.

Nine seals have been counted among the Arabian Gulf Type (Fig. 13.5-10, 19). Of these, special mention should be made of Fig. 13.5, which is of the rare type with bull and Indus text, of Fig. 13.19, which is made of shell but clearly imitates the characteristic profile of the Arabian Gulf Type (cf. Kjærum 1994: Fig. 1723) and of Fig. 13.21, which could not be located but is referred to by Lowe (1986: 80) as having been found in a mound adjacent to that of seal no. 13.4.

The cylinder seal in Fig. 13.18 has been counted among the seals of the Dilmun Type (Fig. 13.11-17) because of similarities in the style of its carvings as well as the presence of the familiar "four dot and circle" iconography on both its ends (Denton & Al-Sindi 1996: Fig.1-2).

The distribution of the three types of seals is structured in agreement with the theoretical border of the proto-cemetery and thus strongly corroborates the proposed chronological development (Fig.14). Hence, the four atypical stamp seals of "Pre-Gulf Type" are all found within the proto-cemetery, in close proximity to seals of Arabian Gulf Type that also, with one exception (Fig. 14.7), appear exclusively within the confines of the proto-cemetery. Significantly, this new evidence unambiguously testifies to a distinct chronological separation of the Dilmun and Arabian Gulf Type seals (*contra* Crawford 1998: 87-90), and the abrupt typological shift certainly adds a strong point in favour of any argument which claims the presence of a central authority behind the introduction of the Dilmun seal proper.

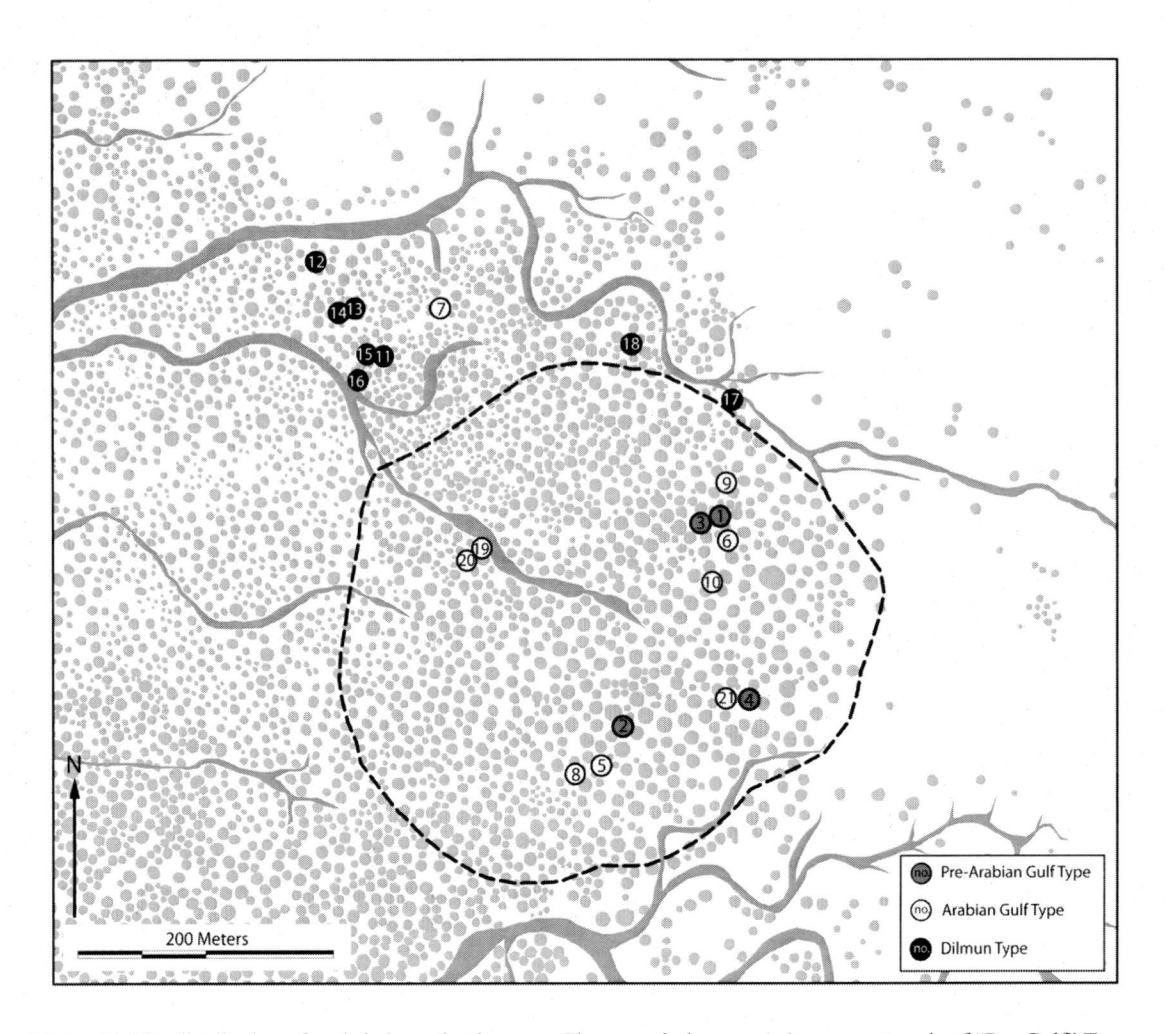

Figure 14. The distribution of seals in investigation area. The grey circles nos. 1-4 represent seals of "Pre-Gulf" Type; the white circles nos. 5-10 and nos. 19-20 represent seals of Arabian Gulf Type; and the black circles nos. 11-18 represent seals of Dilmun Type.

The eight seals of mature Dilmun Type are all found to the north of the proto-cemetery and, while this reconfirms the general chronological pattern, it is actually possible to distinguish a further stylistic subdivision of this group. The seals of Fig. 13 (nos. 12-14) that are found in close proximity exhibit striking similarities in motifs as well as glyptic execution. They depict gods with one "neck curl" wearing horned head-dresses and tiered skirts, seated on chairs above a single animal – either a bull (Fig. 13.12, 14) or a lion (Fig. 13.13). In addition, the goods are flanked by different elements such as horned quadrupeds (*Capra* or *Ibex*). Although these three seals must be fairly contemporary, it is more difficult to determine whether the resemblance can be used as chronological maker in general or if it is the product of three individuals buried in close proximity with similar seals because of affiliation with a particular social group, such as a lineage.

Imported pottery

Prior to the appearance of the Early Dilmun cemeteries, imported pottery from Mesopotamia and the Oman peninsula completely dominated the assemblage from the Early Type mounds. The homogeneity of this early account of Dilmun's overseas relations is, however, contrasted by the wide range of foreign ceramics that has been uncovered in the mounds of the emerging cemetery (Figs. 15-16).

The small Mesopotamian vessel with pointed base (Qala'at M11) that previously dominated the grave assemblage (Lombard 1999: Figs. 7-8) goes out of use simultaneously with a sudden decline in the general frequency of Mesopotamian pottery in the graves. On the whole this vessel type, which appears in Mesopotamia from the Old Akkadian to the Ur III period (see the following section), is only attested from the proto-cemetery in a single case in the form of a related though larger and round-based variant (Fig. 15.1) found in a Radial Wall Type mound (Lowe 1986: Fig. 6). From a neighbouring mound, also of Radial Wall Type, comes a Mesopotamian bowl (Fig. 15.2) with curved rim of a type that is generally assigned to the Ur III-Old Babylonian period (McCown & Haines 1967: Pl. 82.19-20). In Bahrain, however, this type (Qala'at M15) is found at Qala'at al-Bahrain as early as per. Ib-IIa (Højlund & Andersen 1994: Fig. 388), and this renders a date in the first half of the general spectra, i.e. Ur III, somewhat more favourable. Finally, amongst the Mesopotamian vessels from a large mound of Early Type came a small fragmented beaker (Fig. 15.3) originally dated to the Kassite period by Srivastava (1991: 21). Though admittedly the fragment is difficult to date, the overwhelming amount of indirect evidence which points to a date much earlier than the Kassite period should not be disregarded.

With the emergence of the cemeteries, the frequency of the Oman peninsula black-on-red vessels that previously dominated the assemblage declines in the same abrupt way as the Mesopotamian pottery. Three vessels are, at this point, all that testify (at varying levels of confidence) to the continuation of the formerly so persistent ceramic influence from the Umm an-Nar culture (Fig. 15.4-6). The origin of the globular vessel no. 15.4, in particular, is quite enigmatic; it bears open diamonds around its body that are filled with zoological painted motifs including possibly a turtle, an ibex, a goat and a peacock. Although hardly the product of a true Maganite or for that matter Marhashian potter, the vessel is included here because the horizontal lines and chevron hatching suggest influence from the Oman peninsula or Iranian Baluchistan/Kerman. There can be no doubt that the two black-on-red vessels (Fig. 15.5-6) have their origins in the Oman peninsula, and their appearance in mounds of Late Type represents the only authentic Umm an-Nar pottery recorded in our investigation area.

With the emergence of the cemeteries, comes further change as pottery of south-west Iranian origin suddenly makes its appearance in the form of three vessels in the investigation area (Fig. 15.7-9).[9] The brown-on-buff flask (Fig. 15.7) is probably manufactured somewhere in Bushehr, Kohgiluyeh, or western Fars province. Although no direct parallels to the characteristic shape have been located its distinct decoration holds a strong general resemblance to that of Kaftari Buff ware from the Lama Cemetery (Rezvani et al. 2007: e.g. Figs. 50.3-4, 52.1), Tal-e Malyan (*Anshan*) (Nickerson 1983: Figs. 58.a-i, 59.p, 61.i) and Tol-e Nurabad (Weeks et al. 2006: Fig. 3.183.TNP 179 & 3.187, bottom centre). The black-on-green vessel (Fig. 15.8) comes from a mound of Radial Wall Type and mention must be made of an almost exact, though brown-on-buff, parallel from a burial mound in the Aali Cemetery (unpublished). The decorations of both these vessels are, as for the above mentioned flask, generally reminiscent of what Petrie et al. (2005) term "Kaftari-related" pottery and the same west Iranian provenance and parallels as suggested for Fig. 15.7 seem warranted. Another possible Kaftari vessel was found in the Dar Kulayb Cemetery (Carter 2003a: 34-35 referring to a photo in Crawford 1999). The shape of this vessel is identical to Kaftari vessels uncovered in the Tell Abraq tomb (Potts 2000:116-117), and their contexts indicate a date around or just before 2000 BC. The 2200-1600 BC timeframe, which Sumner (1989) offers for the early, middle and late Kaftari phases, is of limited help in this connection but does not exclude a broad date to around 2000 BC for Figs. 15.7 and 15.8. The recent sequence of radiocarbon dates from Tol-e Nurabad and Tol-e Spid (Petrie el al. 2006: Fig. 7.1), show a post 2000 BC date for the levels with Kaftari pottery at these sites. However, Petrie et al. (2006: 179) emphasise that some of the general chronological confusion surrounding Kaftari pottery may be the product of regional variation and chronological development in the Fars ceramic tradition.

---

[9] I would like to express my warmest thanks to Dr. Cameron Petrie, Dr. Lloyd Weeks and Prof. Dan Potts for their generous help in suggesting and providing me with the relevant literature on the Kaftari-related ceramics.

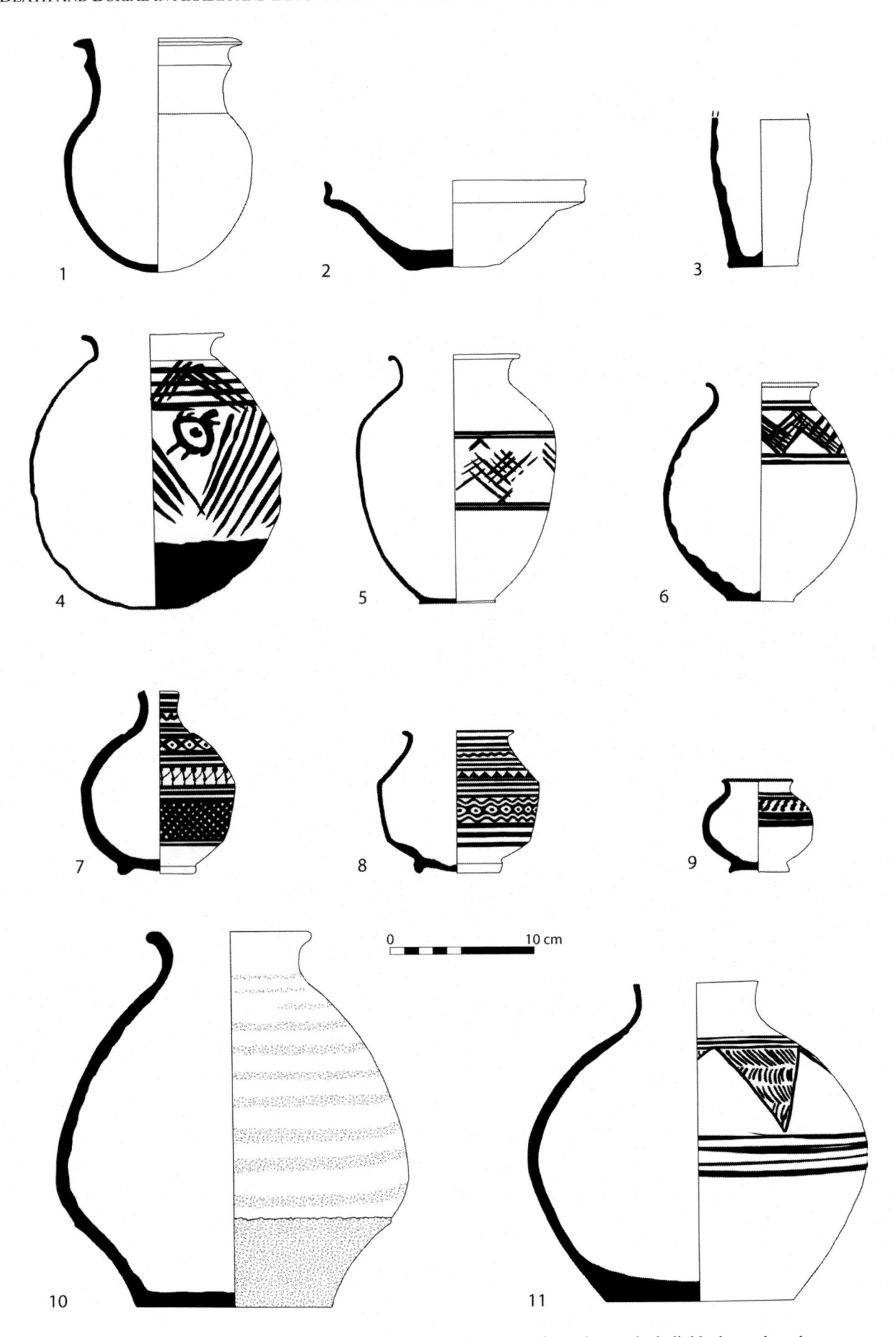

Figure 15. The imported pottery found in the investigation area. Information on the individual vessels and drawings is listed in Appendix 1.

Figure 16. The distribution of imported pottery in the investigation area. The black mounds are of Radial Wall Type. Information on the individual vessels and drawings is listed in Appendix 1.

The small Black-on-grey vessel (Fig. 15.9) derives from a mound of Late Type and it corresponds to Emir Grey Type 2 (Wright 1984: Fig. 3.29) to such an extent that it even exhibits the distinctive exterior surface shaving reported for these vessels (Wright 1984: 132). From eastern Arabia, vessels identical or similar to our exampleare reported from sites including Ajman Tomb B (al-Tikriti 1989: Pl. 43.A), Umm an-Nar Island Grave II (Frifelt 1991: Fig. 120), Hili Tomb B (al-Tikriti 1981: Pl. 81.E), al-Sufouh (Benton 1996: Fig. 123) and Tomb A Hili North (Méry 2000: Fig. 119.6-7). The production centres of Emir Grey pottery have conventionally been sought in the eastern borderlands of Iran (Wright 1984: 149) and, though Type 2 has the widest distribution overall it concentrates in the Bampur Valley (Wright 1984: 139) where it appears in *locus classicus* until phase VI, the end of which B. de Cardi (1970: Fig. 39.392) initially set at c.1900 BC. While the chronology of the Bampur sequence is still controversial, D. Potts (2003: 8) has in this connection recently argued in support of a late terminal date for the related black-on-grey canisters which could be suggestive of a date for this vessel (Fig. 15.9) of c.2200-2000 BC.

By far the most exotic additions to the ceramic inventory, which appear simultaneously with the emerging cemeteries, are those of possible Indus Valley origin (Fig. 15.10-11). The large mould-base jar (Fig. 15.10) comes from a mound of Radial Wall Type and in particular its low centre of gravity and crude join find close parallels in the Mehrgarh per. VIII cenotaphs (Santoni 1988: Fig. 1). Fragments of mould-bases are also known from Qala'at al-Bahrain (Højlund & Andersen 1994: 118-121; E3, Fig. 330, 331, and E7, Fig. 350).

The black-on-orange vessel (Fig. 15.11), which was found in a mound of Late Type to the north of the proto-cemetery, also has some affinity with the pottery of the Indus Valley or Eastern Iran as pointed out by Crawford (1999: Fig. 87). The vessel has an exceptional decoration, consisting of horizontal lines framing pendant triangles filled-in with horizontal rows of brushstrokes, for which a compatible decoration is attested from Tell Abraq on two fragments of similar looking vessels found on virgin soil, just next to the circular tomb (Potts 1994: Fig. 53.4-5), and on a vessel from the Dhahran South Cemetery in Saudi Arabia (Frohlich & Mughannum 1985: Pl. 29.A) that was suggested as parallel to the Tell Abraq fragments by Potts (2000: 73). With reference to sherds from Sibri near Mehrgarh (Santoni 1988: Fig.1), Potts (1994: 618) has further argued that the vessel fragments from Tell Abraq may originate in Pakistani Baluchistan. An unpublished fragment of a similar type of vessel was found at Qal'at al-Bahrain excavation 520 in a layer (520TM) outside the city wall that can be dated to period IIa to IIc.

Chronology

The chronology of the proto-cemetery is of fundamental importance to our general understanding of the emergence of compact cemeteries and the major changes in socio-political organization with which they are affiliated. The well-structured distribution of mounds of Radial Wall Type and the small area occupied suggest that the proto-cemetery was relatively short-lived. Through studies of the development of local pottery within a "sample trench" it has been possible to isolate the proto-cemetery cluster from the neighbouring burial mounds and indirectly confirm the chronological validity of the proposed spatial boundaries.

Seals of Arabian Gulf Type that have been assigned to Qala'at al-Bahrain per. IIa (Kjærum 1994: 341) make their first appearance in, and remain intimately associated with, the proto-cemetery and this readily offers a c. 2050-2000 BC duration for this phase. The fact that Dilmun burial jars are found exclusively in mounds of Late Type, together with the northerly distribution of both subtypes, indicates that they were introduced late in the proto-cemetery phase and first gained popularity afterwards (Fig. 12). Accordingly, the Dilmun burial jar represents an important transitional constituent for the proto-cemetery phase. Only a single rim of a burial jar (B73) is attested from Qala'at al-Bahrain per.IIa. But the type gains modest frequency in Qala'at per. IIb (Højlund & Andersen 1994: Fig. 388), corresponding with its earliest appearance and highest popularity in the equivalent Saar Settlement pottery period II (as type S39; Carter 2005: 255). The fact that these two well established settlement chronologies jointly agree that the burial jar was introduced around 2000 BC is not contradicted by the late appearance of the first subtype in the proto-cemetery phase. Further, a tentative date of c. 2025 BC for the first subtype finds support in the fact that Arabian Gulf seals, which supposedly came into vogue around 2050 BC, appear to have been introduced prior to the first burial jars, as seen in the contrasting northern and southern distributions of burial jars (Fig. 12) and seals of Arabian Gulf type (Fig. 14).

The globular Mesopotamian jar (Fig. 15.1) from a Radial Wall Type mound represents the late development of a type (M11) which at Qala'at al-Bahrain is found exclusively in per. Ib (with a single earlier exception). In the preceding mounds of Early Type, the classic pointed-base version of this vessel type was the exotic burial vessel *par excellence* and in Mesopotamia it appears not only in Akkadian and Ur III contexts – e.g. at Umm el-Jir (Gibson 1972a: Figs. 5 and 42.j), Nippur (McCown & Haines 1967: Pl. 80.18), Kish (Gibson 1972b: Fig. 34.G), Uruk-Warka (Van Ess 1988: Abb. 12.102) and Ur (Woolley 1934: Pl. 254 type 44a; Pollock 1985: Fig. 2) – but also in neighbouring Susa (Gasche 1973: Pl. 16 group 15b). Collectively, it would appear that our morphologically later vessel can be ascribed to the later parts of the Ur III period c. 2050-2000 BC. Parallels to our variant with round base are known from Ur (Woolley 1934: Pl. 253 type 44b) and from Bahrain in Mackay's mound 18 in the Aali Cemetery (Mackay 1929: Pl. VII.15). The bowl (Fig. 15.2), which also comes from a Radial Wall Type mound, finds parallels at Qala'at al-Bahrain (M15) that with a single later exception are found exclusively in per. Ib (Højlund & Andersen 1994: Fig. 388). This renders an Ur III date (c. 2100-2000 BC) plausible, although the circulation of the type admittedly was chronologically much wider (Ur III-Old Babylonian) in Mesopotamia (McCown & Haines 1967: Pl. 82.19-20).

The black-on-red jar (Fig. 15.6) from the proto-cemetery has a number of excellent parallels in the pit-grave Mowaihat Tomb B (al-Tikriti 1989: Pl. 39.D, F; Haerinck 1991: Figs. 7, 9) which can be dated to the later parts of the Umm an Nar sequence, c. 2150-2000 BC. At Qala'at al-Bahrain, Umm an-Nar black-on-red vessels (e.g. U3) are recorded from per. Ia-b and less frequently in per. IIa (Fig. 15.6), which, together with the evidence from Mowaihat, suggests that the vessels should be dated to c. 2100-2000 BC (Laursen 2009: 142-149, fig.8).

The transition to the "post-proto-cemetery" phase is, among other things, marked by the distribution of burial jars of the second subtype; the distribution of which barely overlaps with the proto-cemetery. This distribution indicates that the "classic" burial jar replaced the earlier, short-lived, first subtype around 2000 BC.

Given the systematic replacement in the investigation area of Arabian Gulf seals by those of Dilmun Type, which at Qala'at al-Bahrain are dated to c. 2000-1850 BC, it would be reasonable to expect that our sample holds Dilmun seals with dates ranging from the very transition and well into the 20th century BC.

In conclusion, based on a fairly consistent body of chronological evidence, it would seem that the proto-cemetery emerged around c. 2050 BC and was "populated"/used until c.2000 BC, after which massive encroachment on the area appears to have gradually forced new burials into the more vacant surroundings. At this juncture the enigmatic Radial Wall Type mounds seemingly disappeared, possibly because the transitory social rank system which they reflected had outlasted its function in society.

Discussion

In this paper, I have presented some significant material correlates of the proto-cemetery phase and the following account of this critical juncture has been deduced from the extant evidence. The sudden clustering of burial mounds on Bahrain, which eventually leads to vast cemeteries, can be related to the emergence of a hypothetical system of larger and more permanent villages. Regardless of the peripheral position of these undoubtedly kin-based polities in relation to the central fortified settlement at Qala'at al-Bahrain and its paramount elite, it is nonetheless to be expected that the promotion of new low-level rank systems in the villages was a specific response to the general organizational change within Early Dilmun society. Thus, as the small and scattered ring mounds ceased to be built around 2050 BC, the traditional elite and its relatively flat hierarchical structure appears to have been replaced by a new central authority, as manifested in the much larger "royal" ring mounds (Laursen 2008) and in the appearance of the Arabian Gulf seal. It is likely that a situation arose during these critical times in which the dynamic combination of a thriving trade economy and a disintegrating social hierarchy instigated the redefinition of rank systems and, by implication, the renegotiation of social positions down to a village level. The larger diameters and longer chambers suggest that entombment in mounds with radial walls signifies affiliation with a social group of particularly prominent rank within such a low level village hierarchy. The relatively frequent appearance of Arabian Gulf seals (Fig. 13.5, 8, 20) and exotic pottery (Fig. 15.1, 2, 8, 10) furthermore suggest that the individuals entombed in these special mounds belonged to a more potent economic class – perhaps associated with long-distance trade.

From an archaeological perspective, the proto-cemetery mounds and the artefacts presented offer an unusually accurate account of the situation surrounding the rise of the cemeteries and thus constitute a small but nonetheless precious supplement to our existing picture of when, how and why Early Dilmun society was fundamentally restructured. The synchronous change in the influx of both Mesopotamian and Umm an-Nar pottery support the conventional theory based on economic texts which links the rise of Dilmun to the decline of the Ur III temple economy and the consequent collapse of Magan's monopoly on direct copper trade with Mesopotamia (Oppenheim 1954, Leemans 1960). From the islands along the Emirate Coast and the ceramic sequence of Tell Abraq we get attestations that the maritime network, which formerly had brought the Magan traders past Bahrain, witnessed a directional turn-over simultaneously with the emergence of the cemeteries (per. IIa). R. Carter (2003b) has thus presented a convincing case for the existence of a system of Dilmunite way-stations located on well suited islands, more or less evenly spaced at c.50 km intervals along the coast between Qala'at al-Bahrain and Tell Abraq (Carter 2003b: Tab. 3). Dilmun pottery, generally in small quantities, from these island sites indicates that this system of way-stations was established at the beginning of Qala'at al-Bahrain per. IIa (c.2050 BC). Additional evidence indicating that the longstanding relational asymmetry of Gulf trade at this point in time swung to favour Dilmun over Magan is plainly detectable in the ceramic sequence of Tell Abraq, more specifically in the presence of relatively large quantities of native Bahraini (Grave et al. 1996) red-ridge pottery within the late third and in particular the earliest second millennium levels of this sequence (Potts 1990). Overlying parts of the sealed up/abandoned Umm an-Nar Tomb (that was situated at the base of square OI (7.69-8.00 m.) were multiple levels of Wadi Suq occupation (8.07-7.27m.) that held numerous Barbar red-ridged sherds (Potts 1990: 56-65). In conjunction with the fact that Wadi Suq pottery did not replace the previously frequent Umm an Nar Black-on-red pottery in Bahrain, the evidence from Tell Abraq suggests that it was now merchants from Dilmun who conducted business *in persona* at this vital Magan port.

The synchronism between the major reorganization in Dilmun and the decline in Magan is further detectable in the remarkable discovery at Tell Abraq of several Dilmun ceramic imports and two seal imitations from the circular tomb. These finds, which constitute perfect parallels to some of the material correlates of the proto-cemetery phase, include a Dilmun burial jar (Potts 2000: 120) equivalent to the first subtype, which corresponds accurately to the later half of proto-cemetery phase (c. 2025-2000 BC) at Karzakkan. In this connection, mention should be made of two Dilmun burial jars of the first subtype reported from the Unar 2 tomb, Ra's al-Khaimah (Carter 2002: Fig. 4.6) and from Bandar-e Taheri, south-west Bushehr, Iran (Carter 2003a: 35), respectively.

Also included in the ceramics from the Tell Abraq Tomb are three Dilmun red-slipped, pear-shaped vessels (Potts 2000: Figs. p. 69, 107, 120) of a type that also first appeared with the emerging cemeteries (c. 2050 BC). Finally, an ivory seal has been found (Potts 2000: 122), which clearly imitates the Arabian Gulf Type that is also intimately connected with the proto-cemetery phase. The Dilmun objects from the Tell Abraq tomb exhibit close contemporaneity with the emerging cemeteries in Bahrain and, seen in conjunction with the synchronous appearance of Dilmunite way-stations along the Emirates coast, indicate unmistakably a directional shift in the relation between these two vital nodes in the regional network.

Though the cuneiform texts from Mesopotamia offer a tempting supplement to the archaeological evidence of the changes in the Gulf region, great caution must be exercised owing to the difficulties which are connected with the calibration of the two "independent" chronologies. Consequently, the following thoughts on the historical situation are hypothetical and only represent one among several plausible scenarios.

From a tablet dated to 2028 BC (1st year of Ibbi-Sin), we hear of a business venture destined for Dilmun and, thus, get the first solid indication that Magan's monopoly on the Gulf trade during the third dynasty of Ur was weakening (UET III 1507). There is a broad scholarly consensus that the decline of the Ur III state, and its consequent downfall under Ibbi-Sin (2004 BC), was brought about by the emergence of the Shimashkians in western Iran, most notably Kindattu (Steinkeller 2007).

New relations between Dilmun and western Iran in the period of surmounting opposition in Anshan and Shimashki in late Ur III times could be indicated by the sudden appearance of possible Kaftari-related pottery during our proto-cemetery phase. It would be tempting to view these objects as an early indication of the relations which Dilmun appears to have had with, for example, Liyan and Susa during the first third of the second millennium BC (Potts 1990: 228). This interpretation is by no means contradicted by the fact that Indus Valley pottery and seals with Indus text simultaneously make their first appearance at this juncture, indicating that the gateways to the east had also swung wide open. In connection with the changes in the Gulf trade, it is also significant that around 2000 BC Anshan and Shimashki came to constitute a geopolitical wedge between southern Mesopotamia and Marhashi that was, effectively, to put and end to 500 years of mutual diplomacy between these states (Steinkeller 2006; Potts 2002). If one takes Magan's strong cultural and no doubt political and economic affiliation with Marhashi during the Umm an-Nar period (Potts 2005; Steinkeller 2006) into consideration, it would then be reasonable to expect that the inter-state diplomacy not only protected Babylonia's eastern flank and strengthened Marhashi as suggested by Steinkeller (2006:11) but also ensured the stable transhipment of goods from Magan – most importantly copper – to the cities of the Ur III state. If this in fact was so, then we are offered another essential reason why post-Ur III Magan appears to have been left politically decapitated and relationally isolated and why the Oman peninsula failed to re-establish direct trade with post-Ur III Babylonia in the early Wadi Suq period. Potentially, the collapse of Marhashi's diplomacy with the Ur III state was one of the strongest factors contributing to the opening of the Gulf trade. This opening was, in turn, the main reason why the semi-complex Dilmun society c. 2050-2000 BC was able to more or less completely take over Magan's previous position after 2000 BC.

The standardized Dilmun Type seal, which came to symbolize Bahrain's final consolidation of her newly found status as hub of the Gulf trade, could very well have appeared shortly after the fall of the third dynasty of Ur III, as a response to the vacuum caused by its collapse. Be that as it may, the organizational level of early Dilmun society clearly rose in the second millennium BC, beyond the transitory phase of the proto-cemetery and its burial mounds with radial walls discussed in this paper.

Acknowledgements

I would like to thank the following for various support and assistance without which this study could not have been completed: Shaikha Mai bint Muhammad Al Khalifa, Carolyn & Scott Dollar, Rob Carter, Anna S. Hilton, Flemming Højlund, Dushanthi Jayawardena, Niels Nørkjær Johannsen, Poul Kjaerum, Katie Lindstrom, Anthony Lowe, Sophie Méry, Cameron Petrie, Daniel T. Potts, Mustafa Salman, Danielle Simpson, Khalid al-Sindi, Robyn Stocks, and Lloyd Weeks.

Appendix 1. The rows refer to the individual artefacts presented in Figures 9, 11, 13 and 15 while the columns hold general information. The "A no." is the artefact numbering system used in the Bahrain Museum (2009). The "BBM no." refers to the unique Bahrain Burial Mound number each Early Dilmun mound has been given in the Bahrain Burial Mound project – GIS.

Fig. 9	A no.	Ware	Chamber	Mound no.	Area	Season	BBM no.	Mound Type	Drawing
no. 1	4472	Red ware	N/A	1556	BS	1982-83	20,549	N/A	Anna S. Hilton
no. 2	5722	Red ware	Main	238	Main road	1985-86	19,806	Late	Anna S. Hilton
no. 3	5614	Red ware	Main	275	Main road	1985-86	19,386	Late	Anna S. Hilton
no. 4	5504	Barbar ware	Main	287	Main road	1985-86	18,828	Late	Anna S. Hilton
no. 5	N/A	Red ware	Main	1804	BS2	1984-54	19,000	Radial Wall	Srivastava 1991 no.4
no. 6	MR1258	Red ware	Main	287	Main road	1985-86	18,828	Late	Bahrain Museum
no. 7	MR1291	Barbar ware	Main	244	Main road	1985-86	19,939	Early	Bahrain Museum
no. 8	MR1398	N/A	Main	296	Main road	1985-86	18,677	Late	Bahrain Museum
no. 9	MR775	N/A	Main	186	Main road	1985-86	20,179	Late	Bahrain Museum
no. 10	MR644	N/A	SC3	155	Main road	1985-86	20,637	Late	Bahrain Museum
no. 11	MR1265	Barbar ware	SC1	287	BS2	1984-54	18,828	Late	Bahrain Museum
no. 12	N/A	Red ware	Outside	1413	BS2	1984-54	19,559	Radial Wall	Srivastava 1991 no.29
no. 13	MR1115	Barbar ware	SC1	243	Main road	1985-86	19,973	Early	Bahrain Museum
no. 14	N/A	Red ware	Outside	1423	BS2	1984-54	19,526	Radial Wall	Srivastava 1991 no.26
no. 15	MR749	Red ware	Main	195	Main road	1985-86	20,160	Radial Wall	Bahrain Museum
no. 16	N/A	Red ware	Main	1677	BS2	1984-54	19,323	Late	Srivastava 1991 no.25
no. 17	N/A	Red ware	Outside	1414	BS2	1984-54	19,653	Late	Srivastava 1991 no.27
no. 18	N/A	Red ware	Outside	1423	BS2	1984-54	19,526	Radial Wall	Srivastava 1991 no.28
no. 19	MR430	N/A	Main	81	Main road	1985-86	21,660	Late	Bahrain Museum
no. 20	MR250	Red ware	Main	114	Main road	1985-86	21,197	Late	Bahrain Museum
no. 21	MR762	Red-brown ware	SC	150	Main road	1985-86	20,721	Early	Bahrain Museum
no. 22	MR333	Red-brown ware	Main	136	Main road	1985-86	20,881	Late	Bahrain Museum
no. 23	MR654	Brown ware	Main	163	Main road	1985-86	20,593	Late	Bahrain Museum
no. 24	MR660	Brown ware	Main	169	Main road	1985-86	64,571	Late	Bahrain Museum
no. 25	MR409	Brown ware	SC1	154	Main road	1985-86	20,774	Late	Bahrain Museum
no. 26	MR803	Red ware	Main	146	Main road	1985-86	20,851	Late	Bahrain Museum
no. 27	MR344	Red ware	Main	43	Main road	1985-86	22,075	Late	Bahrain Museum
no. 28	MR421	Red ware	Main	81	Main road	1985-86	21,660	Late	Bahrain Museum
no. 29	MR233	N/A	Main	60	Main road	1985-86	21,981	Late	Bahrain Museum
no. 30	MR802	N/A	Main	146	Main road	1985-86	20,851	Late	Bahrain Museum
no. 31	MR86	Red ware	Main	74	Main road	1985-86	21,732	Late	Bahrain Museum
no. 32	MR486	Tan Ware	Main	97	Main road	1985-86	21,547	Late	Bahrain Museum

	A no.	Ware / Seal Type	Chamber	SC	Mound no.	Area	Season	BBM no.	Mound Type	Drawing
no. 33	MR373	Red ware		Main	21	Main road	1985-86	22,354	Late	Bahrain Museum
no. 34	MR251	Barbar ware		Main	114	Main road	1985-86	22,354	Late	Bahrain Museum
no. 35	MR85	Red ware		Main	74	Main road	1985-86	21,732	Late	Bahrain Museum
no. 36	MR6	Red ware		Outside	30	Main road	1985-86	22,303	Late	Bahrain Museum
no. 37	MR527	Yellow Ware		Main	113	Main road	1985-86	21,143	Late	Bahrain Museum
Fig. 11	**A no.**	**Ware**	**Chamber**		**Mound no.**	**Area**	**Season**	**BBM no.**	**Mound Type**	**Drawing**
no. 1	11430	Orange red ware	Main		158	Main road	1985-86	20,667	Late	Anna S. Hilton
no. 2	5818	Orange red ware	Main		142	Main road	1985-86	20,863	Late	Anna S. Hilton
no. 3	4488	Orange red ware	Main		62	BS3-A	1987-88	20,596	Late	Danielle Simpson
no. 4	4720	Plum slip, orange red ware	Main		1580	BS	1982-83	19,966	N/A	Steffen T. Laursen
no. 5	5373	Orange red ware	Main		1793	BS2	1984-85	18,742	Late	Anna S. Hilton
no. 6	5870	Orange red ware	Main		11	BS3-B	1991	19,822	N/A	Anna S. Hilton
no. 7	4925	Orange red ware	Main		256	Main road	1986-87	19,991	Late	Anna S. Hilton
no. 8	5810	Orange red ware	Main		A154	Main road	1995-96	64,575	Late	Anna S. Hilton
no. 9	5805	Orange red ware	Main		51	Main road	1985-86	21,957	Late	Bahrain Museum
no. 10	9156	Orange red ware	Main		A107	BS3-A	1991-92	21,132	N/A	Steffen T. Laursen
no. 11	5876	Orange red ware	SC3		157	BS3-A	1991	21,672	Late	Steffen T. Laursen
no. 12	4506	Orange red ware	Main		22	BS3-A	1987-88	20,390	Late	Danielle Simpson
no. 13	4934	Orange red ware	Main		893	BS1	1984-85	22,495	Late	Steffen T. Laursen
no. 14	5961	Orange red ware	Main		114	BS3-A	1991-92	21,245	Late	Steffen T. Laursen
no. 15	5807	Orange red ware	Main		39	Main road	1985-86	22,128	Late	Steffen T. Laursen
no. 16	5869	Orange red ware	Main		25	BS3-C	1991	21,240	Late	Steffen T. Laursen
no. 17	5799	Orange red ware	Main		33	Main road	1985-86	22,369	Late	Bahrain Museum
no. 18	5809	Orange red ware	Main		58	Main road	1985-86	21,872	Late	Bahrain Museum
no. 19	5798	Purple slip, buff ware	Main		84	Main road	1985-86	21,599	Late	Anna S. Hilton
no. 20	4933	Purple slip, buff ware	SC2		850	BS1	1984-85	22,178	Late	Anna S. Hilton
no. 21	5796	Orange red ware	Main		73	Main road	1985-86	21,673	Late	Steffen T. Laursen
no. 22	4930	Orange red ware	Main		87	Main road	1985-86	21,604	Late	Anna S. Hilton
Fig. 13	**A no.**	**Seal Type**	**Chamber**		**Mound no.**	**Area**	**Season**	**BBM no.**	**Mound Type**	**Foto/Drawing**
no. 1	N/A	Pre-Arabian Gulf	N/A		1519	BS1	1983-84	20,441	N/A	Poul Kjærum
no. 2	N/A	Arabian Gulf	Main		1657	BS1	1983-84	19,081	Late	Poul Kjærum
no. 3	N/A	Arabian Gulf	N/A		1501	BS1	1983-84	20,393	N/A	Poul Kjærum
no. 4	N/A	Pre-Arabian Gulf	Main		1691	BS	1982-83	19,249	Late	Poul Kjærum
no. 5	N/A	(Indus Text) Arabian Gulf	Main		1757	BS2	1984-85	18,839	Radial Wall	Poul Kjærum

	A no.	Ware	Chamber	Mound no.	Area	Season	BBM no.	Mound Type	Drawing
no. 6	N/A	Arabian Gulf	Main	1518	BS1	1983-84	20,362	N/A	Poul Kjærum
no. 7	13841	Arabian Gulf	Main	203	BS3-A	1991-92	22,010	Late	Martin Ravn
no. 8	N/A	Arabian Gulf	Main	1812	BS2	1984-85	18,789	Radial Wall	Poul Kjærum
no. 9	N/A	Pre-Arabian Gulf	N/A	1526	BS1	1983-84	20,673	N/A	Poul Kjærum
no. 10	N/A	Arabian Gulf	N/A	1492	BS	1982-83	20,038	N/A	Poul Kjærum
no. 11	17572	Dilmun	N/A	81	Main road	1985-86	21,660	Late	Poul Kjærum
no. 12	N/A	Dilmun	Main	26	Main road	1985-86	22,351	Late	Poul Kjærum
no. 13	N/A	Dilmun	Main	61	Main road	1985-86	22,009	Late	Poul Kjærum
no. 14	N/A	Dilmun	Main	60	Main road	1985-86	21,981	Late	Poul Kjærum
no. 15	N/A	Dilmun	Main	79	Main road	1985-86	21,694	Late	Poul Kjærum
no. 16	N/A	Dilmun	Sub 1	94	Main road	1985-86	75,646	Late	Poul Kjærum
no. 17	17642	Dilmun	N/A	19	BS3	1986-87	21,333	N/A	Martin Ravn
no. 18	11754	Dilmun (Cylinder)	Main	20	BS3-D	1991-92	21,739	N/A	Poul Kjærum
no. 19	N/A	Arabian Gulf (shell)	Main	193	Main road	1985-86	20,235	Late	Bahrain Museum
no. 20	17658	Arabian Gulf	Main	195	Main road	1985-86	20,160	Radial Wall	Poul Kjærum
no. 21	N/A	Arabian Gulf ?	N/A	near mound 1691	BS	1982-83	?	Late	N/A
Fig. 15	A no.	Ware	Chamber	Mound no.	Area	Season	BBM no.	Mound Type	Drawing
no.1	6153	Greenish buff	Main	1,684	BS	1982-83	19,066	Radial Wall	Steffen T. Laursen
no.2	19065	Chalky buff	N/A	1773	BS1	1983-84	18,943	Radial Wall	Steffen T. Laursen
no.3	N/A	Chalky buff	N/A	1806	BS2	1984-85	19,098	Early	Srivastava 1991: no.18
no.4	4943	Black-on-red	Main	834	BS1	1983-84	21,759	N/A	Steffen T. Laursen
no.5	4944	Black-on-red	Main	901	BS1	1983-84	22,241	N/A	Steffen T. Laursen
no.6	5893	Black-on-red	Main	36	BS3-B	1991	19,719	N/A	Steffen T. Laursen
no.7	N/A	Brown-on-buff (?)	N/A	1516	BS	1982-83	20,230	N/A	Bahrain Museum
no.8	19069	Black-on-green	Main	269	Main road	1985-86	19,512	Radial Wall	Bahrain Museum
no.9	19070	Black-on-grey	Main	120	Main road	1985-86	21,110	Late	Steffen T. Laursen
no.10	5790	Orange	Main	239	Main road	1985-86	19,835	Radial Wall	Steffen T. Laursen
no.11	14743	Black-on-orange	Main	54	Main road	1985-86	21964	Late	Steffen T. Laursen

References

Amiet, P. 1974. Antiquités du Desert de Lut. *Revue d'Assyriologie et d'Archaeologie Orientale* 88/2: 97-110.

Andersen H. & Højlund F. 2003. *The Barbar Temples.* Højbjerg: Jutland Archaeological Society.

Benton J.N. 1996. *Excavation at al-Sufouh: A third millennium site in the Emirate of Dubai.* Turnhout: Brepols. Abiel I.

Carter R. 2002. Unar 2 and its ceramics: a unique Umm an-Nar period collective grave from Ra's al-Khaimah. *Bulletin of the Society for Arabian Studies* 7: 5-14.

Carter R. 2003a. Restructuring Bronze Age Trade: Bahrain, Southeast Arabia and the Copper Question. Pages 31-63 in H. Crawford (ed.), *The Archaeology of Bahrain: The British Contribution.* Oxford: BAR international series 1189.

Carter R. 2003b. Tracing Bronze Age Trade in the Arabian Gulf: Evidence for Way-stations of the Merchants of Dilmun between Bahrain and the Northern Emirates. Pages 123-132 in D. Potts, H. Al-Naboodah & P. Hellyer (eds), *Archaeology of the United Arab Emirates: Proceedings of the First International Conference on the Archaeology of the U.A.E.* London: Trident Press.

Carter R. 2005. Pottery vessels: typological analysis. Pages 235-278 in R. Killick & J. & Moon (eds), *The Early Dilmun Settlement at Saar.* Ludlow, UK: Archaeology International.

Cornwall P.B. 1943. The Tumuli of Bahrain. *Asia and the Americas* 43: 230-234.

Crawford H. 1998. *Dilmun and its Gulf Neighbours.* Cambridge: Cambridge University Press.

Crawford H. 1999. The house on the edge of the quay: the kingdom's warehouse. Pages 86-100 in P. Lombard & K. Al-Sindi (eds), *Bahrain - The Civilisation of the Two Seas.* Ghent: Institute Du Monde Arabe.

Crawford H. 2001. *Early Dilmun Seals from Saar: Art and Commerce in Bronze Age Bahrain.* Ludlow, UK: Archaeology International.

de Cardi B. 1970. Excavations at Bampur, a Third Millennium Settlement in Persian Baluchistan, 1966. *Anthropological Papers of the American Museum of Natural History* 51/3: 233-355.

Denton B. & Al-Sindi K. 1996. An unusual cylinder seal from the cemetery of Hamad Town on Bahrain. *Arabian Archaeology and Epigraphy* 7/2: 188-194.

Frifelt K. 1991. *The Island of Umm an-Nar - volume 1 - Third Millennium Graves.* Højbjerg: Jutland Archaeological Society.

Frohlich B. 1986. The human biological history of the Early Bronze Age population in Bahrain. Pages 47-63 in H. al-Khalifa & M. Rice (eds), *Bahrain Through the Ages - The Archaeology.* London: Kegan Paul.

Frohlich B. & Mughannum A. 1985. Excavations of the Dhahran burial mounds 1404/1984. *Atlal - The Journal of Saudi Arabian Archaeology* 9: 9-40.

Gasche H. 1973. *Mémoires de la Délégation Archéologique en Iran - Tome XLVII - Mission de Susiane - Ville Royale de Suse I - La Poterie Élamite - Du Deuxième Millénaire a.C.* Belgium: E. J. Brill.

Gibson M. 1972a. Umm el-Jīr, a Town in Akkad. *Journal of Near Eastern Studies* 31/4: 237-294.

Gibson M. 1972b. *The City and Area of Kish.* Miami: Field Research Projects.

Grave P., Potts D.T., Yassi N., Reade W. & Bailey G. 1996. Elemental characterization of Barbar ceramics from Tell Abraq. *Arabian Archaeology and Epigraphy* 7: 177-187.

Haerinck E. 1991. The rectangular Umm an-Nar period grave at Mowaihat (Emirate of Ajman, United Arab Emirates). *Gentse Bijdragen, tot de Kunstgeschidenis en Oudheidkunde* 29: 1-30.

Hallo W.W. & Buchanan B. 1965. A "Persian Gulf" seal on an Old Babylonian mercantile agreement. *Assyrological Studies* 16: 199-209.

Højlund F. 1987. *Failaka/Dilmun: The Second Millennium Settlements - The Bronze Age Pottery.* Højbjerg: Jutland Archaeological Society.

Højlund F. 1989. The formation of the Dilmun state and the Amorite tribes. *Proceedings of the Seminar for Arabian Studies* 19: 45-65.

Højlund F. 1999. Qal'at al-Bahrain in the Bronze Age. Pages 73-76 in P. Lombard & K. al-Sindi (eds), *Bahrain: the Civilisation of the Two Seas.* Ghent: Institute du Monde Arabe.

Højlund F. 2007. *The Burial Mounds of Bahrain - Social Complexity in Early Dilmun.* Aarhus: Jutland Archaeological Society.

Højlund F. & Andersen H. 1994. *Qala'at al-Bahrain - The Northern City Wall and the Islamic Fortress.* Højbjerg: Jutland Archaeological Society.

Højlund F. & Andersen H. 1997. *Qala' at al-Bahrain - The Central Monumental Buildings.* Højbjerg: Jutland Archaeological Society.

Højlund F., Hilton A., Juel C., Kirkeby N., Laursen S. & Nielsen L. 2008. Late third-millennium elite burials in Bahrain. *Arabian Archaeology and Epigraphy* 19: 144-155.

Killick R. & Moon J. 2005. *The Early Dilmun Settlement at Saar.* Ludlow, UK: Archaeology International.

Kjærum P. 1980. Seals of the "Dilmun type" from Failaka, Kuwait. *Proceedings of the Seminar for Arabian Studies* 10: 45-54.

Kjærum P. 1994. Stamp-seals, seal impressions and seal blanks. Pages 319-350 in F. Højlund & H. Andersen (eds), *Qala' at al-Bahrain - The Northern City Wall and the Islamic Fortress.* Højbjerg: Jutland Archaeological Society.

Kveiborg J. 2007. Animal bones from the Aali, Saar and Dar Kulayb mound cemeteries. Pages 149-154 in F. Højlund (ed.), *The Burial Mounds of Bahrain - Social Complexity in Early Dilmun.* Højbjerg: Jutland Archaeological Society.

Laursen S. 2008. Early Dilmun and its rulers: new evidence of the burial mounds of the elite and the development of social complexity, c. 2200-1750 BC. *Arabian Archaeology and Epigraphy* 19: 156-167.

Laursen S. 2009. The decline of Magan and the rise of Dilmun: Umm an-Nar ceramics from the burial

mounds of Bahrain, c.2250–2000 BC. *Arabian Archaeology and Epigraphy* 20: 134-155.
Leemans W.F. 1960. *Foreign Trade in the Old Babylonian Period - as revealed by the texts from Southern Mesopotamia.* Leiden: E. J. Brill.
Lombard P. 1999. *Bahrain: The Civilisation of the Two Seas.* Ghent: Institut du Monde Arabe.
Lowe A. 1986. Bronze Age Burial Mounds on Bahrain. *Iraq* XLVIII: 73-84.
Mackay E.J.H. 1929. The Islands of Bahrain. Pages 1-35 in E.J.H. Mackay, L. Harding & F. Petrie (eds), *Bahrain and Hamamieh.* London: British School of Archaeology in Egypt..
McCown D.E. & Haines R.C. 1967. *Nippur 1: Temple of Enlil, Scribal Quarter, and Soundings.* Chicago: University of Chicago Press.
Méry S. 2000. *Les céramiques d'Oman et l'Asie moyenne - Une archéologie des échanges à l'Âge du Bronze.* Paris: CNRS.
Nickerson L.R. 1983. *Intrasite Variability During the Kaftari Period at Tal-e Malyan (Anshan), Iran,* Unpublished PhD dissertation, Ohio State University.
Oppenheim A.L. 1954. The seafaring merchants of Ur. *Journal of the American Oriental Society* 74: 6-17.
Petrie C.A., Chaverdi A.A. & Seyedin M. 2005. From Anshan to Dilmun and Magan: The Spatial and Temporal Distribution of Kaftari and Kaftari-Related Ceramic Vessels. *Iran* XLIII: 49-86.
Petrie C.A, Weeks L.R., Potts D.T. & Roustaei K. 2006. Perspectives on the Cultural Sequence of Mamasani. Pages 169-196 in D.T. Potts & K. Roustaei (eds), *The Mamasani Archaeological Project Stage 1: A report on the first two seasons of the ICAR- University of Sydney expedition to the Mamasani District, Fars Province, Iran.* Tehran: Iranian Cultural Heritage and Tourism Organisation.
Pollock S. 1985. Chronology of the Royal Cemetery of Ur. *Iraq* 47: 129-158.
Potts D.T. 1990. *A Prehistoric Mound in the Emirate of Umm al-Quiwain U.A.E. - Excavations at Tell Abraq in 1989.* Copenhagen: Munksgaard.
Potts D.T. 1994. South and Central Asian elements at Tell Abraq (Emirate of Umm al-Qaiwain, United Arab Emirates), c. 2200 BC - AD 400. Pages 615-621 in A. Parpola & P. Koskikallio (eds) *Proceedings of the Twelfth International Conference of the European Association of South Asian Archaeologists held in Helsinki University 5-9 July 1993 Volume II.* Helsinki: Annales Academiae Scientarium Fennicae Ser. B271.
Potts D.T. 2000. *Ancient Magan - The Secrets of Tell Abraq.* London: Trident Press.
Potts D.T. 2002. Total prestation in Marhashi-Ur relations. *Iranica Antiqua* XXXVII: 343-357.
Potts D.T. 2003. Tepe Yahya, Tell Abraq and the chronology of the Bampur sequence. *Iranica Antiqua* 38: 1-24.
Potts D.T. 2005. In the beginning: Marhashi and the origins of Magan's ceramic industry in the third millennium BC. *Arabian Archaeology and Epigraphy* 16: 67-78.

Rezvani H., Roustaei K., Azadi A. & Ghezelbash E. 2007. *Final Report of the Archaeological Excavations at Lama Cemetery.* Tehran: Iranian Center for Archaeological Research.
Santoni M. 1988. *Memoires de la Mission Archéologique Francaise en Francaise en Asie Centrale 1.* Paris: Diffusion de Boccard.
Srivastava K.M. 1991. *Madinat Hamad: burial mounds - 1984-85.* Manama: Ministry of Information, State of Bahrain.
Steinkeller P. 2006. New Light on Marhashi and its contacts with Makkan and Babylonia. *Journal of Magan Studies* 1: 1-17.
Steinkeller P. 2007. New Light on Šimaški and its Rulers. *Zeitschrift für Assyrologie und vorderasiatische Archäologie* 97: 215-232.
Sumner W.M. 1989. Anshan in the Kaftari Phase: Patterns of Settlement and Land Use: Pages 135-161 in L. de Meyer & E. Haerinck (eds), *Archaeologia Iranica et Orientalis: Miscellanea in Honorem Louis Vanden Berghe.* Ghent: Peeters.
al-Tikriti W.Y. 1981. *Reconsideration of the Late Fourth and Early Third Millennium BC in the Arabian Gulf, with special reference to the United Arab Emirates.* Unpublished PhD Dissertation, Trinity College, Cambridge.
al-Tikriti W.Y. 1989. Umm An-Nar culture in the northern Emirates: third millennium BC tombs at Ajman. *Archaeology in the United Arab Emirates* 5: 89-100.
Velde C. 1998. The Dilmun Cemetery at Karanah and the change of burial customs in late City II. Pages 237-244 in C. Phillips, D. Potts & S. Searight (eds), *Arabia and its Neighbours.* Brepols.
Weeks L.R., Alizadeh K., Niakan K., Alamdari K., Zaidee M. & Khosrowzadeh A. 2006. Excavations at Tol-e Nurabad. Pages 31-88 in D.T. Potts & K. Roustaei (eds), *The Mamasani Archaeological Project Stage 1: A report on the first two seasons of the ICAR- University of Sydney expedition to the Mamasani District, Fars Province, Iran.* Tehran: Iranian Cultural Heritage and Tourism Organisation.
Woolley C.L. 1934. *Ur Excavations -The Royal Cemetery.* Oxford: The British Museum and the Museum of the University of Pennsylvania.
Wright R.P. 1984. *Technology, style and craft specialization: spheres of interaction in the Indo-Iranian Borderlands, Third Millennium B.C.* Unpublished PhD thesis, Harvard University.

Author's Address
Steffen Terp Laursen
Section of Prehistoric Archaeology
Institute of Anthropology, Archaeology and Linguistics
University of Aarhus
Moesgaard Museum
DK-8270 Højbjerg, Denmark
Farkstl@hum.au.dk or
Steffen@terp-laursen.dk

Probing the Early Dilmun funerary landscape: a tentative analysis of grave goods from non-elite adult burials from City IIa-c

Eric Olijdam

Summary
This contribution deals with the distribution of grave goods from published non-elite adult interments dating to the City IIa-c period from mound fields at 'Ali, Saar, Karzakkan, Malikiyah, Dar Kulayb and Umm Jidr and from the Southern Burial Complex at Saar. Additionally, unpublished data are included from subterranean cemeteries at Karranah as well as a few published graves from Shakhura. The distribution of grave goods is examined in light of increasing social complexity and provides some tantalising insights into the socio-political cohesion of Dilmun during the City IIa-c period.

Keywords: Early Dilmun period, funerary practices, grave goods, Bahrain

Introduction

Before the rapid urbanisation of the past decades, Bahrain's countryside beyond the fertile coastal zones was dominated by large tracts of burial mounds. The mound fields were not only vast, covering an area of 30 km², but also displayed an exceptional density of burial mounds. Original estimates ranged from 100,000 (Bibby 1954: 132) to more than 170,000 (Larsen 1983: 45). Cornwall (1946: 37) was the first to attribute these mounds to an indigenous Bronze Age population and subsequent archaeological research has vindicated his claims as nearly all were produced during the Early Dilmun period (*ca.* 2200-1700 BC). The painstaking work of the *Bahrain Burial Mound Project*, initiated in 2006 by the Directorate of Culture and National Heritage in Bahrain and Moesgård Museum in Denmark, has resulted in a reduction of the original number of Early Dilmun mounds to 75,000: 28,000 Early Type mounds (*ca.* 2200-2050 BC) and 47,000 Late Type mounds (*ca.* 2050-1800 BC) (pers. comm. Steffen Laursen, adjusting the initial estimates in Laursen 2008: 159).

Early Type mounds, consisting of a crudely built low, flat mound of rocky fill with an irregular shaped burial chamber without capstones, date to City I according to the Qal'at al-Bahrain sequence and are scattered along wadis in a broad band around Rifa'a (Fig. 1). At the beginning of City II there is a clear break: Early Type mounds are no longer built and the geographical and topographical setting of the tombs shifts dramatically.[1] Late Type mounds are now built, distinguishable by a high, conical mound of sandy soil and small limestone chips with a burial chamber covered by several large capstone slabs. Their original shape, however, was cylindrical with a stone ring-wall and a flat top. They are grouped in a number of mound fields located on barren limestone outcrops and on the northern and western slopes of the Alat and Khobar formations. Over time these cemeteries grew and amalgamated into at least 10 mound fields: Isa Town North, Isa Town South, Saar, Janabiyah, 'Ali, Buri, Karzakkan, Malikiyah, Dar Kulayb

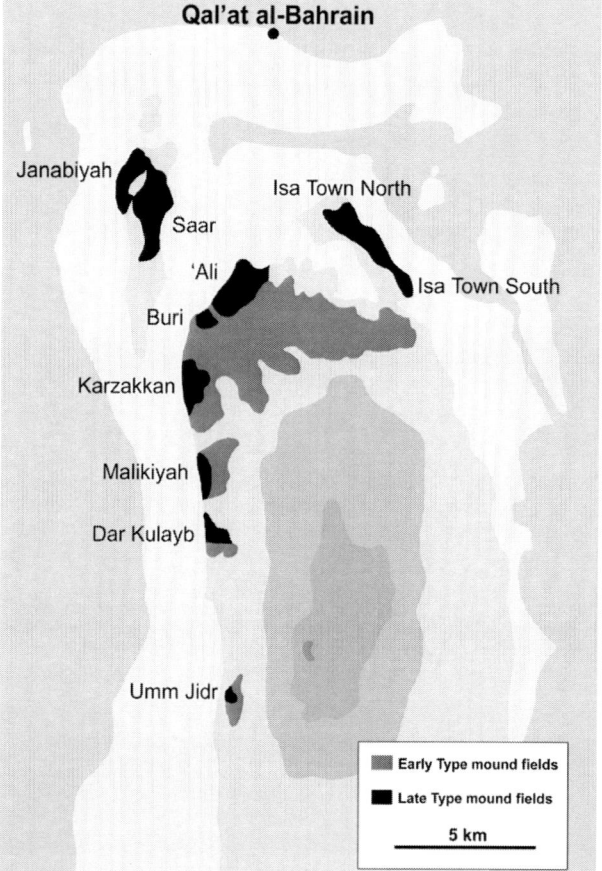

Figure 1. Early Dilmun mound fields (after Laursen 2008: Fig. 4).

and Umm Jidr (Laursen 2008).[2] The fields at Saar and 'Ali are by far the largest; further south the mound fields become progressively smaller. Late Type mounds are completely absent from the southern and south-eastern parts of the island.[3] The total amount of Late Type mounds translates to an average population between

---

[1] Some Early Type mounds have grave goods dating to City IIa. Originally, Intermediate Type mounds were identified but these have been abandoned as a separate category (Frohlich & Littleton 2007).

[2] A small number of Late Type mounds may be located on the main island of the Hawar Islands (Crombé, de Dapper & Haerinck 2001: 251).

[3] A map produced by Glob (1968: 15) indicates burial mounds near Mattalah, much further south, but nothing is known about these mounds (pers. comm. Flemming Højlund).

12,250 and 14,000.[4] Overall, the mound fields closely match the distribution pattern of Early Dilmun sites and appear to be territorially organized (Fig. 2). There are, however, two noticeable exceptions: 1) the fertile northern plain, where Qal'at al-Bahrain and other major settlements and religious centres are located, generally lacks Late Type mounds; 2) the small number of Late Type mounds at Umm Jidr seem inadequate given the cluster of sites in the southernmost habitation zone.

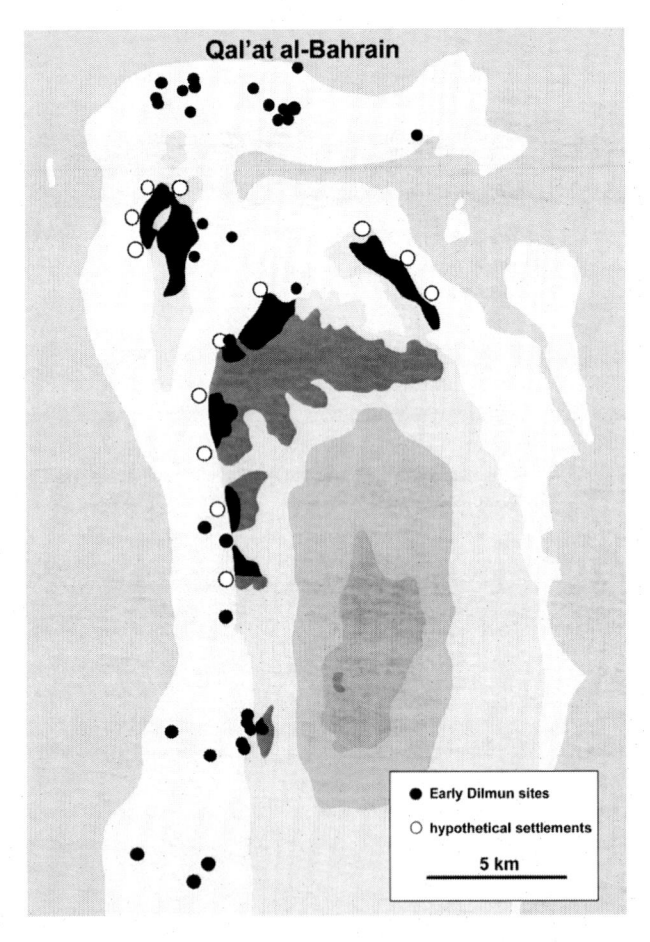

Figure 2. Early Dilmun sites and mound fields (after Højlund 2007: Fig. 265; Laursen 2008: Fig. 4; Larsen 1983: Fig. 11; Velde 1989; Denton 1999; Crawford & Moon 1997; Killick & Moon 2005: Fig. 1.2).

On the adjacent coast of Saudi Arabia, three Late Type mound burial fields were located near Dhahran along the slopes of the Dammam Dome. These mound fields, already under threat in the 1940s, displayed a high density of mounds. Based on aerial photographs it is calculated that the Dhahran South/'Ain as-Saih group consisted of 2551 Late Type mounds (Laursen 2008: 161 n. 3). Construction of the tombs, associated grave goods and topographical location clearly indicate a close affiliation between Dhahran and Bahrain (Cornwall 1946; Zarins, Mughannum & Kamal 1984; Frohlich & Mughannum 1985). The northern periphery of the Dilmun orbit is characterised by an absence of Late Type mounds despite large numbers of small Early Dilmun sites between Dhahran and al-Jubayl, on the Saudi coast, and extensive long-term occupation on various parts of Failaka, in Kuwait.

Other burial structures have been encountered on Bahrain that are contemporary with the Late Type mounds. Although these are far less common, their existence highlights diversity in burial practices. They adhere to the same principle burial practice of interring one individual with grave goods in a burial chamber, which is then sealed by large limestone capstones after which the burial monument is completed.

The best known are the burial complexes, which are confined to the south-eastern part of the Saar mound field. Three have been identified and partially excavated.[5] A burial complex is an organic structure made up of scores of small interconnected tombs. These tombs have a burial chamber and stone ring-wall similar to the burial mounds. However, because they are built against existing tombs their ring-wall is only partial – similar to subsidiary burials built against the primary Late Type mounds. The principal difference between the two is that the shape of burial complex tombs is not semi-circular but much less uniform and precisely built.

The other type are rectangular subterranean graves consisting of a shaft dug into the soil until bedrock, in which a smaller burial chamber is cut. The burial chamber was sealed by placing large capstones on the bedrock and filling the shaft back in. Small clusters of subterranean graves have been reported in a broad band along the Budayyah Highway, with a heavy concentration in the Karranah/al-Hajjar/al-Maqsha area. The subterranean grave is the dominant burial type in the fertile and densely populated northern coastal plain.[6]

Aim of this contribution

Frohlich & Littleton (2007) produced a preliminary inventory of grave goods in City I and II, based on 1,148 Early Type mounds and 2,208 Late Type mounds, excavated between 1978 and 1986. It shows significant differences in grave goods between adult and subadult burials. The grave-inventory also demonstrates a remarkable chronological consistency for adult burials, with two notable exceptions (i.e. an increase in metal

---

[4] The formula is taken from Frohlich (1986: 60). Life expectancy for adults is 35 to 40 years; the time-span for the construction of Late Type mounds is only 250 years (2050-1800 BC) as the total number of mounds constructed in the post-IIc period is quantitatively insignificant (pers. comm. Steffen Laursen).

[5] Besides the Southern Burial Complex (Ibrahim 1982; Mughal 1983) and the Northern Burial Complex (Crawford & Moon 1997: 19; Killick & Moon 2005: 2-3) at least one more has been found, i.e. the 'Small Complex'. This heavily damaged complex, consisting of at least 60 child-size tombs, is briefly discussed by Ibrahim (1982: 28-29) but not included in his catalogue.

[6] The absence of tumuli on Failaka might be explained if people were buried in subterranean graves. However, over the years countless sweet-water holes have been dug on the island without discovering burials, nor has the electro-magnetic prospecting carried out in different parts of the island discovered any Early Dilmun burials (pers. comm. Steffen Laursen; Frohlich 1986: 62; Frohlich & Lancaster 1986: 1419-1420; KSAM 2009).

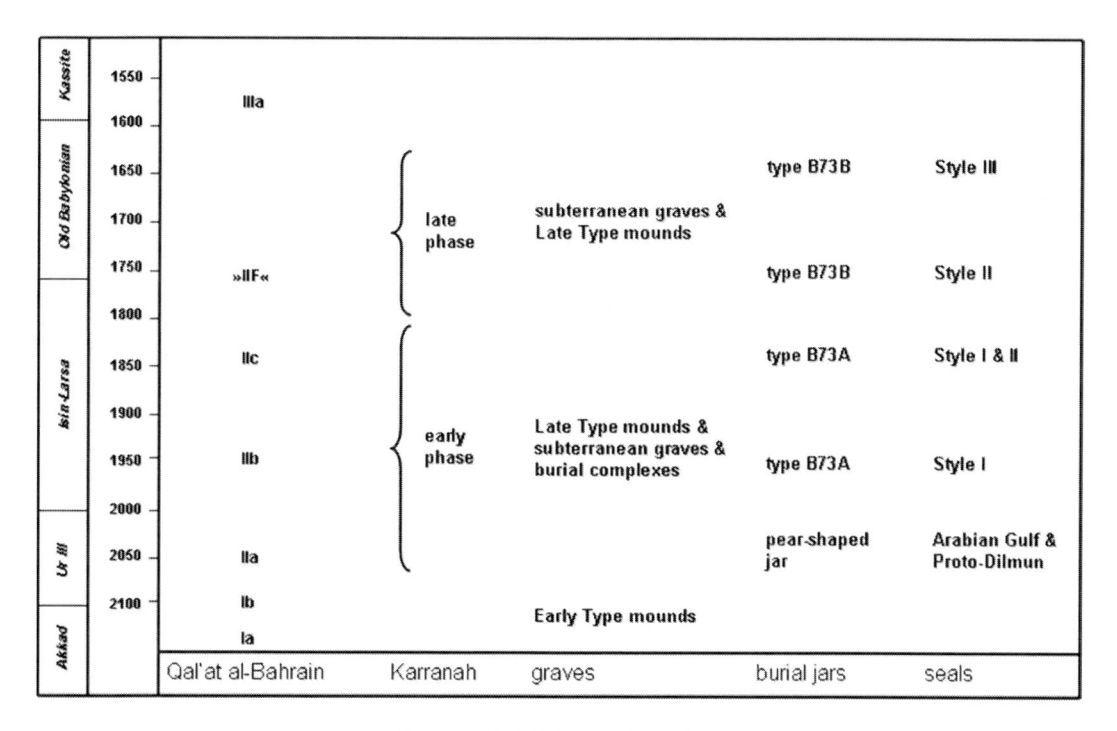

Figure 3. Early Dilmun chronology.

items and animal bones), while subadults display major increases in nearly all categories.

In their analysis, City I and II are presented as two horizons based on differences in tomb structure. These horizons correspond to what has been called the first and second social formations (Højlund 2007: 123-127). The latter was extremely dynamic, resulting in a division into three phases: City IIa, IIb-c and post-IIc (Fig. 3). In funerary practices, the post-IIc period represents a major break with the previous periods and saw the inception of a new dominant burial tradition, exemplified by multiple interments per grave (Velde 1998), and is therefore excluded from this analysis.[7]

It has already been established that City IIa-c graves exhibit a large variation in size, construction and grave goods, which relates to differences in prestige, rank and status. There is also a clear chronological trend towards the construction of larger tombs (Højlund 2007: 131-135) and there appear to be differences between burial fields, possibly linked to availability of raw materials (Velde 1994: 72). In recent analyses a distinction is made between commoners and the ruling lineage, who were buried in two-tiered mounds (Højlund 2007: 136). The funerary record does suggest that Early Dilmun society was much more diverse during the City IIa-c period.

These commoners can, on the basis of the amount of labour and resources invested in the construction of the burial structure, be divided into three main groups (cf. Velde 1994: 72-76): 1) those buried in mounds with a ring-wall diameter of up to 7 m; 2) those buried in mounds with a ring-wall of 7 m and more; 3) those buried in one-tiered shaft burials.[8] This division is also reflected by an increase in the types, quality and quantity of the grave goods interred in each group. The one-tiered shaft burials dating to City IIb-c, most likely represent a local elite not only because they represent a major increase in terms of investment but also because their external appearance and shaft entrance emulate the contemporary 'Royal Mounds'. Their prominence is also confirmed by their placement within the cemeteries (Velde 1994: 77-79; Laursen & Johansen 2007: 145-147; Laursen 2008: 162-164). This three-tier system with a powerful local elite accords much better with the territorial organisation of the burial fields and Dilmun's political identification during City IIa-c as an Early State (cf. Claessen 2001).[9]

In this contribution only the grave goods from the first two groups – the non-elite – are examined, most of which have a ring-wall diameter under 7 m (Fig. 4). Analysis is not limited to mound burials but also includes data from the other burial types. The burial complexes and rock-cut

---

[7] The conclusion that burial mounds and subterranean graves are not only contemporary but also follow a parallel development is conclusive evidence that both burial types belong to the same socio-cultural setting. Interestingly, post-IIc burials in the Southern Burial Complex do not contain multiple interments – some contain two burials of which the post-IIc burial is separated from the original City IIa-c burial by a thick layer of sand. In the post-IIc period, subterranean graves are also attested in areas that were occupied during City IIa-c, i.e. inside domestic (e.g. al-Hajjar) and religious buildings (e.g. Diraz).

[8] The fourth group consisting of large shaft burials with double burial chambers (Velde 1994: 75-76) is excluded from this analysis because the one-tiered examples date to the post-IIc/IIIa periods, while the two-tiered ones belong to the ruling lineage. Laursen & Johansen's (2007: 141-146) tripartite division of the tumuli is based on the modern mound diameter rather than the original ring-wall diameter, while their 7-13 m group also includes small mound clusters (Ibrahim's Type III) and shaft burials.

[9] Note that the differences between mounds with a ring-wall diameter up to 7 m and those of 7 m and more (cf. Velde 1994: 72-75) indicate that even the lowest tier was far from homogeneous.

subterranean graves represent culturally acceptable variants as far as the shape of the burial structure is concerned. The deposition of the body, the placement of the grave goods and the grave goods themselves clearly indicate that the people buried in these variants belong to the same cultural and funerary tradition. Interestingly, both variants only represent the non-elite element of Dilmun society, as indicated by the overall dimensions of the grave-structure, the length of the burial chambers and the absence of 'elite' grave goods.

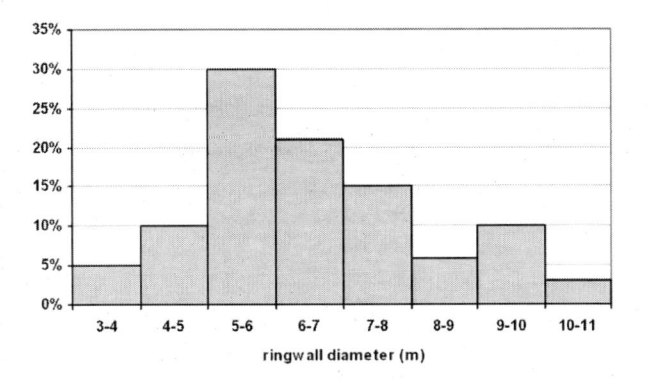

Figure 4. Ring-wall diameter of non-elite burials from City IIa-c.

Database

According to a recent study, of the 55,000 Early Dilmun burial mounds destroyed on Bahrain in the past decades nearly 8,000 have been properly excavated (Højlund 2007: 7). The content of only about 400 individual tombs have been published (Mackay 1929; During Caspers 1980; Cleuziou, Lombard & Salles 1981; Ibrahim 1982; Mughal 1983; Srivastava 1991; Daems, Haerinck & Rutten 2001; Højlund 2007; Højlund et al. 2008). The database is therefore nothing more than a palimpsest, which, in order to deal with the distribution of grave goods from non-elite adult burials dating to the City IIa-c period, has to be filtered resulting in an even greater reduction.

A significant portion of the published data consists of elite burials, i.e. shaft burials and/or burials with four alcoves. Additionally, numerous one-tiered shaft burials date to the post-IIc period, because they have multiple interments in the chamber, have more than one burial chamber within the ring-wall and/or have plastered walls. Finally, a small number are Early Type mounds or Late Type mounds that have been re-used in Middle Dilmun times.

Late Type ring-walled mounds can have one or more smaller burials built against them. Characteristic of these subsidiary burials are a partial ring-wall and a significantly smaller burial chamber.[10] The length of these burial chambers strongly suggests a correlation with the age of death and are thought to belong to children under the age of 15 (Frohlich 1986: 58). Subsidiary tombs had a smaller and less diverse set of grave goods than primary tombs (Frohlich & Littleton 2007). This is also true for the burial complexes, where children were interred in a special area of the complex or in a separate complex altogether, and for the subterranean burials, where children were buried in shallow pits dug in the subsoil.[11] Conditions on Bahrain are generally unfavourable for skeletal remains resulting in a poor preservation of Early Dilmunites, especially children. Nonetheless, remains of some 15 to 18 year olds have been identified in primary burials (Frohlich 1986: 59; Højlund 2007: infra), possibly indicating that in Early Dilmun society social adulthood was reached around that age. The co-occurrence of females aged 15 to 18 with infants in a few primary burials may suggest that the transition into social adulthood was correlated to sexual maturity and for girls possibly with marriage (cf. Leick 1994: 88 for Mesopotamia). This analysis includes only data from the primary tombs, i.e. of social adults.

Finally, tombs lacking any grave goods are excluded because all scholars agree that during the City IIa-c period adults were buried with grave goods – even those interred in the smallest burials. By eliminating 'empty' tombs, percentages can be calculated for the presence of each category of grave goods within the various burial assemblages.

Systemic plundering of grave goods

Any discussion dealing with the presence/absence of Early Dilmun grave goods is seriously affected by the large-scale ancient plundering of tombs. With the exception of burials re-used during the post-IIc and City IIIa periods, forced entry into burial chambers was aimed at obtaining grave goods.[12] It is estimated that as much as 99% of the Early Dilmun burial mounds are plundered (Lowe 1986: 82). It has been suggested that the mounds were a more favourable target for robbers (Mughal 1983: 16), but this has been refuted because virtually all chambers of the Southern Burial Complex and subterranean tombs were plundered. Ergo, plundering was extensive, rigorous and probably even systemic.

The precise date for this is unknown. One theory is that it took place after the decline of the Dilmun culture when many of the old traditions ceased to be respected and upheld, i.e. during the socio-economic and political upheaval of the post-IIc period or, perhaps more likely, in the Middle Dilmun period (Højlund 2007: 36). If this were the case, one would expect large-scale recycling of

---

[10] Numerous tombs from small mound clusters usually referred to as subsidiary are in fact primary burials: they have a complete ring-wall and an adult-size burial chamber. Published cross-sections from Saar, Karzakkan and Umm Jidr show that these clearly precede the subsidiary tombs in the cluster (cf. Velde 1998: 65-66).

[11] Their spatial distribution within the cemeteries is impossible to ascertain as these shallow graves are only preserved in areas covered by Tylos burial mounds which protected them from later erosion.
[12] This is a major difference with the published Late Type mounds from Dhahran South where the original mound was typically opened from one side and the structure was altered in order to accommodate successive burials over a long period of time (Zarins, Mughannum & Kamal 1984; Frohlich & Mughannum 1985).

Table 1: Database of non-elite adult burials from City IIa-c.

	City IIa	City IIb-c	City IIa-c
tumuli			
'Ali	*Mackay 1929*: 18; *Hojlund 2007*: 227, 228, 229, 231, 233, 234, 235, 237, 238, 239, 240, 243, 244, 245, 246, 247, 248.	*Mackay 1929*: 5, 14, 16, 19, 21, 24, 26, 27, 31, 32; *Hojlund 2007*: 206, 207, 209, 210, 211, 212, 213, 214, 215, 216, 217, 218, 219, 220, 222, 223, 224, 225.	*Mackay 1929*: 9, 11, 13, 17, 20, 22, 23.
Saar	*Ibrahim 1982*: 116a, 126, S-7, S-17, S-18, S-41, S-97, S-100, S-113, S-123, S-13/1, S-44/1, S-137.3; *Mughal 1983*: 117.	*During Caspers 1980*: Higham 23, Jefferson; *Ibrahim 1982*: 115, S-180, S-181, S-193, S-199, S-223, S-377, S-232.1, S-238.1, S-394.2; *Hojlund 2007*: 513.	*Ibrahim 1982*: 3, 15, 106, 119, 120, 221, S-23, S-48, S-50, S-51, S-54, S-98, S-106, S-109, S-114, S-124, S-132, S-136, S-138, S-148, S-203, S-240, S-258, S-261, S-137.1, S-137.6, S-137.10, S-238.3, S-245.3, S-248.1, S-248.2, S-253.4; *Mughal 1983*: 143, 144, 146.
Karzakkan	*During Caspers 1980*: Higham 5; *Srivastava 1991*: 1414, 1415, 1809, 1407, 1791, 1844, 1749, 1818, 1757, 1758, 1795, 1406, 1424, 1680, 1812, 1396, 1423, 1742, 1798, 1804, 1425, 1753, 1677, 1413.	*During Caspers 1980*: Higham 32; *Srivastava 1991*: 1434, 1755, 1793, 1417.	*Srivastava 1991*: 1416, 1747, 1837b, 1746b, 1833, 1746, 1817, 1792, 1395, 1767, 1794, 1803, 1761, 1397, 1746a, 1394, 1676, 1421, 1401, 1675, 1797.
Malikiyah Dar Kulayb Umm Jidr	*During Caspers 1980*: Higham 31; *Hojlund 2007*: 252, 253. *During Caspers 1980*: Higham 27; *Cleuziou, Lombard & Salles 1981*: 4, 1a, 1b, 1c.	*During Caspers 1980*: Higham 6. *During Caspers 1980*: Higham 7, Higham 11. *Hojlund 2007*: 251.	*During Caspers 1980*: Higham 30. *Cleuziou, Lombard & Salles 1981*: 2, 3.
Burial Complex			
Saar (South)	*Ibrahim 1982*: A/A1.2, C/A1.1, B/A2.9, B/A3.8, D/G1.1, D/G1.4; *Mughal 1983*: 3, 14, 19, 23, 32, 49, 56, 62, 66, 69, 91, 100, 121, 122, 126, 131, 135, 137a.	*Ibrahim 1982*: C/G1-2.18; *Mughal 1983*: 5, 43, 48, 53, 55, 59, 63a, 77, 84, 94, 105, 106, 113, 134, 137, 139.	*Ibrahim 1982*: TT2.2, TT2.5, TT2.6, TT2.7, TT2.8, C/G1-2.6, C/G1-2.9, C/G1-2.11, C/G1-2.16, C/G1-2.19, A/D5.6, A/D5.8, A/D4.7, A/D3.7, A/D3.5, A/D2.8, A/D2.6, A/D1.6; A/A3.6; A/A2.7. A/A1.7, C/A3.5, C/A2.8, C/A1.5, C/A1.9, B/A1.4; *Mughal 1983*: 7, 16, 16a, 18, 22, 26, 27, 28, 31, 33, 34, 35, 36, 36a, 37, 38, 44, 47, 50, 51, 52, 54, 57, 58, 61, 63, 64, 68, 69a, 70, 72, 75, 76, 78, 79, 82, 88, 92, 93, 96, 97, 99, 102, 107, 108, 109, 110, 111, 111a, 111b, 114, 115a, 118, 120, 124, 125, 125a, 127, 128, 128a, 129, 133, 136, 141, 142, 147, 148, 149a.
subterranean tombs			
Karranah 1		*Velde unpublished*: C I-2, B II-3, B II-8, B III-7, B III-5, B III-3, C III-5, C III-7, C IV-4, C IV-3, D IV-7, D IV-8, B IV-4, C V-8, B V-14, A IV-11, A IV-9, A V-6, A V-3, B V-13, B V-9, B V-10, B V-11, B V-12, B VI-7, C V-3, C VI-5, D V-4, D V-7, D VI-4, C V-5, C II-3, C IV-4, C V-4. *Olijdam unpublished*: A08, A10, A15, A19, A21, A26, A29, A33, B05, B06, B07, B10, B13, B17, C09, D10, D16, D21, D26, E04, E07, E09, E12, E13, E14, E18, E21, E22, E23, E24, E28, E32, E34, E35, E36, E41, H09, H12, H13, J04, J05, J06, J08, J09, J10, J11, J18, J21.	*Velde unpublished*: C 1-3, D V-6, B IV-3, D VI-5, A IV-10, A IV-8, A IV-6, B VI-8, C VII-3, C VI-6, A III-1, A IV-4, A V-4, B V-3, B VI-5, C II-1, C II-2, C II-4, C III-6, D II-1, D II-2, D III-6, B II-2, C V-9, B II-1. *Olijdam unpublished*: A06, A07, A09, A11, A12, A13, A27, A28, A30, A36, B11, B12, B15, C10, D12, D13, D15, D18, D20, D24, D25, D28, E05, E10, E15, E19, E20, E29, E37, E39, E42, F02, F04, F05, H08, H11, H15, H17, H20, H21, H22, H24, H25, H26, H27, H28, H29, H31, H32, H33, H34, J12, J13, J14, J15, J17, J19, J20, J22.
Karranah 2	*Olijdam unpublished*: H03.		
Shakhura A-3	*Daems, Haerinck & Rutten 2001*: 5, 10, 1, 3.		

145

grave goods but the post-IIc and IIIa ceramic, seal and stone vessel assemblages are radically different from those of the City IIa-c periods (Denton 1997; 1999; Velde 1998). The other theory is that they were plundered not long after the actual funeral. In many cultures it is believed that grave goods only have ceremonial significance as long as there is still flesh on the bones of the deceased (pers. comm. Timothy Taylor). Preliminary examination has indicated that when the skeletal remains were disturbed they were no longer held together by tissue or ligaments but that the silting process had not yet set in, i.e. that it took place within a few years after the funeral (Frohlich & Mughannum 1985: 26). Another tantalising clue that the plundering took place within living memory of their construction and use is the *modus operandi* employed by the robbers in the Southern Burial Complex which suggests they were familiar with the particular architectural make-up of these burials (Crawford & Moon 1997: 19).

Grave goods were concentrated in the alcove and in the top corner of the burial chamber next to the face – where most robbers entered the tomb. This demonstrates that they specifically targeted the cluster of grave goods located in this area. Personal items, such as jewellery/adornments and seals, usually placed on the body and/or clothing, on the other hand, are often still present. Additional evidence for this selective targeting is the fact that a significant portion of the burials excavated yielded undisturbed skeletons (Frohlich & Mughannum 1985: 26). It appears as if the plundering, though systemic, was done covertly and in some considerable haste, as exemplified in the breakage and spillage of grave goods, the lack of a complete and/or systematic removal of specific groups of objects in the burial chamber and the disturbance of the skeletal remains, though the latter may also be attributed to rodents and other burrowing animals (cf. Kveiborg 2007: 150).

It is important to remember that Dilmun was devoid of nearly all raw materials and that by placing grave goods in burial chambers precious resources were removed from circulation. Large-scale plundering of burials to retrieve objects and/or materials is therefore hardly surprising, even in times of economic prosperity, which would have benefitted only a small portion of Dilmun's largely rural population. The extensive plundering means that the original furnishings cannot be determined for individual burials. The premise of this analysis is that all burials are plundered approximately to the same extent: robbers targeted specific items, i.e. copper/bronze tools and implements, soft-stone and alabaster vessels as well as ostrich eggs, and materials such as ivory, precious metals and semi-precious stones. Therefore only the presence/absence is registered for (already established) categories of grave goods.

Mounds, burial complexes and subterranean burials

Using one methodology and applying the same criteria for each grave enables direct comparison between burial types as well as between burial fields. The inventories of

	Σ		Pottery		Beads		Metal		Seals		Bitumen		Stone		Shell		Animal	
tumuli	183		123	67%	25	14%	40	22%	16	9%	24	13%	4	2%	22	12%	101	55%
Burial Complex	135		111	82%	21	16%	55	41%	28	21%	35	26%	19	14%	33	24%	7	5%
subterranean tombs	171		162	94%	23	13%	48	28%	13	8%	52	29%	7	4%	31	18%	2	1%
Total	489		396	81%	69	14%	143	29%	57	12%	111	23%	30	6%	86	18%	110	22%
tumuli																		
Ali	54		39	72%	6	11%	18	33%	2	4%	10	19%	3	6%	10	19%	29	54%
Saar	62		46	74%	4	6%	13	21%	7	11%	11	18%	1	2%	7	11%	25	40%
Karzakkan	52		27	52%	13	25%	7	13%	5	10%	1	2%	0	0%	5	10%	43	83%
Malikiyah	2		1	-	0	-	1	-	0	-	0	-	0	-	0	-	0	-
Dar Kulayb	5		5	-	0	-	0	-	0	-	0	-	0	-	0	-	2	-
Umm Jidr	8		5	-	2	-	1	-	2	-	2	-	0	-	0	-	2	-
Burial Complex																		
Saar (South)	135		111	82%	21	16%	55	41%	28	21%	35	26%	19	14%	33	24%	7	5%
subterranean tombs																		
Karranah 1	59		55	93%	5	8%	19	32%	3	5%	26	44%	4	7%	16	27%	1	2%
Karranah 2	108		103	94%	16	15%	29	27%	10	9%	25	23%	3	3%	15	14%	1	1%
Shakhura A-3	4		4	-	2	-	0	-	0	-	1	-	0	-	0	-	0	-

Table 2: Database of non-elite adult burials from City IIa-c.

489 non-elite adult burials from City IIa-c have been analysed: 183 burial mounds, 135 from the burial complex and 171 subterranean graves (Tab. 1). Included are data from six mound fields ('Ali, Saar, Karzakkan, Malikiyah, Dar Kulayb and Umm Jidr), one burial complex (Southern Burial Complex from Saar) and three subterranean cemeteries (Karranah 1, Karranah 2 and Shakhura A-3).

The most notable result is a strong differentiation between the various burial types (Tab. 2). It was already clear that there were major differences between the grave goods from the burial mounds and the Southern Burial Complex (cf. Velde 1994: 76) but by eliminating the elite and post-IIc mound burials, this distinction has become even more pronounced. The two appear to be each other's opposites, with significantly higher scores for the presence of metal items, seals, bitumen-coated vessels, stone vessels and unworked shells for the burial complex. Subterranean graves closely follow the percentages of the burial mounds, except for bitumen-coated vessels and unworked shells. The largest variance is recorded for animal bones, which are found in 55% of the burial mounds as opposed to 5% of the burial complex and 1% of the subterranean graves.

There are not only differences between the burial types, but also between the burial fields. Three mound fields yielded sufficient data to allow comparison: 'Ali has the most metal items, stone vessels and unworked shells, Karzakkan the most beads and animal bones; 'Ali has the lowest number of seals, Karzakkan has few stone vessels. There are also differences between the subterranean cemeteries even though they are located only a few meters from one another: Karranah 1 yielded much more bitumen-coated vessels and unworked shells, Karranah 2 has more beads. Finally, graves from the Southern Burial Complex have a more diverse and larger set of grave goods than the burial mounds from the same area of the mound field.

Chronology

Velde's (1998) division of City II funerary practices into an early and a late phase, each with a specific ceramic assemblage, is widely accepted. A more detailed typology and chronology of the major artefact groups from funerary contexts still has to be established. Recently, a solid start was made in differentiating the early phase into City IIa and IIb-c based on a number of dating criteria (Højlund 2007). The starting point for this division are two very common types of funerary jars: the Dilmun burial jar (type B73A) – already appearing at Qal'at al-Bahrain in City IIa but concentrated in IIb-c – and the pear-shaped jar, which is combined with rim type B9, found at Qal'at al-Bahrain in IIa-c. In the various burial fields the two display different distributions and are rarely associated with each other (Lowe 1986: 79; Højlund 2007: 21), suggesting that the pear-shaped jar was most popular as a grave good in City IIa and was succeeded by the Dilmun burial jar around the beginning of IIb (Højlund 2007: 22). The excavations at Qal'at al-Bahrain have also established a secure date for the first stages of the local stamp seal tradition: Arabian Gulf and Proto-Dilmun style seals date to City IIa, Mature Dilmun IA seals to IIb-c (Kjærum 1994). By association, several types of imported and utilitarian pottery can be assigned to IIa or IIb-c and the same applies to the construction of a group of burial mounds: Late Type mounds with radial walls between the burial chamber and the ring-wall date to City IIa.

According to these criteria 246 of the 489 non-elite adult burials can be assigned to either City IIa or IIb-c: 95 to IIa, 151 to IIb-c. Broken down according to burial types the results are striking: 64% of the burial mounds can be assigned (66 to IIa, 51 to IIb-c), 30% of the burial complex (24 to IIa, 17 to IIb-c) and 51% of the subterranean graves (5 to IIa, 83 to IIb-c). The low number of datable graves – particularly from the burial complex – is primarily due to the way in which the pottery is published. A systematic and detailed analysis of all pottery sherds is conducted only for the burial mounds excavated by the Danish Archaeological Expedition (Højlund 2007) and the subterranean cemetery at Karranah 1 (Velde 1998; unpublished database). Detailed examination of the pottery from other excavations should result in a significant increase of datable graves, particularly since the Dilmun burial jar is executed in a distinct ware so recognisable that even a small fragment may suffice to assign a grave to IIb-c.

City IIa burials

The beginning of City II saw the inception of the Late Type mounds and a different organisation of the burial fields. Concomitantly, other burial types emerged: the burial complexes at Saar and subterranean graves in different areas of the northern fertile plain (Tab. 3). With regard to grave goods there is a strong differentiation between the burial types, especially when pottery and seals, the principal chronological diagnostic categories, are excluded: the Southern Burial Complex has substantially higher scores for beads, metal items, bitumen-coated vessels, stone vessels and unworked shells. Subterranean graves are too few to allow reliable comparison, but the number of burials with beads, metal items and bitumen-coated vessels appear to follow the percentages of the burial mounds. The largest variance is recorded for animal bones: they are encountered in 64% of the tumuli but are completely absent from the burial complex (and subterranean cemeteries).

Differences also exist between burial fields. Three mound fields yielded sufficient data to allow comparison: Saar has the highest percentages of metal items and unworked shells, Karzakkan has the most beads; 'Ali has considerably lower amounts than the other mound fields for most of the categories. Here too the largest variance is recorded for the animal bones: at Karzakkan and 'Ali they are found in 85% and 78% of the tombs, respectively; at Saar this is only 29%.

When the Southern Burial Complex is compared to the

Table 3: Grave-goods in non-elite adult burials from City IIa.

tumuli	Σ	Pottery		Beads		Metal		Seals		Bitumen		Stone		Shell		Animal	
	66	49	74%	11	17%	11	17%	10	15%	2	3%	1	2%	4	6%	42	64%
Burial Complex	24	18	75%	7	29%	13	58%	12	50%	7	29%	13	58%	6	25%	0	0%
subterranean tombs	5	5	-	4	-	2	-	2	-	2	-	0	-	0	-	0	-
Total	95	72	76%	22	23%	26	27%	24	25%	11	12%	14	15%	10	11%	42	44%
tumuli																	
'Ali	18	12	67%	0	0%	1	6%	0	0%	0	0%	0	0%	0	0%	14	78%
Saar	14	12	86%	1	7%	4	29%	3	21%	0	0%	1	7%	2	14%	4	29%
Karzakkan	26	18	69%	8	31%	5	19%	5	19%	0	0%	0	0%	2	8%	22	85%
Dar Kulayb	3	3	-	0	-	0	-	0	-	0	-	0	-	0	-	2	-
Umm Jidr	5	4	-	2	-	1	-	2	-	2	-	0	-	0	-	0	-
Burial Complex																	
Saar (South)	24	18	75%	7	29%	13	54%	12	50%	7	29%	13	54%	6	25%	0	0%
subterranean tombs																	
Karranah 2	1	1	-	2	-	2	-	2	-	1	-	0	-	0	-	0	-
Shakhura A-3	4	4	-	2	-	0	-	0	-	1	-	0	-	0	-	0	-

Table 4: Grave-goods in non-elite adult burials from City IIb-c.

tumuli	Σ	Pottery		Beads		Metal		Seals		Bitumen		Stone		Shell		Animal	
	51	45	88%	8	16%	20	39%	2	4%	12	24%	3	6%	11	22%	22	43%
Burial Complex	17	14	82%	5	29%	7	41%	12	70%	8	47%	0	0%	6	35%	0	0%
subterranean tombs	83	80	96%	14	17%	28	34%	10	12%	28	34%	5	6%	17	20%	1	1%
total	151	139	92%	27	18%	55	36%	24	16%	48	32%	8	5%	34	23%	23	15%
tumuli																	
'Ali	29	23	79%	6	21%	16	55%	2	7%	10	34%	3	10%	10	34%	13	45%
Saar	13	13	100%	1	8%	3	23%	0	0%	1	8%	0	0%	0	0%	4	31%
Karzakkan	5	5	-	1	-	1	-	0	-	1	-	0	-	1	-	5	-
Malikiyah	1	1	-	0	-	0	-	0	-	0	-	0	-	0	-	0	-
Dar Kulayb	2	2	-	0	-	0	-	0	-	0	-	0	-	0	-	0	-
Umm Jidr	1	1	-	0	-	0	-	0	-	0	-	0	-	0	-	0	-
Burial Complex																	
Saar (South)	17	14	82%	5	29%	7	41%	12	70%	8	47%	0	0%	6	35%	0	0%
subterranean tombs																	
Karranah 1	34	34	100%	3	9%	11	32%	3	9%	15	44%	2	6%	9	26%	1	3%
Karranah 2	48	46	96%	11	23%	17	35%	7	15%	13	27%	3	6%	8	17%	0	0%

burial mounds from the same area of the Saar mound field a clear pattern emerges: the burial complex has much higher percentages for all categories, except animal bones which are completely absent.

The picture emerging from the database of non-elite adult burials dating to City IIa is thus quite different from the conclusions drawn by Højlund on the basis of the Danish excavations, where "[t]he burial gifts are few in numbers, mostly consisting of one, or rarely two pottery jars, very infrequently a bitumen-coated jar or a copper object, and a ... sheep or more often goat .... The internal variation between the ordinary burials ... is rather limited with respect to burial gifts ..." (Højlund 2007: 131).

City IIb-c burials

What is immediately obvious from the data is that the differentiation between the burial types in City IIb-c is much less pronounced than in IIa (Tab. 4). The burial complex still has the highest number of beads, bitumen-coated vessels and unworked shells, but there is a dramatic decline of stone vessels and metal items. Subterranean graves closely follow the percentages of the burial mounds, except for bitumen-coated vessels and animal bones. Once again, the biggest difference is formed by animal bones – found in 43% of the burial mounds, in 0% of the burial complex and 1% of the subterranean graves – even though bitumen-coated vessels also show a large variance with 26%.

The distribution of grave goods between the various burial fields also displays patterns unlike those observed for City IIa. Only two mound fields yielded sufficient data for comparison: 'Ali now has many more beads, metal items, bitumen-coated vessels, stone vessels and unworked shells than Saar, while animal bones are also more common. The two subterranean cemeteries show differences as well: Karranah 1 has higher percentages of bitumen-coated vessels and unworked shells, Karranah 2 yielded more beads.

Finally, there is still a strong differentiation between the Southern Burial Complex and the burial mounds from Saar, except for stone vessels which are now completely absent from the datable graves.[13]

The picture that emerges from the database of non-elite adult burials dating to City IIb-c suggests a shift in the burial practices, exemplified by substantial changes in the percentages of the categories – with a positive trend for burial mounds and a mixed trend for the burial complex (Tab. 5). An increase in the number and diversity of grave goods as well as differences between various mound fields have already been alluded to by Højlund (2007: 133-134) in his review of City IIb-c funerary practices.

	tumuli			Burial Complex			subterranean graves			overall		
	IIa	IIb-c	trend	IIa	IIb-c	trend	IIa	IIb-c	trend	IIa	IIb-c	trend
beads	17%	16%	- 1%	29%	29%	0%	n.d.	17%	—	23%	18%	- 5%
metal	17%	39%	+ 22%	58%	41%	- 17%	n.d.	34%	—	27%	36%	+ 9%
bitumen	3%	24%	+ 21%	29%	47%	+ 18%	n.d.	34%	—	12%	32%	+ 20%
stone	2%	6%	+ 4%	58%	0%	- 58%	n.d.	6%	—	15%	5%	- 10%
shell	6%	22%	+ 16%	25%	35%	+ 10%	n.d.	20%	—	11%	23%	+ 12%
animal	64%	43%	- 21%	0%	0%	0%	n.d.	1%	—	44%	15%	- 29%

Table 5: Grave-goods in non-elite adult burials from City IIa and IIb-c (excl. pottery and seals).

---

[13] The complete absence of Mature Dilmun IA seals in the tumuli from Saar stands in stark contrast to the nearby burial complexes. It is even more remarkable since many additional Mature Dilmun IA seals come from burial complex graves not included in the catalogues and have therefore not been included in the analysis.

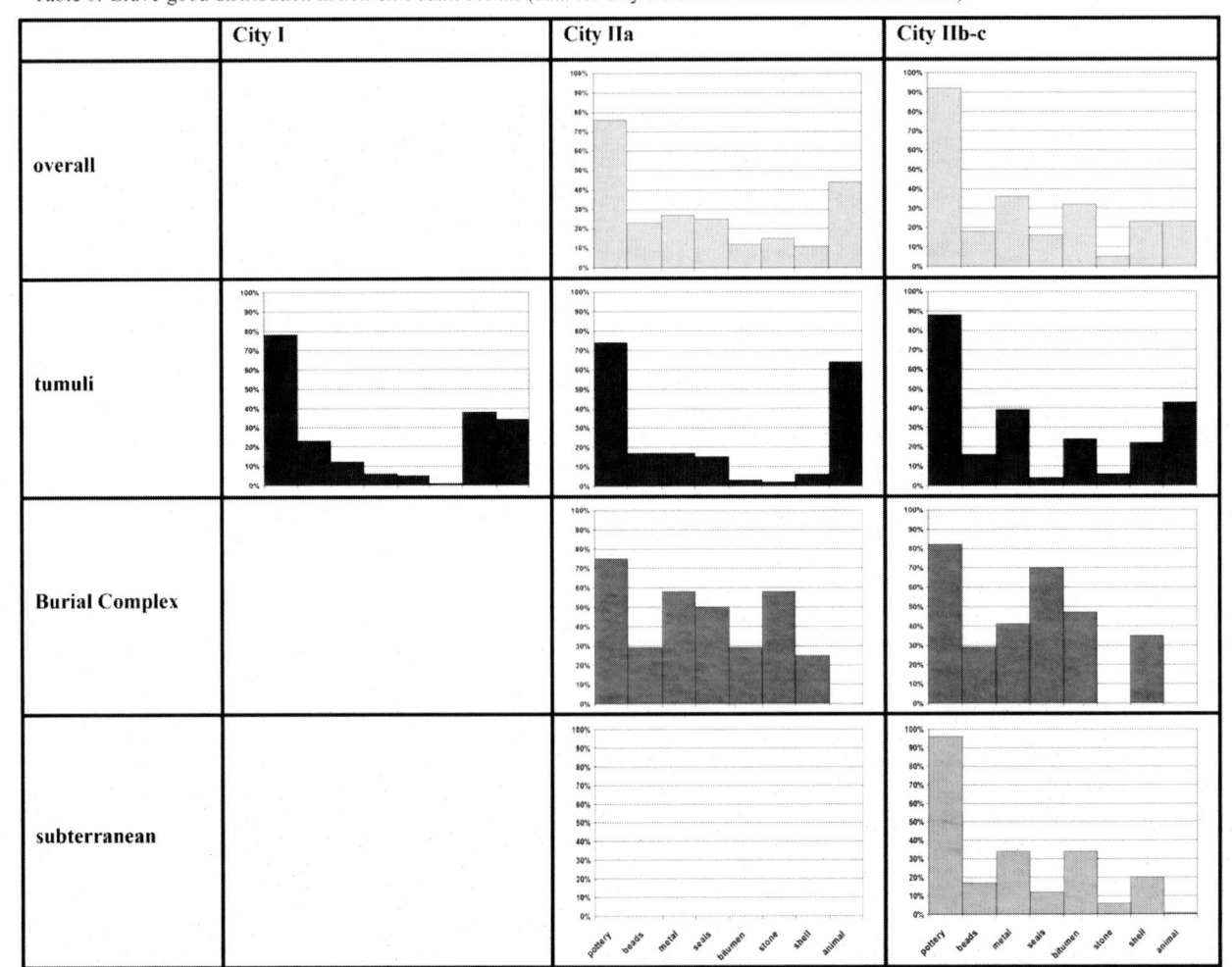

Table 6: Grave-good distribution in non-elite adult burials (data for City I are from Frohlich & Littleton 2007).

	City I	City IIa	City IIb-c
overall		[bar chart]	[bar chart]
tumuli	[bar chart]	[bar chart]	[bar chart]
Burial Complex		[bar chart]	[bar chart]
subterranean		[bar chart]	[bar chart]

Categories (x-axis): pottery, beads, metal, seals, bitumen, stone, shell, animal

What does it mean?

During City IIa-c there was one funerary tradition, but it was not rigid and allowed the existence of parallel expressions in the burial structure above and beyond socio-economic differences expressed primarily in the investment of labour and resources. It would be premature to attempt to explain the co-existence of three burial types for the non-elite element of Early Dilmun society. Do they indicate different professional, social, religious and/or political factions? Whatever the answer, it is clear that the Early Dilmun attitude towards death and the dead was complex and this is even more apparent when grave goods are included (Tab. 6).

Each item was carefully selected and placed in the grave, illustrating the status of those who organise the funeral at least as much as they do the status of the deceased. Clear differences between burial types and/or burial fields indicate that there were specific preferences.

The only grave good produced specifically for funerary use is the Dilmun burial jar; the rest appear to have been items used in everyday life. Apart from pottery and jewellery/adornments, i.e. beads and the majority of metal items, none of the categories appear to have been a regular component of the funerary assemblage. Some have been tentatively associated with females, i.e. jewellery/adornments and bivalve shells (Mughal 1983: 35), and males, i.e. animal bones (Srivastava 1991: 12), but such one-dimensional correlations seem highly improbable given the results from this analysis and the sexual make-up of the funerary record (cf. Laursen & Johansen 2007: 142).

Even taking into account that several categories are underrepresented in the extant database due to the large-scale plundering, it appears that the results are primarily dictated by unique sets of choices as many grave goods may represent alternative items for similar purposes. This is clear for high end alternatives such as ostrich eggs and alabaster vessels – which are found almost exclusively in IIb-c mound burials, with a clear predominance in the 'Ali mound field. Most ceramic, stone and basketry vessels served to hold food and/or liquids required for the journey to the afterlife or for the afterlife itself, while others may have contained oils and ointments probably used in funerary rituals/ceremonies, such as libations, cleansing and anointing the corpse. Residue analyses may provide more information on the interchangeability of grave goods, but until now only a few unworked shells have been analysed, indicating they contained cosmetic substances (Frohlich & Mughannum 1985: 29; cf. Mughal 1983: 36).

The placement of the grave goods might also provide information as it strictly adheres to rules identical for all burial types. The alcove was the focal point for grave goods and appears to have been built specifically for this purpose. Subterranean graves have no alcove and the placement of the grave goods followed that of other burials lacking alcoves. Pottery vessels were placed close to the head of the deceased, funerary jars were usually placed in the alcove or near the wall; bitumen-coated vessels were grouped in the alcove or in the corner of the grave; unworked shells were carefully arranged in most cases in the alcove and sometimes close to the body; seals and stone vessels were placed close to the body, generally in front of the face; jewellery/adornments were found on the deceased, indicating that people were buried fully clothed with their personal ornaments, except for the seals which are only sparsely represented in the funerary record; animal remains were normally confined to the alcove, but in a limited number of cases they were placed very close to the head of the deceased.

Of the grave goods, animal bones show the largest variance – both synchronic and diachronic – between burial types as well as between burial fields. Variations in the number of graves containing animal bones reflect differences in a key grave-side *rite de passage* as the remains of a young goat or sheep (cf. Kveiborg 2007: 153) likely represent remnants of a communal meal.[14]

Final remarks

The *Bahrain Burial Mound Project* is a great initiative and has already produced important results, not only for the study of Early Dilmun funerary practices but also on economic and socio-political developments in Early Dilmun society by placing the funerary practices in their historical context. In this contribution, another potential avenue for the study of Early Dilmun socio-political cohesion has been explored with some intriguing results. However, the conclusions drawn from the extant database of non-elite adult burials from City IIa-c – with all its faults and limitations – should be considered nothing more than tentative. The various idiosyncrasies can only be countered by a massive increase of the database. It is therefore sincerely hoped that the remainder of the 8,000 excavated graves, stored in the Bahrain National Museum, will be published and/or made accessible for study in the form of a national digital database before most of the information is lost.

Acknowledgements

Jean-François Salles graciously allowed me to study and use the information available at the *Maison de l'Orient* of the Early Dilmun cemetery at Karranah 2 excavated in 1986 and 1987 by a team of the University of Lyon. Special thanks are due to Vincent Bernard and Jacqueline Gachet for their work and for providing access to the field notes and drawings of all diagnostic sherds and small finds. I would like to express my gratitude to Pierre Lombard for organising my stay in Lyon in 2004 as well as for his long-term friendship and interest in my work. Christian Velde is greatly acknowledged for many stimulating conversations and for sharing the database and drawings of diagnostic pottery from the Early Dilmun cemetery at Karranah 1 excavated in 1992 and 1993 by a team of the University of Göttingen. Flemming Højlund, Steffen Laursen and Judith Littleton kindly provided valuable comments and suggestions resulting in several improvements and corrections.

References

Bibby T.G. 1954. Five among Bahrain's Hundred Thousand Grave-mounds. *Kuml* 1954: 116-141.

Claessen H.J.M. 2001. Was the State Inevitable? *Social Evolution & History* 1: 101-117.

Cleuziou S., Lombard P. & Salles J.-F. 1981. *Fouilles à Umm Jidr (Bahrain)*. Paris: Editions Recherche sur les Grandes Civilisations.

Cornwall P.B. 1946. Ancient Arabia: Explorations in Hasa, 1940-41. *The Geographical Journal* 107: 28-50.

Crawford H. & Moon J. 1997. Early Dilmun and the Saar Settlement. Pages 13-22 in H. Crawford, R. Killick & J. Moon (eds), *The Dilmun Temple at Saar. Bahrain and its Archaeological Inheritance*. London: Kegan Paul International.

Crombé P., de Dapper M. & Haerinck E. 2001. An archaeological survey of Hawar Island (Bahrain). *Arabian Archaeology and Epigraphy* 12: 143-155.

Daems A., Haerinck E. & Rutten K. 2001. A burial mound at Shakhoura (Bahrain). *Arabian Archaeology and Epigraphy* 12: 173-182.

Denton B.E. 1997. 'Style III' Seals from Bahrain. *Arabian Archaeology and Epigraphy* 8: 174-189.

Denton B.E. 1999. More Pottery, Seals, and a Face-Pendant from cemeteries on Bahrain. *Arabian Archaeology and Epigraphy* 10: 134-160.

During Caspers E.C.L. 1980. *The Bahrain Tumuli. An Illustrated Catalogue of Two Important Collections*. Leiden: Nederlands Historisch-Archaeologisch Instituut te Istanbul.

Frohlich B. 1986. The human biological history of the Early Bronze Age population in Bahrain. Pages 47-63 in Shaikha H.A. al Khalifa & M. Rice (eds), *Bahrain through the Ages: The Archaeology*. London: Kegan Paul International.

Frohlich B. & Mughannum A. 1985. Excavation of the Dhahran Burial Mounds. *Atlāl* 9: 9-40, Pl. 1-29.

Frohlich B. & Lancaster W.J. 1986. Electromagnetic surveying in current Middle Eastern archaeology: Application and evaluation. *Geophysics* 51: 1414-1425.

Frohlich B. & Littleton J. 2007. *Bahrain: A new look at the Early Dilmun burial mounds*. Paper presented at

---

[14] The clear predominance of goats over sheep in non-elite adult graves (cf. Kveiborg 2007: Tab. 2) concurs with the association of sheep with higher social strata.

the Twenty Years of Bahrain Archaeology (1986-2006) Conference, 9th-13th December 2007, Bahrain.

Glob P.V. 1968. *Al-Bahrain. De danske ekspeditioner til oldtidens Dilmun*. Copenhagen: Gyldendal.

Højlund F. 2007. *The Burial Mounds of Bahrain. Social Complexity in Early Dilmun*. Aarhus: Jutland Archaeological Society.

Højlund F., Hilton A.S., Juel C., Kirkeby N., Laursen S.T. & Nielsen L.E. 2008. Late third-millennium elite burials in Bahrain. *Arabian Archaeology and Epigraphy* 19: 143-154.

Ibrahim M.M. 1982. *Excavations of the Arab Expedition at Sār el-Jisr, Bahrain*. State of Bahrain.

Killick R. & Moon J. 2005. Saar, Dilmun and the London-Bahrain Archaeological Expedition. Pages 1-6 in R. Killick & J. Moon (eds), *The Early Dilmun Settlement at Saar*. Ludlow: Archaeology International.

Kjærum P. 1994. Stamp-seals, seal-impressions and seal blanks. Pages 319-350 in F. Højlund & H.H. Andersen (eds), *Qala'at al-Bahrain. Vol. 1: The Northern City Wall and the Islamic Fortress*. Aarhus: Jutland Archaeological Society.

KSAM 2009. *Kuwaiti-Slovak Archaeological Mission (KSAM). Geophysics*. Downloaded on 13-02-2009 from www.kuwaitarchaeology.org/geophysics.html.

Kveiborg J. 2007. Animal bones from the Aali, Saar and Dar Kulayb mound cemeteries. Pages 149-153 in F. Højlund, *The Burial Mounds of Bahrain. Social Complexity in Early Dilmun*. Aarhus: Jutland Archaeological Society.

Larsen C.E. 1983. *Life and Land Use on the Bahrain Islands*. Chicago:. University of Chicago Press.

Laursen S.T. 2008. Early Dilmun and its rulers: new evidence of the burial mounds of the elite and the development of social complexity, *c*. 2200-1750 BC. *Arabian Archaeology and Epigraphy* 19: 156-167.

Laursen S.T. & Johansen K.L. 2007. The potential of aerial photographs in future studies of mound cemeteries. Pages 137-148 in F. Højlund, *The Burial Mounds of Bahrain. Social Complexity in Early Dilmun*. Aarhus: Jutland Archaeological Society.

Leick G. 1994. *Sex and Eroticism in Mesopotamian Literature*. London & New York: Routledge.

Lowe A. 1986. Bronze Age Burial Mounds on Bahrain. *Iraq* XLVIII: 73-84.

Mackay E.J.H. 1929. The Islands of Bahrain. Pages 1-35 in E.J.H. Mackay, G.L. Harding & W.M.F. Petrie, *Bahrein and Hemamieh*. London: British School of Archaeology in Egypt.

Mughal M.R. 1983. *The Dilmun Burial Complex at Sar. The 1980-82 Excavations in Bahrain*. State of Bahrain.

Srivastava K.M. 1991. *Madinat Hamad Burial Mounds – 1984-85*. State of Bahrain.

Velde C. 1994. Die Steinernen Türme. Gedanken zum Aussehen der bronzezeitlichen Gräber und zur Struktur der Friedhöfe auf Bahrain. *Iranica Antiqua* XXIX: 63-82.

Velde C. 1998. The Dilmun Cemetery at Karanah 1 and the change of burial customs in late City II. Pages 245-261 in C.S. Phillips, D.T. Potts & S. Searight (eds), *Arabia and its Neighbours*. Turnhout: Brepols.

Zarins J., Mughannum A.S. & Kamal M. 1984. Excavations at Dhahran South – The Tumuli Field (208-91), 1403 A.H./1983. A Preliminary Report. *Atlāl* 8: 25-54, Pl. 18-59.

Author's address
Eric Olijdam
Adriaan Butijnweg 1
NL-4411 BT Rilland
The Netherlands
olijdam@zeelandnet.nl

The Bahrain bead project: introduction and illustration

Waleed M. Al-Sadeqi

Summary: Beads are small finds with enormous archaeological potential to shed light on various aspects of ancient cultures and their environments. Those of Bahrain have not been sufficiently studied. A bead typology for Bahrain is indispensible in this regard, and must be produced before such study can commence. In this paper, the rudimentary steps in formulating a bead typology have been set out, with a focus on "form" and "material" as an example of the features involved in its construction. The final third of the paper provides an illustration of the use to which the bead typology can be put by comparing samples from two broad epochs of Bahrain's past, the Dilmun and Tylos eras, in terms of the features already discussed. Some basic conclusions are reached by this comparison, though more detailed insight must await the completion of the typology.

Keywords: Bahrain, bead, Dilmun, Tylos, typology

Introduction

Beads represent a distinct type of small find that possesses enormous potential in shedding light on the social, economic, as well as political environment in which an ancient culture existed and participated. Those found amongst the burial assemblages of Bahrain are no different. Unfortunately, however, the beads of Bahrain have seen almost no study whatsoever. A great many beads have been published (i.e., During Caspers 1980: 6, 13-15; Lombard 1989: 79; Mughal 1983: 68-69; and Srivastava 1991: 30-32). Nonetheless, publication is one thing and study another. For the latter, the nature of the small find in question must first be assessed. Its different features must be taken into consideration and the complexities of its nature as well as the significance of such complexities must be determined well before any analysis can be made. In short, a typology of beads particular to the area concerned must first be formulated before any serious study can be performed. Such a typology for Bahrain is currently being constructed through the examination of beads from the Islands. Indeed, Dr. Flemming Højlund has mentioned the need to establish the same in his *Burial Mounds of Bahrain* (2007: 10). It is in this regard – that is, in illustration of the method whereby such a typology can be produced and the importance of its application – that the present paper will proceed.[1]

The Beads of Bahrain: Archaeological Background

A small amount of beads have been found in the excavations of settlements and non-burial sites on Bahrain (i.e., Højlund 1994a: 391-393; Moon 2005: 81-87). However, the majority of those being studied to create a typology are from the cemeteries scattered upon the northern parts of the Islands (Fig. 1). The smallest and most southerly of these is that of Umm-Jidr, comprised of less than a thousand tumuli (Cleuziou, Lombard, and Salles 1981: 21; Højlund 2007: 119). A very sizable amount of the beads examined comes from the mounds at

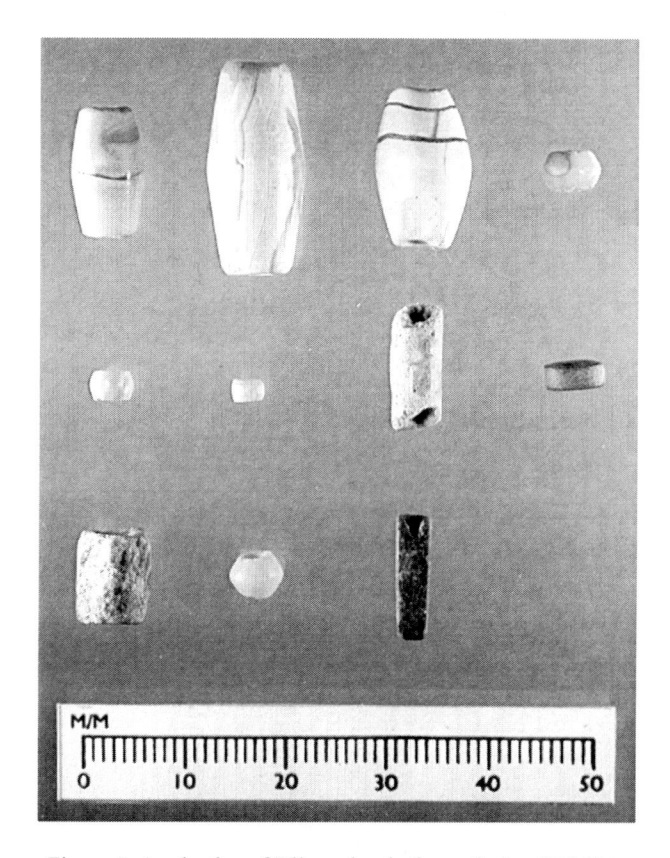

Figure 1. A selection of Dilmun beads (in particular, B1360 to B1370 according to the numbering system of the Bahrain Bead Project) illustrating the variety found amongst the burial assemblages of the Islands.

Saar, the field of which once extended for 3.3 km² from its plateau downwards (Laursen & Johansen 2007: 137-138). The greatest quantity of beads used, however, comes from the tumuli fields of Hamad Town, with the third largest being the contribution of the Aali cemetery. Thereafter come the beads from Janabiya, followed by various other cemeteries of prominence, all of which are located for the most part in the northern half of Bahrain.[2]

---

[1] The present study is part of a PhD that is entering its second year and bears the title of "Bahrain Bead Project". It is a study within which the formation of a typology forms an intrinsic part and which was born out of the necessity to better understand the importance of this type of small find.

[2] The numbers recorded will assuredly be increased as the present year unfolds and the cataloguing of beads as part of this project continues.

Of equal importance to where the beads of Bahrain have come from are the various periods through which the Islands have passed and from which the small finds derive. The two main epochs involved are those of the Dilmun cultures (c. 2300-400 BC) and the Tylos era (c. 400 BC-600 AD). Determining to which period a bead belongs is particularly relevant from the standpoint of constructing a bead typology.[3] Unfortunately, it has been rather difficult to ascertain the period from which many of the beads have come due to the scattered nature of many of the find assemblages from the burial mounds. The majority of the beads have, nonetheless, been placed within context, mainly by way of the style of mound from which they were obtained or through the use of distinct diagnostic pottery types. The presence or absence of glass has moreover been crucial, especially as regards beads from the Tylos era, along with a decrease in carnelian and other materials or the abrupt change in quality as far as bead manufacture goes. Thus one finds that from the total of 1,541 beads excavated from burial sites, 761 have been confirmed to belong to the Dilmun cultures while 373 are certainly Tylos; 407 beads have yet to be dated.[4]

Formulating a Typology: Purpose, Method, and Factors

The benefits of putting together a new bead typology for Bahrain are fourfold: (1) it provides a "standard" for bead definition; (2) it presents a "tailored" system by which researchers in the field can easily define beads found on the Islands; (3) features of a distinct importance can readily be perceived, as well as any discrepancies or absences in this regard; and (4) these same features, and the types defined thereby, can be used to shed light on additional aspects of the cultures to which they belong. An example of this last are such avenues of study as the role of status and wealth in the Dilmun cultures or the extent of Bahrain's trade contacts in the Tylos period. Bahrain being, as is generally accepted, a major maritime trading centre in the region for most of its past, it need not be added that understanding the importance and role of beads on the Islands will also provide a glimpse into the part they play in other neighbouring localities (Andersen 2007: 232; Carter 2003: 31; Crawford 1998: 3; Weisgerber 1986: 135).

Horace C. Beck, in his paper on "The Classification and Nomenclature of Beads and Pendants" (1928), in attempting to mold a universal typology for beads, looked to the very "features of distinct importance" alluded to above. "To describe a bead fully," he wrote, "it is necessary to state its form, perforation, colour, material,

and decoration" (Beck 1928: 1). Peter Francis Jr., writing about three-quarters of a century later, touched on Beck's very words, but added the qualities of "manufacture" deemed relevant by W.G.N. van der Sleen and suggestions of "size" and "diaphaneity" (Francis 2002: 13-15; Van der Sleen 1973: 16). "Size", however, is inherent in Beck's description of bead shapes. All these aspects have been taken stock of in formulating a bead typology for Bahrain. The only exception is Francis' suggestion of "diaphaneity" which, while undeniably relevant, will be applied in the near future to a select sample of beads.

In order to provide an understanding of the method involved in putting together a typology, it may suffice to examine that most crucial of features: the "form" of beads. It should be mentioned that "material" is also essential to the shapes in which beads come, and this last will be turned to in exception below. With regard to "form", however, Beck's own typology was deemed a comprehensive and useful framework. His definitions and technical jargon were moreover observed to be accurate; enough so that slight variations, as for instance between a "bicone" and "truncated bicone", can be distinguished through the use of his system. Objections may be raised that such a typology as Beck's is too complex to be used satisfactorily in the field, as Sir Leonard Woolley did in the past and which prompted him to formulate his own "simplified" system for use in Mesopotamia (Woolley 1934: 366-375). Nonetheless, it should be pointed out that the present undertaking also aims at a simplified system, but one which is to be the end-result of a process that first requires the use of a more comprehensive framework, such as Beck's. Out of the turmoil of all this will appear the final result: a typology suited to Bahrain and the region, being "simple" in its special and localised nature.

It should not, however, be assumed that Beck's system has been applied wholesale. There is much room for expansion and adaption. For example, while Beck makes mention of seven-faceted beads as "polygonal", and part of his "Groups" for "regular faceted beads", this distinction is very broad and does not specify as with some of his other types the exact shape of a specimen; that it does indeed have seven facets (Beck 1928: 6). This cross-sectional type has thus been termed "septagonal" and included in the new typology for Bahrain.

Despite shortcomings of this sort, Beck's system for the classification of most bead shapes (that is, "form") is nonetheless based, in not so many words, on the following salient features: (1) size; (2) cross-sectional shape; and (3) profile shape (Beck 1928: 8-9). These same qualities were therefore deemed essential to defining bead shapes (Fig. 2). The string of qualities can be applied thus to a particular bead; for instance, a "short, circular, truncated bicone" where "short" determines the size, "circular" the cross-sectional shape, and "truncated bicone" the profile shape. Similarly, another bead may be described as a "long, elliptical, barrel", with the relevant features once again presented. In this, one has an accurate, concise method by which bead shapes can be

---

[3] It is currently one focus of the ongoing work upon the Bahrain beads.
[4] The figures, however, do not represent the evaluation of beads scheduled for the coming year, where particularly diagnostic materials (such as carnelian for the Dilmun periods and glass for the Tylos era) will be statistically examined for frequency in burial assemblages and within the context of independent collections (such as necklaces) and the results applied to undated cases. Where enough beads are concerned, as in collections of an adequate size and from a single burial, reliable assumptions can thus be made about the period to which these undated specimens belong.

Bead Shapes Encountered on Bahrain

Cross-sectional Shapes

Circular	Circle and Flat	Ellipse and Flat	Ellipsoid	Hexagonal	Lenticular

Hexgonal Lenticular	Plano-convex	Rectangular	Semicircular	Septagonal	Square

Profile Shapes

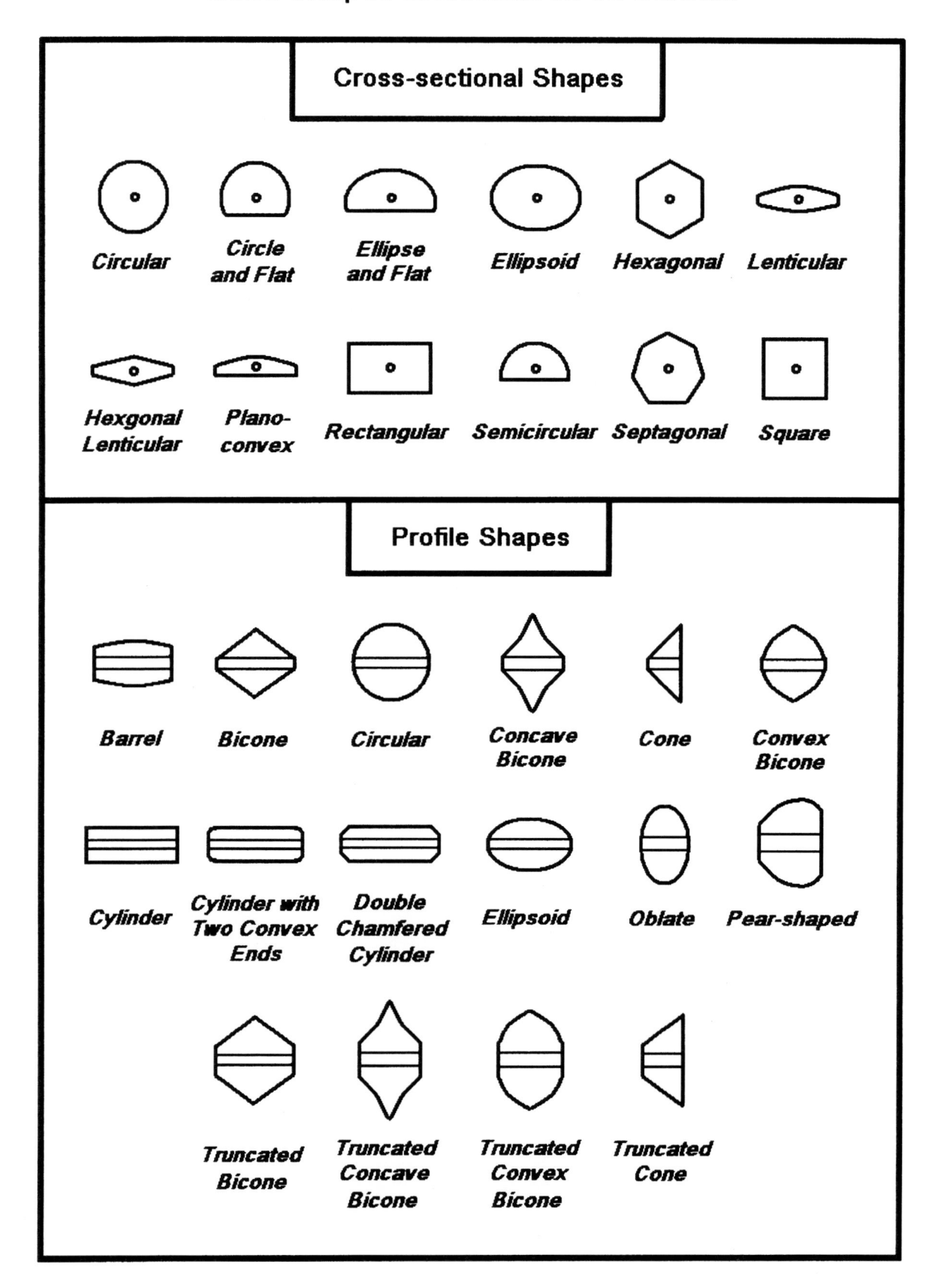

Barrel	Bicone	Circular	Concave Bicone	Cone	Convex Bicone

Cylinder	Cylinder with Two Convex Ends	Double Chamfered Cylinder	Ellipsoid	Oblate	Pear-shaped

Truncated Bicone	Truncated Concave Bicone	Truncated Convex Bicone	Truncated Cone

Figure 2. "Ideal" renderings of the different bead cross-sectional and profile shapes referred to in this paper. Some examples, such as the "septagonal" cross-section, are particular to the Bahrain typology being developed and are not found amongst Beck's classifications for regular beads (Beck 2008: Plates I-III).

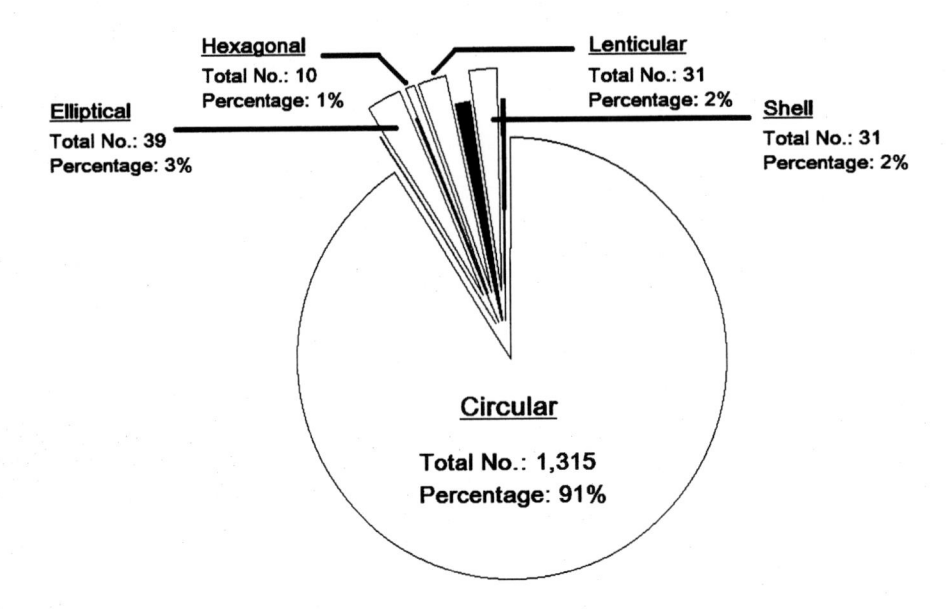

Figure 3. The highest percentages of cross-sectional shapes encountered amongst the burial beads of Bahrain. The term "shell" refers to such types as are slight modifications of natural shell forms.

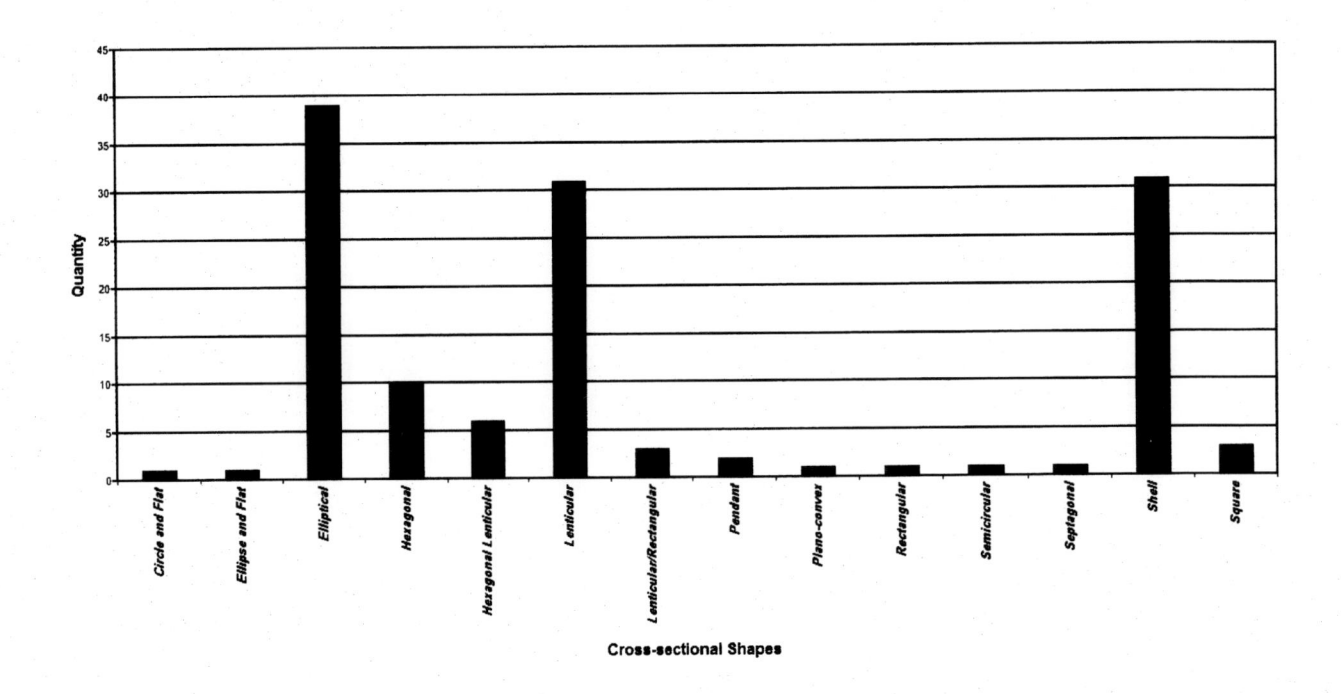

Figure 4. The different bead cross-sectional shapes found amongst the burial assemblages of Bahrain, and excluding the circular variety that is the most common. "Shell" and "pendant" refer respectively to modifications on natural shell shapes and "unique" pendant shapes specifically fashioned for this type of bead.

defined. A full-fledged typology will only be the extension of this method to those kinds found in Bahrain.

The tripartite system of bead description has been employed to great effect on Bahrain. Thus one observes that with regard to the first quality to be examined, that of "size", all four kinds were found. Most burial beads from Bahrain were of the short variety, with 585 examples. Excluding undetermined cases, there were 342 long, 316 disc, and 115 standard beads as well.

With regard to cross-sectional shapes, fifteen different varieties have been noted so far, with circular sections being the most dominant by a vastly wide margin. In fact, out of the 1,541 different specimens from Bahrain's

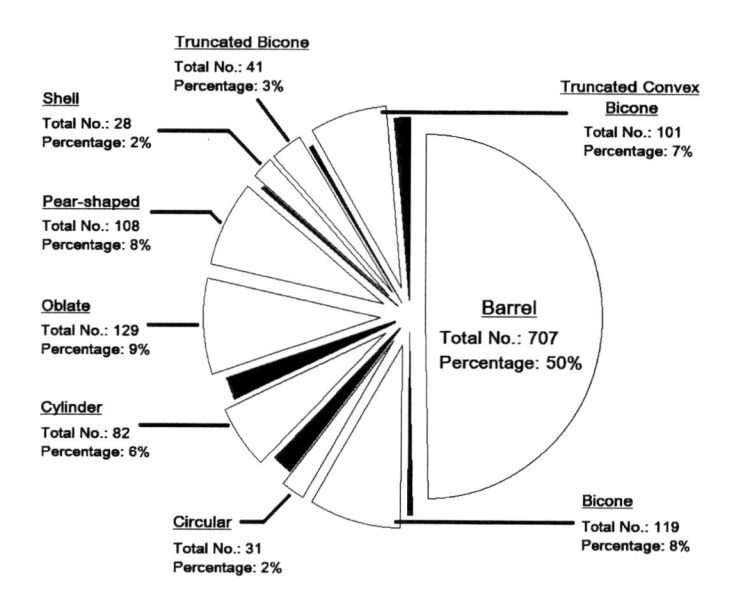

Figure 5. The highest percentages of profile shapes encountered amongst the burial beads of Bahrain.

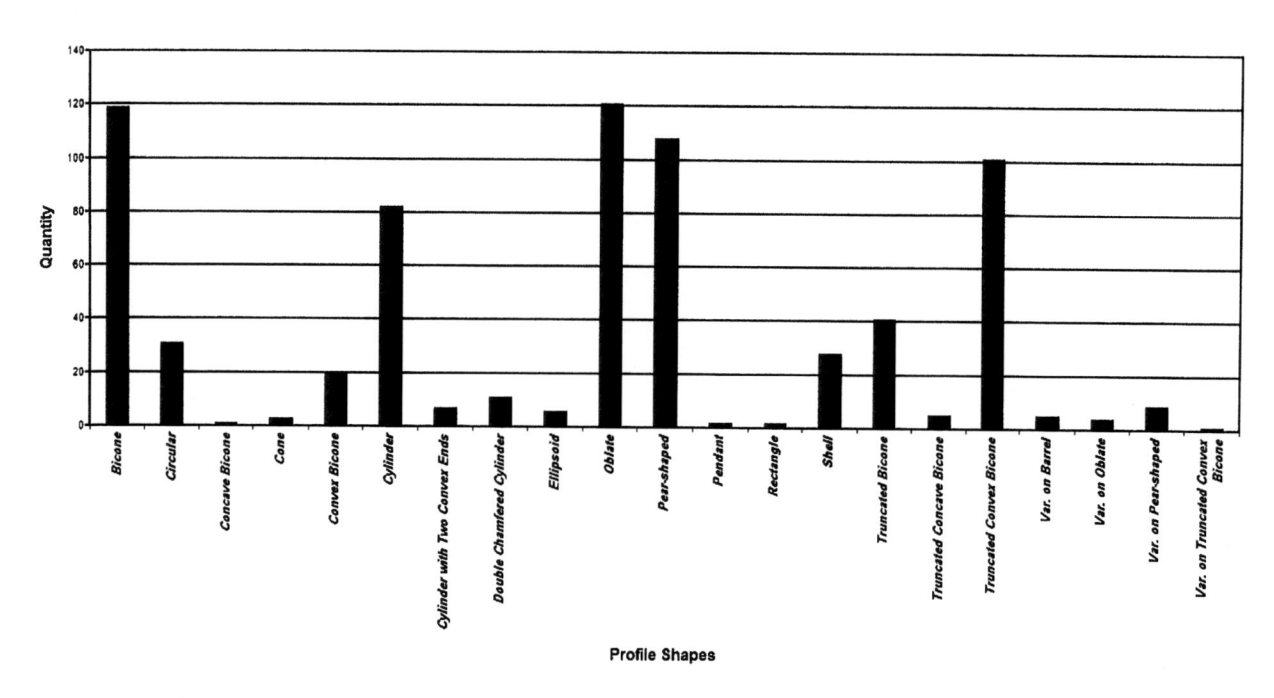

Figure 6. The different profile shapes found amongst the burial assemblages of Bahrain, and excluding the regular barrel variety that is the most common. Variations on this shape (indicated by "Var. on Barrel") have been included nonetheless. Variations on other shapes have been included as well. These represent minor deviations from the standard and have been, for the sake of clarity, presented in this paper under a single heading.

burials, 1,315 circularly cross-sectioned beads were found (Fig. 3). The most common cross-sectional shapes thereafter are the elliptical and lenticular varieties at 39 and 31 cases respectively. Naturally occurring shell cross-sections were also noted 31 times, with all other varieties following in decreasing numbers (Fig. 4).

As far as profile shape is concerned, the different types involved in producing the burial beads total at twenty-two thus far, the barrel being (like the circular cross-section) the most dominant with a wide margin between its 707 occurrences and those of the oblate and bicone, at 121 and 119 cases each (Fig. 5). Thereafter come the pear-shaped, truncated convex bicone, and cylinder shapes at 108, 101, and 82 occurrences each. Other kinds follow with again ever-decreasing numbers (Fig. 6).

Turning now to the sole exception to our cursory look at "form", namely that of "material", it cannot be denied that the same greatly influences the shape and manufacture of beads. It is thus very relevant to the forms in which beads come. Twenty-one different materials have so far been recorded in the study of the 1,541 burial beads, ranging from quartz, alabaster, and onyx to

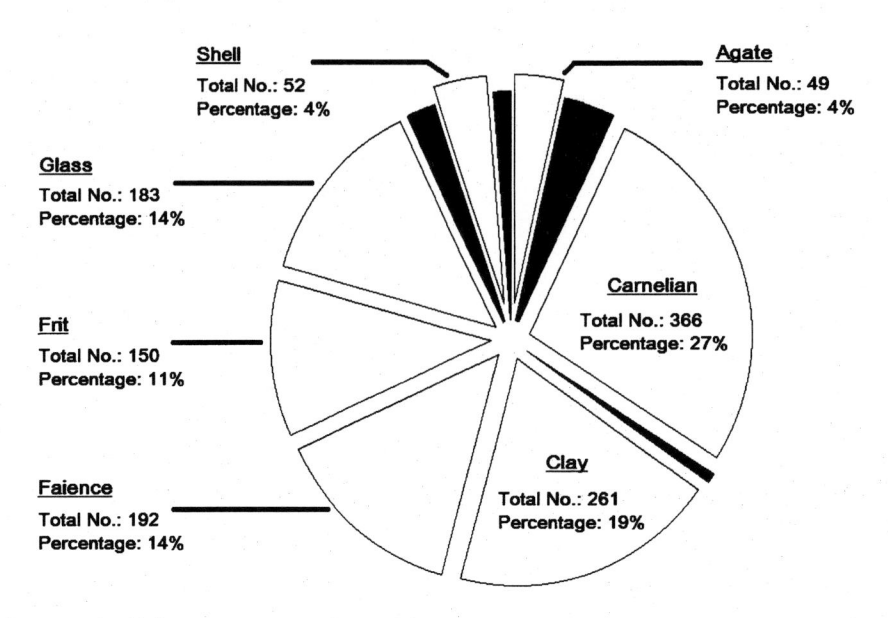

Figure 7. The highest percentages of materials encountered amongst the burial beads of Bahrain.

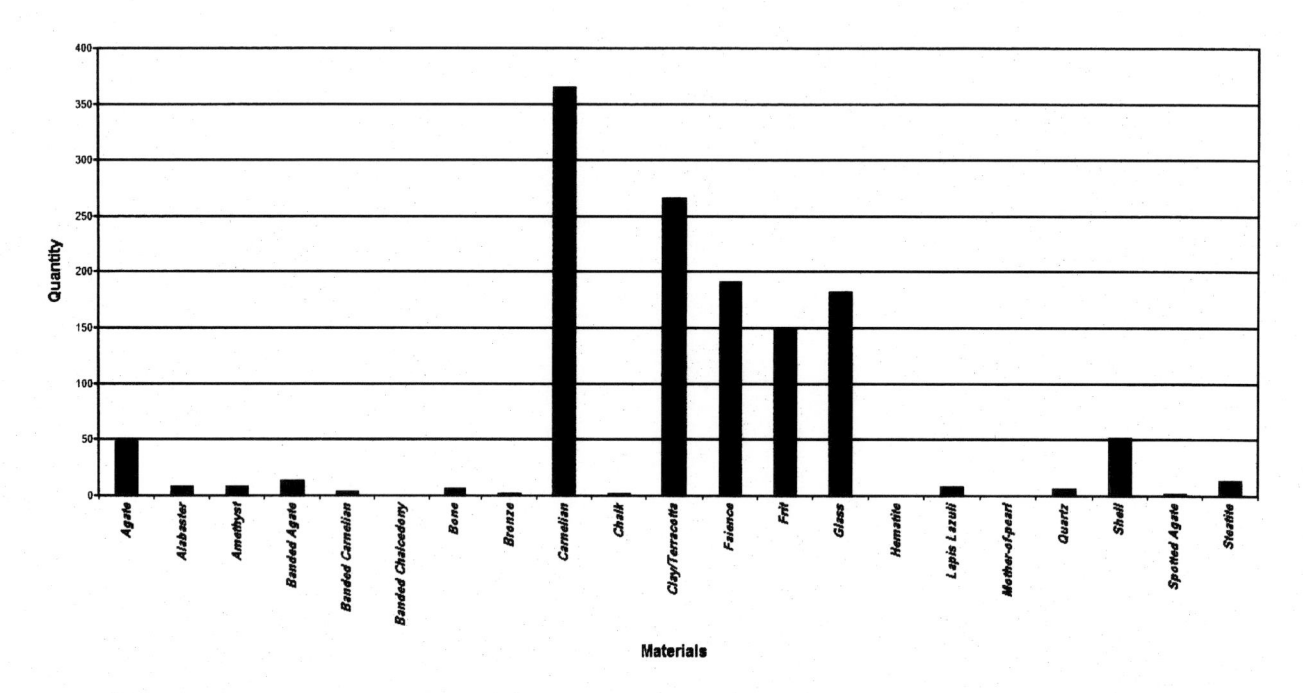

Figure 8. The different materials found amongst the burial assemblages of Bahrain. Since carnelian, which is naturally the most encountered material, does not significantly outnumber the other kinds and inhibit clarity, it has been included herein for the sake of comparison.

copper, shell, and bone, with carnelian forming the largest sub-group. 366 different specimens of carnelian beads, etched or otherwise, were counted while clay came in at second with 261 specimens. Then come faience, glass, and frit at respectively 192, 183, and 150 beads.[5] While these may seem relevant in their abundance, such may likely be explained by the relatively cheap means of producing glass and, by extension, the other materials

(Francis 1999: 54; Lankton 2003: 45; Renfrew & Bahn 2003: 345). Generally speaking, these are the same substance subjected to varying levels of heat (Renfrew & Bahn 2003: 344-345; Van der Sleen 1973: 19). This is particularly true of glass during the Tylos era. During the Bronze Age, the use of glass was more weighty and represented a "prestige technology" (Lankton 2003: 45; Renfrew & Bahn 2003: 345). Nonetheless, it is the preponderance of carnelian that most catches one's eye (Fig. 7). However, given the well-documented trade that was on-going between the Indus and Mesopotamia in the 3rd and 2nd millennia BC and in which Dilmun acted as middleman, and given that the vast majority of the

---

[5] The terms "faience" and "frit" have often been used interchangeably in archaeological literature. However, W.G.N. van der Sleen indicated a slight difference in texture, with frit being coarse and faience otherwise (Van der Sleen 1973: 17). The same distinction is held throughout this paper.

carnelian beads studied here come from the cultures comprising ancient Dilmun, it is no surprise that they dominate (Cleuziou 1986: 153; Dubin 1987: 44-45; Joshi 1986: 72-75; Lankton 2003: 33; Possehl 2002: 217; Weisgerber 1986: 135, 138-139). All other materials, in both the Dilmun and Tylos cultures, are found in relatively decreasing numbers despite their variety amongst the 1,541 burial beads (Fig. 8).

The above is a general overview of the sizes, cross-sectional shapes, profile shapes and materials (excluding undetermined cases) taken into consideration as part of forming a bead typology for Bahrain. The additional features suggested by Beck, Francis, and Van der Sleen, as well as others, have also been examined, though not included here for reasons of space. Nonetheless, the Bahrain bead typology is being produced out of the combination of these features, in compounds of ever-increasing complexity, until final definitive types have been reached.

Comparing Dilmun and Tylos Beads: An Illustration

Having described the basic process being employed in formulating the bead typology for Bahrain, one may wonder about the kind of use to which this typology can be put. An adequate and, at the same time, simple task to illustrate its application would be a comparison between beads from Dilmun burials and those from Tylos graves. Since only 373 Tylos beads have thus far been catalogued, and these from five different graves, it is evident that a similar amount of Dilmun beads will also be required from a comparable number of burials. This will keep the parameters of the comparison in a roughly controlled state. Of course, it need not be mentioned that the Dilmun beads to be employed here come from burials spanning the three periods of Early (c.2300-1700 BC), Middle (c.1700-1000 BC), and Late Dilmun (c.1000-400 BC). It is no dilemma that this is so, as far as the present comparison is simply for the sake of illustrating how the bead typology of Bahrain can be used. Nor is the sampling method involved, of 373 beads from five different burials without regard for site or type of grave, along with other circumstances (such as the re-use of beads), to be considered irksome for much the same reason.

The total number of beads, 746 in all, come therefore from ten burials. The five Dilmun ones are Captain Higham's Grave 36; the respective S-267.3 and 144 burials of the Arab and 1980-82 Expeditions at Saar; and the Bahrain National Museum's Hamad Town Mound 1 and Janabiya 81A.6 burial (During Caspers 1980: 14-15; Ibrahim 1982: 83-85; Mughal 1983: 383-384). The Tylos-period graves are Captain Higham's Grave 46; the German Expedition's Mound 1.2; and the Bahrain National Museum's Saar 1.4 and 5.4-9 burials, along with its 1982 main grave at Aali (During Caspers 1980: 13). To examine the beads from these burials, the most self-evident course of action would be to pursue the various factors important to constructing a bead typology. The full-fledged typology need not be applied, however, and only certain essential features, such as three of those already dealt with in the examination of bead "form", are enough to avoid abstruseness.

In terms of cross-sectional shape, six distinct kinds exist amongst the beads from the Dilmun burials. The most prevalent is the circular cross-section, at 342 cases, followed by a breakdown of the various other types as follows: 10 elliptical cases; 7 lenticular cases; 6 hexagonal ones; 4 of a variety described as hexagonal lenticular (and not found amongst Beck's categories); and single examples of a crescent-shaped, rectangular, and septagonal cross-section. The Tylos burials, however, provide five kinds of cross-sectional shapes, with the circular type being once again the most dominant at 365 cases. Following this, four elliptical cross-sections, along with a circle-and-flat and a naturally occurring shell example, were observed. The remaining two Tylos specimens, out of the 373 total, were undefined due to the irregularity of their cross-sections.

It therefore seems that out of the comparison of this small amount of Dilmun and Tylos beads, respectively, the variety in bead cross-sectional shapes has diminished. The number of circular examples increases in the Tylos period, and while the elliptical kind is still second (in terms of frequency) it is not found in as great a number. What is also intriguing is that the hexagonal lenticular variety, which possesses parallels in Mesopotamia (as at Ur for example), seems to disappear completely (Woolley 1934: 368). It would appear that contact between these two has been reduced, or else that such a style has fallen out of favour in Bahrain or its neighbours. Before any assessment of exchange in Tylos as opposed to Dilmun can be made, however, it will be necessary to move on to the examination of other factors involved in the Bahrain typology.

With regard to profile shapes, the most prominent type in the Dilmun cultures on the basis of five burials is the barrel, there being 240 such examples. Thereafter come the regular bicone at 53, the truncated convex bicone at 27, and the cylinder at 19 instances. Circular beads, those that are described as spherical since they are so in conjunction with a similar cross-section, number at 11 cases. Nine other profile shapes were also observed, in lessening degrees of frequency. There was only a single case where the shape was undetermined. One can compare these figures to the profile shapes of the Tylos sample, where the barrel variety is once again dominant at 217 cases; less than the total from the Dilmun sample and yet still the most numerous type. The three kinds most readily encountered thereafter, however, are no longer the bicone, truncated convex bicone, and cylinder shapes; these occur only at 2, 4, and 5 cases respectively. Rather, the barrel is followed by the pear-shaped bead at 87, the oblate at 22, and a variation on the pear-shape at 9 instances. Even the circular variety has been reduced to 4 cases.

On the whole, however, the variety of profile shapes does not seem to diminish or alter much in the Tylos period;

15 types, in comparison to the Dilmun total of 14, with only 6 undetermined occurrences. Thus one observes that while the sum of profile shape types remains more or less constant, excluding the barrel, preference seems to have switched to pear-shaped beads and variations thereon as well as the oblate kind. This reflects the corresponding shift in manufacture from one based mainly on exploiting semi-precious stone, and particularly carnelian, to the overwhelming use of glass observed in the Tylos period. And while the barrel shape is still predominant, the amount of this sort apparently decreased in proportion to the rise in the glass-associated types mentioned above.

Such a shift, with all its ramifications, may be more readily observed when one examines the beads from both the Dilmun and Tylos samples from the standpoint of material. With respect to the first of the two samples, faience seems to be the most widely appearing material at 189, followed by carnelian at 121. Faience, as mentioned above, was the precursor of glass and cheaply produced. This, along with the large number in which it is found in the five Dilmun burials, does indeed indicate that faience was a frequently used material in terms of the Bronze Age Bahrain beads. However, whilst it seems to outnumber carnelian, this is only an illusory conclusion arrived at by the limitations of the present sample. The earlier analysis of material totals in the collection being studied to form the typology displays carnelian as the most widely encountered type in the Dilmun periods, with faience coming in at third alongside clay. This puts things into perspective, especially as regards acomparison with the Tylos sample. All other materials, such as agate, amethyst, quartz, bronze, lapis lazuli, and the like appear in smaller quantities ranging from 6 cases for the first two to only a single specimen of the last.

With regard to the Tylos sample, these other materials are further reduced in quantity, with only agate remaining at 6 examples. Faience still outnumbers carnelian at 85 to 18; and this is a more accurate representation of Tylos owing to the prevalence of glass-making technology as well as the same being drawn from a less-biased collection than the Dilmun sample obtained to match it. Carnelian is still present and was widely traded during this period. This is to be expected due to sources existing in Iran and in different parts of Asia (Simpson 2003: 64-65). Both materials, however, have been superseded in the Tylos sample by glass and terracotta, with 155 and 96 examples respectively. The appearance of the former in large numbers is no surprise for the boom in glass-making and usage already mentioned. What is surprising, however, is the relegation of faience from those shapes now dominated by glass to pear-shaped and only this last. The cause is of course the similarity between glass and faience in production method, where the former would naturally overtake the latter due to its being an improved material with results of a better quality. Both glass and faience are produced from crystalline matter (usually crushed quartz or sand) to which an alkali is added before heating; the difference between the two is determined solely by the amount of heating applied, this of course improving with the advancements in furnace technology marking the Tylos period (Francis 1999: 54; Lankton 2003: 45; Renfrew & Bahn 2004: 345; Van der Sleen 1973: 19). Pear-shaped beads from Bahrain tend to be poorly produced examples, with a lack of care given to shaping the same, and the usage of faience only points out a similar neglect in forming the material (or else represents poorer quality in its production). Glass is also cheap to produce (Francis 1999: 54; Lankton 2003: 45; Renfrew & Bahn 2004: 345). Clay, being the second most numerous material, was probably used frequently for a similar reason.

Dilmun Bead Quantities Based on Type

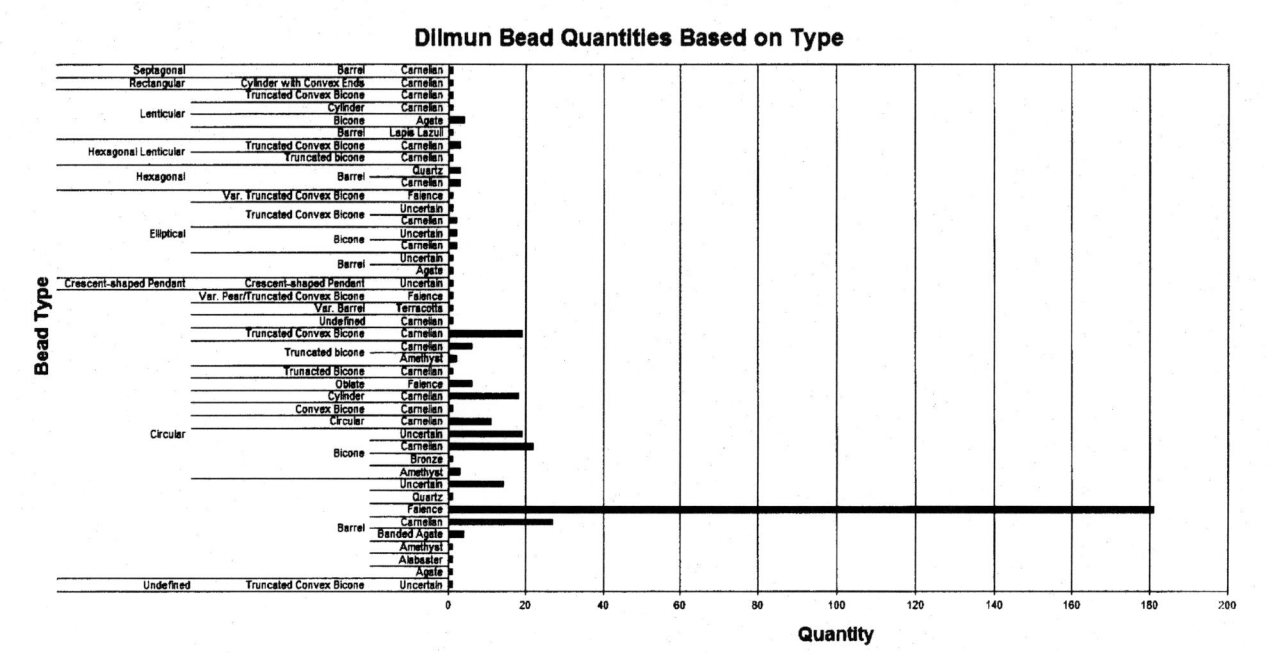

Figure 9. The variety of cross-sectional shapes, profile shapes, and materials involved in the "break-down" of the beads from the Dilmun sample, including those cases that have yet to be defined.

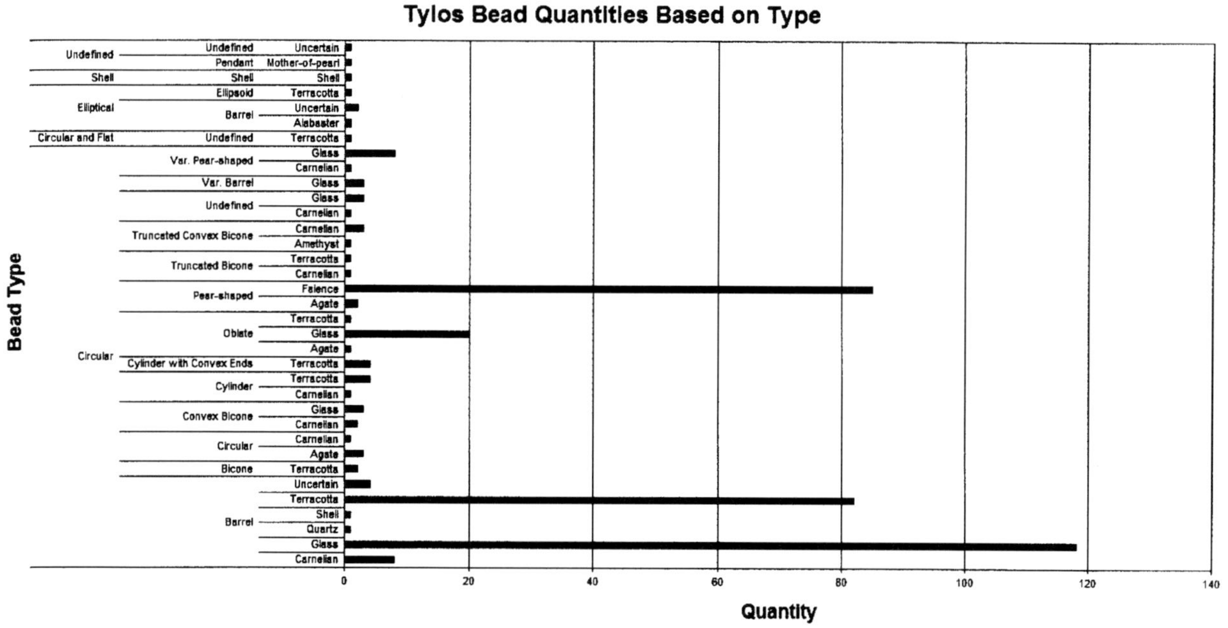

Tylos Bead Quantities Based on Type

Figure 10. The variety of cross-sectional shapes, profile shapes, and materials involved in the "break-down" of the beads from the Tylos sample, including those cases in these three categories that have yet to be defined.

Thus, in Tylos as opposed to Dilmun, there is an increase in employing such materials rather than focusing on more expensive semi-precious materials from abroad. This does not mean a lack of trade, as the existence of foreign materials hint at ongoing contact and exchange, but there does seem to be a lessening thereof as indicated by the beads. Contact with the Indus, if not some nearer source of carnelian, is definitely attested to by the presence of the stone, both in its typical form and in the guise of its near cousin, agate. Other materials, such as amethyst and alabaster also indicate outside contact; though this, as has already been stated, must not have been quite so extensive as it was during the Dilmun periods.

Putting cross-sectional and profile shapes together, along with the material used in manufacturing the beads, the most prevalent type from the Dilmun sample is the faience circular barrel with 181 examples. It is a shape easily produced with prototypical glass-working technology. This is followed by carnelian, however; the Dilmun material *par excellence*. There are 27 circular barrels, 22 circular bicones, 19 circular truncated convex bicones, and 18 circular cylinders all of this material. Other combinations are found with less frequency. In the Tylos sample, glass takes over at the top of the range in circular barrel form, with 118 examples. Thus it replaces faience in this fashion, which appears in circular pear-shaped form with 85 instances of the same. Circular barrels produced of terracotta are next at 82 examples, with glass reappearing in circular oblate form with 20 such cases. Carnelian appears amidst the collection of combinations to follow, many being of other semi-precious stones though some glass and terracotta beads are still stumbled upon. The different combinations for both the Dilmun and Tylos samples appear in Figures 9 and 10, which present the break-down of shape and material in a slightly more straightforward fashion.

Some Conclusions

In comparing the separate factors that have gone into the production of a bead typology for Bahrain along with the combination of some of these into a rudimentary set of classifications, some basic assertions can be made.[6] During the Dilmun periods, extensive trade with its economic neighbours, in particular Mesopotamia and the Indus, is visible both in the bead shapes favoured in Bahrain as well as the diversity of semi-precious stones that went into the production of these. Harriet Crawford has observed that, "lapis and turquoise may have come... from Afghanistan and north-eastern Iran, via the Indus valley, while the carnelian may have originated in the Indus" (1998: 102). Recent studies show that north-eastern Iran and Afghanistan, as with the other materials, were also prominent sources of carnelian (Simpson 2003: 64-65). A more local source, closer to Bahrain, also existed in Ras al-Khaimah (De Waele 2007: 305). Indeed, carnelian was obviously the most favoured material during the Dilmun periods, and the beads produced thereby along with their modifications were likely obtained from its neighbours both in raw form and as finished products. Dilmun, acting as middleman in the trade that existed between these neighbours and which involved such items, could readily have benefited from its position in this way (Dubin 1987: 44-45; Kenoyer 2008: 23; Jyotsna 2000: 6-7). At present this may be taken as most probable, but no statement can be made with certainty about whether the said beads, as finished products, were from the Indus or some other foreign source (Dani 1983: 385).[7] One must also allow the possibility that they were locally produced. However, if the beads did come from the Indus and were finished

---

[6] The classifications are, of course, far from their final form.

[7] Not without further work on the bead typology and comparison with materials in other lands with which the Bahrain Islands had contact. Such will be carried out in the near future.

there, the examples from Bahrain are much cruder in shape than their counterparts found in the former. Perhaps those of a poorer quality were exported to Bahrain, or the beads might have been cut elsewhere. For instance, while most carnelian beads from Ur were manufactured in the Indus, nodules from the site indicate that some local production did indeed take place (Kenoyer 2008: 25-26). Similar locally-produced beads might well have been sent to Bahrain. Despite such speculations, the Dilmun era represents a time of relative prosperity (decline in the Middle and Late Dilmun periods aside), particularly when compared to the Tylos culture, in terms of the value of materials used and the large quantities in which they are found.

In the Tylos era, there seems to be a "diffusion" of trade interests; called this because a greater variety of materials appear in relatively small numbers. Such diffusion is not unfounded, based on Bahrain's possible role as a "Babylonian emporium" in the Achaemenid empire and its subsequent economic activity (with fluctuations) under the presence of the Seleucids, Parthians, and Sasanians (Andersen 2007: 232, 241-242; Højlund 1994b: 480). As far as beads are concerned, this is quite possible given the trade in such objects across the Sasanian empire (Lankton 2003: 68; Simpson 2003: 68). The bulk of beads from the Tylos sample indicate a focus on more cheaply produced glass and terracotta, the former of the two being a mark of the times though neither necessarily indicates a Bahrain more conservative in its trade. Certain materials seem to be favoured, and while it is not impossible that glass beads were produced on the Islands themselves (though there is no evidence), international trade in the same was not unheard of (Andersen 2007: 18-19). The Roman expansion is considered to be one of the great periods of glass-making, and this material was often traded alongside the spread of Roman influence, whether by direct contact or indirectly through exchange (Dubin 1987: 55). Indeed, trade on an international scale is definite and many imports were brought to the Islands (Andersen 2007: 239).

On the whole, however, all assertions made above are based on small samples of beads compared as part of an illustration of how the bead typology of Bahrain can be used. For greater accuracy and more reliable information, the typology will have to be expanded. Related analysis, such as the testing of material compounds by the Raman method or the microscopic study of external and perforation casts to detect finishing and drilling techniques by their serrations, are also being considered for the near future. The results of such studies can then be combined with the bead typology and the whole directed on a larger scale to understanding the nature of the political, social, and economic waters into which Bahrain sailed from the 3rd millennium BC to beyond the mid-1st millennium AD.

Acknowledgments

The author would like to acknowledge those whose advice and support have made the Bahrain Bead Project possible. In particular, Dr. Derek Kennet (Durham University, United Kingdom) whose untiring patience and supervision has aided every step of this PhD project; Dr. Flemming Højlund (Moesgaard Museum, Denmark) who first suggested the need to study Bahrain's beads and provided the impetus to do so; Dr. St John Simpson (the British Museum, United Kingdom) for allowing the E.P. Jefferson and Captain Higham beads stored at the British Museum to be examined as part of this project, and for giving additional advice and feedback; Prof. Tony Wilkinson (Durham University, United Kingdom) who has also been kind enough to supervise the author; Steffen Terp Laursen, MA (Aarhus University, Denmark) for his invaluable suggestions when discussing some of the more difficult issues involved in studying beads; Eric Olijdam, MA (Durham University, United Kingdom) for making known materials and avenues through which the examination of Bahrain's beads can proceed; and the staff at the Bahrain National Museum and Directorate for Culture and National Heritage for their continuing archaeological work and aid. Sincerest thanks are extended to all the individuals concerned, whether in Bahrain or abroad.

References

Andersen S. 2007. *The Tylos Period Burials in Bahrain, Volume 1: The Glass and Pottery Vessels.* Kingdom of Bahrain: Directorate of Culture & National Heritage.

Beck H. 1928. Classification and Nomenclature of Beads and Pendants. *Archaeologia or Miscellaneous Tracts Relating to Antiquity* LXXVII: 1-76.

Carter R. 2003. Restructuring Bronze Age trade: Bahrain, southeast Asia and the copper question. Pages 31-42 in H. Crawford (ed.), *The Archaeology of Bahrain: The British contribution.* Oxford: Archaeopress.

Cleuziou S. 1986. Dilmun and Makkan during the third and early second millennia B.C. Pages 143-156 in H. Al Khalifa & M. Rice (eds), *Bahrain through the ages: the Archaeology.* London: KPI Limited.

Cleuziou S., Lombard P. & Salles J. 1981. *Fouilles a Umm Jidr (Bahrain).* Paris: Éditions A.D.P.F.

Crawford H. 1998. *Dilmun and its Gulf neighbours.* Cambridge: Cambridge University Press.

Dani A. 1986. Bahrain and the Indus civilisation. Pages 383-388 in H. Al Khalifa & M. Rice (eds), *Bahrain through the ages: the Archaeology.* London: KPI Limited.

De Waele A. 2007. The beads of ed-Dur (Umm al-Qaiwain, UAE). *Proceedings of the Seminar for Arabian Studies* 37: 297-308.

Dubin L. 1987. *The History of Beads: From 30,000 BC to the Present.* London: Thames & Hudson.

During Caspers E. 1980. *The Bahrain Tumuli: An Illustrated Catalogue of Two Important Collections.* Leiden: Nederlands Instituut voor het Nabije Oosten.

Francis P. 1999. *Beads of the World.* Atglen: Schiffer Publishing Ltd.

Francis P. 2002. *Asia's Maritime Bead Trade: 300 B.C. to the Present.* Hawai'i: University of Hawai'i Press.

Højlund F. 1994a. Other finds. Pages 361-416 in P. Mortensen (ed.), *Qala'at al-Bahrain, Volume 1: The Northern City Wall and the Islamic Fortress.* Moesgaard: Jutland Archaeological Society.

Højlund F. 1994b. Summary and conclusions. Pages 463-481 in P. Mortensen (ed.), *Qala'at al-Bahrain, Volume 1: The Northern City Wall and the Islamic Fortress.* Moesgaard: Jutland Archaeological Society.

Højlund F. 2007. *The Burial Mounds of Bahrain: Social complexity in Early Dilmun.* Moesgaard: Jutland Archaeological Society.

Ibrahim M. 1982. *Excavations of the Arab Expedition at Sār el-Jisr, Bahrain.* Bahrain: Ministry of Information.

Joshi J. 1986. India and Bahrain: A survey of culture interaction during the third and second millennia. Pages 73-75 in H. Al Khalifa & M. Rice (eds), *Bahrain through the ages: the Archaeology.* London: KPI Limited.

Jyotsna M. 2000. *Distinctive Beads in Ancient India.* Oxford: Archaeopress.

Kenoyer J. 2008. Indus and Mesopotamian Trade Networks: New Insights from Shell and Carnelian Artifacts. Pages 19-28 in E. Olijdam & R. Spoor (eds), *Intercultural Relations between South and Southwest Asia: Studies in commemoration of E.C.L. During Caspers (1934-1996).* Oxford: Archaeopress.

Lankton J. 2003. *A Bead Timeline, Volume I: Prehistory to 1200 CE.* Washington, DC: The Bead Society of Greater Washington.

Laursen S. & Johansen K. 2007. The potential of aerial photographs in future studies of mound cemeteries. Pages 137-148 in F. Højlund (ed.), *The Burial Mounds of Bahrain: Social complexity in Early Dilmun.* Moesgaard: Jutland Archaeological Society.

Lombard P. 1989. The Late Dilmun Period. Pages 51-80 in P. Lombard & M. Kervran (eds), *Bahrain National Museum Archaeological Collections, Volume I: A Selection of Pre-Islamic Antiquities from Excavations 1954-1975.* Bahrain: Ministry of Information.

Moon J. 2005. Tools, weapons, utensils and ornaments. Pages 163-234 in R. Killick & J. Moon (eds), *The Early Dilmun Settlement at Saar.* Ludlow: Archaeology International Ltd.

Mughal M. 1983. *The Dilmun Burial Complex at Sar: The 1980-82 Excavations in Bahrain.* Bahrain: Ministry of Information.

Possehl G. 2002. *The Indus Civilization: A Contemporary Perspective.* Walnut Creek: AltaMira Press.

Rao S. 1986. Trade and cultural contacts between Bahrain and India in the third and second millennia B.C. Pages 376-382 in H. Al Khalifa & M. Rice (eds), *Bahrain through the ages: the Archaeology.* London: KPI Limited.

Renfrew C. & Bahn P. 2004. *Archaeology: Theories, Methods, and Practice.* New York: Thames & Hudson Inc.

Simpson S. 2003. Sasanian Beads: the evidence of art, archaeology and history. Pages 59-78 in C. Glover & H. Hughes Brock & J. Henderson (eds), *Ornaments from the Past: Bead Studies after Beck.* London: the Bead Study Trust.

Srivastava K. 1991. *Madinat Hamad: Burial Mounds – 1984-85.* Bahrain: Ministry of Information.

Van der Sleen W. 1973. *A Handbook on Beads.* York: George Shumway Publisher.

Weisgerber G. 1986. Dilmun – a trading entrepôt: evidence from historical and archaeological sources. Pages 135-142 in H. Al Khalifa & M. Rice (eds), *Bahrain through the ages: the Archaeology.* London: KPI Limited.

Woolley C. 1934. *Ur Excavations, Volume II: The Royal Cemetery.* London: The British Museum Press.

Author's Address
Waleed M. Al-Sadeqi,
Durham University
Dept. of Archaeology
South Road
Durham DH1 3LE
United Kingdom
waleed.alsadeqi@dur.ac.uk

The burial mounds of the Middle Euphrates (2100-1800 B.C.) and their links with Arabia: the subtle dialectic between tribal and state practices

Christine Kepinski

Summary

The burial mounds correspond in the Middle Euphrates, to an exceptional funerary practice. Well known in several regions of the East and particularly in Arabia, they are often situated at cross-roads and river crossings, on islands and hilltops and often represent territorial markers. We hypothesize that they are revealing indicators of the presence of pastoralists in the process of settling down. The Middle Euphrates was one of the meeting points between nomads and sedentary people and both the cohabitation and the alternation between the two subsistence patterns can be observed. Following periods of settling down, the nomadic populations were pushed out towards the steppe and the Arabian Desert with which they maintained constant relations and shared values.

Keywords: Burial mound, Middle Euphrates, Arabia, Amorites, nomadism

Introduction

Within the inventory of burial practices and associated beliefs in Arabia and neighbouring regions, this paper introduces several cemeteries from the Middle Euphrates, focussing mainly on the two isolated Iraqi graveyards of 'Usiyeh and Shuweimiyeh. These cemeteries revealed burial practices that were unknown in the world of Mesopotamian towns, that is to say burials with visible markers. Burial mounds are, however, well attested in several regions of the East, notably in the Arabian Peninsula. The Middle Euphrates is at the crossroads of routes linking Mesopotamia to the Levant and those leading out towards the steppe and Arabia. In this article we will attempt to analyse the reasons for the similarities that have been found and to see in what ways these graves may or may not have belonged to one and the same tradition.

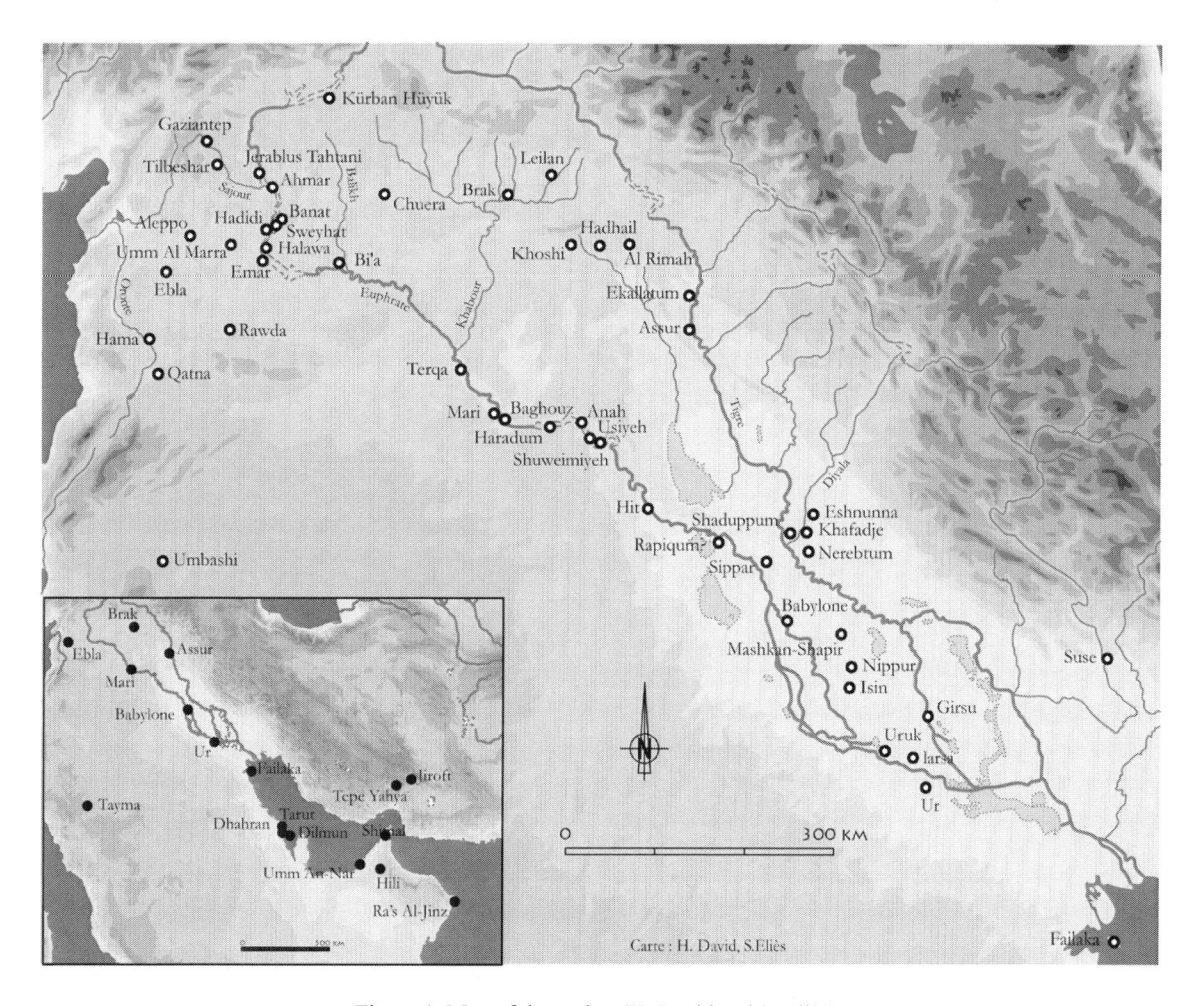

Figure 1. Map of the region (H. David and S. Eliès).

Figure 2. The cemetery of Shuweimiyeh (photo C. Kepinski).

The burial mounds of the Iraqi Middle Euphrates

The cemeteries of 'Usiyeh and Shuweimiyeh were brought to light in the frame of a rescue excavation program in the Haditha area by the Iraqi Department of Antiquities and a Japanese team headed by Prof. Fuji from the Kokushikan University.[1] They include several burial types: jar burials, collective graves and burial mounds with which we are particularly concerned here. Shuweimiyeh is located in a meander of the Euphrates and excavations started there in 1980 (Fig. 1). The cemetery dates mostly from the beginning of the second millennium and the beginning of the first millennium, which in Mesopotamia corresponds to two transitional periods often called Dark Ages. These two periods revealed a world of nomadic origin that is generally invisible from the archaeological point of view – that of the Amorites followed by that of the Aramaeans.

Fifteen burial mounds were excavated in Shuweimiyeh (Fig. 2). Under the artificial mound there is a circular wall in the middle of which lies a rectangular grave and sometimes there are benches. The grave is built of mud brick covered by a corbelled vault and there is a small stone-built platform against the circular wall. There are some variations, for instance, a major grave can be associated with the smaller ones around it. The other cemetery, 'Usiyeh, is also located in a meander of the Euphrates. It includes eighty burial mounds of which thirty were excavated. The ceramic assemblages belong to the beginning of the second millennium B.C.

The burial mounds of the Syrian Middle Euphrates

Tumulus graves are attested elsewhere along the Euphrates, particularly in the neighbourhood of Mari and in the Tabqa dam area, however in Iraq, the tumulus graves from Shuweimiyeh and 'Usiyeh remain exceptional. Actually, according to the survey around Mari, undertaken by Bernard Geyer and J-Y Monchambert, (Geyer & Monchambert 20003), similar graves exist, that are quite different from the graves in the town of Mari itself (Jean-Marie 1999, Margueron 2004). These graves belong to a series of burial grounds of different periods, all situated in dominating positions on high ground and in some cases they are accentuated by the presence of a tumulus. Around Dura Europos there are at least a thousand tumuli. They represent several categories of inhumation from diverse periods, going from a simple shaft grave to a hypogeum, from the Bronze Age to the Roman period. The majority of these graves have not been excavated. The two largest necropolises are those of Es-Susa and Baghouz, neither of which is directly related to a settlement site. At Es-Susa, a cemetery 6 km north of Baghouz, most of the graves belong to the Early Bronze Age but since they were revealed after a bulldozer had passed through, we do not know if there had once been visible mounds. Haddama, in the opposite side of the river, displays a group of seven tumuli.

---

[1] Shuweimiyeh is not published, see Excavations in Iraq 1979-80, *IRAQ* 43, 1981: 196, 198; Excavations in Iraq 1983-84, *IRAQ* 47: 224, 226. For Usiyeh, see Fujii *et al*. 1984-1985, Fujii et Matsumoto 1987, Oguchi and Oguchi 2006. See also Kepinski 2006: 89 and Kepinski 2007: 127-128, fig. 2.

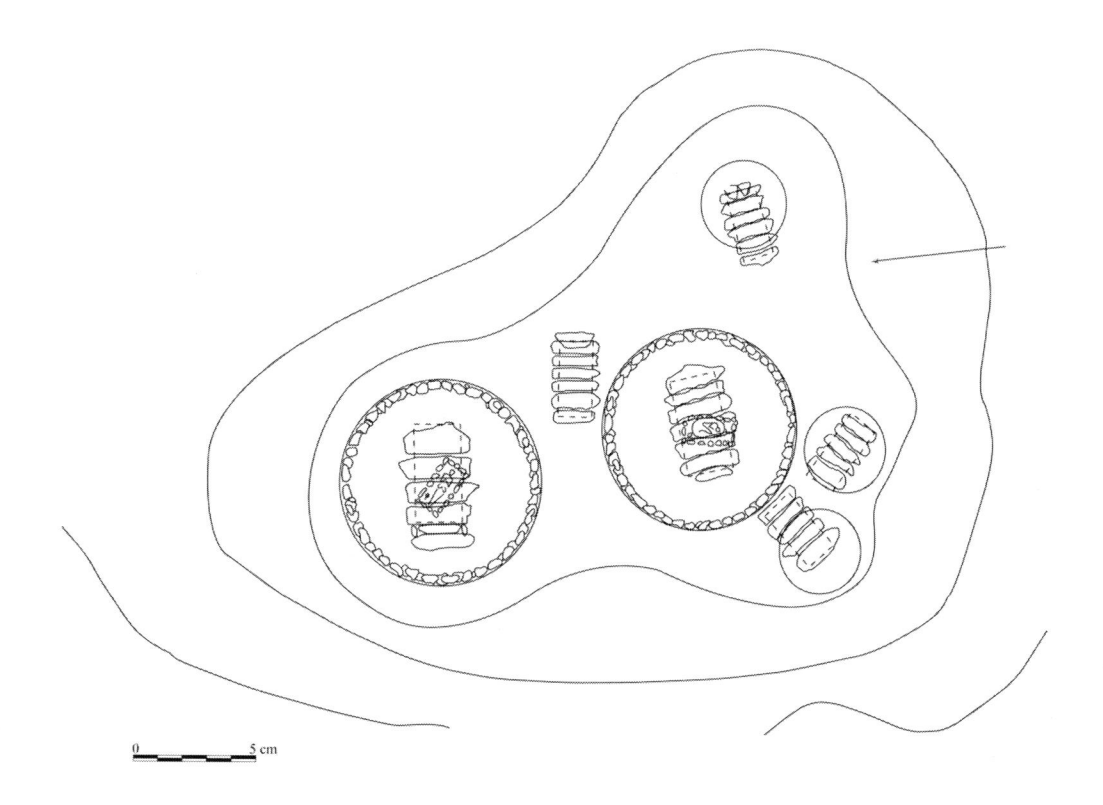

Figure 3. The burial mounds of Baghouz (from du Mesnil du Buisson 1948: Pl. XL).

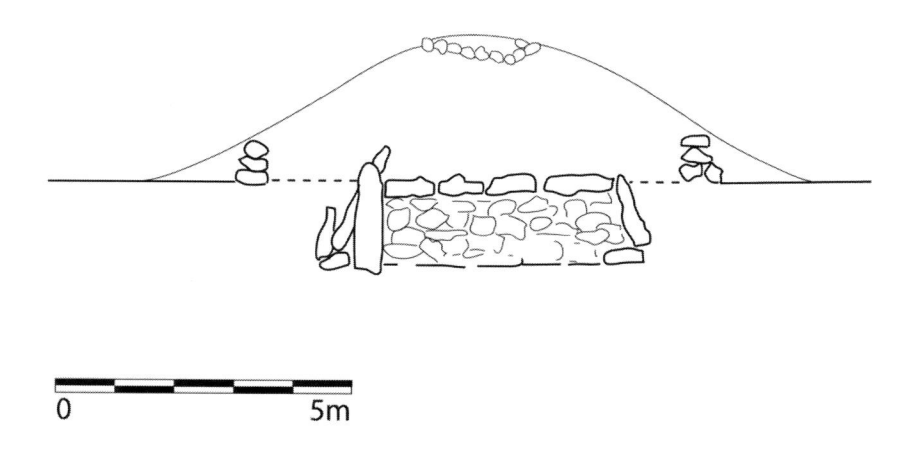

Figure 4. Baghouz elevation (from du Mesnil du Buisson 1948: Pl. XL).

However, the best known Middle Bronze burial mounds are in the Baghouz cemetery. It is also an isolated cemetery, excavated by Du Mesnil du Buisson in 1934 and published in 1948. Contrary to the two Iraqi cemeteries, the graves here were built of stone. Several graves of different sizes, with a diameter between 7 to 8 m, are often grouped around a main grave on top of a small hill (Fig. 3 and du Mesnil du Buisson 1948: Pl XL). Each grave was surrounded by a circle of stones and was covered by a mound that today has, more often than not, disappeared (Fig. 4). However, in the areas most sheltered from the wind, the mounds are preserved and suggest that all the graves were most probably covered in the same way - under a visible tumulus.

Burial mounds are well attested in the Tabqa dam area upstream. They are mentioned in various surveys by Maurits Van Loon (Van Loon 1967) and Adnan Bounni (Bounni 1980), but none have been excavated. West of the Euphrates, the regions stretching from Rawda to the Levant, as well as the Syro-Jordanian desert, provide some other examples (Nicolle, Steimer et Humbert 2001, Steimer-Herbet 2004, Zohar 1992, Cohen 1992).

Main characteristics of the burial mounds from the Middle Euphrates

Several particular characteristics distinguish these graves and associate them directly with the world of pastoralists, a world governed by clan links: 1) they have a visible sign, the tumulus, and are often located on high points in the landscape or at crossing points; 2) they are often grouped in a bunch around a main tomb; 3) they are in isolated cemeteries; 4) they are in regions where a pastoral economy is particularly important; 5) the graves are for individuals; 6) the Mesopotamian corpus of the Euphrates valley and its neighbourhood is very homogeneous and the ceramic assemblages clearly date these grave-mounds to between 2100 and 1800 B.C.

Graves with visible signs are completely foreign to Mesopotamian tradition. However they have ancient roots in northern Syria such as, for example, the tombs of the 3rd millennium at Jerablus Tahtani (Peltenburg 1999), Tawi (Kampschulte & Orthmann 1984: 39-41), Tell Banat (Mc Clellan & Porter 1999) or Halawa (Orthmann 1981: 51). They accompany an important period of foundation of towns in Upper Mesopotamia before the middle of the 3rd millennium BC (Porter 2002). However, the 'White Monument' of Tell Banat, tomb 302 from Jerablus Tahtani (Peltenburg 2008: 31), and the hypogeum of Til Barsib (Thureau-Dangin & Dunand 1936, Roobaert & Bunnens 1999) are collective tombs directly associated with a settlement even though they may be located outside the site.

Mari and Bahrain

The burial mounds along the Euphrates find parallels not only in the Levant and the Syro-Jordanian desert, but also in the Arabian Peninsula. Here they are well attested in several places, in Saudi Arabia at Dhahran and Tema (Zarins, al-Moghannum and Kamal 1984, Frolich and al-Moghannum 1985), in Yemen (Steimer-Herbet 2004) and in Bahrain (Bibby 1986, Boucharlat 1995, Potts 1990: 212). In the Arabian Peninsula of course, graves with visible signs have a long tradition and show a great diversity, but the burial mounds with individual graves in Bahrain follow the tradition of collective graves and accompany the creation, for the first time, of a state system and of an urban way of life. In other words, they go together with the process of the settling down of nomads.

To underline the relations between the Mari area of the Euphrates valley and the Arabian Peninsula, Bahrain in particular, is not new. Several elements show the tight links between the two regions - iconographic motifs (Amiet 1975, Buchanan 1965, Zarins 1978, Potts 1986), shared prestige goods, raw materials, copper from Oman, seashells from the Gulf, bitumen from Mesopotamia and ceramics (Højlund and Andersen 1994: 103, 109, 106, Højlund and Andersen 1997: Fig. 100, 283, 547d). Written sources make abundant mention of international trade and the diplomatic relations maintained with Dilmun (Højlund 1989, Potts 1990: 219-226, Glasssner 1999 and 2002).

Even though numerous elements underline the exchanges of an interlocking oriental world, there is clearly no reason to associate burial practices with trade. Burial practices are not imitated, are not exported; they are shared between communities linked by blood and shared values. Identical burial practices imply related ideologies. Through a similar process of evolution, different regions of the East espouse a certain identity that brings together several human groups across a wide territory.

The role of the Amorites; for a common heritage and against a unique origin

It must be remembered that these graves in the Euphrates valley form a homogenous corpus, foreign to the Mesopotamian world; they appeared during a particular period which brought forward a new element, that represented by the Amorites of nomadic origin (Buccellati 1966, Hojlund 1989, Durand 1992 et 2004, Liverani 1973, Whiting 1995). Moreover it was a troubled period, a period of instability marked by deep changes. Even if the apocalyptic hypothesis developed some years ago is no longer current, it cannot be replaced by one of a peaceful period without changes (Dalfes et al. 1997). If one looks at the elements of continuity, certain regions are indeed deserted, some towns abandoned, while numerous others remained occupied but their size was often reduced (Kuzucuoglu and Marro 2007). It was really a period of transition which, like all transitional periods, highlights the role played by flexible groups of nomadic origin. It is undeniable that the movements of the Amorites at the end of the third millennium and their confrontations with the major powers of the time played an essential role (Charpin, Edzard & Stol 2004: 57). Territorial problems dominated conflicts and the Euphrates valley was precisely one of the areas in which they met, precisely the area where groups that came from the Syro-Arabian desert in successive and constant waves converged.

We hypothesize that the tumulus graves are an illustration of the complex interactions between the Middle Euphrates valley and the island of Bahrain and the Amorites. The Amorites infiltrated progressively into both the Mesopotamian towns and those of the Gulf. In the 22nd century BC, Magan was directed by a figure with an Amorite name. Later, it was another Amorite who reigned over Failaka and the land of Bahrain and Amorite proper names are frequent there at the beginning of the 2nd millennium (Zarins 1986, Glassner 2002).

However, the hypothesis of a unique origin for all the occurrences of these graves has long since been disproved (Aharoni 1982, Kenyon 1966, Lapp 1966). In each region the material from the graves is comparable to that from the settlements in the vicinity and so it varies from one region to another. Similarity over long distances does not equate to borrowing or diffusion, but to elements derived from similar conditions. There was no displacement from one place to another, but rather a belonging to flexible and mobile groups unified by clan links (Kepinski 2006).

To the multitude of dialects revealed by the historical sources there corresponded a great variety of groups of pastoralists linked to each other (Charpin & Ziegler 2003:

30-32). They recognized one another through a shared symbolic language, demonstrated, amongst other things, by their burial practices and their rites. Information about the Amorites is so prolific that we cannot develop the theme here. The recognition and individualization of a common ancestor to whom the grave in the middle of the cluster of tombs might belong, legitimized the membership of a clan. The bunched graves of Bahrain clearly illustrate this process. All forms of power, all power struggles and all alliances were founded on these blood links, be they real or imaginary. They represent an alternative to state practices and centralized administration. In an unstable environment, such as that illustrated by the periods of transition, blood links, rituals and symbolism gave structure to the communities, legitimized the balance of power and presided over alliances (Godelier 1984; D'Hont 2004; Hodder 2001). Remodelling of the alliances between the various nomadic tribes led to the need to establish territorial limits and rights of passage (Durand 2005: 106, 115, 125).

Elements confirming the hypothesis

From the prolific documentation concerned with relations between the Amorites, Dilmun and the Arabian Peninsula, we will focus on three references in particular that might help to confirm our hypothesis. The Amorites were constantly dividing into several branches which maintained special relationships whilst also being closely linked with the settled populations. During the Amorite period it seems that all the Mesopotamians could claim affiliation to a tribe, although some were perceived as being more 'bedouin' than others and the written sources distinguish between the two of them (Charpin and Durand 1986, Durand 2004). The townsfolk of Mesopotamia perceived the Amorites as strangers, drawing a hostile picture of them and describing them as populations that did not even bury their dead. Their nomadic lifestyle was frowned upon: an Amorite was someone "who lives in a tent (…) who has no house during his lifetime and on the day of his death will not be buried" (Charpin 2004: 59, Cooper 1983: 31-33). In fact, it must be remembered that the Mesopotamians buried their dead near their dwellings and very often under the floor of their houses. The concept of an isolated cemetery is unknown in their traditions.

Also, amongst the texts that tell of diplomatic relationships between Samshi-Addu, king of Upper Mesopotamia and Dilmun (Charpin and Ziegler 2003: 140 note 529, Charpin, Edzard and Stol 2004: 191), there is one that is often mentioned, in which this king asks his son Yasmah-Addu of Mari to send a burial urn to the king of Dilmun (Gröneberg 1991, Tsukimoto 1985). This receptacle was for libations of oil and it suggests that the two regions shared an identical burial system.

Finally the cultural ties that associated these groups of nomadic origin could equally well be illustrated by a very specific group of arms, daggers, socketed spearheads and fenestrated axes that one finds from 2100 BC onwards in a geographic area comparable to that of the burial mounds, and notably in Baghouz, in the Levant and in the Arabian Peninsula (Gernez 2006).

Conclusions

Burial mounds are spread across several regions of the East and are revealing indicators of the presence of pastoralists in the process of sedentarization. They are often situated in areas of contact, of conflict and of exchange between sedentary populations and nomads. The circular graves with rectangular chambers and individual inhumations must be distinguished from other varied megalithic monuments dedicated to collective burials that are spread across the desert and in the East. They represent territorial markers bordering the routes used by a mobile people who have a close relationship with the sedentary world, international trade and long distance exchange networks. They are often situated at cross-roads and river crossings, on islands and hilltops.

The middle Euphrates was one of the meeting points between nomads and sedentary people and both the cohabitation and the alternation between the two subsistence patterns can be observed. Following periods of settling down, the nomadic populations were pushed out towards the steppe and the Arabian Desert, areas with which they maintained constant relations. The adoption of a burial practice that was common to the Euphrates valley and the Arabian Peninsula proves a kind of interdependence between different groups of nomadic origin, before their absorption into the sedentary world. The methods of subsistence and similar activities associated with an identical use of space define, over long distances, a certain identity. Burial mounds in relation with individual inhumation clearly illustrate the interconnection of local, tribal and state practices.

References

Aharoni Y. 1982. *The Archaeology of the Land of Israel*. Westminster: Philadelphia.

Amiet P. 1975. A cylinder seal impression found at Umm an-Nar. *East and West* 25: 425-426.

Bibby T.G. 1986. The origins of the Dimun Civilization. Pages 108-115 in H.A. al-Khafija & M. Rice (éds), *Bahrain through the Ages*. Londres-New York-Sydney: KPI.

Boucharlat R. 1995. Archaeology and artifacts of the Arabian Peninsula. Pages 1335-1353 in J.M. Sasson (éd.), *Civilizations of the Ancient Near East* (volume II). New York: Simon and Schuster MacMillan.

Bounni A. 1980. Les tombes à tumuli du Moyen Euphrate. Pages 315-325 in J.-Cl. Margueron (éd.), *Le Moyen Euphrate. Zone de contacts et d'échanges* (Actes du colloque de Strasbourg 10-12 mars 1977). Leiden: E.J. Brill.

Buccellati G. 1966. *The Amorites of the Ur III Period*. Naples: Studi Semitici.

Buchanan B. 1965. A dated "Persian Gulf" seal and its implications. Pages 204-209 in *Studies in Honor of*

Benno Landsberger on his Seventy-Fifth Birthday April 21, 1965. Chicago: The University of Chicago Press.

Charpin D. & Durand J.-M. 1986. « Fils de Sim'al » : les origines tribales des rois de Mari. *Reallexikon der Assyriologie und Vorderasistischen Archäologie* 80: 141-148.

Charpin D. & Ziegler N. 2003. *Mari et le Proche-Orient à l'époque amorrite: essai d'histoire politique.* (Florilegium Marianum V, Mémoires de NABU 6). Paris: Editions Recherche sur les Civilisations.

Charpin D. Edzard D.O. & Stol M. 2004. *Mesopotamien. Die altbabylonische Zeit.* (Orbis biblicus et orientalis 160/4. Fribourg: Academic Press-Göttingen, Vandenhoeck and Ruprecht.

Cohen R. 1992. The nomadic or semi-nomadic Middle Bronze Age I settlements in the central Negev. Pages 105-131 in O. Bar-Yosef & A. Khazanov (éds), *Pastoralism in the Levant. Archaeological Materials in Anthropological Perspectives.* Madison: Prehistory Press. Monographs in World Archaeology N°10.

Cooper J.S. 1983. *The Curse of Agade.* Baltimore-Londres.

Dalfes H.N., Kukla G. & Weiss H. (éd.) 1997. *Third Millenium BC Climatic Change and Old World Collapse.* Springer. NATO ASI Series I: Global Environmental Change, vol. 49.

Durand J.-M. 1992. Unités et diversités au Proche-Orient à l'époque amorrite. *Compte Rendu de la Rencontre Assyriologique internationale* 38: 97-128.

Durand J.-M. 2004. Peuplement et sociétés à l'époque amorrite (I) les clans Bensim'alites. Pages 111-197 in C. Nicolle, *Nomades et sédentaires dans le Proche-Orient ancien.* Paris: Editions Recherche sur les Civilisations. Amurru 3.

Durand J.-M. 2005. *Le culte des pierres et les monuments commémoratifs en Syrie amorrite.* Paris: Société pour l'Etude du Proche-Orient Ancien. Florilegium Marianum VIII, Mémoires de NABU 9.

Frohlich B. & al-Moghannum A. 1985. Excavations of the Dhahran burial mounds, Eastern Province, 1404/1984. *Atlal* 9: 9-40.

Fujii H., Okada Y., Matsumoto K., Oguchi H., Oguchi K. & Numoto H. 1984-85. Preliminary report on the excavations at Area A and Area B of 'Usiyeh. *Al-Râfidân* 5-6: 111-150.

Fujii H. & Matsumoto K. 1987. Usiya Area A. *Archiv für Orientforschung* 34: 166-173.

Gernez G. 2006. Armement et société au Moyen-Orient: l'exemple des lances à douille à la fin du Bronze Ancien et au début du Bronze Moyen. Pages 67-85 in C. Kepinski, O. Lecomte & A. Tenu (eds), *Studia Euphratica. Le moyen Euphrate iraquien révélé par les fouilles préventives de Haditha.* Paris: de Boccard. Travaux de la Maison René-Ginouvès 3.

Geyer B. & Monchambert J.-Y. 2003. *La basse vallée de l'Euphrate syrien du Néolithique à l'avènement de l'islam.* (2 volumes). Beyrouth: Institut Français du Proche-Orient. Mission archéologique de Mari VI/Bibliothèque Archéologique et Historique, 166.

Glassner J.-J. 1999. L'onomastique "amorrite" dans la péninsule arabique. Pages 123-127 in L. Milano, S. de Martino, F.M. Fales & G.B. Lanfranchi (eds), *Landscapes, Territories, Frontiers and Horizons in the Ancient Near East.* Padoue: SARGON. XLIV Rencontre Assyriologique Internationale, Venezia, 7-11 July 1997.

Glassner J.-J. 2002. Dilmun et Magan: le peuplement, l'organisation politique, la question des Amorrites et la place de l'écriture. Point de vue de l'assyriologie. Pages 337-381 in S. Cleuziou, M. Tosi &J. Zarins (eds), *Essays on the Late Prehistory of the Arabian Peninsula.* Rome: Istituto italiano per l'Africa e l'Oriente.

Godelier M. 1984. *L'idéel et le matériel. Pensée, économies, sociétés.* Paris: Fayard.

Gröneberg B. 1991. Le Golfe arabo-persique vu depuis Mari. Pages 69-80 in J.-M. Durand (éd.), *Florilegium Marianum, Mémoires de NABU* 1: 69-80. Paris: Société pour l'Etude du Proche-Orient Ancien

Hodder I. 1982. *Symbols in Action.* Cambridge: Cambridge University Press.

Højlund F. 1989. The formation of the Dilmun state and the Amorite tribes. *Proceedings of the Seminar of Arabian Studies* 19: 45-59.

Højlund F. & Andersen H.H. 1994. *Qala'at al-Bahrain 1. The Northern City Wall and the Islamic Fortress.* Aarhus: Aarhus University Press. Jutland Archaeological Society Publications XXX:1.

Højlund F. & Andersen H.H. 1997. *Qala'at al-Bahrain 2. The Central Monumental Building.* Aarhus: Aarhus University Press. Jutland Archaeological Society Publications XXX:2.

D'Hont O. 2004. Entre sédentarité et nomadisme: éléments pour une définition de ces deux termes pris dans l'histoire du peuplement de la moyenne vallée de l'Euphrate depuis l'avènement de l'islam. Pages 13-24 in C. Nicolle (ed.), *Nomades et sédentaires dans le Proche-Orient ancien.* (Amurru 3). Paris: Editions Recherche sur les Civilisations.

Jean-Marie M. 1999. *Tombes et nécropoles de Mari.* Beyrouth: Institut Français du Proche-Orient. Bibliothèque Archéologique et Historique 153.

Kampschulte I., Orthmann W. 1984. *Gräber des 3. Jahrtausends v. Chr. Im syrischen Euphrattal. I. Ausgrabungen bei Tawi 1975 und 1978.* Bonn: R. Habelt. Saarbrücker Beiträge zur Altertumskunde, Bd 38.

Kenyon K.M. 1966. *Amorites and Canaanites.* London: Oxford University Press.

Kepinski C. 2006. Mémoires d'Euphrate et d'Arabie, les tombes à tumulus, marqueurs territoriaux de communautés en voie de sédentarisation. Pages 87-128 in C. Kepinski, O. Lecomte & A. Tenu (eds), *Studia Euphratica. Le moyen Euphrate iraquien révélé par les fouilles préventives de Haditha.* Paris: de Boccard. Travaux de la Maison René-Ginouvès 3.

Kepinski C. 2007. Tribal links between the Arabian Peninsula and the Middle Euphrates at the beginning of the second millennium BC. *Proceedings of the Seminar for Arabian Studies* 37: 125-134.

Lapp P.W. 1966. *The Dhahr Mirzbaneh Tombs: Three Intermediate Bronze Age Cemeteries in Jordan.* New Haven: American Schools of Oriental Research.

Liverani M. 1973. The Amorites. Pages 100-133 in D.J. Wiseman (ed.), *Peoples of Old Testament Times*. Oxford: Clarendon Press.

Margueron J.-M. 2004. *Mari. Métropole de l'Euphrate au IIIe et au début du IIe millénaire av. J.-C*. Paris: Picard/Editions Recherche sur les Civilisations.

McClellan T.L. & Porter A. 1999. Survey of excavations at Tell Banat: funerary practices. Pages 107-116 in G. del Olmo Lete & J.-L. Montero (eds), *Archaeology of the Upper Syrian Euphrates, the Tishrin Dam Area*. Sabadell: AUSA. Aula Orientalis, Supplementa 15.

Mesnil du Buisson R. du 1948. *Baghouz, l'Ancienne Corsâté. Le Tell archaïque et la nécropole de l'Âge du bronze*. Leiden: E.J. Brill.

Nicolle C., Steimer T. & Humbert J.-B. 2001. Marajim, implantation rurale du IIIème millénaire en Jordanie du nord. *Akkadica* 121: 77-86.

Oguchi K. & Oguchi H. 2006. 1997. Japanese excavations at 'Usiyeh. Pages 157-189 in C. Kepinski, O. Lecomte & A. Tenu (eds), *Studia Euphratica. Le moyen Euphrate iraquien révélé par les fouilles préventives de Haditha*. Paris: de Boccard. Travaux de la Maison René-Ginouvès 3.

Peltenburg E. 1999. The living and the ancestors: Early Bronze mortuary practices at Jerablus Tahtani. Pages 427-442 in G. del Olmo Lete et J.-L. Montéro (eds), *Archaeology of the Upper Syrian Euphrates, the Tishrin Dam Area*. Sabadell: AUSA. Aula Orientalis, Supplementa 15.

Peltenburg E. & Wilkinson T. 2008. Jerablus and the land of Carchemish: excavation and survey in Syria. *Current World Archaeology* 27: 24-32.

Porter A. 2002. The dynamics of death: ancestors, pastoralism, and the origins of a third-millennium city in Syria. *Bulletin of the American Schools of Oriental Research* 325: 1-36.

Potts D.T. 1986. Dilmun's further relations; the Syro-Anatolian evidence from the third and second millennia B.C. Pages 389-398 in H.A. al-Khafija & M. Rice (eds), *Bahrain through the Ages: the Archaeology*. London-New York-Sydney: KPI.

Potts D.T. 1990. *The Arabian Gulf in Antiquity. Volume I. From Prehistory to the Fall of the Achaemenid Empire*. Oxford: Clarendon Press.

Roobaert A. & Bunnens G. 1999. Excavations at Tell Ahmar-Til Barsib. Pages 163-178 in G. Del Olmo & J.-L. Montero-Fenollos (eds), *Archaeology of the Upper Syrian Euphrates. The Tishrin Dam Area. Proceedings of the International Symposium Held at Barcelona, Jan. 28th-30th 1998*. Sabadell: AUSA. Aula Orientalis, Supplementa 15.

Steimer-Herbet T. 2004. Classification des sépultures à superstructures lithique dans le Levant et l'Arabie occidentale (IVe et IIIe millénaires avant J.-C.). Oxford: Archaeopress. British Archaeological reports International series 1246).

Thureau-Dangin F. & Dunand M. 1936. *Til-Barsip*. Paris: P. Geuthner.

Tsukimoto A. 1985. *Untersuchungen zur Totenpflege (kispum) im alten Mesopotamien*. Kevelaer, Butzon & Bercker and Neukirchen-Vluyn: Neukirchener Verlag. Alter Orient und Altes Testament 216.

Van Loon M.N. 1967. *The Tabqa Reservoir Survey 1964. Direction Générale des Antiquités et des Musées*. Damascus.

Whiting R.M. 1995. Amorite tribes and nations of second-millennium Western Asia. Pages 1231-1242 in J.M. Sasson (ed.), *Civilizations of the Ancient Near East* (volume II). New York: Simon and Schuster MacMillan.

Zarins J. 1978. Steatite vessels in the Riyadh museum. *Atlal* 2: 65-94.

Zarins J. 1986. MAR-TU and the land of Dilmun. Pages 233-250 in H.A. al-Khafija & M. Rice (eds), *Bahrain through the Ages: the Archaeology*. London-New York-Sydney: KPI.

Zarins J., Mughannum A.S. & M; Kamal 1984. Excavations at Dhahran South: The Tumuli Field (208-92), 1403 A.H./1983. A Preliminary Report. *Atlal* 8: 41-42

Zohar M. 1992. Megalithic cemeteries in the Levant. Pages 43-63 in O. Bar-Yosef & A. Khazanov (eds), *Pastoralism in the Levant. Archaeological materials in Anthropological Perspectives*. Madison: Prehistory Press. Monographs in World Archaeology No. 10.

Author's Address
Dr Christine Kepinski
UMR 7041 ArScAn
Maison René-Ginouvès
21, allée de l'Université
92023 – Nanterre Cedex
christine.kepinski@mae.u-paris10.fr

Reuse of tombs or cultural continuity? The case of tower-tombs in Shabwa governorate (Yemen)

Rémy Crassard, Hervé Guy, Jérémie Schiettecatte and Holger Hitgen

Summary

During a preventive archaeological survey along the Yemen LNG pipeline route, a cemetery was discovered, and was at first dated to the Bronze Age period. After excavation, these tombs were not clearly datable to this period, as typical Iron Age material was discovered inside them. The ^{14}C dating of three typologically similar tombs reveals two distinct occupation phases. The first one starts from the beginning of the 3rd millennium BC, and the second one from the first half of the 1st millennium BC. What can be concluded? Are we facing a reuse of ancient tombs by later populations, or do we have enough data to think that there was a cultural/technical continuity in building tower-tombs?

Keywords: Yemen, Bronze Age, tombs, Shabwa, South Arabian kingdoms

The survey, architecture and findings

In 2006, an archaeological survey took place along the Yemen LNG pipeline from Ma'rib to Bālhāf (Crassard & Hitgen 2007), by the *Centre Français d'Archéologie et de Sciences sociales de Sanaa* (CEFAS), the *Deutsches Archäologisches Institut* in Sana'a (DAI) and the General Organization for Antiquities and Museums. In the governorate of Shabwa, the plateau area is covered by hundreds of burial places. Several of these were recorded during the survey, most of which are 'tower-tombs'. This type is often dated to the Bronze Age due to architectural typology and comparisons (Steimer-Herbet 2004).

The Bronze Age period (from the early 3rd millennium to the first half of the 2nd millennium BC) has been defined thanks to the discoveries of numerous tombs and cemeteries characterized by megalithic architecture (de Maigret 2002; de Maigret & Antonini 2005). A strong symbolism appears sometimes in the funerary architecture of this period bearing elements which remain poorly understood such as tomb "tails" (Steimer-Herbet 2004) or drawings inside dolmen-like structures (Braemer et al. 2003). Associated domestic architecture is scarcely found and is best represented in the Yemeni highlands (de Maigret 2002).

Nevertheless, the terminology and the chronology used for this period are not accepted by all scholars working in Yemen. The term Bronze Age has its origin in European archaeology and refers to precise cultural concepts that are not equivalent to those in Yemen. The concept of a Yemeni Bronze Age is simply used to qualify a period following the so-called "Neolithic" and preceding the period pertaining to the South Arabian kingdoms. This Bronze Age in Yemen appears as an amalgam of very different cultures with their own material culture and socioeconomic systems. Moreover it is different in many ways from Bronze Age societies in Mesopotamia or Western Europe.

Nonetheless, the burial structures are in general very similar in types during this period of time. The tombs discovered along the pipeline route are of three different types that are already published elsewhere (Crassard & Hitgen 2007; Hitgen et al. 2008): cists, wall-tombs and tower-tombs. These include one main type, the tower-tomb, characterized by a circular tomb with an orthostat-lined funerary chamber. The initial structure of these monuments is not immediately perceptible. At first sight, they look like tumuli with a central funeral chamber. But this is not the case. Excavation showed that they had a more structured architecture than first thought. They are cylindrical in shape with a flat or ribbed cover (Fig. 1).

The absolute date of such structures remains an issue. The dwelling structures detected during the preventive survey along the pipeline route were not excavated. A few small soundings demonstrated that no stratigraphic remains were present on sites. The date for these structures is thus indeterminate and it remains difficult to confirm whether they are contemporaneous with the circular tombs. Our sole evidence comes from the tombs themselves.

The human remains from the tombs

Physical anthropology, thanks to precise archaeological recording, analyses the position of bones in a grave in order to decipher the movements that a corpse has undergone, so as to work out the initial position of the body in its grave and to apprehend a possible structure or perishable container which may have contained the body. Moreover, anthropology allows us to characterize a skeletal population. First we estimate the sex and the age of the skeletons. Then we measure the bones and note abnormalities, which are then examined meticulously to see if they indicate diseases, ill-treatment or nutritional deficiencies. Taken together these observations permit us to define a population of skeletons in terms of demography, morphology and health.

The 2006 Yemen LNG excavation campaign gave us the opportunity to investigate 6 megalithic collective graves at first dated to the South Arabian Bronze Age. They are dry stone built tombs and the burials are successive. The graves were all robbed in the past, probably near to the time when they were built. There were doubtless several episodes of looting. Human remains were found in only three of the graves (T6, T7 and T1).

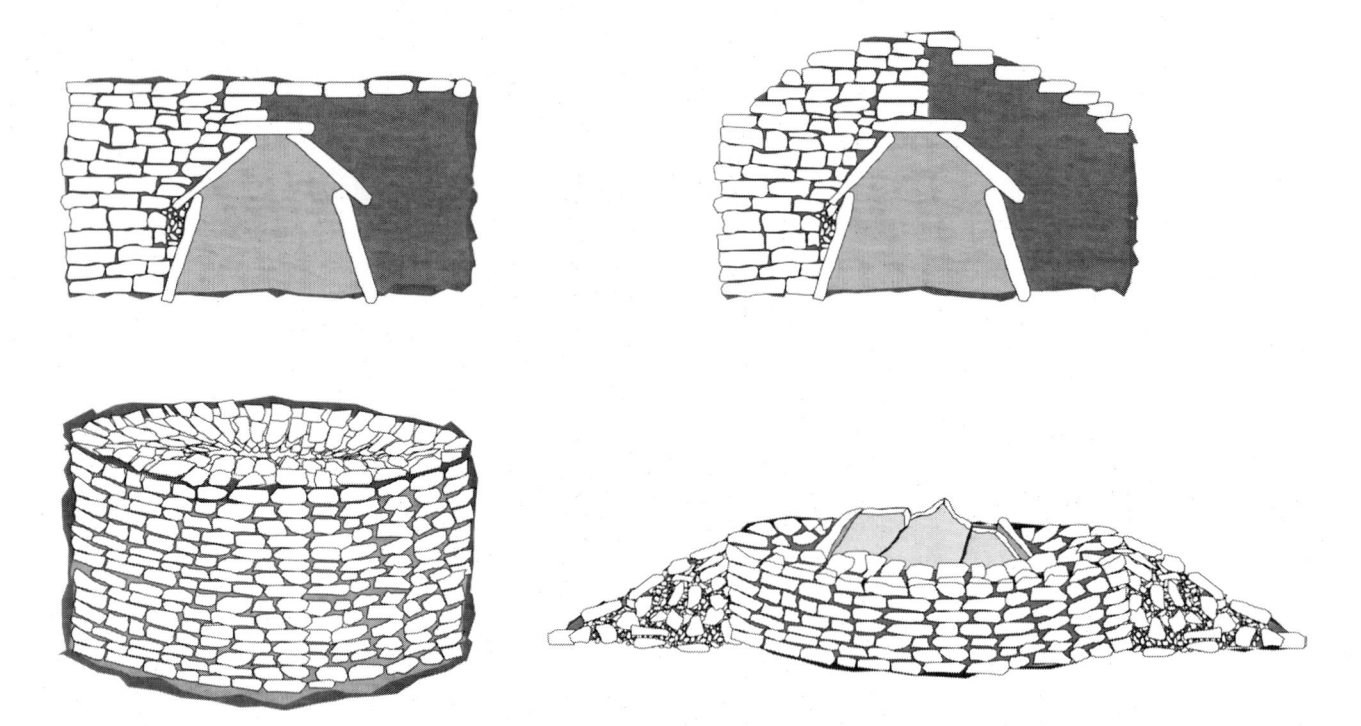

Figure 1. Top: two possible simplified sections of the excavated tower-tombs. Bottom: two views of the structure in elevation before and after robbing and collapse.

Site & Tomb	Peri-natal	IM1	IM2	IM3	IM4	IM5	Total IM	Adult Male	Adult Female	Undet. sex	Total Adult	TOTAL
YLNG 09 T1	0	0	0	0	0	0	*0*	0	0	1	*1*	1
YLNG 09 T2	0	0	0	0	0	0	*0*	0	0	0	*0*	0
YLNG 10 T5	0	0	0	0	0	0	*0*	0	0	0	*0*	0
YLNG 10 T6	0	0	1	3	1	1	*6*	1	0	2	*3*	9
YLNG 10 T7	0	1	2	1	0	0	*4*	1	1	2	*4*	8
YLNG 10 T9	0	0	0	0	0	0	*0*	0	0	0	*0*	0
TOTAL	0	1	3	4	1	1	10	2	1	5	8	18

Tab. 1. Distribution by age and by grave; perinatal: before and near birth, IM1: 0-1 years old, IM2: 1-4 years old, IM3: 5-9 years old, IM4: 10-14 years old, IM5: 15-19 years old.

The preservation of the bones is poor, from both a quantitative and a qualitative point of view, as only half of the graves contained human bones. In the end, after sieving and cleaning, 366 bones were identifiable, most of them fragments. Overall, 52 belonged to immature subjects (14.2 %), and 314 to adults. The distribution by age in each grave is summarised in Table 1.

In spite of a very small sample size, we can put forward some hypotheses. The ratio of immature individuals to adults is 10:8, that is to say 1.25. Ordinarily, this figure indicates a relatively high infant mortality rate, which corresponds to what are called "archaic" populations (Bocquet-Appel & Masset 1996; i.e. before the invention of the smallpox vaccine and the adoption of hygienic obstetric methods, Masset 1973). It also usually indicates a rather high rate of population increase (Bocquet-Appel 2008). Indeed considering that all the children were not found, we would be inclined to postulate that the ratio of immature individuals to adults could have approached 1.5.

In concrete terms, if this figure proves to be correct, we would face a population that renewed itself rapidly. Women's fertility rate would then have been probably around 6 children for each 3 reaching the age of reproduction. This kind of demographic "explosion" is a rare, rather brief moment (it happens in 1 to 3 centuries) in the history of a society. It corresponds generally to a period of deep change in social, economic, and technological organisation. At such a time demographic pressure forces a society to adapt (Boserup 1981). We

Figure 2: The three aligned children in grave 6, lying on a corbel stone, before and after collapsing.

acknowledge that the statistical data from Shabwa governorate discussed here are rather meagre. Nevertheless, we are not very far from what has already been observed in the vast Jabal Jidrān necropolis in the Ramlat as-Sabʿatayn (Steimer-Herbet 2001). At Jabal Jidrān, as in the case of the gas pipeline graves we are likely dealing with family units, where one or two generations of adults were buried with their children (Braemer *et al.* 2001).

The poor general preservation of the bones, in terms of both number and quality, limits the possible measuring and morphological observations. At most we see a very moderate degree of dental wear. In Jabal Jidrān, dental wear was greater, but the "sandy" environment of this site would easily explain this fact. We also noticed the presence of one remarkable detail, the complete ankylosis (or stiffness) of an adult's left wrist and radius.

Finally, in grave 6, one of the stones of the first level of the corbelling was found lying horizontally near the centre of the chamber. On this stone were the remains of 3 young children (being 3 to 6 years old). The bones show a loose but coherent anatomical organization between the principal anatomical pieces (Fig. 2 left). These three children were found lying on their left sides. We can reasonably suggest that they were put in a sort of burial chamber reserved for young subjects, as indicated in Fig. 2 (right). They were probably buried together having died at the same time.

Discussion

Besides cists or wall-tombs, the burial places on the plateau area are mainly circular tombs with wall enclosures and an inner burial chamber. According to the results of the excavations carried out there, based on artefact study and ^{14}C dating, this type of tomb was a common burial structure for many hundreds of years. Contrary to the opinion formed by some researchers, these tombs were used not only during the Bronze Age (3rd and 2nd millennia BC) but also during the Iron Age (first half of the 1st millennium BC).

Eight samples of bone were collected for radiocarbon dating (AMS ^{14}C). The collagen inside the bones was preserved enough for analysis, and it was possible to date at least two burial phases in three different tombs from the YLNG-010 site (Tab. 2: T5, T6 and T7). These dates reveal a first period of occupation between 3030-2670 cal BC (beginning of the 3rd millennium BC), and a second occupation phase during the 1st millennium BC (between 810-360 cal BC). Are we then facing a reuse of ancient tombs by later populations? Or is it possible that there was a cultural continuity in building tombs over several millennia?

The few objects left in the excavated tombs by the looters can help in answering this question. In the tombs dated to the 1st millennium BC, most of the objects pertain to the same material culture. For instance, the obsidian

Designation	Nature	14C Age BP	Calibrated Age 1σ BC	Calibrated Age 2σ BC
YLNG 10 T5 #1	Bone	4310 ± 40	3010-2880	3030-2870
YLNG 10 T5 #2	Bone	4225 ± 35	2900-2760	2910-2670
YLNG 10 T6 #3	Bone	2370 ± 30	510-390	540-380
YLNG 10 T6 #4	Bone	2340 ± 30	415-380	510-360
YLNG 10 T6 #5	Bone	2390 ± 30	510-400	730-390
YLNG 10 T7 #6	Bone	2555 ± 35	800-590	810-540
YLNG 10 T7 #7	Bone	2710 ± 30	895-820	920-800
YLNG 10 T7 #8	Bone	2250 ± 30	390-230	400-200

Table 2: Radiocarbon dates from three tombs from the YLNG-10 site

geometric microliths (a few also made from chert) are good cultural and chronological markers. They consist of a small flake of obsidian or chert abruptly retouched on three edges and un-worked along one edge which acts as the active surface. The common shapes of geometric microliths in Yemen include trapezoids, rectangles or squares. These composite tools can also take the form of a half-circle. The majority of those collected in the tombs are trapezoidal in shape. These objects have been found on the surface of several sites and from a few excavated contexts (Inizan & Francaviglia 2002; Crassard 2008). They are present in many different regions of Yemen and have been collected from the Red Sea coast (Tihama) to the Western Highlands, and from the central desert of the Ramlat as-Sabʿatayn to the plateaus of Ḥaḍramawt. These geometric microliths appear to date to the same period of time, starting from the appearance of the South Arabian kingdoms (1st millennium BC), but most probably earlier in Tihama (Khalidi 2006). At YLNG-10 site, the radiocarbon dating confirms this hypothesis, but does this necessarily mean that these tombs are much more recent than was thought before and were effectively built during the 1st millennium BC?

Some iron object fragments have been found in the Tomb 7, which further demonstrates the later date suggested for the burials. Nevertheless, prior to excavation, Tomb 7 was found in a very poor state of preservation, which could indicate an intrusive context for these iron elements.

In sum, at least Tomb 6 and Tomb 7, which were chronometrically dated, are well associated to a later period than originally thought. In opposition, Tomb 5 is dated to the beginning of the 3rd millennium, which coincides with the dating of the typologically similar tombs at Jabal Jidrān and Jabal Ruwaik (Steimer-Herbet 2004; these tombs have doors, unlike those at YLNG-10). Despite its imposing dimensions, Tomb 5 contained only few beads in shell and cornelian and three tiny pieces of bronze (possibly rivets), which allowed no clear chronological attribution. The absence of obsidian microliths, which were numerous in the later dated tombs, is an interesting fact for the confirmation of the chronometric dating. The typology of Tomb 5 is strictly identical to that of Tombs 6 and 7, although the material culture and the ^{14}C dates are very dissimilar.

Because the material from the tombs dated to the Iron Age could also be dated to the Bronze Age, excepting the geometric microliths and the iron pieces, it is very probable that these tombs are testimonies of reuse of the original Bronze Age funerary structures. The builders of such tombs were possibly an indigenous, nomadic population group who adhered to the same way of life and traditions for a long period, lasting long after the development of the Iron Age caravan kingdoms.

Acknowledgements

We would like to thank Lloyd Weeks for his invitation. We also warmly thank the staff of Yemen LNG, especially Robert Hirst and Mohammad Sinnah, the President of the General Organization of Antiquities and Museums Abdullah Bawazir, the director of GOAM, Shabwa branch, Khairan Mohseen al-Zubaidi and the directors of the German Archaeological Institute (DAI Sana'a) Iris Gerlach and of the French Centre for Archaeology and Social Sciences in Sana'a (CEFAS), Jean Lambert, for their support and assistance during the fieldwork. The excavations were directed by Rémy Crassard and Holger Hitgen and carried out by ʿIssa ʿAlī Ibn ʿAli, Mohammad ʿAmin, ʿAbd al-Karīm al-Barakani, Rabiaʾ Abdullah al-Batful, Sylvain Bauvais, Ueli Brunner, Julien Espagne, Hervé Guy, Sarah Japp, Olivier Lavigne, Jürgen Malsch, Jamāl Mukrit, Jérémie Schiettecatte and Mike Schnelle. Rémy Crassard thanks the Fondation Fyssen for financing his stay at the University of Cambridge.

References

Bocquet-Appel J.-P. 2008. *La paléodémographie: 99,99% de l'histoire des hommes ou la démographie de la préhistoire*. Paris: Errance.
Bocquet-Appel J.-P. & Masset C. 1996. Paleodemography: expectancy and false hope. *American Journal of Physical Anthropology*. 14: 107-111.
Boserup E. 1981. *Population and technology*. Oxford: Blackwell.
Braemer F., Cleuziou S. & Steimer-Herbet T. 2003. Dolmen-like structures: some unusual funerary monuments in Yemen. *Proceedings of the Seminar for Arabian Studies* 33: 169-182.
Braemer F., Steimer-Herbet T., Buchet L., Saliège J. F., & Guy H. 2001. Le Bronze Ancien du Ramlat As-Sabatayn (Yémen). Deux Nécropoles de la première moitié du IIIe millénaire à la bordure du désert: Jebel Jidrân et Jebel Ruwaiq. *Paléorient* 27: 21-44.
Crassard R. 2008. *La Préhistoire du Yémen. Diffusions et diversités locales, à travers l'étude d'industries lithiques du Hadramawt*. BAR International Series 1842. Oxford: Archaeopress.
Crassard R. & Hitgen H. 2007. From Sāfer to Bālḥāf - Rescue excavations along the Yemen LNG pipeline route. *Proceedings of the Seminar for Arabian Studies* 37: 43-59.
de Maigret A. 2002. *Arabia Felix: An Exploration of the Archaeological History of Yemen*. London: Stacey International.
de Maigret A. & Antonini S. 2005. *South Arabian Necropolises - Italian Excavations at Al-Makhdarah and Kharibat al-Ahjur (Republic of Yemen)*. Rome: Istituto Italiano per l'Africa e l'Oriente IsIAO - Centro Scavi e Ricerche Archeologiche.
Hitgen H., Crassard R. & Gerlach I. 2008. *Rescue excavations along the Yemen LNG pipeline from Marib to Balhaf*. Sana'a: Yemen LNG Company/CEFAS/DAI.

Inizan M.-L. & Francaviglia V.M. 2002. Les périples de l'obsidienne à travers la mer Rouge. *Journal des Africanistes* 72/2: 11-19.

Khalidi L. 2006. *Settlement, Culture-Contact and Interaction along the Red Sea Coastal Plain, Yemen: The Tihamah cultural landscape in the late prehistoric period, 3000-900 BC*. Unpublished PhD Dissertation, Department of Archaeology, University of Cambridge.

Masset C. 19731. La démographie des populations inhumées: essai de paléodémographie. *L'Homme* 13: 95-131

Steimer-Herbet T. 2001.Results from the excavation of one high and circular tomb in Jabal Jidrān. *Proceedings of the Seminar for Arabian Studies* 31: 221-226.

Steimer-Herbet T. 2004. *Classification des sépultures à superstructure lithique dans le Levant et l'Arabie occidentale (4e et 3e millénaires avant J.-C.)*. BAR International Series 1246, Oxford: Archaeopress.

Authors' Addresses
Dr. Rémy Crassard
Leverhulme Centre for Human Evolutionary Studies
The Henry Wellcome Building
University of Cambridge
Fitzwiliam Street
Cambridge CB2 1QH
United Kingdom
Corresponding author
E-mail: rcrassard@prehistoricyemen.com

Mr. Hervé Guy
Institut National de Recherches Archéologiques Préventives
Direction interrégionale Méditerranée
24 avenue de la Grande-Bégude – Bâtiment Le Mozart 3
13770 Venelles
France
E-mail: herve.guy@inrap.fr

Jérémie Schiettecatte
Post-doctoral Researcher
CNRS - UMR 8167 "Orient et Méditerranée"
27 rue Paul Bert
94204 Ivry-sur-Seine Cedex
France
jeremie.schiettecatte@mae.u-paris10.fr

Mr. Holger Hitgen
Deutsches Archäologisches Institut
Sana'a Branch of the Orient Department
Embassy of the Federal Republic of Germany
PO Box 2562
Sana'a, Yemen
E-mail: hitgen@y.net.ye

A reverence for stone reflected in various Late Bronze Age interments at al-Midamman, a Red Sea coastal site in Yemen

Edward J. Keall

Summary

An investigation of the Red Sea (Tihāmah) littoral is centred on the city of Zabīd. To appreciate Zabīd's medieval prosperity, the Canadian Archaeological Mission's enquiry addressed all aspects of the Holocene. Remains of megalithic uprights were first documented in 1997, dating likely to the early second millennium BC. Infant bodies were placed ceremonially beneath some of the uprights. No grave goods were associated with these possibly sacrificial burials. Later in the second millennium, vast numbers of uprights were removed – it is argued, with reverence, not through wanton destruction – to build monumental temples. Some skeletal remains were displaced in this process. Recycled stone was also used for a cemetery of individual circular stone-lined graves. Grave goods included whole ceramic vessels. The pottery typology and technology is identical with that of the vessels documented for the entire domestic settlement. Overall, the site imparts a strong sense of deep reverence for stone in an area entirely devoid of stone. An enigmatic activity involved the emplacement of a block of stone on top of a fire, along with pottery and grindstones. Defying explanation, these features have been described as "fire-cracked stone-heaps." Stylistic parallels for the monumental architecture and other cultural material suggest that the site flourished in the second millennium, terminating towards 900-800 BC.

Keywords: Yemen Tihāmah, ceremonial uprights, infant sacrifice, ceramic grave goods, fire-cracked stone-heaps

Preamble

This paper deviates somewhat from the core theme that was consistently addressed in presentations at the conference. To be sure, presented here are some factual details concerning human interment at an archaeological site of the 2nd millennium BC at the southwestern corner of the Arabian peninsula (Keall 1997; 1998; 2000; 2004; 2005). These factual details may serve as a useful basis in their own right for cultural comparanda concerning burial practices in Arabia in general. But more than that, their unique character may serve as a valuable indicator that not all of the burial practices in Arabia are consistent with one another. The standards for "death and burial" that are observable for late Prehistory in the southwestern corner of the peninsula, as documented by the Canadian Archaeological Mission in Yemen, appear to have very little in common with those in its eastern part.

Apart from this observation, however, it is appropriate to point out that this paper deviates somewhat from the main theme of the conference in so far as part of the presentation includes various "commemorative" practices that are not directly connected with human interment. These actions involved seemingly deep reverence for stone. Although these acts may be judged to be a reflection of what may be called a belief in the animistic properties of stone, they do not directly address one of the conference's other underlying themes, namely the concept of the "transition to the afterlife." Indeed, animistic beliefs are generally taken to reflect spirituality in this world, rather than the next. Yet since the site presented here does include instances of human interment, including feasibly infant sacrifice, this discourse on human spirituality can hopefully be judged to be compatible with the conference theme.

The archaeological site of al-Midamman

The archaeological site of al-Midamman lies some two kilometres inland from the Red Sea coast of Yemen (Fig. 1). The remains of the site are scattered across some five square kilometres of terrain. Today the area is a dune and scrub wasteland, and it is conceivable that significant features that have not yet been identified so far lie hidden beneath sizeable sand dunes. In other parts of the site, severe wind erosion has left much of the site record badly deflated. To the immediate south and southeast of the archaeological site lie date palm groves cultivated by the residents of the modern settlement of al-Midamman. Ancient cultural features may easily have been obliterated through the planting of these groves. To the southwest there are extensive scatters of abraded pottery fragments, carried there through intermittent surface sheet-wash run-off.

The exposed nature of the main part of the identifiable settlement enabled extensive surface reconnaissance and strategic soundings to be made. It should be stressed that the five square kilometres of archaeological remains designated on the map in Figure 1 as HWB, HWA, HWN, BNF and WWW in no way represent dense and contiguous settlement. Rather, the dwellings of the settlement were made of ephemeral materials and somewhat distanced from one another. All of the commemorative monuments were outside of the settlement clusters.

To appreciate the original material record it has been hypothesized that an environmental anomaly provided a temporary window of opportunity for settlement in the region in the mid-Holocene (Keall 2005: 97; 2004: 43). Following the standard principle of heightened monsoon seasonal precipitation during the 5th-4th millennia BC (Wilkinson 1999: 190), it is argued here that the rains falling in the Wādī Zabīd watershed ran off largely unchecked from the steep hillsides. Sediments transported

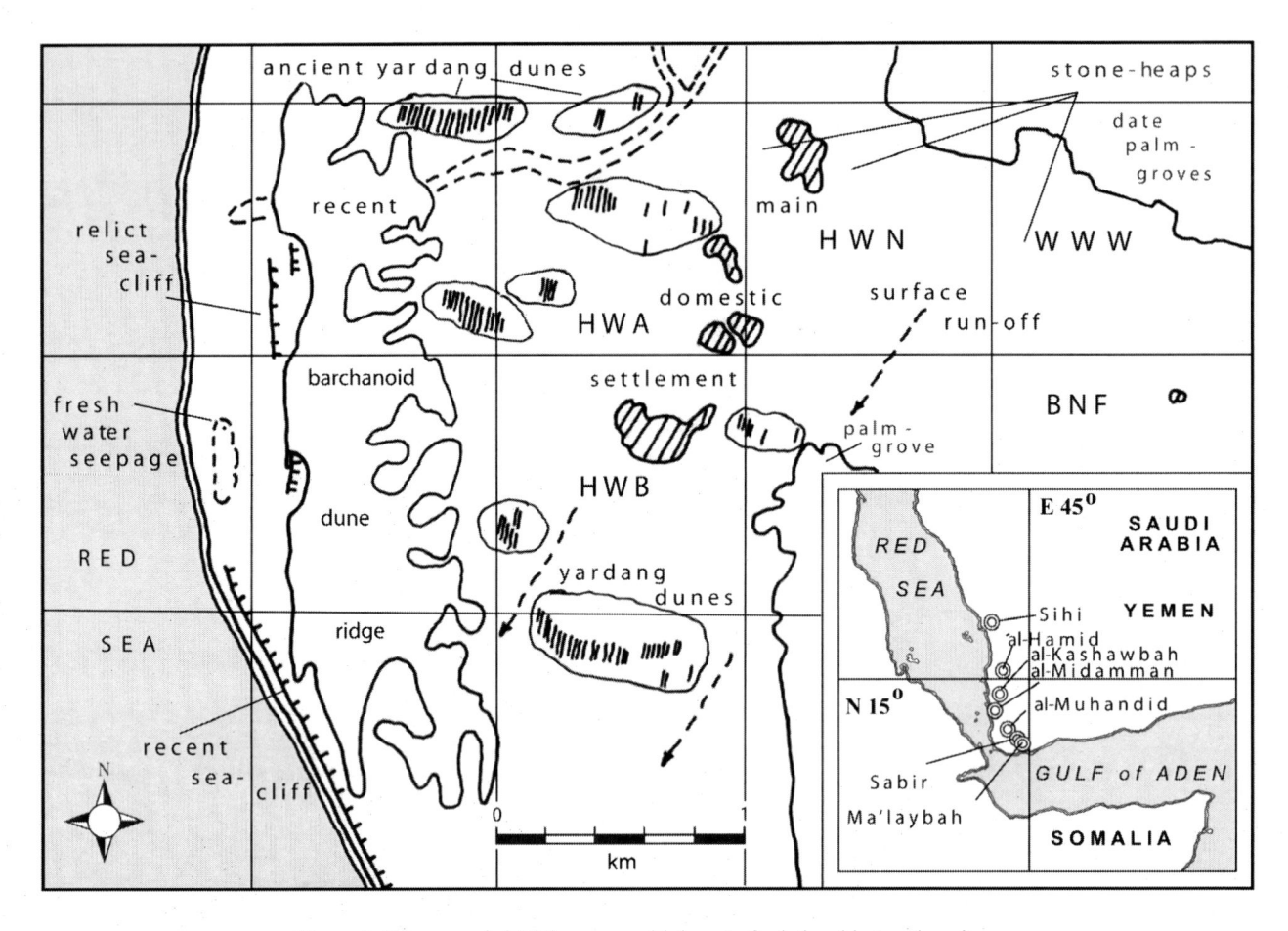

Figure 1. Site map of al-Midamman, with insert of relationship to other sites.

Figure 2. Sea-cliff with Holocene sediments exposed.

by the wadi spate reached regularly as far as the sea, forming a classic flood delta. No longer supplemented on a regular basis for three millennia, the accumulated sediments have for a long time been eroding away through the action of the sea, with the concomitant exposure of a dramatic sea-cliff in which the profile of the previously deposited sediments can be observed (Fig. 2).

Proof of the fact that the sediments were deposited in relatively recent times is derived from the evidence exposed beneath them. Buried at the base of the sediments, at the back of the storm beach, are the traces of a peat environment. A whole (apricot?) fruit buried in the peat furnished a 2-sigma calibrated radiocarbon date of 5220-4950 cal. BC (Beta Analytical INTCAL98: 7170-6900 cal. BP). It is hypothesized that the peat represents a mangrove swamp environment that once supported the life-cycle of Terebralia gastropods that were harvested for food during the Neolithic. Some time after around 5000 BC the swamps began to be buried. Two Terebralia mollusc shells scattered elsewhere inland furnish 2-sigma calibrated radiocarbon dates of 7320-7300 cal. BC (Beta Analytic INTCAL98: 9270-9250 cal. BP), and 5040-4760 cal. BC (6990-6710 cal. BP). Almost all of the shells of this kind recovered in the region are preserved with their points broken off, a clear indication of their having been harvested. The act of breaking the terminal point would have severed the muscle that attached the gastropod to its shell.

The focus of this paper is upon human activity that occurred while the sediments were being deposited above the former mangrove swamp. This natural regime could have helped sustain a community that, beginning around the end of the 3rd millennium, would have been able to take advantage of the vegetation that thrived on the moist and fertile sediments. It is furthermore highly plausible that the community was aware of the regular deposition of the alluvium and may have taken measures to ensure that the flood-waters flowed in directions where they were useful. A classic model for the description of early spate manipulation maintains that the initial exploitation of flood-water normally occurs first down stream where the force of the water is relatively gentle (cf. Francaviglia 2002: 111-114). It is only later that attempts are made to harness the floods upstream through introducing engineered devices. So it is not surprising to find a community exploiting the flood deposits at the point where spate velocity was reduced as they reached the sea.

It would have been only a small step to move to the deliberate farming of these sediments. It must be admitted, however, that in spite of efforts to find them, no archaeological traces of farming were found. There is certainly no trace of any physically engineered structure that one could connect with the classic tradition of Old South Arabian flood irrigation agriculture. Yet this is not surprising, for the absence of most cultural traits normally associated with the classic Old South Arabian cultures is also most noticeable at the site. It is surmised that the settlement at al-Midamman ceased to function in the early 1st millennium BC, because of deteriorating environmental conditions. Those changing conditions brought an abrupt end to the possibilities of settlement in the way that had occurred before. There is no indication of any abrupt end due to outside hostility.

Two words of caution must be introduced here. Firstly, that the current standard interpretation of the ending of the so-called mid-Holocene moist interval during the 3rd millennium BC does not on its own help explain the high volume of flood water reaching the coast in the 2nd millennium BC. We may certainly accept the idea of the on-set of drier climatic conditions. But this trend had already started some centuries earlier before the site of al-Midamman experienced extensive settlement. Perhaps vegetative cover had not reached sufficient maturity on the steep slopes to retard run-off, so that streams ran unchecked and were able to reach the coast several times a year, in spite of current acceptance of the generally increasing on-set of aridity by 3000 BC.

In addition, it is hypothesized that on the western escarpment of Yemen, unlike on the eastern sides of the mountains, man-made terraces and engineered water-harvesting devices had not yet then been set in place. According to that scenario, it would have been the engineering of devices along the flanks of the flood course to trap and divert water, inland, perhaps beginning around the 9th-8th centuries BC, which would have substantially reduced the amount of the free-flowing spate.

The second word of caution is that, conceivably, the methodology applied by CAMROM to identify traces of arable agriculture in the archaeological record failed. It had been expected that through the sectioning of areas where there were good depositions of humic soil, ploughed furrows could be observed; or, at least that "disturbed crusts of mud", which are unmistakable traits of the ploughing of formerly saturated sediments, could be observed in cross-section (cf. Hehmeyer 1989: 444, Fig. 3 – image upside down). None were found, in spite of concentrated efforts to do so. Yet such traits would not so easily have been preserved if farmers were using hoes to break the soil, African style. This is highly feasible, given the other tentative suggestions that these people had African connections (Keall 2004: 53).

It is not within the scope of this paper to address these issues extensively here. However, the environmental conditions that allowed people to sustain a lifestyle in the region over the course of perhaps a millennium are fundamental for the appreciation of what the people accomplished while they were there.

Theoretical framework of the archaeological project

Archaeological excavations began at the site of al-Midamman, immediately following an accidental encounter in March 1997 with previously undocumented giant standing stones in the heart of what was later defined as an archaeological settlement site (Keall 1998).

A strategy had to be improvised in order to deal with the reality of the newly discovered site. For, at the time of the chance encounter, the resources and energies of the Canadian Archaeological Mission of the Royal Ontario Museum (CAMROM) were being directed towards an attempt to understand a medieval Islamic port site on the coast, just to the south of al-Midamman.

The March 1997 campaign had as its mandate the task of defining the relationship of that port site (al-Fāzzah) to the inland regional capital city of Zabīd – the central focus of the CAMROM program. The onset of strong monsoon winds made the continuation of that work untenable, and the project was prematurely aborted. However, transportation of the camp equipment back to the home base in Zabīd led to the unexpected encounter with the standing stones of al-Midamman. Work at the newly-found site at that time was feasible because al-Midamman lay just inland from the coast, with some protection from the strong winds afforded by a range of high dunes between the site and the exposed sea-shore.

In spite of the serendipitous discovery of the site, the call to work at al-Midamman and the immediate transfer of the permit were justified on the basis that CAMROM had adopted a mandate from the very beginning to address the issue of the history of medieval Zabīd. But in order to appreciate how and why Zabīd had flourished in medieval times, it was important to learn what had gone on before. Since irrigation agriculture formed the main sustenance of Zabīd's urban economy, it was essential to attempt to ascertain when engineered irrigation systems first began to be set in place. In other words, although the original encounter with the megaliths of al-Midamman had been accidental, it was possible fortuitously to merge the discoveries with the mandate of the parent project and address the issue of what was the landscape like before the emergence of Zabīd's prosperity.

As a consequence, besides attention to the dramatic standing stones of al-Midamman, considerable attention was paid during CAMROM's activities at the site in 1997, and in the two subsequent seasons of 1999 and 2001, to try to assess how the people of the settlement sustained themselves. Simply put, how were they able to indulge in the luxury of hauling giant stones from miles away for spiritual purposes? What were the resources that made this possible?

Many of the physical features presented here have already been reported in other conference papers (Keall 1998; 2000; 2004; 2005). Not all of these reports, however, are easily accessible by everyone. So it is useful to present some of those facts again. But more importantly, the assigned theme of the conference as defined here in the publication of its proceedings, forced this writer to reflect upon the implications of the previously reported results. For the most part, what was extraordinary about the other papers presented at the conference was how utterly different are the findings from al-Midamman, even in comparison with sites from contemporaneous eras in the Arabian peninsula.

In other words, the record of the cultural activity at al-Midamman – on the edge of the Red Sea in the second millennium BC – is quite different from that now being amply documented for the eastern segment of the Arabian peninsula. At the time of their discovery in 1997 the features of al-Midamman were completely unexpected, as was the possibility of finding anything at all from the Bronze Age in the coastal area of Yemen. A decade later the presence of these features is not quite so surprising, given the slowly growing number of reports of related finds. But the enigma still remains concerning who were the people that were responsible for the erection of these remarkable remains during a limited moment of Late Prehistory.

The megalithic culture of al-Midamman

The background explanation for the presentation of an Arabian site by this writer to a conference on burial practices is that a community of people settled near the Red Sea coast during the second millennium BC. They had no relationship to the hunter-gatherers who had exploited the resources of the area during the Neolithic. These hunter-gatherers used projectiles belonging to the so-called Arabian bifacial tradition. As described above, they harvested Terebralia molluscs from nearby mangrove swamps (Keall 2005: 96-97).

Figure 3. The largest of the upright markers, part of a major alignment at al-Midamman (area HWB).

Figure 4. Remains of a child's skeleton (area HWA) once laid ceremonially beneath an upright marker.

Figure 5. Traces of a child's skeleton partially destroyed through removal of a former marker (area HWA).

Settling in the area to take advantage of naturally occurring flood-deposit conditions, the newcomers brought with them a tradition of using obsidian microliths. Their other utilitarian material possessions were of exceptional quality too. Ceramic vessels and metal tools reflect well-developed manufacturing traditions (cf. Ciuk & Keall 1995; Giumlia-Mair *et al.* 2002). Yet they lived very modestly in terms of the homes they constructed, which were very likely similar to the huts of palm fronds made by today's fishermen along the coast.

This makes even more remarkable the phenomenon of the standing stones (Fig. 3; and Giumlia-Mair *et al.* 2000: 38, Fig.1; Keall 1997: 13, figure), which give testimony to an extraordinary investment of time and energy to transport giant stones from the distant mountains. It must be emphasized that there is no stone of any kind in the alluvial surroundings of the site of al-Midamman. Also, the variety of stone types represented in the monumental record underlines how the stones were hauled from a number of locations, not from just one quarry site. The closest of the mountains are more than forty kilometres away; they are never visible from the coastal reaches, except under exceptional atmospheric circumstances. Searching for stone at a considerable distance underlines how the community must have had a strong reverence for stone when the settled at al-Midamman. Stones found in the mountains are derived from a wide variety of sedimentary, metamorphic and volcanic rock, but by definition their sources are far apart. Collecting them was not a simple matter of exploiting a single quarry or mountainside.

Figure 6. Numerous former uprights laid in the footings of a monumental (temple) structure (area BNF).

The earliest use of the giant stones involved setting them upright as markers (Giumlia-Mair *et al.* 2002: 198, Fig. 2). Use of the term "commemorative" is justified by the fact at least some of the stones were set up over deposits buried deliberately beneath the emplacement. The deposits included infant bodies (Fig. 4), in which case one should not discount the possibility of human sacrifice. In another scenario a cache of metal tools was set around a large core of obsidian (Giumlia-Mair *et al.* 2002: 199, Fig. 3; 2003: Fig.4; Keall 1997: 14-15, figure; Weeks *et al.* 2009). Regrettably, at present there is no archaeological proof of either similarity or dissimilarity of age for the two different actions. The infant burials were disturbed through removal of the uprights at a later time (Fig. 5, and see below). The bones sent for radiocarbon analysis had no measurable collagen preserved.

Others of the uprights are hypothesized to have once formed parts of alignments. Full assessment of this possibility is hampered by the fact that at some point many of the uprights were pulled down (Keall 2005: 92, Fig.4; 1997: 16, figure, right), to be used in monumental building and grave construction. There is no evidence to suggest that this act of demolition reflected wanton destruction, for enormous effort was expended on setting enormous numbers of these giant stones in place in the foundations of what can be best described as temples (Fig. 6). Sun-dried brick could just as effectively have been used for these purposes. Also, the material artifacts associated with both phases of the settlement are identical. In other words, there is no indication that outsiders were involved in the cultural change, other than perhaps through a general influence on cultural expression. Destructive invasion is a completely inappropriate explanation for the change. It appears that, due to some evolution in their thinking, people simply started to build temples for their spiritual expressions rather than setting up giant uprights. From a midden context adjacent to one of the monumental buildings (area HWA) a charred fruit furnished a 2-sigma calibrated radiocarbon date of 1320-970 cal. BC (3260-2920 cal. BP).

At some point the community moved away, in all likelihood in response to deteriorating ecological conditions. The terminal horizon of the site is defined by a band of volcanic ash that can be traced consistently, albeit intermittently, right across the site. There is no indication that this was a catastrophic event that caused the settlement to be abandoned. But the volcanic ash horizon does define a distinct change between the deposition of sediments that defined the occupational opportunities and the wind-blown sands, which accumulated at some time following the ash fallout. That these sands started to accumulate centuries ago – not recently – is attested by the fact that traces of an AD 15th century medieval villa have been identified on top of one of these ancient dunes.

Commemorative acts of interment: infant burials

This term is applied to the phenomenon of skeletal remains of young children having been unearthed from contexts where it can be stated categorically that they had originally been interred beneath stone uprights. In one instance the partial remains of the skeleton were unearthed close to the base of a toppled upright (Fig. 4).

Figure 7. A stone-lined grave in a communal cemetery (area HWN), employing pieces of former ceremonial uprights.

Figure 8. Ceramic grave goods in the communal cemetery (area HWN).

In other instances, the disarticulated bones of children were found in situations where the most plausible explanation of their presence is that when the upright markers were re-used for the construction of monumental buildings, the body once interred beneath them was disturbed (Fig. 5). Some disarticulated bones of different individuals were found in the foundation trench of the monumental building (area HWA, Building A; Keall 2005: 94, Fig. 6) where the former uprights were dragged to form part of the footings (Keall 1998: 143, Fig. 5).

Commemorative acts of interment: cache of tools

A cache of copper-alloy tools set surrounding a large core of obsidian was unearthed in a context where it had clearly once been set deliberately beneath a large upright (Giumlia-Mair *et al.* 2002: 199, Fig. 3). Curiously, all of the evidence for the setting up of these uprights points to an almost cavalier disregard for solid footings (Fig. 3). Rather one may rationalize that this very neglect of built footings adds to the spiritual character of the act. It reads almost as though a successful setting up of an upright was auspicious, its collapse inauspicious. Clearly, the interment of precious items beneath the stones was a conscious part of a propitious act.

Stone grave markers: cemetery with circular graves

A cemetery was unearthed in which the individual graves consisted of circular stone-lined features in which ceramic grave goods were preserved (Figs. 7 & 8). The graves had been robbed. No skeletal remains were recovered. It is hypothesized that all of the rhyolite that provided the medium for the stone lining of the graves was derived through the recycling of former uprights.

Figure 9. The flexed skeleton of an isolated male burial, without grave goods, but marked by stone (area HWA).

Stone grave markers: solitary burial

The long bones of an adult male buried in a flexed position were found in an isolated context, without burial goods (Fig. 9). The grave was identified by the presence of pieces of rhyolite stone preserved on the surface of the ground. It is assumed that the stone had originally been used elsewhere as an upright commemorative marker before being newly employed as a grave marker.

Stone markers: fire-cracked stone-heaps

The phenomenon consists of an isolated fire having being built in an area adjacent to, but not contiguous with a settlement. There is nothing to indicate that these were utilitarian fires, such as those that might have been devised, for instance, for the barbecuing of a piece of meat. Rather, the emplacement of stone on top of the fire, which was fractured and discoloured by the heat – sometimes in conjunction with the additional emplacement of grinding stones and fragments of ceramic vessels – smacks of ceremonial activities. Sectioning of the heaps revealed consistently a burnt layer at the bottom on the open ground, with fractured stone slivers above (Fig. 10; and Keall 2005: 92, fig. 4; 1997: 16, fig., right). One can only resort to conjecture for their explanation – namely that the lighting of these ceremonial fires reflects celebration or an act of propitiation, perhaps somehow connected with the cycle of the annual floods. These fire-cracked stone-heaps were normally found loosely clustered away from the settlements, and generally in the northern parts of the settlement (areas HWN, WWW) though it is conceivable that clusters of heaps were more easily identifiable amongst the dunes than single, isolated ones.

Reverence for stone: buildings A, B & C

Building A

Building A was constructed using irregularly shaped lumps of granite in the foundations (Keall 2005: 94, Fig. 6). In all likelihood they are pieces of stone from smashed-up former standing stones. In addition, found dragged down into the foundation trench were the occasional intact monolith of basalt that had once been set up nearby as commemorative uprights. As described above, some disarticulated human bones from commemorative interments were dragged down into the trench while dragging the heavy stones. The building blocks above ground were comprised of roughly hewn pieces of rhyolite. These, too, are surmised as having been recycled from their original role as former commemorative markers.

Significantly, the interior divisions of the monument, such as may have been appropriate for the emplacement of wooden roof supports, were made of sun-dried brick. The brick as unearthed in the excavations was of good quality, and well preserved, in spite of the high saline content from millennia of sea-mist saturation. Appropriate mud is readily available for the making of sun-dried brick in the vicinity of the site. The presence of this good quality brick helps justify the suggestion that the use of stone in these buildings was not an act of cavalier or wanton destruction. Rather, it is argued that the extra efforts that were expended to re-use the stone reflect a deliberate act of veneration.

Building B

A surprising number of once upright pillars were reused to form the foundations of a second temple structure (Fig. 6; and Keall 2005: 95, fig. 8). Most of them are naturally-shaped slender pillars. A special feature was the inclusion amongst them of a naturally water-worn block of stone. It must have been recovered from a flood course. But it is

Figure 10. Section through a so-called cracked-stone fire-heap (area HWN).

exceptional – in so far as it has an L-shaped profile – and a profile that could have been seen as representing an animal head. Hypothetically it represents inclusion in the temple foundations of a former idol.

As in the case of Building A, the internal divisions of this second temple were built using sun-dried brick – again emphasizing the principle that the construction of buildings using sun-dried brick was both feasible and practical.

Building C

The building blocks of this structure were comprised exclusively of rhyolite. Not enough of the structure is preserved to define definitively its original layout. Yet monumentality is attested by the preserved mass of collapsed masonry on the south side of the compound.

Highly significant is the preservation of fragments of decorations that once adorned the walls. These decorations are identical with those from the famous so-called Banāt ᶜĀd sites, from al-Sawdāᶜ, in the interior of Yemen (Arbach & Audouin 2004). It is important to acknowledge that the decorative fragments from al-Midamman do not just echo the classic Banāt ᶜĀd themes, those few pieces that have been recovered mimic them exactly (Keall 2004: 47-49, Figs. 15-18). This paper does not pretend to address the issue of what society produced these images, and in what era. However, some of the ceramics found at the site are judged to be 10th-9th century BC in date, much earlier than was previously attached to the building (Arbach & Audouin 2004: 4-5). A great deal more research is needed before the cultural context and age of the images even of the al-Sawdāᶜ temple complexes can be properly understood. And, because of their distance from the interior of Yemen, the al-Midamman examples are even more unfathomable. The presentation of some of their details here serves merely to underline the extraordinary attention to stone given by the residents of a settlement far from the source of any natural rock.

Conclusions

The burial practices observable at al-Midamman are largely an anomaly in the context of this conference where much of the material presented is connected with the eastern part of the Arabian peninsular. It may be entirely appropriate to underline this fact, when addressing the issue of the identity of the inhabitants of the entire peninsula during the 3rd-1st millennia. Certainly, one must acknowledge that the character of settlement at al-Midamman during the 2nd and 1st millennia BC is unique, as far as we know it. Yet signs are emerging that more traces of the culture are to be found in this stretch of the Tihamah coast of Yemen (cf. Khalidi 2005).

Without question, one must acknowledge that there are some definite material culture parallels to be found for al-Midamman in the Red Sea and Gulf of Aden coastal areas. Significantly, those sites that have been so far identified as having parallels all lie within the southwestern littoral regions of the Arabian peninsula, facing the Horn of Africa (Fig. 1, insert). Yet while the sites of Sihi, al-Hamid, al-Kashawbah, Sabir, and Maᶜlaybah have valid comparanda by way of ceramic vessels and metal tools, none of them have commemorative stone uprights. On the other hand, the site of al-Muhandid (Hajār al-Ghaymah/Wādī al-Hāmilī) has an avenue of upright stones, but no material artifacts have ever been associated with them to allow us to make any useful connection with the remains of al-Midamman. In its overall make-up, al-Midamman is unique, even in Yemen.

But, as is the case with these sites just mentioned that lie on the edges of the ocean – where there is little obvious connection to the interior of Arabia – one may postulate about a cultural complex that encompasses both sides of the Red Sea, a connection in fact between Arabia and the Horn of Africa. Unfortunately, in spite of valiant attempts to identify the mechanisms of those connections, or even to produce convincing parallels, no solid evidence has yet been presented to support such a case (Keall 2004).

Significantly, there are many indications that at al-Midamman the material culture represented in the archaeological record arrived in the region fully developed. There is no sense for instance in the preserved ceramic record that the pottery made and used underwent either significant evolution or decline. Vessels were made applying the techniques of a potting tradition already adequately established; the shapes of vessels reflected serious attention to specific functions that must have been part of the community's way of life for a long time. The same can be said of the obsidian microliths made and used by the community. One may usefully extend that line of thought and, while emphasizing that the technology involved in the production of these microliths does not belong to an Arabian tradition, one may propose that they reflect an as yet unclearly defined African heritage.

Apart from the ephemeral domestic dwellings at al-Midamman, the site is characterized by extensive use of stone, both in original contexts and in recycling situations. Certainly in the first instance, but also to a degree in the second case, the use of this stone in an otherwise sand-desert landscape underlines for it the notion of sacredness. The act of choosing to use stone for seeming spiritual purposes implies an extraordinary commitment on the part of the community to source and deliver the stone from long distances away. To be sure, these spiritual beliefs were modified likely under the influence of attitudes then being currently expressed elsewhere in Arabia and the Near East in general. But the new structures that were erected to replace the upright markers – monumental temples – were built using stone from earlier commemorative monuments. The action of reusing the stone for a variety of cultic purposes seems to imply deep reverence for the stone, and hints at the origins of the people in a mountainous homeland. Spirituality, in other words, was deeply embedded in stone.

Acknowledgements

The Canadian Archaeological Mission has operated formally since 1987 under a licence from Yemen's General Organization for Antiquities and Museums, directed by author Keall. Funding for the work described here was received from the Royal Ontario Museum Foundation and the Social Sciences and Humanities Council of Canada. A three-year SSHRCC award was made to applicant Keall (along with the cited collaboration of I. Hehmeyer) in 1999, in support of "The changing ecology of Southern Arabia in the Holocene."

References

Arbach M. & Audouin R. 2004. *Nouvelles découvertes archéologiques dans le Jawf (République du Yemen). Opération de sauvetage franco-yémenite du site d'as-Sawdāʾ (l'antique Nashshān). Temple intra-muros I. Rapport préliminaire.* Sanaa: Fonds social de développement/Centre français d'archéologie et de sciences socials de Sanaa.

Ciuk C. & Keall E. 1996. *Zabid Pottery Manual 1995. Pre-Islamic and Islamic Ceramics from the Zabid area, North Yemen.* Oxford: British Archaeological Reports, International Series 655.

Francaviglia V.M. 2002. Some Remarks on the Irrigation Systems of Ancient Yemen. Pages 111-144 in Cleuzio S., Tosi M. & Zarins J. (*eds*), *Essays on the Late Prehistory of the Arabian Pennsula.* Roma: Istituto Italiano per l'Africa e l'Oriente. Serie Orientale Roma 93.

Giumlia-Mair A., Keall E.J., Shugar E.J. & Stock S. 2002. Investigation of a Copper-based Hoard from the Megalithic Site of al-Midamman, Yemen: an Interdisciplinary Approach. *Journal of Archaeological Science* 29: 195-209.

Giumlia-Mair A., Keall E.J., Stock S. & Shugar E.J. 2000. Copper-based implements of a newly identified culture in Yemen. *Journal of Cultural Heritage* 1: 37-43.

Hehmeyer I. 1989. Irrigation Farming in the Ancient Oasis of Mārib. *Proceedings of the Seminar for Arabian Studies* 19: 33-44.

Keall E.J. 2005. Placing al-Midamman in Time. The Work of the Canadian Archaeological Mission on the Tihama Coast, from the Neolithic to the Bronze Age. *Archäologische Berichte aus dem Yemen* 10: 87-100.

Keall E.J. 2004. Possible connections in antiquity between the Red Sea Coast of Yemen and the Horn of Africa. Pages 43-55 in Lunde P. & Porter A. (eds), *Trade and Travel in the Red Sea Region.* Oxford: British Archaeological Reports International Series 1269. Society for Arabian Studies Monographs 2.

Keall E.J. 2000. Changing Settlement along the Red Sea Coast of Yemen in the Bronze Age. Pages 719-729 in Mattiae P., Anea L., Peyronel L. & Pinnock F. (eds), *Proceedings of the First International Congress on the Archaeology of the Ancient Near East. Rome, May 1998.* Rome.

Keall E.J. 1998. Encountering megaliths on the Tihamah coastal plain of Yemen. *Proceedings of the Seminar for Arabian Studies* 28: 139-147.

Keall E.J. 1997. Do you want to see the stones? *Rotunda* (Royal Ontario Museum) 32: 12-19.

Khalidi L. 2005. Megalithic Landscapes: the development of the late prehistoric cultural landscape along the Tihāmah coastal plain (Republic of Yemen). Pages 359-375 in Sholan A.M., Antonin S. & Arbach M. *Sabaean Studies. Archaeological, Epigraphical and Historical Studies in honour of Yūsuf m. 'Abdullāh, Alessandro de Maigret and Christian J. Robin on the occasion of their 60th birthdays.* Naples/Sanaa: Il Torcoliere.

Weeks L., Keall E., Pashley V., Evans J. & Stock S. 2009. Lead Isotope Analyses of Bronze Age Copper-Base Artefacts from al-Midamman, Yemen: towards the identification of an indigenous metal production and exchange system in the southern Red Sea region. *Archaeometry* 51/4: 576-597.

Wilkinson T. 1999. Soil Erosion and Terraced Agriculture in Highland Yemen: a Preliminary Statement. *Proceedings of the Seminar for Arabian Studies* 29: 183-191.

Author's Address
Dr. Edward J. Keall
Royal Ontario Museum
100 Queen's Park
Toronto, Ontario M5S 2C6
Canada
edk@rom.on.ca

The Arabian Iron Age funerary stelae and the issue of cross-cultural contacts

Jérémie Schiettecatte

Abstract

Studies on South Arabian anthropomorphic funerary stelae often suggest that there is North Arabian influence in their iconography, and some claim that there was a migration of North Arabian populations, bringing their own practices. The issue of northern influence will be debated here through the study of two types of South Arabian stelae: *Eye stelae* from the Jawf valley and *square stelae* from Qatabān. The paper demonstrates that neither onomastics nor chronology yield evidence for a northern origin or influence. This is followed by a wider discussion of the origins of South Arabian culture. Two hypotheses are discussed: the first is the acculturation of southern populations by northern groups, or even the migration of people from Southern Levant or North Arabia and the second is endogenous development. The second hypothesis appears to be more convincing.

Keywords: Arabia, funerary stelae, South Arabian culture, cultural contacts, acculturation.

Introduction

The deceased were often represented on funerary stelae in South Arabia in the 1st millennium BC. These anthropomorphic stelae have been found in three areas: the Jawf valley, which corresponded roughly to the ancient kingdom of Maʿīn, the site of Maʾrib, capital city of the ancient kingdom of Sabaʾ, and the site of Ḥayd Ibn ʿAqīl, the cemetery of Tamnaʿ, capital city of the ancient kingdom of Qatabān (Fig. 1). The stelae have common features: the main elements of the face are schematically represented, either in relief or incised. Nevertheless, all these representations have their own unique qualities. North Arabia has also yielded anthropomorphic stelae, whether funerary or not, that show close iconographic and onomastic parallels with those of South Arabia. Therefore, it has been argued that the origin of these South Arabian funerary stelae can be explained either by an acculturation process, or by the settlement of North Arabian populations in the south of the Peninsula (e.g. Garbini 1976: 313; Garbini 1977: 378, n. 18).

The recent acquisition by the National Museum of Sanaa of 581 funerary stelae and the discovery of several others during the excavation of a necropolis at Barāqish (Antonini and Agostini, this volume) makes it possible to reopen the discussion on iconographic and wider cultural links between South and North Arabia.

As the different categories of Arabian funerary stelae have already been detailed elsewhere (see Arbach & Schiettecatte 2006 and Arbach, Schiettecatte & al-Hadi 2008 for the Jawf stelae; for the Arabian funerary stelae in general see Schiettecatte in press), only the possible

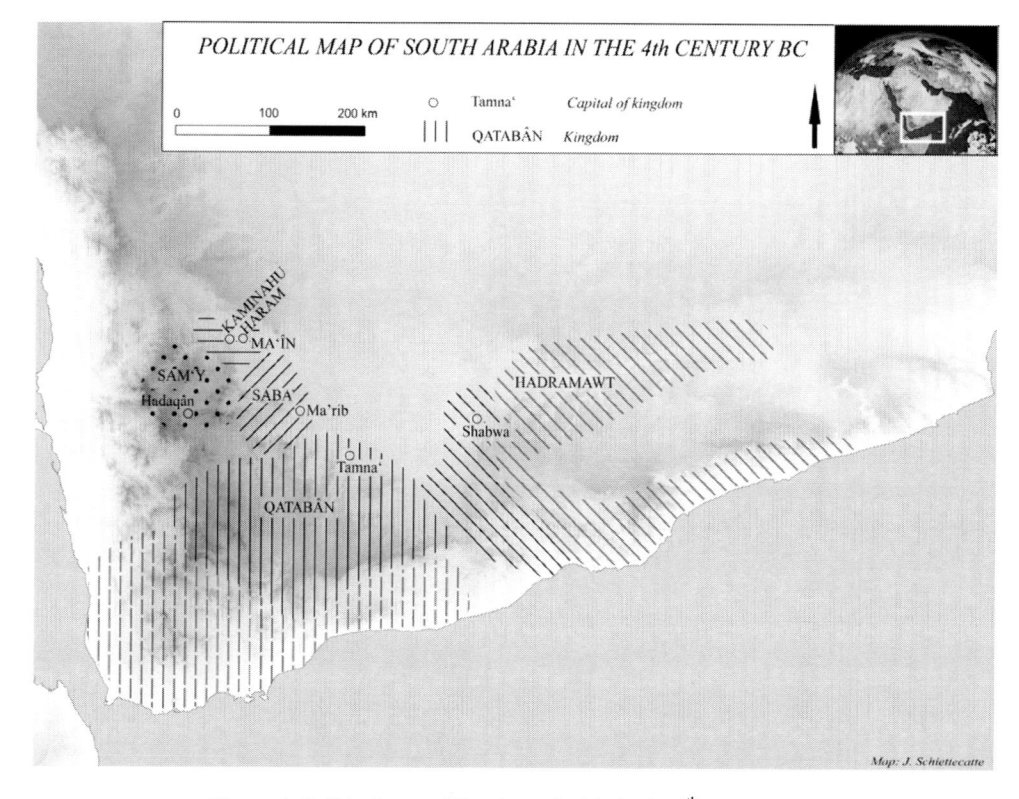

Figure 1. Political map of Southern Arabia in the 4th century BC.

Figure 2. Different types of anthropomorphic funerary stelae from the Jawf (Yemen): a – Eye stela (YM 28033, Arbach, Schiettecatte & al-Hadi 2008, fig. 2 p. 37); b – Bas relief stela (YM 26595, Arbach, Schiettecatte & al-Hadi 2008, fig. 37 p. 49); c – Stela with incised face elements (YM 28353, Arbach, Schiettecatte & al-Hadi 2008, fig. 330 p. 147); d – High relief stela (YM 29120, Arbach, Schiettecatte & al-Hadi 2008, fig. 400 p. 171).

northern origin of South Arabian stelae will be discussed here.

There are two categories of stelae, for which a North Arabian origin has been postulated: *Eye stelae* from the Jawf valley and Qatabānian *square stelae* (Garbini 1976; Garbini 1977; Antonini, Arbach & Sedov 2002). These categories will be presented and then the chronological and onomastic arguments for a northern origin will be reconsidered in the light of the recent discoveries. Next we will turn to the larger issue of the formation and development of the South Arabian culture, as it has been suggested in the past that South Arabian culture was the result of a strong northern influence, or even of incoming populations (e.g., Knauf 1989; Sedov 1996; Nebes 2001; Garbini 2004). The study of funerary stelae, together with linguistic and archaeological evidence, leads to an alternative hypothesis – an endogenous culture.

Anthropomorphic funerary stelae from the Jawf

Description

The stelae from the Jawf are carved from roughly shaped rectangular stone slabs. The material is hard limestone, or less frequently sandstone or alabaster. Four main types can be distinguished in the Jawf valley:

Eye stelae (Fig. 2a): this category was documented by C. Rathjens' '*Augenstelen*' (1955: 81). They only show a pair of eyes, incised or in relief.

Bas relief stelae (Fig. 2b): the whole face is represented in a low, generally sunken relief, the stone being cut away around the ornament, which is left in slight relief.

Stelae with incised face elements (Fig. 2c): this type adopts the iconography which developed on the *bas relief stelae*; it is an incised, less time-consuming variant.

High relief stelae (Fig. 2d): these consist of plain rectangular slabs with a high relief representation of the face. Some of these are sculpted in the round, probably to be inserted in a niche, as were the alabaster portraits of the Awwām temple at Maʾrib (Gerlach 2002).

The alleged North Arabian origin of the *Eye stelae*: a reconsideration

Two arguments have been put forward to suggest that *Eye stelae* came from or reflect North Arabian influence: the use of names that differ from the South Arabian onomastic tradition and the anteriority of the North Arabian anthropomorphic stelae in relation to that of South Arabia. Recent work does not support these differences.

The onomastic issue

The anthroponymy of Jawf funerary *Eye stelae* was first studied by G. Garbini in 1976. Because the only known names on inscriptions were written in the so-called North Arabian languages, Garbini inferred that there was a strong North Arabian component in the onomastics of these stelae, and consequently in the ethnic fabric of the Jawf.[1]

Several points contradict this hypothesis. Firstly, the geographic or ethnic origin of a name does not necessarily reflect the geographic or ethnic origin of its bearer. Examples are legion in our modern societies. Of course, a name can sometimes be associated with an ethnic group or a territory, such as when it includes the name of a local deity, but these cases are rare and do not appear in Garbini's study.

Secondly, even when a name is reflective of the geographic origin of its bearer, one cannot compare the names attested in the Ancient South Arabian inscriptions (Hadramitic, Sabaic, Qatabanic or Madhabic), called by default "South Arabian names", to those mentioned in the so-called North Arabian inscriptions (Lihyanite, Thamudic and Safaitic), considered "North Arabian names", without taking chronological and geographical considerations into account. Indeed, such a comparison would imply names attested in languages that are not necessarily in use at the same time. For example, most inscriptions in Safaitic were written at a time when Madhabic was no more in use. Similarly, Thamudic inscriptions are often considered North Arabian yet they are found throughout the western half of the Peninsula, from Yemen in the south to the extreme north of Arabia.

Thirdly, the significance of such comparisons is limited by the fact that they are most often based on G. Lankester Harding's practical but now dated and very incomplete index (1971). For example, three out of the five names defined by G. Garbini as exclusively North Arabian have now been attested in South Arabian inscriptions.[2] Therefore, the proposed connection between the names attested on the Jawf *Eye stelae* and North Arabian onomastics are no proof of a North Arabian onomastic tradition in South Arabia, even less of an ethnic North Arabian fabric.

Having discussed the problems with the previously held theory, how can the Jawf *Eye stelae* data be understood? A study of 381 names displayed on funerary stelae (Arbach, Schiettecatte & al-Hadi 2008), led Arbach and the author to point out some singularities of the Jawf onomastics. These are the scarcity of mimations and nunations at the end of the names (11%) and the rarity of family names (8.9%), both very frequent features in the monumental inscriptions in the Jawf.

These observations can be explained two ways: by an external influence or by a difference in social status. As these peculiarities are frequent in the Central and North Arabian onomastic tradition, it is tempting to interpret the data as the evidence for a northern influence. Yet, this feature may also reflect the tradition of a lower social class, which is rarely represented in the large monumental inscriptions from the Jawf area, the only onomastic source until the recent discovery of the stelae. As the percentage of stelae names that are only attested outside South Arabia is very low for the 381 stelae (2.9%) and zero for *Eye stelae*, the theory that these individuals belong to a different social class appears to be more probable.[3]

---

[1] Garbini (1976: 313): "Appare pertanto innegabile la forte componente nordarabica nell'onomastica (ed evidentemente nel tessuto etnico) yemenita non-sabea nel periodo più antico della documentazione."

[2] These are *Ḥzf* (al-Kāfir 14); *Mrdn* (*Mrd* in CT 22, *RÉS* 2761, Maʿīn 94, *Mrdm* in MuB 717, Aylward 1); *ʿnbr* (*RÉS* 4994 and Antonini, *AAE* 9, fig. 11; *ʿnbrm* in BAQ 4+2).
[3] See Arbach, Schiettecatte & al-Hadi 2008: 15. A. Avanzini had already put forward the hypothesis that the presence or absence of mimation/nunation could mark a social differentiation between the names used by the ruling classes and those used by the rest of the population (Avanzini 1979: 218).

The chronological issue

Regarding the anthropomorphic funerary stelae, G. Garbini suggested in a second study (1977) a direct influence of North Arabian cultural trends in the Jawf region. His explanation, amongst others, was the anteriority of North Arabian anthropomorphic stelae from Taymāʾ in relation to the South Arabian *Eye stelae*.[4] Leaving aside the clear stylistic differences between these two groups, the hypothesis of this anteriority requires closer examination.

Dating the *Eye-stelae* from the Jawf

There are two ways to date the stelae: their archaeological context and/or a palaeographic analysis of their inscriptions. For most of the stelae, the excavation data is absent as they come from illegal excavations. Only the excavations of Barāqish yielded provisional dating for the funerary stelae in the Jawf. They are thought to date to the last two centuries BC, although the excavation data are still under study and the precise chronological span remains to be determined.[5] No *Eye stela* has been found so far in this site. All the stelae discovered at Barāqish are *Stelae with incised face elements* or *Stelae in relief*.

In order to date the *Eye stelae*, it is therefore necessary to rely on a palaeographic study of the inscriptions. It must be highlighted that some limits are inherent in such dating methods. In general the funerary stela inscriptions are roughly carved; their texts were probably not inscribed by trained stone-cutters. The dating possibilities are therefore limited to the proportions of the letters in respect to one another, the flared footings at the end of the vertical strokes or the evolution of the curved shape of the letters. Therefore, the stelae can only be dated palaeographically to within a range of one or two centuries.

M. Arbach and the author have carried out the palaeographic classification of 446 stelae (including 17 *Eye stelae*) from the Jawf region, now in the Sanaa National Museum (Arbach & Schiettecatte 2006; Arbach, Schiettecatte & al-Hadi 2008). The chronological distribution of the different stela types and their palaeographic dating is represented in Fig. 3.

The *Eye stelae* are all dated between the 8th and 4th centuries BC. They tend to become rarer from the 5th century BC onward. Concurrently, other types of funerary anthropomorphic stelae develop. This chronological distribution also applies to the 21 *Eye stelae* published by G. Garbini showing written forms characteristic of the period lasting from the 8th to the 6th century BC. This is also the case for two out of the three *Eye stelae* housed in the Aden Museum, NAM 244 and NAM 1721, whereas stela NAM 95 seems to have been produced in a later period, c. 3rd century BC (Aqīl 1984: 58-59, 62, fig. 3-4, 11). *Eye stelae* thus appear to be an archaic form of the anthropomorphic stelae. They are mainly known from the 8th to the 5th century BC and not later than the 4th-3rd centuries BC.[6]

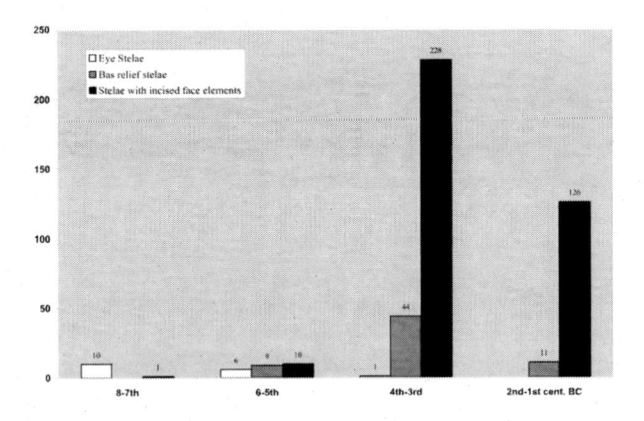

Figure 3. Chronological distribution of the stelae against their palaeographic dating (based on stelae published in Arbach & Schiettecatte 2006; Arbach, Schiettecatte & al-Hadi 2008)

Are there earlier North Arabian funerary stelae?

The Taymāʾ stelae mentioned by G. Garbini are the *Aramaic stelae*.[7] These are rectangular slabs with a rather standardized face representation (Fig. 4). The inscription they bear reveals Imperial Aramaic script, which is dated from the 6th/5th to the 4th/3rd centuries BC (Edens & Bawden 1989: 62, footnote 44). In the seventies G. Garbini, an advocate of a short chronology for South Arabia which dated the most ancient South Arabian stelae no earlier than the 5th century BC, could only postulate the anteriority of the North Arabian stelae to the South Arabian ones. Yet since then adherence to the short chronology has been abandoned by almost all scholars for a longer chronology in which the earliest South Arabian monumental inscriptions and stelae are dated to the 8th century BC. Therefore, there is no evidence which confirms the anteriority of the *Aramaic stelae* from Taymāʾ. Despite this, G. Garbini's northern influence theory is still regularly accepted in works dealing with funerary practices in South Arabia.[8]

Other North Arabian stelae may be considered. A second category of Taymāʾ stelae was discovered after G. Garbini published his paper. It includes two coarse stelae

---

[4] Garbini (1977: 378): "... si tratta di categorie monumentali funerarie di evidente origine settentrionale, introdotte in Yemen, presumibilmente, da gruppi etnici nord-arabici e da quei minei che per ragioni commerciali erano in più stretto contatto con questi ultimi [...] Le Augenstelen trovano il loro immediato precedente nelle stele funerarie aramaiche di Teima."

[5] The excavation of the cemetery of Barāqish was conducted by S. Antonini in 2005, as part of the Italian Archaeological Mission directed by Alessandro de Maigret. She kindly communicated some of the main results to the author.

[6] The latest examples are NAM 95 and the wooden stela *RÉS* 4746 (*Hamburg Museum für Völkerkunde*): Rathjens 1955: phot. 245, Höfner 1964: fig. 1.

[7] See Degen (1974: 89, 93), al-Rāshad (dir.) (2003: 107), Abu Duruk (1986: pl. LI).

[8] Note alongside the contribution of A. de Maigret in the catalogue of the exhibition held at the Institut du Monde Arabe (Robin & Vogt (eds) 1997: 167). See also Roux (1997: 209) and Vogt (2002: 184).

Figure 4. Aramaic Stelae from Taymāʾ (Photographic acknowledgment: William Facey): a – Taymāʾ Museum WF. 00808; b – Taymāʾ Museum WF. 00813; c – Taymāʾ Museum WF. 00871; d – Taymāʾ Museum WF. 00861

much more similar to the South Arabian ones from an iconographic point of view. The first comes from the "Industrial Site" graveyard at Taymāʾ (Abu Duruk 1989: pl. 8), dated between the 2nd millennium and the second half of the 1st millennium BC. It is not possible to determine whether it was produced earlier or later than the South Arabian stelae. The other (TA 514) was found at Taymāʾ (Area S) by the Saudi-German archaeological joint project, in a disturbed stratigraphical context (Tomb T. 1007). Radiocarbon dates place the occupation of the area between the 9th and the 5th centuries BC.[9] The stela is a simple limestone slab on which the face elements are roughly pecked. As with the previous example, nothing

---

[9] Unpublished data provided by Dr. Arnulf Hausleiter (DAI, Orient Abteilung). Concerning the datings, see Eichmann 2009: 62-63, footnote 14.

Figure 5. Qatabanian stelae: a – Square stelae with face representation (TC 1668, Cleveland 1965, pl. 37); b – Rectangular stelae with face representation (TC 1692, Cleveland 1965, pl. 38); c – Non figurative stelae (TC 2183, Cleveland 1965, pl. 74); d – Stelae with bull head (TC 1686, Cleveland 1965, pl. 65); e – Stelae with head sculpted in the round (TC 1884, Cleveland 1965, pl. 24); f – Stelae with high relief representation of the deceased (TC 1557, Cleveland 1965, pl. 45).

indicates whether this stela is older or younger than the *Eye stelae* from the Jawf.

Finally, there are often parallels drawn between the stelae from Petra (Roche 1985; Moutsopoulos 1990), wādī Ramm (Grohmann 1963: Abb. 31), and Madāʾin Ṣāliḥ (Grohmann 1963: Abb. 30) and the South Arabian stelae.[10] The influence of one region on the other is not usually mentioned, though this could be considered. These stelae generally represent the eyes and nose on a stone slab in a very schematic way (Fig. 7a). They differ from the South Arabian or Taymāʾ stelae because they are not funerary stelae but betyls, i.e. representations of deities. Those found in stratigraphical context date at the latest to the first centuries of Christian era[11] and therefore cannot be the forerunners of earlier South Arabian stelae.

Thus, there is no North Arabian anthropomorphic funerary stela which can be clearly dated prior to the 8th century BC, the time of the appearance or the Jawf *Eye stelae*. No influence from North to South can be mapped out so far.

Anthropomorphic Qatabanian square stelae

Description

Hundreds of funerary stelae were unearthed at Ḥayd ibn ʿAqīl, the graveyard of the Qatabānian capital Tamnaʿ

---

[10] For example: Cleveland (1965: 16-17) or Roche (1985: 143-144, 153-154).
[11] The anthropomorphic betyls discovered in stratigraphical context are dated between the 1st and the 4th centuries AD: stela from the Temple of the Winged Lions in Petra dated to the 1st century AD (Baratte 1978: 42); a betyl discovered in the destruction level of Haus III – Raum XXI dated to the end of the 1st century AD (Bignasca, Desse-Berset, Fellmann Brogli et al. 1996: 26-30, 337-38, Abb. 943-44); another in a 4th century context in Petra (Zayadine 1974: 147-148).

Figure 6. Qatabanian Square Stelae: a – TC 1366 (Cleveland 1965: pl. 39); b – TC 2039 (Cleveland 1965: pl. 39); c – TC 920 (Cleveland 1965: pl. 38); d – TC 1604 (Cleveland 1965: pl. 39); e – TC 1822 (Cleveland 1965: pl. 37); f – TC 1668 (Cleveland 1965: pl. 37); g – Van Lesen 11 (Bron 1992: 24); h – Hon 8 (Honeyman 1962: pl. 8).

(Jamme 1952; Cleveland 1965; Antonini, Arbach & Sedov 2002). This corpus is divided into six categories:[12]

- Square stelae with face representation (Fig. 5a)
- Rectangular stelae with face representation (Fig. 5b)
- Non figurative stelae (Fig. 5c)
- Stelae with bull head (Fig. 5d)
- Stelae with head of the deceased sculpted in the round (Fig. 5e)
- Stelae with high relief representation of the deceased as head-and-shoulders or full-length portraits (Fig. 5f)

The first category, the Qatabānian *Square stelae*, show close similarities with some Taymanite and Nabataean stelae, and are worth closer examination. About 80 examples are known so far.[13] This category has been divided up into two types by R. L. Cleveland (1965: 16-20, pl. 36-40). In type A, the facial features are elegantly stylized, with the nose forming a thin vertical band connected to the eyebrows and almond-shaped eyes. Type B is extremely simplified and limited to the symbolic U-shaped representation of the eyes, to which a nose, represented by a vertical line, is sometimes added. However, the distinction between these two types is not always clear. A synoptic presentation of several of these artefacts reveals the stylistic continuity between types A and B (Fig. 6). It is not possible to decide whether the U-shaped eyes are an ancient and archaic production evolving toward the type A form, or whether the simplified treatment reflects an economy of means.

An alleged North-Arabian origin: reconsideration

S. Antonini published two of these stelae, suggesting that they were produced at the turn of Christian era, had Arabian names, and were evidence for the arrival of nomadic tribes in South Arabia from northwestern Arabia, where similar stelae have been found.[14]

The onomastic issue

Antonini does not specify the basis on which she considers the names to be Arabian and therefore a few comments are necessary. With regard to these two names, Arbach indicates in the same volume that the first of these names is partly reconstructed and that it is the name of the lineage *Rdmt*, attested as a personal name in the Qatabānic inscriptions, but which is unknown to the Arab tradititonists (Antonini, Arbach & Sedov 2002: 77). The second is a theophoric name, *Lhyᶜm*, that comprises the name of the main deity of the Qatabānian pantheon, ᶜAmm, which is therefore characteristic of the Qatabānian sphere. It is followed by the patronymic *Ḥdmt*, not attested yet in the Qatabānic texts but known in South Arabia as a Sabaean lineage name (Ir 69, Ja 567). In both cases, the onomastics suggest that the names on the stelae are not Arabian.

Furthermore, the inscriptions born by other stelae in this category show several compound names using the name of the Qatabānian deity ᶜAmm (ᶜmkhl, *Lhyᶜm*). Patronymics and names of common lineages in the Qatabān area (*Sˡflyn*, *Ḡrbm*, *Ṣlfn*, *Ṯbw*, etc.) also appear regularly. All these pieces of evidence tend to support the hypothesis of a local onomastic tradition.

---

[12] The four first categories have been identified by Antonini, Arbach & Sedov (2002).
[13] Lankester-Harding (1964: 48, pl. XLIII), Cleveland (1965), Aqîl (1984), Robin & Vogt (eds) (1997: 173), Antonini, Arbach & Sedov (2002: 4-5, tav. IIIc-d), Avanzini (2004: n° 382, 636, 658, 777, 780, 781, 931, 1057, 1066).

[14] Antonini, Arbach & Sedov (2002: 4-5): "Questo tipi di stele, entrato in uso nel costume funerario sudarabico intorno all'era di Cristo, [...]. I nomi dei defunti sono arabi, e testimoniano l'arrivo di nuove tribù di nomadi in Arabia meridionale, probabilmente dal nord-ovest della Penisola arabica, dove sono state trovate stele molto simili a queste."

Figure 7. Jordanian anthropomorphic stelae: a – Betyl from Petra (Petra archaeological Museum, Bienkowski (ed.) 1991: fig. 49); b – Betyl from the Temple of the winged lions, Petra (Amman archaeological Museum, Bienkowski (ed.) 1991: fig. 47); c – Anthropomorphic stela from Khirbet Rizqeh (Amman archaeological Museum, Bienkowski (ed.) 1991: fig. 50).

The chronological issue

The important issue is whether Qatabānian *Square stelae* appear at the turn of Christina era, as postulated by S. Antonini. Do they appear earlier or later than the North Arabian productions bearing iconographic parallels and can they be the result of any North Arabian influence?

Dating these productions is not easy. There is no information regarding the precise stratigraphic context of the square stelae from the Ḥayd ibn ʿAqīl necropolis. Moreover, the frequent lack of inscriptions on *Square stelae* with U-shaped eyes or the coarse written form of the inscriptions makes any palaeographic study difficult.

It is not clear why Antonini dated the two stelae so late. Especially as Arbach dates them, in the same volume, to an earlier period according to the written form of the inscriptions, one dating to the 2nd century BC and the other to the 1st century BC (Antonini, Arbach & Sedov 2002: 77, 81).

As a whole, it is difficult to date the inscriptions on the stelae. All the stelae the author could gather were examined by Arbach who dated them from the 5th to the 1st century BC. They are representative of a written form that is characteristic of the second half of the 1st millennium BC, but it is not possible to be more precise. The only reliable chronological limits for this type would be the *terminus post quem* given by the beginning of the occupation of the necropolis (7th-6th centuries BC) and the *terminus ante quem* of the date of abandonment of the site, at the beginning of Christian era (Glanzmann 1997: 171). Although there is no strong evidence that this type of stela appears after the turn of Christian era, Tamnaʿ, the city linked to the Ḥayd ibn ʿAqīl necropolis, may not have been abandoned until the 2nd century AD (de Maigret 2003).

Three areas have yielded comparable anthropomorphic stelae in North Arabia: Taymāʾ (*Aramaic stelae*), Petra in Jordan (stela from the temple of the winged lions) and Khirbet Rizqeh in southern Jordan (Figs. 4 and 7).

As we established earlier, Taymāʾ *Aramaic stelae* should be dated from the 6th/5th to the 4th/3rd centuries BC. Qatabānian *Square stelae* should be dated to the second half of the 1st millennium BC. Therefore there is no evidence that the latter appear later than the former. Furthermore, Qatabānian U-shaped-eyes *Square stelae* (Fig. 6a-6d) are a simplified version of face representation *Square stelae* (Fig. 6e-6h). If these U-shaped-eyes stelae can be interpreted as "cheap" funerary stelae, contemporaneous to the finer productions, it is also possible to think them as an archaic form leading to more carefully carved productions —many of them bear no inscriptions and therefore cannot be dated. If this were the case, they could date back to the beginning of the occupation of the Ḥayd ibn ʿAqīl necropolis in the 7th century BC, and therefore may have appeared two centuries earlier than the Taymāʾ stelae. If this were the case it would not be possible that the North Arabian stelae were older.

The iconography of a stela from Petra (Fig. 7b) is very similar to the Taymāʾ Aramaic stelae and the Qatabanian square stelae. It has been found in the Temple of the Winged Lions at Petra and it is dated to the 1st century AD (Baratte 1978: 42). However, this stela did not have a funerary purpose; it was a betyl representing the goddess Hayyan. Due to the different function and the later date, it is highly probable that these stelae reflect South Arabian or Taymanite influence rather than the opposite, solely from an iconographic point of view.

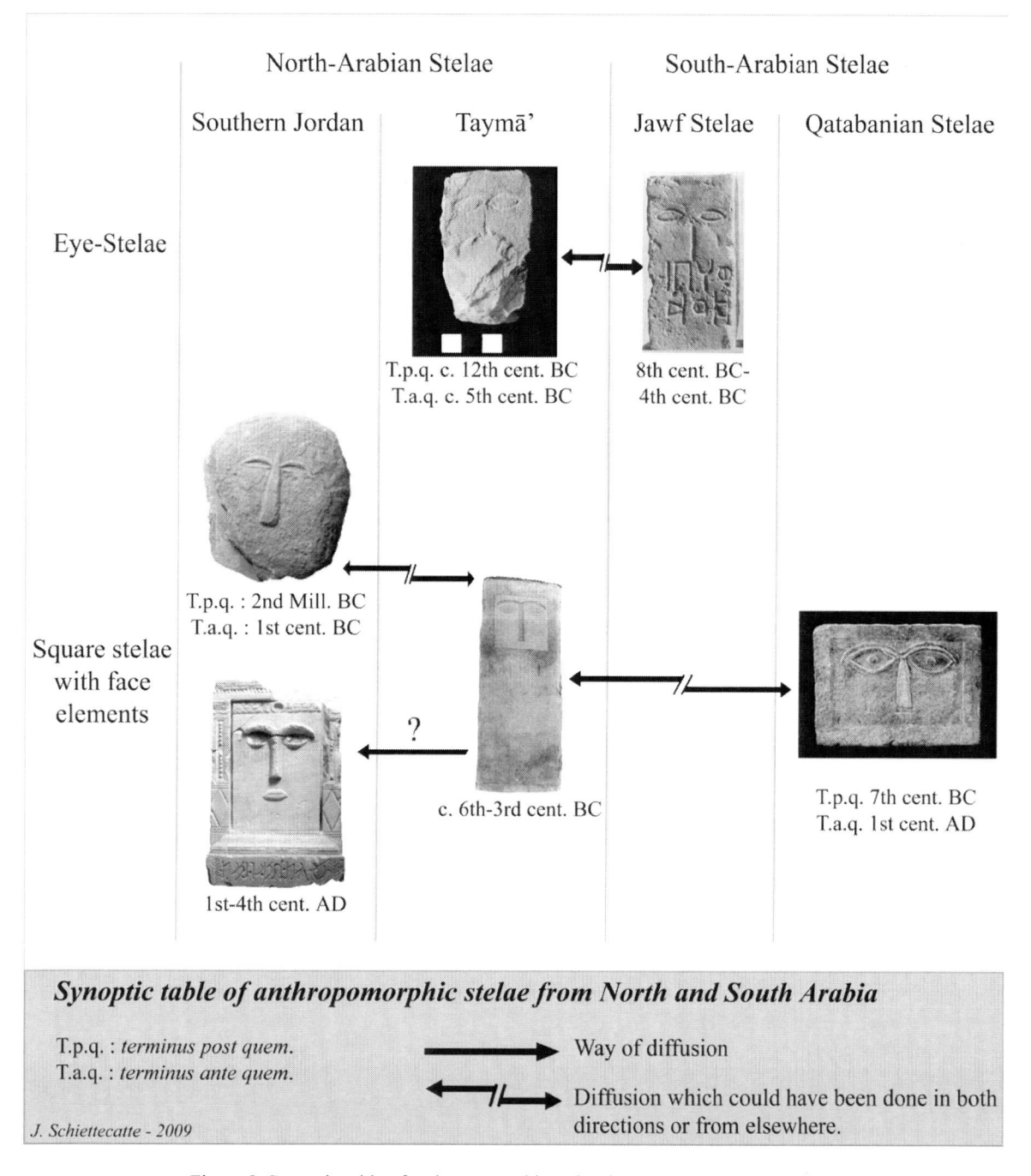

Figure 8. Synoptic table of anthropomorphic stelae from North and South Arabia

The final anthropomorphic stelae to be compared to the *Qatabanian square stelae* come from the Jordanian site of Khirbet Rizqeh (Fig. 7c) (Kirkbride 1960; 1969; Bienkowski (ed.) 1991: fig. 50). They are full-length statues with the eyes and nose simply represented, which have a similar iconography to the Aramaic stelae of Taymāʾ or of the *Qatabanian square stelae*.

These stelae, set in a circle, form what D. Kirkbride has interpreted as a sanctuary devoted to an ancestors' cult. Fragments of these stelae were reemployed in later graves. Therefore, they appear not to have had a funerary purpose. As for their dating, the only known element is the setting of the sanctuary, which dates the production of the stelae to between the Chalcolithic and the end of the 1st millennium BC (Kirkbride 1960; 1969; Schiettecatte in press). Nothing supports a dating to the 1st century BC/AD as it has been suggested elsewhere (Bienkowski (ed.) 1991: fig. 50). Without any precise dating, it is problematic to suggest that there is a link between the southern Jordanian stelae and the South Arabian ones.

Thus, it cannot be maintained that Petra, Khirbet Rizqeh, or Taymāʾ stelae were made earlier than the Qatabān ones – or even the stelae from the Jawf – and that they influenced the South Arabian examples. On the contrary, the connections that have been established all indicate contemporaneousness or that the South Arabian stelae pre-date the North Arabian examples.

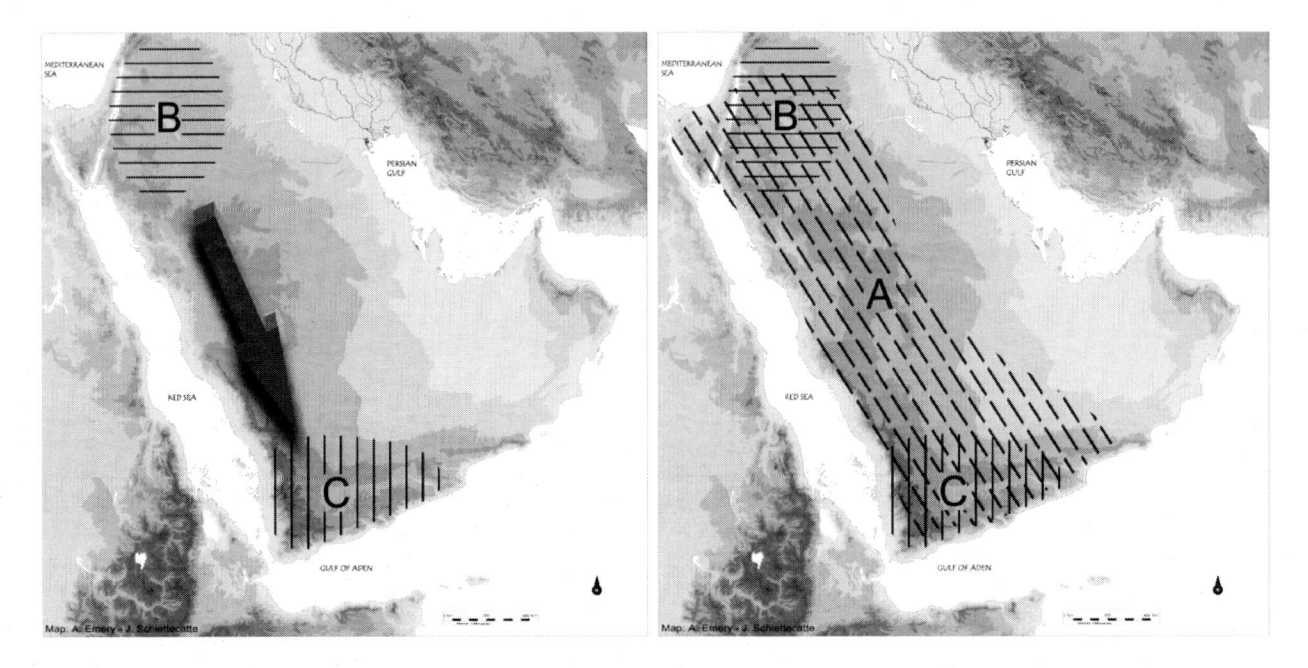

Figure 9. Map a: South Arabian Cultural Area (C) resulting from acculturation or migration from the North (B); Map b: South Arabian Cultural Area (C) and North Arabian Cultural Area (B) as the legacy of a common cultural background (A).

Acculturation versus endogenous evolution

The available chronological data for the dating of the stelae from South and North Arabia (Fig. 8) does not support cultural diffusion, either from North to South or the other way around. The only observation that can be made at this point is the general contemporaneity of many of these artefacts. As was discussed above, the onomastics also do not support the hypothesis of a North Arabian origin for the South Arabian anthropomorphic stelae. Therefore this discussion should be taken further. The idea of a formation of the South Arabian culture at the beginning of the 1st millennium BC by acculturation or adoption of northern cultural elements has been regularly put forward not only for the anthropomorphic funerary stelae, but also for South Arabian culture as a whole. By the 8th century BC, South Arabians were living in fortified cities surrounded by vast irrigated areas. The use of an alphabetic script, the construction of monumental stone architecture, and the production of original artistic works was well established. These major developments appear to have taken place rather suddenly around the beginning of the first millennium BC.

How are we to explain this leap forward? The 20-year-old debate on this issue is still dominated by a diffusionist approach that maintains South Arabian culture was the product of northern innovations, brought with the migrations of South Levantine or North Arabian populations, who arrived in South Arabia and came into contact with local populations. The arguments put forward for this migration theory are of a linguistic and archaeological nature, and include the transmission of a South Semitic alphabet originating in the southern Levant and a series of ceramic parallels between pottery from the Ḥaḍramawt and Northern Arabia (Knauf 1989; Sedov 1996; Nebes 2001; Garbini 2004).[15]

However, this settlement process remains largely hypothetical. It was suggested largely because of the absence of documents from Central Arabia and, until recently, due to gaps in the South Arabian archaeological data.[16] Without denying that there were contacts with North Arabian populations and that foreign influences impacted on South Arabia, a migratory settlement model should be treated with caution, as very recently put forward by A. Avanzini,[17] especially as the theory is based only on the transmission of an alphabetical order.[18] This diffusionist pattern sees the 1500 kilometres separating the southern Levant and South Arabia as a cultural void without any capacity for indigenous innovation.

---

[15] Concerning ceramic parallels: Sedov (1996: 74-76, 1997: 45); concerning migrations: Sedov (1996: 86).

[16] These gaps were filled in by a series of studies insisting on the continuity of settlement between the Bronze Age and the Iron Age: in the Tihāma (Vogt, Buffa & Brunner 2002; Keall 2004; Khalidi 2006), in the Lowlands (Brunner 1983, 1997; Overstreet & Grolier 1996), in the Ḥaḍramawt (McCorriston 2000; Benoist, Mouton & Schiettecatte 2007), or in the Highlands (Wilkinson, Edens & Gibson 1997; Wilkinson & Edens 1999).

[17] Avanzini (2009: 206): "Much of the Near East historiography which has emerged in recent years has deemed the exogenous model for the formation of a culture methodologically obsolete."

[18] Avanzini (2009: 207-208): "[Garbini] has not altogether abandoned his idea of several groups of nomads from Mesopotamia stopping first in Palestine and then happily arriving in that desolate area bordering the desert at the foot of the Yemeni high plateau to find their Arabia Felix […]. Even if we accept the alphabetical order as a north-western creation, it does not mean that south Arabian culture was brought by groups who came from Palestine. Nobody has ever attributed the origin of the Greeks to a mass movement of peoples from the East despite the alphabetical order of Greek clearly deriving from Phoenician."

Yet, recent archaeological research within this previously insufficiently-explored area has begun to sketch the progressive appearance of a common cultural background. Several observations support this idea:

- Bronze age architectural similarities between the Yemeni Highlands (de Maigret 1990), the Jawf valley (Cleuziou, Inizan & Robin 1988), the Rajājil area in North Arabia, Be'er Resisim in the Negev (Cohen & Dever 1980) and Sheikh Awad, Nabi Salah and Sheikh Muhsen in the Sinai (Beit-Arieh 1974; 1981; Zarins 1992).
- Shared Bronze Age funerary practices in Sinai, the southern Levant, and western and southern Arabia (Newton & Zarins 2000; Steimer-Herbet 2004).
- A convergent development of Bronze Age pottery in the Yemeni Highlands and in Palestine (Edens 1999: 125).
- Similarities between domestic tripartite South Arabian architecture of the first half of the 1st millennium BC and that of Palestine, built around the 11th century BC and possibly inspired by nomadic populations in the South Arabian and Levantine steppe (Fritz 1980: 122; de Maigret 2005).
- The possible existence of a '*proto-western verb system*', shared by populations settled in the western half of the Arabian Peninsula, from Syria to Yemen (Avanzini 2009).

Thus, rather than explaining the formation of South Arabian culture by a migratory model implying an acculturation of autochthonous populations to the culture of North Arabia or South Levantine groups of population (Fig. 9: left), the hypothesis of cultural convergences between groups B and C, made possible by a pre-existing West Arabian common cultural background – of which groups B and C are direct cultural heirs – should be proposed (Fig. 9: right). Although the caravan incense trade was clearly a means by which technical, cultural and artistic innovations were transmitted from Mesopotamia and the Levant to South Arabia, it is equally clear that South Arabian funerary stelae – and South Arabian culture in general – cannot be understood solely through the lens of this "northernisation".

Acknowledgments

I wish to express my gratitude to Mounir Arbach for the palaeographic analysis he provided for me, as well as Dr Arnulf Hausleiter and Mrs Sabina Antonini-de Maigret for having informed me of the results of recent unpublished fieldwork. I sincerely thank Prof. Michael Macdonald for giving me access to photographs of unpublished stelae from the Taymāʾ Museum, and Mr William Facey for allowing me to use some of them here. Finally, I thank Dr Astrid Emery for her thorough reading of this paper.

References

Aqīl A.A. 1984. *Les stèles funéraires du Yémen antique*. Paris: Université Paris 1. [unpublished master's dissertation].

Abu Duruk H.I. 1986. *Introduction to the Archaeology of Taymaʾ. A Critical and Comparative Discussion of Certain Ancient Monuments (part of the City-wall, Qasr ar-Radm, and Qasr al-Hamrâʾ), in the North-Arabian City of Taymâʾ in the light of evidence furnished by excavations*. Riyadh: Deputy Ministry of Antiquities and Museums.

Abu Duruk H.I. 1989. Preliminary Report on the Industrial Site Excavation at Tayma, First Season, 1408/1987. *Atlal* 12: 9-19.

Antonini S., Arbach M. & Sedov A.V. 2002. *Collezioni sudarabiche inedite. Gli oggetti dalla missione archeologica italo-francese a Tamnaᶜ, Yemen (1999-2000)*. (Supplemento n. 91 agli ANNALI - vol. 60-61). Naples: Istituto Universitario Orientale.

Arbach M. & Schiettecatte J. 2006. *Catalogue des pièces archéologiques et épigraphiques du Jawf au musée national de Ṣanʿāʾ*. Sanaa: UNESCO.

Arbach M., Schiettecatte J., al-Hadi I. 2008. *Ṣanʿāʾ National Museum. Part III. Collection of Funerary Stelae from the Jawf Valley*. Sanaa: Printart.

Avanzini A. 1979. Alcune Osservazioni sulla documentazione epigrafica preislamica dell'oasi di al-'Ulā. *Egitto e Vicino Oriente* II: 215-224.

Avanzini A. 2004. *Corpus of South Arabian Inscriptions I-III. Qatabanic, Marginal Qatabanic, Awsanite Inscriptions*. (Arabia Antica 2). Pise: Edizioni Plus.

Avanzini A. 2009. Origin and Classification of the Ancient South Arabian Languages. *Journal of Semitic Studies* 54.1 (Spring 2009): 205-220.

Baratte F. 1978. *Un royaume aux confins du désert, Pétra et la Nabatène*. Lyons: Muséum de Lyon.

Beit-Arieh I. 1974. An Early Bronze Age II site at Nabi Salah in Southern Sinai. *Tel Aviv* 1: 144-156.

Beit-Arieh I. 1981. A Pattern of Settlement in Southern Sinai and Southern Canaan in the Third Millennium BC. *Bulletin of the American Schools of Oriental Research* 243: 31-55.

Benoist A., Lavigne O., Mouton M. & Schiettecatte J. 2007. Chronologie et évolution de l'architecture à Makaynûn: la formation d'un centre urbain à l'époque sudarabique dans le Hadramawt. *Proceedings of the Seminar for Arabian Studies* 37: 17-35.

Bienkowski P. (ed.). 1991. *Treasures from an Ancient Land: The Art of Jordan*. Stroud: Alan Sutton Publishing.

Bignasca A., Desse-Berset N., Fellmann Brogli R. et al. 1996. *Petra. Ez Zantur I. Ergebnisse der Schweizerisch-Liechtensteinischen Ausgrabungen 1988-1992*. (Terra Archaeologica II). Mainz: Philipp von Zabern.

Bron F. 1992. *Memorial Mahmud al-Ghul*. Paris: P. Geuthner.

Brunner U. 1983. *Die Erforschung der antiken Oase von Mārib mit Hilfe geomorphologischer Untersuchungsmethoden*. (ABADY II). Mainz: Verlag Philipp von Zabern.

Brunner U. 1997. Geography and Human Settlements in Ancient Southern Arabia. *Arabian Archaeology and Epigraphy* 8: 190-202.

Cleuziou S., Inizan M.-L. & Robin Ch. 1988. *Premier rapport préliminaire sur la prospection des vallées nord du wādī al-Jawf. République Arabe du Yémen.* [Unpublished circulated report].

Cleveland R.L. 1965. *An ancient South Arabian Necropolis. Objects from the Second Campaign (1951) in the Timna Cemetery.* (Publications of the American Foundation for the Study of Man IV). Baltimore: The Johns Hopkins Press.

Cohen R. & Dever W.G. 1980. Be'er Resisim. *Israel Exploration Journal* 30: 228-231.

Degen R. 1974. Die aramäischen Inschriften aus Taimāʾ und Umgebung. *Neue Ephemeris für Semitische Epigraphik* 2: 79-98.

Edens Ch. 1999. The Bronze-Age of Highland Yemen: Chronological and Spatial Variability of Pottery and Settlement. *Paléorient* 25/2: 105-128.

Edens Ch. & Bawden G. 1989. History of Taymāʾ and Hejaz trade during the first millenium BC. *Journal of the Economic and Social History of the Orient* 32: 48-103.

Eichmann R. 2009. Archaeological evidence of the pre-Islamic period (4th–6th c. AD) at Taymāʾ. Pages 59-66 in J. Schiettecatte & Ch. Robin (eds), *L'Arabie à la veille de l'Islam. Bilan clinique.* (Orient et Méditerranée 3). Paris: De Boccard.

Fritz V. 1980. Die kulturhistorische Bedeutung der früheisenzeitlichen Siedlung auf der Hirbet el-Msas und das Problem der Landnahme. *Zeitschrift des Deutschen Palästina-Vereins* 96: 121-135.

Garbini G. 1976. Iscrizioni sudarabiche. *Annali dell'Istituto Universitario Orientale di Napoli* 36 (N.S. XXVI): 293-315.

Garbini G. 1977. Su alcuni tipi di stele e statuette sudarabiche con iscrizione. *Annali dell'Istituto Universitario Orientale di Napoli* 37 (N.S. XXVII): 375-381.

Garbini G. 2004. The origins of South Arabians. Pages 203-209 in A.V. Sedov (ed.), *Scripta Yemenica. Studies in Honor of M.B. Piotrovkij.* Moscow.

Gerlach I. 2002. Der Friedhof des Awām-Tempels in Mārib. Bericht der Ausgrabungen von 1997 bis 2001. Pages 41-91 in I. Gerlach & B. Vogt (eds), *Archäologische Berichte aus dem Yemen* IX. Mainz: Philipp von Zabern.

Glanzmann W.D. 1997. Le cimetière de Tamna. Pages 171-177 in Ch. Robin & B. Vogt (eds), *Yémen, au pays de la reine de Sabaʾ, catalogue de l'exposition présentée à l'Institut du Monde Arabe.* Paris: Flammarion.

Grohmann A. 1963. *Kulturgeschichte des alten Orients – Arabien.* Munich: C.H. Beck'sche Verlagsbuchhandlung.

Höfner M. 1964. Altsüdarabische Stelen und Statuetten. Pages 217-232 in E. Haberland, M. Schuster & H. Straube (eds), *Festschrift für A.E. Jensen.* Munich: K. Renner.

Honeyman A.M. 1962. Ephigraphic South Arabian Antiquities. *Journal of Near Eastern Studies* 21: 38-43.

Jamme A. 1952. *Les pièces épigraphiques de Heid bin ʿAqīl, la nécropole de Timnaʿ (Hagar Kohlān).* (Bibliothèque du Muséon 30). Leuven: Publications universitaires.

Keall E. 2004. Possible connections in antiquity between the Red Sea coast of Yemen and the Horn of Africa. Pages 43-56 in P. Lunde & A. Porter (eds), *Trade and Travel in the Red Sea Region. Proceedings of Red Sea Project I Held in the British Museum, October 2002.* (BAR International Series 1269, Society for Arabian Studies Monographs No. 2). Oxford: Archaeopress.

Khalidi L. 2006. *Settlement, Culture-Contact and Interaction Along the Red Sea Coastal Plain, Yemen: The Tihamah cultural landscape in the late prehistoric period, 3000-900 BC.* University of Cambridge. [Unpublished PhD Dissertation].

Kirkbride D. 1960. Khirbet Rizqeh. *Revue Biblique* LXVII (1960): 232-235.

Kirkbride D. 1969. Ancient Arabian Ancestor Idols, part I. *Archaeology* 22.2 (April 1969): 116-121; part II. *Archaeology* 22.3 (June 1969): 188-195.

Knauf E.A. 1989. The Migration of the Script, and the Formation of the State in South Arabia. *Proceedings of the Seminar for Arabian Studies* 19: 79-91.

Lankester-Harding G. 1964. *Archaeology in the Aden Protectorates.* London: Her Majesty's Stationery Office.

Lankester-Harding G. 1971. *An index and concordance of pre-Islamic Arabian names and inscriptions.* (Near and Middle East Series 8). Toronto: University of Toronto Press.

de Maigret A. 2003. Tamnaʿ, ancient capital of the Yemeni desert. Information about the first two excavation campaigns (1999-2000). Pages 135-140 in M. Liverani & F. Merighi (eds), *Arid Lands in Roman Times. Papers from the International Conference (Rome, July 9th-10th 2001).* (Arid Zone Archaeology, Monographs 4). Rome: Edizioni all'insegna del Giglio.

de Maigret A. 2005. Some Reflections on the South-Arabian Bayt. Pages 101-110 in I. Gerlach (ed.), *Archäologische Berichte aus dem Yemen* X. Mainz: Verlag Philipp von Zabern.

de Maigret A. (ed.) 1990. *The Bronze Age Culture of Khawlan at-Tiyāl and al-Hadāʾ (Republic of Yemen), A First General Report.* (Memoirs and Reports XXIV). Rome: IsMEO.

McCorriston J. 2000. Early Settlement in Hadramawt: Preliminary report on prehistoric occupation at Shiʿb Munayder. *Arabian Archaeology and Epigraphy* 11: 129-153.

Moutsopoulos N.C. 1990. Observations sur les représentations du panthéon nabatéen. Pages 53-75 in F. Zayadine (ed.), *Petra and the Caravan Cities.* Amman: Department of Antiquities.

Nebes N. 2001. Die Genese der altsüdarabischen Kultur: Eine Arbeitshypothese. Pages 427-435 in R. Eichmann & H. Parzinger (eds), *Migration und Kulturtransfer. Der Wandel vorder- und zentralasiatischer Kulturen im Umbruch vom 2. zum 1. vorchristlichen Jahrtausend*, Berlin-Bonn.

Newton L.S. & Zarins J. 2000. Aspects of Bronze Age art of southern Arabia: The pictorial landscape and its relation to economic and social political status. *Arabian Archaeology and Epigraphy* 11: 154-179.

Overstreet W.C. & Grolier M.J. 1996. Summary of Environmental Background for the Human Occupation of the al-Jadidah Basin in Wadi al-Jubah, Yemen Arab Republic. Pages 337-429 in M.J. Grolier, R. Brinkmann & J.A. Blakely (eds), *The Wādī al-Jubah Archaeological Project, vol.5: Environmental Research in Support of Archaeological Investigations in the Yemen Arab Republic, 1982-1987*. Washington: American Foundation for the Study of Man.

Al-Rāshad S. (ed.). 2003. *Atār manṭaqat Tabūk*. Riyadh: Ministry of Knowledge, Antiquities and Museums.

Rathjens C. 1955. *Sabaeica. Bericht über die archäologischen Ergebnisse seiner zweiten, dritten und vierten Reise nach Südarabien. II. Teil. Die unlokalisierten Funde*. (Mitteilungen aus dem Museum für Völkerkunde, 24). Hamburg.

Robin Ch. & Vogt B. (eds). 1997. *Yémen, au pays de la reine de Saba', catalogue de l'exposition présentée à l'Institut du Monde Arabe*. Paris: Flammarion.

Roche M.-J. 1985. *Niches à bétyles et monuments apparentés à Pétra*. Unpublished PhD dissertation, University of Paris 10.

Roux J.-C. 1997. Le monde des morts. Pages 205-215 in Ch. Robin & B. Vogt (eds), *Yémen, au pays de la reine de Saba', catalogue de l'exposition présentée à l'Institut du Monde Arabe*. Paris: Flammarion.

Schiettecatte J. In press. Considérations sur les stèles funéraires sudarabiques, leurs origines et la formation de la culture sudarabique. *Arabia* 4.

Sedov A.V. 1996. On the Origin of the agricultural settlements in Hadramawt. Pages 67-86 in Ch. Robin & I. Gajda (eds), *Arabia Antiqua, Early Origins of South Arabian States, Proceedings of the First International Conference on the Conservation and Exploitation of the Archaeological Heritage of the Arabian Peninsula*. (Serie Orientale Roma LXX, 1). Rome: IsMEO.

Steimer-Herbet T. 2004. *Classification des sépultures à superstructure lithique dans le Levant et l'Arabie occidentale*. (BAR International Series 1246). Oxford: Archaeopress.

Vogt B. 2002. Death and Funerary Practices. Pages 180-186 in St J. Simpson (ed.), *Queen of Sheba. Treasures from Ancient Yemen*. London: The British Museum Press.

Vogt B., Buffa V. & Brunner U. 2002. Maʿlayba and the Bronze Age Irrigation in Coastal Yemen. Pages 15-26 in I. Gerlach & B. Vogt (eds), *Archäologische Berichte aus dem Yemen IX*. Mainz: Verlag Philipp von Zabern.

Wilkinson T.J. & Edens Ch. 1999. Survey and Excavation in the Central Highlands of Yemen: Results of the Dhamār Survey Project, 1996 and 1998. *Arabian Archaeology and Epigraphy* 10: 1-33.

Wilkinson T.J., Edens Ch. & Gibson McG. 1997. The Archaeology of the Yemen High Plains: A preliminary chronology. *Arabian Archaeology and Epigraphy* 8: 99-142.

Zarins J. 1992. Pastoral nomadism in Arabia: ethnoarchaeology and the archaeological record - a case study. Pages 219-240 in O. Bar-Yosef & A. Khasanov (eds), *Pastoralism in the Levant, Archaeological Materials in Anthropological Perspectives*. Madison: Prehistory Press.

Zayadine F. 1974. Excavations at Petra (1973-74). *Annual of the Department of Antiquities of Jordan* XIX (1974): 135-150.

Author's Address
Jérémie Schiettecatte
Post-doctoral Researcher
CNRS - UMR 8167 "Orient et Méditerranée"
27 rue Paul Bert
94204 Ivry-sur-Seine Cedex
France
jeremie.schiettecatte@mae.u-paris10.fr

Sabaean stone and metal miniature grave goods

D'arne O'Neill

Summary
From 1997-2001 the German Archaeological Institute excavated part of the 1st millennium BC Sabaean Awām sanctuary cemetery in the Mārib Oasis Yemen. Over 3000 miniature grave goods were recovered representing two thirds of all pottery and small finds. While most miniatures were pottery, there were also 1006 stone and 126 metal miniatures. Miniatures are well known in the Near East but the presence of miniatures in South Arabia is less well attested with no secure presence so far known before the 8th century BC. Miniatures as a class are generally under studied in the archaeological literature with definitions often arbitrary. Cultural meanings are usually interpreted as either toys or symbolic objects. Miniatures are particularly suitable to function in ritualistic and supernatural environments because objects do not need to function practically or realistically to successfully fulfill their role in such environments. However, the role of miniatures in the burial traditions of mid 1st millennium BC Saba is not known with any certainty as yet.

Keywords: South Arabia, Saba, Mārib, Awām, mortuary, miniatures, stone, metal

Introduction

Miniaturisation of both animate and inanimate objects is a well known phenomenon in the Near East. Even a cursory survey of published miniatures shows their ubiquitous nature across both time and place in nearly all domains including the profane as well as the magical and religious. A particularly significant miniature presence is known from Egypt (Allen 2006; Schiestl 1996; Bárta 1995; Petrie 1937) with around 45,000 ceramic miniatures recorded in just three seasons at the Old Kingdom site of Abu Roash (Allen 2006: 20). Nevertheless, even though miniaturization as a technique is well known in Near Eastern archaeology its analysis has tended to be somewhat fragmentary. There has been little examination of the extent to which miniatures as a class of objects are able to contribute to an interpretation and understanding of the material culture to which they belong. They have been generally under-utilised as an explanatory tool when compared to other small find groupings such as seals, coins, jewellery, beads, figurines or scarabs, often with little or no discussion beyond noting their presence (e.g. Tobler 1950: 208). Even where miniatures constitute a major part of a cultural repertoire, as they did in Old Kingdom Egypt, they still tend to be under studied (Bárta 1995: 15). This may be partly because of their often fragmentary find nature and conservative long-lived forms which make them difficult to date. It may also be partly because they are ambiguous artefacts found mostly in symbolic environments such as temples, sanctuaries and graves which can make them difficult to understand. Finally, it may be partly because of their small size and often generic morphology, which has tended to make them appear less useful for interpretative purposes than other classes of material culture.

From 1997 to 2001 the German Archaeological Institute partially excavated the 1st millennium BC Awām cemetery in the Mārib oasis, some 130 kilometres east of Sana'a in Yemen (Gerlach 2003, 2002, 1999; Hitgen 1998a and b; Japp 2005, 2002; Röring 2005, 2002; Bessac & Breton 2002; Nebes 2002). Over five and half thousand pottery vessels and sherds as well as small finds were recovered (Fig. 1). Of these, nearly two thirds were miniatures, mostly pottery but 1006 stone and 126 metal miniatures were also recovered. This paper looks at the stone and metal miniature repertoire of the Awām cemetery as currently known and the notion of miniaturisation and its possible roles in 1st millennium BC Sabaean mortuary contexts.

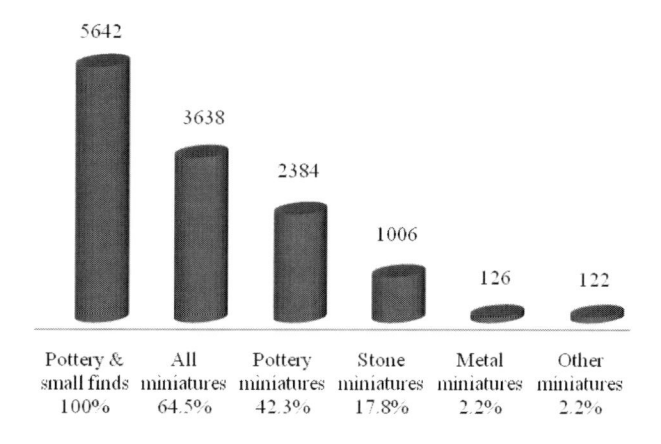

Figure 1. Miniature grave goods recovered from the Awām cemetery showing raw numbers and percentages of the total pottery and small finds.

The Awām Sanctuary Cemetery

The Awām sanctuary cemetery was part of the 1st millennium BC Sabaean settlement infrastructure of the Mārib oasis. The oasis was strategically situated in a transition zone between the highlands and the desert fringe. This allowed access to monsoon floodwater run off from the highlands for irrigated agriculture and exploitation with camels of the flat desert fringe for trade. The oasis included Mārib itself, as well as other major Sabaean sites such as the Bar'ān temple and the Mārib dam. Estimates based on the accumulation of irrigated silts in the north oasis place the beginning of irrigation in the Mārib oasis possibly as early as the mid-3rd millennium BC (Brunner 2005: 116), and definitely by the 2nd millennium BC (Kitchen 1994: 131). The Awām cemetery was part of the Awām sanctuary located 3.5

kilometres southeast of Mārib. Based on inscriptional evidence and ground penetrating radar (GPR) results, connection between the two was likely through a road, perhaps a processional passage (Ibrahim 2006: 202; Maraqten 2006: 53; 2004: 157-63; Moorman *et al.* 2001: 185-86). The sanctuary and its temple made up the main state shrine and the primary pilgrimage site of the Sabaean state. The cemetery was located south of the temple, is around 1.7 hectares in size, and extends irregularly in shape for about 80 to 100 metres alongside the southern half of the Awām temple wall. The spatial relationship of the cemetery to the temple was direct, with a door leading from the temple area directly into the cemetery (Zaid 2008). As well as the cemetery, a mausoleum was situated on the northeast side of the temple wall and along with the South Tombs was partially excavated by the American Foundation for the Study of Man in 1951-1952 (Albright 1958: 215-286). Cemetery architecture consisted of monumental limestone multi-storied tombs with sub and super structures constructed around a narrow orthogonal street grid (Gerlach 2002: 51-54; Röring 2005; 2002). Some were very elaborate, with pillared porticoes replicating temple podium architecture. Bone fragments point to some 20,000 people buried in the cemetery over the 1000 years or so of its functioning (Gerlach 2002: 57). Both adults and children were buried in the cemetery and sex determination from pelvic fragments shows both females and males present although adult males made up 60-70% of the total burial population (Gerlach 2003: 89). The monumental architecture and position of the cemetery next to the state temple point to an elite cemetery population although the basis for inclusion in the elite is as yet unknown. The graves seem to have been well furnished with grave goods including standard full-size ceramic stone and metal vessels, symbolic artefacts such as figurines, memorialising objects such as ostraca, grave stele and heads, personal items such as jewellery and imported objects such as scarabs (Gerlach 2002: 54-56). Cemetery inscriptions generally give no indication of the social rank of the deceased although where they do they refer to senior administrative personnel, family or tribal heads and private individuals (Gerlach 2002: 57, 52; Nebes 2002: 162-163).

The cemetery is severely deflated and has been badly looted in both ancient and modern times so little stratigraphy remains. As a result most of the Awām grave goods including the miniatures were found either as surface finds or in a top debris layer of at least 4 metres (Hitgen 1998a: 121). This distribution pattern and the practices of collective inhumation and the reutilisation of former graves make it impossible to link the grave goods to different graves or to differentiated population cohorts based on status, age, ethnicity or gender. Neither can the presence of miniaturization be taken necessarily as an indicator of elite status. For example, stone miniatures were recovered from a group of non-monumental contemporary graves in the Wadi Jufainah in the Mārib Oasis dated between the 8th and 6th centuries BC (Hitgen 2005: 326). It is likely that the quantities of miniatures deposited in graves and the use of stone but more particularly metal as the preferred miniature material are better indicators of elite status than the presence of miniatures *per se*.

Chronology

Given the almost complete destruction of the cemetery's stratigraphy, dating of the Awām cemetery is provisional and relies completely on evidence from the Awām sanctuary temple. While neither the earliest nor latest occupation is as yet certain (Ibrahim 2006: 201, 211; Glanzman 2003: 186-193) inscriptions (CIH 957) currently allow estimations that the temple operated in some form for over 1000 years from the 7th century BC until the end of the 4th century AD (Ibrahim 2006: 199, 201, 211; Glanzman 2002: 189; Maraqten 2002: 211-213; Kitchen 2000: 163). Where the miniatures are concerned, the best current dating estimate based on ceramic parallels is between the 7th century BC and the first centuries AD (Japp 2005: 70, 2002: 146). So far there is no published evidence of a miniature presence in South Arabia in general prior to the 8th century BC.

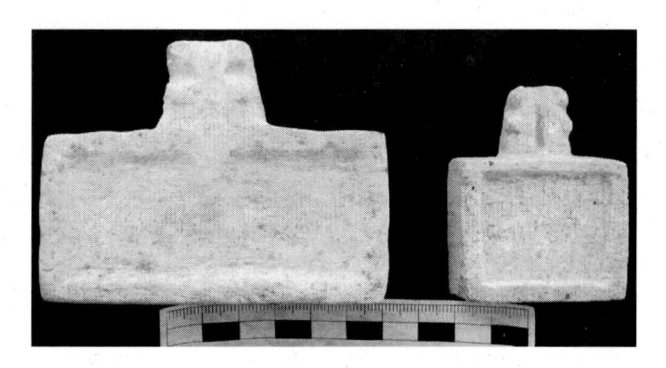

Figure 2. Two miniature limestone offering tables from the Awām cemetery repertoire (Deutsches Archäologisches Institut (DAI) field numbers Aw00 B1105, Aw00 D45). © D. O'Neill.

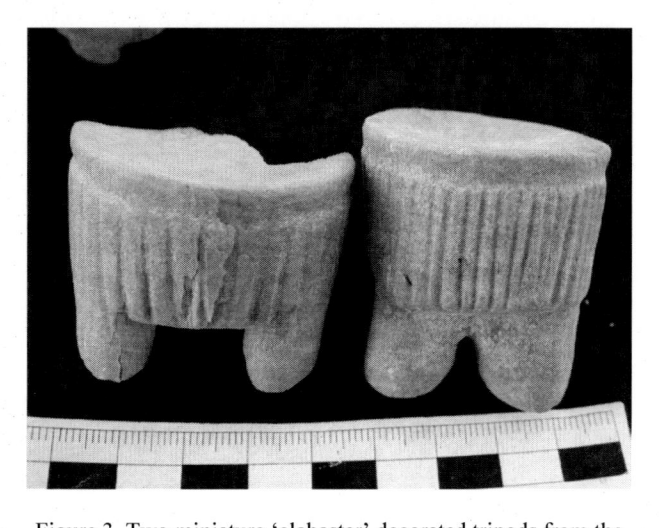

Figure 3. Two miniature 'alabaster' decorated tripods from the Awām cemetery repertoire displaying the most frequent decorative style in the repertoire of incised parallel vertical wall lines with a concentric horizontal line below the rim. Such decoration is found on a range of morphologies in the repertoire (DAI field numbers Aw01 E12, Aw01 B1930). © D. O'Neill.

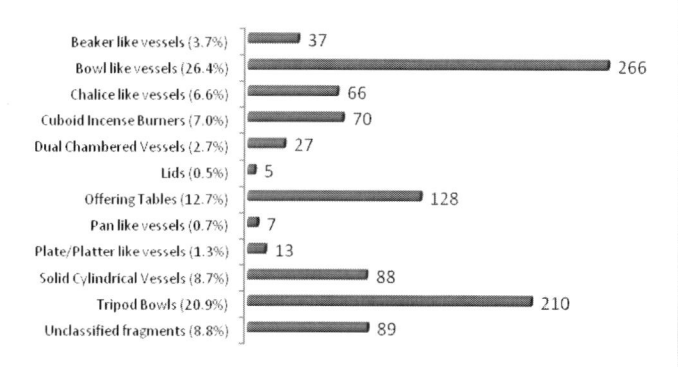

Figure 4. Frequency groupings of the Awām cemetery stone miniature repertoire showing raw numbers and percentages.

Figure 5. Detail of a bull's head on a miniature limestone (?) offering table from the Awām cemetery repertoire (DAI field number Aw00 B946). © D. O'Neill.

The Repertoires

The stone repertoire

Where the stone miniatures are concerned the repertoire is known from full-sized equivalents in mortuary, temple and settlement contexts. The forms include various standard vessel shapes and well known forms such as cuboid incense burners, offering tables and tripod bowls (Figs. 2 and 3). The three most frequent miniature groups are bowls, tripod bowls and offering tables which together make up nearly 60% of the total stone miniatures recovered (Fig. 4). Over half (56%) of the miniatures are not decorated but geometric, figurative and architectural elements exist on decorated vessels (Figs. 3, 5 and 6). Eight different materials make up the stone repertoire but the overwhelming presence of 'alabaster'[1] is clear (Fig. 7). Sources for the main stones used in the miniatures include limestone quarries adjacent to the Mārib oasis in the surrounding hills and travertine quarries in the nearby Wadi Jufainah in the north oasis (Harrell 2007: 188-90). However, recent German Archaeological Institute research suggests that the travertine for the 'alabaster' miniatures and for decoration in general as opposed to building material may have been sourced from the al Machdarah quarry to the west near Ṣirwāḥ, as it tends to be more stable and homogenous than the travertine from Wadi Jufainah (Weiss *et al.* 2009).

Figure 6. Miniature limestone footed cuboid incense burner from the Awām cemetery repertoire displaying three vertical rows of recessed false windows on the top half of the walling above a row of toothcut frieze (DAI field number Aw01 F17). © D. O'Neill.

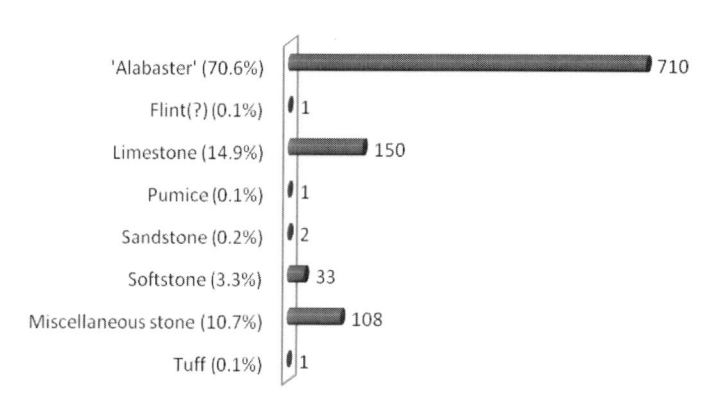

Figure 7. Stone miniature materials of the Awām cemetery repertoire showing raw numbers and percentages.

---

[1] The 'alabaster' referred to here is not geological alabaster, that is gypsum, but calc-sinter travertine composed of calcite. The incorrect designation of calc-sinter travertine as 'alabaster' is a well known and long standing confusion in Near Eastern archaeological literature. Many terminological solutions have been suggested including travertine, calcite, calcite-alabaster, Egyptian alabaster, Arabian alabaster and Yemenite alabaster. All South Arabian 'alabaster' is calc-sinter travertine, as that was the only calcareous sinter exploited in Yemen in antiquity (Harrell 2007: 184). While Yemenite alabaster would suit most of the references to 'alabaster' from Yemen it is not suitable for references to the stone outside of Yemen. In this article calc-sinter 'alabaster' is placed in quotation marks to distinguish it from geological alabaster.

Currently published miniature parallels exist from the Awām temple (Albright 1958: 274-275, Catalogue 106, 123, 126, 127, 129, Pls. 194.106, 195.129) and the Jawf (Arbach & Schiettecatte 2006: 77, 04.73-04.75, Pl. 22.77, 78). Rathjens (1955: 169, 276-285) also published unprovenanced miniature parallels likely from the Jawf. Further away from Saba the closest and most numerous stone miniature parallels are those from the Ḥayd ibn ʿAqīl necropolis at Tamnaʿ (Antonini 2005: 9; de Maigret 2002: 93-97; Cleveland 1965) and to a lesser extent from the tomb and settlement contexts at Hajar ibn Ḥumayd (Van Beek 1969: 272-278, 323-327, Figures 118-121, 129-130, Pls. 50, 57). However, currently miniature recovery in general seems to be fragmentary across South Arabia and parallels are rather generic. Full-size parallels exist from the Jawf for at least the Awām miniature tripods, flat base cuboid incense burners, some plate-like vessels and some softstone bowl-like vessels (Arbach & Schiettecatte 2006: 76-83, 04.69-04.71, 04.77-04.104, Pls. 22.73-74, 23.80-85, 24.86-94, 25.95-103, 26.104-107). As well as Tamnaʿ and Hajar ibn Ḥumayd, full-size parallels for the miniaturised Awām cemetery forms are known from a number of South Arabian sites (e.g. Sedov & Graznevich 1996; Roux 1991; Breton & Baṭayā 1991; Caton Thompson 1944). Full-size parallels from across the Near East and Ethiopia are also known, particularly for well known forms such as the cuboid incense burners, offering tables and tripod bowls (Hassell 2005; Cleuziou and Tosi 1997: 59-68, Figures 6-7; Davies & Friedman 1998: 191; Anfray 1990; O'Dwyer Shea 1983). Intercultural links or borrowings are shown by two full-size examples. A full-size Levantine middle 2nd millennium BC carinated bowl – thought to be an Egyptian copy of a Syrian form – is a close parallel for one of the Awām footed carinated miniature bowls (Sparks 2007: 122, Figure 45: 3, Catalogue 1463). Intercultural links or borrowings are also indicated by a direct Sabaean full-size tripod parallel from Lachish (Tufnell 1953: 238, Pls. 42.7, 57.36). Recovered from plundered tomb 1007, it is made of calcite ('alabaster') and dated between c. 550-350 BC. The tripod is less 'chunky' than the typical Sabaean miniature examples but nevertheless displays the unmistakable grouped parallel vertical incised lines around the body of the vessel that are the most common form of decoration found on the miniature stone repertoire from the Awām cemetery.

The metal repertoire

The 126 metal miniatures are bronze, except for two iron miniature swords (Fig. 8). They show a wide variety in their morphology, including two miniature swords, although the single most common group is bowls (Figs. 9 and 10). Very little decoration is evident but the typical South Arabian crescent and moon motif is present. Parallels for the metal miniatures are known from the Awām temple and the mausoleum (Albright 1958: 275, Catalogue 137, Pl. 195.137) but metal miniatures in South Arabia in general are sparse. The Tamnaʿ necropolis has the most metal miniatures currently published in South Arabia although not all currently

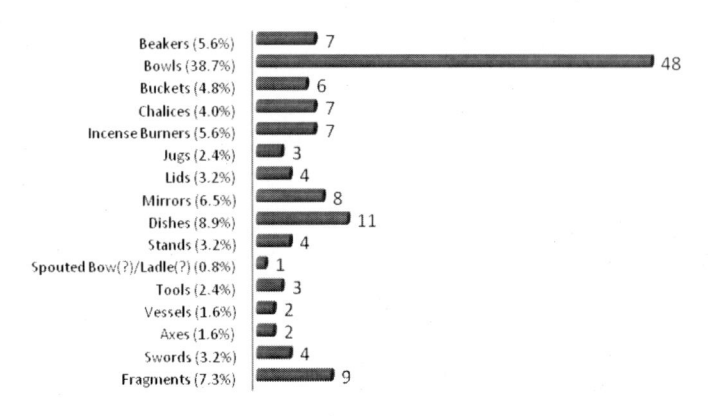

Figure 8. Frequency groupings of the Awām cemetery metal miniature repertoire showing raw numbers and percentages.

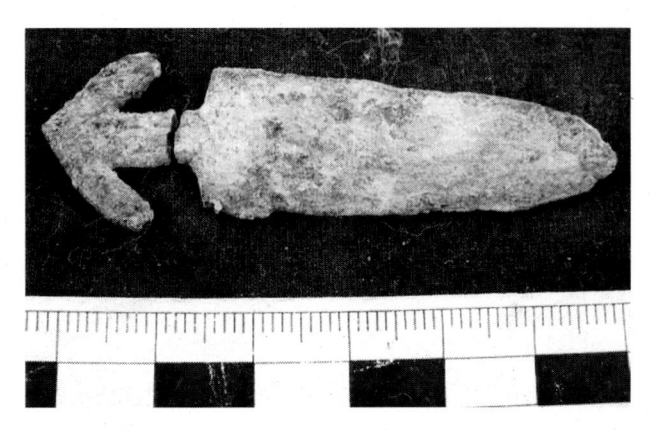

Figure 9. Corroded miniature bronze sword from the Awām cemetery repertoire (DAI field number Aw98 A2101). © D. O'Neill.

Figure 10. Corroded round-base miniature bronze bowl from the Awām cemetery repertoire with steep walls and two opposing handles attached below the vessel top (DAI field number Aw98 A2099). © D. O'Neill.

known metal miniatures at the two cemeteries can be paralleled (Cleveland 1965: 121-128, Pls. 91-93). Other parallels from ritual or symbolic contexts are known, such as a 2nd century BC miniature concave walled beaker-like vessel from the Haram temple (Seipel 1998: 289, Catalogue 147, photo 288) and two parallel chalice-like vessels, one a miniature and one full-size from the 1st century AD grave 3 at Wadi Dūra^c (Breton & Bāfaqīh 1993: 30-31 Numbers 39 & 41, Pls. 15.40, 28.84, 85). Cleveland (1965: 122, TC1040, Pl. 92) publishes a similar although larger (10cm) bronze base from the Tamna^c necropolis.

Miniaturisation

Defining a miniature is a little like defining time. We know with absolute certainty what it is until we try to define it. The problem is compounded because there is a lack of evidence beyond the existence of the objects themselves for any indigenous construction of 'miniature' as an emic category of meaning. Sizing in antiquity was not necessarily standard and size graduation within artefact classes was frequent. For example, Levy and Kansa (2006: 395) identify a miniature to full-size range as well as a tri-modal range of small, medium and large among the pottery vessels at Chalcolithic Gilat. The 1st millennium BC shallow carinated bowls from Wadi al-Jubāh, Yemen, seem to possess a graduation in diameter from a miniature of 7 cm through a small to medium size of 13-25 cm to a large size of 29-30 cm (Glanzman 1994: 137). The small rounded shoulder jar from the same site is also present in two sizes with a smaller diameter of c. 11-16 cm and a larger diameter of c. 21-29 cm (Glanzman 1994: 169). However, whether the smallest objects were conceptualised in the same way as the modern construct of miniature is unclear and their relevance to indigenous conceptions of material culture is unknown. Nevertheless if the term miniature is used because it provides a useful analytical or interpretative category it should at least be used in accordance with its modern definition. The New Shorter Oxford English Dictionary defines a miniature as an

> 'n. image or representation on a small scale'. adj. represented, designed etc, on a small scale; much smaller than normal; tiny'

and to miniaturise is to 'produce in a smaller version; make small' with miniaturisation as 'the process or an instance of miniaturising something'. The existence of something reproduced at a reduced scale is inherent in the modern meaning of 'miniature'.

This is a useful definition as it enables a crucial distinction to be made between miniatures and other similar sized tiny but nevertheless full-size objects such as ointment pots or cosmetic jars, and between small and miniature objects. Tiny and small objects are miniatures only if they are a reduced-scale copy of an original larger object. Some ambiguity may remain about what constitutes a miniature where reduced scale copies of an original full-size object are produced in more than one size. However, generally miniatures could be expected to have the largest reduction within an artefact class of a particular culture. It is also recognised that archaeologically it may not always be possible to uncover the complete range of full-size shapes that miniatures copy so some tiny and small objects may need to have a provisional miniature status until confirmation is possible.

However, the existence of a larger copy of an object as a necessary condition for a miniature lessens some of the often arbitrary nature surrounding what constitutes a miniature, as it reduces reliance on absolute dimensions as the sole defining criterion for miniature. Such reliance makes miniature definition difficult in two ways. First, miniature dimensions including the amount of reduction employed to produce a miniature are variable across both time and space. For example, Bárta (1995: 15) sees vessels with either a width or height of up to c. 10 cm as miniature in the Old Kingdom. Richard's (2000: 401, 405) miniature cups from the Early Bronze IV site of Khirbet Iskander in Jordan have diameters of 6-7 cm and miniature jar forms are 4.5-9.5 cm in height. Hassell (2005: 139) in his discussion of mainly 1st millennium BC cuboid incense burners from Tell Jemmeh in the northwestern Negev desert defines miniature as 'where at least two of the three measurements are less than 3 cm'. In the Awām cemetery most miniatures have diameters and heights of less than 5 cm. A bronze chalice in the Awām repertoire with a height of 3.3 cm is paralleled by a small surface find from Wadi Dura with almost twice its height of 6.0 cm (Breton & Bāfaqīh 1993: 31 Number 41, Pls. 15.40, 28.85), and both are reduced scale copies of a full-sized parallel piece from grave 3, Wadi Dura with height of 21.7 cm (Breton & Bāfaqīh 1993: 30 Number 39, Pls. 8.16, 28.84). The amount of reduction used to produce a miniature can also vary between cultures and artefact classes. For example, at Chalcolithic Gilat miniature churns were reduced by eight times but beakers by 42 times (Levy and Kansa 2006: 428). In the Awām cemetery preliminary work seems to suggest that most miniatures were reduced from between six to around 14 times if compared to their full-size counterparts in the cemetery, but the smallest of the miniature offering tables from the Awām cemetery were reduced by more than 30 times if compared to some of the larger South Arabian offering tables.

Second, even within single cultural horizons miniature definition using dimension is often arbitrary and necessarily subjective especially when distinguishing between miniatures, and tiny and small but nevertheless full-size vessels. Green (1993: 111) for example, points out in the Abu Salabikh excavations that a jar with a height of 7.1 cm was termed miniature while another of 6.9 cm was not. It is very much the case that one archaeologist's miniature may well be another's small vessel even within a single cultural horizon.

Given the problems associated with using dimension alone as a defining tool function has often also been used to define a miniature. There is a common argument that a tiny artefact cannot be classed as a miniature if it has a utilitarian function (Stillwell and Benson 1984: 309). A tiny tool for example, copied from a larger version and used for very fine and delicate working is not seen as a miniature but a tool in its own right (Haerinck & Overlaet 1985: 409). While non-utilitarian functions may define most miniatures there is evidence from the Awām that at least some miniatures may have had some utilitarian function. Rare residues from the Awām miniature corpus especially from a tripod bowl and a dual chambered vessel suggest utilitarian use of miniatures should not be ruled out in all cases of miniature function. Lipids in a miniature (7.0 cm high with full-size copies of 15.0 cm in height known) unguentaria from Adranon, a 5th century BC Sicilian necropolis, point to a probable utilitarian use as a container (Agozzino et al. 2007). Allen (2006: 21) also argues that miniatures can be both tiny and functional at the same time with 'the potential of containing small amounts of liquid or perhaps grain'.

Miniature Function

Without doubt the most frequently addressed issue in the literature is miniature function. The actual functions miniatures either perform or have attributed to them across time and place are innumerable. However, while objects may always have an embedded social meaning, it is rarely self-explanatory. Miniatures are particularly difficult subjects as they are often found in non-literal, symbolic contexts and are therefore ambiguous and elusive objects to understand, often with multiple interpretative functions. The doll for example, may be a toy miniature but it may also be 'the dangerous instrument of the magician and the witch' (Ariès 1973: 67). Due to their small dimensions miniatures lend themselves easily to symbolic interpretations. The two most frequently cited are as toys and ritual vessels.

Toys

Miniatures are often interpreted as toys because they are small, often not well made and therefore as one writer put it they 'look like children's toys rather than serious adult offerings' (Thompson 1952: 150). As a result miniatures are seen as suitable 'only' for children on the assumption that 'small pots equal small people'. However, the revival of interest in exploring childhood in the archaeological record has brought re-examination of the material culture associated with childhood (e.g. Baxter 2005; Kamp 2001). At its best, identification of toys is made through archaeological research and the application of specific physical and intellectual criteria associated with children (Park 1998; Smith 1998; Wacher 1995). For example, Bagwell (2002) and Crown (2002) apply criteria such as the ability to use coiled construction relating to children's cognitive development to identify children's products in the archaeological record. Lacking such criteria, construing miniatures as toys is often no more than a default position. Ethnographic analogy is also used to identify miniatures as toys. In still other cases miniatures are interpreted as toys because they seem to resemble objects used as such in modern cultures. Moorey's (2003:

7) warning in his discussion of terracotta figurines about the 'conceptual hazards' associated with seeing figurines as toys is directly applicable to miniature interpretation. This is not to deny that both figurines and miniatures were toys in some places at certain times, but an ethnographic or modern cultural analogy is not a reliable indicator by which to identify a toy, as societies structure the 'ages of life' and their associated material culture very differently.

Symbolic objects

Miniatures are frequently designated as ritual or cultic objects as they often occur in the non-literal environments of mortuary and temple contexts. Miniatures are particularly suitable to function in ritualistic and supernatural environments because they do not need to function practically or realistically to fulfil their role there as they can retain their purpose through magic means. Certainly in South Arabia most miniatures so far have been found in such contexts. For example, miniature pottery vessels interpreted as offering substitutes were found just outside the forecourt wall of the Bar'ān temple in the Mārib oasis (Robin & Vogt 1997: 142). Taken in conjunction with the miniature grave goods of the Awām cemetery this suggests miniaturisation's close connection to and identification with Sabaean symbolic life. There are only rare miniatures so far published from settlement contexts and their use either in settlement temples or as part of domestic rituals cannot be ruled out. Indeed Hassell (1997: 275) suggests that small objects, unlike their larger and more public counterparts, may have been for personal use in domestic and mortuary contexts.

The Awām sanctuary cemetery stone and metal miniature assemblage is a specialist body of consciously produced artefacts for deliberate deposition with the deceased as part of the correct performance of Sabaean mortuary rites. Mortuary miniatures were used consciously and deliberately because they acted as symbolic substitutes for objects that were regarded as important by the Sabaeans. Given the tiny volume capacity of the Awām miniature vessels, whatever storage, cooking, eating, drinking or ritual vessel functions they represented would have been enacted and sustained through magic. However, the repertoire does not have a specialised mortuary morphology. Instead it references full-size standard objects from everyday life. The elite Sabaeans in the Awām cemetery were buried with many of the same vessels, albeit miniaturised, as surrounded them in their daily life. What sets the miniatures apart as grave goods are their reduced sizes, not their morphologies. In the Awām cemetery banal everyday morphologies were ritualised through miniaturisation and deposited in the highly symbolic and supernatural context of a mortuary environment. While miniaturisation in the Awām cemetery may be seen as a pragmatic response to a crowded mortuary environment or perhaps as a response to limit looting, the use of miniatures in other ritual contexts suggests a well established symbolic tradition in the use of miniatures. However the plundered Awām cemetery lacks much of the archaeology necessary to give an account of Sabaean mortuary beliefs. Ostraca, stele and grave wall inscriptions in the Awām typically only provide information relating to grave ownership and construction. Direct physical links between the deceased and miniatures that could help clarify their representational role are also lacking. South Arabian texts do not provide any information relating to mortuary beliefs and only very limited information relating to mortuary practices.

Conclusions

Lévi-Strauss (1966: 23) in *The Savage Mind* sees miniaturisation, a 'reduction in scale', as a kind of enabling technique to make an object less formidable, more susceptible to control and hence more understandable. As he succinctly puts it, 'by being quantitatively diminished, it seems to us qualitatively simplified'. This view of miniaturisation accords well with the general interpretation of mortuary practices as an attempt to ritually lessen, simplify or gain control over the impact of death on individuals and the community. However, the working out of such ritual mechanisms is culturally specific and since there are only situated and contextualised objects, the meaning and function of grave goods can only be understood within their own specific cultural milieu. Unfortunately, the culturally specific representational role of the Sabaean miniatures is difficult to capture. While it is likely the Sabaeans believed in an after life, their belief system is currently unknown. The miniatures by themselves in the graves are not sufficient evidence to confirm Sabaean belief in an after life as they may be purely items of remembrance. It is clear the mortuary miniatures were symbolic signifiers. What is not clear so far is exactly what kind of Sabaean symbolic belief system to do with death they are signifying.

Acknowledgements

The author would like to acknowledge the following institutional and financial support: The German Archaeological Institute, Sana'a; University of Sydney Postgraduate Research Support Scheme (PRSS), Grants-in-Aid, Near Eastern Archaeological Foundation (NEAF) Grant-in-Aid and 2008 Leone Crawford Travel Grant, and PhD Research Travel Grants; Australian Government Postgraduate Award (APA); Society for Arabian Studies.

References

Agozzino P., Avellone G., Donato I.D. & Filizzola F. 2007. Identification of organic compounds in fictile unguentaria from two Sicilian necropolis of Greek age (5th century B.C.) by GC-MS Analysis. *Annali di Chimica* 97/9: 859-865.

Albright F.P. 1958. Excavations at Mārib in Yemen. Pages 215-286 in R.L. Bowen Jr. & F.P Albright (eds), *Archaeological Discoveries in South Arabia*. Baltimore: The Johns Hopkins Press.

Allen S. 2006. Miniature and model vessels in Ancient Egypt. Pages 19-24 in M. Bárta (ed), *The Old Kingdom: Art and Archaeology*. Prague: Academia.

Anfray F. 1990. *Les anciens Ethiopiens*. Paris: Armand Colin.

Antonini S. 2005. The first two campaigns at Ḥayd Ibn 'Aqīl, the necropolis at Tamna' (2003-2004). Pages 1-19 in Sholan A.M., Antonini S. & Arbach M. (eds), *Sabaean Studies. Archaeological, Epigraphical and Historical Studies in honour of Yūsuf M. 'Abdallāh, Alessandro de Maigret and Christian J. Robin on the occasion of their 60th birthdays*. Naples and Sanaa: Il Torcoliere.

Arbach M. & Schiettecatte J. 2006. *Catalogue des Pièces Archéologiques & Épigraphiques du Jawf au Musée National de Ṣanʿâʾ*. Sanʿâʾ: Centre français d'archéologie et de sciences sociales de Sanʿâʾ.

Ariès P. 1973. *Centuries of Childhood*. Harmondsworth, Middlesex: Penguin.

Bagwell E. 2002. Ceramic form and skill: attempting to identify child producers at Pecos Pueblo, New Mexico. Pages 90-107 in K. Kamp (ed.), *Children in the Prehistoric Puebloan Southwest*. Salt Lake City: University of Utah Press.

Bárta M. 1995. Pottery inventory and the beginning of the IVth Dynasty. *Göttinger Miszellen* 149: 15-24.

Baxter J.E. 2005. *The Archaeology of Childhood: Children, Gender, and Material Culture*. Walnut Creek, CA: AltaMira Press.

Bessac J.-C. & Breton J.-F. 2002. Note technique sur la nécropole d'Awām à Mā'rib (Yémen). *Archäologische Berichte aus dem Yemen* IX: 117-136.

Breton J.-F. & Bāfaqīh M.A.Q 1993. *Trésors du Wādī Ḍura' (République du Yémen). Fouille franco–yéménite de la nécropole de Hajar am-Dhaybiyya*. Paris: Librairie Orientaliste Paul Geuthner.

Breton J.-F and A Baṭayā'. 1991. Les Autels de Shabwa. *Syria* 68: 365-78.

Brunner U. 1983. Die Erforschung der Antiken Oase von Mārib mit Hilfe Geomorphologischer Untersuchungsmethoden. *Archäologische Berichte aus dem Yemen* II.

Brunner U. 2005. The Beginnings of Irrigation. Pages 115-116 in A.C. Gunter (ed.), *Caravan Kingdoms. Yemen and the Ancient Incense Trade*. Washington: Smithsonian Institution.

Caton Thompson G. 1944. *The Tomb and the Moon Temple of Hureidha (Hadramaut)*. Oxford: The Society of Antiquaries.

Cleuziou S. & Tosi M. 1997. Evidence for the use of aromatics in the Early Bronze Age of Oman: Period III at RJ-2 (2300-2200 BC). Pages 57-81 in Avanzini A. (ed.), *Profumi d'Arabia. Atti del Convegno*. Roma: "l'Erna" di Bretschneider.

Cleveland R.L. 1965. *An Ancient South Arabian Necropolis. Objects from the Second Campaign (1951) in the Timna' Cemetery*. Baltimore: The Johns Hopkins Press.

Crown P. 2002. Learning and teaching in the Pre-Hispanic American south-west. Pages 108-124 in K. Kamp (ed.), *Children in the Prehistoric Puebloan Southwest*. Salt Lake City: University of Utah Press.

Davies V. & Friedman R. 1998. *Egypt*. London: British Museum Press.

Gerlach I. 1999. Die Grabungen des Deutschen Archäologischen Instituts im sabäischen Friedhof des Awâm-Tempels in Ma'rib. Pages 113-123 in W. Daum, W.W. Müller, N. Nebes & W. Raunig (eds), *Im Land der Königin von Saba*. München: I.P. Verlagsgellschaft, International Publishing.

Gerlach I. 2002. Der Friedhof des Awām-Tempels in Marib. Bericht der Ausgrabungen von 1997 bis 2000. *Archäologische Berichte aus dem Yemen* IX: 41-91.

Gerlach I. 2003. The Cemetery of the Awam Temple in the Oasis of Marib. In I. Gerlach (ed.), *25 Years Excavations and Research in Yemen 1978-2003*. Berlin: Deutsches Archäologisches Institut Orient-Abteilung Aussenstelle Sanaa: 86-95.

Glanzman W.D. 1994. *Towards a Classification and Chronology of Pottery from HR3 (Hajar ar-Rayhani), Wadi al-Jubah, Republic of Yemen*. Unpublished PhD dissertation, University of Pennsylvania.

Glanzman W.D. 2002. Some notions of sacred space at the Mahram Bilqīs in Mārib. *Proceedings of the Seminar for Arabian Studies* 32: 187-201.

Glanzman W.D. 2003. An examination of the building campaign of Yada''il Dharīḥ bin Sumhu'alay, mukarrib of Saba', in light of recent archaeology. *Proceedings of the Seminar for Arabian Studies* 33: 186-198.

Green A. (ed.) 1993. *The 6G Ash-Tip and its contents: culti and administrative discard from the temple?* London: British School of Archaeology in Iraq. Abu Salabikh Excavations. Vol.4.

Haerinck E. & Overlaet B. 1985. Armes et outils miniatures en Afghanistan et en Iran à l'Age du Bronze et à l'Age du Fer. Pages 389-416 in Huot J-L., Yon M., & Calvet Y. (eds.), *De L'Indus Aux Balkans*. Paris: Editions Recherche sur les Civilisations.

Harrell J.A. 2007. Building and ornamental stones of the Awam (Mahram Bilqis) Temple in Marib, Yemen. *Arabian Archaeology and Epigraphy* 18: 182-192.

Hassell J. 1997. Alabaster beehive-shaped vessels from the Arabian peninsula: interpretations from a comparative study of characteristics, contexts and associated finds. *Arabian Archaeology and Epigraphy* 8: 245-281.

Hassell J. 2005. A re-examiniation of the cuboid incense-burning altars from Tell Jemmeh. *Levant* 37: 133-62.

Hitgen H. 1998a. The 1997 excavation at the Cemetery of Awam in Marib. *Proceedings of the Seminar for Arabian Studies* 28: 117-124.

Hitgen H. 1998a. The 1997 excavations of the German Institute of Archaeology at the cemetery of Awām in Marib. *Proceedings of the Seminar for Arabian Studies* 28: 117-124.

Hitgen H. 2005. The Ancient Cultural Landscape of the Wādī Ğufayna in the Oasis of Ma'rib. Pages 321-340 in Sholan A.M., Antonini S. & Arbach M. (eds), *Sabaean Studies. Archaeological, Epigraphical and Historical Studies in honour of Yūsuf M. 'Abdallāh, Alessandro de Maigret and Christian J. Robin on the occasion of their 60th birthdays*. Naples and Sanaa: Il Torcoliere.

Ibrahim M.M. 2006. Report on the 2005 AFSM excavations in the Ovoid Precinct at Maḥram Bilqīs/Mārib preliminary report. *Proceedings of the Seminar for Arabian Studies* 36: 199-216.

Japp S. 2002. Die Miniaturkeramik aus der Nekropole des Awam-Tempels in Marib. *Archäologische Berichte aus dem Yemen* IX: 137-159.

Japp S. 2005. Selected Pottery from the Cemetery of the Awām Temple in Marib – Observations on Chronology and Provenience. *Archäologische Berichte aus dem Yemen* X: 69-86.

Kamp K. 2001. Where Have All The Children Gone? The Archaeology of Childhood. *Journal of Archaeological Method and Theory* 8/1: 1-29.

Kitchen K.A. 1994. *Documentation for Ancient Arabia. Part I. Chronological Framework & Historical Sources*. Liverpool: Liverpool University Press.

Kitchen K.A. 2000. *Documentation for Ancient Arabia. Part II. Bibliographical Catalogue of Texts*. Liverpool: Liverpool University Press.

Lévi-Strauss C. 1966. *The Savage Mind*. London: Weidenfeld and Nicolson.

Levy T.E. & Kansa E. 2006. Gilat's Ceramics: Cognitive Dimensions of Pottery Production. Pages 394-506 in Levy T. (ed.), *Archaeology, Anthropology and Cult. The Sanctuary at Gilat, Israel*. London: Equinox.

Maigret A. de 2002. *Arabia Felix. An exploration of the archaeological history of Yemen*. London: Stacey International.

Maraqten M. 2002. Newly discovered Sabaic inscriptions from Maḥram Bilqīs near Mārib. *Proceedings of the Seminar for Arabian Studies* 32: 209-216.

Maraqten M. 2004. The processional road between Old Mārib and the Awām temple in the light of a recently discovered inscription from Maḥram Bilqīs. *Proceedings of the Seminar for Arabian Studies* 34: 157-163.

Maraqten M. 2006. Legal documents recently discovered by the AFSM at Maḥram Bilqīs, near Mārib, Yemen. *Proceedings of the Seminar for Arabian Studies* 36: 53-67.

Moorey P.R.S. 2003. *Idols of the People. Miniature Images of Clay in the Ancient Near East*. Oxford: Oxford University Press.

Moorman B.J., Glanzman W.D., Maillol J.-M. & Lyttle A.L. 2001. Imaging beneath the surface at Maḥram Bilqīs. *Proceedings of the Seminar for Arabian Studies* 31: 179-187.

Nebes N. 2002. Die 'Grabinschriften' aus dem 'Awām-Friedhof Vorbericht über die Kampagnen 1997 bis 2001. In *Archäologische Berichte aus dem Yemen*. Vol. IX: 161-164.

O'Dwyer Shea M. 1983. The small cuboid incense-burners of the ancient Near East. *Levant* XV: 76-109.

Park R.W. 1998. Size counts: the miniature archaeology of childhood in Inuit societies. *Antiquity* 72/276: 269-281.Petrie M.W.F. 1937. *The Funeral Furniture of Egypt. Stone and Metal Vases*. London: British School of Archaeology in Egypt.

Petrie W.M.F. 1937. *The Funeral Furniture of Egypt. Stone and Metal Vases*. London: British School of Archaeology in Egypt.

Rathjens C. 1955. *Sabaeica Bericht über die archäologischen Ergebnisse seiner zweiten, dritten und vierten Reise nach Südarabien. Vol. 2. Die unlokalisierten Funde.* Hamburg: Appel.

Richard S. 2000. Chronology versus Regionalism in the Early Bronze Age IV: An Assemblage of Whole and Restored Vessels from the Public Building at Khirbet Iskander. Pages 399-417 in L.E. Stager, J.A. Greene & M.D. Coogan (eds), *The Archaeology of Jordan and Beyond. Essays in Honor of James A. Sauer.* Winona Lake, Indiana: Eisenbrauns.

Robin C.J. & Vogt B. (eds.) 1997. *Yémen. Au pays de la reine de Saba.* Paris: Flammarion. Institut du monde Arabe.

Röring N. 2002. Grabbauten im Friedhof des Awām-Tempels als Beispiele Sabäischer Sepulkralarchitekur. *Archäologische Berichte aus dem Yemen* IX: 93-115.

Röring N. 2005. The Facade of Monumental Tombs and Temples in Comparison. *Archäologische Berichte aus dem Yemen* X: 153-159.

Roux J-C. 1991. La Tombe-Caverne I de Shabwa. *Syria* 68: 331-63.

Schiestl R. 1996. *Modellgefasse der pra-und fruhdynastischen zeit in Agypten.* Unpublished MPhil Dissertation. Vienna: University of Vienna.

Sedov A.V. & Griaznevich P.A. 1996. *Raybūn Settlement. (1983-1987 Excavations). Preliminary Reports of the Soviet-Yemeni Joint Complex Expedition. Volume II.* Moscow: Vostochnaya Literatura.

Seipel W. (ed.) 1998. *Jemen. Kunst und Archäologie im Land der Königin von Saba'.* Wien: Kunsthistorisches Museum.

Smith P.E. 1998. *When Small Pots Speak: The Stories They Tell.* Unpublished MA Thesis, McMaster University.

Sparks R.T. 2007. *Stone Vessels in the Levant.* Leeds: Palestine Exploration Fund, Maney.

Stillwell A.N. & Benson J.L. 1984. *Corinth. Volume XV. Part III. The Potters' Quarter. The Pottery.* Princeton, New Jersey: The American School of Classical Studies at Athens.

Thompson D.B. 1952. Three centuries of Hellenistic terracottas. *Hesperia* 21/2: 11-164.

Tobler A.J. 1950. *Excavations at Tepe Gawra, II: Levels IX-XX.* Philadelphia: The University Museum, University of Pennsylvania Press.

Tufnell O. 1953. *Lachish III. The Iron Age.* London: Oxford University Press.

Van Beek G.W. 1969. *Hajar Bin Ḥumeid. Investigations at a Pre-Islamic Site in South Arabia.* Baltimore: The Johns Hopkins Press.

Wacher J. 1995. *The Towns of Roman Britain.* London: Taylor and Francis.

Weiss C., O'Neill D., Koch R., (delete comma) and Gerlach I. 2009. Petrological characterisation of 'alabaster' from the Marib province in Yemen and its use as an ornamental stone in Sabaean culture. *Arabian Archaeology and Epigraphy* 20/1:54-63.

Zaid Z. 2008. The architecture of the Awâm Temple/Mahram Bilqis, Ma'rib. Unpublished paper delivered to the Rencontre Sabéenne 12th May 2008, Rome.

Author's address
D'arne O'Neill
Department of Archaeology A14
University of Sydney
NSW 2006
Australia
done6778@sydney.edu.au

Excavations of the Italian Archaeological Mission in Yemen: A Minaean Necropolis at Barāqish (Wadi Jawf) and the Qatabanian Necropolis of Ḥayd bin ᶜAqīl (Wadi Bayḥān)

Sabina Antonini and Alessio Agostini[1]

Summary

During two archaeological campaigns at Barāqish/*Yathill*, a number of pit graves has been excavated in a necropolis located approximately 200 meters west of the city walls. This is the first time that Minaean graves have been investigated, offering a unique opportunity to study Minaean funeral customs. Further, a significant number of stereotype inscribed stelae was discovered *in situ* and the study of the iconography and onomastics has provided interesting information regarding the origin of the people who habitually visited the region between the 3rd century BC and the 1st century AD. The rather modest crafting and typology of the pit graves, very different from the tombs of the other large caravan cities such as Tamnaᶜ, show that *Yathill* was populated also by a nomadic community, residing seasonally outside the city walls. The graves we investigated presumably belong to this community.

The necropolis of Tamnaᶜ is situated about 2 km north of the city, on the western side of the hill named Ḥayd bin ᶜAqīl. The tombs were investigated in two excavation campaigns at the foot of the hill and on the hillside, and are contemporary of those of Barāqish. The funerary monuments are multiple-roomed family tombs, and numerous inscribed stelae suggest that it was largely Qatabanians residing in Tamnaᶜ who were buried in the cemetery.[2]

Keywords: southern Arabia, Barāqish, Tamnaᶜ, tombs, stelae, onomastics

The Excavation

Barāqish

Over the last 10 years the Italian Archaeological Mission, under the direction of Prof. Alessandro de Maigret, has excavated the two sites of Barāqish and Tamnaᶜ. In both cases attention has focused above all on the urban settlement, although recently the scope has been enlarged to include the respective necropolises. The necropolis of Ḥayd bin ᶜAqīl was already known to scholars from the excavations carried out in the 1950s by the mission of the American Foundation for the Study of Man (Cleveland 1965), while the one at Barāqish had never been excavated.

The recent archaeological activity at Barāqish has involved the excavation of a series of tombs (Antonini & Agostini 2010) and stratigraphic probes both within the ancient city near the temple of Nakraḥ (de Maigret in press) and just outside the city walls (Fedele in press). This has produced interesting data concerning the Minaean occupation of Barāqish, which overlay a pre-existing Sabaean settlement. Our findings originate from the stratigraphic probes, the material culture (primarily the pottery), the epigraphy and from radiocarbon dating. The latest results confirm what had been deduced in the early 1990s thanks to the excavation of the temple of Nakraḥ, which stands inside the city wall (de Maigret & Robin 1993). The history of the necropolis seems to be closely linked to the events that had affected the city of Barāqish. Excavating the tombs enabled us to identify for the first time the typology of the tombs and the funerary customs of the Minaeans, and also to establish at last the archaeological context for the Minaean stelae, which were previously known to scholars only from the antiquarian market (Antonini 1998, 2005*a*; Arbach & Schiettecatte 2006; Arbach *et al.* 2008; Garbini 1977; Höfner 1964).

The necropolis is situated about 200 m west of the main city gate (Fig. 1). It is a small mound of anthropic origin, with fragments of funerary stelae and pottery dating from pre-Islamic times. Excavation of the mound revealed a first, thick layer totally devoid of structures, comprising stratified levels of debris from the late-Minaean period (1st/2nd centuries AD) which in turn covered a sandy aeolian layer that had been deposited on the funerary structures. This seems to show that the area of the burials was reused as a tip after the necropolis had been abandoned and covered by wind-blown sand. The Minaean tombs were built on top of some mud-brick structures having a different orientation from Sabaean times (i.e. beginning of the 1st millennium BC), as evidenced by the pottery, characterized by a thick burnished dark red slip, and radiocarbon analyses.

In spite of evident and repeated episodes of looting in the area (in ancient times as well as recently), a series of contiguous pits were brought to light. These were rather small (sides measuring 50-70 cm), square, oval or round in shape, and surrounded either by a row of barely fashioned limestone blocks or by little walls in mud-bricks. The burial area must have been enclosed, to judge from a thick wall conserved to the height of two courses discovered on the south-western edge of the excavation area (Fig. 2). We believe that each pit was marked by an anthropomorphic funerary stela (Fig. 3), even though no tomb was found intact and no stelae in the original position. The personal grave goods found were scant (some shells, beads, bronze fragments and pot shards),

---

[1] Sabina Antonini is the author of the "The Excavation" section and Alessio Agostini of the "Onomastic Analysis" section.
[2] The translation of "The Excavation" section was done by Dr Mark Weir, Lector at "L'Orientale", Naples.

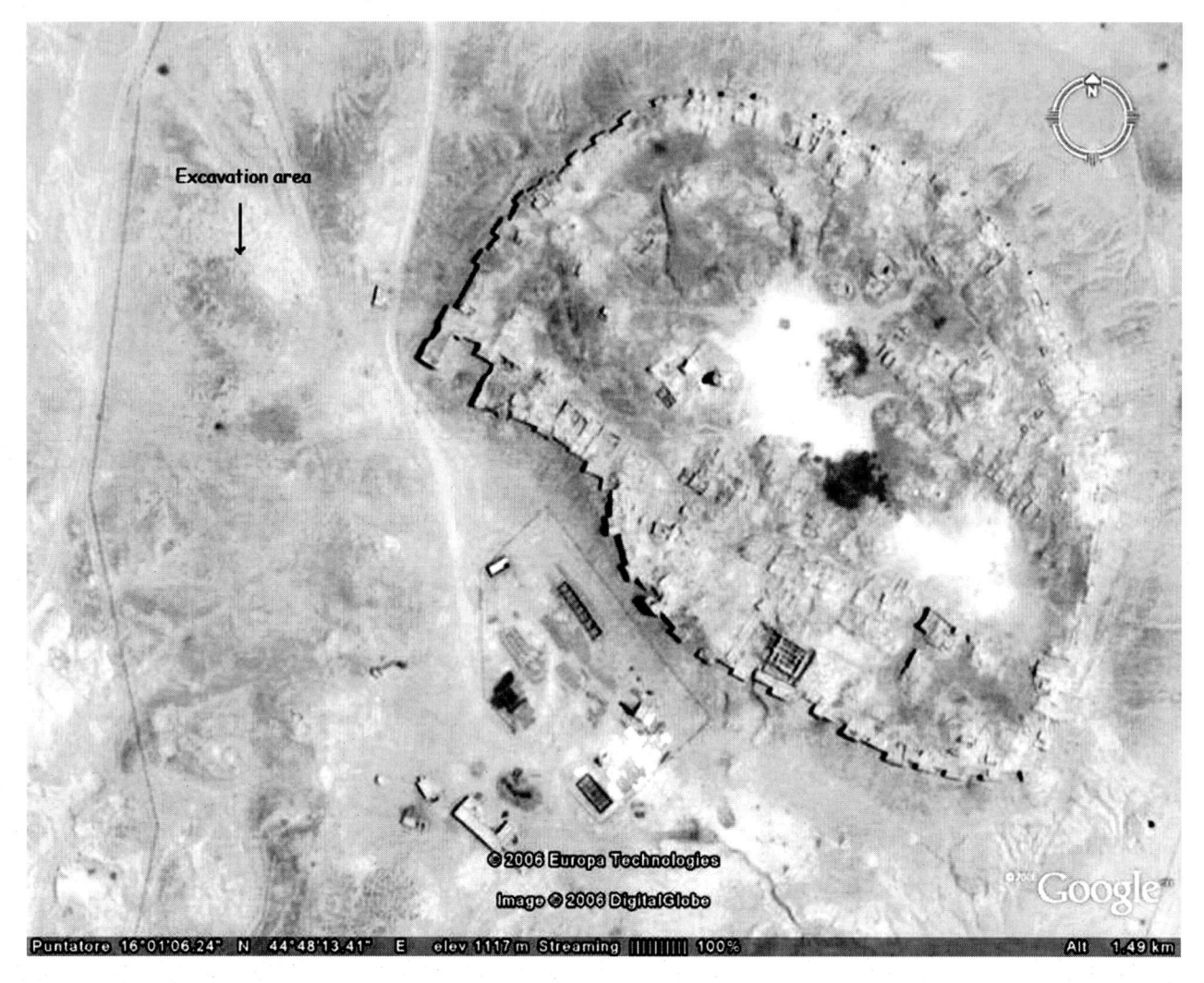

Figure 1. Barāqish: satellite view of the ancient city and the location of the Minaean necropolis.

Figure 2. Barāqish: general view of the excavation area and the location of the pit-graves (from NE).

B.05.D.O/26

Figure 3. Limestone funerary stela with male face in high relief, from Barāqish necropolis.

and marked with a seal imprint or incised marks. This type of jar is found in Southern Arabian contexts between the 2nd century BC and the first centuries AD. Both the wavy rim bowls and jars were widespread in different archaeological sites of the Inner Yemen as well as of the plateau and coast, proving some circulation of local products.

From an art historical evaluation of the portraits, when we observe the male heads carved in high relief on the Minaean limestone stelae (Fig. 3), then we recognize a style familiar to the Qatabanian and Sabaean alabaster heads sculptured in the round, pointing to a common Southern Arabian artistic language. This fact, together with both the analysis of the archaeological material, including the pottery, and the palaeographical study of the inscriptions on some of the stelae, enabled us to date these tombs to a period between the 2nd and the end of the 1st century BC. This period corresponds to the latest phase (phase A) of the temple of Nakraḥ (de Maigret 2004: 21-23; de Maigret & Robin 1993: 450-458).

The small size of the *loci* rules out the customary burial by deposition of the corpse. Either a different type of burial was used, possibly in a crouching position, or other funerary rites were involved such as cremation, although in this case urns should have come to light. The latter hypothesis can surely be discarded because to date no evidence for such a rite has ever been found in the Southern Arabian civilization. The first hypothesis does seem plausible, although no human remains came to light in any of the trenches or nearby areas. There is no doubt that the structures were pillaged, as indeed is the case for all the tombs we investigated at Ḥayd bin ʿAqīl, but in the latter context many traces of bones came to light, and one complete skeleton was found still *in situ*. The suggestion that Barāqish was not in fact a burial area can be immediately rejected because some forty funerary stelae were found *in situ*. It is still too early to give definitive answers, since further excavations may unearth human bones, but given our findings we suggest that these tombs should be interpreted as cenotaphs. The study of the onomastics (see below) established that most of the names incised on the stelae of Barāqish, as well as on those found in other sites of Jawf (Arbach *et al.* 2008), have similarities with North-Arabic names. At Tayma, Madāin Ṣāleh and Petra there are baetyles inside *naiskoi* with schematic eyes or faces, or that are aniconic, which recall the Minaean or certain Qatabanian stelae. These, however, are generally identified with the deities of the Nabataean pantheon. The Minaean stelae, on the contrary, have a funerary function, as they represent the symbolic portraits of the deceased, rendered in a peculiar, autochthonous way. Therefore, the hypothesis that the tombs of Barāqish could be related to caravaneers and to people of a rather lowly social status, of both southern and northern Arabian origin, cannot be totally ruled out when one considers the role played by the Minaeans in the caravan trade, and by Barāqish as a major staging post in the Jawf.

either on account of the violations or because of the poverty of the tombs themselves; nonetheless we did find fragments of offering tables and incense burners associated with documented Southern Arabian religious practices. Amongst the common local pottery, of mediocre quality, we found the characteristic bowls with wavy rims, known as Bayḫān bowls, and jars with everted rim used for transportation, i.e. pottery that was present in other contemporary sites in Southern Arabia. The polylobate bowls appear at Barāqish towards the end of the Later Sabaean occupation (late 7th century), continuing into the Final Sabaean (early-mid 6th century; Fedele in press). The latest examples are documented in the late-Minaean period. Regarding the jars, they have fairly thick rim, sometimes concave inside to take a stopper in terracotta or stone, specifically fashioned in lenticular shape. The jars were then sealed with the addition of plaster which completely covered the stopper,

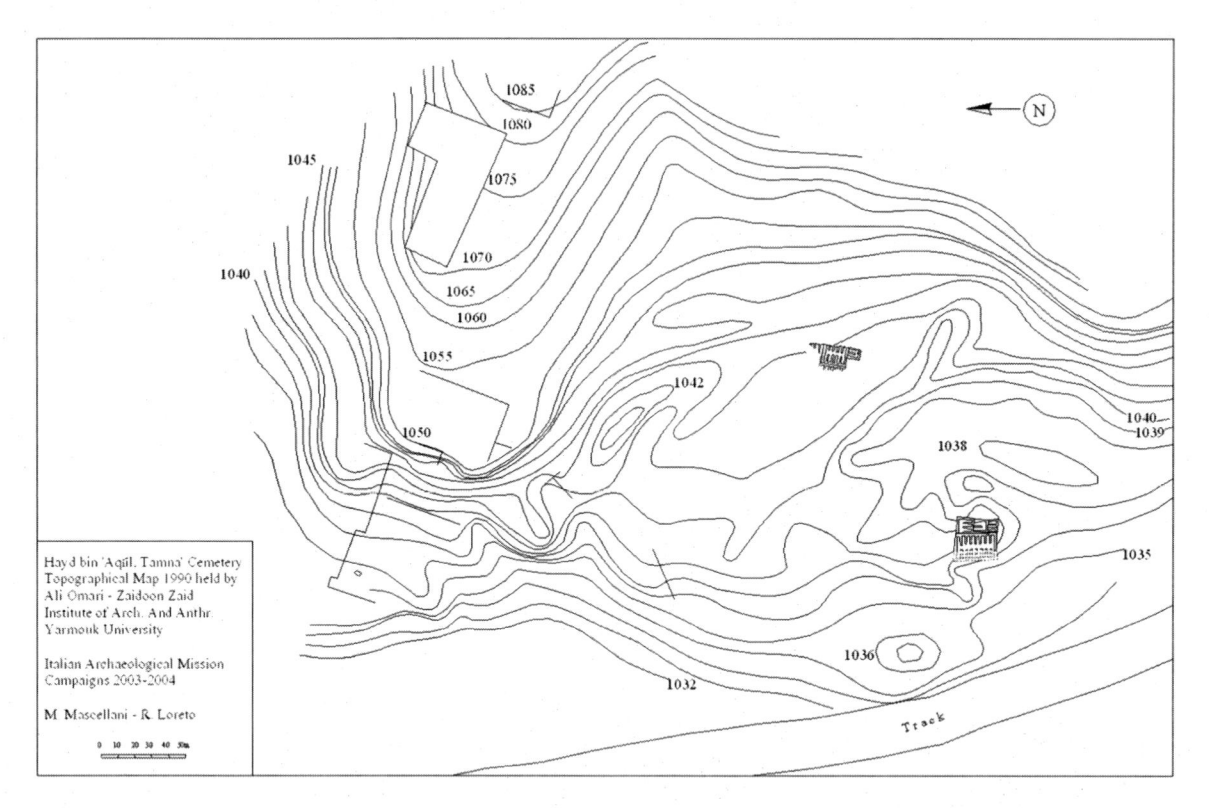

Fig. 4. Ḥayd bin ʿAqīl: topographical plan of the Qatabanian necropolis (by ʿAlī Omari e Zaydūn Zaid 1990, Yarmouk University) and the location of the tombs excavated by the Italian Mission.

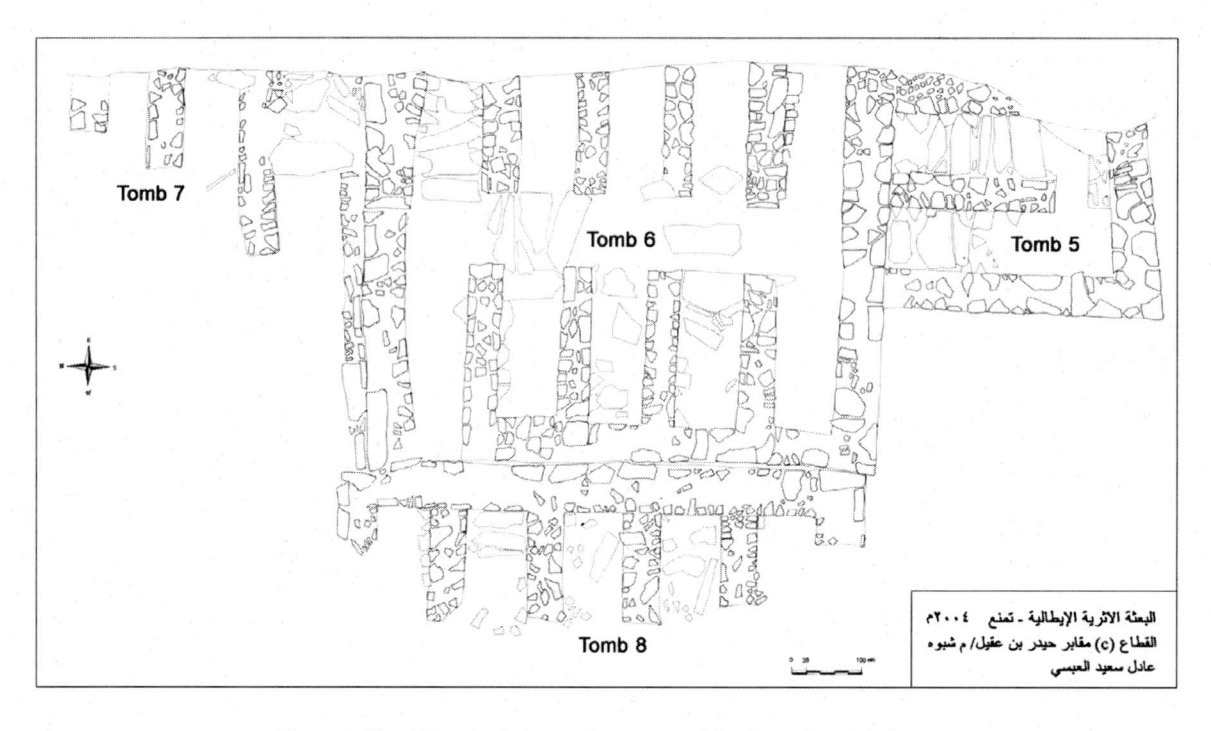

Figure 5. Ḥayd bin ʿAqīl: the tombs excavated by the Italian Mission.

Ḥayd bin ʿAqīl

Ḥayd bin ʿAqīl is the hill where the necropolis of Tamnaʿ is located, about 2 km north of the ancient city (Fig. 4). The tombs, which are on the western side of the hill, comprise masonry structures built from irregular blocks of granite and schist (Antonini 2005: 2-7). The layout is organized in quarters in which it is possible to isolate some groups of tombs where the funerary chambers (*loci*) can be recognised. These were funerary monuments involving multiple depositions, square or rectangular in shape, and we have identified three types of tombs (Fig. 5). The most common type has *loci* disposed in a herringbone pattern separated by a central corridor. The second type has a series of funerary chambers opening to a common corridor. The third type comprises a series of *loci* with no corridor. It seems that none of the tombs was isolated; the original structure was subsequently extended by setting further tombs against it, exploiting more than one of its external walls. The internal space of each tomb was divided into several adjoining *loci* (the number of *loci* varies depending on the length of each tomb) and each *locus* is vertically partitioned with slabs of schist used to form up to three *loculi*, each taking one deposition (Fig. 6). Some of these slabs were built into the side walls, while others rested on ledges made of short flat stones projecting 15–20 cm from the side walls. Since each *loculus* was about 1 m high, a monumental tomb must have been over 3 m in height. On the basis of the recognisable structures we were able to identify points of access to the tombs in the upper part of one of the external walls, but no means of communication between one tomb and another. Each funerary quarter (composed of several tombs) was clearly separated from the others by open spaces which may well have been criss-crossed by pathways.

The tombs in Ḥayd bin ᶜAqīl had evidently been looted (in ancient as well as in modern times), but nonetheless we found examples of grave goods, comprising symbolic human portraits in alabaster, offering tables, incense burners, Qatabanian pottery, sporadic personal objects (beads, utensils, shells) and funerary stelae (Antonini 2005: 8-9). The stelae are made of alabaster and may be of the aniconic (Fig. 7), anthropomorphous or zoomorphous type (bovine stelae). In general the name of the deceased is clearly visible either on the stela itself or on a base (made of limestone or alabaster) built to take the stela. The study of the funerary goods allowed us to date the latest burials in the range of the 1st century BC and the 1st century AD. Specifically, several vase types are recurrent amongst the ceramics found in the tombs, including the wavy rim bowls, which are commonly used both in domestic and cultual contexts. There are close parallels between the pottery of Ḥayd bin ᶜAqīl and the pottery found in precise stratigraphic profiles of the temple of Athirat and the houses excavated in the Market square of Tamnaᶜ (Antonini & Buffa, in preparation). Moreover, the typical funerary thin-walled jars found in the tombs of Ḥayd bin ᶜAqīl, characterized by flaring rim, globular body, flat bottom and finished with brown burnished slip, are precisely dated by the discovery of this type of jar in the hypogean tombs of Kharibat al-Ahjur (Antonini 2005c: fig. 47, no. 5-6; fig. 62, no. 2-3) together with 10 coins of ʾAmdān Bayyin Yuhaqbiḍ, king of Saba and dhū Raydān (80-100 AD) (Davidde 1992) and imported objects of Roman origin (Antonini 1992). However, some older objects together with those from this period suggest that the tombs were in use over a long period of time, and also that some objects may have been reused. The results we achieved studying the cultural material are confirmed by the palaeographical study of the inscriptions.

Figure 6. View of the tombs built against the rock face on the hillside (from NE).

Figure 7. Alabaster aniconic stela found in the excavation at Ḥayd bin ʿAqīl.

The proper names on these stelae can be subdivided into three groups according to the pattern, or onomastic formula, used:

a. Single Names (20 in total)
b. Double Names juxtaposed to each other (11 in total)
c. Single Name preceded by the relative ḏ- (2 in total)

As indicated, they can be distributed according to their number, taking into account all the stelae for which we can identify this pattern, even if the name is not entirely legible.

What is evident at first is the high number of single names. In these cases, it is highly improbable that the individual could have been identified even by his contemporaries. This onomastic model has been frequently observed in the abundant material recently published from the Jawf valley (Arbach & Audouin 2007; Arbach & Schiettecatte 2006; Arbach et al. 2008), and was previously recorded by Gonzague Ryckmans in some Saudi Arabian rock inscriptions (Ryckmans 1957). Whilst Ryckmans hypothesised that in such cases the individual would have been of low social class,[3] Beeston thought that the use of single personal names meant that those persons were "in process of being integrated into a tribe; and [...] there may have been in the towns a floating population of 'unattached' individuals with no family or clan background" (Beeston 1978: 16).

The presence of single names introduced by the relative pronoun is particularly unusual, because the relative is generally used to express affiliation to a family or group and follows the first name. For analogous cases, Beeston pointed out that such individuals may have been some kind of head of that group, however the presence of the relative pronoun as an indication of aristocracy can be recognized with certainty only in the late Himyarite period (Beeston 1978: 15-16). What follows is a comparison of our newly found names with the already known onomastic documentation divided according to its provenance. This is performed only for those names for which a complete reading is possible and not taking into account the number of homonyms.

Onomastic Analysis

An analysis of the onomastics found on the stelae of the two necropolises is an important tool in achieving a deeper knowledge of the individuals for whom these burials were intended. The first analysis of these data from Barāqish (Agostini 2010) and Ḥayd bin ʿAqīl (Agostini in preparation) was largely from a linguistic perspective. Some aspects of their historical implications are outlined here. The differences between these two near contemporaneous cemeteries can also be stressed, thanks to the comparison between these two groups of proper names. The material is not abundant enough to let us think that our conclusions will not receive some future correction, but what is of particular value here is that these names come from an archaeological context, and for the Minaean kingdom, for the first time, they do not come from the antiquities market.

Barāqish

Barāqish has yielded numerous inscriptions, most of which were set into the circuit of city walls or found inside the site. These are mostly official inscriptions in which the people named, who are the subjects of the texts, must have occupied a leading role in the society of this Minaean city. Thus our knowledge of the onomastics of Barāqish chiefly concerns the upper social class, and must not be taken as being representative of the population as a whole.

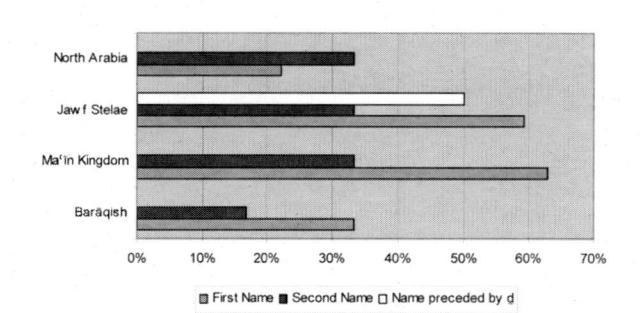

Figure 8. Percentage of matches between the names found in the Barāqish necropolis and the rest of the Minaic documentation.

---

[3] This explanation could be surely adapted in these more recent cases, even though I would like to stress that in others, like those of graffito names, the scribe probably wrote his name in an extemporaneous way, without any intention to stress his familial and social background with great precision.

In observing the comparisons between these names and those already known in Minaic, we can see a difference between first and second names (Fig. 8). The first names show more connections with the known Minaic documentation (comprising the Jawf stelae). This is easily understandable as these are some of the most common names in use, and are thus shared by individuals from different areas and social classes. Other connections can be found within the Barāqish documentation, the other Jawf funerary stelae and even with the Minaic texts from the north of the Arabian Peninsula. This indicates that the first names found in this necropolis were also in use across the Minaean area of influence. The funerary stelae from Jawf have been set apart because of their peculiarity and uncertain origin, as they all come from an unknown context. However, the fact that such onomastics present many similarities with this particular group is noteworthy.

The case of second names, which are of greater importance for the identification of the bearer's affiliation, is more complex. For these names the comparisons are very few, not only due to their numerical scarcity, but also because only one of the names is attestated in the known Minaic documentation.

The presence of some homonyms in the group of second names is also to be stressed; three stelae are recorded in which the second name is *Mḫḍr*.[4] This is one of the names for which we have not been able to find exact matches in the Minaic onomastics. As already pointed out, we can advance the hypothesis that the excavated structures were intended for someone who was not effectively buried there, since no bones were found in any grave (see above). If we add the fact that the names used (in particular the second names) have no strict connection with the Minaic onomastics, we can hypothesise that such individuals were connected in some way with the town of Barāqish, but that they were not in effect members of the community. The most plausible idea is that they were caravaneers engaged in commerce throughout the western side of the Peninsula, thus explaining why they used onomastics with some clear links to the Minaic tradition, but also to the Northern tradition, especially Safaitic (Agostini 2010: 69). The fact that three stelae bear the same group name could suggest that members of the same family were engaged in the same economic activity.

Ḥayd bin ʿAqīl

There is a greater quantity of data from Tamnaʿ, primarily due to the abundant epigraphic material from stelae found during excavation and on the antiquarian market. There are then some 70 inscriptions from the city itself, which form a reasonably comprehensive account of the names of the inhabitants of Tamnaʿ.

The Qatabanian necropolis has revealed the following modalities in proper name composition:
a. Single Names (2 in total)

b. Double Names juxtaposed to each other (9 in total)
c. Double Names, the second being introduced by the relative *ḏ-* (3 in total)

Most of the names on these Qatabanian stelae are double (personal name + family name), but we note a difference in the onomastic formula used. The name of the family group may be either simply juxtaposed or linked to the personal name by the relative pronoun *ḏ-*. In this case we have not encountered the phenomenon of single names introduced by the relative as in Barāqish (see above). The presence of single names is moreover not as numerous as in Barāqish. Jamme (1952: 15-16) conjectured that these names belonged to members of the community who had not yet been fully integrated into the life of the city, such as individuals who had died young and who had thus not yet become fully-fledged-members of the town.[5]

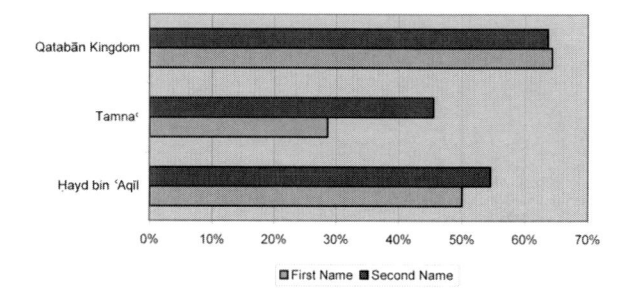

Figure 9. Percentage of matches between the names found in the Ḥayd bin ʿAqīl necropolis and the rest of the Qatabanic documentation.

The coherence between our documentation and that already known in the necropolis, in the town of Tamnaʿ and, more generally, to Qatabanian onomastics, is considerable (Fig. 9). This is true for both first and second names. For this reason we can argue that such onomastics are totally in line with those already known as true "Qatabanian", and we conclude that these graves were intended for the inhabitants of Tamnaʿ.

Thanks to abundant material coming both from the town and the necropolis itself, and to the previous American excavation campaigns, we are able to carry out more extended comparisons and recognise consequently, among those buried in the cemetery, some of the family groups that feature in the inscriptions from the city. Jamme himself recognised four major families, which he called "les grand clans": *Ḏrʾn*, *Ḏrḫn*, *Ygr*, *Ġrbm* (Jamme 1952: 30-97). These groups can be very numerous and extended, and the palaeographic variations in the inscriptions that allude to the same family show them to have been strikingly long-lived. In the tombs we excavated in Ḥayd bin ʿAqīl we found three more attestations involving the *Ḏrʾn* family,[6] all of them coming from the same structure (Tomb 1).

---

[4] Stelae No.: B.05.D.O./11; B.05.D.O./23; B.06.D.O./27.

[5] Both of the stelae bearing single names are very small, and one was found very close to Tomb 4, which was surely intended for three young persons, as shown by the small dimensions both of the *loci* and of the bones.

[6] Stelae No.: T.03.C.T1.O./32; T.03.C.T1.O./36; T.03.C.T1.O./38.

Closer scrutiny of the findings reveals further interesting aspects. The three stelae which bear the same second name were found very close to each other,[7] so we can suppose that the original burials were also very close by. The onomastic formula used is different, since the use of the relative pronoun is only seen in one case. This suggests that the presence or absence of the relative was not a matter of social status, but probably due to other factors, such as the availability of space on the stela or, more simply, that there was no fixed pattern to be followed (Avanzini 2004: 319-320; Jamme 1952: 8; 25-26). We can hypothesise that in funerary contexts simplifications tended to be used, on account of having limited space for lettering, whereas in the case of official public inscriptions (like those put up in the city) the onomastic formula is invariably more extended and articulated. In the latter case, those responsible for a major construction or recorded as signing a legislative decree obviously had every interest in being identified in the most unequivocal way possible. This could explain why we have not found more complex formulas here, such as the presence of the patronymic, for instance, which is more frequent on monumental inscriptions. So, if the presence of a patronymic is an indicator of distinguished social status, the presence or absence of the relative indicating family affiliation may be a consequence of the type of text.

Near the stelae belonging to the $Dr^{\jmath}n$ family there is another which bears the second name Hrn,[8] which we know from other inscriptions to have been somehow related to the $Dr^{\jmath}n$ family. All these texts come from Tamna[c] (RES 3566 and VL 5) or from Ḥayd bin ᶜAqīl (Ja 350) and are all dated between the 1st century BC to the 1st century AD. These data suggest that Tomb 1 at least was primarily intended for members of the same enlarged family, including those affiliated after marriage. The large amount of material brought to light by the Americans cannot be investigated in the same way, because we do not know the exact position in which the stelae were discovered. This could have been of great help in confirming the use of these structures as "family chapels". However, it can be recognized that one family (like that of $Dr^{\jmath}n$) could have had different burial structures in different parts of the necropolis (since the areas excavated by the Americans and those we are studying here are distant from each other), and this could be the consequence of a chronological distance, i.e. depending on the availability of burial spaces over time. Besides, such large groups were probably divided into various sub-groups whose members, as time passed, no longer felt strong bonds even though they bore the same family name.

Conclusions

With regard to the Ḥayd bin ᶜAqīl cemetery, it may be assumed that it was mainly used for the families living in Tamnaᶜ, as demonstrated both by the onomastics and the necropolis' architecture and layout. It is in fact possible to identify quarters of tombs which could be interpreted as genuine "funerary chapels", intended for members of the same family. The architecture of the tombs, planned for subsequent extensions, is further evidence for this use. In the same way, the tomb plans correspond perfectly to what can be termed a modality of spatial organization informed by a single overall approach which has given shape to different kinds of structures. As de Maigret pointed out: "the South Arabian schema of the tripartite private house seems to be reflected, as well as in religious architecture, also in funeral architecture" (de Maigret 2002: 106).

At Barāqish, on the contrary, the cemetery plan is much less homogeneous, and the lack of an overall design can be primarily seen in the disorderly manner in which the pit-graves were built up. It is almost as if each new structure (which cannot be properly described as a "burial" in the absence of corpse) was simply made next to an earlier one, without any preordained criteria.

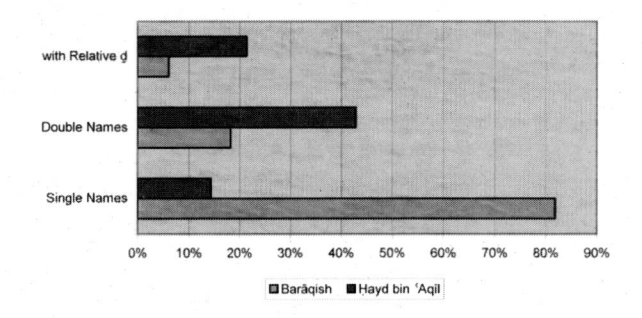

Figure 10. Comparison between the distributions of onomastic formulae used in the two investigated necropolises.

Moreover, whereas the onomastics have enabled the recognition some of those buried in Ḥayd bin ᶜAqīl as citizens of Tamnaᶜ, the onomastics of the Minaean stelae suggest groups coming from elsewhere, in view of the many cross-references with northern Arabian onomastics. The absence of human bones remains an open question: if the necropolis of Barāqish is considered as a sort of cenotaph, this makes the identification of the ethnic background of the deceased even more difficult. As we have noted, there are many common elements with names from the north of the peninsula, and the lack of bodies strengthens the hypothesis that we are dealing with people who died beyond the borders of Minaean territory. But did they die elsewhere because they were not Minaeans or because they were Minaeans who happened to be elsewhere at the moment of their death? In the first case they would have been foreigners who certainly had some sort of contact with the inhabitants of Barāqish, otherwise why would they have had such a monument? In both cases it is likely that they were people engaged in commerce, perhaps caravaneers who, whether Minaean

---

[7] All come from Locus 2 in Tomb 1. Since the tomb has been looted we cannot be totally sure of their original collocation, but we can suppose that they should not have been put very far away from the position in which have been discovered.
[8] Stela No.: T.03.C.T1.O./35.

or not, had developed relationships with the sedentary inhabitants of the city but did not "officially" belong there.

What is shown by the study of these two cemeteries is that at the turn of the millennium two of the most important South Arabian centres probably exhibited different forms of social and ethnic complexity: the capital of Qatabān was probably occupied by a society composed of large and long-lived family groups, whereas Barāqish, like other cities of the Jawf, was more exposed to the influence of small groups that originated from northern Arabia. This differentiation is revealed also by the two onomastic patterns: the family affiliation is clearer in the Tamnaᶜ necropolis, while in the cemetery from Barāqish this kind of specification is virtually absent (Fig. 10). This scenario suggests that we have not yet discovered the actual burial site of the urbanized citizens of Minaean *Yathill*.

Sigla

Ja 350   Published by Jamme (1952: 195-199, pl. 8b).
RES 3566   Published in *Répertoire d'épigraphie sémitique*. Paris: Imprimerie nationale (see also Avanzini 2004: 293-298).
VL 5   Discovered by major Van Lessen and published by Bron (1992: 20-22).

References

Agostini A. 2010. Funerary Stelae from Barāqish. Study of the Onomastics. In S. Antonini & A. Agostini (eds), *A Minaean necropolis at Barāqish (Jawf, Republic of Yemen). Preliminary Report of the 2005-2006 archaeological campaigns*. (Reports and Memoirs N.S. IX). Rome: IsIAO.

Agostini A. In preparation. La necropoli di Ḥayd bin ᶜAqīl. Le iscrizioni. In A. de Maigret & Ch.J. Robin (eds). *Gli scavi Italo-Francesi a Tamnaᶜ (Repubblica dello Yemen). Rapporto finale* (Reports and Memoirs).Rome: IsIAO.

Antonini S. 1992. Oggetti d'importazione dalle tombe di Kharabat al-Ahjur (Dhamār). *Yemen. Studi archeologici, storici e filologici sull'Arabia meridionale*, 1: 3-12. Rome.

Antonini S. 1998. South Arabian Antiquities in a Private Collection in ar-Riyaḍ (Saudi Arabia). With a note by G. Mazzini. *Arabian Archaeology and Epigraphy* 9: 261-272.

Antonini S. 2005*a*. Alcune stele inedite dal Jawf (Yemen). Pages 308-313 in A. V. Sedov & I. M. Smilijanskaja (eds), *Arabia Vitalis. Studies in honour of Vitalij Naumkin in occasion of his 60th anniversary*. Moscow.

Antonini S. 2005*b*. The first two archaeological campaigns at Ḥayd Ibn ᶜAqīl, the necropolis of Tamnaᶜ. Pages 1-19 in A. Sholan, S. Antonini & M. Arbach (eds), *Sabaean Studies. Archaeological, epigraphical and historical studies in honour of Y. M. ᶜAbdallāh, A. de Maigret and Ch .J. Robin*. Naples-Ṣanᶜā: Il Torcoliere.

Antonini S. 2005*c*. The Hypogean Tombs of Kharibat Al-Hajur. Pages 53-90 in S. Antonini & A. de Maigret (eds), *South Arabian Necropolises. Italian Excavations at Al-Makhdarah and Kharibat al-Ahjur (Yemen)*. (Reports and Memoirs, N.S. IV). Rome: IsIAO.

Antonini S. 2010. The excavation and the archaeological materials. In S. Antonini & A. Agostini (eds), *A Minaean necropolis at Barāqish (Jawf, Republic of Yemen). Preliminary Report of the 2005-2006 archaeological campaigns*. (Reports and Memoirs N.S. IX). Rome: IsIAO.

Antonini S. In preparation. La necropoli di Ḥayd bin ᶜAqīl. Lo scavo e i materiali. In A. de Maigret & Ch.J. Robin (eds). *Gli scavi Italo-Francesi a Tamnaᶜ (Repubblica dello Yemen). Rapporto finale* (Reports and Memoirs). Rome: IsIAO.

Antonini S. & Buffa V. In preparation. The Qatabanian pottery assemblage of Tamnaᶜ. In A. de Maigret & Ch.J. Robin (eds). *Gli scavi Italo-Francesi a Tamnaᶜ (Repubblica dello Yemen). Rapporto finale* (Reports and Memoirs). Rome: IsIAO.

Arbach M. & Schiettecatte J. 2006. *Catalogue des pièces archéologiques et épigraphiques du Jawf au Musée National de Ṣanᶜā*. Ṣanᶜā.

Arbach M. & Audouin R. 2007. *Ṣanᶜā National Museum. Collection of Epigraphic and Archaeological Artefacts from al-Jawf Sites*. Ṣanᶜā: UNESCO - SFD.

Arbach M., Schiettecatte J. & al-Hādī I. 2008. *Ṣanᶜā' National Museum. Part III. Collection of Funerary Stelae from the Jawf Valley*. Ṣanᶜā: UNESCO - SFD.

Avanzini A. 2004. *Corpus of South Arabian Inscriptions I-III: Qatabanic, Marginal Qatabanic, Awsanite Inscriptions*. Arabia Antica 2. Pisa: Edizioni Plus.

Beeston A.F.L. 1978. Epigraphic South Arabian Nomenclature. *Raydān* 1: 13-21.

Bron F. 1992. *Mémorial Mahmud al-Ghul. Inscriptions sudarabiques*. (Centre Français d'Etudes Yéménites - Ṣanᶜā. L'Arabie Préislamique 2). Paris : Paul Geuthner.

Cleveland R.L. 1965. *An Ancient South Arabian Necropolis. Objects from the Second Campaign (1951) in Timnaᶜ Cemetery*. Publication of the American Foundation for the Study of Man IV. Baltimore: The John Hopkins Press.

Davidde B. 1992. Le monete di ᵓAmdān Bayyin Yuhaqbiḍ rinvenute nelle tombe di Kharibat al-Ahjar, presso Waragah (Dhamār). *Yemen. Studi archeologici, storici e filologici sull'Arabia meridionale*, 1: 41-54. Rome.

de Maigret A. 2002. Some reflections on the South Arabian bayt. *Archäologische Berichte aus dem Yemen* X: 101-110. Mainz-on-Rhine: Verlag Philipp von Zabern.

de Maigret A. 2004. *Barāqish, Minaean Yathill. Excavation and Restoration of the Temple of Nakraḥ*. Papers of the Yemeni-Italian Centre for Archaeological Research – National Museum of Ṣanᶜā 1. Naples: Il Torcoliere.

de Maigret A. in press. A "Sabaean" Stratigraphy from Barāqish. *Arabia. Revue de Sabéologie* 4.

de Maigret A. & Robin Ch.J. 1993. Le temple de Nakraḥ à Yathill (aujourd'hui Barāqish), Yémen, résultats des deux premières campagnes de fouilles de la Mission Italienne. *Comptes Rendus de l'Académie des Inscriptions et Belles Lettres*: 427-498.

Fedele F. G. in press. Barāqish, over-wall excavations 2005-2006: stratigraphy, environment and economy of the Sabaean-Islamic sequence. *Arabia, Revue de Sabéologie* 4.

Garbini G. 1977. Su alcuni tipi di stele e statuette sudarabiche con iscrizione. *Annali dell'Istituto Orientale di Napoli* 37 (N.S. 27): 376-381.

Höfner M. 1964. Altsüdarabischen Stelen und Statuetten. Pages 217-232 in E. Haberland, M. Schuster & H. Straube (eds), *Festschrift für A.E. Jensen*. München.

Jamme A. 1952. *Pièces épigraphiques de Ḥeid bin ʿAqīl, la nécropole de Timnaʿ (Hagr Koḥlān)*. Bibliothèque du Muséon 30. Louvain.

Ryckmans G. 1957. Graffites sabéennes relevés en Arabie Saḵudite. *Rivista degli Studi Orientali* 32: 557-563.

Authors' Addresses
Dr Sabina Antonini PhD
Via Case sparse, 25
I-06019-Umbertide (Perugia)
sabantonini@tiscali.it

Dr Alessio Agostini PhD
c/o Università degli Studi di Firenze
Dipartimento di Linguistica
Piazza Brunelleschi 3-4
I-50121 Florence

Funerary monuments of southern Arabia: the Iron Age – early Islamic traditions

Juris Zarins

Summary

This study focuses on a particular set of funerary monuments found in southern Arabia and often called boat or ellipse graves. Their distribution is noted throughout much of Dhofar, Oman, the Mahra Governorate of Yemen and Socotra. They can occur in isolation, small groups or larger clusters. Limited excavations since 1952 have determined they are the interments of single individuals generally without grave goods. Constructed in a fairly uniform manner of large stone blocks, they are generally dated from the post-Classic period (c. 400 CE) until 1000 CE based on stratigraphy, C-14 dates, and associated site ceramics.[1] Often identified with the people of 'Ad as their ancestors and the geographical region of *al-Ahqaf* by modern MSAL speakers, their construction may reflect differing aspects of socio-political, religious and ethnic status in the region.

Keywords; Boat/ellipse graves, Southern Arabia, MSAL speakers, 'Ad, Ahqaf

Introduction

The Arabian Peninsula has long intrigued travellers and scholars by its enigmatic historical and archaeological remains. One such category has been monuments which have generally been defined as containing human burials, a focus of this conference. Human burials, as is generally acknowledged, can be a focal point of human settlement patterns, helping identify ritual, religious, economic, political, kinship and even ethnic/linguistic trends.

Our attention here is focused on a particular set or type of tomb found in the Dhofar Governorate, Southern Oman, and the Mahra Governorate of Yemen belonging particularly to the late Iron Age-Early Islamic periods (Fig. 1). This grave type is often referred to as "boat-(shaped)" or elliptical. A study of this grave type is made all the more interesting and compelling since it could represent ideas developed over the course of six difficult centuries (400-1000 CE) with their shifting political, economic, ethnic and religious beliefs. More specifically, this grave type could reflect local lineage kinship, ancestor definition, and ritual associations expressed in local funerary customs fused with the arrival and spread of first Judaism, then Christianity followed by Islam in ancestral MSAL groups.

Definition of a Corpus

The late 19th century travellers, Theodore and Mabel Bent, passing through Dhofar, noted the large megalithic stones forming an ellipse, often grouped together in clusters (Bent & Bent 1900). Thomas, some thirty years later, referred to them as "giant ovoids" (Thomas 1932: 39). The AFSM group led by W. Phillips and F. Albright in 1952 was the first to examine the ellipse monuments over a wider scale and excavated a small number.

The ellipse-shaped tombs are defined by a single or double row of semi-dressed blocks outlining the ellipse or "boat-shape," hence the name (Fig. 2). In a number of cases, larger monolithic blocks define the end of the long axis – sometimes orientated north-south. The interior of the ellipse is filled with pebbles, gravel or transverse-placed slabs. The graves occur singly or more commonly in clusters with linked or common outer walls (Figs. 3-4). These clusters vary in number/size from 3-4 to over 50 graves (Figs. 3-5).

Individual ellipses also vary in size tremendously ranging from 2 to 12 m long to 1-3 m wide. On occasion, some tombs are over 18 m long. Some of the ellipses were constructed level to the ground, but more often, the megalithic blocks and the ellipse fill rise more than 1 m above ground level. The tombs are often situated on lower wadi terraces overlooking lagoons, above steep scarps overlooking promontories or as an integral part of settlement sites (Al-Shahri 1991, 1992; Zarins 1997: 652; 2001: 90) (Fig. 5). Despite our definition and the apparent similarity to boats/ships, the original *intent* of such a specific type of construction still eludes us.

Geographical Distribution

The geographical range and distribution of the ellipse monuments in Dhofar is largely confined to four locales – the Salalah Plain, the higher foothill front range, the plains and harbours of the Mirbat-Hasik area called the *Solot* by the Shahra, and the northern hills (or *Qatn*). Few if any such tombs have been noted in the greater Nejd. In the Mahra Governorate of Yemen, they have been reported from the coastal plain and the upland *jol* wadis (Fig. 1 and Tab. 1).

Survey and Excavations

At least twelve ellipse tombs have been excavated and examined since 1952. We can briefly analyze the results to determine possible cultural affiliation and date. In 1952, Albright noted a large ellipse graveyard containing over 250 graves at the base east of the Sumhuram fort (Khor Rori). He noted that their size and orientation varied greatly. He excavated one large example near the base of the fort. Orientated to the west, the length of the

---

[1] All cited C-14 dates are uncalibrated. The use of the term *Classical* is here understood to mean the period between 500 BCE and 400 CE in Southern Arabia.

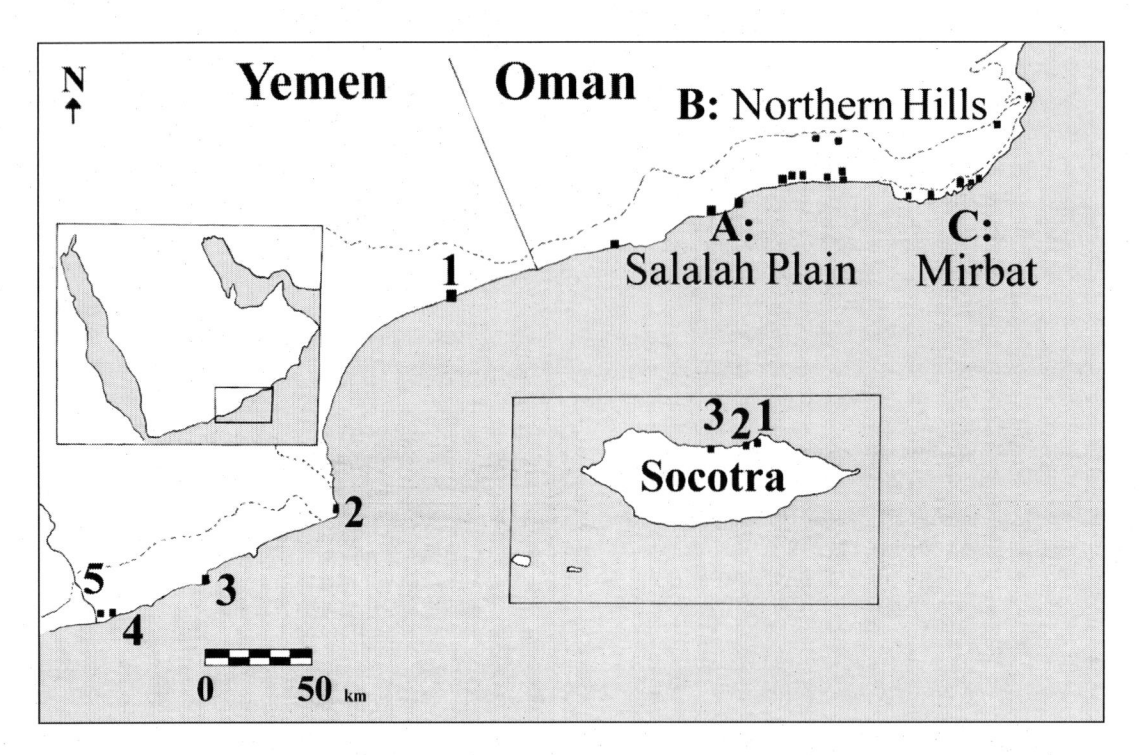

Figure 1. Geographical distribution of ellipse tombs in Southern Arabia.

Salalah Plain	Northern Hills (*Qatn*)	Mirbat-Hasik Plain (*Solot*)
1. Khor Rohri (TA 92:46, KR-48, 62) [Phillips 1972: 111; Albright 1982:40; Cremaschi and Perego 2008]	1. TA 92:26	1. Hinu
	2. DS-08-001 (Dtheethmaad)	2. Old Hasik
	3. DS-08-005 (Jibjat Plain)	3. Ras Jinjali
2. Wadi Darbat (TA 95:255, KR 55/56) [Bonacossi 2002:43-45]	4. DS-08-040 (Aztah)	4. Sadh [Albright 1982:82]
3. Khor Sowli (TA 92: 6) [Al Shahri 1991:187]	5. DS-08-043	5. DS-08-003
4. Sinur (TA 95:5)	6. Wadi Dikur [Thomas 1929: 108].	6. DS-08-018 (Qinqari area)
5. Ain Razat (TA 92:61, TA 93:158)	7. Mahmula/Milwah al Aud [Thomas 1932:39]	7. DS-08-021
6. Ain Humran (TA 94:204) [Zarins 2001:89, fig. 34]		8. DS-08-025
7. Wadi Dahariz [Zarins 2008]		9. DS-08-026 (Lagga Shalyon)
8. Salalah [Zarins 2008]		10. DS-08-028
9. Raysut [Phillips 1972: 160-161, Albright 1982: 81]		

Table 1. Geographical Location of Recorded Ellipse/Boat-Shaped Graves in Dhofar.

tomb was 2.8 m. The interior of the grave contained cross-laid stone slabs. The central box inside the ellipse was 1.65 m long and over 70 cm deep. Lined with slabs, one adult skeleton was inside, lying on his back with pelvis and legs turned slightly to the right side. The head was at the western end of the tomb. The forearms were placed over the stomach. Albright suggested that the tomb was "non-Islamic", dating to the latter part of the city's habitation (post-300 CE). This hypothesis was reinforced by noting the close proximity of the cemetery to the fort (as well as a number of other large ellipse graves surrounding the Classical period settlement). In addition, a later date for the tomb is indicated by the re-use of Sumhuram architectural elements into the tomb's construction including a limestone stair-step block. Albright thought the date of the burial should bracket the classical end of Sumhuram and the arrival of Islam. No grave goods were found inside (Phillips 1972: 111-112; Albright 1982: 40).

An extremely large ellipse grave, over 18 m in length, constructed and placed by itself, was also examined in 1952. This tomb was constructed of large vertical megalithic slabs on the interior, the edging provided by smaller erect slabs. Large stone slabs covered the tomb's interior. The grave box was also stone-lined. No grave goods were recovered (Albright 1982: 83).

Figure 2. An ellipse tomb at Ain Humran. Photo by Lynne Newton.

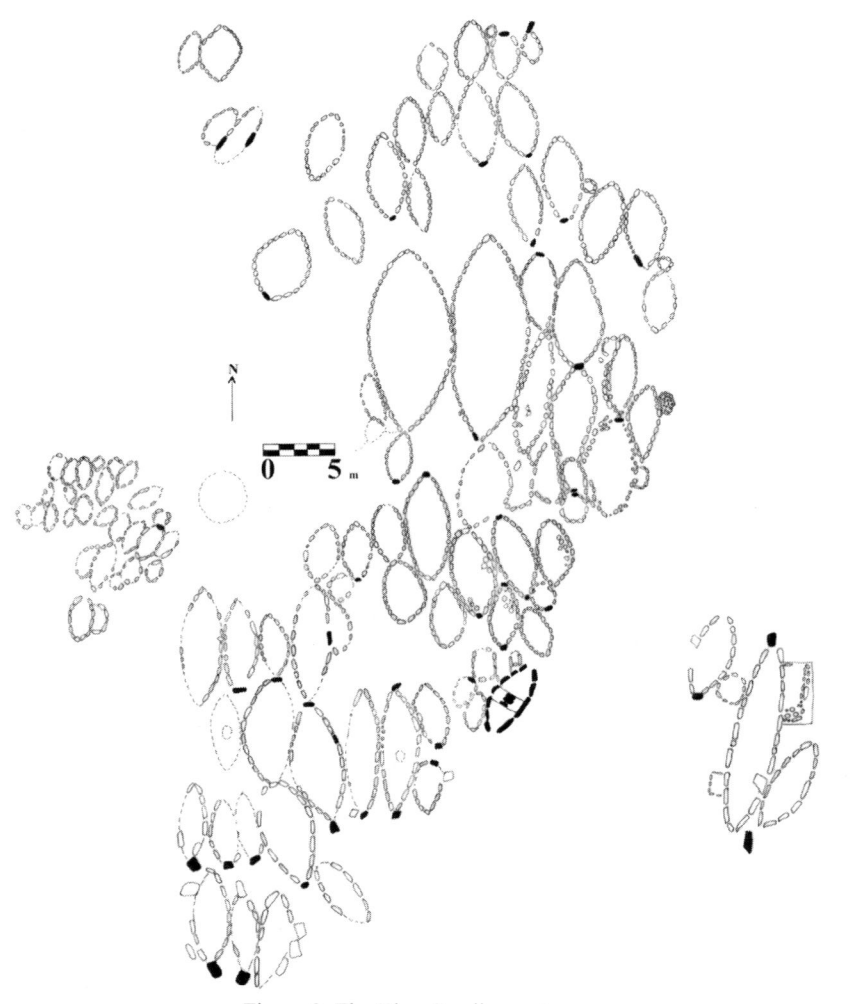

Figure 3. The Khor Sowli cemetery.

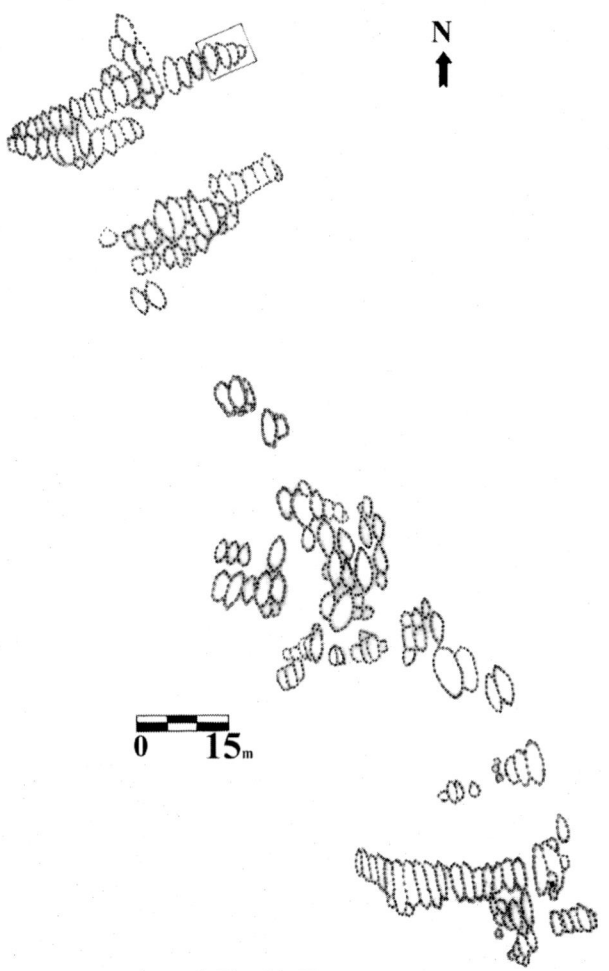

Figure 4. The Ain Humran cemetery.

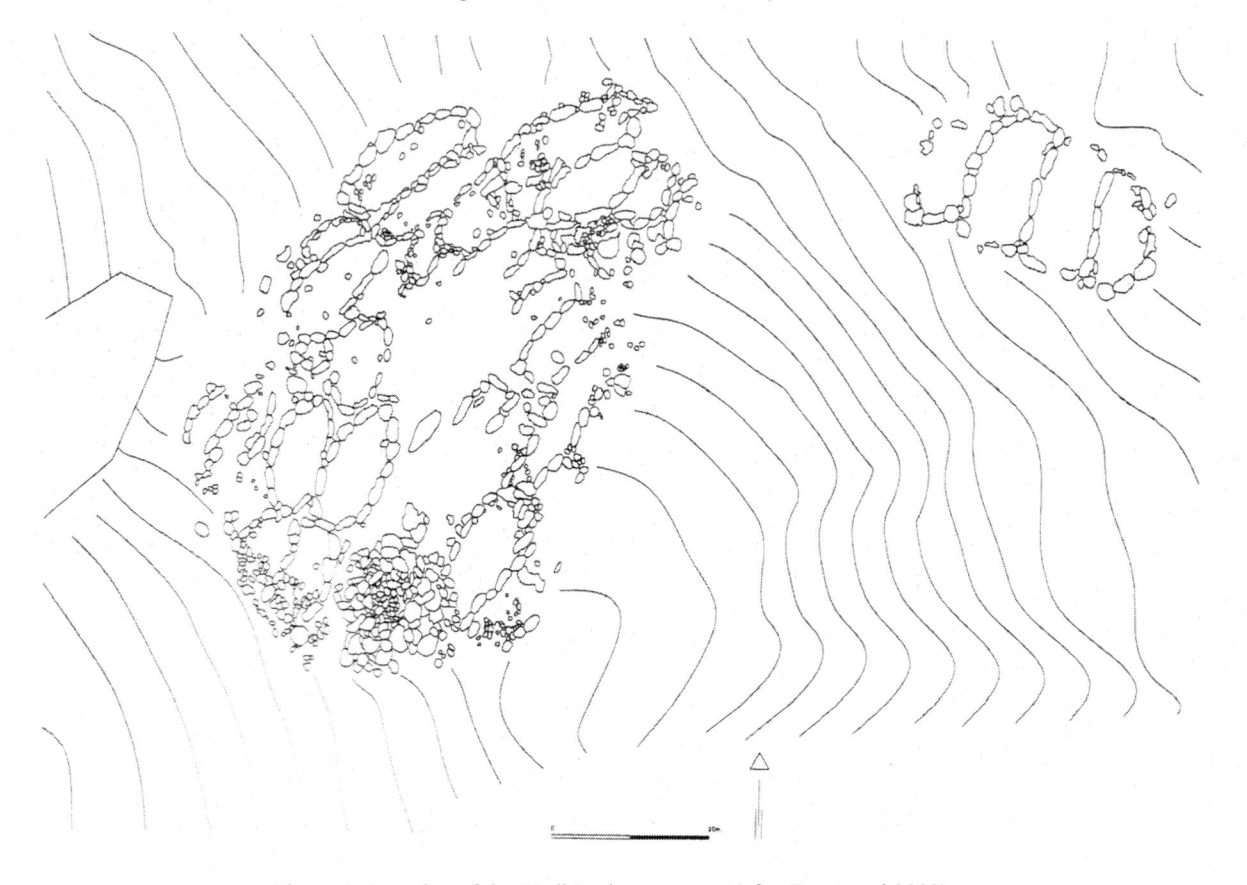

Figure 5. A portion of the Wadi Darbat cemetery (after Bonacossi 2002).

Figure 6. An excavated ellipse tomb at Wadi Darbat (KR 55/56) (after Bonacossi 2002).

Figure 7. An excavated ellipse tomb inside Khor Rohri (after Avanzini and Orazi 2000).

In 1997, an ellipse tomb was excavated at the very large 500 grave cemetery northwest of Sumhuram on the high terrace of Wadi Darbat (TA 95:255; KR-55/56) (Avanzini & Orazi 2001: 59-62; Bonacossi 2002: 43 and Pl. 9.1) (Fig. 5). This large cemetery undoubtedly was associated with the large post-Classic settlement at Khor Rohri (Rougeulle 2008). The typical monolith-ended tomb selected for excavation measured over 5 m in length. The 25 cm fill of pebbles/earth covered four limestone slabs which, in turn, covered the burial box of a single person (Bonacassi 2002: Pl. 9.2 and 10.1) (Fig. 6). The adult lay in a flexed position on the right side, face to the west. No grave goods were found (Bonacassi 2002: 43).

In November of 2000, The Italian Mission to Oman working inside the Sumhuram fort/city, found next to a monumental square and building of the Classical period, a floor level (US 54) which was interpreted as the last living surface in this part of the city. A small "boat-shaped grave" was found in the northeast corner of the trench. The grave box was rectangular and there were two rows of pavement stone outlining the ellipse (see parallel construction from Socotra) (Fig. 7). The date of the ellipse was indicated by its stratigraphic, in situ placement when this part of the city was already in a state of neglect, but the surrounding buildings were still intact just after the abandonment of US 54. Paralleling the reuse of Sumhuram architecture blocks as noted earlier in Albright's excavation, a limestone Classical period incense burner was found in the ellipse stone wall. The tomb was empty and no grave goods were found. Based on near-by, excavated ceramics, the excavators assigned the tomb to the end of the third city phase, ca. 300-350 CE (Avanzini & Orazi 2000: 6-9).

In 1995, the Transarabia team cleaned and excavated three ellipse tombs on the eastern arm of Khor Sowli which were located on a 5 m terrace above the current wadi (TA 92:6) (Fig. 3). The largest megalithic ellipse grave was over 6 m long. Large megalithic pillars were placed on both ends. Inside the ellipse, a gravel/earth layer, 30cm thick, was cleared. Below it were stone transverse slabs. The stone box was cut 1.3 m below the interior surface. The body inside lay on its back. No grave goods were found. Two other graves were cleared to confirm the structural pattern (Zarins 1997: 652; 2001: 90). In 1994, the Transarabia team also cleared a large ellipse grave located at the south base of Ain Humran (TA 94:204) (Fig. 4). A typical local rice-ware vessel was found outside on top of the tomb (Zarins 2001: 90 and Fig. 33b.209.1).

At Salalah itself, a very large cemetery with ellipse-shaped graves was found on the high terraces of the Wadi Dahariz (DS-08-103) and smaller ellipse graves inside Salalah itself north of al-Baleed in 2008 (DS-08-102). To the west, other ellipse graves were excavated at Raysut in 1952. The tomb field was located west of the promontory fort in the Wadi Adhonib. Two cemeteries with a total of 160 tombs were identified. One excavated stone-lined slab box contained one individual 1 m below the surface. The head was at the north end, the right cheek facing west. A second tomb was similar with the slab-lined box 1.10 m below the surface with the head at the north end. No grave goods were found in either tomb (Albright 1982: 81).

At Mughsayl, which is technically not part of the Salalah

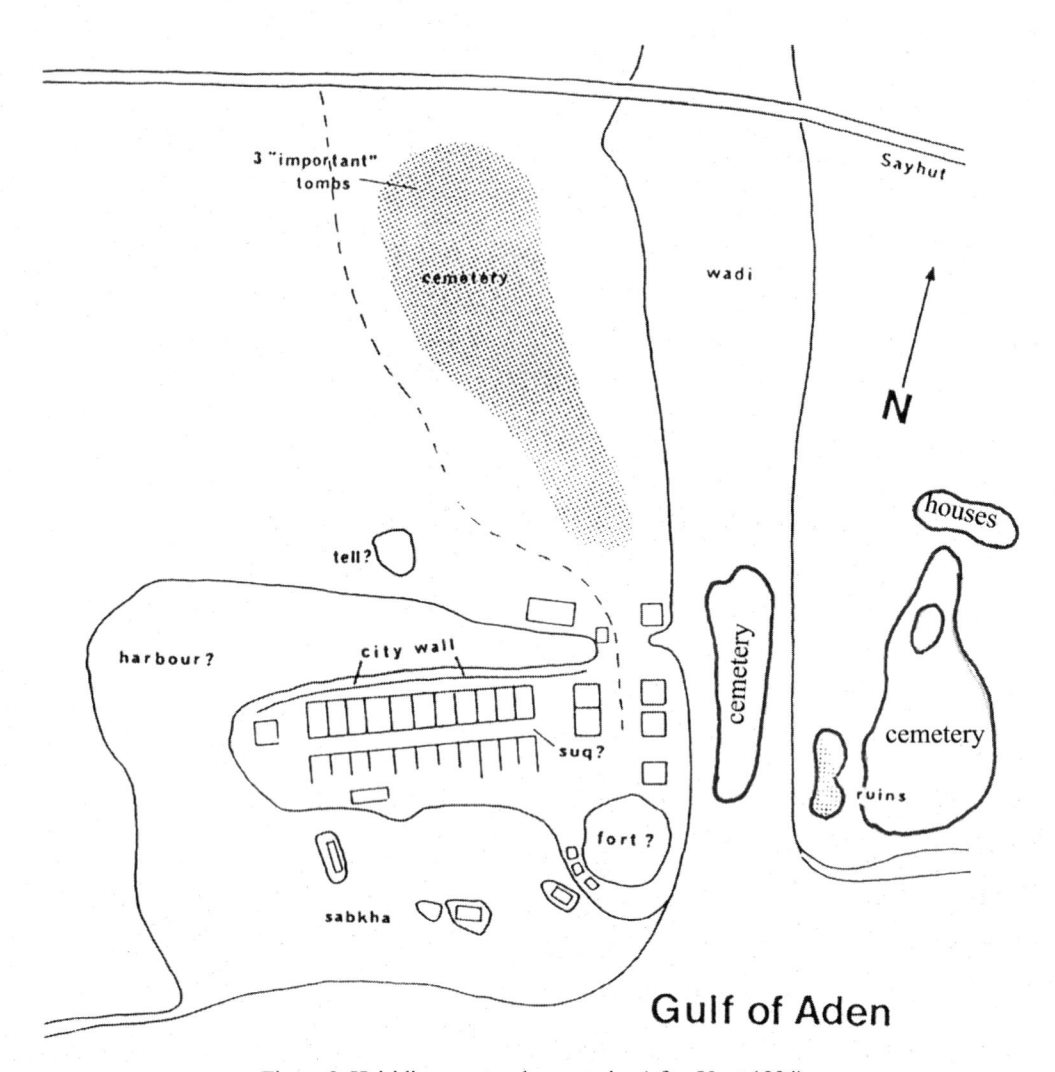

Figure 8. Hairidj seaport and cemeteries (after Vogt 1994).

Plain, west of Raysut, a small settlement was located on the adjoining lagoon. It consists of a small formal settlement (perhaps later converted into a mosque) and an adjoining promontory investigated by Brigham Young University in 2007-2008 (Johnson et al. 2007, 2008). There is a large cemetery near the sea west of the village site. As at Ain Humran, the older sections, determined by the patination of the stones, are separated from the newer, more modern part. Albright excavated two ellipse/boat-shaped graves here. One, 2.3 m long, was filled with stones and earth. The internment box was placed 1.10 m below the surface. The head was orientated 16° east. The body of a child was on its back, knees flexed, face up and arms crossed. A second grave, with a north-south orientation, was that of an adult. The body lay on its face with the head towards the north. No objects were found in either grave (Albright 1982: 79).

Mahra Governorate of Yemen

Before we turn to a discussion of dating the ellipse grave monuments of Dhofar, several key sites from the adjoining Mahra Governorate in Yemen and Socotra can be briefly examined to shed further light on these structures. At Damqut, a typical set of archaeological materials parallels those found at Mughsayl and Raysut. The lagoon mouth is dominated by a promontory fort, below which is a village complex and adjoining cemetery of boat-shaped graves (MAP Sites 2-71-74) (Fig. 1/1).

Further to the west, at the eastern base of Ras Fartak, at Khalfut two main graveyards are located to the north and south of the main settlement and fort (Rougeulle 2001: 210 and Fig. 60) (Fig. 1/2). The ellipse tombs numbering in the hundreds are mainly found in the north cemetery (Rougeulle 2001: 209).

At Sharwayn, a large promontory protecting the town of Qishn and the site of a safe anchorage from the southwest monsoon, the main cemetery lies north of the city across the wadi (Fig. 1/3). The majority of the graves are of the ellipse/boat-shaped variety. Some are as large as 3.5 m long. In the words of the excavator, the tombs consist of a "filling of pebbles and stone fragments bordered by a line of horizontal or vertical blocks, the extremities are sometimes marked by two prominent blocks or slabs" (Rougeulle 2001: 207). She remarks that they seem to be typical of pre-and/or Early Islamic sites in this region (Rougeulle 2001: 207).

At al-Qisha, located upstream of the Wadi Masila, we found a typical fort on a promontory, a village and cemetery (Fig. 1/5). The latter is found on the east bank. The mosque and saint's tomb are surrounded on the southeast by an extremely large ellipse-grave tomb field (Newton 2007: Fig. 2).

Finally from Socotra, archaeological work in 1985 and 1987 defined the standard grave type characteristics of the island. The majority are rectangular tombs outlined in stone slabs (Fig. 9). Four megaliths mark the corners. The slab-lined burial pit cut underground usually contains one person, usually lying on its back. The orientation of the long axis varies (Sedov 1993: 88-109, Figs. 4.3a-c, 4.6, 4.10b). At the large village site of Hajyra, south of Suq, the settlement is dominated by a very large building perhaps identified as a cathedral/church (Sedov 1993: 112, Fig. 4.13a). The east side of the site is a vast cemetery (Sedov 1993: Fig. 4.13c-d) (Fig. 1/Socotra 2). Here, as elsewhere, the larger percentage of graves belongs to the typical rectangular type, outlined in stone slabs, with the body laid on its back. The tombs, on average, are 2.4 m long. These tombs form chains or clusters of 3-4 or at times 8-12 individual tombs. Sedov notes that the graves in the eastern part of the cemetery are somewhat different, with an orientation of northeast-southwest, smaller and oval (ellipse type) (Sedov 1993: Fig. 4.13b). [Note that the caption says it is an Islamic grave]. While they have the appearance of being rather haphazardly planned, they still are linked in clusters of 2-3 graves. I assume no grave goods were found.

A third cemetery on Socotra at Mobrhim shows a similar pattern (Fig. 1/Socotra 2). The excavator notes that one cemetery contained between 35-40 graves, orientated largely east-west. Some of them have a rectangular stone slab outline (Fig. 1/Socotra 3) and others have an *oval* stone slab wall surrounding them (Sedov 1993: 102). Near Hajyra, another cemetery of ten graves also contains either an oval or rectangular stone slab outline. Here in a number of cases, the slab ring is defined by a second slab line or even a third. The Islamic identification is made certain by the attachment inside the grave of two or three anthropomorphic type slabs.

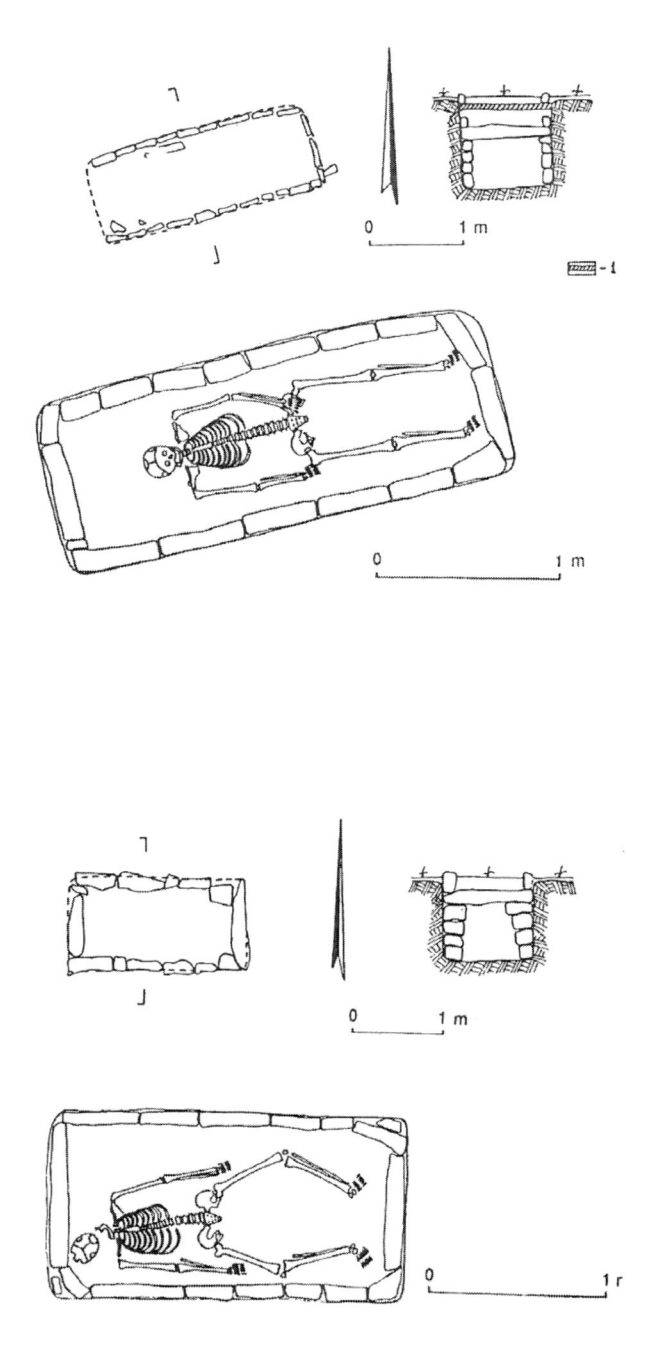

Figure 9. Socotran rectangular graves (after Sedov 1993).

Christians and Muslims on Socotra

Sedov remarks on the characteristics of what he calls the *Pre-Islamic* grave shapes and their similarity to the later *Islamic* grave type. The latter, he notes, are usually nearly *oval* in shape (Sedov 1993: 124). What then are the differences between Islamic and "Pre-Islamic" graves? They include the shape of the slab outline wall, the position of the body, the practice of collective burials and grave goods.

In spite of ample later historical documentation (Ibn Mujawir 1220 CE, Smith 1985: 85-86; 1995: 10-11; Nicolo 1422 CE, Major 1857: 20; Ibn Majid 1488 CE, Tibbetts 1981) and the presence of churches on Socotra (Doe 1970: 42-43, 91; Sedov 1993: 116, 131-133), Sedov never states that any of the "Pre-Islamic" *rectangular*

Hairidj is a seaport located on the east bank of a small wadi, 10 km east of Wadi Masila in western Mahra Governorate (Vogt 1994) (Fig. 1/4). The harbor is mentioned in several early Islamic texts of the 9th-10th centuries CE (Rougeulle 1999: 130 n. 8). Abbasid barbotine blue, Chinese white porcelains of the 11th century CE and Indian RPW's have been collected (Rougeulle 2001: 211). Vogt remarks on the numerous graves numbering in the thousands found at the site (Vogt 1994: 138 and sketch map 3). As in other cases already described, the tombs occur on both sides of the wadi and on an island in the middle (Fig. 8). Our inspection of the site confirmed that hundreds of ellipse tombs were located primarily on the east side of the wadi (cf. Rougeulle 2001: 207).

graves may be Christian (Fig. 9). However, Christianity is attested on the southern mainland as early as the 4th century CE at Qana (Sedov 1992, 1995:18), by the 6th century CE in the Hadramaut (Shahid 1979: 26, 52; Arbach 2007: 4) and in Himyar by the same time (Yule 2008). Their early mid-1st millennium presence on Socotra is reputed to come from remnant Greek populations (*bakiyat al Yunan*, according to Abu al-Fida, *Takwim al Buldan*; cf. also the same account in Mas'udi, *Muruj al-Dhahab* sec. 37, Lunde & Stone 2007: 62-63; Peutz 2008). Here, based on Sedov's dating of the early ceramics on Socotran sites to the early to mid-first millennium CE, and the appearance of Christianity on the island, a hypothesis suggesting that the rectangular outlined graves, in part, could be Christian can be entertained.

In addition, Sedov underestimated the early impact of Islam on the Socotran population. It occurred earlier than generally thought and not as late as 12-13th centuries CE. A Muslim presence on the island certainly extends back to the First Oman Imamate, since at least 750 CE (Wilkinson 1988: 135 and n. 16; Ministry of Information, Oman 1995: 169).

Dating

From Dhofar, we have only one direct date for the ellipse graves, that of 1070±50 BP (880 CE uncalibrated) from bone collagen extracted from tomb at KR-55/56 at Khor Rori (Bonacossi 2002: 45 n. 38) (Fig. 6). That being the case, one could assume that some if not the majority of boat-shaped graves from Khor Rori were contemporary not to the fort at Sumhuram but to the Jebel Taqa/Mirbat promontory occupation at the lagoon. These two settlements have three associated C-14 dates of 1130±60 BP [GX-27886], 1190±100 BP [GX-27587], and 1010±60 BP [GX-27588] (Avanzini & Orazi 2000; Rougeulle 2008) which are contemporary to the date from the KR-55/56 cemetery. The boat grave excavated by Avanzini in 2000 (Fig. 7) inside the last phase of the city can now be re-dated somewhat later to the fifth construction phase at Khor Rori or to the last occupation when most of the buildings were abandoned (GX-26642, 1580±50 BP). More recently, other dates from Area F may confirm a post-6th century CE date for the ellipse tomb indirectly (GX-30987: 1560±70 BP; GX-30989: 1240+50 BP; GX-30985: 1020±50 BP; Avanzini 2008: 727-731). Together with Albright's ellipse tomb, at the exterior base of the fort, both of which reused Classical Sumhuram worked blocks or artifacts, the dates for the ellipse tombs could in reality belong to a period of 400-900 CE or even later into the Early Islamic period.

The terminal use of the earlier round or circular cairn tombs in the immediate area, for example, can be seen at Taqa 60, where the latest occupation date is 1670±60 BP [Beta-83798] (Zarins 2001: 73 and fig. 30). This date fits well within the Khor Rori Sumhuram occupation as well. This suggests that ellipse graves at Khor Rori and the general Dhofar area are post 350-400 CE.

The only direct date of a body from Socotra also supports a later or an Abbasid date (875-1200 CE). Grave goods from a rectangular tomb on Socotra were radiocarbon dated to 1230±140 BP [LE-4317] confirming them to be contemporary with the Early Abbasid date at Jebel Mirbat. From the Hajyra town excavations the date is similar, 1190±140 BP (Sedov 1993: 120 and n. 4).

Indirect dating of the ellipse tombs is difficult to say the least. At Ain Humran, a local rice-ware vessel rim was found on top of the cleared graves (see above). At Khor Sowli, the ellipse tombs were constructed *over* an earlier settlement which contained Late Iron Age lithics and incised wares including rice ware. Since shell middens at Khor Rohri and the Taqa 60 site are similar (without rice ware) and are dated to 2340-2135 BP, the date for the rice ware is also post-400 CE and of probable "local origin" (Zarins 2001: 83-85 and Figs. 33b-d). In Wadi Dhahabun at survey site DS-08-89, three boat graves are built above triliths – the latter dated to before 300 CE. The latter generally ceased to be built by 300 CE based on radiocarbon dates (see below). From Fazaiyah west of Mughsayl, boat graves (survey site DS-08-145) were also built over existing older stone circles and structures.

The ellipse graves at Hinu (TA93-101), Hasik (TA94-117), and Jinjali (TA95-121) support this date as well. The ceramic corpus at these sites consists of Abbasid imports and local incised wares (including rice ware and dot/circle), red wares with a black slip, paddle stamp etc. A date of 700-1000 CE is generally suggested (cf. Hamr Al Sharqiya at Khor Rohri, Rougeulle 2008).

At Raysut, Phillips's assessment of the ellipse/oval tombs as Early Islamic (1972: 161) is supported by the ceramic material from the promontory fort at Raysut (TA92-1) generally being Abbasid or earlier. At Mughsayl, the ellipse graves belong also partially to the Abbasid period and perhaps earlier. Excavations at KM-2 and KM-3 produced a four-phase occupation sequence which could span the time period 600-1400 CE. The excavators suggest the rice ware and dot/circle ceramic types could be dated to the late pre-Islamic period (Johnson et al. 2007, 2008).

In the adjoining Mahra Governorate of Yemen, at Khalfut and Sharwayn the dates for the ellipse tombs are based on the date for the settlement occupation. Rougeulle suggests a late pre-Islamic and early Islamic occupation spanning 500-1100 CE (Rougeulle 2001). At Hairidj (Fig. 8), and al-Qisha near Wadi Masila, two radiocarbon dates of 1220± 50 BP (Beta-107757) and 1070±90 BP (A-11679) respectively and an inscribed date for the local saint's tomb associated with the cemetery (411/1020) also support an Early Islamic date (Newton 2007).

On Socotra, the date for the ellipse tombs at Hayjra is partially based on ceramic evidence. This includes three periods: pre-Islamic South Arabic/Classical period, Abbasid, and Early Medieval (including the large al-Baleed red ware slip amphora with handles) (Sedov 1993: Fig. 4.14c/1).

Interpretation

Based on the body of evidence presented above, what conclusions can we draw? In Dhofar, circular-type cairns gave way to the ellipse/ovoid/boat-shaped type sometime after the end of the classical period, c. 400 CE and during the Himyarite expansion. Based on their distribution in Dhofar, the Mahra Governorate and Socotra, we can suggest they can largely be identified with MSAL speakers. A post-Classic date would also suggest that local belief systems were for the first time influenced by Judaism and/or Christianity (Arbach 2007: 4).[2] This hypothesis perhaps can be supported by noting the parallels of the supine body position at Khor Rohri, Raysut and Mughsayl to those similarly interred on Socotra. The lack of grave goods, often interpreted as sign of only Islam, may, however, equally apply to Judaic-influenced, Christian (and pre-Islamic) graves as well.

By 630 CE, Islam was introduced into the area (cf. Al Tabari, Donner 1993: 105). Gradually more ellipse graves began to conform to the Islamic tradition of north-south axis orientation, the head to the north, the body lying on the side with the head/face facing west. The limited number of excavated tombs suggests a majority conforming to the Islamic tradition, but still with a number deviating from it. This would be expected as populations wrestled with the religious and political differences taking place along the South Arabian coast (al-Shahri [2000: 207-218] notes the various local traditions associated with these graves which included defining them as belonging to "monotheists, abusers, Jinns, prophets" etc.). In addition, local populations experienced the first northern Arab migrations eastward through the region, perhaps as early as 250 CE putting pressure on land rights and product trading (Jamme 1962; Arbach 2007:4). Grave interments could be a reflection of many of these changes.

The presence of large, formal ellipse graves in Wadi Dahariz and the recovery of similar graves inside modern Salalah firmly place a 400-700/1000 CE human presence at al-Baleed. This mortuary evidence is supported by al-Baleed Phase I city walls and ceramic materials. (The earliest radiocarbon date from al-Baleed thus far is 1000±35 BP [KL-4369]).

In terms of economic change, as Bonacossi remarked (2002: 45 n. 40) in her analysis of the Khor Rohri ellipse graves, there is clear evidence of a large group of people participating in a vast trade network extending along the South Arabian coast from Hasik to Wadi Masila. This network included maritime trade linked to the interior. An early phase of this network culminated in the Abbasid period, providing wealth and prosperity to its local participants. In the succeeding period, 1000-1500 CE, the smaller coastal settlements were integrated into much larger and fewer centers such as al-Baleed/Zafar (Costa 1981; Zarins 2007) and al-Shihr (Hardy-Guilbert 2004, 2005).

The post 1000/1200 CE period in the region also saw a change in funerary customs. Post- 1000/1200 CE graves in Dhofar differ from the earlier ellipse style. They are constructed from stone slabs to form a smaller box. The small head stones are largely not inscribed but do bear a wide variety of incised geometric decorations. Many have an additional two or three stones placed in the middle of the box signaling the gender of the deceased. This tomb style is well documented at al- Baleed and elsewhere in the region (Serjeant 1949; Oman 1983, 1989; al-Shahri 2000: 71).

Who constructed the ellipse/boat-shaped graves? In 1991, al-Shahri summarized his studies of grave monuments found in Dhofar. He assumed the Shahra, as one of the oldest MSAL language/ethnic groups in Dhofar (see Johnstone 1975; Simeone-Senelle 1997), had a direct link to the majority of these tombs. Al-Shahri categorized the ellipse tombs as Type 2 and referred to them as *enfi* (pl. *enfo*). He understood the term to refer to Shahri *enfe'en* – our ancestors. Another local term for the ellipses was *hadeeta/hadite* meaning "ancient local people," or "too old to trace its origin or history" (al-Shahri 1991: 183, 194, n. 4; 1992: 23-25). More recently, he noted that the local people assigned the boat graves to the work of the *Jinn* (al-Shahri 2000: 66, 211-212).

However, since the graves have a much wider distribution than just the Dhofar region, we must consider this idea more carefully. Al-Shahri noted in his study of the ellipse graves that the term for them outside Dhofar was *adite*, literally "of the time of 'Ad" (al-Shahri 1991: 194 n. 4). In all probability, the terms *adite* and *hadeeta/hadite* are one and the same term derived from the basic 'Ad, reflecting only dialectal usage. Thus, the term 'Ad requires a brief explanation. Its occurrences in the Quran (Suras 7/65-72, 11/50-60, 26/123-140, 46/21-26 and other references, see Muhammed Ali 2002: 343 n. 65a) define a people living essentially in South Arabia preceding and contemporary to the Prophet Hūd and later the Prophet Mohammed himself, encapsulating the period of late Antiquity. The term was commented on by numerous later Arab historians. In Sura 46 called *Al-Ahqaf,* v. 21, the brother of 'Ad is linked with the region of *al-Ahqaf* (Mohammed Ali 2002: 983 and n. 21a). In 1220, Ibn Mujawir quotes al-Wasiti who noted that the Mahra originated from the remnants of the people of 'Ad (see commentary and genealogies by Carter 1982: 43, 59-60; the earliest independent attestation of the term *Mahra* occurs at al-'Uqla, in the vicinity of Shabwa c. mid 3rd century CE as part of an official delegation to the Hadrami kings, Jamme 1963; Pirenne 1990: 90-125; Muller 1991:80). When God destroyed this people, those who believed in the Prophet Hūd were saved and lived in the mountains of Dhofar, on the island of Socotra and

---

[2] For Christian influence/presence in Dhofar, see the limestone disk inscribed with *IHS* found at Sumhuram/Khor Rohri (Albright 1982: 50, 105) and the clay chalice with crosses excavated in 1994 at Ain Humran (TA 92-55.904/1570). Shahid (1979: 52-53, n. 79) suggested that a location called Atephar in the accounts of *Vita Sanctii Gregentii*, dated to 500-520 CE, is al-Baleed/Zafar and Legmia, east of Zafar, as possibly Khor Rohri.

Masira (Smith 2008: 268-269). Thus, based on the Quran, the people of *'Ad* became synonymous with the geographical region known as *al-Ahqaf* – a region spanning Dhofar and as far west as Wadi Masila. We may state then that the people of *'Ad* and *al Ahqaf* represent the ancestors of the modern MSAL populations in a more generic way as suggested by Ibn Mujawir. He noted in 1220 that the region's famous triliths were made by the *'Ad* people (Smith 2008:256-257). Since the construction of the triliths is now assigned to a bracketed date of c. 300 BCE – 300 CE (Zarins 1997: 673-675), the term *'Ad* can be applied to people of the later Iron Age. Therefore, a tentative link between the Iron Age and the Early Islamic period tomb monuments in Dhofar and the ancestral MSAL speakers can be suggested (see a summary of the arguments in Zarins 1997: 639-642).

If the dating of the ellipse graves is largely correct and is to be associated with the *'Ad* people, kinship considerations associated with the ellipse/boat graves probably can be associated with groups such as the Shahra – by consensus the oldest living Dhofari MSAL group (Janzen 1986: 136 and nn. 32-33; Carter 1982: 16, 29, 58, 81 "The people of *'Ad* represented today by the Batahara, and Shahara…"). Disregarding modern political boundaries and extensions into ecological zones probably never occupied by the Iron Age MSAL speakers of Dhofar, the Shahra north-south land strip divisions (Janzen 1986: 97; Map 2 al-Shahri 2000:26) may go back to the Iron Age; note that Pliny in 70 CE uses two MSAL/Shahri terms *kharf* [carfiathum] and *dote* [dathiathum] for the seasons of autumn and spring respectively which suggests his sources were acquainted with MSAL speakers (Rackham 1988: 42-43). In the somewhat later *Periplus* [150 CE], the author refers to a high quality incense gum as *mokratu*. It is identified with the Shahri term *megert* referring to the frankincense tree (Casson 1989: 127; Miller & Morris 1988: 78-81).

Perhaps Pliny's mention of 3000 families who retained a right in trading frankincense (Rackham 1986: 38-39) could represent an ancestral form of the living Shahra thirteen clan [*bayt* or *fakdh*] groups (Tabuki 1982: 53 and 56 n. 2; Peterson 2004: 261) who still live in the Dhofar area (Johnstone [1975: 94]; Carter [1982: 59] and Janzen [1986: 140 n. 4] cite figures of 5000 families living in the Dhofar hills in the 1960s). These clans are further subdivided into 48 lineages (sub-clans) of *substantially differing sizes* (al-Shahri 2000:26-29; Tabuki 1988:127). Some have as few as one sub-group while others ten. According to him, the thirteen clans are traced back to three eponymous ancestors: Uz/Aus, Offer, and Barah (al-Shahri 2000: 31-35 and map 3) who occupied larger portions of the Dhofar landscape. Keeping in mind the mechanisms of fictive kinship (Carter 1982: 14) and the need to identify communal territorial rights, Al-Shahri suggests the three eponymous ancestors or sons are descendents of Joktan, a son of Noah (Al-Shahri 2000: 30-31). Unfortunately, the framework of *Genesis* and the *Book of Job* cannot be precisely placed within the *'Ad/Aqhaf* chronology. At best, a general Iron Age date can be entertained for these accounts. From a strictly linguistic viewpoint, MSAL languages are thought to have separated from the Central Semitic grouping (including Arabic) by at least 1000 BCE if not earlier (Zohar 1992; Rose & Petraglia 2009).

How does this relate to the boat graves? Very large single ellipse tombs represent the burials of powerful clan or lineage individuals (*kaair*) (Fig. 3). Buried with these persons were other deceased clan/ lineage relatives in radiating order outward. Larger discrete group clusters (Fig. 4) may represent different subsections within the overall cemetery complex. Which specific group is represented at least in Dhofar can be ascertained perhaps by examining in detail the territorial map produced by al-Shahri (2000: 26 map 2). The full scope of understanding the micro-territories of the MSAL speakers is beyond the scope of this paper, but would involve an investigation to produce similar territorial maps for the ancestral clan groups of the Mahra in the Mahra Governorate of Yemen (Dostal 1967: 123-135; Muller 1991: 80) as well as other groups in the Hadramaut *jol* (McCorriston 2005).

In conclusion, it would appear that the boat-shaped graves were typical of much of south Arabia (*al-Ahqaf*) and most were constructed sometime between 400-1000 CE. Their occurrence as a series of clusters suggests Shahri-type, lineage-based groups who buried their dead in accordance with established guidelines tempered by changing economic, political, ethnic and religious beliefs over the course of least six or more centuries.

Acknowledgements

This study was made possible by the dedicated support of H.E. Abdul-Aziz bin Mohammad al-Rowas, both as former Minister of Information and now Advisor to HM the Sultan for Cultural Affairs. Most of the data utilized here came from the 1991-1995 Transarabia Expedition surveys, the al-Baleed excavations (2005-2008) and the new archaeological survey of Dhofar instituted by H.E. in 2008. Thanks are also due to his staff in both Muscat and Salalah, particularly Dr. Said al Salmi, Hassan al Jabberi and Ghanim al Shanfari. Survey and excavation work in the Mahra Governorate of Yemen (1997-2001) were made possible by Dr. Yusuf Abdullah of GOAMM and his staff, especially Ahmed Shemsan, Muamar al Amri, Abdul Basit al Noman and Samir al Qaddasi. The project in Yemen was supported financially by George Hedges of The Archaeology Fund, and by the Seaver Foundation, both of Los Angeles CA, USA. Any textual and interpretive errors are solely those of the author.

Sigla

DS	Dhofar Archaeological Survey - Oman, 2008-2009
ESA	Epigraphic South Arabic
KR	Khor Rohri Archaeological Survey - Oman, 1997- 2005
MAP	Mahra Archaeological Project - Yemen, 1997-2001
MSAL	Modern South Arabic Language(s)

TA   Transarabia Archaeological Expedition - Oman, 1990-1995

References

Albright F.P. 1982. *The American archaeological expedition in Dhofar, Oman, 1952-1953*. Washington DC: The American Foundation for the Study of Man [AFSM].Vol. 6.

Arbach M. 2007. Les visiteurs de Shabwa du vii^e s. av. J.-C. au iii^e s. ap J.-C. Pages 1-4 in *Shabwa IV*. Paris: Paul Geuthner.

Avanzini A. (ed.) 2008. *A port in Arabia between Rome and the Indian Ocean (3rd c. BC-5th c. AD). Khor Rohri Report 2*. Rome: Erma di Bretschneider.

Avanzini A. & Orazi R. 2000. Preliminary report, October-November 2000. MID-Missione Italiana in Dhofar, Sultanate of Oman, University of Pisa. Salalah: unpublished file report.

Avanzini A. & Orazi R. 2001. Excavations and restoration of the complex of Khor Rohri, interim report (October 2000-April 2001). *Egitto e Vicino Oriente* 24: 5-63.

Bent T. & Bent M. 1900. *Southern Arabia, Soudan and Socotra*. London: Smith, Elder and Co.

Bonacossi D. M. 2002. Excavations at Khor Rohri: The 1997 and 1998 campaigns. Pages 29-69 in A. Avanzini (ed.), *Khor Rohri Report No. 1*. Pisa: Edizione Plus.

Carter J. 1982. *Tribes in Oman*. London: Peninsular Publishing.

Casson L. 1989. *The Periplus Maris Erythraei*. Princeton: University Press.

Costa P. 1981. The study of the city of Zafar (al-Balid). *Journal of Oman Studies* 5: 111-150.

Cremaschi M. & Negrino F. 2002. The frankincense road of Sumhuram: palaeoenvironmental and prehistorical background. Pages 325-363 in: Avanzini, A. (ed.), *Khor Rohri Report I*. Pisa: Edizioni Plus.

Cremaschi M. & Perego A. 2008. Patterns of land use and settlements in the surroundings of Sumhuram. Pages 563-607 in A. Avanzini (ed.), *Khor Rohri report no. 2*. Rome: Erma di Bretschnieder.

Doe B. 1970. *Socotra, an archaeological reconnaissance in 1967*. Coconut Grove, Florida: Henry Field.

Donner F. 1993. *The history of al-Tabari, vol. X. The conquest of Arabia, the Riddah Wars*. Albany, New York: SUNY Press.

Dostal W. 1967. *Die Beduinen in Sudarabien*. Wien: F. Berger and Sohne Horn.

Hardy-Guilbert C. 2004. Al Shihr, porte du Hadramawt sur l'ocean Indien. *Annales Islamologiques* 38: 95-157.

Hardy-Guilbert C. 2005. The harbour of al Shihr, Hadramawt, Yemen: sources and archaeological data on trade. *Proceedings of the Seminar for Arabian Studies* 35: 71-85.

Jamme A. 1962. *Sabaean inscriptions from Mahram Bilqis (Marib)*. Baltimore: The John Hopkins Press.

Jamme A. 1963. *The al-'Uqla Texts*. Documentation Sud-Arabe III. Washington D.C.: AFSM.

Janzen J. 1986. *Nomads in the Sultanate of Oman*. Boulder, CO: Westview Press.

Johnson D., Brown S.K., Phillips W. & Rempel S. 2007. *Excavations at Khor Mughsayl, Brigham Young University, 2007*. Salalah: file report.

Johnson D., Brown S.K., Glanzman W., Rempel S. & Gudrian G. 2008. *Excavations and survey around Khor Mughsayl, Brigham Young University, June-July 2008*. Salalah: file report.

Johnstone T. 1975. The modern South Arabic languages. *Afroasiatic Linguistics* 1/5: 93-121.

Lunde & Stone, see Mas'udi.

Major R.H. ed. 1857. *India in the fifteenth century*. London: Hakluyt Society.

Mas'udi [trans. Paul Lunde & Caroline Stone]. 2007. *From the meadows of gold and mines of precious gems*. [*Muruj al-dhahab wa ma'adin al-jawhar*]. London: Penguin.

McCorriston J. 2005. Roots of Agriculture (RASA) Project 2005: A season of excavation and survey in Wadi Sana, Hadramawt. *Bulletin of the American Institute for Yemeni Studies* 47: 23-28.

Ministry of Information, Oman. 1995. *Oman in History*. London: Immel Publishing.

Miller A. & Morris M. 1988. *Plants of Dhofar*. Edinburgh: Holmes McDougall Ltd.

Muhammed Ali M. 2002. *The Holy Qur'an*. Ohio, USA: Ahmadiyya Anjuman Isha'at Islam Lahore, Inc.

Muller W. 1991. Mahra. Pages 80-84 in the *Encyclopaedia of Islam*, Second Edition. Leiden: E.J. Brill.

Newton L. 2007. Al Qisha: archaeological investigations at an Islamic period Yemeni village. *Proceedings of the Seminar for Arabian Studies*, 37: 171-186.

Newton, L.S. and J. Zarins 2010. Preliminary results of the Dhofar archaeological survey. *Proceedings of the seminar for Arabian Studies* 40: in press.

Oman G. 1983. Preliminary epigraphic survey of Islamic material in Dhofar. *Journal of Oman Studies* 6/2: 277-289.

Oman G. 1989. Arabic-Islamic epigraphy in Dhofar in the Sultanate of Oman. Pages 193-198 in P. Costa & M. Tosi (eds), *Oman Studies*. Rome: Istituto Italiano per il Medio ed Estremo Oriente.

Peterson J. 2004. Oman's diverse society: southern Oman. *Middle East Journal* 58/2: 254-269.

Peutz N. 2008. Reorienting heritage: poetic exchanges between Suqutra and the Gulf. *Revue des Mondes Musulmans et de la Mediterranee* 121/122: 163-182.

Phillips W. 1972. *History and archaeology of Dhofar*. Unpublished Ph.D. thesis, University of Brussels. Faculty of Philosophy and Letters.

Pirenne J. 1990. Temoins ecrits de la region de Shabwa et l'histoire. Pages 95-120 in *Fouilles de Shabwa I*. BAH 134. Paris: Paul Geuthner.

Pliny, *Natural History,* (see Rackham, H. 1986).

Rackham H. 1986. *Pliny, natural history*. Volume IV, Libri XII-XVI. Cambridge, MA: Harvard University Press.

Rose J. & Petraglia M. 2009. Tracking the Origin and Evolution of Human Populations in Arabia. In J. Rose & M. Petraglia (eds), *The evolution of human *populations in Arabia: palaeoenvironments, prehistory and genetics*. New York: Springer.

Rougeulle A. 1999. Coastal settlements in Southern Yemen: the 1996-1997 survey expeditions on the Hadramawt and Mahra coasts. *Proceedings of the Seminar for Arabian Studies* 29: 123-136.

Rougeulle A. 2001. Notes on pre-and early Islamic harbors of Hadramawt (Yemen). *Proceedings of the Seminar for Arabian Studies* 31: 203-214.

Rougeulle A. 2008. A medieval trade entrepot at Khor Rohri? The study of the Islamic ceramics from Hamr al-Sharqiya. Pages 645-667 in A. Avanzini (ed.), *A Port in Arabia between Rome and the Indian Ocean (3rd c. BC-5th c. AD). Khor Rohri Report 2*. Rome: Erma di Bretschneider.

Sedov A. 1992. New archaeological and epigraphical material from Qana (South Arabia). *Arabian Archaeology and Epigraphy* 3/2:110-137.

Sedov A. 1993. Chapter 4. Archaeology of Socotra. Pages 84-134 in V. Naumkin (ed.), *Island of the Phoenix. An ethnographic study of the people of Socotra*. Ithaca: Cornell University Press.

Sedov A. 1995. Qana' (Yemen) and the Indian Ocean – the archaeological evidence. Pages 11-35 in J.-F. Salles & H. Ray (eds), *Tradition and archaeology, early maritime contacts in the Indian Ocean*. New Delhi: NISTADS.

Serjeant R. 1949. The cemeteries at Tarim (Hadramawt). *Le Museon* 62: 151-160.

Shahid I. 1979. Byzantium in South Arabia. *Dumbarton Oaks Papers* 33: 23-94.

Shahri Ali A. M. al- 1991. Grave types and 'triliths' in Dhofar. *Arabian Archaeology and Epigraphy* 2: 182-195.

Shahri Ali A. M. al- 1992. Dhofar tombs: fact or fiction? *PDO News* 3: 22-28.

Shahri Ali A. M. al- 2000. *The language of Ad*. Abu Dhabi: National packaging and printing.

Simeone-Senelle M.-Cl. 1997. The Modern South Arabian Languages. Pages 378-383 in R. Hetzron (ed.), *The Semitic Languages*. London: Routledge Kegan.

Smith G.R. 1985. Ibn al-Mujawir on Dhofar and Socotra. *Proceedings of the Seminar for Arabian Studies* 15: 79-92.

Smith G.R. 1995. Magic, jinn, and the supernatural in medieval Yemen: examples from Ibn Mujawir's $7^{th}/13^{th}$ century guide. *Quaderni di Studi Arabi* 13: 7-18.

Smith G.R. 2008. *A Traveler in thirteenth-century Arabia, Ibn al-Mujawir's Tarikh al-Mustabsir*. London: Hakluyt Society.

Tabuki S. 1982. Tribal structures in south Oman. Pages 51-56 in R. Serjeant & R.Bidwell (eds), *Arabian Studies* VI.

Tibbets G.R. translator. 1981. *Arab navigation in the Indian Ocean before the coming of the Portuguese. A translation of Ahmad b. Majid al-Najdi, Kitab Al-Fawa'id*. London: Royal Asiatic Society of Great Britain and Ireland.

Thomas B. 1929. Among some unknown tribes of south Arabia. *Journal of the Royal Anthropological Institute* 59: 97-111.

Thomas B. 1932. *Arabia felix. Across the Empty Quarter of Arabia*. New York: Charles Scribner's Sons.

Vogt B. 1994. A lost late Islamic port on the south Arabian coast. *Bulletin of Archaeology, The University of Kanazawa* 21: 137-158.

Wilkinson J.C. 1988. The Omani and Ibadhi background to the Kilwah Sirah: the demise of Oman as a political and religious force in the Indian Ocean in the $6^{th}/12^{th}$ century. Pages 131-148 in A. Irvine, R.B. Serjeant & G.R. Smith (eds), *A miscellany of Middle Eastern articles in memoriam of Thomas Muir Johnstone, 1924-83*. London: Longman.

Yule P., Franke K., Meyer C., Mebe G., Robin C. & Witzel C. 2008. *Zafar, capital of Himyar, Ibb province, Yemen*. Bonn: R. Habelt.

Zarins J. 1997. Persia and Dhofar: aspects of Iron Age international politics and trade. Pages 615-689 in G. Young, M. Chavalas & R. Averbeck (eds), *Crossing boundaries and linking horizons*. Bethesda, MD: CDL Press.

Zarins J. 2001. *The land of incense*. Muscat: Sultan Qaboos University.

Zarins J. 2007. Aspects of recent archaeological work at al-Baleed, Sultanate of Oman. *Proceedings of the Seminar for Arabian Studies* 37: 309-324.

Zohar M. 1992. Pastoralism and the spread of Semitic languages. Pages 165-180 in O. Bar-Yosef & A. Khazanov (eds), *Pastoralism in the Levant*. Madison: Prehistory Press, pp. 165-180.

Author's Address
Juris Zarins
Office of the Advisor to HM the Sultan for Cultural Affairs
P.O. Box 1, Al Hafa, Al-Baleed
PC 216, Salalah
Sultanate of Oman
email: dr.zarins@gmail.com

Burial contexts at Tayma, NW Arabia: archaeological and anthropological data

Sebastiano Lora, Emmanuele Petiti and Arnulf Hausleiter

Summary
The contribution presents the results of investigations on the burial ground of Tal'a, located some 2 km south of the ancient oasis of Tayma (Northwest Arabia). This cemetery, most probably to be dated to the mid-1st millennium BC, consists of stone cists, most of them rectangular, which can be attributed to two groups of collective burials (average MNI 5.3) of altogether 64 individuals. Preliminary palaeo-pathological analysis identified the individuals as belonging to one group, characterised by a number of epigenetical traits, certain degenerative diseases and occupational markers, probably caused by the environmental conditions in antiquity. Characteristic patterns of the distribution of grave goods have been identified at a number of juvenile/infant burials.

Keywords: Saudi Arabia, Tayma, Iron Age, graveyard, head injures, grave good distribution, physical anthropology

Introduction

Tayma is well known as a site of historical and archaeological interest, since it was one of the important locations on the so-called incense road connecting South Arabia, the Levant and Syro-Mesopotamia. Less known, though accessible through publications, is the significance of its burial grounds or cemeteries. Numerous graves occur mainly outside the walled 950 ha site, mostly in two shapes: cairns with built structures and stone cists clustering together. Some of these graves have been published in the journal ATLAL, such as those from the Industrial Site/Sana'iye (Abu Duruk 1996, al-Hajri 2006). Recently, results of archaeological investigations of the burial ground at Rujum Sa'sa' have been published (al-Hajri 2002; al-Hajri et al. 2005; al-Taimā'i 2006). A very general dating of the cairns to the 3rd/2nd millennia BC and of the stone cists to the late 2nd/early 1st millennia BC may be occasionally found in the literature, but it is by no means based on archaeological or stratigraphical evidence, nor on C14 dates. It seems that, in the case of the cairns, their round shape has been compared to the 3rd millennium BC burials in the eastern part of the Arabian Peninsula (al-Taimā'i 2006; cf. Steimer-Herbet 2004).

The work of the Saudi-German Joint archaeological project active at Tayma since 2004 is aimed at investigating the development of human occupation at the oasis through time (Eichmann et al. 2006; in press; Eichmann 2008a; Hausleiter 2006). So far, a total of six occupational periods has been identified through excavation and surface findings, focusing on the Bronze and Iron Ages and the Islamic period. In the framework of this project, well known sites with burial grounds have been re-visited and new locations with graves have been discovered. One of the latter is the site of Tal'a, located *extra muros* with no apparent direct connection to burial grounds already known, but generally located south of the area of Sana'iye. The necropolis at Tal'a has been attributed to Occupational Period 3 (Iron Age) based on several C14 dates covering a period from the 9th to 5th centuries BC (cf. Eichmann 2008b) and the occurrence of a characteristic painted pottery, dubbed Sana'iye Pottery by the Saudi archaeologists (al-Anizy 2005; Hashim 2007: 139-169).

Figure 1. Area O, general view of a part of the area showing three late 1st millennium BC graves in different phases of excavation, from west.

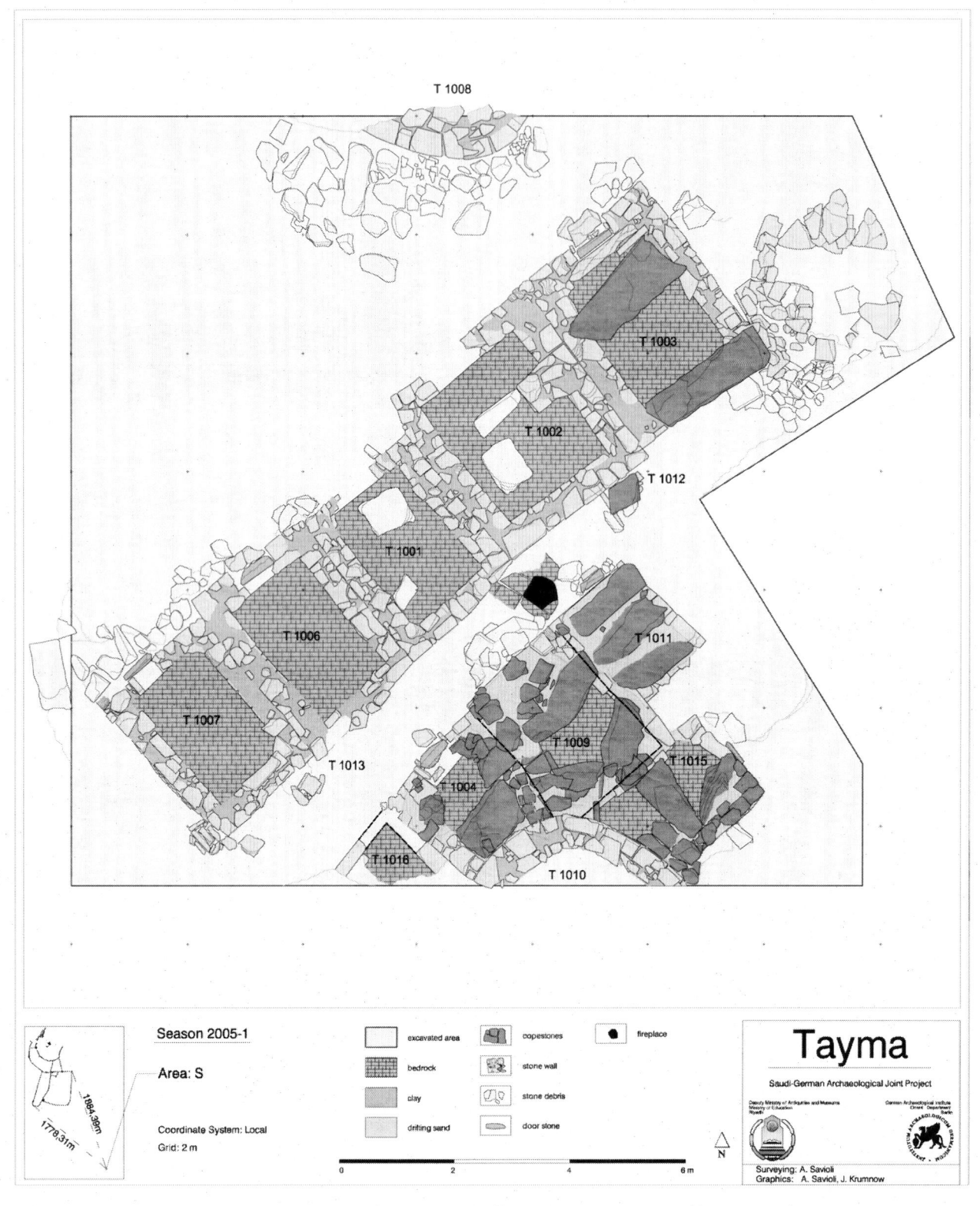

Figure 2. Plan of the Tal'a necropolis (Area S).

Also *within* the walls of Tayma new evidence for burials has come to light at three different locations. Firstly, possible cairns – looted and nowadays represented by accumulations of human bones at the surface – have been identified in 'Compound A' (Eichmann et al. 2006; cf. Bawden et al. 1980).

Secondly, between the outer and the inner walls, in a large area labelled 'Compound C' by Bawden et al. (1980), a cemetery has been found covering remains of at least one public building dating to the Early Iron Age (Area O of the Saudi-German excavations). According to C14 analysis it seems possible to date the cemetery in the last third of the 1st millennium BC, although dated objects have not yet been recovered from these graves. These

Figure 3. General view of grave T. 1006, showing the remains of an adult burial, on the left, from south-west.

graves were subsequently disturbed by looting activities, probably at a time around 500 AD, as suggested by a first series of optically stimulated luminescence (OSL) dates. So far, a total of eighteen graves (nine of them excavated) have been identified. They do not show a uniform orientation but exhibit a very similar construction technique: at first, a large pit was dug into existing deposits down to the natural bedrock which occurs at some 0.7 m below surface; thereafter, a smaller one, of about human size, was cut into the bedrock. The individual was laid down inside it and the pit was then covered with large stone blocks mortared with mud. In grave O-g3 one of the blocks was a re-used eye stele bearing an Aramaic inscription; a re-used stele with Aramaic inscription (but without eyes) also covered O-g11. Finally the large pit was refilled with soil (Fig. 1).

Thirdly, remains of several burials have been found at the surface next to the southern outer wall to which 'Compound A' was later added. In the vicinity, remains of occupation including several sherds of the so-called Qurayyah Painted Ware were discovered. At the present time, however, there is no connection between these architectonic remains and the burials.

Area S

The necropolis of Tal'a is located less than 2 kilometres to the south-east of the central archaeological site of Tayma, over the northern slope of a small hill, now a military area. A salvage excavation took place in autumn 2004 and spring 2005 in cooperation with the local administration to preserve the archaeological remains during the installation of public services.

In the area a total of 14 collective graves (T. 1001-1011, T. 1014-1016) and two individual graves (T. 1012-1013) has been brought to light and investigated (Fig. 2). Graves are grouped in two clusters, a northern one made of a single row of five NW-SE-oriented rectangular cists built in rough stone masonry. They were roofed by two or three large slabs, and an entrance, closed with a stone slab, is present on the northern side. All the graves are composed of a single chamber, apart from grave T. 1002 which is divided in two rooms by a 30 cm thick NE-SW-oriented wall. Two c 0.70 x 0.50 m single cists T. 1012-1013, each containing an individual infant burial are attached to the southern side of graves T. 1002 and T. 1007. Both the sides and the coverings were made of stone slabs. Only the individual grave T. 1012 was recovered intact and it will be discussed in detail below.

The southern cluster of graves, only partially investigated in spring 2005, is made of a central circular structure completely surrounded by at least five rectangular graves. They are similar to the northern ones for dimensions and building materials and technique. Heavy plundering activities disturbed the remaining exposed graves resulting in looting of grave goods, especially in the southern group, and in scattering of the human remains all around the surrounding area. A substantial layer (SU 402) of loose sand and fragmented bones, the result of the plundering, covered the structures. Graves were filled with sandy silt and commingled human remains in secondary deposition. Part of the chest and of the vertebral column of an adult burial was recovered in primary deposition in grave T. 1006; the body had been laid down directly on the bedrock (Fig. 3). Remains of a fireplace, external and, on general stratigraphic grounds, probably contemporary to the northern cluster of graves, have been radiocarbon dated to 762-412 cal BC (2 σ range) (Eichmann 2008b; Eichmann et al. in press).

Methods of Osteological Analysis

The osteological material is fragmented and characterized by deep surface erosions due to chemical and weathering factors, which are characteristic of arid/semiarid environments, such as in Tayma. The presence of longitudinal and transverse fragmentation, chromatic alteration (heterogeneous white-yellow colour) and depauperation of the bone tissues (weight and density loss) seems to indicate exposure to secondary cremation or post-depositional burning (Reverte Coma, 1985 and 1996). However, since warping, twisting and shrinking patterns are not present, the alterations observed are only superficial, as described by Asmussen (2009), and are the result of climatic conditions, as is the almost complete absence of teeth.

An anthropological analysis was carried out following Buikstra and Ubelaker's (1994) *Standards* for the recording of commingled human remains. The human remains were dry-cleaned and, when possible, restored with Plexol D in a 1:10 solution. The sample was catalogued and the Minimum Number of Individuals (MNI) was estimated for each grave. Age and sex were determined, when possible, from single diagnostic fragments. The presence of non-metrical traits and of markers of occupation stress (MOS) was also recorded. A preliminary paleopathological analysis was carried out on recorded evidence. Poor preservation status of the bones prevented the recording of anthropometrical data. An MS Access 2003 database was created to manage the collected data and a GIS system (made in ESRI ArcView 8.1) allowed the analysis of the spatial distribution of the human remains.

The osteological sample

The minimum number of individuals (MNI) has been estimated on the recurrence of the most represented bone element in each grave, resulting in a total of 64 individuals; 50 adults and 14 juveniles (Fig. 4). Excluding the incompletely investigated grave T. 1010 and the two single infant graves, which are not significant in this analysis, the data show a large variation of the MNI values in the two groups of burial structures. In the northern cluster of graves MNI values range from a minimum of at least 2 individuals in graves T. 1001 and T. 1003 to a maximum of at least 10 individuals in grave T. 1002. In the southern group the MNI range is narrower, from at least 4 individuals in grave T. 1004 to at least 9 in grave T. 1011. The mean value in the northern cluster is of at least 4.5 individuals/grave, in the southern of at least 7.3 individuals/grave while the global value is of at least 5.3 individuals/grave.

These data should be considered as an indication of the minimum number of individuals present in each grave since the plundering activities which targeted the graves in the past consistently removed an unknown portion of the osteological sample. The large span in the minimum/maximum MNI rating recorded in the northern and southern groups, and especially in the graves of the northern one, seems to be the result of looting, which hit one structure harder than the others, rather than a difference connected to the funerary practice or customs in the use of a specific grave. Furthermore, there seems to be no correspondence between dimensions or relative topographic position of the graves and the number of buried individuals. The largest grave T. 1002 (4.6 m^2) presents indeed the highest MNI (10), but smaller graves such as T. 1011 (1.3 m^2) and T. 1015 (0.9 m^2), show a close MNI (9) in a smaller burial space.

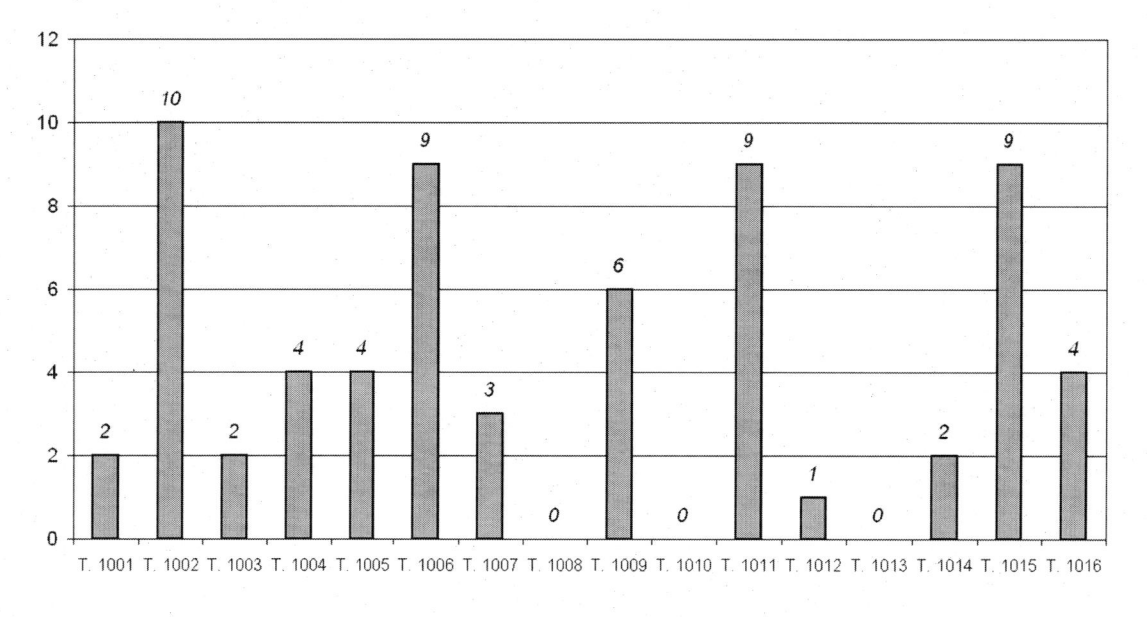

Figure 4. Chart of the minimum number of individuals (MNI) present in graves from Area S.

The poor state of preservation of the sample and the lack of complete individuals limited the analysis of sex and age class distribution to some general indications. The minimum number of males and females has been calculated taking into account both sex determination carried out on the diagnostic bone elements (skull and pelvis fragments mainly) in each grave and the MNI of each burial.

The most significant data come from graves with a high MNI. In graves T. 1002 and T. 1006 at least two males and two females were buried, while in graves T. 1011 and T. 1015 it was possible to identify at least three males and one female. In graves with fewer individuals, sex information lowers accordingly, with the exception of graves T. 1004 and T. 1007, where one male and one female and two males and one female respectively are present. The age of adult individuals was determined based on the analysis of the few preserved pubic symphyses. It was thus possible to identify one young adult male in grave T. 1007, two senile adult males (grave T. 1002) and two females (one in grave T. 1001 and one in grave T. 1005). One young adult of unknown sex was identified in grave T. 1004, one in grave T. 1006 and one senile adult in grave T. 1009.

Absence of teeth and lack of complete bones have restricted age determination in juvenile individuals to only recording the presence of non-adult specimens in each grave. Burial of juvenile individuals was not limited to the cists attached to the main structures (T. 1012 and T. 1013) but occurred also in most of the collective graves belonging to both groups. Presence of juvenile remains varies from grave to grave, ranging from a minimum of one individual (T. 1001, T. 1004, T. 1007, T. 1011 and T. 1016) to a maximum of 4 individuals (T. 1002) per grave. The presence of male, female and not adult individuals in most of the graves suggests that no distinction based on gender or age was made in the choice of the burial place. This seems to point towards a family-relationship-based use of the graves, where probably each unit owned its own funerary structure.

Tomb No.	Septal opening, Humerus			Os Trigonus, Talus			Double facet, Calcaneus		
	presence	total	occurrence	presence	total	occurrence	presence	total	occurrence
T. 1001									
T. 1002		2	0.0%	0	5	0.0%	5	7	71.4%
T. 1003									
T. 1004				1	2	50.0%			
T. 1005	2	3	66.7%						
T. 1006		3	0.0%	1	7	14.3%	2	3	66.7%
T. 1007	1	3	33.3%	1	8	12.5%	1	4	25.0%
T. 1008									
T. 1009	1	4	25.0%						
T. 1010									
T. 1011		5	0.0%	7	15	46.7%	7	11	63.6%
T. 1012									
T. 1013									
T. 1014		1	0.0%	0	2	0.0%	0	1	0.0%
T. 1015	5	12	41.7%	0	9	0.0%	1	5	20.0%
T. 1016				0	3	0.0%			
Total	9	33	27.3%	10	51	19.6%	16	31	51.6%

Table 1. The occurrence of non-metrical traits.

Epigenetic variation

On the assumption that the composition of the sample is not ideal for analysing epigenetic variations, relevant data have nevertheless been collected according to Buikstra and Uberlaker's (1994) *Standards*, with the aim of obtaining information on existing family-relationships between the individuals buried in each grave and within the whole group. Skull district variation data were not consistent and thus ignored. Therefore, the analysis focussed on the septal opening on the humerus, *Os Trigonus* on the talus, and the double facet of the calcaneus as the three most represented traits in this sample (Tab. 1).

It was possible to record the presence of the septal opening in the 27.3% (9 out of 33 cases) of the humeri where the diagnostic area was preserved. Most of the cases were recorded in grave T. 1015, where the trait was present in the 41.7% (5 out of 12 cases, 2 left and 3 right humeri) of the sample and in the at least 3 out of 7 (42.8%) humerus-based MNI. In the rest of the sample this trait is less represented, but it recurs in half of the graves where humeri are present, i.e. graves T. 1005 (66.7%, 2 out of 3), T. 1007 (33.3%, 1 out of 3) and T. 1009 (25%, 1 out of 4). It is completely absent in graves T. 1002 (0 out of 2), T. 1006 (0 out of 3) and T. 1011 (0 out of 5).

The presence of *Os Trigonus* was recorded in the 19.6% (10 out of 51 cases) of the tali where the observation of this trait was possible. It is attested mainly in grave T. 1011, which shows the highest rate of presence in the sample with 46.7% (7 out of 15 cases, 2 on left tali and 5 on right ones); in this burial, at least 5 individuals out of 7 show this trait. This trait is almost absent in the other graves, appearing only in T. 1004, T. 1006 and T. 1007 (one case each).

The presence of double facets of the calcaneus is the most frequently attested epigenetic trait, occurring in 51.6% of those bones where it was preserved. This trait is highly represented in grave T. 1002, where it has been recorded in 71.4% (5 out of 7 cases) of the sample and in at least 75.0% (on 3 of the 4 left calcanei on which the MNI is based) of the individuals. It also appears in grave T. 1006 in 66.7% of the sample (2 out of 3 cases; 2 out of 3 calcaneus-based MNI); grave T. 1011 in 63.3% of the sample(7 out of 11 cases; 5 out of 6 calcaneus-based MNI); grave T. 1007 in 25% of the sample (1 out of 4 recovered calcanei); and grave T. 1015 in 20% of the sample (1 out of 5). It is absent in grave T. 1014 (0 out of 1).

The discussion of these data considers the limits caused by the poor state of preservation of the sample, the lack of a closed context, the impossibility of recovering complete individuals and, consequently, the incomplete knowledge of the group composition. Septal opening shows a high ratio in T. 1015, while *Os Trigonus* is very frequent in T. 1011. In contrast, the presence of the double facets of the calcaneus is relevant in three graves: T. 1002, T. 1016 and T. 1011, both for the ratio and the absolute number of cases. It is significant also considering the whole group-pool, where it is present in more than half of the recorded sample. Of course, these data do not confirm the existence of family-relationships between individuals in graves with a high recurrence of a single trait, but the high recurrence of this set of traits in the studied sample remains remarkable. Also in the light of the group-composition, the data outline a homogeneous population which shares, at least, a narrow pool of epigenetic traits and which consists of a limited number of family units.

Fig. 5. General view of the infant burial in the individual cist grave T. 1012, from south east.

Grave T. 1012

The single infant grave T. 1012 is the only undisturbed burial found in Area S thus far. The well preserved skeleton was not affected by weathering and it has been recovered complete. The grave is a cist made of stone slabs where a 5 to 7-year-old child was buried. The skull has slightly shifted to the left; the right arm lies along the body, while the lower left arm is bent with the hand in the pelvic region; the legs are flexed (Fig. 5). Next to the right shoulder, two geometric painted beakers had been stacked, the upper one containing dark brown compact soil. Chemical analysis of the contents is still in progress but it is possible that the material was once connected to the funerary practice.

Grave No.	Juveniles	Beakers
T.1001	1	3
T.1002	4	
T.1003		
T.1004	1	
T.1005	1	
T.1006	2	4
T.1007	1	2
T.1008		
T.1009	2	
T.1010		1
T.1011	1	
T.1012	1	2
T.1013		
T.1014		
T.1015		
T.1016	1	

Table 2. Presence of juvenile individuals and beakers.

Similar complete, or almost complete beakers have also been recovered from three collective graves of the northern group: three beakers from T. 1001; four from T. 1006 (where one beaker also contains soil similar to the one in grave T. 1012); and two from T. 1007. In contrast, they are completely absent in the graves of the southern group. In the northern graves containing these beakers infant or juvenile individuals are also present with beaker to individual ratio of two to one (Tab. 2): at least one infant in grave T. 1001, two infants in grave T. 1006, and one infant in grave T. 1007 (Fig. 6).

In the light of the context of grave T. 1012, we should then suppose a connection between this kind of beaker and the infant funerary practice. In grave T. 1001, in grave T. 1002 and in the graves of the southern cluster this association is not confirmed due to the lack of complete beakers, while infants are present. Even if it is probable that the lack of beakers was caused by plundering activities, which seem to have been more systematic in this group of graves, we cannot exclude other hypotheses, such as a change in funerary practice or a difference in customs between the two groups.

Other grave goods from the collective graves in secondary deposition include: a complete terracotta figurine of a camel (*dromedarius*) from grave T. 1003 (cf. Jantzen 2009); a partially fragmented bronze blade from grave T. 1006; elements of personal jewellery, such as beads made of glass-paste from graves T. 1001 (2), T. 1006 (3), T. 1007 (1), and two rings made of shell, one from grave T. 1006 and one from grave T. 1007. Lack of primary deposition context and of the direct connection between the objects and a specific individual prevent us from identifying any patterns of ancient funerary customs. As similar objects are not present in juvenile burial T. 1012, we can suppose they should be connected to the burials of the adult members of the group.

Preliminary paleopathology

"Anthropologists often obtain data on health, disease and death from ancient populations, using the methods of paleopathology, the study of ancient disease. By looking at populations in different environments over time we may be able to gain insights into the long-term relationships of human biology, culture and disease" (Grmek 1989: 5).

Based on a significant sample, paleopathological methods can help to provide important information about life and health status of ancient populations; in fact, in a global perspective, there is a tight connection between environment, material production, biological traits (sex ratio, stature and also life-style and diseases, among others) and, finally, culture. This methodological approach leads to two orders of programmatic questions; the first regarding the biological structure of this population, and the second regarding their main adaptive strategies.

The *post-mortem* changes on the bone surface and structure can, in fact, feign new bone proliferation and resorption linkable to pathological status during the life of the individual, especially when the skeletal remains are poorly preserved. Additionally, the lack of complete individuals and the forced limits in the excavation of the graves imply that the sample is not fully representative of a complete population. However, this preliminary paleopathological analysis was necessary in order to generate initial data on the health status of the Iron Age human group which chose Tal'a as their burial ground, to develop some preliminary hypotheses and, especially, to plan further investigations in the area.

Three different classes of pathological indicators have been sampled: degenerative, traumatic and non-specific indicators. The degenerative diseases are pathologies of the articular joints, connected both to physical stress factors and physiological aging process of the individuals. Even if the evidence is not consistent for a statistical approach, 42 indicators of DJD (degenerative joint disease) were recorded. Most of them (75%) affected the column (spondiloarthritis), 18% the lower limbs, and a very low percentage (11%) the upper limbs. In general, most of these pathological signs seem to be due to age-related diseases. Even supposing that post-

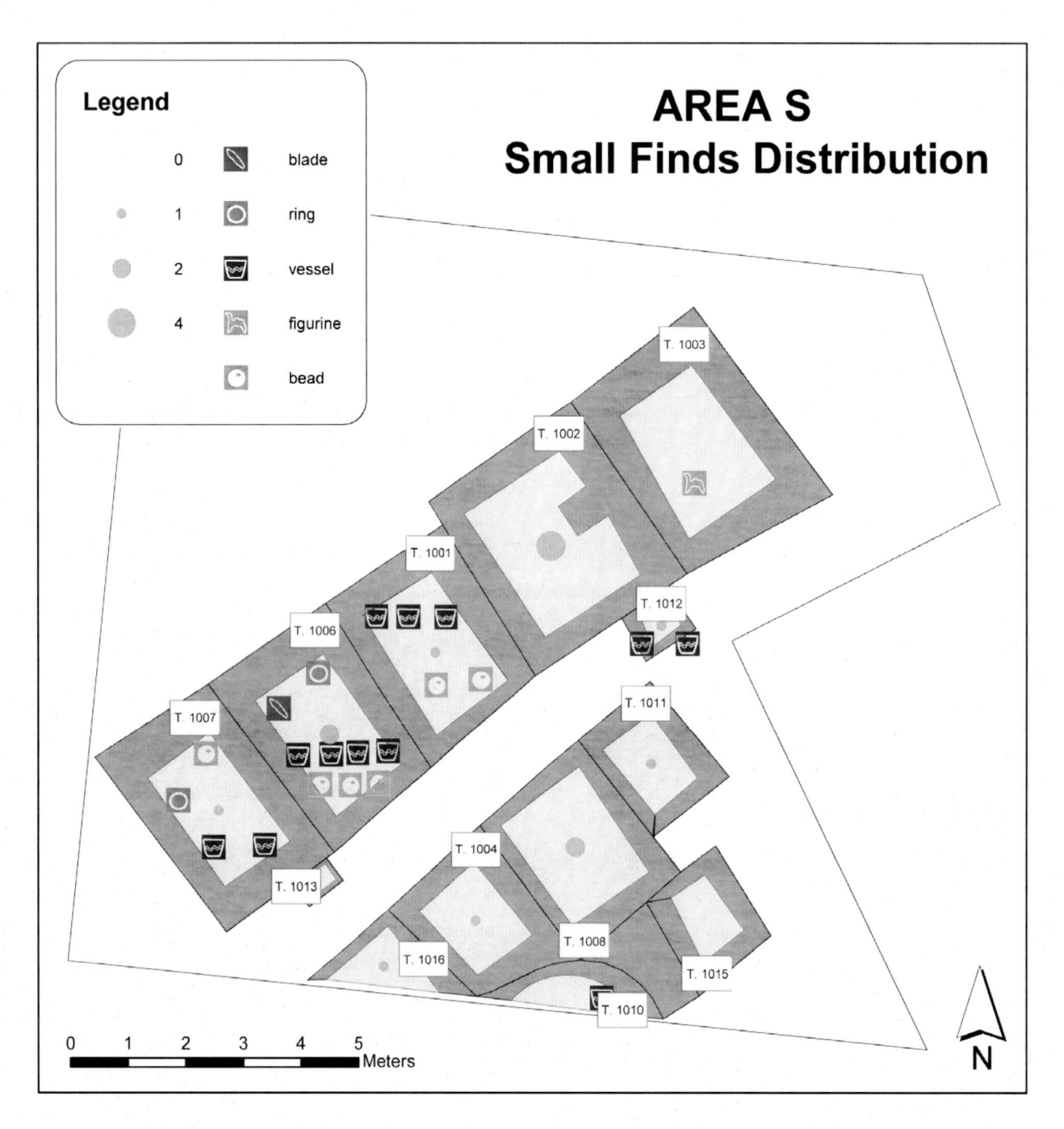

Figure 6. Distribution of minimum number of juvenile individuals and grave goods.

depositional factors played an important role, there is evidence for heavy and, probably, continual working activities related to a strong use of the column and of the lower limbs (to walk or to ride for long distances, for example).

It will be very important to correlate the evidence of osteoarthritis with the occupational markers, and with the activities-induced changes on the bone surface due to the different workload on specific muscles during the life of individuals (Angel 1982). Nevertheless, so far no statistical significance emerges from the analysis of MOS (markers of occupational status), as enthesopathies are present on just 0.7% of all the bones.

The non-specific indicators (bone-resorption or formation of new bone) outline an "abnormal" situation in the physiological equilibrium of the individual, caused by the presence of a non-identified pathological agent or stress factor. *Cribra orbitalia*, *cribra cranii* and *cribra palatalia* (irregularities on the bone surface of the frontal bone, the vault and the maxilla) were recorded in 6 individuals. The frequent absence of the cranial district prevented a statistical approach, but five different individuals, in four different graves, show traces of *cribra orbitalia* or *cribra palatalia*, while the last one shows contemporary evidence of *cribra cranii* and *cribra orbitalia*.

An etiological investigation should consider the following factors as possibly responsible for these three types of *cribra*: genetic disease (emolithic congenital anaemia), poor nutritional status (sideropenic anaemia and anaemic-like diseases), or bad hygienic conditions, with parasitic infestation (e.g. by Parelminthes, etc.). Further anthropological and palaeoecological investigations are needed to narrow the diagnosis from the recorded evidence.

Traumatic diseases have been identified in five cases. Apart from a poorly preserved healed trauma near the distal epiphysis of a right radium in grave T. 1009, all the traumas (1 from T. 1006, 2 from T. 1011, and 1 from T. 1016) are located on the skull district. A healed, rounded-shaped blunt trauma has been identified on a bone fragment of left parietal, near the bregmatic area, from grave T. 1011. A second healed blunt trauma, of a more elongated shape, has been recovered again on a bone fragment of left parietal, near the lambda, from grave T. 1016. Both were probably inflicted by a blow from a stick, cudgel, or similar object, according to the most common standards in paleopathological and forensic diagnostics. These traumas can lead us to suppose the existence of events of interpersonal violence, caused probably by right-handed aggressors. In fact, the presence of cranial trauma on the left side of the vault "fits the expected pattern of injury sustained by a weapon held by a right-handed person during a face-to-face encounter" (Larsen 1999: 144).

Figure 7. Healed piercing trauma on a parietal bone of unknown side from grave T. 1011.

A circular healed trauma with a 2 mm diameter has been identified on a right parietal from grave T. 1011, probably caused by the hard impact of a small pointed object, such as an arrow. The strike location, on the top area of the calvarium, is consistent with the flight pf an arrow coming from above with a parabolic trajectory (Fig. 7). In all these cases, X-Ray analysis confirmed the pathological diagnosis. Around the injuries, some new bone tissue had healed long time before death in all the three bone elements, although traces of infective processes were still present.

Fig. 8. Partially healed blunt trauma on two fragments of a parietal bone of unknown side from grave T. 1006.

The last case is a trauma on two un-restorable fragments of a parietal bone from grave T. 1006. The injury is circular or elliptical, with a maximum diameter of c. 5 cm and is located next to the lambda. Unlike the others, the trauma is only partially healed, as slight bone reactions are visible on the blunt edges (Fig. 8). The presence of new bone formation could indicate that this individual survived the traumatic event, probably helped by some kind of basic surgical intervention, such as the cleaning of the injured area. Nevertheless, the trauma proved too severe and the individual died no more than days after sustaining it.

This evidence, although unique, is very important both as remarkable paleopathological evidence and as a striking episode of interpersonal violence which caused the death of one of the members of the group. We may then assume that the presence of these kinds of traumatic lesions means that some members of the group buried at Tal'a necropolis were exposed, during their life, to episodes of interpersonal violence, sometimes fatal.

Conclusions

Even though looting activities in the past and the consequent poor preservation status both of commingled human remains and of the archaeological context of Tal'a necropolis limited the data collection, a first analysis on the funerary practices and on the composition of human group has been carried out. The structure of the graves and the contemporary presence of both genders and of adult and juvenile individuals suggest a use of the single graves based on familial units. The results of the analysis of epigenetic traits do not contradict this hypothesis. The comparison of the distribution of one class of grave goods and anthropological data outlines the important role of these objects in the funerary practice, in particular for juvenile burials.

Significant recurrence of MOS on the vertebral column and on the lower limbs suggests functional loads probably connected to human mobility rather than specific work activities. However, a wider osteological sample and a deeper knowledge of the local economic framework are fundamental for a more precise understanding of physical occupational patterns in the area.

Evidence of various kinds of *cribra* attests that the human group was probably affected by environment-related diseases, but more data and further multidisciplinary investigations are needed since the information gathered thus far is not sufficient to reconstruct the general health status of the population. The high rate of trauma on the skull seems to indicate that interpersonal violence episodes may have occurred, even though it was not possible to identify any specific martial weapon. Lack of information on the sex and age of the people who sustained the injuries prevents us from describing possible violence patterns in the group.

In conclusion, apart from the context limits, information collected by the archaeological and anthropological analysis describe human remains from Tal'a as a homogeneous group with a codified funerary practice in which family relationships probably played an important role. Hopefully, this analysis will represent the foundation for further investigations in the area in order to collect a better preserved sample and to improve the knowledge of the human groups that lived in Tayma in the past.

Acknowledgments

The authors are indebted to the Saudi Commission for Tourism and Antiquities, Riyadh, the German Archaeological Institute, Orient-Department, Berlin, for general support and to the German Research Foundation (Deutsche Forschungsgemeinschaft) for funding the research project at Tayma. Radiocarbon analysis was carried out by the Leibniz laboratory of Kiel University; OSL analysis was provided by Helmut Brückner and colleagues, Marburg University, Faculty of Geography. Further thanks go to Ricardo Eichmann and Andrea Intilia for discussion.

References

Abu Duruk H.I. 1986. *Introduction to the Archaeology of Tayma*. Riyadh: Department of Antiquities and Museums.
Abu Duruk H.I. 1989. A preliminary report on the Industrial Site excavation at Tayma, first season 1408 AH/1987 AD. *ATLAL* 12: 9-19 [Arabic version: pp. 9-24].
Abu Duruk H.I. 1990. A preliminary report on Industrial Site excavations at Tayma, second season 1410 AH/1989 AD. *ATLAL* 13: 9-19 [Arabic version: 9-21].
Abu Duruk H.I. 1996. A preliminary report on the Industrial Site excavation at Tayma, third season 1411 AH/1990 AD. *ATLAL* 14: 11-24 [Arabic version: 11-22].
Al-Anizy M. 2005. *Painted pottery from the tombs at Sana'iye*. Riyadh: King Saud University [MA thesis] [in Arabic].
Al-Ansary A. & Abu al-Hasan H. 2002. *Tayma. Crossroads of Civilizations*. Riyadh: Dar al-Qawafil.
Buhl F. & Bosworth C.E. 1999. Taymā'. Pages 430-431 in *The Encyclopedia of Islam*. (2nd edition). i. Leiden: Brill.
Angel J.L. 1982. "Osteoarthritis and occupation (ancient and modern). Pages 443-446 in Novotný V.V. (ed), *Proceedings of the II Anthropological Congress dedicated to Dr. Aleš Hrdlička, held in Prague and Humpolec, September 3–7, 1979*. Prague: Universitas Carolina Pragensis.
Asmussen B. 2009. Intentional or incidental thermal modification? Analysing site occupation via burned bone. *Journal of Archaeological Science* 36: 528-536.
Aufderheide A.C. & Rodriguez Martin C. 1998. *Cambridge Encyclopedia of Human Paleopathology*. Cambridge: Cambridge University Press.
Bawden G., Edens C. & Miller R. 1980. Preliminary archaeological investigations at Tayma. *ATLAL* 4: 69-106.
Bergeron R.T. & Rumbagh C.L. 1971. Skull Trauma. Pages: i:763-818 in Newton T.H. & Potts D.G. (eds), *Radiology of the Skull and Brain: The Skull*. (Volume 1). St Louis: Mosby.
Berrymann H.E. & Haun S.J. 1996. Applying forensic techniques to interpret cranial fracture patterns in archaeological specimen. *International Journal of Osteoarchaeology* 6: 2-9.
Buikstra J.E. & Ubelaker D.H. (eds) 1994. *Standards for Data Collection from Human Skeletal Remains, Proceedings of a Seminar at The Field Museum of Natural History*. (Arkansas Archeological Survey Research Series, 44). Fayetteville: Arkansas Archaeological Survey.
Campillo D. 1988. Herniated intervertebral lumbar disks in an individual from Roman era, exhumation from the 'Quinta de San Rafael' (Terragona, Spain). *Journal of Paleopathology* 2: 88-94.
Campillo D. 1993. *Paleopatologia: los primeros vestigios de las enfermedad*. (Primera parte). Barcelona: Fundaciòn Uriach 1838
Campillo D. 1994-1995. *Paleopatologia: los primeros vestigios de las enfermedad*. (Segunda parte). Barcelona: Fundaciòn Uriach 1838
Capasso L., Kennedy K.A.R. & Wilczak C.A. 1999. *Atlas of occupational markers on human remains*. Teramo: Edigrafital.
Eichmann R. 2008*a*. Tayma - Oasis and trade center on the frankincense caravan route. *Adumatu* 17: 17-26.
Eichmann R. 2008*b*. Archaeological evidence of the pre-Islamic period (4th to 6th cent. AD) at Tayma. Pages

55-69 in Robin C. & Schiettecatte J. (eds), *L'Arabie à la veille de l'Islam*. Paris: De Boccard.

Eichmann R., Hausleiter A., al-Najem M. & al-Said S. 2006. Tayma - Spring 2004. Report on the Joint Saudi-Arabian-German archaeological project. *ATLAL* 19: 91-116 [Arabic version:191-216].

Eichmann R., Hausleiter A., al-Najem M. & al-Said S. In press. Tayma – Autumn 2004 and Spring 2005. 2nd Report on the Saudi-German Joint Archaeological Project. *ATLAL* 20.

Eichmann R., Schaudig H. & Hausleiter A. 2006. Archaeology and Epigraphy at Tayma, Northwest-Arabia. *Arabian Archaeology and Epigraphy*. 17: 163-176.

Fornaciari G., Mallegni F., Bertini D. & Nuti V. 1981. Cribra Orbitalia and Elemental Bone Iron in the Punics of Carthage. *Ossa*. 8: 63-77.

Grmek M. 1989. *Diseases in the Ancient Greek World*. Baltimore/London: Johns Hopkins University Press.

Grmek M. 1994. *Les maladies à l'aube de la civilisation occidentale*. Paris: Payot.

al-Hajri M. 2002. Tayma excavation, Rujoum Sasa, first season 1418. *ATLAL* 17: 23-25 [Arabic version: 43-67].

2006. Brief preliminary report on the excavations at the Industrial Site in Tayma. *ATLAL* 19: 21-26 [Arabic version: 49-82].

Al-Hajri, M., al-Mutlaq M., Hashim A., al-Shaman S., al-Najam S., al-Helwa S. & al-Radhiyan S.

2005. Archaeological excavations on the site of Rujoom Sa´sa´ - Tayma (second season 1421 AH/2000 AD). *ATLAL* 18: 23-27 [Arabic version: 55-67].

Hausleiter A. 2006. Tayma, North-West Arabia. The context of archaeological research. Pages 160-182 in Gong Y. & Chen Y. (eds), *Collection of papers on Ancient Civilizations of Western Asia, Asia Minor and North Africa*. [Special Issue of Oriental Studies] Beijing: Peking University.

Hengen O.P. 1971. Cribra orbitalia: Pathogenesis and probable etiology. *Homo* 22: 57-75.

Jantzen H. 2009. *Eisenzeitliche Dromedarterrakotten aus Tayma in Nordwestarabien. Attributanalyse und Implikationen für die Oasensiedlung Tayma*. Unpublished MA Thesis, Freie Universität Berlin.

Knight B. 1991. *Forensic Pathology*. Oxford: Oxford University Press.

Manchester K. 1983. *The Archaeology of Disease*, Bradford: Bradford University Press.

Larsen C. S. 1999. *Bioarchaeology: interpreting behaviour from the human skeleton*. Cambridge: Cambridge University Press.

Ortner D. J. 2003. *Identification of pathological conditions in human skeletal remains*. Washington: Academic Press.

Parr P.J. 1997. Tayma. Pages 160-161 in Meyers E.M. (ed), *The Oxford Encyclopaedia of Archaeology in the Near East* vol. V. New York/Oxford: Oxford University Press.

Reverte Coma J.M. 1985. *Tecnica del estudio de las cremaciones*. Madrid: Universidad Complutense.

Reverte Coma J.M. 1996. Estudio de las cremaciones. Pages 31-39 in Villalaìn Blanco J.D., Gòmez Bellard C. & Gòmez Bellard F. (eds), *Actas del II Congreso Nacional de Paleopatologìa*. Valencia: Asociacìon Española de Paleopatologìa.

Roberts J. & Manchester K. 1995. *The archaeology of diseases*. Ithaca, NY: Cornell University Press.

Robledo B., Trancho G.J. & Brothwell D. 1995. Cribra orbitalia: health indicator in the late Roman population of Cannington (Sommerset, Great Britain). *Journal of Paleopathology*, 7: 185-193.

Steimer-Herbet T. 2004. *Classification des sépultures à superstructure lithique dans le Levant et l'Arabie occidentale (IV e et III e millénaires avant J.-C.)*. (British Archaeological Reports International Series, 1246). Oxford: Archaeopress.

Wells C. 1967. Pseudopathology. Pages 5-19 in Brothwell D & Sandison A.T. (eds), *Diseases in Antiquity: A Survey of Diseases, Injuries and Surgery of Early Populations*. Springfield, Illinois: Charles C. Turner.

Authors' Addresses

Dr. phil. Sebastiano Lora
Deutsches Archäologische Institut Orient-Abteilung
Podbielskiallee 69-71
14195 Berlin, Germany
sl@orient.dainst.de

M.A. Emmanuele Petiti
Department of Evolutionary Biology
Laboratory of Anthropology
University of Florence
via del Proconsolo 12
50122, Firenze, IT
emmanuele.petiti@gmail.com

Dr. phil. Arnulf Hausleiter
Deutsches Archäologische Institut Orient-Abteilung
Podbielskiallee 69-71
14195 Berlin, Germany
arh@dainst.de

Feasting with the dead: funerary marzeaḥ in Petra

Isabelle Sachet[1]

Summary

Funeral banquets in Petra are evidenced primarily by archaeological remains. The many banquet halls in the Necropolis of Petra reflect a common practice in the Nabataean capital. These rooms can be associated with a series of tombs or they may be dedicated to one monumental tomb in particular, especially in the case of a funerary complex. The banquet halls are mostly rock-cut rooms with arrangements generally well preserved. Inside the room, the benches for guests differentiate the banquet room from any other type of room. Other arrangements are also sometimes visible inside the banquet hall: graves (*loculi*) or simple niches, designed to house a statue. The study of these installations and their location inside the banquet hall provides information on the organization of banquets and even the guests who were being honoured, whether a living person, a deceased person or a deity.

Keywords: Nabataean, Petra, banquet, funerary practices.

Introduction

Banquets in Classical Antiquity have been a widespread theme in Mediterranean historical research and several studies have been published discussing the topic in the Greek and Roman worlds (Donahue 2004; Murray 1994; Nielsen I. & Nielsen H.S. 1998; Scheid 1985; Slater 1991). Unfortunately, studies regarding ancient meals in the Near East area are not so numerous (see Alster 1980), especially concerning the classical periods (Dentzer 1982).

The Nabataeans had their own banqueting tradition, probably of nomadic origin, mixed with Hellenistic and Mediterranean tradition. Nabataean meals are described by ancient authors but those testimonies only concern royal banquets. Nabataean epigraphy also gives evidence for *marzeaḥ*, or banquets, but neither the texts nor the inscriptions describe a meal in a funerary context. Starting with the same idea, Dennis Pardee recently reconsidered banquets in the Ugaritic inscriptions and he was not able to recognize a general tradition of funerary meals in Ugarit. In fact, only one text mentions a funerary meal and this text is associated with the funeral of a king of Ugarit (Pardee 1996). In the Bible too, the term *mrzḥ* appears only twice, in *Amos* 6,7 and in *Jeremy* 16,5. The study of the various drafting stages allows Virginie Alavoine to state that the *mrzḥ* was not explicitly used in the Old Testament to designate a funerary meal (Alavoine 2000).

In Petra, the existence of funerary meals is, however, attested by archaeological remains. Banquet rooms are numerous in the city: one hundred and eleven rock-cut triclinia are known in Petra and twenty-five of them, i.e. nearly one quarter at the total, are in a funerary context (Tarrier 1995; Tarrier 1988: 99, corpus based on Dalman 1908). We will examine some of the banquet rooms cut in the necropolises of the city and we will try to determine what ceremonies were held there and who took part in those ceremonies for the dead.

Literature and epigraphy

The testimonies of ancient writers provide information on the banquets in Nabataea. These descriptions always come from a source outside the Nabataean world and they do not describe an ordinary banquet but a royal banquet in conjunction with diplomatic activity. There is, unfortunately, no Nabataean literature, and Nabataean epigraphy also gives few details on the participants in these banquets.

Literary sources and the royal Nabataean banquet

The munificence and characteristics of Nabataean banquets have been described by non-Nabataean authors from all around the Mediterranean. Ancient sources consistently describe banquets organized by Nabatean rulers as "orgies of luxury". In fact, these banquets were held for a diplomatic purpose; they were intended to honour dignitaries and to demonstrate the power of the Nabataean hosts.

Strabo (c. 63 BC-21/25 AD), a Greek geographer and historian who travelled with Aelius Gallus in the Near East, described a drinking ritual taking place in Nabataea. According to him, the royal Nabataean banquet, or *symposium*, was a common meal for several groups of thirteen people invited by the king, with festivities including musicians and a drinking ritual (*Geographica* 16.4.26). A particular attitude of the Nabataean king is quoted by Strabo who seems to find it unusual for a monarch. Sometimes, the Nabataean king himself served the rest of the group. That attitude prompted Strabo to say that the monarch was particularly close to the people, δημοτικός. Although the ancient Greek banquet had a tradition of equality among the guests too (Dunbabin 1998: 90-98), the somewhat surprising statement from Strabo indicates that this tradition was lost in the Greek world at the end of the 1st century BC. The position of the king during a banquet was then to be served and not to serve his guests.

From another point of view, Tacitus (ca. 55-ca. 120), senator and Roman historian, focused on the wealth of the Nabataean monarchs when he described a specific banquet taking place in 18 AD. Germanicus (15-19 AD),

---

[1] I would like to thank Laurent Tholbecq for his remarks and Zbigniew Fiema who kindly read and corrected my English; any remaining mistakes are my own.

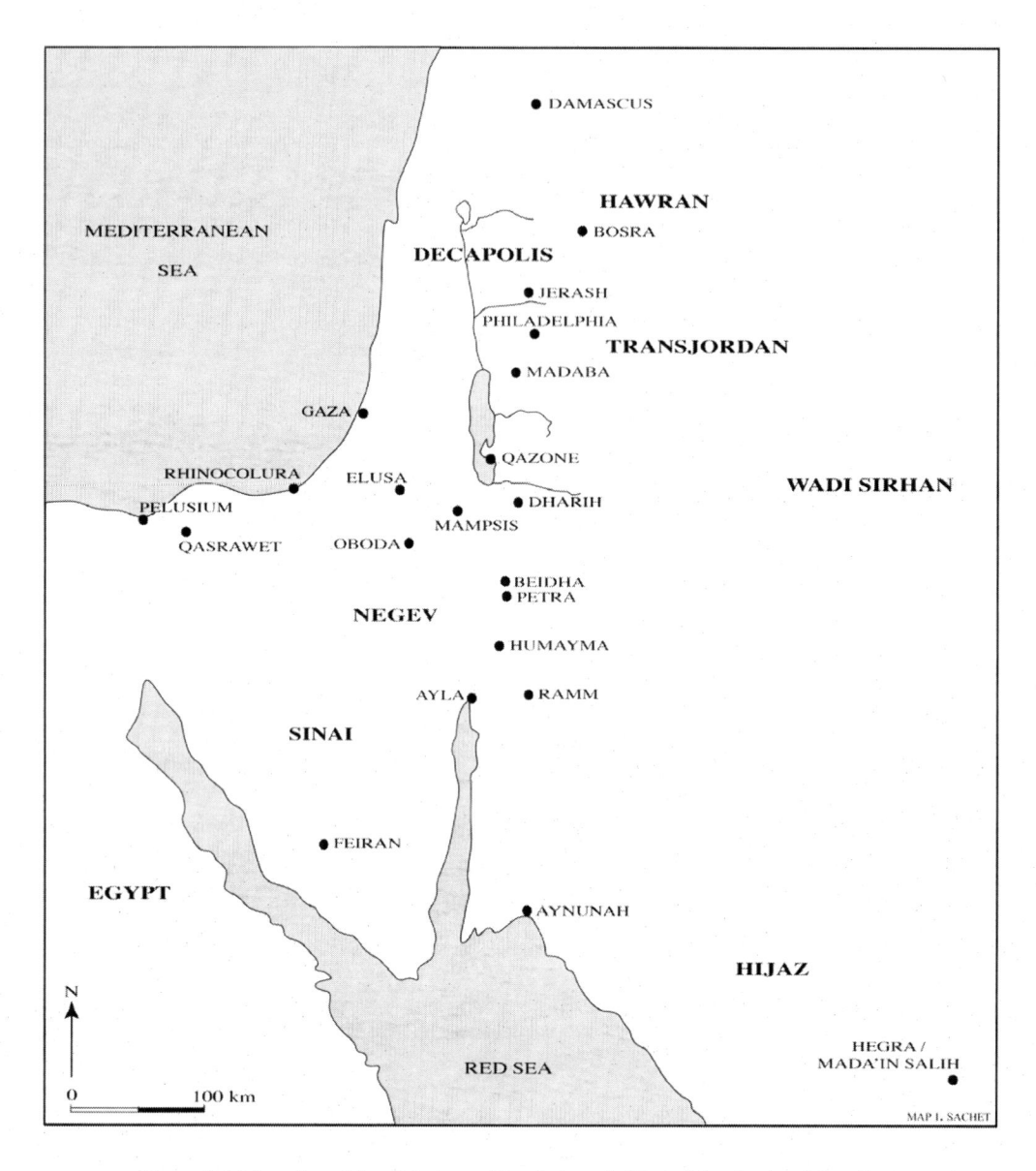

Figure 1. Major sites of the Nabataean Kingdom and cities of the Ancient Near East.

Tiberius' adopted son, and his wife Agrippina, were invited by Aretas IV (9 BC-40 AD), king of the Nabateans. The splendour of the ceremony and the heavy golden crowns offered by Aretas to Germanicus aroused the jealousy of Piso, the governor of Syria, who received a lighter crown, and made a long speech against luxury.[2] The offerings of golden crowns were traditional in Greek ceremonies (Hackl, Jenni & Schneider 2003: 619), but they were far from Roman customs. The Nabataean king was following a ceremonial tradition unfamiliar to the Romans at the beginning of the 1st c. AD, who were still influenced by Republican values and reluctant to accept excessive demonstrations and wealth.

Royal Nabataean banquets were sumptuous, and valuable gifts were offered to the guests. However, the king was not in any higher position than his guests as he was taking part in the ceremony and he even served his guests sometimes. Depending which classical author is cited, it is interesting to note what he considers the most remarkable in the Nabataean banquet. The Greek historian Strabo seems to be most struck by the fact that the Nabataean king himself serves its guests, which must be unthinkable in the Greek custom at the end of the 1st century BC. Tacitus, the Roman historian, is shocked by the luxury of the ceremony, especially the offering of golden crowns for guests, a custom probably of Greek origin but still unusual in the eyes of the Romans.

Epigraphic sources

Nabataean *symposia* are mainly described by historical sources from the perspective of an outsider. Written sources from the Nabatean kingdom are only epigraphic, but some inscriptions carved by Nabataeans in the mountains around Petra provide additional information on banquets and their participants.

An inscription from Beida (Fig. 1), 5 km to the North of Petra, dated to the first half of the 1st century AD, mentions a person named Ganamu, who is *rb mrzḥ*, chief

---

[2] "(…) abiecitque simul coronam et multa in luxum addidit", *Annals* 2, 57, 4.

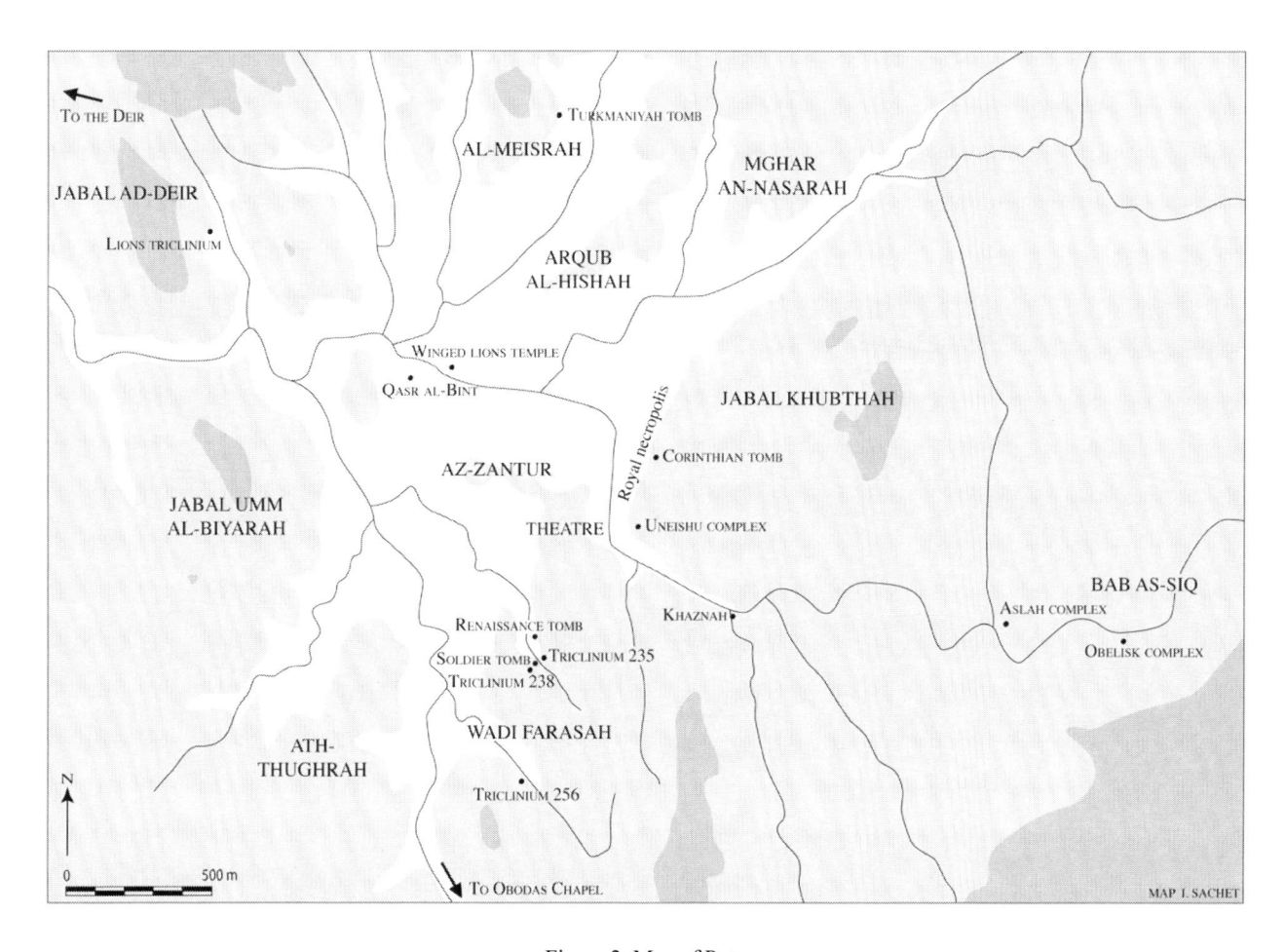

Figure 2. Map of Petra
(Turkmaniyah, Deir, Obodas Chapel, Khaznah, Corinthian Tomb, Lions triclinium, Aslah triclinium, Wadi Farasah East/West).

of the *marzeaḥ*, or *symposiarch* (Zayadine 1976). The inscription may refer both to a worship organization and to its main participant, the chief of the *symposium*. The *marzeaḥ* is the usual word to designate the cultic meals in Semitic inscriptions, for example in Palmyra (Milik 1972: 149). The members of the Nabataean *marzeaḥ* were *bny mrzḥ*, so named in another inscription from Oboda in the Negev, commemorating a gift from the association of the *marzeaḥ* of the god Dushara (Negev 1963: 113-117).

Another Nabataean inscription written on the cliff near the Deir monument (Fig. 2) mentions a banquet: *dkyr ʿbydw br wqyhʾl wḥbrwhy mrzḥ ʿbdt ʾlhʾ*, "In memoriam ʿObaidu, son of Waqyhʾel and his companions from the *marzeaḥ* of the God ʿObodat" (RES 1423, revised by Savignac 1913: 440). Scholars sometimes assumed that the inscription refers to a funerary meal (Niehr 1998: 228), perhaps on the assumption that the named god Obodas was the dead deified king Obodas III. As a matter of fact, nothing indicates that the members of the *marzeaḥ* mentioned in the Deir inscription were attending a funerary meal. The term *dkr*, to remember, is often seen in *graffiti*, engraved by people who wrote their names in a particular place, especially along caravan roads, to indicate that they stopped at the place (Cantineau 1932: 82). The words *slm* or *dkyr* were indifferently used by the travellers before their signatures, as attested by many inscriptions (*CIS* II, 2.1). *Dkyr* does not specifically refer to the memory of a dead person.

Consequently, there is no indication in Nabataean epigraphy of a specific use of the word *mrzḥ* in a funerary context, but this does not mean that there is no evidence in Nabataean inscriptions for funerary meals. Actually, a banquet room, *smkʾ*, is mentioned in the funerary inscription of the Turkmaniyah tomb in Mʿeisrah necropolis in Petra as part of the installations built inside the funerary complex (Fig. 2). The whole complex of the Turkmaniyah tomb, including the banquet room, is sacred and placed under the protection of the god Dushara: *qbrʾ dnh wṣryḥʾ rbʾ dy bh (...) wgnt smkʾ (...) wšʾryt klʾ ṣlʾdy bʾtryʾ ʾlh ḥrm wḥrg dwṣrʾ (...)*, "This tomb and the large burial chamber within it (...) and triclinium-garden (?) (...) and all the rest of the property which is in these places are sacred and dedicated to Dushara (...)" (Healey 1993: 238-239).

The word *smkʾ* is attested in other Semitic languages. For example, in Syriac, it means "couch, banquet". In the Turkmaniyah inscription, the term *smkʾ* is associated with *gnt*, meaning "garden" in Aramaic. J. Healey proposed to translate the term *gnt smkʾ* as "triclinium-garden", possibly a garden for reclining (Healey 1993: 240). In architectural terms, a triclinium-garden was an open air banquet room, certainly unroofed. Consequently, the *gnt smkʾ* of the Turkmaniyah complex was most likely an "hypaethral triclinium" built in a garden, meaning an outside banquet room dedicated to the funerary ceremonies. Hypaethral triclinia were common in Nabataean religious contexts. The most spectacular of them was cut at the top of the Madhbaḥ mountain, dominating the city of Petra (Augé & Dentzer 1999: 80-81). During his recent excavations in the Obodas Chapel, Laurent Tholbecq discovered a new open air triclinium built in front of the rock-cut triclinium of the Obodas sanctuary (Fig. 2) (Tholbecq & Durand 2005: 303, fig. 11 ; Tholbecq, Durand & Bouchaud 2008: 238-240, fig. 6). In the Turkmaniyah complex, the banquet room was, unfortunately, not preserved. Other funerary complexes, including a tomb and a triclinium, are however still visible in Petra.

Banquets bringing together groups of people under the protection of a deity and under the auspices of a personality, a *rbʾ* (chief), took place in Petra and its environs. The funeral banquets are evidenced by the mention of an hypaethral triclinium, or *gntʾ smkʾ*, among the components of the Turkmaniyah's Tomb and by other remains for funeral banquets still preserved in the cemeteries of Petra.

Architectural remains

Banquet rooms associated with a funerary complex are numerous in the cemeteries of Petra; there are at least twenty-five according to D. Tarrier (Tarrier 1988: 99). They can be open rooms or *hypaethral triclinia*, but the well preserved *triclinia* are covered halls carved into the rock. There are three types of funeral banquet rooms in Petra: single rooms, rooms with burials, and rooms with a niche.

Simple triclinia

Simple banquet rooms are rectangular with benches carved into the rock. The well preserved simple funerary *triclinia* in Petra are rock-cut monuments found in the necropolises around the city center, associated with one or several tombs.

The triclinium BD 238, located in Wadi Farasah East, is a 6 m² room (Fig. 2). Its entrance is a few meters above the Soldier tomb and the access to it was through separate stairs, on the right side of the monumental stairs leading to the Soldier tomb complex from the valley. The two buildings were perhaps not directly associated despite their proximity. The triclinium BD 238 was associated with another funerary ensemble: a series of pit tombs excavated by S.G. Schmid that were cut in the adjacent rocky plateau (fig. 3) (Schmid & Barnasse 2006). The pit tombs were organised in two sets: a first series of a dozen of pit tombs aligned against the mountain, and a series of four pit tombs overlooking the valley, inscribed in a rock-cut circle engraved in the ground. The latter series of tombs was probably surrounded in the past by a building of c. 4 m diameter, possibly a *tholos*, according

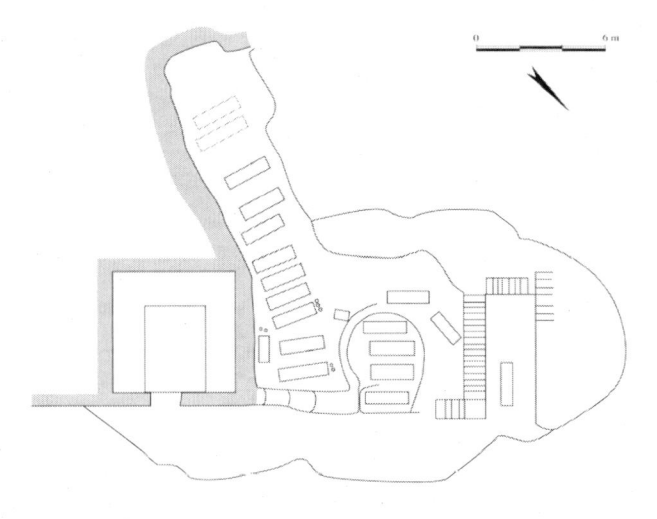

Figure 3. Triclinium BD 238 in Wadi Farasah East (Sketch by I. Sachet after Dalman 1912 and Schmid & Barnasse 2006: Fig. 7).

to the form of the marks on the ground. Rock-cut *tholoi* are found in Petra at the top of the most sumptuous monuments of the city: the Khaznah, the Corinthian tomb and the Deir. The triclinium BD 238 may thus have functioned with a monumental funerary *tholos*, built in front of it, indicating the southern entrance of the Wadi Farasah East.

Figure 4. Façade of the Lions triclinium (photograph I. Sachet).

About fifty tomb façades adorn each side of the processional way running east from Petra to the Deir monument. The Lion's triclinium was built at the entrance of the necropolis, at the beginning of the stairs (Fig. 2). Two lions carved on both sides of the door gave the name to the monument (Fig. 4). Immediately to the left of the façade, there is a betyl that placed the monument under the protection of a god. Despite its carefully executed façade with sculptures, the interior of the monument is roughly dressed. A rock-cut bench is still visible on the left side of the room but it was removed on the right side. In Judith McKenzie's classification, the Lion's triclinium belongs to her group

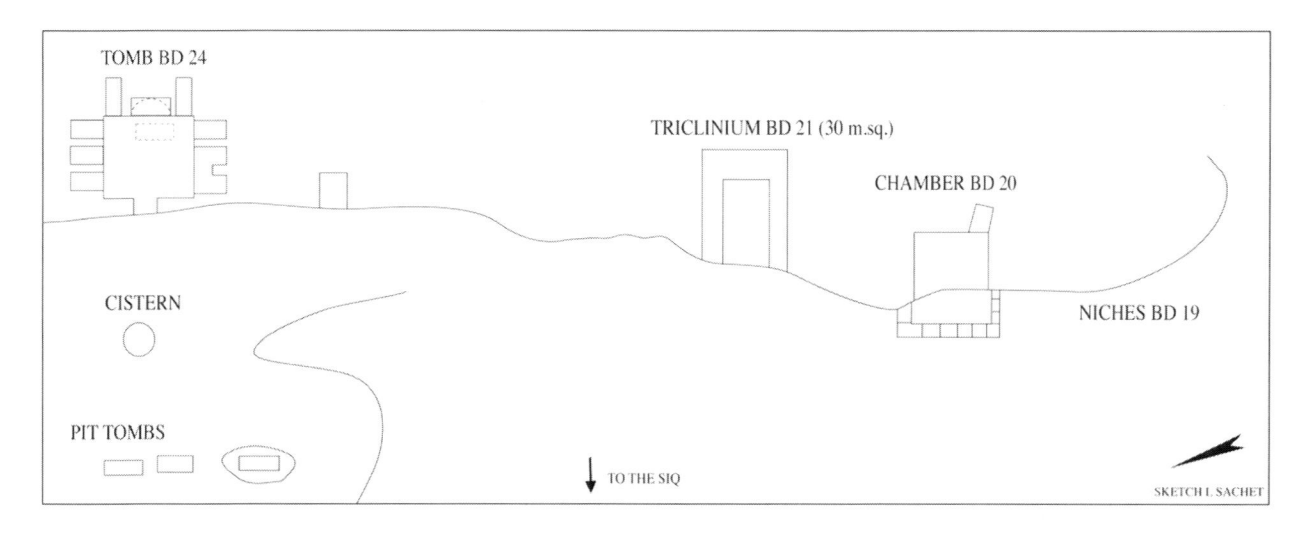

Figure 5. Aslah triclinium at the entrance of the Siq.

D, dated from the reign of Malichos II (40-70 AD) (McKenzie 1990: 45-46, 52). The Lion triclinium is not associated with one tomb but with the adjacent necropolis of façade tombs. The whole necropolis was not for one family but presumably it belonged to a group, whether a Nabataean tribe or a professional or religious congregation.

The Aslah triclinium, situated in the hill east of the entrance to the Siq and facing it, is the oldest *triclinium* in Petra and is dated by an inscription from 96/92 BC (Fig. 2) (McKenzie 1990: 33-34; Hackl 2003: 219-220). The monument is a rectangular chamber measuring ca. 30 m^2 with an inscription in the back wall (*RES* 1432):

ᵓln ṣryḥyᵓ wgbᵓ dy ᶜbd ᵓṣlḥ br ᵓṣlḥ ldwšrᵓ ᵓlh mnktw ᶜl ḥyy ᶜbdt mlk nbṭw br ḥrtt mlk nbṭw šnt I

These are the rooms and the cisterns made by ᵓAṣlaḥ, son of ᵓAṣlaḥ, ... for Dūšara, god of Manbaṭū, for the life of Obodat, King of the Nabataeans, son of Aretas, King of the Nabataeans, in his first year

The rooms and the cistern made by ᵓAṣlaḥ are still visible few meters to the north of the triclinium and a series of decorated niches are also cut at its entrance. In front of the cistern, the chamber tomb BD 24 was designed to contain at least 10 persons. The niches, the hydraulic installation, the tomb and the banquet room were then associated in one funerary complex (Fig. 5). A wall, or *krk*, as mentioned in the inscription of the Turkmaniyah, could perhaps close the Aslah complex (Healey 1993: 238-240). In 2005, the team of the French Geophysical Survey used a GPR (Ground Penetrating Radar) to investigate the area but no signal was recorded in the ground (Martinaud & Sachet 2005). It is possible that the rocky cliffs on both sides of the Aslah complex were a natural barrier enclosing the complex.

The burial chambers associated with the banquet halls in Petra are nearby, usually within a few meters or tens of meters of each other. The single banquet rooms have a well defined function in the funerary complex: to host the living for a banquet which honours the dead located nearby.

Banquet rooms with funerary places

In the necropolises of Petra, the facilities reserved for the dead are near the facilities for the living. This reality is sometimes pushed to the extreme in some funerary complexes where graves have been arranged inside the banquet hall meaning that the room had a mixed function for banquets and burials. But it is not certain that the graves and the seats were used at the same time. From our contemporary perspective, the first idea that comes to mind is generally to assume that the tombs were constructed *a posteriori*. It is difficult to verify that assumption in a cave where the relative chronology for the construction of the various installations is much more difficult to establish than in a masonry-built monument. However, the banquet rooms in Petra equipped with burials are sufficiently numerous to doubt that *loculi* were systematically built after benches. This category of banquet rooms needs to be carefully studied in order to determine whether the graves and the seats were built at the same time.

The triclinium of the Obelisk Tomb (BD 34) was cut in the mountain of Bab as-Siq, at the entrance of Petra (Fig. 2), under a chamber tomb crowned by three obelisks, or monumental *nefeshes*, that gave name to the monument. People had easy access from the wadi to the triclinium and they had to climb stairs, on the eastern part of the monument, to visit the tomb (Fig. 6). The triclinium BD 34 is flanked by three funerary chambers, one above it and two on its right and left sides. The triclinium itself also had a funerary function as two *loculi* were cut in its back wall (Fig. 7). The quantity of the places for the dead, at least 15 individual places cut in the four chambers of the funerary complex, suggest the placement in the chambers of an increasing number of the dead with time. Consequently, the triclinium could have

Figure 6. Obelisks Complex (photograph I. Sachet).

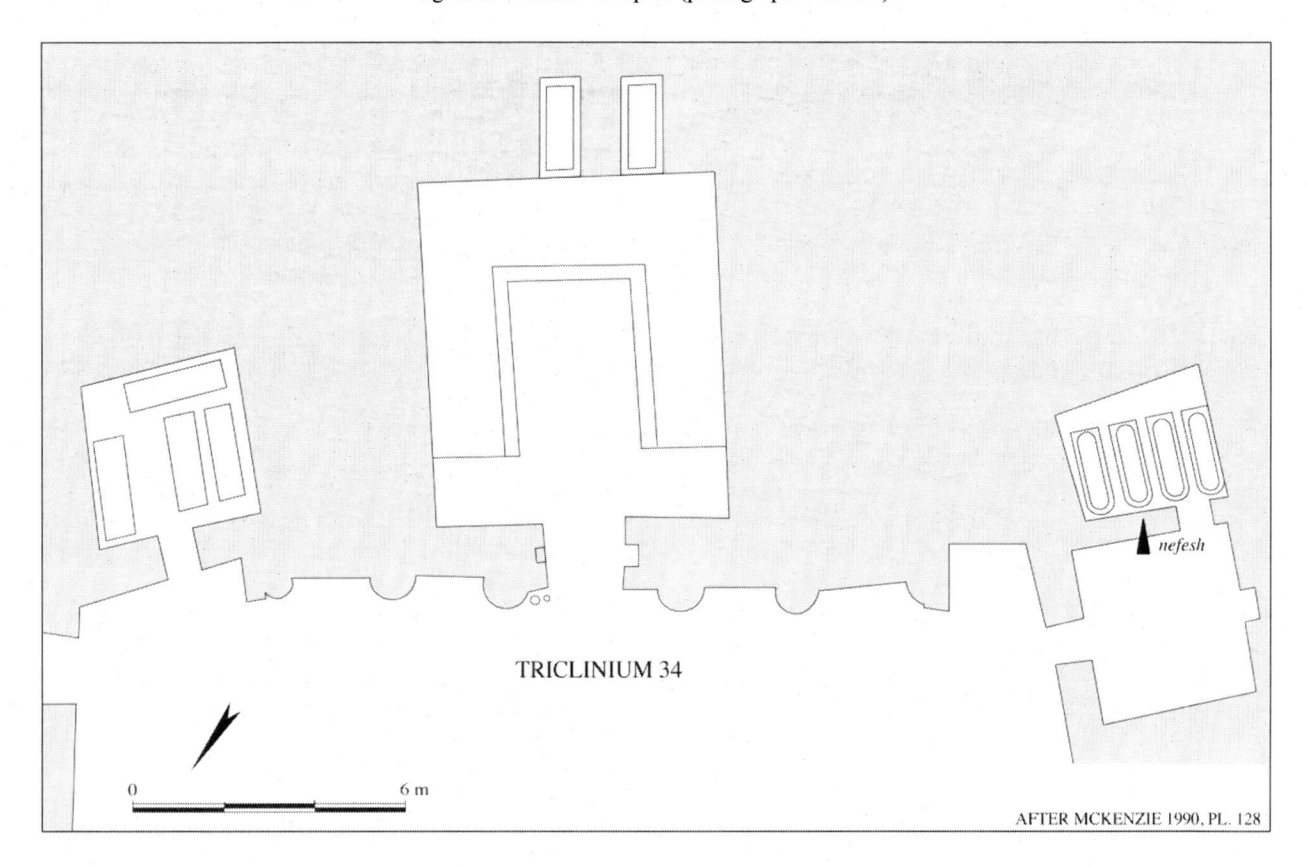

Figure 7. Triclinium of the Obelisks Tomb (after McKenzie 1990: Pl. 128).

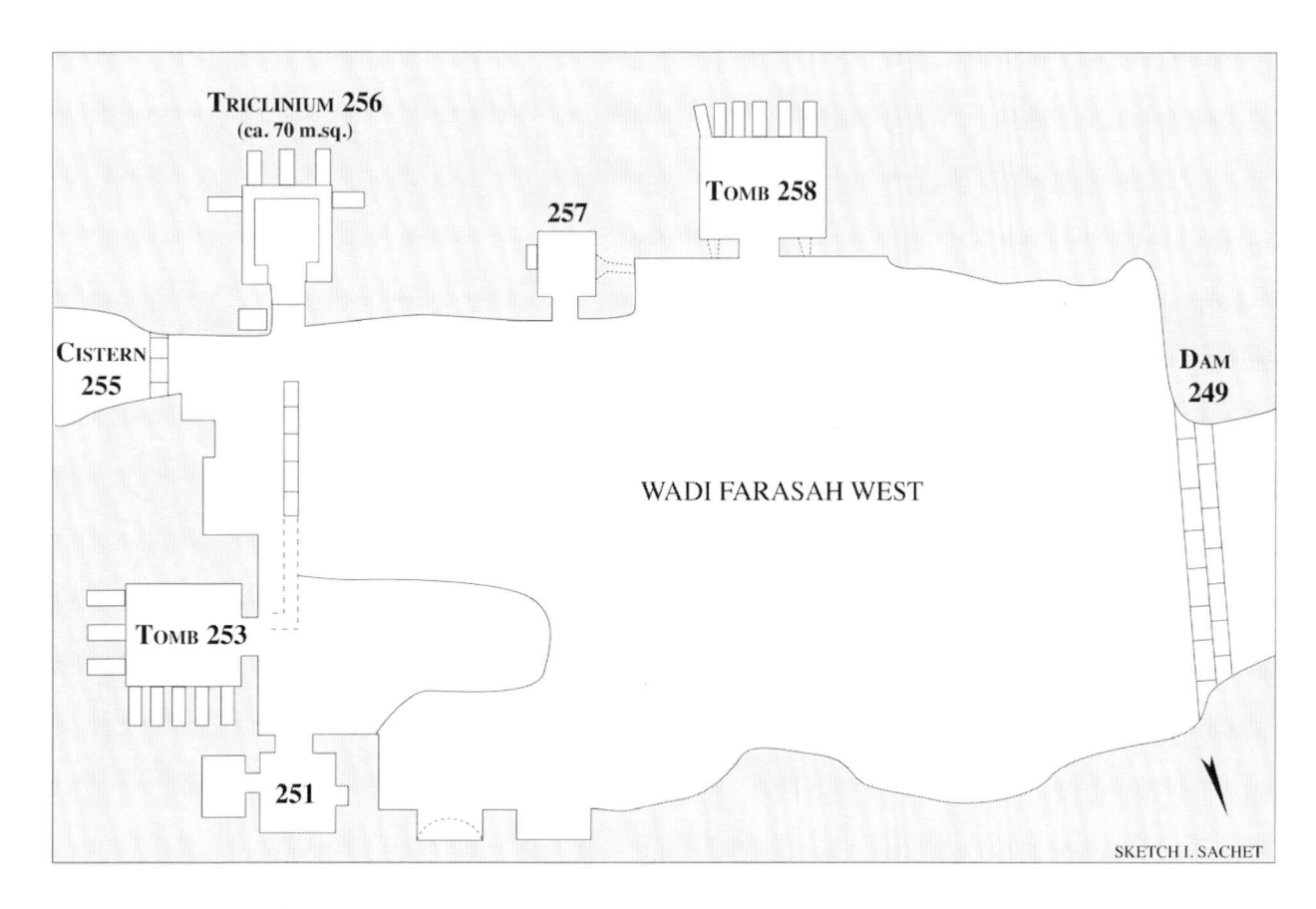

Figure 8. Wadi Farasah West Complex.

Figure 9. Interior view of Triclinium BD 256 before cleaning of the room, with stone slab *in situ* closing the loculus (photograph L. Nehmé).

been reused into a tomb to accommodate a larger number of dead. Given the difficulties in establishing a relative chronology for rock-cut monuments, it is not possible to ascertain the anteriority of the benches on the *loculi* in the banquet room of the Obelisk Tomb.

In Wadi Farasah West, the mountain was not as over-exploited as in the Obelisk complex and more space was available in the funerary complex (Fig. 2). The organization of the Wadi Farasah West funerary complex resembles to the organisation of the Wadi Farasah East, i.e. the Soldier Tomb Complex, with a dam upstream and series of tombs and rooms organised around a central space (BD 251 to BD 258; Fig. 8). The complex appears like a smaller copy of the Soldier tomb complex in the nearby wadi. The façade of the tomb BD 258 is stylistically similar to the Soldier tomb (see Schmid 2007), but without statues, and the façade of the tomb BD 253 resembles the Renaissance Tomb, dated by excavations to the third quarter of the 1st century AD (Schmid, Huguenot & B'dool 2004). The funerary complex of the Wadi Farasah West should therefore be dated between the construction of the Soldier tomb, at the end of the 1st century BC (Schmid & Barnasse 2004), and the end of the 1st century AD. Funerary spaces would have been cut anywhere around the triclinium BD 256.

Thus, it was certainly a deliberate choice to associate funerary places and benches for banquets. Moreover, the funerary spaces were cut in a place difficult to reach, high on the walls of the chamber (Fig. 9). Referring to the construction techniques of the Nabataean tombs, stone cutters were digging from the ceiling to the floor and Nabataean workers did not use any scaffolding (Bessac 2007: 89, 266, fig. 95). Consequently, the *loculi* were certainly cut during the execution of the chamber and necessarily a short time before the benches.

In the al-Khubtah massif, the tomb of Uneishu (BD 813), associated with triclinium BD 812, is located a hundred metres south of the royal necropolis (Fig. 2). The monument is a funerary complex with a tomb and a triclinium organised around a colonnaded courtyard (Fig. 10). The triclinium is a large chamber measuring c. 75 m^2 with stairs giving access to the benches on both sides of the door. The *loculi* cut in the chamber were not in a high position, under the ceiling as in BD 256, but at the same height as the benches. Each one of the three *loculi* had three superposed places, with an additional place at the bottom of the western loculus. In total, ten persons were planned to be buried there. In the Uneishu complex, it is highly probable that the *loculi* and the benches were cut at the same time. The

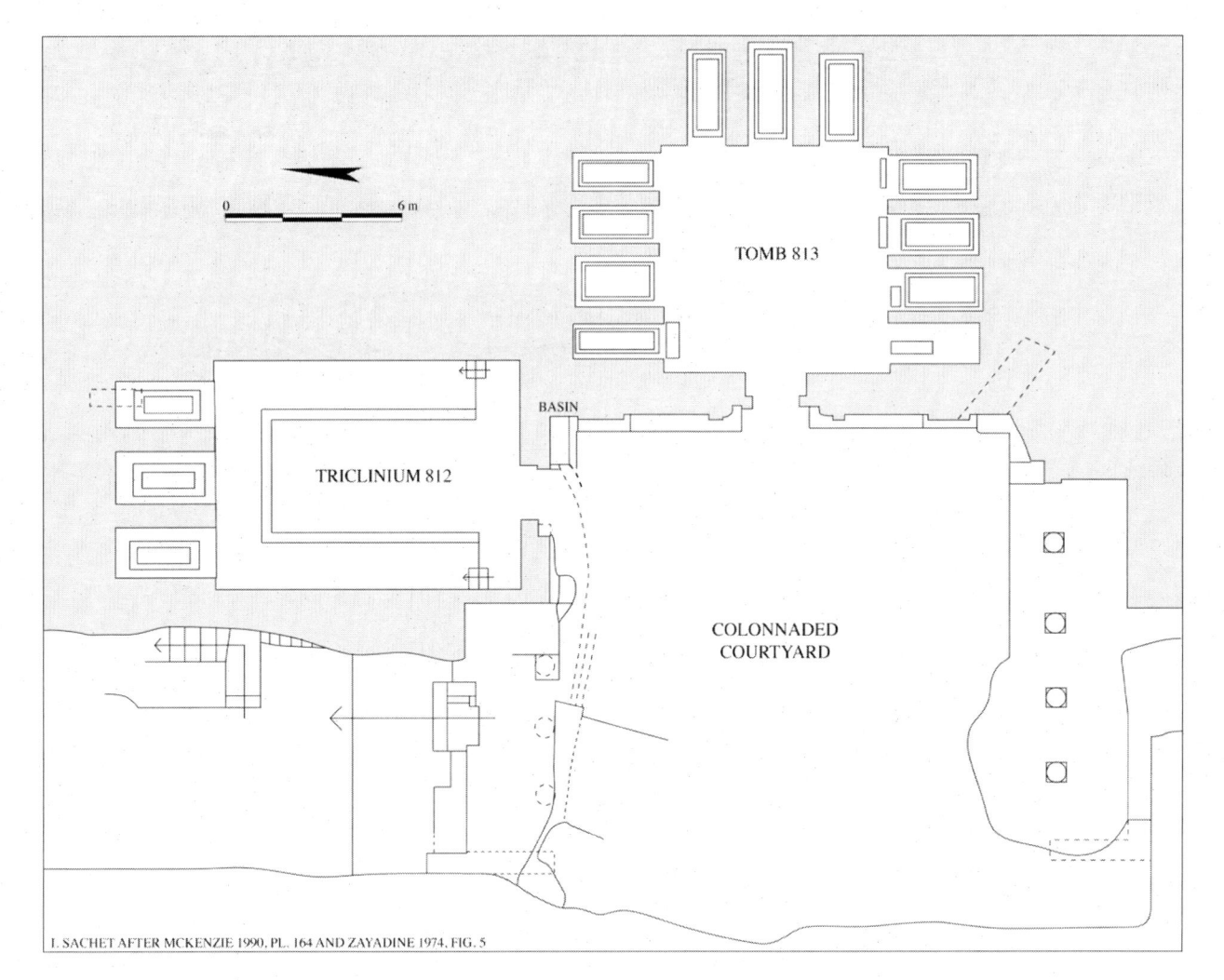

Figure 10. Plan of the Uneishu Tomb Complex (I. Sachet after McKenzie 1990: Pl. 164, and Zayadine 1974: Fig. 5).

architecture of the whole complex is homogeneous, with *loculi* cut in the three walls of the tombs, and *loculi* with the same shape and three superposed places cut in the triclinium. The only additional loculus in the Uneishu complex built after the construction of the complex is the one on the right side of the façade tomb, cut obliquely in order not to perforate the wall of the chamber.

In summary, graves were cut in some banquet rooms in Petra and were in use together with the other installations for religious meals. Thus, ceremonies were held near the deceased buried in the walls of the room. In Petra, the living and the dead symbolically feasted together and such proximity was frequent.

Funerary banquet rooms with a central niche

Other banquet rooms were not equipped with *loculi* but niches that were too small to receive a body. Cut in the center of the back wall of the banquet room, these niches were more likely to house a statue.

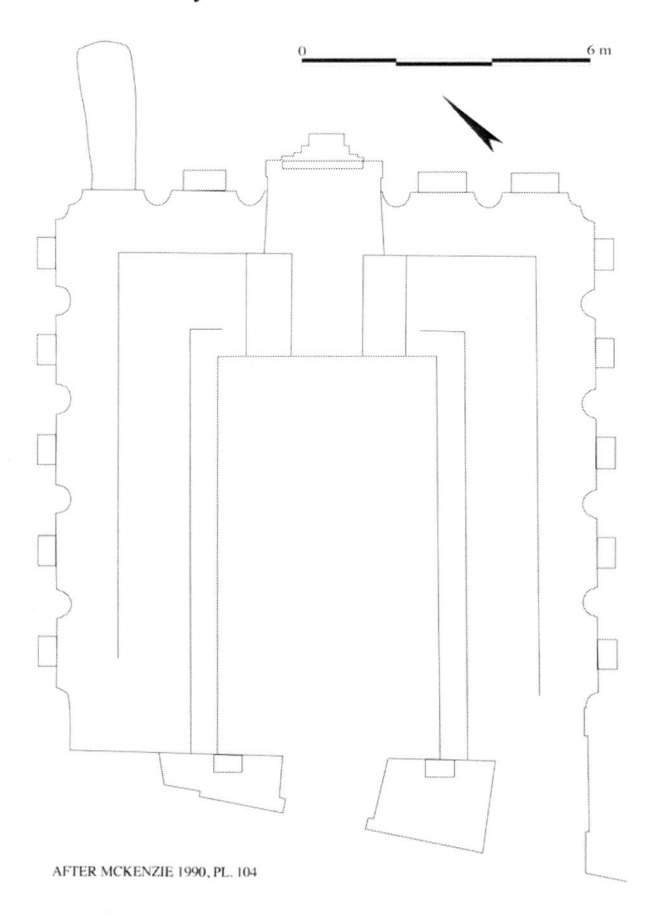

Figure 11. Plan of triclinium BD 235 in the Soldier Tomb Complex (I. Sachet after McKenzie 1990: pl. 104).

In Wadi Farasah East, the triclinium BD 235 faces the Soldier tomb (Fig. 2). They were built on opposite sides of a colonnaded courtyard, brought together in a large funerary complex (see Schmid 2007, figs 9-11). The funerary complex of the Soldier tomb, excavated by S.G. Schmid, was built at the beginning of the 1st century AD with additional rooms built in the middle of the century (Schmid & Barnasse 2004: 340). The banquet room (Fig. 11) is richly decorated with engaged half-columns, niches and painted stuccos. A loculus was carved in the northern corner of the room but its rough cut suggests that it belongs to the late reuse of the room. In the back wall of the triclinium, a niche was cut and the bench was discontinued in front of it. The niche is actually empty but it is likely that a statue formerly stood in it. No guest was allowed to sit in front of this statue, as the bench is discontinued there. Facing the door entrance and benefiting from the view to the Soldier tomb, the statue was given the honourific place in the banquet room. No inscription nor any fragment of statue was found in the triclinium BD 233 but, in the Obodas chapel, a niche was also cut in the back wall of the triclinium and the head of a statue identified with the God Obodas was found in front of the niche, probably having fallen from it (Nehmé 2002: fig. 10). In Wadi Farasah East, the banquet ceremonies may have been placed under the protection of a god image, as they were in the Obodas Chapel.

We must now consider the function of the largest rock-cut monument in Petra, the Deir monument. Was the Deir used as a religious monument or a burial place? First, the facade of the monument is comparable to other tombs in Petra, especially the Palace Tomb in the royal necropolis. Secondly, the great temples of Petra were not carved, but built, as the Qasr al-Bint and the Temple of the Winged Lions. There is therefore no parallel in Petra for a rock temple of the size of the Deir monument while the Palace Tomb and the Corinthian tomb, both cut in the al-Khubthah mountain, are of comparable size. The large niche carved in the back wall of the chamber of the Deir, facing the door, is difficult to interpret (Fig. 12). It is similar to other burial places carved into burial chambers, as in the Soldier Tomb or in the tomb BD 24 of the Aslah complex (Fig. 5). In the Roman catacombs too, the rounded niches, or *arcosolia*, were used to accommodate coffins. The levelled benches on each side of the door also demonstrate the use of the room as biclinium. Thus, banquets were held at the foot of the central niche in which probably something valuable was placed, whether a group of statues or the sarcophagus of an important person, for example a king. The deification of a dead king was a practice known in Nabataea. According to the testimony of Stephanus of Byzantium in the 6th century AD, the king Obodas (c. 96-85 BC) had been deified and he became the subject of a cult (*Ethnica* 482, 15-16). The banquet room of the Deir is the largest banquet room in Petra, c. 135 m² (Table 1). Banquets to honour a royal figure could have taken place there and the royal presence could have been real or symbolic.

According to epigraphic and archaeological sources, Nabataean banquets were placed under the protection of a deity, mainly Dushara or Obodat (*RES* 1423; Healey 1993: 238-239). Beyond its symbolic protection, the deity had also the opportunity to attend the banquet, installed in a niche that had been planned for it inside the banquet hall.

Figure 12. View of the back wall of the Deir (photograph I. Sachet).

Monument	Sector	Number (after Brünnow and Domaszewski 1904)	Characteristics	Size	Date	Method of Dating
Aslah triclinium	Bab as-Siq	BD21	niche	30 m²	96/92 BC	paleographical
Uneishu triclinium	Khubthah	BD812	loculi	75 m²	end of the 1st c. BC	archaeological
Soldier tomb triclinium	Wadi Farasah	BD235	niche	120 m²	beginning 1st c. AD	archaeological
(up to) Soldier Tomb	Wadi Farasah	BD238	simple	35 m²	before beg. 1st c. AD?	archaeological
Farasah West	Wadi Farasah	BD256	loculi	70 m²	after beg. 1st c. AD?	archaeological
Obelisks tomb triclinium	Bab as-Siq	BD34	loculi	50 m²	40-70 AD	paleographical
Lion triclinium	Meisrah	BD452	simple	35 m²	40-70 AD	stylistic
Deir	Deir	BD462	cultic or funerary niche	135 m²	70-106 AD	stylistic

Table 1. Chronology and size of the major funerary banquet rooms in Petra.

Guests for the funerary banquets

According to the various types of installations inside the banquet rooms in the funerary complex from Petra, i.e. graves or niches, it is possible to determine the presence of different actors participating in the meals. The size of the banquet room is also the main indication of the type of ceremony held inside the complex.

Public or private ceremonies

The size of the banquet hall reveals the maximum number of persons that were allowed inside to celebrate the ceremony. In Petra, the banquet rooms can be divided into three categories: small rooms of about 30 m^2, medium ones measuring c. 50 m^2, and large rooms over 70 m^2 (Table 1).

The small *triclinia* were well-suited for small groups whereas large *triclinia* were designed to accommodate more important meetings. In small and medium rooms (i.e. under 50 m^2), people had the possibility to share their meal and talk together. Such banquet rooms contributed to social interaction, conviviality, and the strengthening of group solidarity (Donahue 2003; Dunbabin 1998). They were particularly well suited to family or private group meetings, for example for " ᵓAṣlaḥ, son of ᵓAṣlaḥ and his family" in the complex at the entrance of the Siq (*RES* 1432). On the contrary, large *triclinia* (up to 70 m^2) were designed to receive larger groups of people. In large rooms, communication between members of a group is much more difficult. People can talk with their direct neighbours but cannot interact with someone laying on another bench. Large *triclinia* are designed for meetings centered around a ceremony, perhaps around an entertainment taking place in the middle of the room, for example the musicians described by Strabo at a royal Nabataean banquet (*Geographica*, 16.4.26).

The small *triclinia* of 30 m^2 were planned to allow five to ten persons to lay on the benches. For example, in the 30 m^2 Aslah triclinium, we might guess that the entire family of Aslah, son of Aslah, did not participate in the banquet. Women were involved in the Greek banquet, and children were allowed sometimes to take part in the Roman banquet (H.S. Nielsen 1998: 58). Considering the small size of the familial *triclinia* in Petra, there might have been a kind of selection in the Nabataean banquet. The large banquet rooms offered more space to the participants: twenty-five people at least could have comfortably reclined in a diagonal position on the large benches of the chamber of the Deir. The luxury of the installations indicates that such rooms were owned by rich people from the aristocracy or the royal family. The tomb of Uneishu was a royal or peri-royal property: according to an inscription found in the tomb, Uneishu was the "brother", or minister, of a queen Shaqilat (*CIS* II, 351: ᶜnšw ᵓḥ šqylt). The Soldier tomb was the tomb of an aristocrat, probably a *strategos* or an *eparchos*, a military man of high rank with a significant administrative role. In the large *triclinia*, private ceremonies with families and priests could have taken place, or even public ceremonies when a royal commemoration was involved.

The oldest banquet room in Petra dated by an inscription is the Aslah triclinium, from the first year of the reign of a king Obodas, certainly Obodas I, who became king in 96/92 BC (Starcky 1980) (Table 1). The most recent banquet room would be the Deir. The building shows a strong Roman influence and may have been built during the reign of Rabbel II (70-106 AD) (Schmid 2001: 413). Furthermore, its isolated location may indicate that it was built when it was no longer possible to build a monument of that size in the city center. The highest point of building activities in Petra center was reached during the first half of the 1st century AD and it is highly likely that the Deir was built later. In Wadi Farasah East, two banquet rooms were built close to the Soldier tomb. The first one, BD 238 is a small triclinium of 30 m^2 associated with a group of pit tombs. The second one, BD 235, is a large triclinium measuring 120 m^2 facing the tomb and a part of the funerary complex of the Soldier tomb. The organization of the architectural remains in Wadi Farasah East point to an earlier date for the triclinium BD 238. Indeed, it is difficult to imagine that the descendants of the Soldier tomb's owner would have agreed to the construction of a monument above his tomb. Therefore, we may assume that the triclinium BD 238 was already built when the funerary complex of Wadi Farasah was planned, at the beginning of the 1st century AD.[3]

Chronologically, the small *triclinia* are earlier than the large ones and both categories were still in use within, at least, the 1st and 2nd centuries AD. Small *triclinia* preceded the large banquet rooms in Petra; the first known triclinia are dated by an inscription to the early 1st century BC while larger rooms were built from the early 1st century AD. Both types of installation nonetheless continued functioning simultaneously. The same tendency is observed in Rome and around the Mediterranean Sea, where large *triclinia* of the imperial period succeeded to the small *triclinia* of the Republican era (Dunbabin 1998: 95).

The honoured guests

Considering the large number of architectural remains relating to the funerary banquet in Petra, the practice of meals in honour of the dead should be considered, at least among the richest. We discuss here the funerary complexes that belonged to the wealthier classes of the Nabataean capital, and even to the royal entourage. Indications of funeral banquets in other cemeteries of the Nabataean kingdom are scarce. In Khirbet Qazone, the presence of ceramics above the simple shaft tombs used for single inhumations (Politis, Granger-Taylor 2003: 107) may indicate a funerary meal. However, funerary banquets could have been held above the graves in temporary installations, for example tents, as depicted on Etruscan paintings (Martha 1889: 412).

The dinners in honour of the dead were held in their own space, that is to say, in the necropolises. Sometimes, the banquet was even held in the presence of the dead, in the banquet rooms containing burials. The burials were usually installed in the back wall of the room, facing the door. The deceased were therefore at a place of honour

---

[3] Excavations led archaeologists to date the construction of the Soldier tomb to the early 1st century AD: Schmid & Barnasse 2004: 340.

and lead the banquet.[4] This picture may seem strange to our contemporary sensibilities. The burials, however, were sealed with stone slabs several inches thick cemented in the wall. In the tomb BD 256, closing stone slabs are still visible, collapsed inside the *loculi* (fig. 9).[5] Moreover, recent excavations of the French mission at Madāin Ṣāleḥ, in Saudi Arabia, have established that the bodies of Nabataeans were wrapped in textiles coated with resin to prevent decomposition (Delhopital & Sachet, in press). Thus, the banquet rooms with sealed graves perfectly suited for the activities of the living.

The numerous betyls, anonymous figures of gods, located at the entrance and inside the funerary complexes (Sachet 2010 in press), reflect the degree of religious character in funerary activities. At the entrance of the Lion triclinium for example, a betyl was cut in a niche to protect the monument (Fig. 4). Like the dead, the god could be invited to the banquet. Banquet rooms equipped with central niches were intended to receive statues, for example the statue of the god Obodas, found in the chapel Obodas (Nehmé 2002). The god was then also placed in the position of the honoured guest, facing the door and visible by all other guests.

Conclusion

The *marzeaḥ* is a gathering of guests around a meal. The primary use of the term *mrzḥ* is not only in the funerary context and it applies to any form of religious meal. In the case of Nabataean funerary *marzeaḥ*, family or companions, *bny*, are invited to commemorate the deceased. The ceremony takes place under the patronage of the *rbʾ mrzḥ*, or head of the banquet, who may be the family head or the head of a congregation. The honoured guest sits at a place, visible to everyone, at the back wall opposite the door with a view to the outside. The honoured guest can be either a living person – probably the *rbʾ mrzḥ* – or the deceased himself when graves are located in the back wall of the triclinium, or the tutelary deity placed in a central niche.

Comparing banquet rooms, it appears that the size of buildings increases with time. We see the emergence of small banquet rooms in the early 1st century BC, e.g. the Aslah triclinium, designed to accommodate small groups of up to ten people. According to currently available data, banquet rooms measuring over 70 m^2 and receiving larger assemblies appear from the late 1st century BC onward. With the increasing wealth of Nabataean society, particularly through trade, population grew. Many monumental tombs were built for the richest families from the late 1st century BC to the late 1st century AD. At the end of the major phase of building activity, i.e. presumably in the course of the 2nd century AD, more than 630 decorated façade tombs were carved for Nabataean families in the mountains surrounding the centre of the ancient city. These aristocratic tombs required the construction of facilities for funeral rituals including banquets. The largest banquet rooms belonged to members of the aristocracy and to the royal entourage. Private ceremonies could also take place there, probably with priests, but public ceremonies were certainly held in large banquet halls too. The banquet hall of the Deir had to meet the particular needs of a public ceremony. Its size is indeed comparable to that of other royal banqueting halls in the palaces of the Mediterranean world in the 1st centuries BC/AD, e.g. in Rome, Masada or Jericho (I. Nielsen 1998: fig. 24).

Sigla

CIS II 2.1 1907   *Corpus inscriptionum semiticarum, pars secunda : inscriptiones Aramaicas continens, Tomus II, fasciculus primus*. Ab Academia inscriptionum et litterarum humanorium conditum atque digestum. Parisiis: e reipublicae typographeo.

RES   *Répertoire d'épigraphie sémitique*. Publié par la commission du *Corpus inscriptionum semiticarum*. Paris: Imprimerie nationale. 1900-1968.

Bibliography

Alavoine V. 2000. Le *mrzḥ* est-il un banquet funéraire? Etude des sources épigraphiques et bibliques (*Am*. 6, 7 et *Ier*. 16, 5). *Le Muséon* 113 (1-4): 1-54.

Alster B. (*ed.*) 1980. *Death in Mesopotamia, XXVIe Rencontre assyriologique internationale (Copenhague July 1979)*. (Mesopotamia, 8). Copenhague: Akademisk Forlag.

Augé C. & Dentzer J.-M. 1999. *Pétra. La cité des caravanes*. Découvertes Gallimard Archéologie. Paris: Gallimard.

Bessac J.-C. 2007. *Le travail de la pierre à Pétra. Technique et économie de la taille rupestre*. Recherches sur les civilisations. Paris: Culturesfrance.

Brünnow R.E. & von Domaszewski A. 1904. *Die Provincia Arabia auf grund zweier in den Jahren 1897 and 1898 unternommen Reisen und der berichte früherer Reisender. Band I. Die Römerstrasse von Mâdebâ über Petra und Odruh bis el ʿAkaba*. Strassburg: K.J. Trübner.

Cantineau J. 1932. *Le Nabatéen. II, Choix de textes, lexique*. Paris: Ernest Leroux.

Dalman G. 1908. *Petra und seine Felsheiligtümer*. Leipzig: Hinrichs.

Dalman G. 1912. *Neue Petra-Forschungen*. Leipzig: Hinrichs.

Delhopital N. & Sachet I. In press. Area 5, Work in the Monumental Tombs. In L. Nehmé, D. al-Talhi and F. Villeneuve (*dir.*), *Report on the First Excavation Season (2008) at Madâ'in Sâlih, Saudi Arabia*. Riyadh: Supreme Commission for Tourism.

---

[4] Concerning the place of honour in banquet rooms, see Dunbabin 1998 and I. Nielsen 1998.
[5] Observation made on the field by the author in 2003.

Dentzer J.-M. 1982. *Le motif du banquet couché dans le Proche-Orient et le monde grec du VIIe au IVe siècle avant J.-C.* (Bibliothèque des écoles françaises d'Athènes et de Rome, 242). Athènes; Rome: écoles françaises d'Athènes et de Rome.

Donahue J.F. 2003. Toward a typology of Roman public feasting. *American Journal of Philology* 124: 423-441.

Donahue J.F. 2004. *The Roman Community at Table during the Principate.* Ann Arbor: University of Michigan Press.

Dunbabin K.M.D. 1998. Ut Graeco More Biberetur: Greeks and Roman on the Dining Couch. Pages 81-101 in I. Nielsen and H.S. Nielsen (ed.).

Hackl U., Jenni H. & Schneider C. 2003. *Quellen zur Geschichte der Nabatäer. Textsammlung mit Übersetzung und Kommentar. Mit Beiträgen von Daniel Keller.* (Novum testamentum et orbis antiquus, 51), Freiburg: Universitätsverlag, Göttingen: Vandenhoeck und Ruprecht.

Healey J. 1993. *The Nabataean Tomb Inscriptions of Mada'in Salih.* (Journal of Semitic Studies Supplement 1). Oxford: Oxford University Press.

Lindsay H. 1998. Eating with the Dead: The Roman Funerary Banquet. Pages 67-80 in I. Nielsen I. & H.S. Nielsen (eds), *Meals in a Social context. Aspects of the Communal Meal in the Hellenistic and Roman World.* (Aarhus Studies in Mediterranean Antiquity, 1). Aarhus: Aarhus University Press.

Martha J. 1889. *L'art étrusque.* Paris : Firmin Didot.

Martinaud M. & Sachet I. 2005. Umm al-Biyara and an-Nasara necropolis, Petra Archaeological Park. French Geophysical Survey in Petra's Necropolis. [23rd April-2nd May 2005]. *Munjazat* 6: 57-58.

McKenzie, J.S. 1990. *The Architecture of Petra.* British Academy Monographs in Archaeology 1. Oxford: Oxford University Press.

Milik J.T. 1972. *Dédicaces faites par des dieux (Palmyre, Hatra, Tyr) et des thiases sémitiques à l'époque romaine.* (Bibliothèque archéologique et historique, 92), Paris: P. Geuthner.

Murray O. (ed.) 1994. *Sympotica: a symposium on the "symposion" [held at Balliol College, Oxford, on 4-8 September 1984].* Oxford: Clarendon press.

Negev A. 1963. Nabatean Inscriptions from 'Avdat (Oboda). *Israel Exploration Journal* 13: 113-124.

Nehmé L. 2002. La chapelle d'Obodas à Pétra. Rapport préliminaire sur la campagne 2001. *Annual of the Department of Archaeology in Jordan* 46: 243-256.

Niehr H. 1998. *Religionen in Israels Umwelt: Einführung in die nord-westsemitischen Religionen Syrien-Palästinas von ca. 1500 v. Chr. bis zur Zeitenwende.* (Neue Echter Bibel AT, 5). Würzburg: Echter.

Nielsen H. S. 1998. Roman Children at Mealtimes. Pages 56-66 in I. Nielsen & H.S. Nielsen (eds), *Meals in a Social context. Aspects of the Communal Meal in the Hellenistic and Roman World.* (Aarhus Studies in Mediterranean Antiquity, 1). Aarhus: Aarhus University Press.

Nielsen I. 1998. Royal Banquets: The Development of Royal Banquets and Banqueting Halls from Alexander to the Tetrarchs. Pages 102-133 in I. Nielsen & H.S. Nielsen (eds), *Meals in a Social context. Aspects of the Communal Meal in the Hellenistic and Roman World.* (Aarhus Studies in Mediterranean Antiquity, 1). Aarhus: Aarhus University Press.

Nielsen I. & Nielsen H.S. 1998. *Meals in a Social context. Aspects of the Communal Meal in the Hellenistic and Roman World.* (Aarhus Studies in Mediterranean Antiquity, 1). Aarhus: Aarhus University Press.

Pardee D. 1996. Marziḥu, kispu, and the Ugaritic Funerary Cult: a minimalist view. Pages 273-287 in N. Wyatt, W.G.E. Watson & J.B. Lloyd (eds), *Ugarit, Religion and Culture. Proceedings of the international Colloquium on Ugarit, Religion and Culture. Edinburgh, July 1994. Essays presented in Honour of Professor John C.L. Gibson.* (Ugaritisch Biblische Literatur, 12).

Politis K.D. & Granger-Taylor H. 2003. Nabataeans on the Dead Sea Littoral. Pages 106-108 in G. Markoe (ed.), *Petra rediscovered. Lost City of the Nabataeans.* London: Thames and Hudson.

Sachet I. 2010, in press. Dieux, déesses et démons d'Arabie Pétrée. In C.-J. Robin & I. Sachet (eds), *Dieux et déesses d'Arabie. Images et représentations*, Actes du colloque tenu à Paris les 1er et 2 octobre 2007. (Orient et Méditerrané). Paris: de Boccard.

Savignac R. 1913. Notes de voyage de Suez au Sinaï et à Pétra. *Revue Biblique* 10: 429-442.

Scheid J. 1985. Sacrifice et banquet à Rome. *Mélanges de l'École française de Rome* 97.1: 193-206.

Schmid S.G. 2001: The 'Hellenisation' of the Nabataeans: A New Approach. *Studies in the History and Archaeology of Jordan VII*: 407-421.

Schmid S.G. 2007. The International Wadi Farasa Project (IWFP) 2006 Season. *Annual of the Department of Archaeology in Jordan* 51, 141-150.

Schmid S.G & Barnasse A. 2006. The International Wādi Farasa Project (IWFP). Preliminary report on the 2005 season. *Annual of the Department of Antiquities of Jordan* 50: 217-227.

Schmid S.G., Huguenot C. & B'dool M. 2004. Cleaning and excavation of the Renaissance Tomb at Petra. *Annual of the Department of Archaeology in Jordan* 48: 203-210.

Slater W.J. (ed.) 1991. *Dining in a Classical Context.* Ann Arbor: The University of Michigan Press.

Starcky J. 1980. Pétra et les Nabatéens. *Le Monde de la Bible* 14: 10.

Tarrier D. 1988. *Les triclinia nabatéens dans la perspective des installations de banquet au Proche-Orient.* Unpublished PhD thesis, University of Paris 1.

Tarrier D. 1995. Banquets rituels en Palmyrène et en Nabatène. *Aram Periodical* 7: 165-82.

Tholbecq L. & Durand C. 2005. A Nabataean Rock-cut Sanctuary in Petra. *Annual of the Department of Antiquities of Jordan* 49: 299-311.

Tholbecq L., Durand C. & Bouchaud Ch. 2008. A Nabataean Rock-cut sanctuary in Petra: Second Preliminary Report on the 'Obodas Chapel' excavation, Jabal Nmayr (2005-2007). *Annual of the Department of Antiquities of Jordan* 52: 235-254.

Zayadine F. 1974. Excavations at Petra (1976-1978). *Annual of the Department of Antiquities of Jordan* 19: 135-150.

Zayadine F. 1976. A Nabataean Inscription from Beida. *Annual of the Department of Antiquities of Jordan* 21: 139-142.

Author's Address
Dr. Isabelle Sachet
CNRS - Collège de France (Paris)
Laboratoire des études sémitiques anciennes
UMR 8167 "Orient et Méditerranée"
27 rue Paul Bert
94204 Ivry-sur-Seine Cedex
France

Biomolecular archaeology and analysis of artefacts found in Nabataean tombs in Petra

Nicolas Garnier, Isabelle Sachet, Anna Zymla, Caroline Tokarski and Christian Rolando

Summary

Domestic Nabataean libations and fumigations are described by Classical authors, but concerning funerary contexts, there is no literary evidence for a funerary cult. Still, archaeological remains attest that Nabataeans also conducted fumigations and poured libations to their dead. Altars or ceramics with residues inside, or libation holes are widespread in Nabataean tombs. By implementing a new interdisciplinary approach associating archaeology with chemistry, we have been able to research the organic residues used for rituals, in order to better understand the rites and products involved.

In order to demonstrate the potential of organic analysis, we developed a methodology allowing the characterization of organic amorphous residues preserved as invisible impregnations of libation holes directly carved in the stone. Fluid materials, liquids or burnt and softened solids represent an untapped source of data that can be now be added to the interpretative documentation by using recent technologies, such as gas chromatography coupled to mass spectrometry.

Two types of samples were examined. Firstly, crude residues found in the "Incense Tomb" located under the Khazneh were analysed. Contrary to first expectations based on visual examination and context analysis, the "incense" lumps proved to be slag inclusions, indicating metallurgical activities (preparation of iron, brass, and alloys of iron-manganese). Secondly, libation holes analysed from tombs in Petra (Umm al-Biyarah, ath-Thughrah, Bab as-Siq) revealed several natural products including mainly dairy products, but also vegetal oils, and coniferous resins that may have been used for libations and fumigations. These results obtained by the approach show how to exploit a new source of data, often neglected by archaeologists. Through physicochemical examination, archaeological artefacts can yield new scientific information, allowing the reconstruction what was and is often still considered as an invisible part of human history, the organic component.

Keywords: biomolecular archaeology, chromatography, mass spectrometry, biomarkers, Petra, Nabataeans, funerary practices

Introduction

According to the number of monumental Nabataean tombs in Petra – at least 1179 rock-cut tombs, including 628 tombs with a decorated façade (Nehmé 2003: 157) – the Nabataeans cared about their dead. The rituals practiced at the time of funerals and commemorative ceremonies have been established from the artefacts found inside the tombs. Food was offered on plates, incense was burnt on altars, and libations were poured into libation holes (Sachet 2010). But what food was offered on the plates, what incense was burnt on altars, or what libations were poured to the dead? These artefacts consist mainly of organic amorphous materials that lack identifiable biological structures due to their initial fluid aspect or the loss of microstructures by human processing of the material. Their fluid state makes them labile against environmental degradations (climate, humidity, microorganisms etc.), and difficult to detect by a simple visible observation. Thus, organic materials seem to be definitively lost. However, the recent development of new analytical technologies allows us to investigate such residues, even if only preserved as traces in porous artefacts, such as ceramics, or lithic objects.

In this article, we will present two different studies illustrating the need to use rigorous and cautious approaches. A step-by-step analytical methodology was elaborated and adapted to each sample, in order to extract the most precise chemical data. It consists on several complex steps, including the choice of the artefacts, the sampling, the preparation of the samples, the analysis of the organic extract, and the interpretation of the data that depends on the actual knowledge of the chemical composition of modern materials.

Analytical organic chemistry applied to ancient biomaterials, also named biomolecular archaeology, brings to classical archaeology new tools for the study of objects and the material context of ancient people (Regert 2003: 1620-1630; Evershed 2008: 26-47). Although as early as the 1920s, some fatty residues were discovered in large amounts in two alabaster cups in the tomb of Tutankhamen by H. Carter, and characterized by A.C. Chapman according to his thorough knowledge in chemistry and physics (Chapman and Plenderleith 1926: 2614-2619), neither chemists or archaeologists of this time showed interest in the chemical data retained in invisible organic residues. The field really took of with the pioneering work of F. Formenti who showed that organic constituents, especially fatty acids, can be preserved in the porous sherds of amphorae (Condamin *et al.* 1976: 195-201; Formenti *et al.* 1978: 95-100). These invisible impregnations can be extracted by organic solvents after crushing or milling the potsherds, and identified by separative methods (gas or liquid chromatography) coupled with structural techniques (mass spectrometry) (Evershed 2000: 177-240). Because these first results did not bring to light new relevant significant data for the archaeological field, archaeologists did not ask for organic examinations for another 20 years until technological developments in GC-MS allowed larger identification of biomolecules such as

Figure 1. Four artefacts of the collected and analysed slags.

fatty acids, terpenoids, sterols, phenolics, sugars, proteins.

Today, biomolecular archaeology can deal with a large number of organic residues, even if preserved as tiny traces (ca. several micrograms). It is advantageously implemented with amorphous organic materials that cannot be identified by microscopic examination. By determining the chemical composition of the preserved markers, several natural products of both plant and animal origin can be identified. However, from currently available data, only a few resins, oils, fats, pitches, waxes and dairy products can be correctly identified by their chemistry.

Two factors constrain the relevance of such an innovating approach: 1) the enhancement of selectivity and sensibility of analytical techniques allows the analysis of very small amounts of materials, reaching the level of environmental contaminations. The utmost care and cautiousness is needed for a correct interpretation of data. 2) The choice of a specific methodology, devised to adapt to the artefacts and to the questions put forward by archaeologists, seems to be a crucial starting point for each study. We will show in our first example the unreliability of simple observation by eye; in a second part, we will propose a methodology for the identification of deposits adsorbed in sandstone.

Inclusion slags from the Incense Tomb, Petra

In 2005, the excavations of tombs just in front of the Khazneh, managed by Suleiman Farajat, Qais Tweissi and Sami al-Nawafleh from the Jordanian Department of Antiquities (Farajat, al-Nawafleh 2005), revealed in one of them, the tomb 62A, kilograms of dark brown to greyish residues. After a physical examination by eye, the hypothesis that these residues were from incense was proposed, and the tomb was thereafter named the Incense Tomb. In order to confirm this hypothesis, the decision was made to analyse the sample.

The material was classified by visual examination into three groups: one with a mixed aspect (Fig. 1a), one of bright vitreous nature (Fig. 1b) and one of brownish and dark slag inclusions (Fig. 1c, d). Microscopic observation allowed the recognition of the glassy nature of the material, and to exclude an organic origin such as incense. In order to precisely characterise the inorganic nature of the samples, analysis using electronic microscopy revealed the heterogeneity of samples and of their individual constitution. A study was performed to measure major element composition, by using an Energy Dispersive Spectrometry (EDS) microprobe coupled to a Scanning Electron Microscope (SEM), as usually performed for the examination of ancient metal artefacts. Each sample presented iron derivatives: pure metal, oxides, carbonates, or silicates of iron. The precise study of crystallised structures and of their chemical constitution provided further information about the origin of the residues.

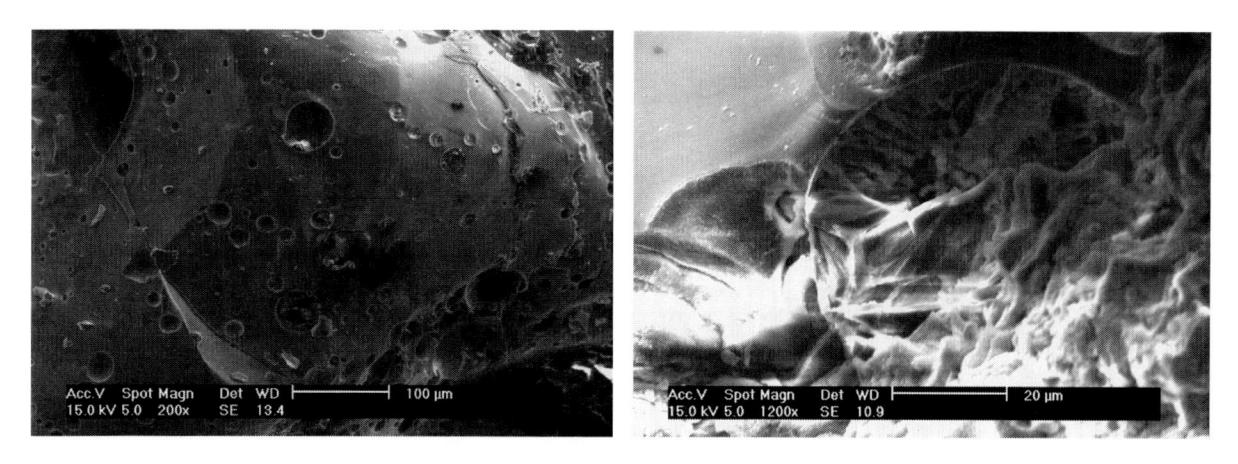

Figure 2. SEM observations of (a) the glassy bubbled surface (left), and (b) a bubble filled with crystallised CaO.

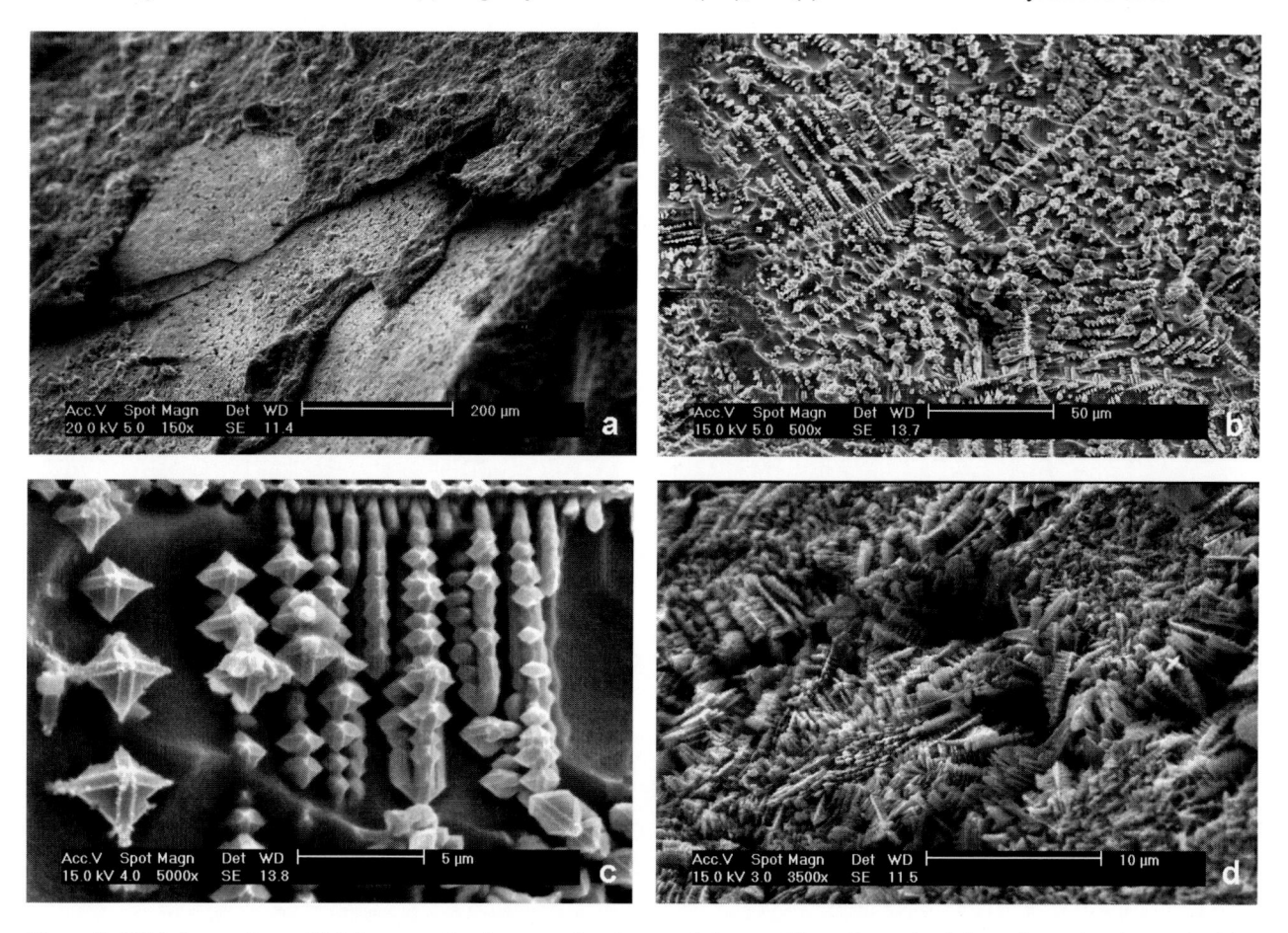

Figure 3. SEM observations of (a) the separation between the glassy and the metallic surfaces, (b, c) three-dimensional growth of the dendrites of reduced iron, and (d) needles of crystallised α-brass.

A first class of residues presented a characteristic vitreous bluish aspect, sometimes scratched or bubbled at the surface (Fig. 2a). The SEM analysis revealed a potassium aluminosilicate global composition, or a mixture of silica and calcium oxide. Some aggregates trapped into bubbles consist of silica, iron compounds, potassium and calcium aluminosilicate, with traces of chlorine and titanium. Although potassium comes from charcoal used for firing and heating the furnace, as shown below, chlorine and mostly titanium are markers of the red sandstone from the Wadi Musa region.[1] In some cases, bubbles were filled with spherical structures, consisting on an external shell made of calcium aluminosilicate, and a core of iron oxide and silica in different proportions. In other cases, bubbles

---

[1] Titanium oxide was identified as intense black crystals in red pigments used for wall-paintings, from the excavations of Leigh-Ann Bedal (Paradeisos, Petra, analyses made by N. Garnier by SEM-EDS in 2005). An independent study dealing with the colours used for Nabatean pottery revealed the presence of titanium in red pigments (analyses by made Maram Na'es and Khayryeh 'Amr, by XRF; personal communication).

can be filled with radial needles consisting on pure calcium oxide (Fig. 2b). This fragment presented also a glassy aspect but the inner sides of the bubbles were covered with very small spherical nodules of a pure iron-manganese mixture. This latter metal could be present with different oxidation states, because of its high electropositivity and the difficulty of reducing it to pure metal or into alloys. Apart from the glass part, a bright region revealed a scratched surface under SEM (Fig. 3a). At higher magnification, crystallised structures appeared as a strongly organized network of dendrites. These structures have grown in three dimensions, along orthogonal directions, and are directly related to the crystallisation of freshly reduced iron (Fig. 3b and 3c). The SEM examination identification of the core of the dendrites as iron oxide in the form of wustite (FeO). Greyish needles of fayalite (2 $FeO \cdot SiO_2$) appeared in the glassy matrix, which has a global composition $CaO \cdot Al_2O_3 \cdot 2\ SiO_2$, corresponding to anorthite. At the surface of the same sample, fine needles give a glassy and coloured aspect to the artefact; the high density of these very fine needles indicate a rapid cooling of the slag. Other metals have been identified: a precise combination of zinc and copper indicates the production of brass, crystallized in its α form (Fig. 3d), giving the glassy artefacts a grey to orange-reddish reflective appearance.

Metallic fragments (Fig. 1c) showed the formation of sponges of iron oxides (Fig. 4a), crystallized in lozenge structures associated with structures of sand roses of $FeO \cdot SiO_2$ (Fig. 4b). Such sponges constituted of lozenge- and whisker-shaped structures indicate a successful reduction reaction of the ore and carbon monoxide into pure iron and CO_2 in

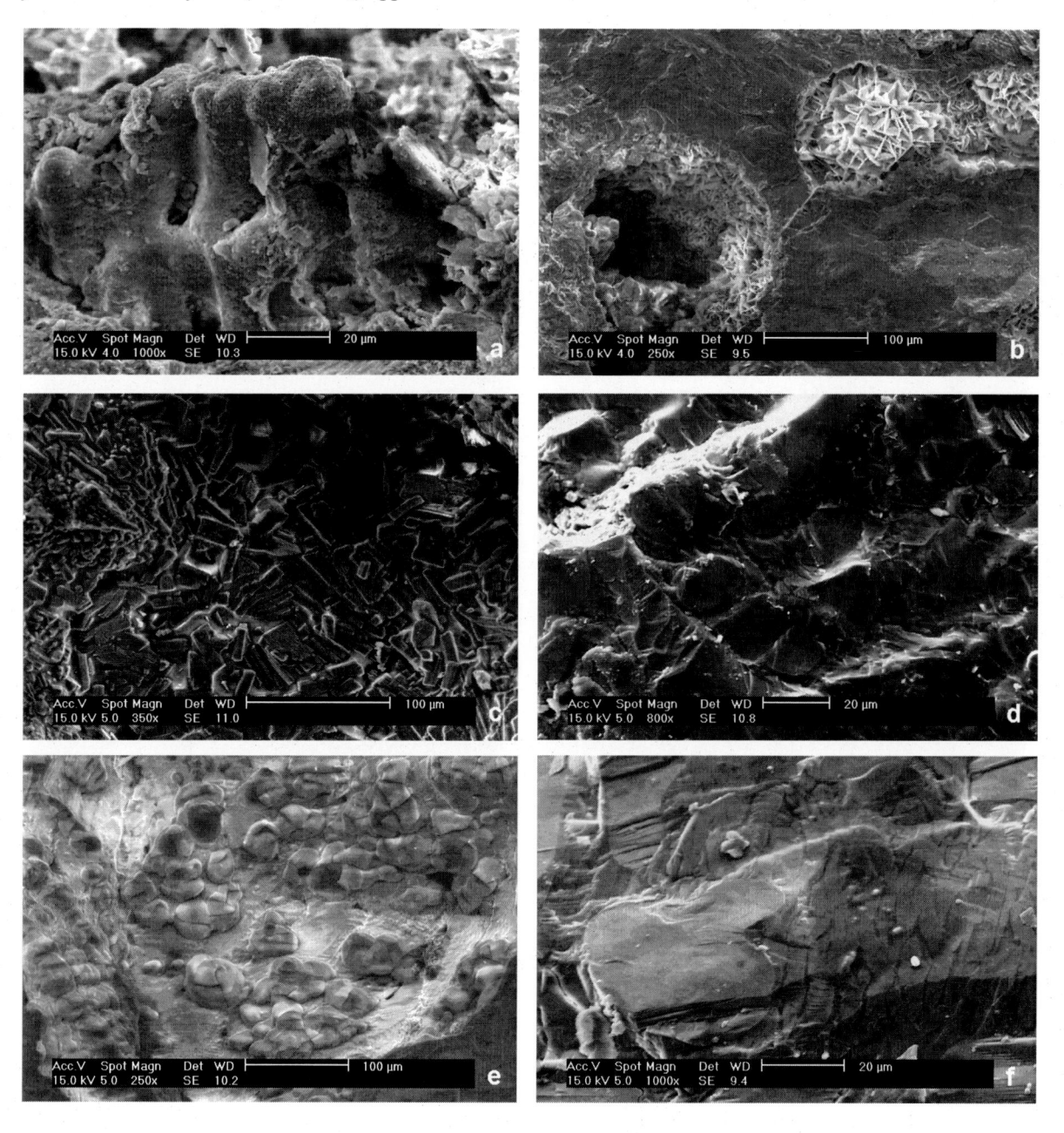

Figure 4. SEM observations of (a) iron sponges with (b) sand roses structures; (c) the eutectic mixture reveals the growth of (d) $FeO \cdot SiO_2$ mixed with calcium oxide, and (e, f) of impurities.

solid phase. Other samples, with a higher proportion of iron, presented different steps of the reduction and crystallisation of iron: the eutectic mixture (Fig. 4c) associated dark crystals of pure iron oxide (FeO), growing as cylindrical structures from which emerge, radially, amorphous structures of $FeO \cdot SiO_2$, mixed with calcium oxide (Fig. 4d). Impurities, usually named "non-reduced compounds" consisting of MgO, Al_2O_3, SiO_2, K_2O and CaO, are present as pillow nodules collected in anfractuosities (Fig. 4e, SiO_2, FeO, Al_2O_3, and CaO) or as scaled surface (Fig. 4f, SiO_2, FeO, Al_2O_3, K_2O and CaO).

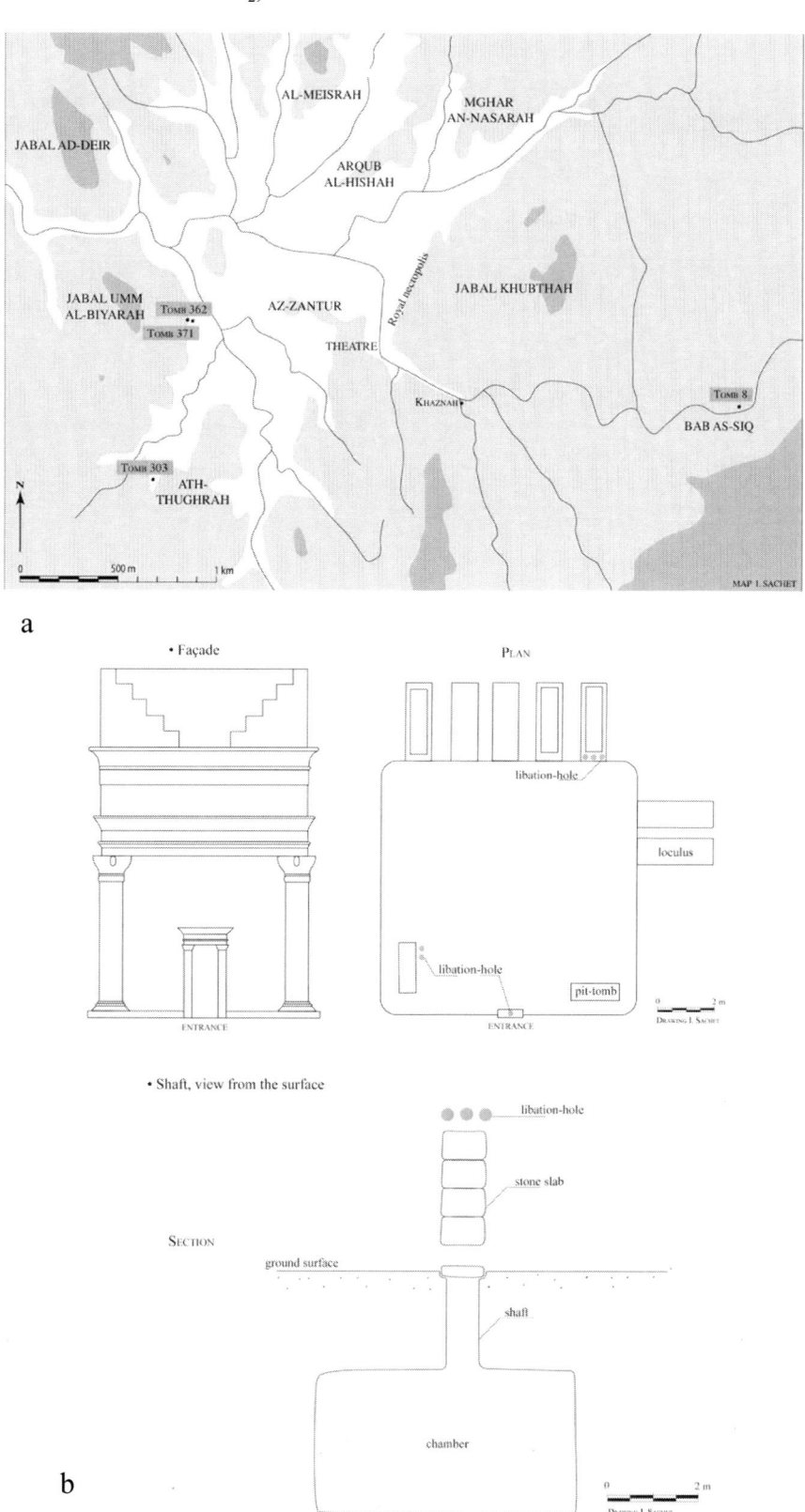

Figure 5. Location of the four samplings in libation holes from Petra (Jordan): (a) map of Petra, and (b) possible locations for libation holes in façade tombs (BD362 and BD371) and in shaft tombs (BD8 and BD303).

Figure 6. Tomb 362 and libation holes.

Thus, the lumps found during excavations consists only of slags, the molten waste material resulting from production sequences to obtain iron by reduction of the ore through a direct process. A part of the metallurgical operations of the bloomery process took place under the melting temperature of the metal. For this reason, some non-metallic second phase particles remained entrapped in the metallic matrix, forming the so called "slag inclusions" containing several compounds from the metallurgical system that were not reduced or that came from the re-oxidation of several elements. Some data could be deduced from the chemical constitution and the crystallised structures observed in the slag inclusions: the furnace was built from local sandstone, containing mainly silica and a portion of clay sufficient in order to bind silica particles together. A slag tapping hole, aperture made at the bottom of the furnace closed during the operation, was regularly opened and allowed slags to be removed at intervals. The furnace or structure was used repeatedly with the aim to produce different metals: pure iron, iron alloys, and pure brass. Thus, the scientific study of the archaeological artefacts allowed us to reconstruct metallurgical activities at the site.

Libation holes, ath-Thughrah, Umm al-Biyarah and Bab as-Siq necropolis, Petra

Circular cavities of c. 20 cm diameter, usually set in twos or threes, are often found inside or arranged on one side of pit-tomb or shaft-tombs at Petra (Fig. 5). These holes were used by Nabataeans to pour libations to their dead (Sachet 2010). In 2005, Isabelle Sachet took samples of sandstones from the bottom of two libation holes in tombs BD362 (Fig. 6) and BD371 in Umm al-Biyarah necropolis, in order to carry out tests on the porosity of Petra sandstone and on its ability to preserve organic traces over archaeological time-scales. Those two samples were taken in rock-cut chamber tombs obviously reoccupied by Bedouins as houses or sheepfolds. In 2006, Michel Mouton made soundings in front of the tower tombs BD8 in Bab as-Siq and BD303 in ath-Thughrah (Mouton 2007; Mouton this volume). Libation holes were uncovered in an open air area in front of both shaft entries to the tombs and samples were taken from two holes.

Organic analysis has never been conduced on such materials, because it was thought that stone is not sufficiently porous to retain organic substances. Moreover, the sandstone samples did not show any visible residues or impregnations. Finally, the context presents adverse conditions in terms of contamination risk, since for BD 8 and BD 303 (Fig. 5b), the space is open and the cups form depressions in the bottom apt to collect all superficial contamination sources (plant degraded materials). Additionally, they are exposed to rains and frost, the latter contributing to the enhancement of natural degradation and loss by lixiviation of organic markers. Moreover, for BD 362 and 371, libation holes were located inside a rock-cut chamber that was re-used by humans for domestic occupation or cattle penning.

The first step of our study was to determine if organic residues retained from libations were preserved in the sandstone. In order to extract and identify the more relevant data from these original samples, we implemented a methodology suited to micro-scaled samples, using very sensitive analytical methods (Garnier and Frère 2008: 61-71).

The methodology implemented was as follows (Fig. 7): sandstone samples were crushed and the resulting powder was extracted by solvents (dichloromethane/methanol 1:1 v/v) under ultrasonication. After centrifugation, the inorganic solid was discarded. The organic extract was separated in two parts, the first one being analysed by GC-MS for the characterisation of volatile molecules, the second one by thermochemolysis coupled to GC-MS (named THM-GC-MS) and nanoESI-MS for the study of high-molecular markers in the liquid state. A further purification by solid phase extraction (SPE) was implemented in order to simplify chromatographic and mass profiles: specific cartridges were used in order to purify and to analyse individually the different chemical families with the most appropriate conditions. Concurrently, the crushed sandstone was hydrolysed with a methanolic solution of potassium hydroxide (protocol of saponification by KOH at 80°C, 40 min). The extract was purified and analysed by HRGC and GC-MS according to the same methodology as outlined above. This double analysis, derived from methodologies recently developed for food analysis (Laakso et al., 2005: 402-410, Moreau et al. 2002: 457-500, Toivo et al. 2001: 631-643), allows the capture of organic matter preserved in a free and extractable form and in the "bound" form. The latter case needs a hydrolysis step allowing the dissociation of organic soluble molecules from inorganic or organic polymeric phases.

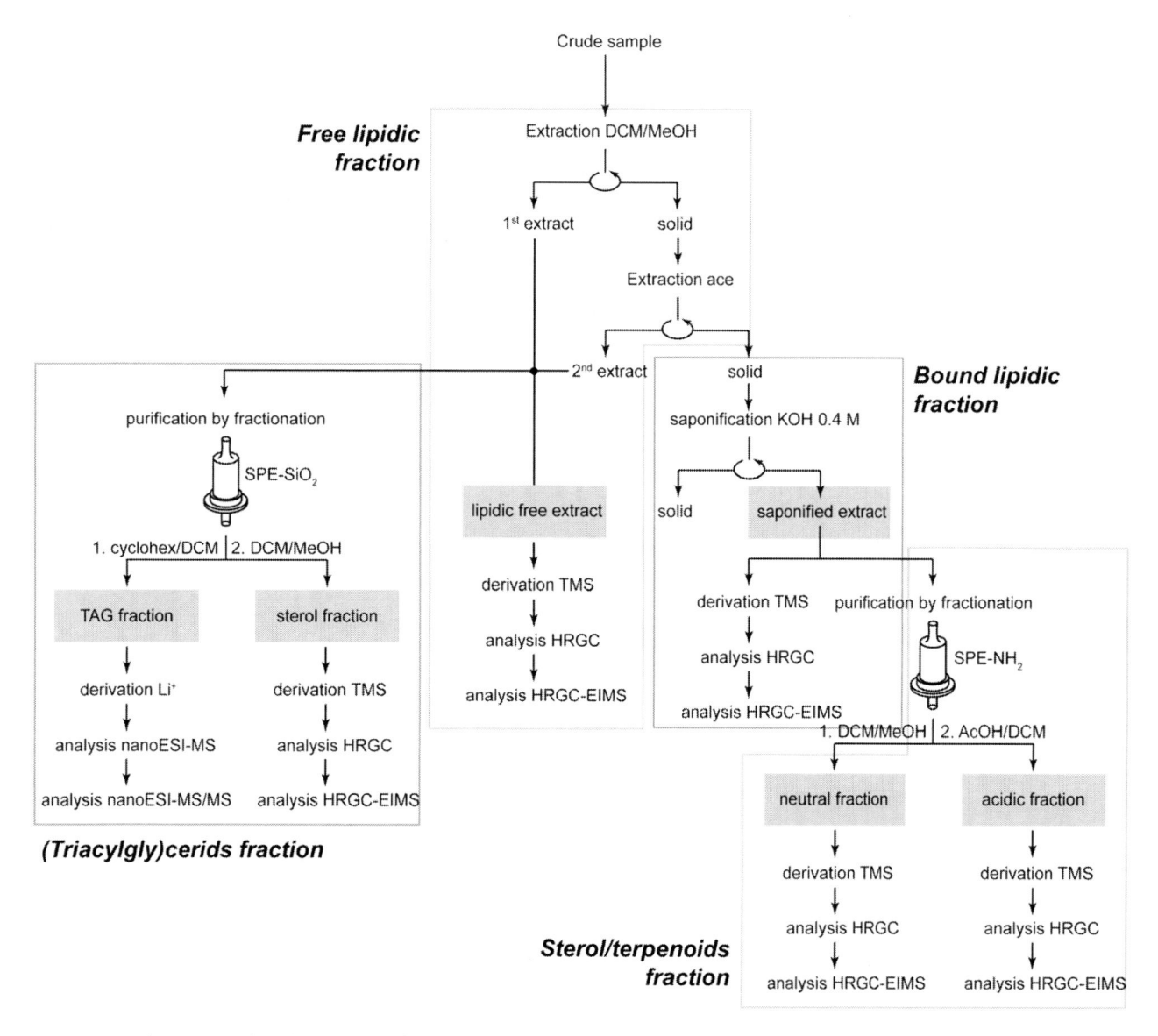

Figure 7. Methodology applied for the characterisation of the molecular structure of archaeological residues.

Although the two samples coming from Umm al-Biyarah (BD362, BD371) presented a very low content of organic soluble matter, the other two from Bab as-Siq (BD8) and ath-Thughrah (BD303) showed a complex chromatographic profile (Fig. 8). The saponified extract of the four samples was more abundant and revealed complementary data (Table 1: BD303). The interpretation of the data requires the identification of each separated marker according to its mass spectrum, and in a second step, the determination of the associations of biomarkers, e.g. of native constitutive molecules, of natural degradation markers and of anthropic degradation markers. Combinations of such categories and their chemotaxonomic value allow the definition of the nature of the original animal or vegetal species and the recovery of information regarding the *chaîne opératoire* and the degradation steps undergone by the material.

The content of fatty acids is relevant for fatty materials such as oils, fats, and waxes. The chromatographic profiles of saponified extracts are more informative than those from soluble fractions. They mainly consist of even-numbered fatty acids, the more present being those with 16 or 18 carbon atoms. Palmitic acid (noted 16:0)[2] dominates in samples BD371 and BD8, although stearic acid (18:0) and oleic acid (18:1) are the more intensive compound in samples BD362 and BD303 respectively. Myristic (14:0) and lauric (12:0) acids are also present. These short-chain acids, associated with *iso*-palmitic, *iso*-stearic acids and even-numbered acids (isomers of 15:0 and 17:0) are characteristic of dairy products. The use of such products seems to be relevant for samples BD362, BD8, and BD303. Lower proportions of odd-numbered fatty acids present as the three isomers *anteiso*, *iso* and *neo*, are considered to be contamination markers coming from the degradation of the cellular walls of bacteria present in the sediment. Oleic acid cannot be systematically interpreted as marker of vegetal oil, as it was in earlier studies (Condamin *et al.* 1978: 195-201), because of its broad distribution in the animal and vegetal

---

[2] The notation *n:i* indicates the carbon length (*n*) of the fatty acid, and its unsaturation number (*i*), each one corresponding to a double bond C=C.

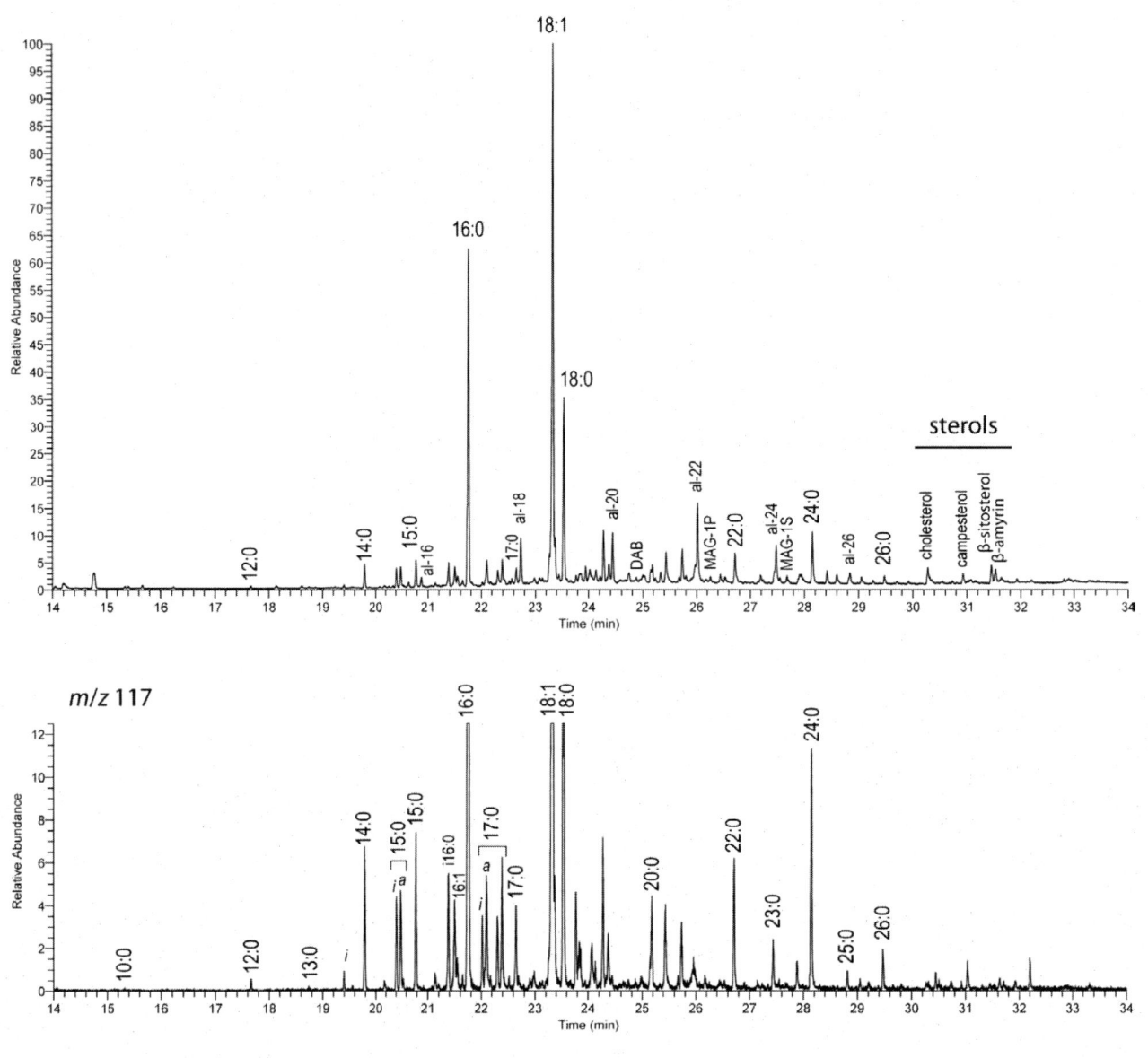

Figure 8. Chromatographic profile of the saponified extract from the sample of sandstone BD303 (top). The reconstructed chromatogram at *m/z* 117 permits a clearer reconstruction of the presence and the distribution of fatty acids (bottom).

kingdom. However, when associated with other unsaturated fatty acids such as palmitoleic (16:1) or linoleic (18:2) acids, it does tend to indicate a plant origin (Belitz and Grosch 1999: 152-236). It is well known that unsaturated compounds are very labile against degradation processes, especially oxidation reactions catalysed by the presence of micro-organisms or metallic salts (iron, manganese, etc., Garnier 2007: 39-58). Such oxidation markers are identified in the extract BD362, where α,ω-diacids (9:0 dioic, 11:0 dioic, and 13:0 dioic) indicate the cleavage of C=C bonds in unsaturated acids, leading to shorter ones. Compared to other samples, the extract BD362 is more degraded and difficult to interpret.

The profile of fatty acids of a natural material is deeply modified by such degradation processes, and no direct identification can be rigorously suggested. In order to mitigate this loss of information, the sterol distribution is studied (Fig. 9). These biomarkers are very stable against degradation, including hydrolysis, heating or oxidation, and lixiviation (Huang and Meinschein 1979: 739-745). They can be classified in three classes: C27-sterols, mainly cholesterol and its degradation markers coprostanol, produced by microbial digestion in the guts of higher animals and considered as a faecal marker; C29-sterols or phytosterols, coming from plants; and C28-sterols specific to plants, fungi, and marine organisms. The animal origin of fatty materials is revealed in samples BD371, BD8, and BD303 by the presence of the native cholesterol (Fig. 9b), and the degradation markers, cholest-3-ene and cholestan-3β-ol. This confirms the presence of dairy products in BD362, BD8 and BD303. A large contamination by fungi is shown by ergosterol; it is correlated to the presence of ramified odd-numbered fatty acids and proves that fungi and micro organisms have settled and proliferated in the tombs (Fig. 9c). Other contaminations are brought to light by the presence of coprostanol and epicoprostanol issued from the reduction of cholesterol by mammals. Vegetal sources are clearly revealed by the presence in the

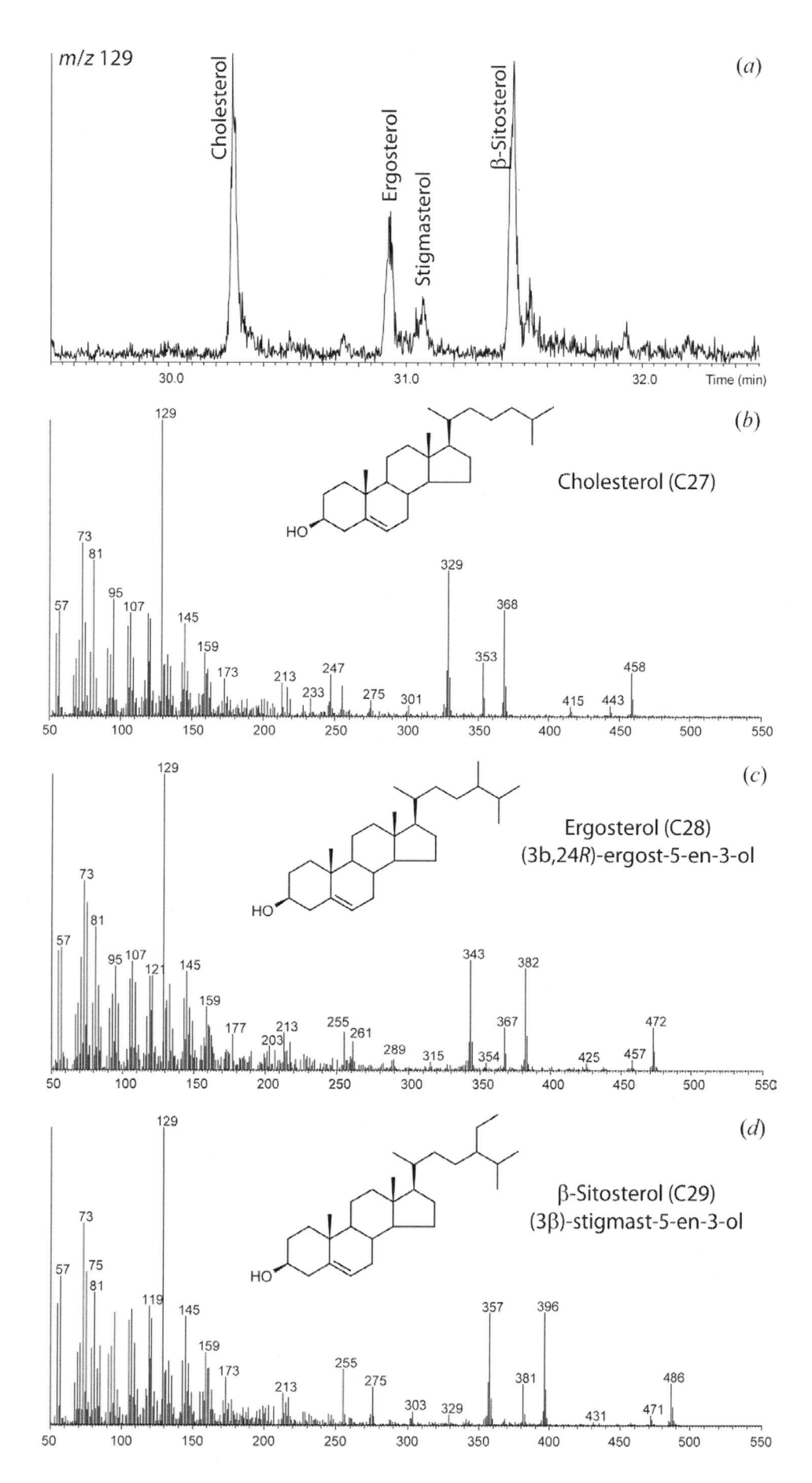

Figure 9. Partial chromatographic profile of the saponified extract BD303, showing the profile of sterols (a), and the characteristic mass profiles of the most important (b, c, and d).

samples of β-sitosterol (Fig. 9d), associated with stigmasterol and stigmastan-3β-ol, reflecting multiple origin fats. If campesterol does not allow the precise identification of the nature of the vegetal oil, traces of brassicasterol in BD303 permit the identification of *Brassica sp.* (cabbage/mustard genus, Normen 2007: 193-201).

With the aim of identifying the biological origin of fatty materials, a process using complementary purification of the soluble extract and analysis by nanospray-mass spectrometry was investigated. This methodology was successfully implemented previously for Nabatean and Roman lamps, revealing the presence of triacylglycerols, native biomarkers of oils and fats (Garnier 2008: 47-56). The mass profile and the structure of each detected triacylglycerol allowed the identification of the use of olive oil and other degraded vegetal oils, sometimes mixed with resin in eight lamps, and the use of pure sesame oil in two other lamps, without addition of any other product.

Concerning our samples BD8, BD303, BD362 and BD371, the first obtained lipidic extract was purified by solid phase extraction (SPE) on a diol-cartridge, a selective phase that allows the successive retention of analytes according their polarity. The phase corresponding to triacylglycerols and cerids is selected and directly injected by infusion in the nanospray source of a mass spectrometer, after doping with a methanolic solution of lithium chloride. In this technique, the high-molecular and non-volatile compounds are lightly ionised and analysed directly from a liquid solution (Hsu and Turk 1999: 587-599). The lithium ion allows a quantitative ionisation of cerids, without any fragmentation; thus, the nanospray-MS spectrum reflects the real composition of the extract. The nano-ESI-MS spectra of the four extracts presented a very low intensity, traducing a very low content in (triacylgly)cerids. No triacylglycerol could be detected; this observation is not incompatible with the presence of oils, but reveals the complete hydrolysis of the native biomarkers. Meanwhile, a series of cerids are detected, each peak being separated by 14 amu from the following one. The complete structure of such cerids could not be determined because of the low intensity of the signal, but the spectrum and the detected markers confirm the presence of vegetal waxes. Since the study of epicuticular waxes is a very recent technique, due to the lack of appropriate methodology and analytical method, no data have been yet published on the molecular structure of cerids and their chemotaxonomic value.

Long-chain odd-numbered fatty acids are present in samples BD371 and BD303. They are associated with a series of odd-numbered *n*-alcohols. These compounds result from the hydrolysis of cerids, characteristic of the epicuticular waxes present on the surface of plant leaves. By hydrolysis, each cerid forms the fatty acid and the *n*-alcohol. This origin is confirmed by the presence of vegetal ramified alcohols, especially phytol, and its oxidation marker, phytanic acid. The association of all these markers indicates either the pollution by degraded vegetation that has grown on the site, or the intensive use of raw plant material. Additional precision can be added by studying diterpenoids: these natural C20-compounds are produced by resinous species. They are derivatives of abietic acid, such as pimaric acid, but their high sensibility to oxidation leads to the formation of the more stable dehydroabietic acid, that can undergo further oxidation resulting in the formation of its 3-oxo derivative (Mills and White 1994: 95-128; Evershed *et al.* 1985: 528-530). Small amounts of dehydroabietic acid have been identified in samples BD362, BD371, and BD8, allowing the precise identification of the use of branches of resinous species. The nature of the botanical species can not be otherwise elucidated by chemistry, since the diterpenoid compounds can be found in several species, even in fresh material. A parallel study in anthracology made by Charlène Bouchaud (PhD student, university of Paris 1) proved the presence of fragments of conifer, Pinaceae (*Abies sp.*), in very small amounts in tomb BD303, that could possibly have been imported from Anatolia.

In conclusion, the study of the four libation holes confirmed that organic matter can impregnate and be conserved in soft stones such as sandstone. Obviously, the amount is very tiny and requires the implementation of very sensitive analytical methods, according to a methodology well-adapted for ancient and degraded organic material.

Evidence for a reoccupation by Bedouins of the Umm al-Biyarah tomb chambers (BD362, BD371) for domestic and cattle breeding uses are confirmed by the presence of coprostanols in the analyses. The libation holes from Umm al-Biyarah also contained a mixture of vegetal oils and dairy products. Animal fats were detected in minor amounts. The purification of sterols and terpenoids confirms the use of several vegetal oils and animal fats. The degraded state of the samples does not allow further determination of the nature of each oil and fat. In the necropolis of ath-Thughrah (BD303), the libation hole analysed revealed a complex composition, consisting of animal fats, especially dairy products. The place where the holes were cut, at the top of the shaft tomb, indicates that no cattle were held there. In this case, it may indicate human pouring of dairy products, probably milk, in the libation holes of tomb BD303. From the tower tomb BD303, vegetal oils were also identified, mixed with a diterpenoid resin coming from an imported conifer showing that this resin may not result from an environmental pollution.

The present study of materials linked to libations provides evidence of the value of chemical analyses for the identification of amorphous residues. Our study has demonstrated that, in the future, light can be thrown on the substances poured on votive stones such as *nefesh* and betyles, if the porosity of the stone is sufficient to trap some traces of the fluid. Even if the molecular structure of biomaterials is very complex, their more stable biomarkers can be isolated and characterised using efficient analytical processes. The procedure for the extraction, purification and the analysis of the extracted markers has to be thought over and carefully explored for each chemical family: fatty acids, sterols, triacylglycerids, cerids, *n*-alcohols and other long-chain compounds or polyaromatic hydrocarbons constituting the lipid class, polysaccharids, proteins, and polyphenols. Chromatography and mass spectrometry revealed all their potential for the research of oils and resins. The knowledge of the chemical structure of modern reference materials allows the relevant identification of ancient artefacts. Nowadays, with such methodologies at hand, it will be interesting to couple this approach with traditional archaeology and botanical examinations to fine-tune the questions and the problematic put forward. Such a combination of complementary disciplines allows new aspects of the everyday life of past civilisations to be revealed.

Acknowledgements

We thank the Department of Antiquities of Jordan and its director, Dr. Fawwaz Khraysheh, for the authorizing excavations and analyses, and the team of Suleiman Farajat, Sami al-Nawafleh and Qais Tweissi. The GC-MS spectrometer used in this study was funded by the Conseil Général du Puy-de-Dôme and the Museum of Ceramics in Lezoux (France). The authors would like to express their gratitude to Elisabeth Dodinet for the English revision.

References

Belitz H.-D. & Grosch W. (eds) 1999. *Food Chemistry*. Berlin, Springer-Verlag.

Chapman A. C. & Plenderleith H. J. 1926. Examination of an Ancient Egyptian (Tutankh-Amen) Cosmetic. *Journal of the Chemical Society* 129: 2614-2619.

Condamin J., Formenti F., Metais M. O., Michel M. & Blond P. 1976. The application of gas chromatography to the tracing of oil in ancient amphorae. *Archaeometry* 18: 195-201.

Evershed R. 2000. Biomolecular analysis by organic mass spectrometry. Pages 177-240 in E. Ciliberto & G. Spoto (eds.), *Modern Analytical Methods in Art and Archaeology*. New York: Wiley-Interscience.

Evershed R. P. 2008. Experimental approaches to the interpretation of absorbed organic residues in archaeological ceramics. *World Archaeology* 40: 26 - 47.

Evershed R. P., Jerman K. & Eglinton G. 1985. Pine wood origin for pitch from the Mary Rose. *Nature* 314: 528-530.

Farajat S., Al-Nawafleh S. 2005. Al-Khaznah Courtyard Excavation at Petra. *Annual of the Department of Archaeology of Jordan* 373-393.

Formenti F., Hesnard A. & Tchernia A. 1978. Une amphore "Lamboglia 2" contenant du vin dans la Madrague de Giens. *Archaeonautica (Paris)* 2: 95-100.

Garnier N. 2007. Analyse de résidus organiques conservés dans des amphores : un état de la question. *LRCW2. Late Roman Coarse Wares, Cooking Wares and Amphorae in the Mediterranean: Archaeology and Archaeometry* I: 39-58.

Garnier N. & Frère D. 2008. Une archéologie de l'évanescent. Pages 61-71 in A. Verbanck-Piérard, N. Massar & D. Frère (eds.), *Parfums de l'Antiquité. La rose et l'encens en Méditerranée*. Mariemont, Musée royal de Mariemont.

Garnier N., Tokarski C. & Rolando C. 2009. Analysis of archaeological triacylglycerols by high resolution nanoESI, FT-ICR MS and IRMPD MS/MS: Application to 5th century BC-4th century AD oil lamps from Olbia (Ukrainia). *International Journal of Mass Spectrometry* 284: 47-56.

Garnier N., Tokarski C. & Rolando C. (in press). Quel combustible pour les lampes nabatéennes de Pétra ? In Salles, J.-F. (ed.), *Lampes antiques du Bilad esh-Sham, de l'Âge du Bronze à la période de transition byzantine-ommeyyade*. Amman, Petra (6-13 Nov. 2005), IFPO Amman.

Hsu F.-F. & Turk J. 1999. Structural characterization of triacylglycerols as lithiated adducts by electrospray ionization mass spectrometry using low-energy collisionally activated dissociation on a triple stage quadrupole instrument. *Journal of the American Society for Mass Spectrometry* 10: 587-599.

Huang W. Y. & Meinschein W. G. 1979. Sterols as ecological indicators. *Geochimica et cosmochimica acta* 43: 739-745.

Laakso P. 2005. Analysis of sterols from various food matrices. *European Journal of Lipid Science and Technology* 107: 402-410.

Mills J. S. & White R. 1994. *The organic chemistry of museum objects,* Oxford, Butterworth-Heinemann.

Mouton M., 2007. Mleiha, à l'origine des traditions funéraires nabatéenne, *Archéologia* 441 : 42-49. Paris: Faton.

Moreau R. A., Whitaker B. D. & Hicks K. B. 2002. Phytosterols, phytostanols, and their conjugates in foods: structural diversity, quantitative analysis, and health-promoting uses. *Progress in Lipid Research* 41: 457-500.

Nehmé L. 2003. The Petra Survey Project. Pages 144-163 in G. Markoe (*ed.*), *Petra rediscovered. Lost City of the Nabataeans*, London: Thames and Hudson; New York: Harry N. Abrams; Cincinnati: The Cincinnati art museum.

Normen L., Ellegard L., Brants H., Dutta P. & Andersson H. 2007. A phytosterol database: Fatty foods consumed in Sweden and the Netherlands. *Journal of Food Composition and Analysis* 20: 193-201.

Regert M., Garnier N., Decavallas O., Cren-Olivé C. & Rolando C. 2003. Structural characterization of lipid constituents from natural substances preserved in archaeological environments. *Measurement Science and Technology* 14: 1620-1630.

Sachet I. 2010. Libations funéraires aux frontières de l'Orient romain : le cas de la Nabatène. Pages 157-174 in J. Rüpke & J. Scheid (eds), *Bestattungsrituale und Totenkult in der römischen Kaiserzeit*. Stuttgart:

Franz Steiner Verlag. Potsdamer Altertumswissenschaftliche Beiträge 27.

Toivo J., Phillips K., Lampi A.-M. & Piironen V. 2001. Determination of Sterols in Foods: Recovery of Free, Esterified, and Glycosidic Sterols. *Journal of Food Composition and Analysis* 14: 631-643.

Authors' Addresses
Nicolas Garnier
Laboratoire Nicolas Garnier
32 rue de la Porte Robin
63 270 Vic-le-Comte
France
Email: labo.nicolasgarnier@free.fr.
Website: www.labonicolasgarnier.eu

Isabelle Sachet
Orient et Méditerranée, UMR 8167
Collège de France
52 rue du Cardinal Lemoine
75231 Paris cedex 05
France
Email: isabelle.sachet@college-de-france.fr

Anna Zymla
Laboratoire Génie et Procédés des Matériaux
Ecole Centrale-Paris
Grande Voie des Vignes
92295 Châtenay-Malabry Cedex
France

Caroline Tokarski
Chimie Organique et Macromoléculaire, UMR CNRS 8009
and Protéomique, Modifications Post-traductionnelles et Glycobiologie, IFR 147
Université des Sciences et Technologies de Lille
59655 Villeneuve d'Ascq Cedex
France

Christian Rolando
Chimie Organique et Macromoléculaire, UMR CNRS 8009
and Protéomique, Modifications Post-traductionnelles et Glycobiologie, IFR 147
Université des Sciences et Technologies de Lille
59655 Villeneuve d'Ascq Cedex
France

The monolithic *djin blocks* at Petra: a funerary practice of pre-Islamic Arabia

Michel Mouton

Summary
At Mleiha, in the Oman Peninsula, the oldest graves, dating to the 3rd-2nd centuries BC, are associated with massive mud brick tower-like monuments, square in plan and decorated with crowsteps. Parallels with Qaryat al-Fau and Levantine monuments have already been discussed (Mouton 1997 and 2006). The closest parallels are found at Petra, in the shape of monolithic towers, generally considered as the earliest expression of Nabataean funerary architecture. But most of such monuments include a funerary chamber, which is never the case at Mleiha. From 2006-2008, excavations were carried out around the six monuments at Petra to check the hypothesis of separate graves originally associated with them, and to find chronological data indicating whether the graves inside correspond in fact to a re-use of the monoliths. Separate graves, mostly underground, have been found associated with five monuments (one could not be completely explored) confirming the closeness of the funerary traditions. Additionally, the collected artefacts indicate two periods of utilisation of the graves; a first one very lightly represented, dating back to the 1st-2nd centuries BC, clearly distinguished in stratigraphy from a second one, much better represented by a large quantity of fine pottery from the 1st-2nd centuries AD.

Keywords: Arabia, funerary practices, Mleiha, Petra, Jordan

Introduction

The discovery of the oldest Late pre-Islamic funerary monuments at Mleiha in the Oman peninsula led us to undertake the survey and cataloguing, and eventually a small excavation, of the area around the monolithic funerary monuments of Petra, commonly known as *djin blocks* or *sahrij*. These monuments showed clear parallels with those found at Mleiha (Mouton 1997 and 2006) which needed to be confirmed by detailed observations. Those parallels are all the more interesting in that both these sites developed at the same time, at opposite ends of Arabia, and that the communities which produced them were related to the world of the nomads (Fig. 1).

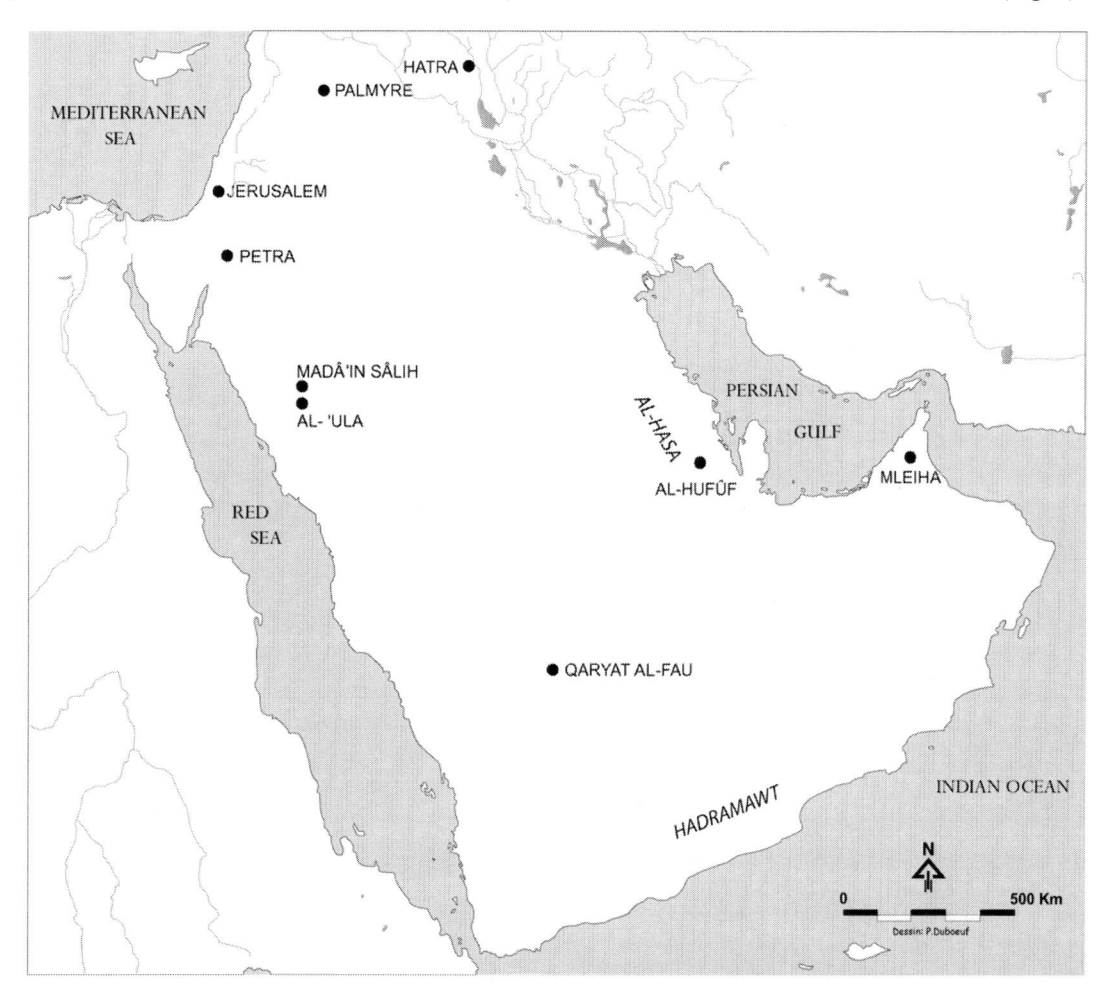

Figure 1. Map of Arabia (P. Duboeuf).

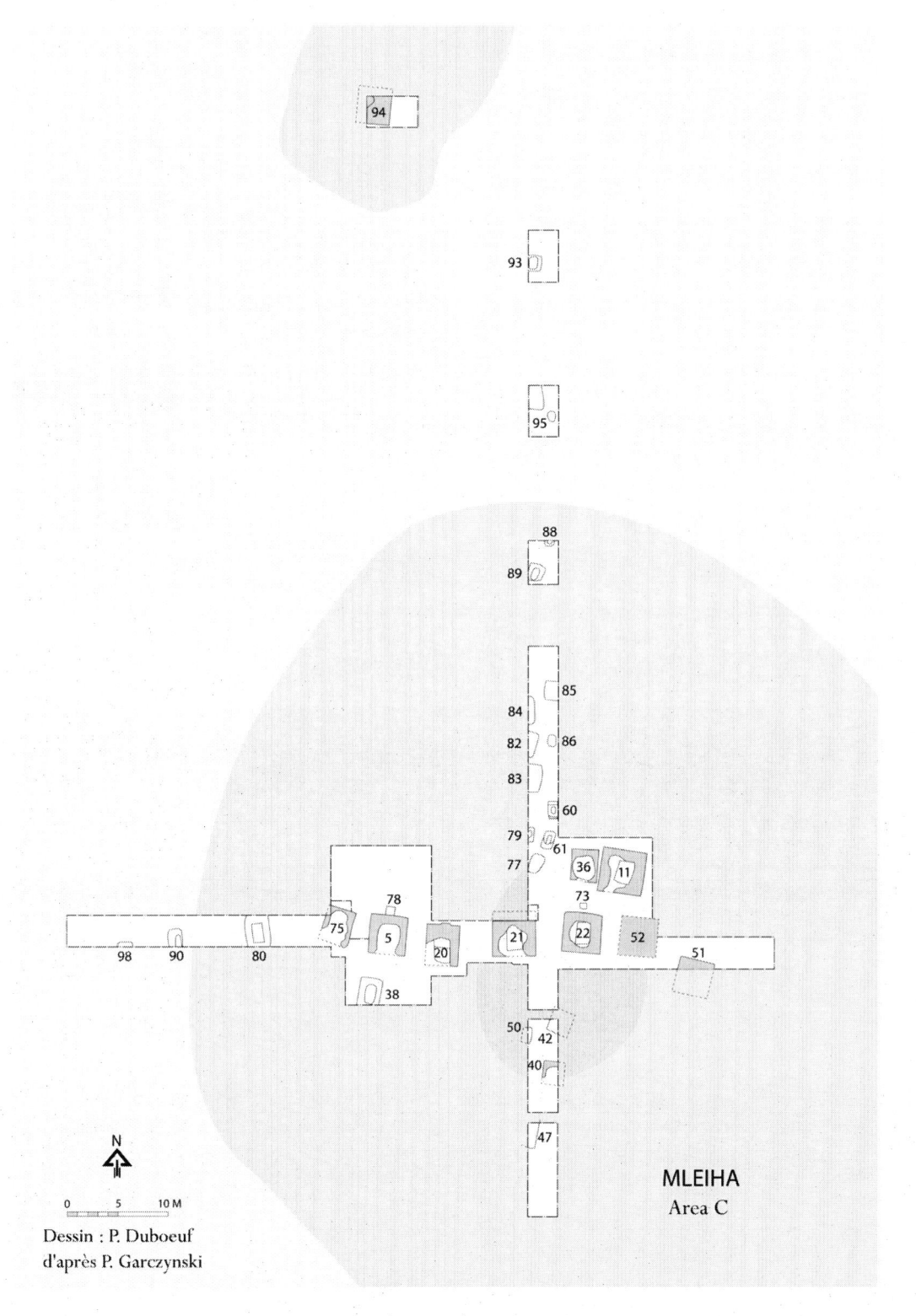

Figure 2. Mleiha. Plan of the cemetery in area C (P. Duboeuf, after P. Garczinsky).

Late Pre-Islamic Funerary Monuments at Mleiha

Mleiha, in the western foothills of the mountains of the Oman peninsula (Sharjah, U.A.E.), was occupied from at least the 3rd century BC and bears witness to a profound cultural change with regard to the preceding Iron Age village communities. The assemblage of artefacts is clearly different, as are also the technology (iron metallurgy, soft stone working etc.), the culture (use of writing and of coins), the lifestyle (dwellings constructed of light materials) and the burial practices (Boucharlat & Mouton 1993; Mouton 2008).

A comparative ethno-archaeological analysis of the development of dwellings at Mleiha from the oldest phase, PIR.A (Pre-Islamic Recent A, from the 3rd to mid 2nd century BC) to the final phase, PIR.D (from mid 2nd to mid 3rd century AD), shows all the characteristics of a process of sedentarisation (Mouton 1999). If one adds to this various other indicators (development on a single site, early pottery collections of mainly small forms, mobile forges and involvement in trans-Arabian exchanges) the most likely hypothesis is that of a mobile population becoming settled.

Whereas the first inhabitants of Mleiha lived in dwellings constructed from light materials, for their dead they built monuments made of mud bricks. This shows that whilst they chose mobile dwellings for themselves they chose to build durable, even ostentatious, monuments to the memory of their dead, as is frequently seen in nomadic populations (tumuli, cairns and other protohistoric funerary monuments, contemporary gipsy tombs, etc.).

The tombs are grouped into cemeteries, forming a necropolis of thousands of burials which border the site to the east and to the south. Several areas have been excavated by the French archaeological team and the Department of Antiquities of the Emirate of Sharjah (Boucharlat & Mouton 1998; Jasim 1999). Each cemetery is a low mound formed by the ruins of the central funerary monuments. The tombs have all been robbed and their contents scattered around. The finds collected from the burial pits and from the spoil heaps of the grave robbers indicate the phases of occupation.

The oldest of the cemeteries excavated is sector C (Fig. 2), to the east, which dates from the PIR.A period, as indicated by the presence of Rhodian *amphorae*, from which three stamped handles have been clearly dated to the end of the 3rd century BC or the first quarter of the 2nd century BC (Boucharlat & Mouton 1998: 18-19); a few finds indicate that its use continued into the following phase, PIR.B (mid 2nd - 1st century BC). The stratigraphic analysis showed that the central tombs are the oldest and that the cemetery developed progressively around them.

These tombs are also the biggest and all display similar features. A rectangular burial pit was dug into the hard marl sediment which lies approximately 1m below the surface and was reached through wide pits dug through the upper sand and gravel deposits. After the funeral (each grave is separate) the burial pit was closed by a layer of mud bricks over a transverse wooden layer, and the whole pit was backfilled to surface level either with the excavated material or mud brick. A rectangular mud brick monument was then erected over the pit, the sides of which vary between 3.75 and 4.25 m (Fig. 3). These constructions were quite tall, as is shown by the volume of their ruins. Whole slabs of collapsed mud brick facings have been excavated, of which the longest is 3.5m. Including the base, the monument from which it fell was therefore more than 4m high and had sides 4.1m long: this reconstruction (Fig. 4) indicates a funerary monument in the shape of a cube or tower.

There is evidence of a stepped base for two of the six central monuments in sector C, which was formed by moving back the rows of mud brick over one or two courses. For two of the others it is clear that there were no steps at the base, and in the two remaining cases the state of preservation makes it impossible to determine whether there were steps or not.

These monuments were all entirely covered either by a thick white coating or by a layer of very dense white gypsum bricks. A single fragment of coating, found at the foot of a later funerary monument in a different cemetery (sector AH from the PIR.C period, 1st to mid 2nd century AD) bears traces of a red pigment.

The white gypsum bricks were also used to make the crowsteps found in the destruction layers. The marks of their removal indicate that for the most part they were meant to be fixed to the facing; others are markedly eroded on both sides and were probably used to crown

Figure 3. Mleiha. Excavations in area C (3rd - mid. 2nd centuries BC): a funerary monument and a crowstep made of gypsum mud brick (photos French archaeological mission in Sharjah).

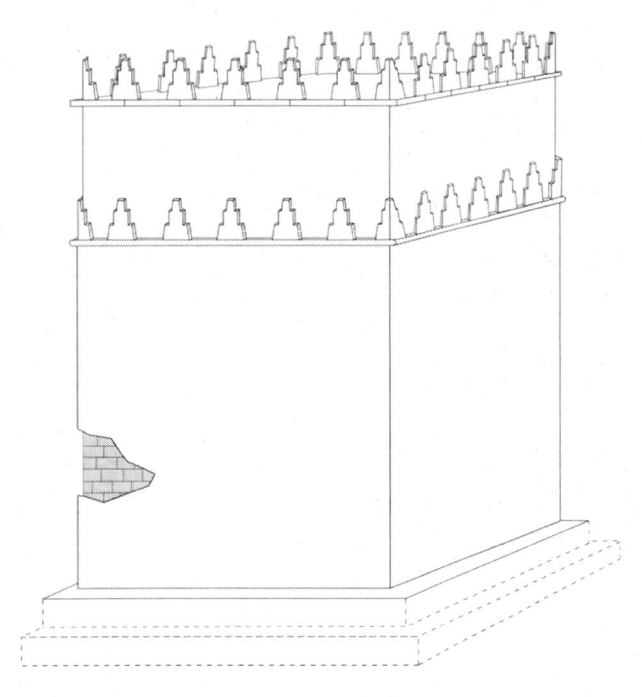

Figure 4. Mleiha. Hypothetical restitution of a funerary monument from the early period PIR.A (3rd - mid 2nd centuries BC) (H. David and P. Duboeuf).

the top of the structures (Boucharlat & Mouton 1998: 25, Fig. 8). Linear mouldings, also of white brick, probably marked the edges of the band of crowsteps.

The characteristics of these monuments may be summarised thus:

- cemeteries built to the south and east of the inhabited area
- each cemetery is arranged around the largest, central tombs
- underground graves contain material dated to the 3rd–2nd centuries BC
- each grave is associated with a solid mud brick monument, square in plan and forming a cube or a tower
- decorated with bands of crowsteps on the façades and/or at the top of the monument
- and horizontal linear mouldings probably along the edges of the bands of crowsteps
- in some cases having a stepped base

These monuments are related to a funerary tradition attested along the northern fringes of Arabia, in particular at Palmyra, in Lebanon and in the valley of the Euphrates (Mouton 1997; Clauss 2002). But clear parallels can be found on two sites which developed contemporaneously with Mleiha: Qaryat al-Fau and Petra (Mouton 2006).

Late Pre-Islamic Funerary Monuments at Qaryat al-Fau and Petra

The excavator of Qaryat al-Fau dates the start of the occupation of the site to the 3rd century BC (al-Ansary 1982; al-Ansary 1988: 109; al-Ansary 1993). Raised monuments, massive and badly ruined, are visible in some areas of the necropolis which borders the site to the east and south. A.R. al-Ansary dismisses any possible correlation with a system of defences, pointing out that there are no traces anywhere else (north or west). On two photographs of the 1982 publication, the towers seem to be of rectangular plan, with sides more than 3m long and preserved elevations of greater size (al-Ansary 1982: 48 Fig. 2, 57 Fig. 4; Mouton 1997: Fig. 11-12). Al-Ansary states that the graves of a single family are grouped around each of the towers and that some of the tombs are decorated with crowsteps (al-Ansary 1988: 109; 1982: 48) or have crenellated decorations (al-Ansary 1993). From this one may deduce that:

- right from the start of the occupation of Qaryat al-Fau, in the 3rd century BC, funerary monuments were linked to collective underground tombs
- they were built to the east and south of the inhabited area
- monuments were solid, brick built, at least 3–4m along each side and had an elevation of more than that, in the shape of a tower
- they were decorated with crowsteps
- a cemetery grew up around each one.

Defined in this way the funerary tradition at Qaryat al-Fau is entirely in keeping with what has been observed at Mleiha.

At Petra, the rocky landscape and the easily-workable sandstone favoured adaptation to the surroundings in the form of cave installations, a large number of which were tombs. Many are decorated with one or two bands of crowsteps (Brünnow & Domaszewski 1904: 137-143; Mouton 2006) which makes them look like sculptural representations of monuments comparable with those of Mleiha. The catalogue of the tombs of Petra shows the varying degrees of relief of the monuments, from a simple sculptured façade to a free-standing monolith. These monoliths, of which there are only six and which are known as *djin blocks*, are found in only two areas of the site, to the east in the Bab as-Siq (BD 7, BD8, BD9, BD30) and to the south at Ras-Suleyman (BD303, BD307). Their characteristics relate them to the funerary monuments which we have described at Mleiha and at Qaryat al-Fau:

- the monoliths are rectangular in plan, with sides varying between 4.5 and 6.5m, and elevations of between 6 and 9m; the shapes are the same but they are carved out of solid rock rather than built of mud brick
- they all have a stepped base
- there are bands of crowsteps sculpted on the façade, framed by horizontal lines in relief (except on two of the monuments which have been reshaped), and crowsteps at the top, preserved on two of them
- they are situated on the eastern and southern approaches to the site.

However, there are two points which need to be emphasised to justify a genuine relationship to the monuments of Mleiha. The first concerns the chronology: given that there is no element by which to date them absolutely, architectural criteria alone have been used for the generally agreed dating of these monoliths to the start of the evolution of rock tombs in Petra (McKenzie 1990: 6, table 1). The only indicator of the age of the monoliths is stylistic: if one accepts that the design of bands of crowsteps pre-dates façades with two large corner half-stacks, which are clearly dated to the 1st century AD at Mada'in Salih (McKenzie 1990; Healey 1993; Sachet 2005), then these monuments date from before the Christian era.

The second point concerns the location of the tomb: the parallels seem to be weakened by the confusion between the monument and the tomb. In four of the cases a tomb has been cut into the interior of the monument, and in one case only roughed out. In order to confirm the relationship with the monuments of Mleiha and Qaryat al-Fau, the significant distinction between the funerary monument as a stele/*nefesh* and the tomb itself, generally subterranean, must be attested at least, in the oldest phase of Nabataean funerary architecture.

The notion of *nefesh* is essential, for it is the foundation of this funerary tradition: the two most ancient funerary inscriptions discovered at Mleiha begin with the formula *nfs wqbr*, "*nefesh* and grave ..." which makes clear the distinction between the monument known as the *nefesh* and the tomb itself. In Semitic languages the word *nefesh* means "breath", "soul", "person"; it appears to express here the belief that the soul of the deceased is incorporated into the monument of its burial, which thus becomes a kind of substitute for the departed person (Teixidor 1992; Starcky & Gawlikowski 1972: 125; Gawlikowski 1972: 5).

The use of this term for a funerary monument appears to go back further in Arabia than in the Levant generally (Kühn 2005: 229). All kinds of monuments, from rough stone to artistic constructions, can be referred to as *nefesh* (Dalman 1912: 77; Will 1949b: 287; Kühn 2005: 136-228; Nehmé forthcoming). They are intended as a repository for the soul, the breath of the deceased, and are the "house of the soul" in the same way that the *betyl* is the "house of the divinity". In theory each *nefesh* can only be linked to the burial of a single individual (Gawlikowski 1972: 10; see also Will 1990: 434) and it is in accordance with this principle that the oldest tombs at Mleiha were built.

In central and eastern Arabia at the beginning of the Christian period, these monuments became open rooms, probably used for prayer and rituals, linked to collective underground tombs (Mleiha: Boucharlat & Mouton 1998; ed-Dur: Haerinck 2001; Qaryat al-Fau: al-Ansary 1982); they never became the tomb itself. In the Levant the word acquired a less precise meaning, referring either to a tomb or to its associated commemorative monument. In the 1st century BC in Jerusalem, *nefesh* simply means a funerary monument erected in memory of one or more people (Rahmani 1982: 46). In Palmyra, in the 1st c. AD it refers to a communal tomb in the form of a tower (Will 1949b: 308; Will 1990: 435; Gawlikowski 1970: 187 and 194).

In Petra, the term *nefesh* designates only pyramid-shaped steles commemorating a deceased person; and no inscription mentioning *nefesh* has been found related to the six monolithic funerary monuments. Only one of them (BD307) has a few words in Nabataean characters inscribed on one of its walls: *dnh qbr'*, "this is the tomb", followed by one or two letters which are difficult to decipher.

Therefore, if one believes that the monuments at Mleiha are related to those in Petra, this implies that they are manifestations of the same funerary tradition which does not allow for confusion between the *nefesh* and the tomb. Our hypothesis is therefore that the tombs built into the monoliths at Petra are indications of re-use of the monuments in later times, when burial customs were modified by Hellenistic and Roman influences (Mouton 2006: 93-94). In only two cases can a separate tomb be linked to a monument: BD30 where an underground room is accessed through an opening in the rock on which the monument rests, and BD8 which is exactly aligned with a pit tomb cut into the top of the rock out of which the monument was carved.

Recent Fieldwork at Petra

In order to investigate these matters, we carried out fieldwork at Petra to look for the tombs linked to the other four monuments and also to search for dating evidence that could confirm the antiquity of the Petra monoliths.

Figure 5. Petra. The monument BD303 at Ras Suleyman, with a detail of the crowsteps preserved at the top (photos French archaeological expedition at Petra).

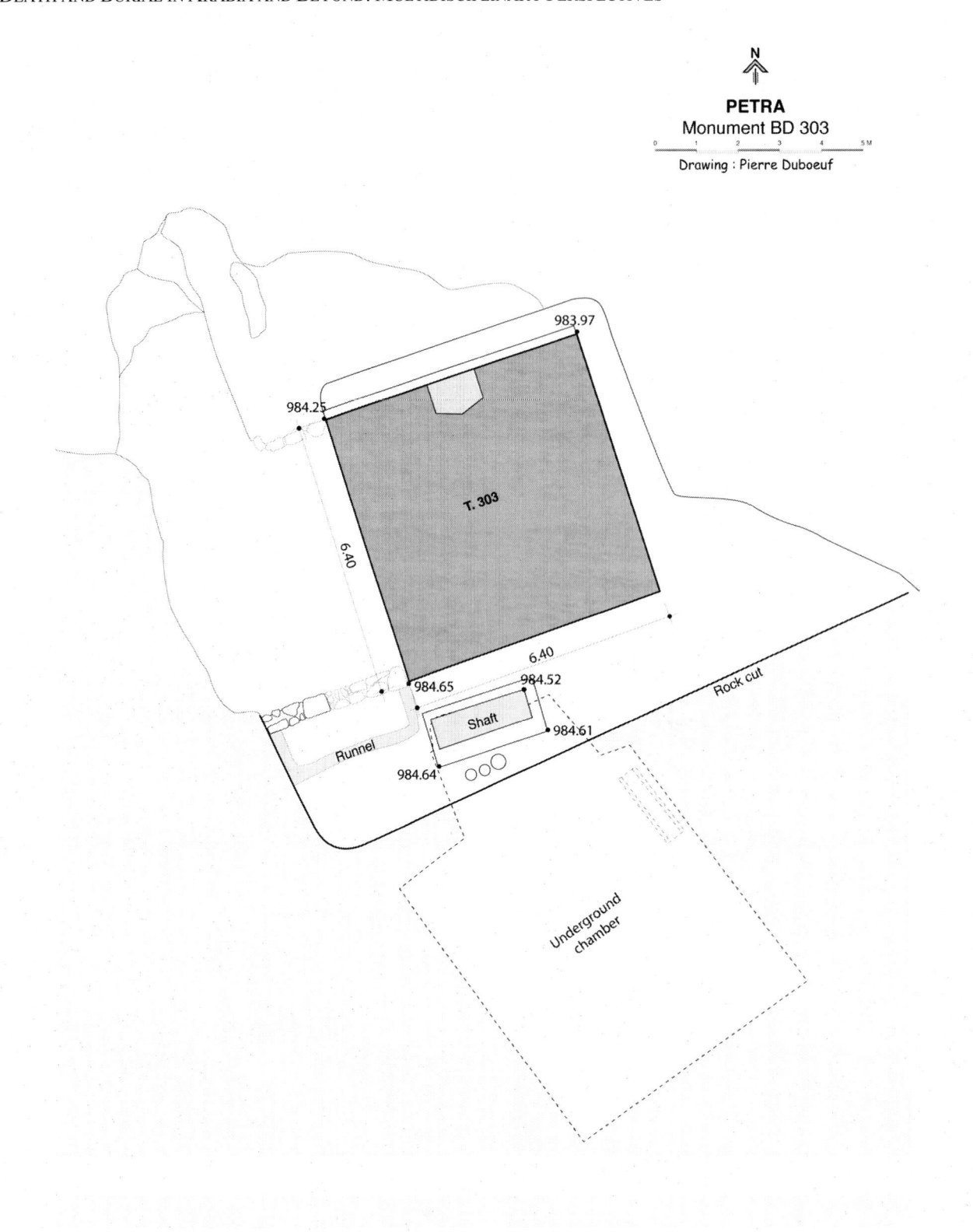

Figure 6. Petra. Plan of the monument BD303 at Ras Suleyman after the excavation carried out in 2006 (P. Duboeuf).

Monument BD303

Two tombs, BD303 and BD307, face each other across the little valley of Wadi ath-Thughrah at Ras-Suleyman, just below the Snake Monument. BD303 (Figs. 5 & 6) stands on an artificial terrace created as a result of its carving (Brünnow & Domaszewski 1904: 289, Fig. 317, Taf. X; Mouton 2006: 84, Fig. 8-11). It is 6.5 m square and a little over 9m high, which gives it a tower shape, and it sits on a two-stepped base. Although it is eroded there are still the remains of a band of carved crowsteps, framed by two horizontal mouldings, 1m below its top. Each face has six stacks of crowsteps (4 steps) framed by two half stacks. At the top, small stone slabs form a border overhanging the façades on which rest crowsteps of the same size and proportions as those which decorate the façades. The top is partially covered by earth and small stones. A doorway for access to an interior room has been roughed out on the north side, cutting into the stepped base, which indicates an intention to re-use the monument that never came to fruition.

The area cleared by the carving of the monument is 2.5–3 m long on the eastern and southern sides and 4.2 m long on the western side, facing the valley. In the space to the south, between the monument itself and the cut away rock face, an access shaft 2.4m long and 80cm wide leading to an underground chamber was revealed by recent looting. The vertical walls of the shaft have steps cut into them to facilitate access to the underground chamber, which measures 6.5 x 7.5 m, and the floor of which is more than 3m below the surface. Only the deposits between the monument and the rock face were excavated to completely clear the access shaft (the chamber itself was partially excavated at a later date by I. Sachet). A large cover slab was preserved at the mouth of the shaft, and three cup holes around its border were presumably intended for libations or offerings. Channels cut into the flat level surface of the rock carried away the rain water so that it did not flow too abundantly into the underground chamber. A wall of a much more recent dwelling, medieval or modern, was found in the south-west.

Figure 7. Petra. The monument BD307 at Ras Suleyman, with a detail of the shaft discovered along its southern side (photos French archaeological expedition at Petra).

Monument BD307

On the same rock formation which closes the valley of Ath-Thughrah stands BD307 (Fig. 7), facing BD303 to the west (Brünnow & Domaszewski 1904: 290, Fig.318-319, Taf.X; Mouton 2006: 84-85, Fig.12). This monument, very similar to the other, has sides of 5.1 to 5.2 m, and stands on a four-stepped base 7.6 m wide at its widest point. The elevation facing the valley is 10.2 m high. Approximately 1 m below the top is a band of crowsteps carved between two horizontal lines. Each side of the monument has five stacks of crowsteps framed between two corner half stacks. As with BD303 the top has small slabs overhanging the walls, carefully cut with rounded edges. There are fragments of inverted crowsteps on the top, mixed up with a little soil and some stones. Inside the monument a chamber approximately 3 m square has been carved out. Access is by a rectangular opening a little over 2 m high cut through the steps of the base facing the valley to the east.

The area created by the carving of the monolith forms a platform 1.2 m wide to the north, 1,5 m wide to the west, 2-3 m wide to the south, more than 6 m wide to the east. The south east corner of this area is partially covered by a deposit of ashy soil. Here, at the foot of the monument, an area 3 x 5 m was excavated (Fig. 8).

The access shaft to an underground chamber was quickly discovered, cut alongside the monument, and measuring 2.20 x 0.78 m. A parapet and a slot cut under the monument made it possible to wedge the cover slabs in place. Deep runnels were cut around the opening and along the bottom step of the monument to drain away the rain water. Six cup holes were cut around the rim of the access shaft and two other smaller cup holes may have been part of a suspension system for descending into the tomb. The stratigraphy of the deposits which covered these remains indicates at least two phases of robbery:

- first robbery: a sandy layer of crumbling sandstone containing a lot of broken pieces of fine ceramic, spread right up to the mouth of the shaft
- second robbery: a more ashy layer spread over the preceding layer, filling the shaft itself, which we did not excavate to any depth. It contained very little material from antiquity, including a few hand made ceramics from Islamic periods and some remains of unarticulated bones from at least three adult individuals.
- and up two clearly differentiated layers, with scattered ashy lenses and very little Islamic or even modern materials, indicating temporary dwellings.

Monument BD30

In the area of Bab as-Siq, on a terrace overlooking the left bank of the Wadi al-Mudlim, stands BD30 (Brünnow & Domaszewski 1904: 203, Fig.232, Taf.III; Mouton 2006: 83-84, Fig.6-7). This monument is 4.5 m square and 8 m high, slightly wider at the base, which has two steps. The

Figure 8. Petra. Plan of the monument BD307 at Ras Suleyman after the excavation carried out in 2006 (P. Duboeuf).

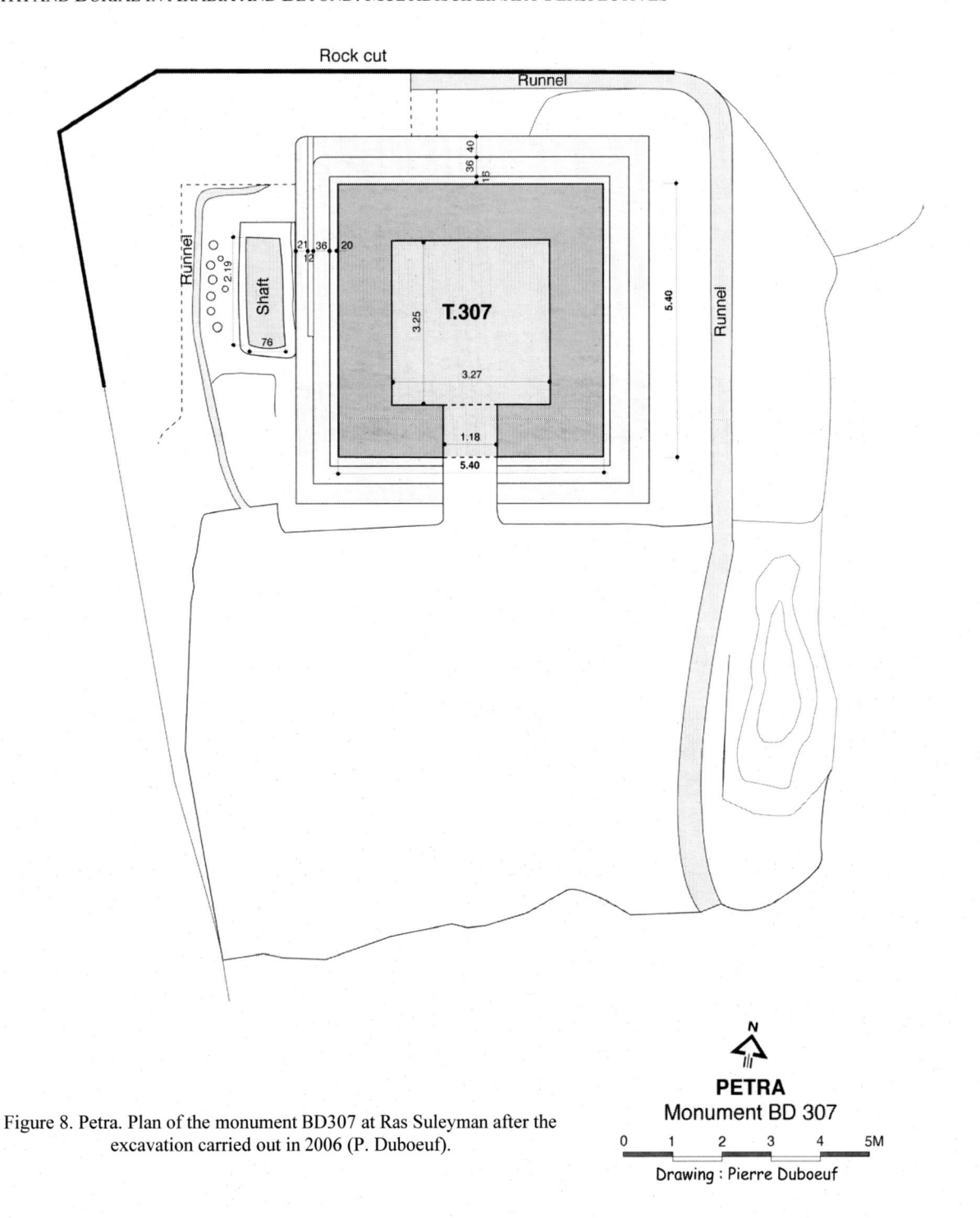

original rock was probably not high enough to allow for the monument to be constructed in the desired proportions, so the stepped base had to be cut deep into the rock on the southern side. The top is irregularly shaped and there is a little pile of earth and small stones on it. About 1 m below the top there is a carved band of crowsteps (4 steps) between two horizontal lines. Each face has five stacks of crowsteps flanked by half stacks at the corners.

To the west, the rock cut below the stepped base forms a wall in which is the access to an underground tomb, with a semi-circle carved above it. The first chamber leads to a narrow vertical shaft through which a deeper underground chamber is accessed. This tomb is clearly separated from the funerary monument decorated with crowsteps, therefore, no excavation was carried out around BD30, but surface material was collected in the surrounding area.

Monument BD7

Further up the Wadi Musa there is a group of three monoliths, known as *djin blocks* on the right (north) bank (Fig. 9). Upstream, BD7 (Brünnow & Domaszewski 1904: 197, Fig.141 and 225, Taf.III; Mouton 2006: 81-82, Fig.2-3) was deeply buried in a very compacted layer of river shingles, cemented together for a depth of 2.2 m

Fig. 9. Petra. The three *djin blocks* at Bab as-Siq; from left to right, BD9, BD8 and BD7
(photo French archaeological expedition at Petra).

on the north side. This deposit is most likely a result of works carried out in Nabataean and Roman times which reduced the flow of water and favoured the deposition of sediments carried by the floods (clearly attested at the Khazneh, beneath which two rock-cut tombs are completely buried; Farajat & Nawafleh 2005).

Two soundings were made, one along the northern face and the other at the north eastern corner of the monument, which enabled us to reconstruct its dimensions. The preserved height of the monument is 7.5 m but two deep incisions made by the stone worker indicate the removal of at least 50 cm of stone from the summit. The monument is 5.20 m square and rests on a three stepped base. Inside, a funerary chamber measuring 2.10 x 2.20 m opens to the east through a doorway which cuts into the upper step of the base. This chamber is almost completely filled with sediment deposited by floodwaters. Near the top of the monument runs a band comprised of 6 crowsteps (4 steps) between two half stacks in the corners, framed between two badly eroded horizontal bands. The carving of the monument created a terrace varying in width between 2.5 and 4.5m. Along the rock face behind the monument run two channels which carried water to the city in antiquity.

The soundings did not reveal any underground tomb related to the monument. The density of the shingle deposits made work extremely difficult and it was not possible to finish clearing them away. Runnels to carry away the rainwater, like those found at BD303 and BD307, and a quite large unexplored area towards the north west corner allows us not to dismiss the existence of an underground tomb.

The stratigraphy shows two main archaeological levels below the river deposits. Firstly, a layer a few centimetres deep of sand and crumbling sandstone blocks, containing very little ceramics, lies on the bedrock around the monument. Above this an uneven layer, up 30 cm deep in places and very black, extends as far as the rock face; it contains a large quantity of broken pieces of fine ware and painted pottery. Above these is a layer of fine sand, which is sealed by a thick accumulation of compacted river shingles, more than 2 m thick to the east. On the surface, a layer of powdery soil containing many hearths and lines of stones corresponds to shelters from the Islamic period which may be very recent.

Monument BD8

Immediately to the west, cut into a rock a few metres further up, is monument BD8 (Brünnow & Domaszewski 1904: 199, Fig. 140 and 225, Taf. III; Mouton 2006: 82, Fig.4) which is 4.5 m square and 6 m high. A parapet around all four sides of the summit leads one to suppose that it has been re-cut. One may, therefore, imagine that it was originally about 1m taller, which would give it proportions comparable to those of the other monoliths (L 6.5 x H 9.m; L 5.20 x H 10 m; L 5.20 x H 8 m; L 6 x H 9 m) and could also explain the lack of decorative band which would have been removed along with the top of the monument. The three-stepped base has been cut into by the entrance to the funerary chamber which was carved out of the centre of the monument. This chamber is square, 2.60 m per side, and contains two burial pits. Five cup holes have been carved out in front of the entrance.

Like BD7, the monument is in the middle of a terrace created by the carving of the rock. The terrace is 4.5 m wide where it overlooks the Wadi Musa and only 1.5 m wide at the back. The area between the back of the monument and the rock face has been filled by rubble to a depth of about 80 cm. Although the tomb associated with this monument is visible on the rock to the north, the excavation of this fill was undertaken in order to gather material.

The stratigraphy revealed two levels containing ceramics which might correspond to two episodes of looting separated by an episode of rock-cutting: the rocky floor of the terrace was covered by a layer about 10 cm thick containing a few pieces of pottery; above this was a layer of about 10-15 cm thick of sand and sandstone fragments, taken to be the layer corresponding to the carving out of the interior room; above this, and covering the cup holes in front of the entrance to the inner chamber, was a third layer, sandy and containing a large quantity of fine painted ceramics which would seem to correspond to an episode of grave robbing; above this a thick layer of rock-cutting debris sealed the whole, consisting of large blocks of cut sandstone which probably correspond to the re-cutting of the top of the monument; on the surface the deposits consist of the usual crumbling occupation layer containing hearths and late pottery; there was also the grave of an infant aged less than 6 months in a shallow pit filled with stones.

Monument BD9

To the west of BD8 stands BD9 (Fig. 10), which differs markedly in its present appearance from the other two monuments. (Brünnow & Domaszewski 1904: 199, Fig. 142 and 225, Taf. III: Mouton 2006: 82-83, Fig. 6; Zayadine 1979: 194-195). Square in plan, 5.8 m per side, it stands approximately 8 m high rising from a stepped base which is so eroded that only a few protrusions indicate its shape. The carving out of the monolith created a space all around the monument, 3.5 m wide to west, 4 to 5 m wide to the north and 6 m wide to the east, covered by rubble.

Each face was decorated with four pilasters topped by capitals embedded in a wide groove where fragments of ashlar blocks are still preserved. Above, a deep horizontal groove held a row of slabs which formed a cornice of which only two embedded pieces remain. The tomb is a rectangular pit hollowed out of the top and was accessed by a ramp cut into the rock face behind the monument. At the end of the ramp notches were cut to steady a removable bridge which would have been placed there to provide access for the burial(s).

The architectural decoration seems entirely comparable to monuments in Jerusalem dating from the early centuries of the Christian era. If one assumes that a pyramidion sealed the tomb at the summit it is then an exact replica of the tomb of Zachariah in the valley of Josaphat (Rahmani 1981: 46-47, 114-115).

It is clear that this monolith has been entirely reshaped: its proportions are identical to those of the other monoliths we have catalogued; two horizontal mouldings are still visible, framing a blank band of the same size as those which bear the crowstep decoration of the other monuments, and at the same distance from the top; the texturing of the band is rougher than that observed on the other surfaces of the monolith in the less eroded areas, and is presumably a result of the later removal of the crowstep motif; the embedded blocks for the construction of the reliefs for the cornices and capitals can only be explained by re-use of the monument – were it not so the reliefs would have been carved out of the solid rock, as they are on all the Nabataean and Roman rock-cut façades in Petra.

In the belief that the extant state of the monument is the result of a later re-use related to the installation of the tomb on its summit, an excavation was undertaken to search for the original tomb with which the monolith was associated. A sounding 2 x 1.5 m was sufficient to reveal the access shaft to an underground tomb dug in the space between the north face of the monument and the cut rock face. As with the other underground tombs, the mouth of the shaft is surrounded by a narrow parapet designed to retain the covering slabs, and a rock-cut runnel diverted the rain water.

The stratigraphy of the 1.2 m of deposits is fairly even, with no evidence of layers corresponding to the looting and very few finds. The deeper layers correspond to a progressive accumulation of wind-blown sands; the upper layers contain more stones and ash, indicating several successive temporary occupations. A column drum has fallen into the filling of the shaft.

Summary and Conclusions

At the end of these explorations, five of the six monolithic funerary monuments of Petra were linked to separate tombs, underground in four instances and on a rock overlooking the monument in the fifth instance. In the case of the sixth monument the possible presence of an underground tomb cannot be dismissed.

The hypothesis that the internal chambers represent re-use and modification of the monuments cannot be clearly demonstrated, but some evidence suggests this interpretation. Firstly, in the case of BD303 the carving of a space inside the monument was undertaken but never accomplished, although an underground tomb exists. Secondly, for BD307, BD7 and BD8 the excavation of the internal chamber cut through the steps of the base: had the original design of the monument included this opening it is very likely that it would have been placed at

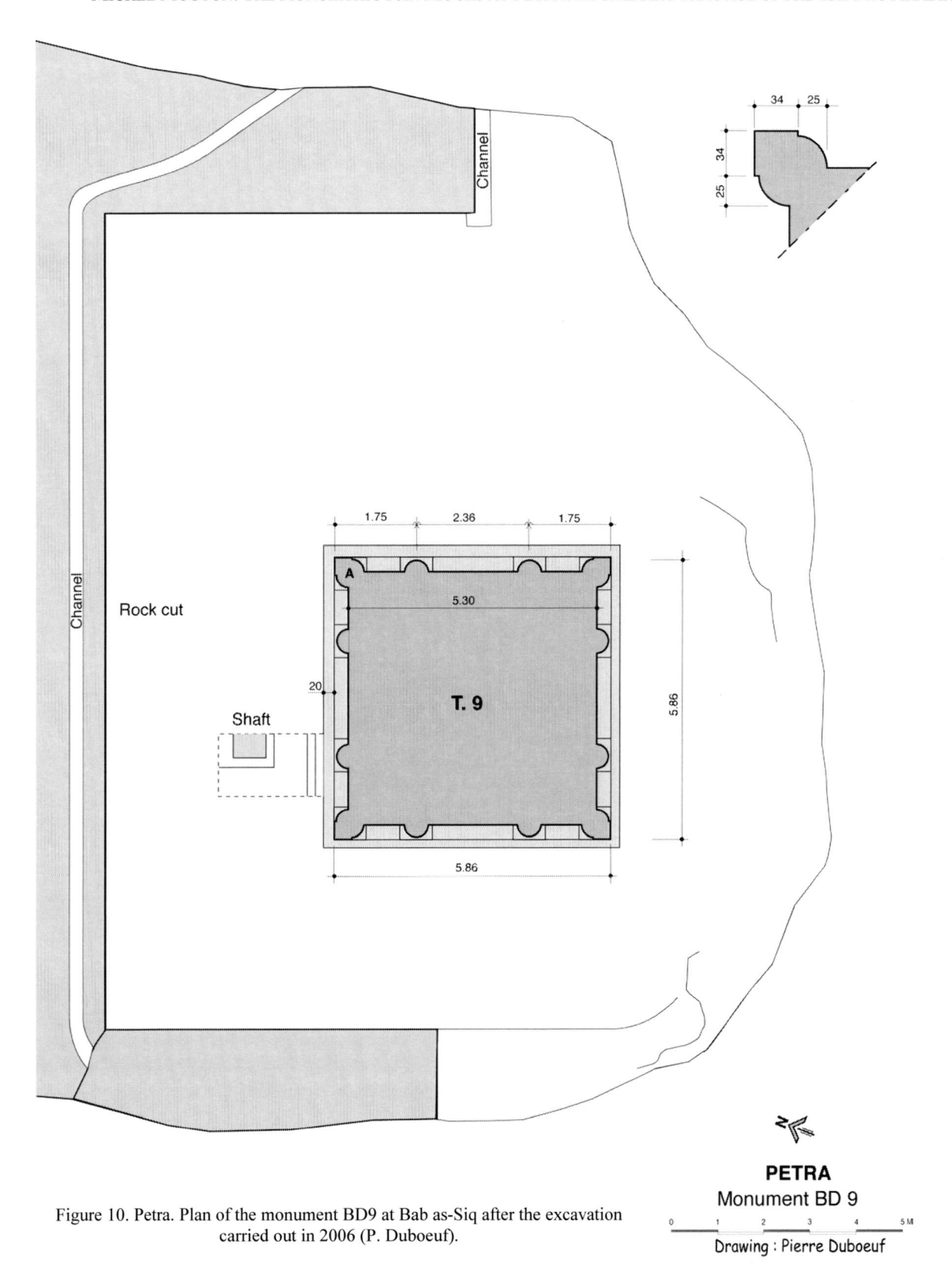

Figure 10. Petra. Plan of the monument BD9 at Bab as-Siq after the excavation carried out in 2006 (P. Duboeuf).

the top of the steps. Thirdly, in the case of BD9 the technical aspects of the decoration support the hypothesis that the monument was re-used, and the stylistic characteristics are clearly of a late period, the beginning of the Christian era. Finally, the pottery finds from around some of the monuments and from the excavations indicate two phases of use (excluding the Islamic finds from the upper levels). Specifically:

BD303: the surface finds were Nabataean ceramics from the 1st-2nd centuries AD and a few sherds more probably from the 1st century BC – a straight-rimmed dish, the rim of a black ceramic bowl and a plate with painted floral motif (S. Schmid's Phase 2a; Schmid 2000: Abb.79-80); the excavation carried out by I. Sachet in the underground chamber produced two fragments of Hellenistic unguentarium and a few sherds of fine painted ware from the end of the 2nd and the 1st century BC (S. Schmid's Phase 1; Schmid 2000: Abb.73-74)

BD30: the surface finds were mainly from the 1st-2nd centuries AD, but a few fragments more Hellenistic in form and one fragment of Rhodian amphora attest to the use of the tomb in the last centuries BC, as do several fragments of painted plates from the second half of the 1st century BC (Phase 2a)

BD7: a looting level containing a large quantity of fine ware from the 1st-2nd centuries AD lay immediately above a level that rested directly on the bedrock, in which only a small amount of pottery was found; it included two fragments of Rhodian amphorae and a double handle from a small, green-glazed jar of Mesopotamian type, which all point to the last centuries BC

BD307, BD8 and BD9: those layers which were cleared only yielded pottery from the 1st-2nd centuries AD; only very few came from BD9, but the excavation of the grave on the top of this monument, carried out by F. Zayadine, yielded a few fragments described as "Nabataean and Byzantine" (1979: 194-195).

Although the excavations undertaken around the monolithic funerary monuments of Petra yielded very little material which could be dated to before the Christian era, by their very presence they confirm an occupation of these tombs as far back as the 2nd - 1st centuries BC. This dating confirms the chrono-stylistic interpretation, given that archaeology has not produced any more ancient tombs in Petra. The underground tombs associated with a monolith decorated with bands of crowsteps would therefore appear to represent the most ancient Nabataean burial practices.

The identification of tombs separated from the monuments and nearly always underground confirms the parallels between the oldest forms of funerary architecture observed in Mleiha and Petra. This funerary architecture in Petra, Mleiha and Qaryat al-Fau thus not only presents morphological but also conceptual parallels which point to a common background. They are the visible indicators of a burial tradition shared by groups that once had a nomadic lifestyle (as is suggested by the archaeological documentation at Mleiha and the testimony of the classical authors at Petra), who settled between the 4th and 3rd century BC on the desert margins of Arabia and who were the founders of regional centres heavily involved in trans-Arabian exchanges.

Aknowledgements

The field work at Petra was carried out in the frame of the French Archaeological Expedition to Petra, financed by the French Ministry for Foreign Affairs and directed by Christian Augé (CNRS/Amman). The architectural drawings were done by Pierre Duboeuf. We are very grateful for the support of Dr. F. Khraysheh, Director of the Department of Antiquities of Jordan, S. Farajat, Director of the Petra National Site, and Mohammed Shawbaki, Director of the archaeological projects at Petra. Finally, I would like to thank my colleagues, Leila Nehmé (CNRS/Paris) for the reading and commentaries on the inscription found during the season of work on monument BD307, Isabelle Sachet (Post-Doctoral Fellow/CNRS Strasbourg) and Nathalie Delhopital (IFPO/Amman) for information about the anthropological and ceramic remains found during the excavation of the underground chamber at BD303, S. Schmid (Humbold Universität/Berlin) and F. Renel (INRAP/Paris) for their help on dating the ceramics. The English translation was done by Isabelle Ruben.

References

Al Ansary A.R. 1982. *Qaryat al-Fau. A Portrait of Pre-Islamic Civilisation in Saudi Arabia*. Riyadh: University of King Saud.

Al Ansary A.R. 1988. [Questions on the History of Pre-Islamic Arabia]. *Al Mukhadarat* 6: 82-121 (in Arabic).

Al Ansary A.R. 1993. [New discoveries at Qaryat al-Fau]. *Al Hayat* january 15th 1993 (in Arabic).

Boucharlat R. & Mouton M. 1993. Mleiha (3e s. avant J.-C.-1er/2e s. après J.-C.). Pages 212-249 in U. Finkbeiner (ed.), *Materialien zur Archäologie der Seleukiden-und Partherzeit im südlichen Babylonien und im Golfgebiet, Ergebnisse der Symposien 1987 und 1989 in Blaubeuren*. Tübingen: Ernst Wasmuth Verlag, Deutsches Archäologisches Institut Abteilung Baghdad.

Boucharlat R. & Mouton M. 1998. Les pratiques funéraires dans la péninsule d'Oman. Répartition et mode de construction des tombes de Mleiha (E.A.U.). Pages 15-32 in C.S. Phillips, D.T. Potts & S. Searight (eds), *Arabia and its Neighbours. Essays on Prehistorical and Historical Developments Presented in Honour of Beatrice de Cardi*. Gent: Brepols.

Brünnow R.E. & Domaszewski A. von 1904. *Die Provincia Arabia*. Strassburg: Verlag von Karl J. Trübner.

Clauss P. 2002. Les tours funéraires du Djebel Baghoûz dans l'histoire de la tour funéraire syrienne. *Syria* 79: 155-194.

Dalman G. 1908. *Petra und seine Felsheiligtümer*. Leipzig: J. C. Hinrichs'sche Buchhandlung.

Farajat M. & Nawafleh S. 2005. Report on the al-Khazna courtyard excavation at Petra (2003 season). *Annual of the Department of Antiquities of Jordan* 49: 373-393.

Gawlikowski M. 1972. La notion de tombeau en Syrie romaine. *Berytus* 21: 5-15.

Gawlikowski M. 1970. *Monuments funéraires de Palmyre*. (Travaux du Centre d'Archéologie Méditerranéenne, 9). Warszawa.

Haerinck E. 2001. *The University of Ghent South-East Arabian Archaeological Project. Excavations at ed-Dur (Umm al-Qiwan, United Arab Emirates). II : The Tombs*. Leuven: Peeters.

Healey J.F. 1993. *The Nabataean Tomb Inscriptions of Mada'in Salih*. Oxford: Oxford University Press.

Jasim S.A. 1999. The excavation of a camel cemetery at Mleiha, Sharjah, U.A.E. *Arabian Archaeology and Epigraphy* 10: 69-101.

Kühn D. 2005. *Totengedenken bei den Nabatäern und im Alten Testament. Eine religionsgeschichtliche und exegetische Studie*. Münster: Ugarit-Verlag.

McKenzie J. 1990. *The architecture of Petra*. British Academy Monographs in Archaeology 1. Oxford: Oxford University Press.

Mouton M. 1997. Les tours funéraires d'Arabie, *nefesh* monumentales. *Syria* 74: 81-98.

Mouton M. 1999a. Mleiha: Description and Dating of the Site. Pages 9-32 in M. Mouton (ed.), *Mleiha I: environnement, stratégies de subsistance et artisanats*. (Travaux de la Maison de l'Orient 29). Lyon: Maison de l'Orient.

Mouton M. 1999b. Éthnoarchéologie et sédentarisation : évolution de l'architecture domestique à Mleiha (Sharjah, E.A.U.). Pages 109-130 in F. Braemer, S. Cleuziou & A. Coudart (eds), *Actes des XIXe Rencontres Internationales d'Archéologie et d'Histoire d'Antibes*. Antibes: Editions APDCA.

Mouton M. 2006. Les plus anciens monuments funéraires de Pétra : une tradition de l'Arabie préislamique. *Topoi* 14/1: 79-119.

Mouton M. 2008. *La péninsule d'Oman de la fin de l'Age du fer au début de la période sassanide*. Society for Arabian Studies Monographs No. 6, BAR International Series 1776. Oxford: Archaeopress.

Nehmé L. Forthcoming. Les inscriptions nabatéennes du Hawrân. In Actes du colloque *Cultures du Hauran : déterminismes géographiques et communautés humaines. Bilan de dix ans de recherches de terrain et perspectives nouvelles, Damas, 8-11 octobre 2007*.

Rahmani L.Y. 1982. Ancient Jerusalem's Funerary Customs and Tombs. *Biblical Archeologist* 45: 43-53, 109-119.

Schmid S. 2000. Die Feinkeramik der Nabatäer: Typologie, Chronologie und kulturhistorische Hintergründe. Pages 1-200 in *Petra. Ez Zantur II. Ergebnisse der Schweizerisch-Lichtensteinischen Ausgrabungen*. Mainz: Verlag Philipp von Zabern.

Sachet I. 2005. Étude sur le développement et l'organisation des nécropoles de Pétra et Madâ'in Salih. Pages 25-41 in D. Sebag (ed.), *Deuxièmes rencontres doctorales d'Orient-Express. Actes du colloque tenu à Paris les 5, 6 et 7 février*. Paris: COREP.

Starcky J. & Gawlikowski M. 1985. *Palmyre*. Paris: Librairie d'Amérique et d'Orient.

Teixidor J. 1992. Une inscription araméenne provenant de l'Emirat de Sharjah (Emirats Arabes Unis). *Comptes Rendus de l'Académie des Inscriptions et Belles-Lettres* 1992: 695-707.

Will E. 1949. La tour funéraire de Palmyre. *Syria* 26: 87-116.

Will E. 1990. La maison d'éternité et les conceptions funéraires des Palmyréniens. Pages 433-440 in M.-M. Mactoux & E. Geny (eds), *Mélanges Pierre Lévêque*. Annales Littéraires de l'Université de Besançon 413. Besançon: Université de Besançon.

Zayadine F. 1979. Excavations at Petra (1976-78). *Annual of the Department of Archaeology of Jordan* 23: 185-197.

Author's Address
Michel Mouton
UMR 7041 / CNRS - Université Paris X
Maison de l'Archéologie et de l'Ethnologie
21 Allée de l'Université
92023 Nanterre cedex
France
michel.mouton@mae.u-paris10.fr

Colouring the Dead: New Investigations on the History and the Polychrome Appearance of the Tomb of Darius I at Naqsh-e Rostam, Fars

Alexander Nagel and Hassan Rahsaz

Summary

During recent conservation work conducted on the monumental façade of the tomb of the Achaemenid ruler Darius I (d. 486 BCE) at Naqsh-e Rostam in Fars (south-west Iran), abundant traces of an earlier polychrome surface coating were discovered. In our paper, we introduce preliminary observations of the colour schemes detected on the façade, and address issues of the history and original polychrome decoration of the tomb. Although the meticulously carved façade of Darius' tomb served as a model for the tomb façades of all following Achaemenid rulers, not only at Naqsh-e Rostam, but also for those above the terrace of the Persepolis-Takht, the colour schemes were remarkably different. Although traces of paint were noticed by earlier visitors in their descriptions of the façades of these tombs, no systematic study of the coloured ornamentation of the Achaemenid tomb façades has been completed. New investigations into the façade of the tomb of Darius I, conducted by the team of the Parsa-Pasargadae Research Foundation between 2001 and 2005 were directed by Hassan Rahsaz. These investigations, originally intended to clean calcareous layers on the tomb façades caused by rainfall from their surfaces, not only exposed traces of the polychromatic decoration, but also revealed evidence of ancient restoration work.

Keywords: Polychromy, Achaemenid Tomb Architecture, Naqsh-e Rostam, Persepolis, Iran

Introduction

The aim of this paper is to introduce observations made during recently conducted conservation work on the sculpted façade of the tomb of the Achaemenid ruler Darius I (d. 486 BCE) at Naqsh-e Rostam, Fars, in south west Iran, and to provide a preliminary report on the colour schemes identified. Parallel to the conservation work, conducted by the Architectural Conservation and Restoration Group of the Parsa-Pasargadae Research Foundation, rather unexpected but important results for our general understanding of both the history and aspects of the earlier polychromatic appearance of the tomb were revealed. The first part of our paper describes previous observations on the colour schemes. The second part will comment on the recent conservation work and provides an interim report with respect to the polychrome decoration detected. The intention is to show that intensified research on colour must be an integral part of ancient Near Eastern archaeology, and that ancient Near Eastern tomb architecture (as well as other environments) often becomes truly comprehensible only when seen with the layers of paint originally attached.

Archaeologists, anthropologists and conservation specialists have long shown an interest in issues of polychromy and surface coatings as important aspects of material culture and non-verbal communication in pre-modern societies. The modern definition of polychromy refers to "the application of paint and other coloured materials to the surface of a sculpture for decorative, practical or ritual purposes" (Marincola 2004: 1318; see also Seidl 2005). In recent years, conventional research on colour has gradually shifted from an earlier focus on colour linguistics to a more systematic identification and interpretation of the pigments themselves as detectable with modern analytical and technological methods (e.g. papers in Davies 2001; Jones & MacGregor 2002; Blänsdorf & Yin 2006; Brinkmann 2008; Panzarelli et al. 2008; Blänsdorf et al 2009), even though much work remains to be done in acknowledging the significance of colour in academic research (Gage 1993; Young 2006; Insoll 2007: 91). Scholars of the ancient Near East have commented on such diverse topics as colour linguistics (Warburton 2007), the role and symbolism of coloured artifacts (e.g. Winter 1999; Weisgerber 2004) and on colour schemes identified on the few preserved wall paintings (e.g. Tomabechi 1985; Nunn 1988), but only briefly on the polychromy of sculpture in relief and in the round (Nunn 1988: 229-234). While documentation on the evidence of an originally rich polychromy of rock-cut shrines in the ancient Near East (e.g. at Petra: Shaer 2003a and 2003b; Phrygia: Berndt-Ersoetz 2006: 32-34) is increasing, the extent and characteristics of colour and polychromy in the Achaemenid period, between c. 550 and 320 BCE, have surprisingly not been a main research agenda. Traces of paint on monuments of the Achaemenid period have frequently been noted and studied, especially at Persepolis (Lerner 1971, 1973; Tilia 1978; Stodulski et al. 1984; Ambers & Simpson 2005), but no systematic and comprehensive study has been conducted (Nagel 2010; in preparation a-b).

Polychrome coatings, especially when found on exterior façades, present an extremely complex and difficult problem for archaeologists and conservators. Any treatment of polychrome sculpture is a complex challenge for a conservation specialist (e.g. Finn 1990), and forces archaeologists to re-think earlier assumptions, to think beyond and break down traditional academic disciplines. The instability of pigments or binders often results in a change in colour (e.g. Lee & Quirke 2000: 104). Before we can answer questions concerning the diversity of the paint palette of the craftsmen working for the Achaemenid rulers, we should understand the role and significance that modern scholars attribute to polychromy in the Achaemenid society, and we need to determine and address practical issues regarding the objective recording of colour and pigments (e.g. Strudwick 2001). Conservation specialists, chemists and archaeologists

Figure 1. General view of royal tombs at Naqsh-e-Rostam with No. III: tomb of Darius I (after Trümpelmann 1992).

Figure 2. Drawing of the facade of the tomb of Darius I (after Seidl 2003).

alike need to work in close collaboration to focus on the identification, protection and preservation of polychromy on the surface of pre-modern monuments. The importance of a systematic documentation of the remains of polychrome coatings left on Achaemenid architectural and sculptural surfaces is unmistakable. Research on the extent and role of colour in Achaemenid Persia can profit especially from fruitful exchanges and dialogues between archaeologists and conservation specialists, the latter specialized in protecting, the former in providing context and historical background.

Approaching the Šumar of Darius I at Naqsh-e Rostam

According to literary evidence the Achaemenid ruler Darius I died late in 486 BCE at the age of sixty-four, after a reign of thirty-six years (Hdt. vii 1.4; Schmidt 1970: 89; Briant 2002: 524; Kuhrt 2007: 236-237). A mountain cliff, some 11 km northeast of Persepolis was chosen as his final resting place (Fig. 1). A tomb chamber complex with an elaborately chiselled façade was carved into the foothills of Husain Kuh ("Mountain of Hussein") at the mountain cliffs at Naqsh-e Rostam; the ancient name of the site, which became the burial place for three subsequent Achaemenid rulers, we do not know of. The šumar[1] or tomb of Darius I is today the only one of the four tomb chamber complexes at Naqsh-e Rostam that can be identified for certain by the available epigraphic evidence: the carved inscriptions on the façade mentioning his name have been described as the *Res Gestae* of this most eminent Achaemenid ruler (Fig. 2; Schmitt 2000). Historic and epigraphic evidence highly suggests that guards and priests were involved in the safekeeping of the Achaemenid ruler's tombs (Henkelman 2003; Kuhrt 2007: 574). The interior layout of the tomb has been studied by earlier generations of archaeologists: three vaulted chambers, each with three tombs inside, all empty when excavated, were probably intended for the burials of Darius and at least two of his five known wives, perhaps Atossa and Artystone (Schmidt 1970: 89). Due to the lack of precise historical sources, information regarding the history of construction and the original appearance of the tomb in the Achaemenid period can be drawn only from a study of the monument itself.

Early modern travellers noted the difficulties in accessing the monument for closer inspection. Drawings from the 19th century prove how those interested in seeing the carvings and inscriptions needed ropes and ladders to obtain access.[2] At least one reference to paint on the façade of the tomb of Darius I is known from the 19th century: Perrot and Chipiez (1890: 643; 1892) noted that an early visitor had "ascertained that the letters of the long inscription on the tomb of Darius at Naks-i-Rustem stood out blue on the natural grey of stone." It is surprising that the pigments originally attached to the inscriptions survived modern interventions like paper-mâché squeezes taken in the 1920s (the squeezes are today in the Freer Gallery of Art and Sackler Gallery Archives in Washington, D.C.: see Herzfeld 1926: 246-247; Hennessey 1992: 134; Nagel 2010).

Archaeological investigations and excavations by an expedition of the Oriental Institute at Chicago between 1933 and 1939 yielded significant information about the early history of the site of Naqsh-e Rostam and provided detailed architectural drawings and measurements of its individual monuments. It is known that the sacred complex of Naqsh-e Rostam was only entered through gates in a fortification wall (Schmidt 1970: 54-58).[3] It was through the work of a team of photographers that colours on the façade of the tomb of Darius I at Naqsh-e Rostam were noted in some detail: Schmidt referred to traces of blue on the bull capitals in the middle register of the tomb's façade, noted traces of paint on the dais and concluded that at least parts of the tomb façade must have been painted in antiquity (Schmidt 1970: 84).[4]

Published photographical documentation of the tomb façade has been limited to the results of few photographic surveys, most notably those of Boris Dubensky, field photographer for the Chicago Oriental Institute mission in 1938 and 1939 (Schmidt 1970), Morteza Rostamy, photographer of the Tehran Archaeological Museum in 1965, and Barbara Grunewald, German Archaeological Institute, Tehran (Schmitt 2000) and has thus been the only way of discussing the tomb façade. Subsequently, the iconography and style of the relief scene carved into the top register of the façade has been discussed (Schmidt 1970: 84-90; Calmeyer 1975*a*, 1975*b*; Root 1979: 162-181; Gall 1989; West 2002). The inscriptions, which constitute a major part of the imagery and iconography of the tomb, have been extensively studied by specialists (Kent 1953; Lecoq 1997; Schmitt 2000), but no further investigations on the colour schemes have been conducted.

---

[1] For the term see Henkelmann 2003: 160-162.
[2] Kawasjee 1889: 137: "I was obliged to go up by the aid of the ropes, but to my cost I found the descent was very difficult, as during the time the man were pulling me up, I suffered most severely, particularly on my face, knees and elbows, on account of every now and then dashing against the projecting stones of the rock." See also Schmidt 1970: 17, pl. 18.
[3] Already Herzfeld 1926: 244: "Zu den weiteren Entdeckungen … gehört die Aufnahme der alten Fortifikation, die einst die Königsgräber umschloss, und diese durch ihre gewaltige Höhe fast völlig unsichtbar gemacht haben muss."
[4] Schmidt 1970: 84: "Traces of blue pigments discovered by Boris Dubensky in some signs of the DNa inscription behind the king's figure are sufficient proof that all characters of at least the Old Persian and Elamite Versions of this inscription were painted blue, and we see no reason to doubt that all inscriptions on the tomb were treated in the same manner. Furthermore, traces of blue, brown red and green pigments found by Boris Dubensky on the ledge beneath the lower row of throne bearers strongly suggest that these figures were painted with distinctive patterns. If so, the reliefs of all persons must have been similarly adorned. Finally, since traces of blue on some of the capitals of the middle register almost certainly indicate that parts, or perhaps all, of the architectural carvings were painted, we must assume that the throne, the altar with its fire, the king's pedestal, the Ahuramazda Symbol, and the moon were also coated with appropriate colours. When newly cut and smoothed, the white or creamy-white rock of the cliff would have provided an effective background without need of paint." Schmidt frankly admitted that further colours may have been overlooked (Schmidt 1970: 92).

The Recent Restoration Work on the Tomb Façade

Since 2001, the Parsa-Pasargadae Research Foundation has organized a great number of research projects and invited international scholars and experts to work on the Persepolis Takht and its surroundings (Talebian 2004, 2007), including a multi-year conservation and preservation program focusing on the monuments and façade s at Naqsh-e Rostam. Between 2001 and 2005, a conservation and restoration project of the tomb of Darius I was conducted under the auspices of Dr. Hassan Rahsaz, prime consultant of the Architectural Conservation and Restoration Group of the Parsa-Pasargadae Research Foundation. The preservation concept developed by Hassan Rahsaz is in accordance with modern international standards of preservation.

In order to give access to the façade, a 50-meter steel-tube-coupling scaffolding was constructed.[5] This construction allowed for close inspection of the monument and observation under the best possible lighting conditions on the different levels of the tomb façade. The first phase of the operation comprised a six-month survey period aimed at taking careful rescue measurements of the façade and documenting damage to all parts of the surfaces severely subsided by natural erosion and humidity. A thorough examination followed by a complete inventory and reassessment of the causes of decay and damage identification was the primary goal of the preparation period. A basic preservation concept for the tomb façade was worked out with guidelines and procedures for restoration and documentation.

Natural erosion, pollution and humidity caused by nearby agricultural activities, and changing weather conditions has resulted in heavy incrustations on the surface of the façade. The greatest cause of concern was erosion that had formed its way through the entire part directly to the right of the central figure of Darius I in the top register. Water, which originally would have dropped off the edges of the top register of the façade, eventually caused washouts in the elaborately carved surface. Plant growth covered some parts of the façade. Humidity retained in the plants and vegetation caused damage to the surface of the rock, while their roots caused the stone to split in some parts. Finally, rainwater damage has resulted in an almost amorphous appearance of the sculpted forms on some parts of the façade, especially on the left of the top register, where fissures have penetrated the surface of the rock itself.

Before starting with any conservation treatment it is necessary to guarantee the reversibility of any interventions and materials. As became evident, the most important objective was to slow down further deterioration as much as possible through the improvement of the structure of the façade, as well as the elimination of the causes of deterioration. The surface of the relief structures was cleaned and prepared by subtle mechanical techniques, and stabilized with lime extract. Loose dust and stone particles in damaged areas were swept away with brushes. Special care was taken in order not to affect the original surface. Plants were carefully removed. Loose rocks above and near the tomb were re-attached to the main body of the mountain with appropriate tools and sustainable materials. Cleaning was undertaken with a brush and water, and technical instruments were used to consolidate the structure of the rock. Steam was used to moisten and clean the identified areas, and gaps were sealed. All conservation work was documented and photographed.

Figure 3. Previously undocumented area of Achaemenid channels above the tomb of Darius I. (Photo: Hassan Rahsaz).

During the restoration work it was also possible to make new observations on the history of the monument itself. Directly above the tomb's façade, for instance, a previously undocumented area of channels was found (Fig. 3). These channels were probably cut into the rock sometime during the preparations for the carving of the façade relief, probably in the early phases. The architects working under the Achaemenid rulers were thus aware of the cracks in the natural rock and built channels to divert the rainwater, preventing it from flowing into the gaps. Such preventive measures demonstrate the high technical standards and knowledge of the Achaemenid craftsmen. A drainage system of channels was also found inside the tomb chamber. Over time, however, these channels clogged and allowed water to attack the tomb's carved façade and the interior. As a result of the new conservation work, these channels were cleaned. The channels above the tomb's façade were directed towards the channels running parallel to the tomb façade, already existing in the early Achaemenid period. The cracks and splits of these channels were filled with a mixture of lime extract, sand and appropriate materials, which are reversible and allow for stabilization.

Closer inspection of the façade brought surprising results for the actual Achaemenid carving progress on the sculptures. In addition to tools such as a flat, toothed and claw chisel, a pointed hammer was also used. Close examination also revealed that some parts of the tomb

---

[5] According to Schmidt, the original height from the bottom to the top of the cliff was about 64 meters (Schmidt 1970: 80). The distance of a visitor at the foot of the façade, today about 6 m, would have been approximately 15 m in Achaemenid times.

underwent restoration in earlier periods. At an uncertain point, parts of the head including the face of the winged figure, conventionally labeled the "man in the winged disk" (Calmeyer 2009: 29), in the top register were stabilized with a clamp. A hole to the left of the "man in the winged disk" was refilled in antiquity. Also, the face of Darius I himself underwent restoration in antiquity. Overall, ancient restoration work seems limited to the top register of the tomb façade.[6]

The Polychromy of the Façade

During the surface cleaning of the sculpted façade rich traces of an earlier polychromy were revealed. While traces of paints had been noted by Erich Schmidt (see above), the new observations allowed for the very first time a more detailed documentation of the state and extent of the paint residues. The exact location and condition of the remaining traces of paint were recorded, photographed, mapped and documented. Documentation of a scientific pigment analysis is the main requirement for a critical investigation and re-examination of the monument, which is so fundamental and of prime importance for our understanding of Achaemenid polychromy. FTIR-Analysis conducted on the pigments identified on the squeezes from Naqsh-e Rostam confirmed the employment of Egyptian blue (Nagel 2010). The pigments identified by personal observation on the tomb's façade correspond to those documented on the monuments at Persepolis and Pasargadae, and the later tombs of Achaemenid rulers (Stodulski et al. 1985; Nagel 2010; Nagel, in preparation b). No scientific analysis has been conducted so far on the pigments remaining *in situ*. This, however, should not limit the value of the photographic documentation carried out.

No traces of paint were identified in the lower register of Darius' tomb. Musche's (2006) hypothesis of a free standing wooden stairway enabling access to the tomb and therefore covering the lower register of the façade provides a convincing explanation for this absence. Abundant evidence of polychrome paint, however, was detected in the middle and top registers. These traces of paint, we would argue, are traces of the original polychromy, applied to the surface of the façade in the months immediately following the carving of the sculptures and inscriptions.[7] The interior of the tomb may have been painted, too, but no evidence has been found thus far.

The central figure in the top register Darius I measures 2.70 m high, and is depicted in profile facing a fire altar

---

[6] Elaborate systems of ancient, probably Achaemenid repairs had already been documented by the Italian conservation team working on the façade of tomb V (= Tomb of Artaxerxes II.?) at Persepolis (e.g. Schmidt 1970: 100; Tilia 1968). The circumstances and the chronology of the repairs of Naqsh-e Rostam need to be clarified further.

[7] Naturally, the paints could also stem from later periods of repainting. It is, however, beyond the scope of this preliminary report to give a detailed account of the arguments. Future investigations and technical analysis may well provide additional information about the existence of possible paint preparation layers or re-paints.

and the "man in the winged disk". Darius is depicted standing with his left foot forward on a three stepped pedestal. The pedestal itself is resting on a throne stage.

Figure 4. Traces of blue pigment on beard of Darius, top register. (Photo: Hassan Rahsaz).

Abundant traces of blue pigment can be identified on the curls of the beard and hair of Darius (Fig. 4). Traces of red pigment can be identified on the eye, the eyeballs, and on the lips. It is almost certain that the black lines, used to accentuate the eyelid, were made from black charcoal or soot/lamp black.

Traces of blue and white pigments have been identified on Darius' headdress, the diadem or *cidaris*, which is crowned with three stepped crenellations resembling the same headdress as carved in relief at Bisotun (Luschey 1977: 72, pl. 33). The Roman author Quintus Curtius Rufus (1st century CE) – thought to have heavily relied on Cleitarchus, a contemporary of Alexander the Great – noted in his description of the appearance of the last Achaemenid ruler, Darius III (c. 380–330 BCE), that the Persian king's headdress "was bound with a blue fillet variegated with white" (transl. Rolfe 1946). On the tomb façade at Naqsh-e Rostam, Darius I is dressed in what scholars have defined as a typical Achaemenid dress, the sleeved *candys*. The detailed painted motifs detected on the monuments at the Persepolis-Takht and meticulously reconstructed by Tilia (1978: 54, fig. 6; Kuhrt 2007: 532, fig. 11.25) may provide a clue to the original appearance of the king as he was depicted on the façade relief at Naqsh-e Rostam. A somewhat dark red pigment was used for the shoes of the ruler, perhaps as a prime layer for an additional coating.

Figure 5. Detail of DNe inscription, top register. (Photo: Hassan Rahsaz).

Figure 6. Decoration scheme of cornice directly above the central doorway, middle register. (Photo: Hassan Rahsaz).

No traces of paint have been identified so far on either the pedestal or the fire altar depicted in the top register in front of Darius. Behind the ruler are inscriptions in Old Persian, Babylonian and Elamite, all bearing abundant traces of blue paint (Fig. 5). The "man in the winged disk" is shown in left profile facing the king. He is wearing a headdress, and has curly hair and a long beard, traits that are similarly associated with Darius. Courtiers and soldiers, representing the two columns of the Achaemenid Empire, are depicted in the flanks, the two top figures left of Darius being Gobryas and Aspathines, identified by their inscriptions, highlighted in blue. The supporting throne stage bearers are arranged in two tiers, carrying the dais of the throne stage. The throne bearers are representatives of the various peoples who were part of the vast Achaemenid Empire in the reign of Darius I. The various peoples can be identified through their legends, again accompanied by inscriptions in three languages (Elamite, Old Persian and Akkadian) highlighted in blue. These labels were framed with fine chiseled lines, filled in with blue. Blue was also found in the leaf-like ornaments which constitute the uppermost part of the throne. Furthermore, the leonine creature which is part of the carrying throne had remnants of blue on the body and mane, red pigment in the mouth.

Traces of paint have also been identified on the entablature, separating the middle and top register. The entablature, measuring 1.60m in height, presumably represents the wooden roof of a palace; three horizontal units project into inverted steps in the form of plain bands. On the dentils in the lower unit traces of red were noticed, while the background was painted in blue. Traces of red, blue and green pigments were identified on the fillet of the tomb. In the tombs by the Persepolis-Takht, these fillets depicted a frieze of eighteen lions arranged antithetically in walking position with a lotus flower in the centre (Schmidt 1970 pl. 75; Calmeyer 2009, pls. 17.3 and 32.1). This painted pattern on the façade of the tomb of Darius I is highly suggestive of the animal frieze found in sculpted form on the later Achaemenid tomb façades at Persepolis. There are traces of green in the fillet's central part indicating the existence of an earlier painted lotus flower.

The middle register evokes an architectural façade featuring four plain columns on rectangular two stepped bases with a torus and bull capitals carrying a beam below the architrave. Already Schmidt had identified traces of blue paint on the bull capitals (see above). This is in accordance with the blue identified on the body of the animal protome capitals of the residential palaces at Persepolis (Nagel, forthcoming). The horns of the bull's protomes carrying the roof on the top register were probably made of a separate material. No details have been observed indicating the type and appearance of these horns.

Traces of original paint coatings were identified on the Egyptianized cavetto cornice in the middle register's central doorway (Figs. 6, 7). The leaves of this cornice were decorated in an alternating blue and red colour

Figure 7. Proposed reconstructed decoration scheme of cornice directly above the central doorway, middle register. (Credit: Alexander Nagel).

Figure 8. Decoration scheme of cornice directly above the central doorway, Tomb V, Persepolis. (Photo: Alexander Nagel).

Figure 9. Proposed reconstructed decoration scheme of cornice directly above the central doorway, Tomb V, Persepolis. (Credit: Alexander Nagel).

scheme, with a fine fin in the centre of the individual leaves - a colour scheme evoking the scheme known as painted leaf from the façades of Egyptian and Mediterranean contemporary Greek monuments (e.g. Brinkmann 2008 figs. 107-8, 119, 179). In our case, the blue leaves were decorated with a red fin, while blue fins correspondingly filled the other scales.

Since the publication of Schmidt's corpus on the Achaemenid tombs at Naqsh-e-Rustam and Persepolis it has been established that the construction of the tomb of Darius I began early in the period of Darius' reign, probably very soon after 520 BCE (Schmidt 1970: 80-89). Darius' tomb became a cultic shrine and a model for all subsequent Achaemenid tombs. The carved iconographic motif of the façade of the tomb of Darius I was repeated on the façade of the tombs of all subsequent Achaemenid rulers. Such was obviously not the case with the polychrome decoration.[8] The Egyptianized cornice of the doorway of the middle register of tomb V (= tomb of Artaxerxes II?) at Persepolis has green and blue leaves rather than the red and blue found on Darius' tomb façade at Naqsh-e Rostam. No painted fins however can be identified on the leaf scheme (Figs. 8, 9).

Preliminary Conclusions: Completing the Picture

Of the many ritualized habits in the ancient world, the coronations and funerals of rulers were certainly the most lavish. In his excavations of the royal tomb chamber of Tutankhamun, Howard Carter was astounded by the hundreds of coloured objects that had been interred with the king. The polychrome decoration of the Achaemenid tomb façades described above in the case of the tomb of Darius I suggests that colours were used abundantly on the façade. The polychrome decoration served not only as adornment, but became an expression of the wealth, and therefore of the status of the buried ruler's dynasty, too. Furthermore, colours highlighted and enhanced dramatic effects, created depth and three-dimensionality. The inscriptions carved into the natural rock became visible from afar only with the colours applied to them as did many of the features of the iconography in the top register. Colour contrast was intended and had obviously been of major importance on Achaemenid tomb façades, too.

Greek and Roman authors have often referred to the colourful world of the Achaemenid court (Nagel, in preparation b). Shining appearances of metals like gold and silver, sometimes directly laid into the carved reliefs and on the monuments would have made a striking visual impact in the palaces at Persepolis, Susa, Babylon and Ecbatana and elsewhere. Inhabitants and visitors alike would have worn colourful dresses documenting status and wealth, birds and vegetation must be taken into account when reconstructing the colourful environment of the individual Achaemenid courts. The famous glazed brick reliefs, excavated in Susa depict soldiers and creatures in the brightest colours and provide an idea of the wealth of colour and texture which adorned the Achaemenid courts. Finally, there is evidence for the craftsmen themselves in the number of paint pots have been found in great numbers at Persepolis itself (Nagel 2010).

The identified traces of paint and colour schemes on the façade of the tomb of Darius I at Naqsh-e Rostam reveal a wide palette of colours, but with a strong focus on blue. Blue was used to highlight the inscribed text accompanying the message of Darius I, the door lintel was painted in a striking blue and red contrast. The bull capitals were covered with an intense blue (for a possible interpretation of the Achaemenid blues: Nagel 2010). A band of red, green and blue hues served as ornament of the architrave separating the registers.

Naturally, the present colours may not be same as those seen in antiquity: pigments may have degraded, produced new colours and have lost their original hues. It must be stated though that the Achaemenid craftsmen used rather thick applications and layers of paint. Additional aspects need to be taken into account when understanding the complex relationships between the colours and their intended meaning: when wet or with seasonal change, the colours themselves become more intense, different light conditions resulted in different perceptions.

More Achaemenid tomb façades need surely to be studied with the focus specifically on the original polychromy. The preliminary results discussed here confirm in part what the investigations by Lerner and Tilia in the 1970s (Lerner 1971, 1973; Tilia 1978) and ongoing research reveals for the site of Persepolis. We hope, however, to have shown that colour should play a significant role in the modern (re)construction of the afterlife in the ancient Near East, too. With the increasing evidence of original plaster and paint decoration at Petra in Jordan (Shaer 2003a), the extent of paint applications in the earlier dynastic tombs of Egypt, as well as from the tomb architecture and funerary stelae of Classical Greece (Davies 2001; Koch & Posamentir 2008; Posamentir 2007), such a tradition of elaborate decoration and polychromy of funerary architecture is interesting also from an anthropological point of view. There are cultures even today, where colour is an important indicator of wealth in the burial traditions. The cemeteries of the Central American regions for instance have still the most elaborate colourization (e.g. Chichicastenango: Lenclos & Lenclos 2004: 109). We hope to have shown that the documentation of the surface treatment of a tomb façade is equally important as the documentation of the architecture itself.

Acknowledgements

The authors express their deepest gratitude to Mohammad Hasan Talebian, Director of the Parsa-Pasargadae

---

[8] Schmidt did not observe any traces of pigments on the tombs of the successors of Darius (Schmidt 1970: 92).

Research Foundation, to Maziar Kahemi, General Manager of Persepolis, and to Kamyar Abdi, Dartmouth College. We are grateful to Fiona Kidd for reading and commenting on an earlier draft of the paper.

References

Ambers J. & Simpson St.J. 2005. Some pigment identifications for objects from Persepolis. *Arta 2005.02 (=www.achemenet.com)*: 1-13.

Berndt-Ersoetz S. 2006. *Phrygian Rock Cut Shrines. Structure, Function, and Cult Practice.* Leiden: Brill.

Blänsdorf C. & Yin X. 2006. A colourful world for the Emperor's soul: the polychromy of the terracotta sculptures at Qin Shihuang's burial complex. Pages 177-183 in D. Saunders, J.H. Townsend & S. Woodcock (eds), *Contributions to the Munich Congress, 28 August - 1 September 2006: The Object in Context: Crossing Conservation Boundaries.* London: International Institute for Conservation.

Blänsdorf C., Pfeffer S., Melzl E., Thiemann L., Höfle E., Reiserer M., Wagner N. & Knidlberger M. 2009. The polychromy of the Giant Buddha Statues in Bamiyan, Afghanistan: a challenge. Preliminary investigations. Pages 129-147 in X. Yin, R. Bo et al. (eds.), *The second international symposium of the terracotta figures and painted cultural relics preservation and research. Conference Abstracts.* Xi'an, China.

Briant P. 2002. *From Cyrus to Alexander. A History of the Persian Empire.* Engl. Transl. P. Daniels. Winona Lake: Eisenbrauns.

Brinkmann V. (ed.) 2008. *Bunte Götter. Die Farbigkeit antiker Skulptur.* Eine Ausstellung der Liebighaus Skulpturensammlung, Frankfurt am Main in Kooperation mit der Stiftung Archäologie, München, 8. Oktober 2008 – 15. Februar 2009. Frankfurt/Main: Liebighaus.

Calmeyer P. 1975a. The Subject of the Achaemenid Tomb reliefs. Pages 233-242 in F. Bagherzadeh (ed.), *Proceedings of the III international Symposium on Archaeological Research in Iran, 1974.* Tehran: ICAR.

Calmeyer P. 1975b. Zur Genese altiranischer Motive: Felsgräber. *Archäologische Mitteilungen aus Iran* 8: 99-113.

Calmeyer P. 1988. Aufreihung-Duplik-Kopie-Umbildung. Pages 101-119 in A. Kuhrt & H. Sancisi-Weerdenburg (eds), *Method and Theory. Proceedings of the London 1985 Achaemenid History Workshop* (= Achaemenid Studies 3). Leiden: Nederlands Instituut voor het Nabije Oosten.

Calmeyer P. 2009. *Die Reliefs der Gräber V und VI in Persepolis* (= Archäologie in Iran und Turan 8). Mainz: Zabern.

Davies W.V. (ed.) 2001. *Colour and Painting in Ancient Egypt.* London: British Museum Press.

Finn C. 1990. The Cleaning of Painted Stone. Pages 214-218 in J. Ashurst & F. Dimes (eds), *Conservation of Building and Decorative Stone.* vol. 2. London: Butterworth-Heinemann.

Gage J. 1993. *Color and Culture:Practice and Meaning from Antiquity to Abstraction.* Boston: Little, Brown and Company.

Gall H.V.1989. Das achaemenidische Königsgrab: Neue Überlegungen und Beobachtungen. : Pages 503-523 in L. De Meyer, & L. Vanden Berghe (eds), *Archaeologia Iranica et Orientalis: Miscellanea in honorem Louis Vanden Berghe.* Gent: Peeters.

Henkelmann W. 2003. An Elamite Memorial: the Šumar of Cambyses and Hystaspes. Pages 101-171 in W. Henkelman & A. Kuhrt (eds), *A Persian Perspective. Essays in Memory of Helen Sancisi Weerdenburg* (= Achaemenid History Workshop 13). Leiden.

Hennessey C. 1992. The Ernst Herzfeld Papers at the Freer Gallery of Art and Arthur M. Sackler Gallery Archives. *Bulletin of the Asia Institute* 6: 131–141.

Herzfeld E. 1926. Reisebericht. *Zeitschrift der Deutschen Morgenländischen Gesellschaft. Neue Folge* V (80): 225-284.

Insoll T. 2007. *Archaeology. The Conceptual Challenge.* London: Duckworth.

Jones A. & MacGregor G. (eds) 2002. *Colouring the Past: The Significance of Colour in Archaeological Research.* Oxford: Berg.

Kawasjee D.K. 1889. *Ancient Persian Sculptures or the Monuments, or the monuments, buildings, Bas-Reliefs, Rock inscriptions, etc. belonging to the kings of the Achaemenian and Sassanian Dynasties of Persia.* Bombay: Education Society's Press.

Kent R. 1953. *Old Persian. Grammar, Texts, Lexicon.* New Haven.

Koch-Brinkmann U. & Posamentir R. 2008. The Grave stele of Paramython. Pages 132-139 in V. Brinkmann (ed.), *Bunte Götter. Die Farbigkeit antiker Skulptur.* Eine Ausstellung der Liebighaus Skulpturensammlung, Frankfurt am Main in Kooperation mit der Stiftung Archäologie, München, 8. Oktober 2008 – 15. Februar 2009. Frankfurt/Main: Liebighaus.

Kuhrt A. 2007. *The Persian Empire: A Corpus of Sources From the Achaemenid Period.* London and New York: Routledge.

Lee L. & Quirke S. 2000. Painting materials. Pages 104-120 in P. Nicholson, & I. Shaw (eds.), *Ancient Egyptian Materials and Technology.* Cambridge: University Press.

Lerner J. 1971. The Achaemenid Relief of Ahura Mazda in the Fogg Art Museum, Cambridge, Massachusetts. *Bulletin of the Asia Institute* 2: 19-35.

Lerner J. 1973. A Painted Relief from Persepolis. *Archaeology* 26: 116-122.

Lenclos P. & Lenclos D. 2004. *Colors of the World: A Geography of Color.* New York: Norton.

Lecoq P. 1997. *Les Inscriptions de la Perse Achéménide.* Paris: Gallimard.

Luschey H. 1977. Studien zu dem Darius Relief von Bisutun. *Archäologische Mitteilungen aus Iran* 10: 63-94.

Marincola M. 2004. Polychromy. Pages 1318-1322 in *The Encyclopedia of Sculpture.* New York and London: Fitzroy Dearbon.

Musche B. 2006. Überlegungen zur Architektur der achaemenidischen Felsengräber von Naqs-e Rostam. *Archäologische Mitteilungen aus Iran und Turan* 38: 325-345.

Nagel A. 2010. *Colors, Gilding and Painted Motifs in Persepolis: The Polychromy of Achaemenid Persian Architectural Sculpture, c. 520-330 BCE*. PhD Dissertation, University of Michigan, Ann Arbor.

Nagel A. Forthcoming. The Colors of Persepolis: New Research on the Polychromy of Achaemenid Sculpture and Architecture. In: K. Abdi et al. (eds.), *Ō Šābuhr kē čihr az yazdān dāšt: Essays in Memory of A. Shapur Shahbazi*. Tehran and Persepolis: Iran University Press and Parsa Pasargadae Research Foundation.

Nagel A. In prep. a. Aspects of Non-Verbal Communication in Persepolis: The Polychromy of Achaemenid Persian Sculpture, c. 520-330 BCE. In P. Jockey et al. (eds.), *Les arts de la couleur en Grèce ancienne. Productions antiques, reproductions modernes et contemporaines*. Bulletin de Correspondance Hellénique, supplements.

Nagel A. In prep. b. Everlasting Blues: Colour and the Epigraphic Habit in Achaemenid Persia, c. 520-330 BCE. In K. Piquette & R. Whitehouse (eds.), *Writing as Material Practice: Surface, Substance and Medium*. Walnut Creek: Left Coast.

Nunn A. 1988. *Die Wandmalerei und der glasierte Wandschmuck im alten Orient*. Leiden: Brill.

Panzarelli R., Schmidt E. & Lapatin K. (eds) 2008. *The Color of Life: Polychromy in Sculpture from Antiquity to the Present*. Malibu: Getty Publications.

Perrot G. & Chipiez C. 1890. *Histoire de l'art dans l'antiquité. Vol. V: Perse*. Paris: Hachette.

Perrot G. & Chipiez C. 1892. *History of Art in Persia*. Transl. from the French. London: Chapman & Hall.

Posamentir R. 2006. *Bemalte Attische Grabstelen*. München: Biering & Brinkmann.

Quintus Curtius, *History of Alexander*. Transl. J. Rolfe. 1946.

Root M.C. 1979. *The King and Kingship in Achaemenid Art: Essays on the Creation of an Iconography of Empire*. Acta Iranica 19. Leiden: Brill.

Schmidt E. 1970. *Persepolis III. The Royal Tombs and other Monuments*. Chicago: University of Chicago Press.

Schmitt R. 2000. *Corpus Inscriptionum Iranicarum. I. 1. The Old Persian Inscriptions: The Old Persian Inscriptions of Naqsh-i Rustam and Persepolis*. London: School of Oriental and African Studies.

Seidl U. 2003. Wie waren die achaemenidischen Doppelprotomen-Kapitelle ausgerichtet? Pages 67-77 in W. Henkelman, & A. Kuhrt (eds.), *A Persian perspective. Essays in Memory of Heleen Sancisi-Weerdenburg*. Leiden.

Seidl U. 2005. Polychromie. Pages 599-600 in *Reallexikon der Assyriologie und Vorderasiatischen Archäologie* 10. Berlin & New York: De Gruyter.

Shaer M. 2003a. *The Decorative Architectural Surface of Petra*. PhD Thesis Munich: Technische Universität, FB Restaurierung.

Shaer M. 2003b. The architectural surfaces of Petra: Techniques of Paint Application. Pages 39-41 in E. Greipl & M. Petzet (eds), *Historical Architectural Surfaces. Lime – Plaster – Colour*. München: Lipp.

Stodulski L., Farrell E. & Newman R. 1984. Identification of ancient Persian pigments from Persepolis and Pasargadae. *Studies in Conservation* 29: 143-154.

Strudwick N. 2001. Problems of recording and publication of paintings in the Private Tombs of Thebes. Pages 126-140 in W.V. Davies (ed.), *Colour and Painting in Ancient Egypt*. London: British Museum Press.

Tilia A.B. 1968. New Restoration Work at Persepolis. *East and West* 18: 67-108.

Tilia A.B. 1978. *Studies and Restorations at Persepolis and other sites of Fars. Part II*. Rome: IsMEO Reports and Memoirs, vol. 18.

Tomabechi Y. 1980. *Wall Painting and Color Pigments of Ancient Mesopotamia*. Unpublished PhD Thesis, University of California, Berkeley.

Trümpelmann L. 1992. *Zwischen Persepolis und Firuzabad: Gräber, Paläste und Felsreliefs im alten Persien*. Mainz: Zabern.

West M. 2002. Darius' Ascent to Paradise. *Indo-Iranian Journal* 45: 51-57.

Warburton D. 2007. Basic color term evolution in the light of ancient evidence from the Near East. Pages 229-246 in R. MacLaury, G. Paramei & D. Dedrick (eds.), *Anthropology of Color: Interdisciplinary multilevel modeling*. Philadelphia: John Benjamins.

Weisgerber G. 2004. Decorative Stones in the Ancient Orient (Lapis lazuli, turquoise, agate, carneole). Pages 64-75 in T. Stöllner (ed.), *Persiens Antike Pracht. Bergbau, Handwerk, Archäologie*. Bochum: Deutsches Bergbau-Museum. vol. 1.

Winter I. 1999. The Aesthetic Value of Lapis Lazuli in Mesopotamia. Pages 43-58 in A. Caubet (ed.), *Cornaline et Pierres Précieuses: La Méditerranée de l'Antiquité à l'Islam*. Paris: Louvre.

Young D. 2006. The Colours of Things. Pages 173-185 in C. Tilley, W. Keane, K. Kuechler, M. Rowlands & S. Spyer (eds.), *Handbook of Material Culture*. London: Sage.

Authors' Addresses

Alexander Nagel (corresponding author)
Kelsey Museum of Archaeology
University of Michigan, Ann Arbor
434 South State Street - Ann Arbor, MI 48109-1390
E-mail: aleos@umich.edu

Hassan Rahsaz
Head of Conservation Centre of the Archaeological Institute of Persepolis
Parsa Pasargadae Research Foundation
MarvDasht, Fars, Iran
E-mail: hassan_rahsaz@yahoo.com

Introduction to the Contributions on Arabia and the Wider Islamic World

Janet Starkey

There may be as many as 1.3 billion Muslims comprising 20% of the world's total population, for whom death is populated with a rich repository of saints, martyrs, religious jurists, and cosmologies, through a range of narratives in many social and cultural contexts. In addition, there are fascinating Jewish and Christian traditions within the region (BBC website). Graves and graveyards are memorials to the dead, with tombstones, marker stones, and even elaborate tombs, which are sites of pilgrimage and veneration. The treatment of death and burial in Middle Eastern "imagined" communities must be understood as syncretism of Islam in its many forms, other religious beliefs and local traditions.

Searching through anthropological literature one winter's evening, I became morbidly fascinated by how reticent anthropologists were about burials in the Middle East, yet European travellers often recorded funeral ceremonies and rituals surrounding death. Classical Arabic authors, as well as European travellers such as Lane (1836; repr. 2005), Klunzinger (1878), Blackman (1927), Kennedy (1978) Hobbs (1989), Rodenbeck (1998), and Sattin (2000) all variously record details of their experiences of death, burials, funerals, memorials and saints. They show how ruins and cemeteries play an active part in the community: they were not exclusively for the dead but were also sites of pilgrimage and veneration, even for European travellers, anthropologists and historians.

As I outlined in a recent paper (Starkey 2009, 14/3: 286–302), there have been few studies which explored the relevance of modern sociological theories on death and dying as they might apply to Islamic communities. Recently, however, there have been several important multi-disciplinary studies. First, the RQAD Project; secondly, the publication of Leor Halevi's excellent study of the topic; and thirdly, through the papers presented at the Arabian Studies Conference on Death and Burial presented here and held at the British Museum in November 2008.

Written on paper, coins and ostrich eggshells, Arabic fragments from the 12th to 15th centuries were found between 1999 and 2003 by a University of Southampton archaeological team in the foundations of a Roman and Islamic harbour at Quṣayr al-Qadīm on the Egyptian Red Sea coast. The principal investigators were David Peacock, Lucy Blue and Stephanie Moser (http://www.southampton.ac.uk/archaeology/research/projects/quseir_alqadim_project.html). As a result, the RQAD project – Reconstructing the Quseiri Arabic Documents – funded by the Arts and Humanities Research Board was set up in 2001 to translate and interpret the fragments in their socio-historical context, a project that involved Arabists, archaeologist and computer experts at the University of Leeds.

On 18 May 2005 Dionisius Agius, Anne Macklin and Francine Stone organised an informal "Study Day on Islamic Burial Practices" at the University of Leeds under the auspices of the RQAD Project. The twelve participants at this multi-disciplinary workshop discussed topics as diverse as burials at Quṣayr al-Qadīm, eulogies following the death of a loved one in medieval Egypt which were written on ostrich eggs, burial practices at sea, Upper Egypt funeral processions in the 1920s, tombs in Central Asia, and so on. The Study Day raised important questions about Islamic burial practices, the spiritual and philosophical study of the symbol of death and the afterlife.

Secondly, **Leor Halevi**'s probing and elegant study of the role of death rites during the pre-modern rise of Islam in *Muhammad's Grave: Death Rites and the Making of Islamic Society* (2007) focuses on the codes of funerary law produced by early Muslim scholars. His book is thoroughly documented and also uses oral traditions and legal rulings. Burial practices in the time of the Prophet Muḥammad (d. AD 632) allowed many interpretations and practices to develop. As Halevi describes, early and medieval jurists, such as Ibn Abī al-Dunyā (d.894), al-Ghazālī (d. 111), Ibn Qayyim al-Jawzī (d. 1350) and al-Suyūṭī (d. 1505), located in different cities or communities, elaborated a Muslim funerary code (Halevi 2004: 120–52). They provided moral lessons to warn believers that they should lead a virtuous life and encouraged believers to think about their own future demise in detail and thus established new social patterns in the eastern Mediterranean that identified Islamic practice from that of religions established earlier in the region.

Halevi focuses on the way in which a body of rituals enabled Islam to create its own, distinct identity and a fascinating link with modern funeral rites and with the development of contemporary Muslim attitudes toward the body. Halevi (2007) provides new approaches to the treatment of a Muslim corpse and associated everyday urban practices. He explores the corpse from its deathbed, its preparation for burial to the grave to reflect on different layers of human interaction. As Walter (1994: 6) reflects, the universal fear of death is faced only with the traditional resources of community, religion and ritual. It was an honour to a pleasure to hear a paper by Halevi presented at the conference and its workshop on Islamic Burials greatly benefitted from his contributions to the discussions.

Thirdly, there are several papers in this volume that illuminate the diverse ethnographic contexts of the topic.

Corinne Fortier in "The Intercessor Status of the Dead in Mālikī Islam and in Mauritania", studies the representations and practices linked to death (*mawt*) through reference to Islamic scripture in Moorish society in Mauritania where the dead mediate between men and God. She outlines Mauritanian funeral practices in detail, and describes the graves and cites relevant Qurʾānic citations. Despite Qur'anic prescriptions, she discovered that for her Mauritanian informants, the sensory perceptions of the dead and hearing in particular, do not cease upon death, nor do sensations linked to comfort or discomfort. In addition, the living seek salvation for the souls of the deceased and try to influence the destiny of the dead through visiting the graves, almsgiving and other commemorative practices, though the final decision rests with God.

Based on anthropological fieldwork, **Anna Tozzi Di Marco** focuses on life in graveyards in her paper, "Cairo's City of the Dead: the cohabitation between the living and the dead from an anthropological perspective". Traditionally, modern Egyptians, whether Copt or Muslim, buried their dead in a room-like "burial cites" so they could live in them during the long mourning period of forty days and visit them annually. This is not just an Islamic practice in Cairo: in the Coptic cemetery behind the Church of the Virgin, at Qaṣr al-Shamʿa, Cairo, silent lanes of desolate burial houses built over the years in wide-range of styles are often marked by graffiti recording annual visits by relatives. Di Marco discusses the interaction between its urbanization which began in the ninth century AD and funerary rituals. It is not only a sacred burial ground but also used as a profane location for of work and habitation, as well as for political parades and even horse races. The paper focuses on the symbolic relationship between the living and the dead and the Cairenes' perception of death, the dead and the afterlife. As Max Rodenbeck (2000:89) reminds us:

> So casual about other things, Cairenes are strikingly punctilious in the rituals of condolence. Friends not only will drop everything to rush to a funeral but will also mark the end of the 40-day mourning period and the anniversary of someone's passing. The death notices in *al-Ahram*, the city's newspaper, run to 30 solid columns a day and often more: the saying is that a person cannot have died if their death goes unmentioned in *al-Ahram*, Ladies of leisure often turn straight to the be back of the paper so as to plan their daily agenda of condolence visits (the form of notices … every member of the bereaved family is listed, along with their place of work and relation to the deceased).

William and Fidelity Lancaster present "Observations on death, burial, graves and graveyards at various locations in Ra's al-Khaimah Emirate, UAE, and Musandam *wilāyat,* Oman, using local concerns" based on information they collected when compiling an archive on "Life before Oil" for HH Shaikh Sultan bin Saqr al-Qasimi, the then deputy Ruler of Ra's al-Khaimah Emirate and Director of the National Museum. They describe the funeral customs, graves, grave goods and graveyards as well as associated structures. They provide a useful catalogue and analysis of specific local traditions of the burial of the dead and reflect on local identity in the light of "orthodox" Islamic tradition.

Lynne S. Newton recently undertook a survey to reveal the presence of over fifty shrines in Dhofar, especially around Salalah, a higher number than had been described in previous reports on the region. These shrines ranged from formal buildings associated with mosques to solitary tombs. Many commemorate the lives of charismatic and respected individuals or saints (*awliyāʾ*), including Islamic scholars (*ʿulamāʾ*), pre-Islamic prophets or descendants of the Prophet Mohammad. Newton provides a preliminary categorization of these shrines and discusses traditional Dhofari shrine architecture. She explores their distribution through the *topos* of cultural landscape, combined with analyses of associated practices and traditions, to explore Dhofari local socio-political and religious institutions. Specifically, she presents case studies on five shrines near the archaeological site of al-Balīd to demonstrate the landscape approach to the study of shrines. A landscape of local shrines provided a people with spiritual help as much as political protection and alliances.

In "Wādī Ḥaḍramawt as a Landscape of Death and Burial", the cultural anthropologist and folklorist, **Mikhail Rodionov**, dynamically describes the sacred landscape of death and burial of the Ḥaḍramawt in South Arabia. An examination of these ritual complexes helps to map the landscape of Ḥaḍramī traditional culture. Drawing upon a range of oral and written traditions including mediaeval and modern vernacular poetry, local traditions of pilgrimage and visitations to graves, he examines the configuration of a cultural space, with its various levels of hierarchy, limits, routes, connections. The well Barhūt at the eastern end of the Wādī is believed to be a gateway to the afterlife. As Newton discovered in Dhofar, tombs of Islamic holy men often stand beside tombs of pre-Islamic prophets and other ruins. Furthermore, Rodionov identifies various pre-Islamic rites such as dancing, chanting, performing poetry, sharing meals, and ibex-hunting and connects pious functions with markets and fairs.

Rodionov points out that practically all the venerated tombs are associated with water possibly due to a pre-Islamic correlation between water and vegetation at the graves as a path to revival. In much the same way, Bedouin of the Eastern Desert of Egypt also try to locate a grave near a permanent water source to reinforce the bonds between living and dead: and visitors there will place a few *ben*-tree needles (*Moringa peregrina*) or other foliage on the tomb. The souls of the dead enter the cemeteries of Upper Egypt in the form of small green birds (Blackman 1927: 127) and as Lane explained: "the souls of martyrs reside, until the judgment, in the crops of green birds, which eat of the fruits of Paradise and drink of its rivers" (Lane 1836: repr. 2005: 71).

James E. Taylor also recognises the association between the commemoration of death and poetry in "Attitudes,

Themes and Images: An Introduction to Death and Burial as Mirrored in Early Arabic Poetry". This poetry especially celebrated the heroic untimely deaths of rich and powerful men and reflected on death's inevitability. Though often concerned more with posthumous reputations than comforting prospects of an afterlife, it was customary to lament the deceased in rhymed prose (*saj‿*), a form of poetry that later developed into the poetic genre known as *rithā*⁾. Through an analysis of this poetry, Taylor discusses blood vengeance and other aspects of death but found no suggestion in the poetry of the deliberate mutilation of the dead on the battlefield nor any reported cases of cannibalism, despite periods of extreme famine and starvation.

Devout Muslims, Christians and Jews can expect to enter Paradise after death, for the "Religions of the Book" extend beyond any worldly utopia and the appointed time of death is known only by God. **Dina Dahbany-Miraglia** describes "Jewish Burial Customs in Yemen" in a fascinating account that describes the interaction between Jews and local Muslim communities, in the allocation of Jewish cemeteries by the local tribal elders, for example. Jewish and Islamic laws require speedy burial and both communities, Yemeni Jews and Muslims, believed that the "human world was crowded with a plethora of unseen beings—spirits, ghosts, demons, and the angry spirits of the dead". Using a delightful perceptive tale about a Jew in a small town in southern Yemen to illustrate her account, the author shows how there are specific religious prescriptions but at the same time individual predilections that often successfully defined or defied local customs. Jewish Yemen was one of the most conservative of Jewish cultures, denying women access to literacy and the religious laws that controlled their lives. Yet individual Jews deliberately challenged religious law and local customs of death and dying.

Not only is this collection of papers concerned with local and Islamic traditions and practices, but it also covers aspects of bioethics. Ethical problems associated with vivisection of what might be considered by some to be inferior forms of life such as anthropoid monkeys and handicapped human beings are considered in a wide-ranging paper, "*In anima vili*: Islamic constructions on life autopsies and cannibalism" by **José Mª Bellido-Morillas and García Fernández-Piñar**. Galen's treaty *De vivorum dissection*, for example, showed that he had no choice but to dissect apes. Medieval Islamic scholars including Yuḥannā ibn Māsawayh later performed vivisections on apes to explore Galen's findings. This paper studies Arabic and Islamic cultural constructions on the meaning of death with reference to these *animae viles*.

Suhad Daher-Nashif also addresses important ethical issues in her powerful paper, "Instituting the Palestinian Dead Body", in which she describes the passage that Palestinian dead bodies that are found in criminal circumstances undergo in the time between the determination of death and their final destination, prior to burial. The paper is based on ethnographic fieldwork at the Palestinian Forensic Medicine Institute (FMI) between 2004 and 2007. The binary discrimination between life and death is confused, so that the body is in a liminal stage betwixt and between in which the corpses become the subject of various national, semi-state or state institutions – Palestinian, Israeli, and sometimes, Jordanian – in a multi-institutional passage dominated by multi-bureaucratic logics. The dead body has a dynamic role in maintaining semi-state institutions and upholding the sovereignty of laws under any jurisdiction.

As Hertz (1960: 51–52, 79–80, 84–86) reflected in his thought-provoking classic, conceptions of afterlife and immortality are constructed on the premise that culture is ongoing and immortal, but as death only effects individuals, an individual death is a threat to culture. Yet, though dead, the body is still a socio-political actor.

References

BBC Website, *Guide: Christians in the Middle East* on-line at http://news.bbc.co.uk/1/hi/world/middle_east/4499668.stm (viewed 5.10.2009)

Blackman W.S. 2000 [1927]. *The Fellāḥīn of Upper Egypt*. London: Harper and Row, 1927; repr. American University in Cairo Press, 2000.

Halevi L. 2004. The Paradox of Islamization: tombstone inscriptions, Qur'anic recitations, and the problem of religious change. *History of Religions* (2004): 120-52.

Halevi L. 2007. *Muhammad's Grave: Death Rites and the Making of Islamic Society*. New York: Columbia University Press.

Hertz R. 1960. *Death and the Right Hand*. Glencoe: Free Press.

Hobbs J.J. 1989 [1960]. *Bedouin Life in the Egyptian Wilderness*. Cairo: American University in Cairo Press.

Kennedy J.G. 2005 [1978]. *Nubian Ceremonial Life*. Cairo: American University in Cairo Press.

Klunzinger C.B. 2001 [1878]. *Upper Egypt*. London: Darf.

Lane E.W. 2005 [1896]. *An Account of the Manners and Customs of the Modern Egyptians written 1833–1835*. New York: Cosimo Classics.

Rodenbeck M. 2000. *Cairo: the City Victorious*. Cairo: American University in Cairo Press.

Sattin A. 2001. *The Pharaoh's Shadow*: travels in ancient and modern Egypt. London: Indigo.

Southampton University, http://www.southampton.ac.uk/archaeology/research/projects/quseir_alqadim_project.html (viewed 5.10 2009)

Starkey J. 2009. Death, paradise and the *Arabian Nights*. *Mortality* 14/3: 286–302.

Walter T. 1994. *The Revival of Death*. London: Routledge.

Author's Address:

Dr. Janet Starkey
School of Modern Languages and Cultures
Durham University
Elvet Riverside
New Elvet
Durham DH1 3JT
UK
j.c.m.starkey@durham.ac.uk

The intercessor status of the dead in Maliki Islam and in Mauritania

Corinne Fortier

Summary
In this article, the representations and practices related to death are studied through references to Islamic texts and also from their lived practice in one specific society, Moorish society in Mauritania. The majority of social and religous practices related to funerals are salutary not only to the deceased, but also for those who carry them out. It thus seems that, in spite of a certain denial by Islam with regard to intercession practices, the dead in this religion are considered as mediators between men and God. Moreover, the living continue after the funeral to seek salvation for the soul of their relative and more generally for all Muslims, which bears witness to the fact that they are able to have an influence on the destiny of the dead, which is decided upon in the final instance by God.

Keywords: Islam, Mauritania, death, body, intercession

Introduction

Representations and practices related to death (*mawt*) will be considered here using Islamic texts, and also from their lived practice in one specific society, Moorish society in Mauritania. Moorish society, as with most societies in North Africa, has for a long time been Islamized. The Maliki rite of Sunni obedience was spread in this area by the Almoravids in the 11th century. Moors regard themselves as Arabs, and speak an Arab dialect, *ḥassâniyya*. They call themselves *biḍân,* an Arabic term which means "white". They are still Bedouins in cultural terms, even though they are now rarely nomadic. Three regions in Mauritania with minuscule cultural variations can be differentiated - Adrar in the north west, Trarza in the south west, and Hawdh in the east. Moorish society is considerably hierarchical in tribal terms; at the top, there are the maraboutic tribes and the warrior tribes, each one of which comprises former tributaries, former slaves, blacksmiths and sometimes griots (musicians).

Initially, detailed analysis of funeral rites and of the status attached to death enable us to precisely examine Islamic sources related to such matters. Subsequently, the connection of local practices with foundational Sunni Islamic texts reveals the subtle interplay that a Muslim society keeps alive with its scriptural references. In order for our approach to be coherent, we limit ourselves to the texts which are the most well-known in Moorish society,[1] and which are most likely to have influenced local funeral practices.

In the service of a pure body

Upon the death of a person, the body is no longer the subject, rather it is the object of intentions and of attentions from its social and religious community. Firstly, in washing it and in blocking all of its orifices, the Muslim ritual of funerary cleaning is aimed at protecting the body from all exterior impurity, so as to prepare its entrance into the beyond. This hypothesis enables us to understand a recommendation of Maliki jurisprudence, according to which any person in a state of impurity must not approach the deceased (Qayrawânî 1968: 105). Moreover, it is required that the person who lifts up the body of the deceased perform minor ablutions (*wudû'*) (Khalîl 1995: 112). Thus, unlike other societies and other religions,[2] in Islam, the dead body (*mayyit*) represents less of a source of impurity for the living, than they do for it.

In Moorish society, the cleaning of the dead body is not reserved for a particular social category, it may be carried out by any individual who knows the required Muslim recommendations. Maliki jurisprudence (Qayrawânî 1968: 107 and Khalîl 1995: 106) has nonetheless determined the type of person who may carry this out, in accordance with criteria related to gender and to kinship with the deceased. In the first instance, it is recommended that this be the spouse; in the second, a close relation and in the third an individual of the same gender.[3] The latter possibility is the one most followed in Moorish society, local codes of modesty between couples and relatives of the opposite sex prevent the persons stipulated in the first two categories being favoured juridically.[4]

Numerous actions in attending to the dead are religiously recognised as meritorious for salvation of the deceased, and also for the person who carries them out. In Moorish society, as in classic Islamic texts, the notion of *âjr* is

---

[1] To appreciate more precisely the corpus of texts taught in Mauritania, notably concerning Maliki jurisprudence, see Fortier (1997: 89-91).

[2] On the other hand, in Judaism, the corpse, through contact, and even its very presence, represent one of the main sources of impurity (Wigoder 1996: 834), just as the whole cemetery does, and those who go there must cleanse when they leave (Wigoder 1996: 223). M. Gaborieau, who worked in a Hindu and Muslim environment, also notes that Islam restricted the impurity related to the corpse to a minimum (1993: 178). This minimum corresponds for instance to the fact that Maliki jurisprudence (Khalîl 1995: 109) recommends that the person who is taking care of the cleaning of the body carries out major ablutions (*ghusl*) once they have finished. Concerning Mâlik's uncertainties on this matter, the corpse is not considered as a source of contamination, see Halevi (2007: 54-55).

[3] Failing this the funerary cleaning may in exceptional cases be carried out by an individual of the opposite sex who by necessity must be a prohibited relation (*muḥaram*). Thus, a man may carry out the funeral cleansing of his wet nurse (Khalîl 1995: 111), considering the milk kinship between them (Fortier 2007).

[4] On the other hand, in Malik's age, in Medina, a wife could legitimately wash her husband's corpse and vice versa (Halevi 2007: 54).

used to refer to "good points" which they believe have been accumulated during this life in preparation for life in the beyond (Fortier 2005).[5] It is for instance meritorious for the believer who knows the rules to complete the funerary cleaning as well as presenting, amongst others, this hadith: "God shall forgive forty times over anyone who washes the dead body and conceals its state" (Nawawy 1991: 258). In Moorish society, a person who is not in any way related to the deceased, but rather has a relationship based on respect, can ask to wash him. This is the ultimate homage that an individual can pay to a person who has died, since they will be the last to see them before a shroud covers the body.

Moreover, it is not uncommon that a significant person might, out of respect for the deceased, wish to carry out their final cleaning; the family of the deceased would be eternally grateful. This practice confirms that the funeral cleaning, although it puts the person performing it in contact with a corpse in a state of putrefaction, has been related in Moorish society, and more generally in Sunni Islam, to a pious practice which honours the person undertaking it religiously and socially – which again constitutes an indication of the "sacred status" of the dead body.

Praying for the body

The body should be buried as quickly as possible, in accordance with prophetic speech: "Bury him the same night!" (Bukhârî 1977, vol. 1: 404). In ancient cities and in encampments in Mauritania, as in a lot of other Muslim countries, the dead body is taken to the cemetery (*maqbara*) on a stretcher (*janâ'iz*) which the men present at the funeral are expected to carry in turns, since this is a meritorious undertaking from the religious point of view. This practise is seen in other Muslim countries, notably in Egypt (Galal 1937: 179, note 2) and in Constantine in Algeria (Breteau and Zagnoli 1979: 305). In general, Muslims considered it a meritorious act to follow processions to the cemetery; jurists represented this deed as one of the five essential duties that Muslims owed one another, and they argued that God would reward participants by forgiving their sins (Halevi 2007: 144).

As for women, in Mauritania, they follow slightly behind the funeral procession, as Maliki jurisprudence advises (Khalîl 1995: 110). It is even recommended "that an old woman or a young girl, of whom there is no fear of temptation, go out to accompany the funeral procession of a relative, such as a father, mother, son, daughter, brother, sister or spouse" (Khalîl 1995: 111). Women going out for funeral processions (*khurûj al-nisâ' 'ala al-janâ'iz*) was associated by traditionalists with temptation, or with civil strife (*fitna*) (Halevi 2007: 128).

The grave, which is of a depth equivalent to the height of a man, is made up of two levels and it is the lowest level (*la'ad*) which receives the deceased. The position of the body, in accordance with Muslim requirements, is stretched out on its right-hand side, feet pointing northward, head turned toward the south, eyes directed toward Mecca (*qibla*) (Qayrawânî 1968: 111).

The body is first of all set down at the side of the grave which has been dug for the occasion, then the funeral prayer is carried out (*ṣalat al-janâ'iz* or *ṣalat al-mayyat*), which requires that the body be situated on the bare ground (Khalîl 1995: 107). This prayer, which has the distinct feature of not comprising inclination, calls for an imam to oversee it, since it is to comply with specific rules.

During this prayer, the imam on four occasions says "God is great" (*Allah akbâr*) (Qayrawânî 1968: 111), yet from the pronunciation of the first *takbîr*, those giving prayer call to God for his protection against Satan "the stoned" (*ta'awudh*), and they recite the first sura of the Qur'an, which is known as *fâtiḥa* (Nawawy 1991: 260). The second *takbîr* "Abraham's prayer" (Nawawy 1991: 260) then follows. The sura *yâ'sîn* (XXXVI) may also be recited in accordance with certain rites, however not that of Mâlik (Qayrawânî 1968: 105). In listening to the invocations which follow this prayer, the assistants reply: amen (*amin*).

Those who know the funeral prayers have a religious obligation to perform them, and may even, according to certain jurists, receive remuneration in compensation (Ould Bah 1981: 105). Moreover, uttering this prayer is part of "collective obligations" (*farḍ al-kifâya*) in Maliki jurisprudence (Qayrawânî 1968: 291), unlike ritual prayer which is the result of "individual obligations" (*farḍ al-'ayn*); in addition, in theory, as soon as two Muslims have carried this out, the others are excused from doing so, yet failing to do so may lead to divine punishment (Qayrawânî 1968: 109), so the majority participate voluntarily.

In the event that numerous persons participate in the funeral prayers, it is necessary for there to be at least three rows (*ṣufûf*),[6] since multiplying the rows of the faithful during this prayer favours its fulfilment, as this hadith shows: "Marthad b. Abdallâh al-Yazani reports that Mâlik b. Hubayra, while conducting a funerary prayer where he considered the congregation to be too few, separated the faithful into three groups then addressed them thus: 'God's envoy' says: 'he who will have gathered three rows of faithful at his funeral services is deserved of paradise'" (Nawawy 1991: 259).

Invoking the body

The funerary prayer concludes with an appeal for divine mercy. The clemency of God is sometimes invoked on behalf of the deceased, and on behalf of all the dead and the living, with this invocation: "My Lord! Forgive us the living, our dead, those present with us, those who are

---

[5] The concept of *thawâb*, is also used in the same sense in classic Islamic texts, yet less commonly used in Moorish society.

[6] Fifteen faithful, for example, will be made up of three rows of five people.

absent, the young and the old among us, men and women…" The more the significance of the number of people who carry out this type of invocation, the greater the chance of it bearing fruit; as a hadith declares: "When a community of Muslims, one hundred in number, carry out the *ṣalat* for a Muslim, and all pray for the forgiveness of sins, this prayer is sure to be answered" (Muslim, *Janâ'iz,* Wensinck and Gardet 1998: 183).

In short, when the body is placed into the grave, the person who carries out the burial, utters a religious invocation requesting that God alleviate the suffering of the dead in the grave (Qayrawânî 1968: 107). Each person present then takes three handfuls of soil, or sand, which they throw on the deceased while reciting a section (*ḥizb*) of the Qur'an, for the salvation of its soul (*rûḥ*). This is a section named *tabarak*, in reference to the first word of the sura cited – although it is known in the Qur'an under the name of the sura of Monarchy (*al-Mulk*) (LXVII) (trans. Blachère 1980: 605).

Participating in the funeral is not only salutary for the dead, but for individuals too, as a hadith asserting that it is meritorious to participate in the funerary prayer suggests, it is still advantageous to be present at the burial:[7] "Anyone who is present at the burial until the funeral prayer is finished will have one *qîrât*. A person who is present until the burying will have two *qîrât*. To anyone asking: 'What are *qîrât*?', the response would be 'The equivalent of two large mountains'" (Nawawy 1991: 259).

The body "quranised"

After the burial, the men present and the Qur'anic pupils from the place, simultaneously read different sections (*aḥzâb*) of the Qur'an for the happiness of the deceased in the beyond. This sacred chorus is called *salka* in regions of the Adrar and of Hawdh, and *khatma* in the Trarza region, a term which refers to the closing of the Qur'anic reading, which is also used in the same context in other countries, notably in Egypt (Galal 1937: 190).

In Tiris, a border region of north-west Mauritania, this ceremony takes place within three days after the burial, according to the custom of their Moroccan neighbours. It is not rare for Muslim societies to carry out the reading of the Qur'an in its entirety, even on the day of the burial, as is the case in Egypt (*ibid.*: 189), or more often afterwards, for example during the first three days which follow the burial in Syrian villages (Jomier 1994: 141); or even on the fourth day in Nepal (Gaborieau 1993: 230). This custom, acknowledged in numerous Muslim societies, does not seem to have any sources in foundational Islamic texts and might even be semi-forbidden in Maliki jurisprudence (Khalîl 1995: 112).

In Moorish society, women who stand outside the dwelling, where this reading is taking place, carry out one thousand *tarkim* at this moment, that is, they rub hundred beans of their rosary, ten times, while repeating the religious phrase: "May God forgive him and grant him mercy" (*Allah raḥmu wa yaghfarlu*). When the reading of the Qur'an is over, they approach the men[8] and invoke with them the salvation of the soul of the deceased. A hadith indeed recommends that the majority approach those who have finished the complete recital of the Qur'an because this moment, which is particularly pleasing to God, favours the fulfilment of wishes: "Being present at a session is recommended where there is a reading of the Qur'an, whether we are those who know how to read it or those who do not know" (Nawawy 1991: 131).

Laying down the body

Local custom consists of setting down branches[9] on the grave, already noted in 1795 by the traveller Mungo Park (1996: 54), and this is also recognized in other Muslim countries, notably in Egypt (Galal 1937: 198; Abu-Zahra 1997: 58), revealing, after analysis of Islamic sources, inspiration from a hadith. The Prophet, passing close to two sepultures whose inhabitants suffered torture, would have taken the branch of green palm tree[10] and, breaking it in two, put each of the pieces on one of the tombs (Bukhârî 1977, vol. 1: 439). To those who questioned him about the finality of such a gesture, Mohammed responded: "In the hope that they will feel some relief as long as these branches are not dried out (*la'allahu an yukhaffafa 'anhumâ mâ lam yaybasâ*)" (*id.*).

The significance of this gesture is found in Mauritania; so, the phrase which makes reference to the recent death of an individual: "There remain branches which are still green" (*mazal zarbu akhẓar*), suggests that as long as the greenery placed on the grave is not dried out, the deceased is supposed to have no worries. Moreover, in Egypt, it is believed that as long as the palms, placed on the tomb, are verdant, they will bring about divine mercy (Galal 1937: 198, note 4).

During this period of time, God is not supposed to hold debts left by the deceased. This is a significant pardon, since their reimbursement, in the sayings of the Prophet, is amongst the major problems which may delay the liberation of the soul: "The soul of the believer is held prisoner as long as their debts have not been settled" (Nawawy 1991: 263). In addition, as a hadith recommends, their heirs must settle them quickly: "It is advisable to settle the debts of the deceased without delay" (Nawawy 1991: 263).

The beneficial nature of this greenery is without doubt due to its implicit association with Muslim paradise,

---

[7] It is the same in Judaism, both for the salvation of the dead and for the living (Gugenheim 1978: 197).

[8] Women continue nonetheless to avoid men seeing them, even hiding themselves behind the canvas of a tent or behind the walls of a house in which the Qur'anic recital has taken place.

[9] Especially acacia branches (*Accacia raddiana*), of the palm tree in ancient cities, or simple twigs which are still green.

[10] In another hadith, reference is made to a piece of green wood (Bukhârî 1977, vol.1: 445).

which is represented in a particularly luxuriant manner, even the term paradise in Arabic literally refers to garden (*janna*). More precisely, the shade that this vegetal protection brings in the time that it remains verdant seems to echo "the extensive shade" of the trees of paradise of which the Qur'an talks about: "The companions of the straight line will be, amongst the jujube trees which have no thorns and acacias lined up in the extensive shade" (LVI, 27-40). The image of the shade of the tree relates to the idea of blessed rest, physical or spiritual, and presents a particularly evocative suggestion of men of the desert who live under a blazing sun, which would appear to be the Moors or the Bedouins of Arabia from the beginnings of Islam.

The body celebrated

In Mauritania, after the burial, a sheep is slaughtered by the family of the deceased for those who have come, sometimes from far away, to be present at the burial. This custom, known in other societies of the Maghreb, is not completely in keeping with what a hadith stipulates, according to which it is strangers to the family, or at the very least, those who are more distant genealogically, who must serve a meal to the closest relations of the deceased. Thus, the close family of the deceased, in honour of those taking part in the funeral, offer a feast considered as an almsgiving (*ṣadaqa*), which is intended to favour the salvation of the soul of their relative.

Condolences ('*azâ*') must be presented to the family within three days. Expressions of praise are then made, with the aim of God, bearing witness to the sentiment of respect that the deceased individual inspires. Moreover, divine clemency is invoked in these terms: "What God takes back and what He gives, are chosen by Him, and each item has a predetermined term in His opinion. Endure with fortitude and hope for divine reward." The most commonly used expression of mercy at the time of condolences: "May God welcome his soul" (*Allah raḥmu*), is also used in a systematic manner since it alludes, in conversation, to the deceased.

Moreover, in Maraboutic tribes, in the same way – and in reverse generational order – that poems, composed at birth, praise the ascendants of the newborn and ask that this intercedes favourably for their parents, funeral orations put into verse[11] in honour of the deceased, praising their qualities, have a propitiatory effect for their descendants. This kind of funeral oration, called *marthiyya*, is a poetic genre which is known in classic Arab literature. We have also shown (Fortier 1998: 207-209) that small children were considered in Islam as intercessors, and it seems that it may be the same for the dead, and for similar reasons related to their unconsciousness, their incapability to do wrong, as well as their power to communicate with the invisible world, and in particular with angels.

The body and the grave

A stone positioned in the ground at head level is used to indicate the position of the grave; a smaller one may also be placed at the feet. Furthermore, it is forbidden by Islam for a building to be constructed above or around the sepulture (Khalîl 1995: 113), signifying that social and economic differences are no longer applicable in the other world.

The Moors, essentially Bedouins, do not have much trouble in conforming to this instruction, unlike their sedentary neighbours in Maghreb who are in the habit of building mausoleums (*qubba*) to the "very close to God" ('*awliyyâ*').[12] In Moorish encampments, it is even the case that the sepultures are not made of distinctive stone, in accordance with prophetic custom.

In Mauritania, although some gravestones do not bear any inscription, in conformance with certain prophetic traditions (Halevi 2007: 32-35) and with the recommendation of Maliki jurisprudence (Khalîl 1995: 113), others bear the name of the buried man, along with that of his father, combined in the epitaph: "Here lies so-and-so, son of so-and-so" (*hadha qabru fulân ibn fulân*) while in another it reads: "May God grant mercy to the son of so-and-so" (*raḥima Allahu fulân ibn fulân*).

Various formulae invoking divine clemency are also used, such as "Entrusted to the kindness of God" (*raḥmatu Allah*). Mention is sometimes made, not just to the father, but also to the mother, who thus benefit from the mercy that God might possibly decide to grant to their child: "May God pardon and grant mercy to the slave of God named so-and-so, and also to his father and mother" (*Allahuma 'aghfir wa raÌam wa tajâwaz 'an mâ ta'lam min 'abdika fulân wa abîhi wa ummihi*).

The stones are engraved by one of the local men who has the neatest handwriting; this man sometimes adds his name beside that of the deceased, in the aspiration that his sins will also be pardoned. In the majority of cases these steles are not dated, however, the name of the engraver, which appears on several of them, enables sepultures from the same epoch to be identified.

The custom of burying an individual in the same place where he dies is consistent with the hadith, which the Prophet, amongst others declared (Wensinck and Mensing 1943, vol.2: 138): "If I had been present at the time of your death, you would have been buried where you died" (*law ḥaḍartuka mâ dufinta illa ḥayzu mita*). So, in Moorish society, when an individual has died far away from their encampment, or from their city, he is buried in the place where he has died. In this case, he has two gravestones, one in the area where his death occurred, and the other in the cemetery where his ancestors are buried. The latter gravestone, which generally consists of a stele, enables his relatives to carry on his memory,

---

[11] The same kind of funeral oration is also shown in Judaism (Wigoder 1996: 310).

[12] This is why we call them '*awliyyâ*' (sg: *walî*) who are set apart from other believers by their prodigies and their religiosity.

meditating not on his body but on his name; something which bears witness, moreover, to a genuine relation between the name and the identity of a person.

Exceptionally, in Chinguetti, for reasons of social and religious prestige, a person there may also be seen to be given two gravestones; one in the courtyard of the big Mosque, the other in the cemetery where they have been buried. In Mauritania, the cemetery is generally located well away from dwelling places, to the east of them, beside sacred space.

The blessed body

When the gravestone of the deceased is located close to the place where his close family members reside, they generally go there each week. Visits to the cemetery are thought to be salutary for the dead and for the living alike. A local expression of "distinction", which makes reference to Jews and to infidels, bears witness that this custom is fundamental for Muslims: "The poorer a cemetery is of Jews and infidels is, it is not visited and no alms are given to it" (*afqar min maqbarat al-yahûd* or *al-kâfar, mâ tanzâr wa lâ yuṣaddaq 'aliha*). The preferred day for visiting the cemetery is a Friday (*yûm al-jum'a*),[13] a blessed day; or even Monday, since the Prophet would arrive there on this day; the time of day is preferentially the time which comes before the sun wanes.

Visits to the cemetery are followed by intercession practices, the deceased are considered as being closer to God than the living.[14] This conception is found in Islamic sources, and more particularly in the hadith where the term which refers to the dead, *ṣâliḥîn*, which refers to the idea of piety and of "holiness".

Visiting the gravestones (*ziyârat al-qubûr*) in Moorish society, as in Islamic society, is moreover designated by a specific term, *ziyâra*, which refers to the quest of blessing (*tabarruk*). This, though less known and less studied than that carried out more especially on the gravestones of those "very close to God",[15] proceeds nonetheless in the same way, by a gesture of contact with the ground[16] of the gravestones. Moreover, when an individual looks for the "blessing of the dead" (*barkat ṣâliḥîn*) not for himself, but for a sick person for example, he brings with him a little bit of this ground which will later be scattered on the head of the person for whom it is destined.

This type of blessing, which is found in many other Muslim societies, does not seem to be explained by the sacred value that Islam grants in particular to the ground of the sepulture. Therefore, in some countries, such as Egypt where the grave of the dead does not amount to one simple stele, but rather is akin to a tomb, other elements may also be preserved, for instance a little piece of fabric or of wood (Galal 1937: 199). It is thus less the ground in itself which serves as a vehicle for the baraka of the dead, but rather any element related to the gravestone, or more precisely, to the body which it contains. In fact, the gravestone, in so far as it extends the presence of the body therein, is only one of the receptacles of the sacred aura of the dead body, in the same way, for example as the mount (horse or camel) which has touched the body when it was alive is a source of baraka in Moorish society.

In addition, it would seems that the notion of "relic", known in late Antiquity to the Christians of North Africa and the Western Mediterranean (Brown 1984: 13), is not alien to the Muslim world. However, it does not concern the fragments of the body of someone who is "very close to God" but instead that which, having been in contact with his body, is endowed with sacred power and serves, as in the world of Christians, as "material support for intercession". We use this expression to emphasise the physical and tactile nature of this form of intercession which is carried out by contact from body to body, by means of a transitional object, itself designed as a substitute for the absent body.

The proximity of bodies

In Mauritania, numerous tales of wonders concern the gravestones of those who are "very close to God". Among these tales, those connected with the gravestone of Sidi wuld Rawth, of the Maraboutic tribe of the Laghlâl, bear witness to the importance of the spatial organisation of bodies in the cemetery; organisation which generally follows that of family ties. When the tomb of Sidi wuld Rawth was dug behind that of his father, in accordance with the custom which respects the codes of behaviour between generations, the earth filled in the grave continuously, while in front of the paternal gravestone, the ground was miraculously half open. Such a wonder, which indicated the place to bury this man, showed that he was superior to his father from a religious point of view.

The position of the dead in the cemetery is moreover decisive for his salvation ; as it is said in a hadith quoted locally:[17] "Bury your dead in the middle of a group of pious men since the dead is wronged by having evil neighbours, in the same way as the living" (*âdfinû mawtâkum wasta qawmîn ṣâliḥîna fa'inna al-mayyita yatâ'adha kamâ yatâ'adha al-ḥayyu*). The notion of a

---

[13] Leor Halevi (2007: 226) has shown the connection between the custom of visiting the graves on Friday and the cyclical supension of the punishment in the grave ('adhâb al-qabr).

[14] Similarly, the conception according to which the dead, in particular those who are in purgatory, may intercede with God for the living was established in Christianity at the end of the Middle Ages (Legoff 1999: 813).

[15] Jews in North Africa also go on a pilgrimage to the gravestone of a person that they consider as being "very close to God", so this intercedes in their favour (Wigoder 1996: 224).

[16] It may also consist of sand, depending on the location.

[17] Leor Halevi (2007: 228) mentioned that in the beginning of Islam, families expected favourable effects by burying their relatives proximate to dead holy men, whose blessings might spread to neighbouring graves. This idea of good or bad neighbourhood appears also in Ibn 'Asâkir (d. 1176) in his history of Damascus: "Bury your dead amidst pious folk, for indeed a dead individual is wronged by a wicked neighbour just as a living person is wronged by a wicked neighbour" (Halevi 2007: 228).

good neighbourhood amongst the living and the dead, seems to be very important in Islam.

The body which is "all ears"

In accordance with certain Islamic representations, the sensory perceptions of the person do not cease upon death, in particular those related to hearing, and this in spite of the verse of the Qur'an (35:22) declaring: "You cannot make hear those who are in their graves". Al-Ghazâlî, who was a mystic and a Sunni jurist (1058-1111, Perse), explicitly asserts in his major work on death and the beyond in Islam, entitled (*The precious pearl for uncovering consciousness of the world to come; ad-durra al-fâkira fî kashf 'ulûm al-âkhira*), that loss of sight precedes loss of hearing (1974: 9): "The last thing which disappears in the dying, is hearing, since sight is lost the moment when the spirit is completely separated from the heart. However hearing is preserved until the soul has been removed." Hearing is not only the last sense to remain alert beyond death, it is also the first to appear in a child (Fortier 1998: 207), which seems to confirm the hypothesis that we have advanced (Fortier 1997: 104), that hearing is one of the senses which is the most fundamental in Islam.

The conception according to which the dead hears, is without doubt inferred from the behaviour of the Prophet who, when he saw the bodies of his dead companions in the battle of Badr, talked to them thus: "'Have you really found what your Lord promised you?' He asked him: 'Are you speaking to the dead?' He replied: 'You do not hear any better than them, yet they cannot reply'" (Bukhârî 1993: 270, par. 689). The dead, in Islam, cannot speak directly to the living except through the medium of dreams.

On the other hand, al-Ghazâlî (1974: 27) reports that Mohammed would have declared: "The dead hear the sound of your footsteps, and if they hear the sound of footsteps, all the more reason for them to hear everything else." In Moorish society, Muslim representation according to which the dead "hears" explains a number of deeds during visits to gravestones.

When an individual goes to meditate at a grave, he positions himself at the level of the stone where it is thought that the head of the dead lies, and recites eleven times in a low voice the first sura of the Qur'an (*fâtiḥa*). This prayer is addressed to the souls of the dead as a locally used expression shows: "He recites the *fâtiḥa* to the souls of the dead" (*aqra al-fâtiḥa 'ala arwah al-mawta*). It is also recommended that the believer recites sura CXII ("the worship") three times, sura CXIV ("the people") three times, and if possible sura XXXVI ("*yâ'sîn*"), since the Prophet would have declared, in connection with this last sura: "Everything has a heart, and the heart of the Qur'an is the sura *Yâ'sîn*. So recite this to your dead" (Sharaf 1987: 76). The traces of these invocations are often visible in the sand, where a series of points forming squares are drawn, with the aim of counting the number of recitals. Then follows, in Moorish society, "an invocation of the dead" (*du'â' 'ala al-mayyat*) in which the person giving prayer calls to God to pardon this person for their sins, so that he receives paradise.

Those who visit the deceased usually adress their invocation more widely to all those buried in the cemetery. This practice, which is found in other Muslim societies,[18] proves, according to our research in foundational Islamic texts, to be of prophetic origin. Mohammed would, essentially, himself implore divine pardon on behalf of all the "inhabitants" of the cemetery:[19] "God's envoy passed in front of the graves in Medina: he made his way toward them, facing them and said: 'Peace be with you, inhabitants of the graves, may God pardon you and also us. You are our predecessors and we are your vestiges'" (Nawawy 1991: 167). The intercession (*shafâ'a*) on behalf of the dead carried out by the Prophet is moreover confirmed by the account of his spouse, 'Aysha, who declared that we go to the cemetery at night to ask God to forgive those who are there of their sins (Muslim, *Janâ'iz*, cited by Wensinck and Gardet 1998: 183).

In Moorish society, the community of inhabitants of the cemetery, like those inhabitants of a place, have an imam. "The imam of the cemetery" (*imâm maqbara*), as he is known, acts as a special intercessor for the living; in general he is a man who has shown great piety, if not extraordinary deeds during his life, that is a man "very close to God". Just as the imam stands in front of the other faithful to oversee prayer, the imam of the cemetery is buried slightly in front of the other deceased in order to better fulfil his role as intercessor amongst them.[20]

The body suffering

The sensory perceptions of the dead are not just auditory but may also consist of corporeal sensations related to comfort and to discomfort. This conception is found in Sunni texts, in particular in an-Nafîs: "The soul which remains continues to perceive and discern, and at the same time experiences pleasure and grief; there are pleasures and grief in the grave [...]" (Savage Smith 1995: 107).

Al-Ghazâlî (1974: 25) moreover recounts several narratives indicating that the dead may recognise physical pain in their grave. He cites for instance the case of a deceased man, who appeared in a dream to one of his relatives, asking about his condition. As this person complained: "I am dead and I am well, except for the moment when you smoothed out the ground above me, a stone broke my rib and I am suffering from that", the

---

[18] This is for instance the case in the countryside of North Tunisia where one beseeches "the inhabitants of the graves" thus: "Salvation for you, oh inhabitants of the graves. You have arrived ahead of us and we will re-join you ..." (Dermenghem 1954: 125, note 1, citing Dornier).
[19] In Judaism, it is the cemetery as a whole which is considered as a dwelling place (Wigoder 1996: 222).
[20] No reference to this practice has been found in the foundational Islamic texts consulted.

veracity of these declarations was certified. These beliefs find their origin in a hadith: "The dead suffers in his grave as do the living in their home" (*id.*).

In addition, to ensure the corporeal well-being of the dead, their family, on the day of the death, prepare "the drink of the dead" (*shrâb al-mawta*) or the "meal of the dead" (*'asha al-mawta*). Though given to a poor person, or similar, such as an orphan or a foreign Qur'anic pupil (Fortier 1997: 96), the dead are supposed to benefit from such charity carried out for them.[21]

The expressions "drink of the dead" or "meal of the dead" refer to a collective, since an individual who gives this sort of alms intends it especially for the person who is recently deceased, but also for all the deceased from their family, and even, more generally, to all dead Muslims. This is no doubt explained by the fact that they recognise one common fate: everyone is waiting for the final Judgement. This state would concern all who died since Adam, except for the Prophet and ten of his companions who, according to a hadith, would have already been reunited in paradise.

This almsgiving, aiming to change the fate of the dead, which is still not permanently sealed, may be repeated indefinitely for several generations. It is carried out the day before the Friday, since on this sacred day its beneficial effect is increased. This practice is considered by Moors as Islamic, and makes reference to the proverbial expression already cited, aimed at differentiating the condition of dead Muslims to that of Jews, just as in this other quote of the same genre: "more thirsty than the dead of the Jews" (*a'tash min mawta al-yahûd*). It is moreover significant that, in this desert society whose main foodstuff is milk, the fundamental needs would make reference to hydration.

As a result, if divine grace is all powerful, the living nonetheless continue during the funeral and afterwards, on a long-term basis, to seek salvation for the soul of their relative and more generally for all Muslims, which bears witness to the fact that they may have an influence on the destiny of the dead, decided in the latter proceedings by God (Fortier 2003).[22] Moreover, funeral conduct describes not just having a salutary effect on the deceased, but also on those who carry it out; it appears that in spite of a certain denial of Islam regarding intercession practices, that the dead in this religion are considered, in the same way as small children, as mediators between men and God (Fortier 2006).

Intercessor status is thus not only the exclusive right of "extraordinary figures" who are remarkable and remarked upon – by believers and by researchers alike – such as those of holy men or heads of brotherhood, but turns out equally to be, in the Muslim world, the common and unnoticed destiny of everybody, at the beginning and at the end of their life.

References

Abu-Zahra N. 1997. *The Pure and Powerful. Studies in Contemporary Muslim Society*. Berkshire, UK: Ithaca Press.

Breteau C.-H. & Zagnoli N. 1979. Aspects de la mort dans deux communautés rurales méditerranéennes: la Calabre et le nord-est constantinois. *Études corses* 12-13. *La mort en Corse et dans les sociétés méditerranéennes*: 291-308.

Brown P. 1984. *Le culte des saints. Son essor et sa fonction dans la chrétienté latine*. Trans. A. Rousselle. Paris: Cerf.

Bukhârî M. 1977. *Les Traditions islamiques*. Trans. O. Houdas & W. Marçais. (4 volumes). Paris: Adrien & Jean Maisonneuve.

Bukhârî M. 1993. *Le sommaire du Sahih al-Boukhari*. (2 volumes). Beyrouth: Dar al-Kutub al-Ilmiyah.

Coran. 1967. Trans. D. Masson. Paris: Gallimard.

Coran. 1980. Trans. R. Blachère. Paris: Maisonneuve et Larose.

Dermenghem É. 1954. *Le culte des saints dans l'islam maghrébin*. Paris: Gallimard (Tel).

Fortier C. 1997. Mémorisation et audition: l'enseignement coranique chez les Maures de Mauritanie". *Islam et sociétés au sud du Sahara* 11: 85-105.

Fortier C. 1998. "Le corps comme mémoire": du giron maternel à la férule du maître coranique. *Journal des africanistes* 68/1-2: 199-223.

Fortier C. 2003. Soumission, pragmatisme et légalisme en islam. *Topique* 85, *Les Spiritualités*: 145-161.

Fortier C. 2005. "Infléchir le destin car la vraie souffrance est à venir" (société maure-islam sunnite). *Systèmes de pensée en Afrique noire* 17. *L'excellence de la souffrance*, D. Casajus (ed.): 195-217.

Fortier C. 2006. La mort vivante ou le corps intercesseur. *Revue du Monde Musulman et de la Méditerranée* 113-114. *Le corps et le sacré en Orient musulman*, B. Heyberger & C. Mayeur-Jaouen (eds): 229-246.

Fortier C. 2007. Blood, Sperm and the Embryo in Sunni Islam and in Mauritania: Milk Kinship, Descent and Medically Assisted Procreation, *Body and Society* 13 (3). Special Issue: *Islam, Health and the Body*, D. Tober & D. Budiani (eds): 15-36.

Gaborieau M. 1993. *Ni brahmanes ni ancêtres, colporteurs musulmans du Népal*. Nanterre: Société d'ethnologie.

Galal M. 1937. Des rites funéraires en Égypte actuelle. *Revue des études islamiques*: 135-285.

Ghazâlî A.H.M. 1974. *La perle précieuse*. Trans. L. Gautier. Amsterdam: Oriental Press.

Gugenheim E. 1978. *Le judaïsme dans la vie quotidienne*. Paris: Albin Michel (Présence du judaïsme).

---

[21] In Egypt, alms are also given to the poor on this occasion, bearing a name which explicitly attests to their beneficial effect with regard to the dead: "the bread of mercy" (Abu-Zahra 1997: 61).

[22] It is the same in Christianity (Legoff 1999: 899), where those who have been punished by the flames of the purgatory fire, and who remain there until final Judgement day, may escape it earlier by prayers, almsgiving, fasting, and offerings to their relatives, or masses they make to declare their intention.

Halevi L. 2007. *Muhammad's grave. Death rites and the Making of Islamic Society*. New York: Columbia University Press.

Jomier J. 1994. *L'islam vécu en Égypte*. Paris: Vrin.

Khalîl M. 1995. *Le précis de Khalîl*. Beyrouth: Dar el-fiker.

Legoff J. 1999. La naissance du purgatoire. Pages 771-1231 in *Un autre Moyen Âge*. Paris: Gallimard (Quarto).

Nawawy I. 1991. *Les jardins de la piété, les sources de la Tradition islamique*. Paris: Alif.

Ould Bah M. 1981. *La littérature juridique et l'évolution du malikisme en Mauritanie*. Publications de l'Université de Tunis, Faculté des Lettres et Sciences humaines de Tunis 19.

Park M. 1996. *Voyage dans l'intérieur de l'Afrique*. Paris: La Découverte (Poche).

Qayrawânî A.Z. 1968. *La Risâla, épître sur les éléments du dogme et de la loi de l'islam selon le rite mâlékite*. Trans L. Bercher. Alger: Pérès.

Savage-Smith E. 1995. Attitudes Toward Dissection in Medieval Islam. *Journal of the History of Medicine* 50: 67-110.

Sharaf S.S.M. 1987. *Le rappel et l'invocation de Dieu*. Kuwait: Dar al-qalam.

Wensinck A.J. & Gardet L. 1998. Shafâ'a. Pages 183-184, vol. 9. *Encyclopédie de l'islam*. Leiden: Brill.

Wensinck A.J. & Mensing J.P. 1943, vol. 2. *Concordance et indices de la tradition musulmane* (7 volumes). Leiden: Brill.

Wigoder G. 1996. *Dictionnaire encyclopédique du judaïsme*. Paris: Cerf et Robert Laffont (Bouquins).

Author's Address
Corinne Fortier
Laboratoire d'Anthropologie Sociale (Collège de France)
52 rue du Cardinal Lemoine
75005 Paris
France
email: corinne.fortier@college-de-france.fr

Cairo's City of the Dead: the cohabitation between the living and the dead from an anthropological perspective

Anna Tozzi Di Marco

Summary
This essay focuses on my fieldwork in Cairo's City of the Dead regarding the cohabitation between the living and the dead. I particularly investigated the interaction between urbanization and funerary rituals, through qualitative analysis and living in the Mameluk burial area for eight years to 2006. The City of the Dead is unique in that it is inhabited and yet continues to be a functioning cemetery. This cohabitation without a clear-cut division has been the main characteristic of this cemetery from the beginning of its urbanization in the ninth century AD. It is represented by several modalities of occupancy of the cemetery for profane activities; as a place for living and working, as well as for political parades, military celebrations, and horse races. I explore the reasons for the physical and social production and reproduction of this necropolis as well as its fruition by residents and visitors. The links between the two categories of the sacred and the profane are analysed, focusing specifically on the symbolic relationship between the living and the dead generated by Cairenes' perception of death, the dead and the underworld.

Keywords: Cairo's al Qarafa, City of the Dead, Islamic funerary rituals, popular piety

Introduction

This essay presents the results of my fieldwork in Cairo's City of the Dead regarding the cohabitation between the living and the dead. In the context of the process of the necropolis's urbanization, I focus particularly on interactions with funerary rituals, examining firstly the historical records, then the data from current anthropological research. Indeed, I began this field research in 1998, living in the Mameluk burial area for eight years to 2006.[1] The data on which this essay is based emerged from participant observation and from unstructured interviews and conversations; in other words from the ethnographic techniques of qualitative analysis.

From an anthropological point of view, the City of the Dead is unique in that it is inhabited and yet continues to be a functioning cemetery. The coexistence between the living and the dead, without a clear-cut division between these two spheres within the spatial and symbolic orders, has been the main characteristic of this cemetery since the beginning of its urbanization in the ninth century AD (Fig. 1). It is represented by the several modalities of the occupancy of the cemetery for profane activities; as a place for living and working, as well as for political parades, military celebrations, and horse races.

In contrast to other social sciences that utilize functionalist interpretations for this complex reality,[2] this anthropological study emphasizes also its symbolic dimensions. It explores the physical and social production and reproduction of this necropolis as well as its realization by residents and visitors, reflecting Cairenes' changing perceptions and representations throughout history. Thus whereas the City of the Dead is a sacred site, I analyse the ties between the two categories; the sacred (investigated at various levels of meaning, i.e. funerary rituals, perception and functions of the tombs, cult of the holy figures, funerary architecture and art, division and structure of funerary space, etc.) and the profane. Specifically I explore the symbolic relationship between the living and the dead resulting from Cairenes' perception of death, the dead and the underworld.

For this task, it is useful to reconstruct the historical process of urbanization of the City of the Dead and the conurbation of its burial zones from its origins up to the present day. The pragmatic target of my research is to contribute to the preservation of the City of the Dead's intangible heritage, specifically its socio-cultural diversity, as the necropolis represents a mirror of Egyptian society in its stratification of traditions throughout the ages. To this end, I initiated an applied anthropological activity of guided tours in order to characterise Cairo's City of the Dead from a socio-anthropological point of view (Tozzi Di Marco 2008: 107-108).

The urbanization and the occupation of the cemetery through history

Cairo's city of dead is named *al Qarafa* or *turbat*[3] by the locals for centuries, as reported in the ancient topographical maps (Fig. 2). It was founded as burial site of the first Arab capital of Egypt, al Fustat, in 642. As for the foundation of Islamic cities, specific foundation myths are associated with the planning of various burial sites in al Qarafa.[4] Afterwards it became so extended that it was divided in the *Greater Qarafa* and the *Lesser Qarafa* (Fig. 3). Throughout the ages it followed the urban development of the city. Nowadays it is 12 km

---

[1] My fieldwork was co-financed by Italian Ministry of Foreign Affairs and Egyptian Ministry of Education for the first year.
[2] The urban studies classify the necropolis as a slum and its community as the urban poor. See also local and foreign sociological analyses, such as Mohammed H. Hafiz's Masters dissertation in sociology based on his research on the community of the cemetery, a study on the characteristics of Bab el Nasr cemetery.
[3] Some scholars have suggested that the term *al Qarafa* comes from the name of the Arab tribe Banu Qarafa, who settled in al Fustat. Every tribe had its own burial ground.
[4] The foundation myths are a common topic in every Mediterranean civilization, and are often fundamental to the choice of where to found a city.

Figure 1. Cohabitation between the living and the dead.

Figure 2. Bertelli's map of Cairo (1575).

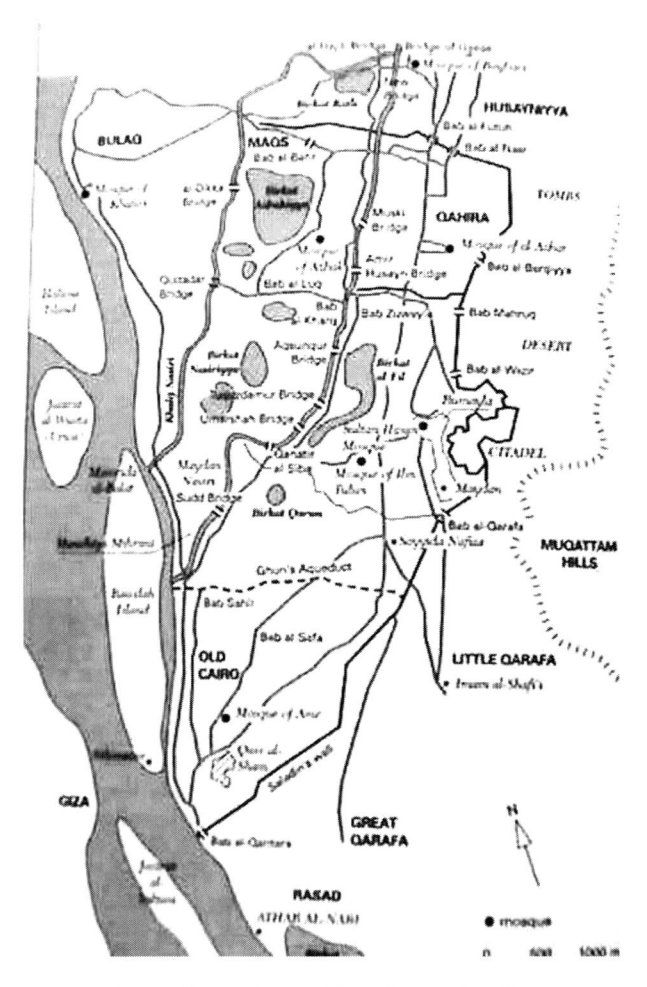

Figure 3. Greater Qarafa and Lesser Qarafa.

Figure 4. The southern cemetery and the city from al Moqattam.

long, stretching from the ancient Fatimid walls in the north to the southern borders of the city at the foot of al Moqattam hills and around Salah el Din's Citadel (Fig. 4), and consisting of seventeen quarters.

During the first Umayyad reign (AD 642-750) the cemetery was shaped according to Islamic law,[5] later the Abbasids (AD 750-1218), built funerary monuments on the pious tombs,[6] whose architectural style was influenced by the Persian and Seljuk cultures. In this period al Qarafa started to be populated by a first nucleus of residents who lived close to the holy places of veneration and the noble tombs, in order to improve their maintenance and service. The independent ruler ibn Tulun's aqueduct (9th century AD), which ran through the Greater Qarafa, facilitated the proliferation of construction and the expansion of its population. Besides the Abbasids, later the Shi'ite Fatimids (969-1171) provided patronage for the building of some saintly edifices such as holy shrines, two kinds of funerary mausolea (the *qubba* and the *mashhad*),[7] and even the holy figures' apocryphal graves.

Figure 5. Sayyeda Nafisa's mosque and tomb.

For example, in the ninth century AD a new burial site arose around Sayyeda Nafisa's tomb (Fig. 5),[8] excavated by herself in her house, because of her power to transmit the *baraka*.[9] During the Fatimid era in particular – because of the spread of *Alid* shrines,[10] and the relatively fervent religious devotion of the population – many aspects of urban infrastructure were developed in al Qarafa in order to fulfil the pilgrims' needs. These included hostels and restaurants as well as charity institutions. For this purpose the Fatimids restored the *waqf* system,[11] which worked to fund many religious establishments. Moreover the necropolis was also

---

[5] Islamic law prescribes two types of orthodox tomb: a grave with a ditch in the centre, and another kind with the ditch at the side. It is forbidden to erect any cenotaph.

[6] The Abbasid dynasty, based in Mesopotamia, moved the capital from Damascus to Baghdad. They ruled for the 500 years and they were great patrons of the arts and learning.

[7] They were two types of monumental mausolea. The *qubba* or *turbe* is a cubical chamber surmounted by a dome, spread in Iran in tenth century, while the *mashhad*, less prevalent, is a large structure with some chambers and one central burial room.

[8] She was the Prophet's great grand-daughter and one of Cairo's three female patron saints. Her ziyara day is on Sunday, which she chose before dying (although during her lifetime Saturdays and Wednesdays were her cultic days). Nowadays, men and women visit her shrine every day on pilgrimage, in a room attached to the mosque. It is believed that at her tomb the prayers are directly accepted in heaven.

[9] The *baraka* is the divine blessing associated with holy figures.

[10] The Alids were the members of Ali's family. He was the cousin and the husband of the Prophet's daughter, Fatima.

[11] The *waqf* (pl. *awqaf*) is an inalienable religious endowment whose incomes are usually allocated for charitable purposes. It also represented the primary resource for the maintenance of funerary mausoleums and pious institutions.

Figure 6. Al Menoufi's tomb in his zawiya in the Mameluk cemetery
(a local holy man lived here during the fourteenth century).

inhabited by the Islamic mystic brotherhoods of Sufi, who lived in the *khanqahs* and the *zawiyas*,[12] often erected around the tomb of a *tariqa's* founder. They often served as hospices for Sufi itinerants and poor students.

The following Ayyubid dynasty (1170-1250) founded a large number of Koranic schools, *madrasas*, and *khanqahs* to spread the Sunni faith, in contrast to the Shi'ite Fatimids. These theological institutes offered also lodging for trainees and teachers. People went to the cemetery to see the Sufi processions from their *khanqahs* to the congregational mosque for Friday prayer, in order to receive their blessing.

During the Mameluk sultanate, the last extension of the City of the Dead occurred (Fig. 6). They founded a new burial site, named Sahara, at the eastern desert fringe of the city and they tried to secularize it with the building of fountains, mills, bakeries, hammans and mosques; the typical elements of infrastructure which characterized the Islamic city. They also patronized many *ribats*; hospices for men, devout old women and widows. The historian al Maqrizi (1950: 450-452) listed six *ribats* as well as some *jawsaqs*, that is large porches of wealthy families, used as resting places when visiting their dead.[13] Some of these pavilions were of considerable size, with fountains, gardens and balconies, such as Qasr al Qarafa, firstly restored by the Fatimid caliph al Hakim who used to observe from the loggia how the Sufi danced below him.

After the Mameluks Egypt became a province of the Sublime Porte (1517-1798). The Ottomans did not change the character of the vast City of the Dead. Few governors built their tombs there, because of their short mandate and consequent return to Turkey, so that the cemetery lost its importance and underwent gradual decay. Under the later French jurisdiction, it was strictly prohibited to dwell among graves,[14] a consequence of Napoleonic edict on the cemeteries,[15] even if the people continued to ignore the ban. During the nineteenth century the government authorized the building of new working class suburbs in empty areas within the cemetery.

In the last century the impoverishment of the country, caused by the World Wars and the Israeli invasion of the Suez peninsula, provoked a massive flow of the poorest rural immigrants and refugees to the capital. They occupied the shelters for the cult of the dead, with the complicity of the guardians who operated as intermediaries between the new dwellers and the owners of the *hawsh-s*. As a result, the resident population grew enormously and the socio-economic profile of al Qarafa changed completely. The burial space was transformed gradually and the environment was ruralised with the newcomers' lifestyle orientation. Because of their very low conditions of life it became a slum like the other peripheral suburbs of the capital. In recent decades, this process of degentrification[16] has come to an end. In fact, increasing occupation of the cemetery by the noble classes had led to the City of the Dead being described as the most popular resort in Egypt (al Maqrizi 1920: 123-124). At present, the majority of its residents belongs to the lower and lower-middle classes (El Kadi 2001: 265).

Recently, Cairo's municipality decided upon a spatial reconfiguration of some burial zones in al Qarafa,

---

[12] The *khanqahs* were large, structured, Sufi retreats organized around a master founder of the brotherhood, while the *zawiyas* were the abode of a holy figure.

[13] Along the main street of the Mameluk cemetery, Sultan Ahmed street, the nobles and the sultans built their palaces to assist every religious and secular ceremony.

[14] The ban concerning the misuse of the tombs, including sleeping or eating inside or in the funerary courtyards, was regularly enacted during medieval times but without any remarkable results.

[15] S. Cloud edict was enacted in 1763 but only definitely approved by the king Luis XVI in 1776.

[16] Degentrification, the opposite of gentrification, is the process by which upper classes abandon a place.

through the construction of large walls at their borders and the demolition of some graves in the Bab el Nasr area.[17] The residents were displaced against their will into new settlements outside the capital, reshaping the entire zone around the Fatimid perimeter wall for touristic purposes. Further it has to be underlined that in spite of Nederosick and Watson's analyses,[18] which subsume the seventeen different suburbs into one social and cultural milieu, the ethnic, religious and economic parameters of neighbourhood organization vary considerably among them. The quarters differ in their landmarks, in their social identities, their residents' quality of life and their potential for collective action and governance.

The relationship between funerary customs and urbanization/settlement[19]

The relationship between funerary customs and the urbanization/settlement of the necropolis must be analysed at various levels of meaning beyond the historical; religious, psychological, sociological, spatial and architectural connections are essential to its comprehension. Regarding the religious aspect of this relationship, a series of ritual events are fundamental to the City of the Dead: the *baraka* complex; the *ziyarat al qubur*, the visititations to the graves; the cult of *awalya* – literally friends of God, saintly figures – with the visitations to their holy tombs; and the funerary cult (Tozzi Di Marco 2008: 87-97).

The physical scenery of the City of the Dead consists of the urbanization and conurbation of different burial areas belonging to the four Arab dynasties' capitals,[20] founded through the ages. As in the historical background described above, the cemetery was, and still is, a holy locality, linked to the sacred geography of Islam through pilgrimages to sacred tombs. In medieval times there was a pilgrimage circuit to the seven famous righteous tombs,[21] renowned all over the Muslim world as reported by the orientalist scholar Massignon (1958: 3). A lot of the "saints"[22] were local but many others were and are notorious to the *Umma* as mentioned in the ancient pilgrimage guides[23] which drew mostly on the oral hagiography. These pilgrimages were and are performed individually or in groups during the weekly gatherings of a Sufi *tariqa* or the annual commemoration of the order's founding master at his grave.

Figure 7. The devotion at the holy grave.

Most of the time, devotees settled for long periods in the relevant structures built at the cemetery. Close contact with the holy deceased, next to his tomb, was thought to lead to a greater benefit from his blessings through a paradigmatic set of prescribed pious acts. Every saint has his precise day of veneration and he/she responds to a specific need. For instance, the present popular devotion at Abou al Su'ud al Jahiri's grave is enacted by women affected by infertility, who go there to receive his *baraka* which is believed to be helpful in healing (Fig. 7.;Tozzi Di Marco 2009). As a result, the graveyard was and is visited throughout the week.

At the present time, the *ziyarat al qubur* toward the ordinary dead, as a part of funerary ritual, are performed on various occasions. Although nowadays the departed is visited weekly on Fridays, until twenty years ago it was customary on Thursday to spend the night at the *bayt al mayyt*, the house of the dead, in the funerary courtyard, the *hawsh* (Fig. 8). It is traditionally believed that God accepts the prayers to forgive sins during nocturnal hours.

---

[17] A large project financed by the Agha Khan Foundation has involved the preservation and the restoration of the heritage of the ancient centre, al Qahira. The government planned to transform the whole area into an open-air museum and undertook the removal of slums and workshops.
[18] There are only two other anthropological studies, besides the present one, on Cairo's City of the Dead: by Watson (1992) and Nedorosick (1997). The first work is fundamentally based on a collection of female storytellings, while the second one relies on the historical and sociological background. Although both the anthropologists attended the necropolis milieu daily, they did not highlight its symbolic dimensions.
[19] The term "urbanization" is used here to mean the activity of building urban infrastructures in a rural or inhabited area, whereas "settlement" means the movement of people into a place to populate it.
[20] Al Fustat was founded under the Umayyad dynasty, Al 'Askar founded by the Abbasids, Al Qata'i founded by the Tulinids and Al Qahira founded by the Fatimids.
[21] The seven tombs belonged to recognized holy figures, and have now mostly disappeared. Maqrizi reported two lists of this circuit.
[22] In the Islamic religion it is improper to use the term saint when speaking about these sacred characters, because of its absolute monotheism.

[23] The most renowned Medieval pilgrimage guides were: Ibn Uthman's Murshid, Ibn al Nasikh's Misbah, and Ibn al Zayyat's Kawakib al Sakhawi's Thufa.

Figure 8. Friday ziyara in a hawsh.

Figure 9. Al 'Eid ziyara.

The funerary ritual, as rite of passage according to Van Gennep, has three stages, to which a conventional set of visitations to the dead are correlated. Immediately after the death, three days' visitations to the tomb are expected. This period corresponds to the sojourn of the soul waiting the two angels, Munkir and Nakir,[24] who will interrogate the deceased on the degree of his faith. During the forty days mourning period the family visits their dead every Friday. The last stage corresponds to a yearly commemoration of the dead which occurs at the anniversary of his death. The cult of the dead includes, in addition, a general annual commemoration on the night of 14th of the month Sha'ban. A popular tradition tells that the tree of life on whose leaves are written the names of the living is shaken during this night. The leaves that fall down indicate the people who will die in the next year. People perform the *ziyarat* also during other religious

---

[24] Munkir and Nakir are mentioned in the Koran. They ask the dead three questions about Allah, Islam, and the Prophet, in order to establish the degree of their faith.

occasions, including the two most important Islamic festivals, *'Eid el Fitr* and *'Eid el Adha* (Fig. 9).[25] The entire family used to spend many days in the accommodations built in the *hawsh*. This custom is still reported in rural areas in Middle Egypt.[26]

Thus, the belief in the regular return of the deceased's soul to the grave – i.e. after three days, forty days, one year, every Friday, during the two 'Eids, and on other important religious dates – explains the frequency of visits to the dead. According to Islamic texts, such visits are considered a desirable thing for instilling the remembrance of death as admonition for good conduct during life. On the other hand, the distinctive nature of the Egyptian *ziyarat*, which resides in their frequency, attendance and typology, characterizes Cairo's City of the Dead. There is a deep rooted credence that the living can communicate with the dead, a belief corroborated by the Prophet Mohammed's habit of greeting the deceased when he passed nearby their tombs. Thus, a sort of reciprocal complex of benefits between the living and the departed substantiates the temporary, brief, and long term sojourns at the graveyard. Through the saint or deceased/client link, God's mercy is provided. The dead are intercessors towards God; the devout pray on their behalf to promote divine blessing.

However this piety can flow into a heterodox performance of venerations, as attested even in the present. In fact, many archaic conceptions and attitudes towards death and the dead still survive. During the Pharaonic age the tomb and the afterlife, because of their eternity, were considered more essential than the house and life, so that the cult of the tomb was very developed. The grave, structured and decorated as the main house, was built during the lifetime. Moreover, archaeological evidence informs us about the workers' custom of living next to the noble tombs in Deir el Medinah.[27] In modern times, the deceased is still perceived as part of the family's life. This symbolic relationship is effected through the partaking of food and almsgiving, especially during religious festivals. These distributions of food and meals at the grave, amongst the relatives of the dead and neighbouring families, reinforce the social cohesion within the family and the wider community, by stressing peoplehood and community.

The sociological aspects of this phenomenon relate to ties between the owner of the tomb and its occupants. Specifically, although landlords of funerary courtyards may occasionally find illicit occupants inside them, they do not contest or reprimand such use due to respect for the Islamic duty of charity. The occupants establish economic relations with the owner of the tomb: they pay

Figure 10. Two kinds of habitations: brick edifices and wooden shelters.

a rent or they work as guardians of the tomb. In both cases they provide hospitality when the landlord's family visits their dead. The interaction between the settlement of the cemetery and the funerary customs in the social field is reflected also at the spatial level in the manners of occupancy. The increase in illegal utilization of the tombs as residences has caused an economic and social discrepancy within the resident community. The former guardians (enriched now as estate agents) inhabited, and their descendants still inhabit, the comfortable residences inside the *awaqf* and also noble graves, in spite of the rural lower class which occupied the crumbly wooden shelters (Fig. 10). Nowadays it is not unusual to see middle class craftsmen and wholesalers living in large and new edifices whereas the poor still inhabit in the funerary courts and work in their houses, shops and factories of traditional handmade products. In addition many owners of the *hawsh* have arranged their productive activity among the tombs. These kinds of activities cause much pollution and for this reason they are established in wider spaces and distant from habitation.

A final aspect of this phenomenon relates to the psychological and emotional orders of understandings of the *hawsh* residence. This implies an intimate level of discourse regarding self identity. Indeed many of the residents are relatives of the dead buried in the *hawsh* where they live. They choose to live close to their dead as a protected symbolic horizon of living. The necropolis is thus perceived as an intermediary place between this world and the underworld. Furthermore, the natives born at the cemetery have a strong feeling of living close to their own roots, that is of their ancestors' family. They share a common sense and way of life based on solidarity and social ties within the community of neighbours.

Conclusions

All of the factors mentioned above are at the base of the transformation of Cairo's first orthodox *al Qarafa* to the later City of the Dead, which is characterized by the cohabitation between the living and the dead. It is also the

---

[25] The celebration of the end of Ramadan and the celebration of Ibrahim's sacrifice.
[26] Elsewhere in Cairo, I attested this custom also in el Minya's cemetery.
[27] During the New Kingdom it was a village populated by the workers and artisans of the noble and royal tombs of Thebes (modern Luxor) on the opposite bank of the Nile.

result of an intersection between top-down and bottom-up forces[28] in different orders of production and representation. The interplay of these forces – previous governmental efforts to urbanize al Qarafa; secular and religious entities for the reproduction of the elite power; and the religious ethos of the Egyptian populace – was fundamental to the settlement of the necropolis, even if it was always contrasted by the ulama class that is the class of law scholars. This lack of definite separation between the world of the living and that of the dead is embedded in archaic death beliefs and the cult of the dead and it is related to the Islamic category of the sacred. This peculiar coexistence, of life and the death intertwined, locates the City of the Dead as a liminal site and its community as liminal component of Egyptian society. For this reason, both the place and its inhabitants are perceived as dangerously deviant from the "true" nature of the religion, based on interpretation of the Holy Scriptures by the leading classes. In the recent years the construction of a high wall that hides the burial landscape in order to avoid the sight of its resident community, in addition to the displacement of this population in some areas, can be viewed as attempts to homologate the cemetery identity, the funerary rituals and the heterodox cult of the saints to the normative religion. As further evidence of these efforts, one can note the construction of new burial sites outside the metropolis that conform to the Islamic orthodoxy.

Author's Address
Anna Tozzi Di Marco
Independent scholar
Vicolo delle Capannelle 31
00178 Roma
Italy
email: anna_tozzi@hotmail.com

References

El Kadi G. 2001. *La Citè des Morts. Le Caire*. Paris: Mardaga.
al Maqrizi A. 1950. *Khittat*. Cairo: IFAO.
al Maqrizi A. 1920. *Al Mawa'iz w'al I'tbar bi dhikr al khitat w'al athar*. Cairo: IFAO.
Massignon L. 1958. *Le citè des Morts au Caire*. Cairo: IFAO.
Nedoroscik J. 1997. *City of the Dead: a History of Cairo's Cemetery Communities*. London: Bergin & Garvey.
Tozzi Di Marco A. 2008. *Il Giardino di Allah. Storia della Necropoli Musulmana del Cairo*. Torino: Ananke.
Tozzi Di Marco A. 2009. Cairo's City of the Dead as a site of ancient and contemporary pilgrimages. In *Proceeding of the IUAES Conference City of Pilgrimages*. Tehran: University of Tehran.
Watson H. 1992. *Women in the City of the Dead*. London: Hurst & Company.

---

[28] The top-down forces pertain to the administrative authorities, therefore to the high culture, while the bottom-up forces are more associated with the population's governance which concerns their conceptualising of the world.

Observations on death, burial, graves and graveyards at various locations in Ra's al-Khaimah Emirate, UAE, and Musandam *wilayat,* Oman, using local concerns

William and Fidelity Lancaster

Summary

The use of local materials as an analytic tool demonstrates that differences in graves come from the following of Islamic practice of using materials immediately to hand, rather than tribal identity. While burial is an Islamic necessity, how the deceased is buried is the concern of the bereaved family. Differences between large graveyards on the coasts and smaller graveyards in the mountains resulted from seasonal movements. Pre-Islamic mounds, described as 'sanam mounds', were associated with several of the old Islamic graveyards in the northern and southern mountains and on the coasts and recognised by tribespeople as funerary monuments and often as graves. Sanam also described Islamic covered graves and tombs. If visited for religious purposes, sanam became mazar or ma'bad, although these need not be built structures. There were no suggestions that larger, more elaborate or visited graves were part of a hierarchy of graves; all were equal before God.

Keywords: Graves; graveyards; tribe; community; Islamic practice; local materials; pre-Islamic mounds; sanam; Islamic sanam

Introduction

Information was collected in the course of compiling an archive on 'Life before Oil' for HH Shaikh Sultan bin Saqr al-Qasimi, the then deputy Ruler of Ra's al-Khaimah Emirate and Director of the National Museum. We are grateful to Shaikh Sultan for the opportunity to make this archive, and to the people of Ra's al-Khaimah and Musandam who were so generous with their knowledge and time in establishing it. The archive is deposited at the National Museum, and a book version is published in Arabic as *'al-'Izz fi al-Qina'ai'*.[1]

The study region (Fig. 1) has varied natural environments; the Gulf coast and coastal plain, the sands, the Ru'us al-Jibal mountains of northern Ra's al-Khaimah and Musandam, and the western Hajar mountains of southern Ra's al-Khaimah. People describe themselves as tribespeople, members of groups defined by male descent and associated with particular resource areas. There are more than twenty tribes, most of which have sections elsewhere in Oman, Saudi Arabia, Jordan, Iran or East Africa. Tribal identity gives a jural persona with claims on tribally-owned resource areas and obligations to fellow tribal members (*qabila,* tribe, derived from *q b y l* 'guarantor, surety').

It might be assumed that the numerous graveyards would be described in tribal terms, as the presence of large, old graveyards in tribal territories is used rhetorically to justify ownership of a locality, and that differences in graves would be associated with tribal identities. However, local people described graveyards in terms of local communities (*jama'a,* 'to assemble'), the people who live, work and marry in a locality, connected by links through women in marriage and from inheritance.

Differences in graves were described as coming from the practices of the families. Local communities on the ground were flexible and fluid. Most families had access to several resource areas to which they moved over the seasons through variously constituted networks made possible by the common cultural homogeneity shared across the wider region and the decentralised political arenas of the region.

Information on traditional burial, graves and graveyards is greater for mountain areas than the coastal plains and towns which are now modernised, but their burial practices and graveyards were similar to those elsewhere. Local concerns start with the obligation to bury the dead in accordance with Islamic practice, with 'the dead' becoming 'the deceased', *mutawaffa'*, a social category replacing the physical state.

Burial

Local people stated that burial must take place before noon, if death occurs after sunset, or by sunset if after noon. The body is washed and wrapped in clean cloth by the women of the family. The grave is dug by male family members, who place the body on its side, with the face towards Mecca; say the prayers; fill in the grave and place a kerb of stones or flat rocks around it, and water it. (As funerals follow closely on death, the family holds a 'house of mourning', *bait al-azha,* for a period so relations and associates unable to attend the funeral can pay their respects.) When the grave has settled, head and footstones may be erected, and/or objects deposited on the grave. Graves of the relatively recent dead are visited by relations at sunset on Thursdays and at the main Islamic feasts if possible. The afterlife was hardly mentioned, the dead living on through their descendants and the consequences of their actions when alive.

The dead were buried 'where they died'. If a person died at a place of habitation, the *farij,* he or she was buried at the *farij.* Many *farij* had graveyards, *muqbara*; others, often small and not lived in for long periods, did not.

---

[1] There are 107 photographs in the full set of illustrations of our Arabian Graves fieldwork. In this paper, reference is made to these photographs using the prefix AG followed by the picture number. A CD copy of all the photographs can be obtained by emailing the authors; a disc copy will cost c. £3.00

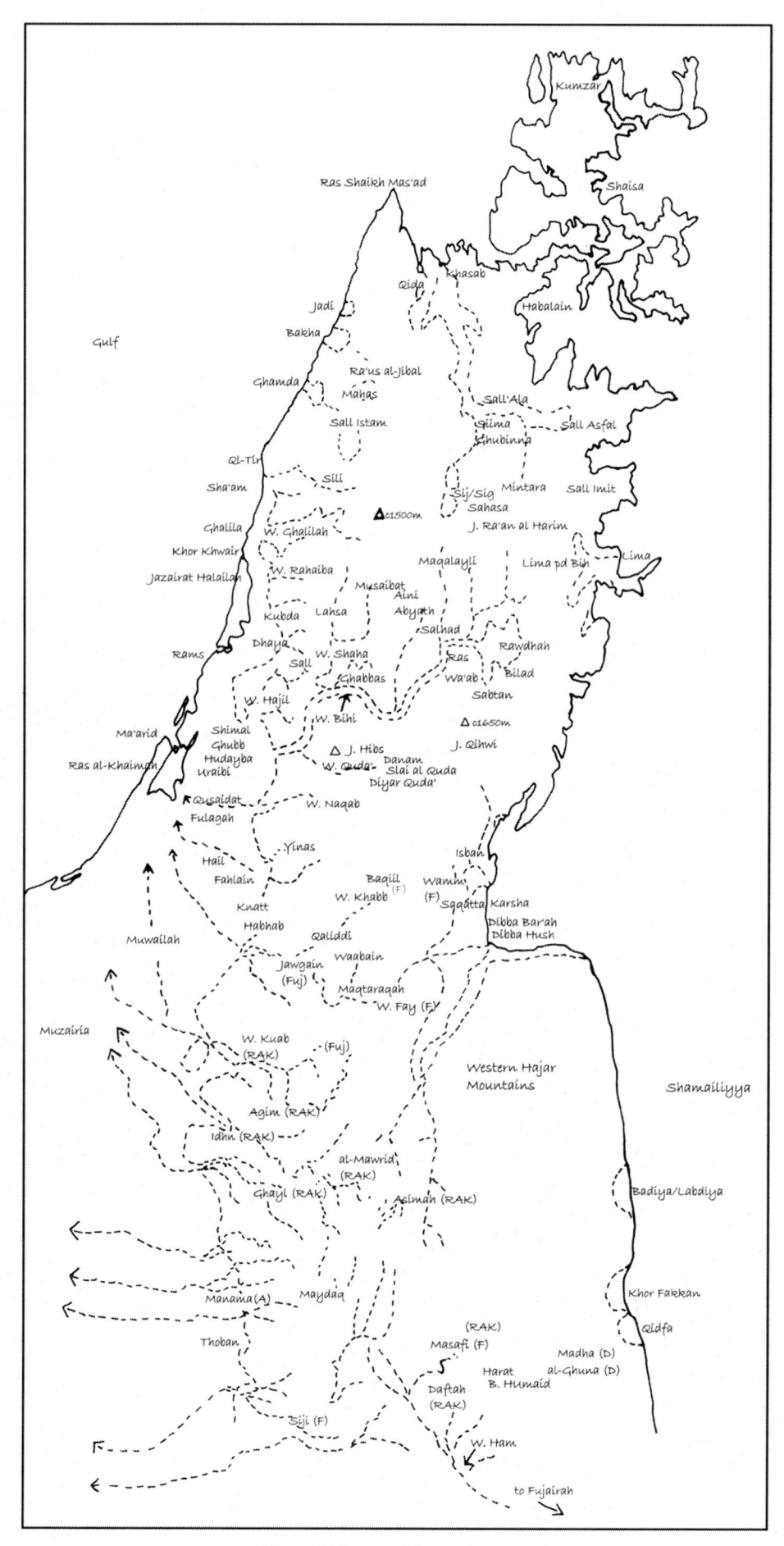

Figure 1. A map of the study area.

Occasionally, a person was buried at a place indicated by them earlier. If death occurred at an isolated field complex, garden, or fishing station, the body was buried there. The dead were sometimes buried close to the family house, at the edge of a garden or field, by the wish of the family; several people recalled dead siblings had been buried very close to home because 'parents wanted their children close to them.' In bad weather, the dead were buried under rock overhangs (AG 1 and 2) because of the difficulty of digging a grave or the impossibility of reaching the graveyard.

Graves

A primary concern in the siting of graves is that the dead should not be disturbed, either by flood flows caused by torrential storms or by animals. Graves were dug on raised ground, shallow slopes at the edges of the mountains, or natural terraces above wadi channels. A few graves had walls to divert flood flows (AG 3). Some had branches or biers left to protect them from animals (AG 4). Such land, unsuitable for cultivation or housing, was not regarded as 'rubbish land' since all land is acknowledged to have been created by God and to have its purpose. All graveyards were at or near clusters of habitation and use: e.g., in northern Ra's al-Khaimah, (AG 5 –Wadi Sha'am, AG 6 – Wasdi Nagab, AG 7 – Wadi Ruhaibah, and AG 8 – Sall Bani Zaid; in Omani Musandam, AG 9 – Sabtan, AG 10 – Lima, AG 11 – Hablain, and AG 12 – Karsha; Dibba Bai'ah: southern Ra's al-Khaimah AG 13 – 'Asimah, AG 14 - Wadi Tuwa, AG 15 – Wadi Sfai, and AG 16 – Daftah). The dead were often seen as beneficent; in southern Ra's al-Khaimah, a man commented "Those fields always grew good crops, because they were overlooked by the graves of the dead."

All graves were made and finished from materials immediately to hand. Blair (1998:196) notes this practice across the Islamic world, and people commented that their practice in the making and finishing of graves was in keeping with their concern to pay attention to what God had provided and to ensure that what they made was pleasing to Him.

Local people described two types of graves: one, a narrow rectangular boxed grave, using thin slabs of rock, and a head and footstone, and seen mostly in the northern mountains; the second, an oval mound of earth or gravel, with a kerb of large stones and a head and footstone, and seen everywhere else. Informants insisted the types had no meaning and represented differences in local conditions and materials. Boxed graves were associated with rocky soils and bedrock close to the surface, typical of the northern mountains; oval, kerbed graves were associated with gravel soils, typical of conditions elsewhere. Many boxed graves look very narrow because it is the body that is marked on the surface, not the grave cavity holding the body. A few multiple graves were seen.

Two exceptions to burial in a dug cavity were seen in the northern mountains One (AG 17) was the grave of a man who fell and broke his leg on his way down from the mountains in high summer and died; his body was not found for some weeks, by which time it was past being handled. His remains had been covered by a mound of stones, but rains one winter washed away part of the burial mound, so a wall had been built round the grave to deflect the water. The second was similar but without the wall.

Sourdel-Thoumine (1978: 352) states that *qabr,* grave, originally meant the burial pit and had the "general meaning of the tumulus or construction covering the grave to bring it to notice, a custom current in Islamic countries from early times." Graves were brought to notice by the erection of head and footstones and kerbs, attested in the Gulf region from the 4th/10th centuries at Siraf on the Iranian Gulf coast (Blair 1998: 196, quoting Lowick). A Shamaili tribesman said kerbs should not be used by proper Muslims, echoing the injunction in *hadith* to make the grave level with the surrounding ground (*taswiya*). Graves with head and footstones only were seen in graveyards at Rams, Ghalilah and Sha'am, coastal towns north of Ra's al-Khaimah town; at al-Bidy north of Dibba Bai'ah; a small group in Wadi Andab off Wadi Bih; and in southern Ra's al-Khaimah at two out of nine graveyards in Wadi Kuub. Head and foot stones were usually set inside and separate from the kerb, although at the graveyard at Danam in Wadi Quda' in the northern mountains, the head and foot stones were larger stones in the kerb. Grave mounds built up by two or three courses of mortared stones were seen at three sites, Wa'ib (AG 18), Salhad, and Jalaba (AG 19) in the northern mountains; at a large graveyard in the date gardens inland of Ra's al-Khaimah town; and at the graveyards of Ghayl and Khadra in the southern part of the Emirate. Graves without head and footstones were seen at Sall Asfal and Wadi Nagab in the north and in graveyards along Wadi Sfai in the south. Apart from graveyards at coastal towns, no large graveyards had all graves the same. Most graves in the northern mountains were boxed and narrow, most everywhere else were oval and kerbed, and most had head and footstones.

Local concerns on the finishing of graves are demonstrated at the graveyard at al-Yahal in the northern mountains (Fig. 2; AG 20-23). Four distinct groups of graves are visible: 1) graves with oval kerbs of grey stones, gravel cover, and head and footstones; 2) oblong box type graves, some covered with black pebbles, and orange coloured slabs of rock for head and foot stones; 3) oval graves without kerbs, gravel cover on the graves, and grey slabs or boulders as head and foot stones; and 4) rectangular box type graves in grey stones, gravel cover, and flat slabs for head and footstones. A local Shihuh with relations buried there stated all the graves were of members of the local community, who were from sections of two tribes – Qiyaishi Shihuh and Khanabila Shamaili. He insisted the differences between the groups of graves had no meaning, the family of the deceased who made and finished the grave did so from stone

Figure 2. Examples of graves from the cemetery at al-Yahal.

immediately to hand, and showed that the differences in stones lined up with changes in the rock outcrop behind the graveyard and with family preferences. He pointed out that these were Islamic graves with no differences between the graves of men, women, and children; differences in the relative heights of headstones and the presence or absence of footstones were irrelevant to the Islamic concern that all are equal before God; it was the family who chose how to finish the grave so that it was pleasing, families do what they want, there were no other connotations.

Other informants said that headstones for men's graves were higher than those for women's, which corresponded to most observations. Another said women had a third stone set in the centre of the grave; this was rarely seen, so presumably a family preference. At a site in Wadi Shaha, a pair of graves (AG 24), one with a higher headstone, the other with a higher footstone, were said to be of a husband and wife. At several graveyards in the central northern mountains, pairs of head and footstones were equal in height while in another, some headstones were much higher than others. Kerbs also varied. A group of seven box type graves above fields (AG 25) were built with little finesse; but a single grave nearby (AG 26) was carefully made with a well defined double kerb. A grave (AG 27) in a wadi below also had a double kerb, but no head or footstones.

Elaboration of graves

Most families finished the grave so it was neat and pleasing to God. Elaboration of graves beyond this is regarded as reprehensible, *makruh,* but not forbidden, and families made their own decisions, and did 'what they wanted.' Some deposited items on the grave, planted aloes, or, in the more distant past and only in a small area of the Ru'us al-Jibal, made carvings on the head or foot stones. At four graveyards, three on or near the coast (Ghubb, two at Dibba Bai'ah), and one in the southern mountains (al-Faqi in Fujairah Emirate near Asimah), most graves had had aloes planted on them. Aloes were also seen at two single graves at different graveyards in the far south of the southern mountains. Again in the south, a Mazari' said white stones on old graves indicated that these graves were before the arrival of Wahhabism.

In the northern mountains, incense burners and a camel stick were seen on graves (AG 28) at Rawdhah and Wadi Banna in the central area, in Khasab (AG 29) at a graveyard where Kumazarah and Hadiya Shihuh were buried after a battle, and at the graveyard at Dibba where the Commanders of the Faithful were buried (Fig. 3). Water pots, fragments of water pots, and tins for carrying water were seen at some graveyards throughout the study area. Watering graves is permitted in Islam, and men were seen sprinkling water on recent graves at Sha'am and Rams. The practice that things taken to a grave

Figure 3. Incense burners in the graveyard at Dibba where the Commanders of the Faithful were buried.

Figure 4. Carved gravestones from central Musandam.

cannot return is common throughout the wider region, illustrated by Mershen (2004) on practices at a cemetery in Ibra, Oman.

A total of 27 carved gravestones, most on headstones but some on footstones, were seen at two graveyards at ar-Rawdhah, Salhad, Wadi Jalaba, Wa'ib, Sabtan, Buthaina and two graveyards at Lima; this number is a tiny proportion of the total number of graves in these graveyards, all in central Musandam (Fig. 4). People of the area said they assumed the carvings were schematic representations of the individual property owned by the deceased, jewellery for women, and date trees and *khanjar,* Omani curved daggers, for men. These were, for people of this area, commercial items, bought as investments and stores of value, not part of livelihood resources from tribally owned assets. The photographs are arranged by graveyard: ar-Rawdhah (AG 30-37); Salhad (AG 38-40); Jalaba (AG 41); Wa'ib (AG 42-44); Sabtan (AG 45-51); Buthaina (AG 52); Lima (AG 53-

55). Photographs AG 30, 36, 47 and 56 show one sort of head ornament, while AG 57 and AG 59 show another, possibly representing an embroidered head covering. While some of the carvings are of recognisable jewellery items, others are more schematic and could represent embroidery patterns on the front panels of women's dresses; the carved pattern on the base of one stone resembles embroidery patterns at the ankles of women's drawers.

Local people said these carvings were made at the family's request or by a family member, represented the deceased's personal property, and perhaps the material blessings of God on the deceased's life; they could be seen as a sort of epitaph in personal terms and as providers of a store of heritable property. Carvings of *qibla*, niches showing the direction of Mecca for prayer, were seen on the kerb of the grave with the headstone showing the man with the spear and shield, and on a few others at Rawdhah (AG 56). Blair (1998: 198) states that epitaphs, *kitaab*, record the name of the deceased and bear witness to his faith; the rare carvings of *qibla* could be epitaphs of piety. Implications of greater wealth or status, or tribal identity, were never suggested by local people; making these carvings was a choice made by a few for unknown reasons, except perhaps as a way of further honouring the deceased. It seems possible that a family member or a member of the local community executed the carvings, as the styles and techniques are like those of the region-wide corpus of rock carvings.

Additional Structures

Additional structures were seen at some graveyards. This large grave (AG 57-59), at Slai al-Quda' in the northern mountains, has a small building of large stone blocks, roofed with stone slabs, at right angles to the grave, and on the same built platform. Tribesmen of the area saw the building as part of the grave, and described the whole complex as 'our ancestor', or 'a sheikh's tomb', which often implies the grave was visited by supplicants.

If a graveyard had a built place for prayer, a *masjid*, then usually there was no other mosque in the locality, and vice versa, although some places had no built *masjid* but prayed in the open (Fig. 5). In the northern mountains, four graveyards in the central area had stone buildings like *masjid* but lacking *qibla* (AG 60). A local Shihuh said these were where mourners had gathered and where a guard had kept watch over newly buried bodies; another remarked that a guard had been necessary because *saḥaar*, magicians, dug up the newly buried to feast on their bodies. Seven *masjid*, including one built in outline only, were seen in graveyards, among them those at Sij (AG 61), Salhad (AG 62), and one at ar-Rawdhah just outside a graveyard (AG 63). In southern Ra's al-Khaimah, eleven stone *masjid*, including four partial or outlines, were seen in three graveyards at Wadi Kuub, and in graveyards at Fara', al-Mawrid, 'Asimah, Wadi Sfuni (AG 64), al-Ghuna, Riyam, Tuwa, and Daftah.

In the northern mountains, at the top of Wadi Haila, a graveyard at a long deserted *farij* had a shallow cistern (AG 65), and two large graveyards at ar-Rawdhah had shallow cisterns very nearby; no-one knew why as the bodies would have been washed at home.

Remains of circular double-walled white structures were seen at or very close to graveyards or small groups of graves at seven places in the lower western area of the northern mountains; Wadi Hajil, al-Yahal (AG 66), Wadi Ghabbas (AG 67-68), north of Haila, Wadi Quda', and possibly at Sabtan. The owner of the building at Wadi Hajil identified it as an old granary, *yanz*, and those at

Figure 5. A *masjid*, or place for prayer, in a graveyard.

Figure 6. Food processing and storage structures near graves at Mayya.

Wadi Ghabbas and al-Yahal had been milling houses, *bait ar-raha*. It seemed possible that others had been communal granaries or milling houses. *Yanz* is the local pronounciation of *janaza*, which now has the meaning of 'funeral' but earlier meant (Lane 1984 [1863]: 470) 'he concealed, hid, collected, gathered it up' and so 'as a man is gathered up in the grave-clothes, or he died.' No-one made this connection but it is interesting that people of the study area who often use old meanings for words, have this word for a granary. In southern Ra's al-Khaimah, *makhzan*, 'store', is used consistently. An association between basic food processing and storage, graves, and graveyards was also seen at Mayya, above Wadi Khabb (AG 69) at the southern edge of the northern mountains (Fig. 6). In the southern mountains, the association was noted at two sites in Wadi Kuub, one of which had a *masjid* adjacent to a threshing floor (AG 70), and the other a ruined 5 m diameter circular double walled structure whose owner said it had been a storehouse or a *masjid*; and in Wadi Ayaili, where a pit seen in among graves (AG 71) was identified by a local Maharse tribesman as a date store.

Many local people commented on the association of graves and graveyards with pre-Islamic mounds seen in many places in Musandam and northern and southern Ra's al-Khaimah (Fig. 7). These mounds are imposing, built from stones immediately to hand on a made platform; in some, a built cavity is clearly visible. Many head and footstones at graves, stones in *masjid* and in field walls look very like the long, flat slabs used to define the cavities of these mounds. The mounds are sited on terraces above the main wadis through which people moved to resource areas e.g. Wadi Bih (AG 72) and at the entrance to some resource areas, e.g. al-Aini (AG 73) in the north. In the south, they lie along the watered wadis such as Wadi Mamduh (AG 74-75), Wadi al-'Ayaili (AG 76), at Rafaq in Wadi al-Qawr (AG 77), and Wadi Mlah (AG 78). A Khatri tribesman from the sands described the Umm an-Nar tomb (AG 79) in Idhn as "our first mosque", while the Amir of Munai'y described the pre-Islamic tomb there to be of "our ancestors"; both qualified their statements as rhetorical, not factually accurate.

Local people across the region called these mounds *sanam, asnam*, literally 'a curved mound'. Arabists stated that *asnam* could only be *aṣnam*, the plural of *sanam*, meaning 'idol' which local speakers denied. Local people regard these pre-Islamic mounds, *sanam*, at least as funerary monuments and often as graves. In the northern mountains, Islamic graveyards are often near *sanam*, for example Mahas (information from a Dhahuri), Sall Bani Zaid/Quda' (AG 80-81), Farij Fra' (AG 82) and Farij Umm Swait in Wadi Shaha (AG 83-84), al-Yima (AG 85), Salhad (AG 86) and at least a dozen other sites. *Masjid* at two graveyards, Sij and Fiduk in Sall Asfal, were almost certainly built by demolishing *sanam* and using the stones. Around the Ru'us al-Jibal coast, one of the three large graveyards at Bukha has a pre-Islamic mound, as do the graveyards at Jiri, and at Sur al Kumazarah and Harat Bani Sanad in Khasab, where a *masjid* and Islamic graves were built on the mound. Both of the large graveyards at Lima have *sanam* with *masjid* built on them (AG 87-88), Hablain graveyard has a *sanam*, the very large graveyard by the beach at Dibba Bai'ah has a mound with Islamic graves on it, and the small graveyard at Saqattah has *sanam* nearby.

Figure 7. Graveyards associated with pre-Islamic mounds in the study area.

In the southern mountains, *sanam* in graveyards were usually rebuilt as *masjid*; for example, in Wadi Kuub (AG 89), Yaruf (AG 90), Mahdah (AG 92), Daftah (AG 93), Sfai (AG 94) and probably in Wadi Mlah (AG 95-96). The building (AG 97-98) in the huge graveyard at Shu'aiba as-Samah, in Wadi Sfai, appeared to follow the same pattern; the local Amir insisted the structure was 'a very, very old house' on a *sanam,* and the *masjid* (AG 99) was at al-Ghaba nearby.

The only domed *sanam* existing today in the study area is Shaikh Mas'ud in Musandam (Fig. 8). Shaikh Mas'ud comprises the domed building over the tomb, a *masjid,* and its graveyard (AG 100-104) and continues to be visited for sacrifice, prayers and burning incense, it is said mostly by Baluch. Domes at or over the graves of people noted for their religious lives and their moral influence in the community existed on the coasts. The Qawasim built one for the spiritual guide of Shaikh Rashid bin Matar al-Qasimi, later destroyed under Wahhabi influence (al-Rashid 1981: 46-7). Whitelock (1844: 46) stated "From Cosaab (Khasab) to Raumps (Rams) there are several ancient buildings of the Persians called Senem (an idol or Image). They used to worship their idols in these buildings until the Wahabees destroyed them some years ago." Dutch documents from the 17th century recorded "pagodas", i.e. domed religious buildings, at Sha'am and Khasab (Slot 1993). Several people in different parts of the study area said that there had been many *sanam* before the arrival of Wahhabi doctrines at the end of the 18th century, and their subsequent destruction.

Figure 8. The domed *sanam* at Shaikh Mas'ud in Musandam.

While *Sanam* as idols, carved or painted stones, were said to have been destroyed a long, long time ago, some local men doubted their existence in the area as no fragments have ever been found, which concurs with Wellhausen's opinion, quoted by Fahd (1978: 5-6), that *Sanam* as a word and thing was imported from the north. Most used *sanam* as a description of pre-Islamic tomb mounds and Islamic covered graves and tombs. If visited for religious purposes, these became *mazar*, although not all *mazar* were built structures. A Khanbuli Shihhi said he had heard of a *mazar* at the top of Wadi Baana which was a large *sidr* tree, under which people left goods for safety. The hot springs at Khatt were also a *mazar*; local people held them in reverence, while visitors from outside the area made offerings. He considered that while some *asnam* had been at tombs of holy men, as for example at Sha'am, others were 'real' *asnam*, a stone that served as a focus or reminder of God. These places with stones, which need not have been buildings, were also called *ma'bad*, defined by Wehr (1974: 486) as 'place of worship; house of God, temple'. In all these places, at graves, *mazar, asnam, ma'bad,* prayers were offered for a boon of some sort – health, pregnancy, safe journey, and so on – all those things with which formal Islam is not concerned. The tomb at Lahsa in Wadi Jiib was a *haram* (AG 105), where passersby could spend the night and leave their goods in safety. A Tunaij from Rams knew *mazar* as a religious memorial or shrine, such as that of Muhallab Abi Suffrah in Dibba Fujairah, but also as the local word for gatherings around a family grave, usually fairly recent, for prayers. A Haslamani Shihhi said that at their high mountain *farij* of Sall Imit, there had been a *sanam* like that at Kumzar (AG 106), where people used to sacrifice, pray and burn incense; other places had *sanam* like the ones at Lima, others were like Shaikh Mas'ud, and one beyond Khasab was a large cairn. He had visited the *sanam, mazar,* of Ayyub in Dhofar.

In southern Ra's al-Khaimah, an elderly Ka'abi at Munai'y said there were several ruined *sanam*, pre-Islamic tomb mounds, in the wadis, citing that in Wadi Mlah. He had heard of *ma'bad* and assumed they were the same as *sanam*. In his opinion, *mazar* were always associated with a person or a tomb, at which or to whom people prayed for help, good luck, or to become pregnant, and he implied there were some in the general area. A ruined mound with many pieces of incense burner on the beach between Murair and Bu Baqra was identified by locals as a *mazar*.

In Wadi Sha'am, Dhahuriyiin drew attention to an area of small cairns (AG 107) which they described as pre-Islamic graves, as they were consistent with local concerns of burial in the earth and the erection of "a simple heap of pebbles" (Sourdel-Thoumine 1987: 352 discussing early Islamic graves) but not orientated towards Mecca – although it is not known when this orientation became standard for Islamic graves. Other groups of cairns that might be graves were seen in other areas: at the top of Wadi Ghabbas, in Wadi Quda' by the graveyard, at two places up Wadi Baqqarah, south of Wadi Mamduh near Islamic graves, and at al-Ghuna, by Islamic graves.

Graveyards on the coasts and plains were much larger than those in the mountains, especially the northern mountains. Within the mountains, the more easily accessible *farij* and those with good fields had more graves and graveyards than those that were at high altitudes or difficult access. That is, the size of graveyard and numbers of graves reflected the numbers (and ages) of people using the area and the amount of time throughout the year that people were there. Many families, though by no means all, left the northern mountains for date growing areas on the coasts and to a lesser extent for date gardens in the wadis of the southern mountains. People who lived from animals in the sands and in the southern mountains moved to date gardens in the southern mountains. Within both mountain areas, but particularly for the northern mountains, families moved between higher and lower *farij* seasonally, and population numbers at any *farij* fluctuated considerably over the year. There are huge graveyards north of Dibba Bai'ah and at Lima; at Ghubb, Hudaiba, Hail, and Shimal inland from Ra's al-Khaimah town and at Rams and Sha'am; and graveyards near the deep wells at Kharrana in Wadi Ghalilah, Shiddu in Wadi Hajil, Burairat near the mouth of Wadi Bih, Rabiya, and Khatt. Date growing places often had many small graveyards on mounds between the gardens, as at Qusaidat, Qida, and Khasab. People died from illnesses more in the summers than in winters, and in the rest of the year, most deaths were from accidents.

A Dhahuri in Wadi Sha'am remarked that his father was buried at Mahas in the mountains, where they had most of their land, but his mother was buried at a graveyard in Khasab, where she had died one summer. Because they were present, and because they behaved properly while they were there, they were part of the community. A Shihhi at Karsha in Dibba Bai'ah commented that both large groups of graves were of Shihuh sections who summered there, and who, while they were there, became part of its community. A Sharqi at a wadi in the southern mountains commented that some of the graves were of his relations, others were of herding Khawatir who had died there during the summers and were part of the community through marriages and economic activities.

Conclusions

The paper has described graves and graveyards in Ra's al-Khaimah Emirate and Omani Musandam. Local concerns with burial of the dead and graves are in accordance with Islamic practice as established by Sourdel-Thoumine (1978). The use of local concerns as an analytic tool demonstrated that the isolated small groups of graves and graveyards represent the decentralised local arenas in which people had lived and moved between and in which community was achieved through cultural solidarity and local identification. There were no suggestions that larger or more elaborate graves had any meaning of stratification, also established in an earlier paper on graves in the Jordanian eastern steppe (Lancaster and Lancaster 1993).

References

Blair S. 1998. *Islamic Inscriptions.* Edinburgh. Edinburgh University Press.

Fahd T. 1995-7. Sanam, *Encyclopedia of Islam,* 2nd edition, vol.ix, 5-6. Leiden: Brill.

Lancaster W. & Lancaster F. 1993. Graves and funerary monuments of the Ahl al-Jabal, Jordan. *Arabian Archaeology and Epigraphy* 4: 151-169.

Lancaster W. & Lancaster F. Forthcoming. *Honour is in contentment; Life before oil in Ra's al-Khaimah and the surrounding areas.* Berlin: de Gruyter.

Lane E. 1984 [1863, 1877]. *Arabic –English Lexicon.* 2 vols. Cambridge: The Islamic Texts Society.

Mershen B. 2004. Pots and tombs in Ibra, Oman: investigations into the archaeological surface record in Islamic cemeteries, and the related burial customs and rituals. *Proceedings of the Seminar for Arabian Studies* 34: 165-79.

Al-Rashid Z.M. 1981. *Su'udi Relations with Eastern Arabia and Uman, 1800-1870.* London: Luzac.

Slot B.J. 1993. *The Arabs of the Gulf, 1602-1784.* Leidenschendam.

Sourdel-Thoumine J. 1978. Kabr – tomb, *Encyclopedia of Islam,* 2nd edition, vol iv, 352-355. Leiden: Brill.

Whitelock F. 1836-8. An account of the Arabs who inhabit the coast between Ras al Khaimah and Abuthubee in the Gulf of Persia, generally called the Pirate Coast. *Transactions of the Bombay Geographical Society* 1: 32-54.

Authors' Address

William & Fidelity Lancaster
Rysa Lodge
Orkney KW16 3NU
Scotland
wolancaster@yahoo.co.uk

Shrines in Dhofar

Lynne S. Newton

Summary

A recent survey conducted by the author has revealed the presence of over 50 shrines in Dhofar. This number is significantly higher than the few discussed by others in previous reports in Dhofar (Costa 2001; Costa and Kite 1985; Oman 1983: 278). The current Dhofar landscape is dotted with shrines of many sorts, from formal buildings with cupolas associated with mosques to solitary open air tombs. Generally speaking, these shrines commemorate the lives of admired and respected individuals, such as for example Islamic teachers (*'ulamā*), pre-Islamic prophets or descendents of the Prophet Mohammad (*sada*). This paper will first briefly offer a preliminary categorization of shrines in Dhofar and a discussion of traditional Dhofari shrine architecture. Second, a landscape approach is utilized to study how their distribution informs the production of the cultural landscape of Dhofar in the Islamic period. Such an approach, combined with analyses of their associated practices and traditions, sheds valuable light on shrine history and the development of local socio-political and religious institutions in the region. Five known shrines in the vicinity of the archaeological site of al-Baleed are presented as a case study to demonstrate this landscape approach to studying shrines.

Keywords: Shrines, Dhofar, al-Baleed, *waliyy, zawiyah,* Cheraman Perumal

The Shrines of Dhofar

Throughout southern Arabia the most studied shrines are in the Hadramaut (e.g. Ho 2004; Rodionov 1997, 2004; Boxberger 2002; Knysh 1993, 1997; Bujra 1971; Serjeant 1949, 1954, 1957, 1962). This body of literature is invaluable for researchers and of course informs the research on shrines in Dhofar. However, while it may be tempting to lump the shrines in Dhofar in with those in the Hadramaut, as there is undoubtedly some Hadrami influence in Dhofar regarding certain social practices and shrine architecture, it is important to acknowledge the uniqueness of Dhofari history and culture. Therefore, the shrines in Dhofar should be studied within their own historical and cultural context. Nonetheless, with this study in its infancy, the concept of the *hawtah* (sacred enclave; e.g. Serjeant 1954, 1962) provides a valuable base of comparison.

Dhofari Shrine Architecture

Architecturally, the majority of shrines in Dhofar traditionally were distinct from their Hadrami counterparts, with the exception of course being the shrine of bin 'Ali in Mirbat (Costa and Kite 1985: 152; Oman 1983: 287), bin 'Afīf (Oman 1983: 284) and Ba 'Alawi (Oman 1983: 285) in Salalah, and the shrines now known to be affiliated with Sheikh Sa'ad in Mudhai (Costa 2001; Costa and Kite 1985: 153).. The latter shrines were originally built with graves inside a formal building with a cupola. The many shrines with cupolas that can be seen in Dhofar now, however, are new constructions and were probably not recognizable as shrines, *per se*, by Costa during his surveys as they did not fit the architectural model of what a shrine should look like (i.e. they did not have formal buildings and/or cupolas). Note that the shrines mentioned above are for Hadrami emigrants to Dhofar, thereby explaining their Hadrami architectural influence.

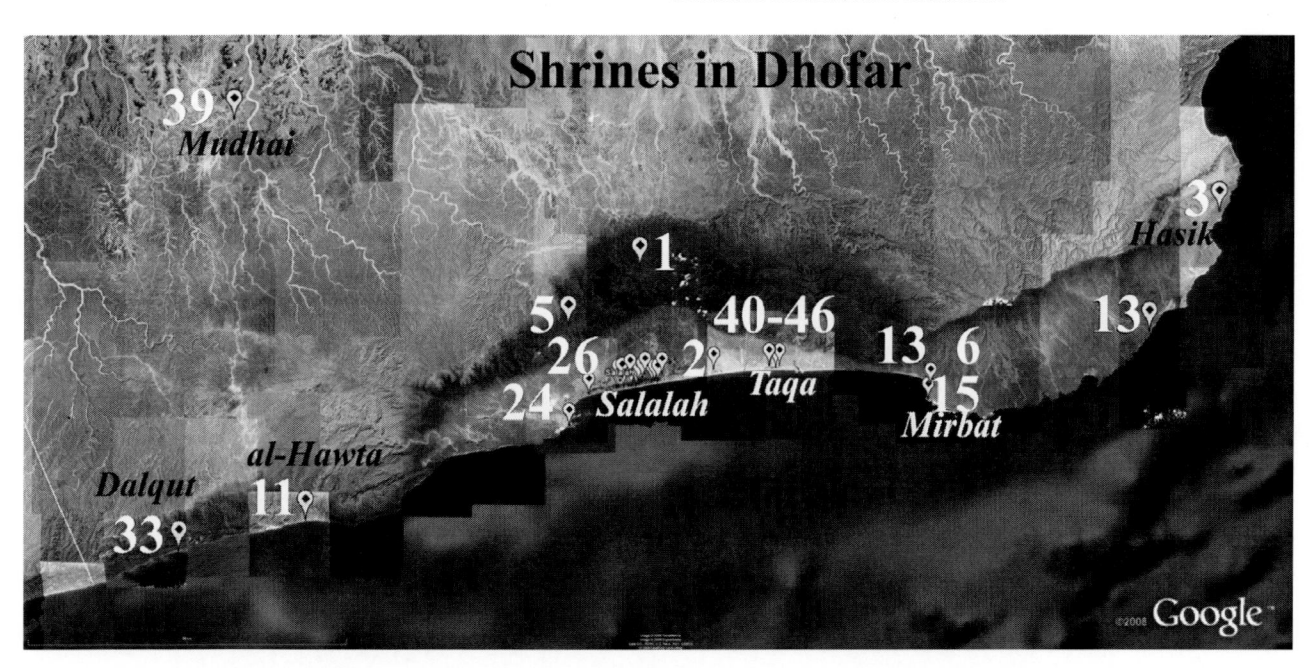

Figure 1. Distribution of shrines in Dhofar. Refer to Tab. 1 for names and additional information.

Because most of the shrines in this survey have been modernized, the original character and traditional architecture have been lost. However, some valuable sources have come to light. It is clear from photos taken before of Hūd bin 'Aber's tomb in Dhofar (al-Shahri 2000:193) (Fig. 3), and 'Amran (Fig. 5), both taken before modernization, and from the description of Samiri's tomb (see below) that they were all originally open-air tombs. Therefore, the cupola, which has been included in the modernization of many of the shrines in Dhofar, is not indicative of traditional Dhofari shrine architecture (see Fig. 4 for modern shrine of Hūd bin 'Aber). Most often they were likely graves without any formal roofing and were known by local inhabitants through oral tradition to be the graves of important people. They were embellished with offerings, be they pieces of fabric, flags, incense and/or food. Local shrines were not associated with formal buildings, but did have variety. For example, the grave of the Prophet Hūd originally was not embellished by a formal building and was similar to surrounding graves, while 'Amran's took much more energy to produce, with its extensive length and outer wall (Fig. 5). Ironically, it is through their modernization that they have become visible to the western eye as shrines. There are still extant examples, however, of open-air shrines (Tab. 1).

With over 50 known shrines in Dhofar, most of them in the Salalah vicinity, it is helpful to categorize them to discuss them in a meaningful way. Architecture is not useful because most of the shrines in Dhofar have been renovated/modernized since the 1970's. However, in some cases there are archaeological indicators on the surface, such as older foundations and artifacts that indicate their historical presence in the landscape (see Tab. 1: e.g. shrines 2, 3, 6, 11, 15, 16, 27 and 47). Traditionally, it is likely that the majority of shrines were open-air tombs constructed in a more conventional Islamic style, such as the original tomb of the Prophet 'Amran in Salalah (Fig. 5). Therefore, this study categorizes these shrines not by architecture, but rather by the status/significance of the individuals interred.

Shrines

Many shrines in Dhofar are of *awliya* (sing. *waliyy*) or what is usually translated into English as "saints." Visitation, *ziyara,* to shrines involves a complex socio-political system centered on mediation, the concept of sacred enclave/territory (*hawtah*), and the people who administer and maintain these inviolable places of protection and veneration. There is a long tradition of shrines in the Hadramaut serving as places of mediation for tribal disputes and for trade (Serjeant 1962; Knysh 1997: 143; Bujra 1971: 26-30). The concept of the *hawtah* as described in Hadramaut is not foreign to Dhofar as Thesiger (1984: 111) mentions Mughshin being one. The extent of its manifestation in the mountains and other areas of Dhofar, however, is not well understood. It is likely, however, that prior to the modernization in Oman some shrines were used as places of mediation in Dhofar (particularly those associated with

Figure 2. Shrines in the vicinity of al-Baleed are indicated by the tear-drop shaped markers and archaeological sites contemporary to al-Baleed are indicated by squares.

the *mashayikh*). They definitely served socio-political functions as some groups in Dhofar, such as the Mahra, traditionally swear innocence on the tombs of saints (Carter 1982: 61) while others visit shrines to ask for help (al-Shahri 2000: 67). Undoubtedly their purposes and uses throughout history have changed and their complexity probably matches the cultural diversity of Dhofar.

The shrines are classified in this study into two major categories: Prophets and Saints (*awliya*). The saints are subdivided into the *sada* (descendants of the Prophet), the *mashayikh* (spiritual, holy families that are not descended from the Prophet Mohammad and traditionally known as shrine conservators, see Carter 1982: 64-65) and the *'ulamā* (pl. of *'ālim*, active participle of *'ālima*, "to know"). A third category is listed as undetermined or other and includes shrines with limited information to date or ones that are known but do not fit into the above to categories. Tab. 1 follows this classification and lists the shrines known to date.

The Shrines of Prophets in Dhofar

The shrines attributed to prophets in Dhofar are mentioned in the Quran and/or relate to pre-Islamic ancestors tied to those mentioned in the Quran. These are the shrines of the Prophet Hūd bin 'Aber, 'Aber bin Hūd, Saleh bin Hūd and the Prophets 'Amran and Job.

Figure 3. The shrine of Hūd bin 'Aber before modernization (al-Shahri 2000: 193).

Figure 4. The shrine of Hūd bin 'Aber after modernization (photo by Nigel Moss).

Figure 5. 'Amran's tomb before modernization. Photo taken in 1960 on display inside the current shrine. Note the pieces of cloth on and around the tomb and the stone wall that surrounds it.

The Three Hūds

In the Muslim world there are three places that claim to possess the tomb of the Prophet Hūd: Damascus, Hadramaut in Yemen (al-Sabban 1998) and the mountains of Dhofar in a place known as Shihait (al-Shahri 2000:192-193; Museum of the Frankincense Land 2007: 100-101). Each place has its reason for laying a claim on the final resting place of the Prophet Hūd as well as an argument for authenticity. Such a discussion is beyond the scope of this paper and is irrelevant as it is impossible to prove a claim of authenticity in this case. Nevertheless, in the mountains of Dhofar there is a sacred place called Hūd bin 'Aber. This shrine exists in the physical and cultural landscape of Dhofar and conveys meaning and importance for those that visit it. It is this social action, the *ziyara*, that this place provokes, and what it provides people in return, that legitimizes it for Dhofaris (Figs. 3 and 4).

In addition to the tomb of the Prophet Hūd himself (known as Hūd bin 'Aber), there are two other shrines, presumably of his sons, known as 'Aber bin Hūd and Saleh bin Hūd. 'Aber bin Hūd is located on the coast east of Salalah and south of Ain Humran. Saleh bin Hūd's tomb is in a very remote part of eastern Dhofar about 20km south of Hasik. In the past it must have been an arduous journey to reach this shrine. Al-Hamdani (c. 950 CE) mentions that the Mahra visit the tomb of the Prophet Hūd (Müller 1993: 83; Serjeant 1954: 122-123). The tomb of 'Aber bin Hūd was visited by Ibn Battuta in 1325 CE (Gibb 2004: 386) and noted that this was an important hospice (*zawiyah*). Archaeological survey in the vicinity of this shrine has revealed the presence of a nearby cemetery, the foundations of many buildings and a very large, formal rock-cut well. The site dates to at least the 14th century CE as many examples of Yemen Yellow glazed redwares (Kennet 2004: 41-42) have been found. Therefore, the occupation determined by archaeology is contemporary with the description provided by Ibn Battuta.

'Amran

The name 'Amran may refer not only to Miriam's father, but may serve to legitimize local genealogy back to Adam, Noah and Abraham (Quran 3: 33-35). This shrine is one of the most well-kept shrines in Dhofar and along with Job's, is among the most visited. The tomb is well known for is length, which measures 29.5 m. A photograph, taken in 1960 illustrates the open-air aspect of the original tomb before it was modernized (Fig. 5). It is important to note the pieces of torn cloth and the small flags seen in this photograph were made as offerings. Even today when visiting many shrines in Dhofar such offerings can be seen; especially common are pieces of red fabric or red flags (Fig. 8; see al-Shahri 2000: 219). The specific meanings of such offerings are not known, but it is possible that they represent the presence of a Sufi brotherhood (J. Starkey, *pers. com.*). Hints of a surrounding cemetery are visible in Fig. 5, and the actual remains of this larger cemetery are still visible to the east of 'Amran's shrine. People have speculated as to the great size of this tomb-suggesting that it is either a collective burial or person of great stature. It is possible that tomb size in Dhofar may be directly correlated with a person's social status – a tradition which clearly extends back into the pre-Islamic period (see Zarins, this volume).

Job

Job, as the central character of the *Book of Job*, lived in the land of Uz, a land which has not been positively identified within the confines of the larger Arabian Peninsula. He is also mentioned in the Quran (e.g. 21: 83-84 and 38: 41-44), and is perhaps best known in both accounts as being a righteous person who suffered under duress, remained patient under trials, and as one who was ultimately delivered from affliction (Ali 2002: 899 footnote 41a). Dhofari tradition states that Job's tomb is located in Baid Zarbij near a spring called Sharsate, that according to legend gushed out after the Prophet Job prayed to God (The Museum of the Frankincense Land 2007: 105). According to Shahra genealogy, this Zarbiji is one of 13 clans in Dhofar (al-Shahri 2000: 26, map 2 area 4). Zarbiji traces its ancestry to an older eponymous ancestor called *Aus*. The location of Job's tomb in this clan area, and the supposition that the ancestral name *Aus* can be identified with the Biblical Uz, the land in which Job lived, is likely the underlying basis for identifying this shrine in Dhofar (al-Shahri 2000: 31, map 3). A crevice near the tomb that is now covered with a lid has what are traditionally believed to be Job's footprints. This phenomenon is a common way in many religious traditions to indicate (or convince others of) the presence of a deity or a spiritual leader (Branfoot 2006: 64).

The Saints of Dhofar

Waliyy (saint) is perhaps best translated as "devotee" or "friend of God," while it can also connote someone protected by a kin relationship (Ernst 1997: 58). Such a designation is applicable to many different types of people and here they are divided into three major categories: the *sada* (descendents of the Prophet Mohammad), the *mashayikh* (holy families) and the *'ulamā* (learned) (Tab. 1). The nature of a *waliyy's* friendship with God is similar in some ways throughout each of these categories as each person is known for being an exemplary Muslim. However, it is how they come to the religious life that distinguishes them. For example, by claiming descent from the Prophet Mohammad, the *sada* claim to have special religious attributes and social status (Bujra 1971: 25). Their history is context-dependent throughout the Muslim world (see Ho 2006: 28, footnote 1) and for example they were established in the Hadramaut in 952 CE when a migrant from Iraq, Ahmad 'Isa, known as al-Muhajir ("the emigrant") arrived (Boxberger 2002: 19; Dresch 2000: 15; al-Sabban 1998: 12; Bujra 1971: 25). One of his descendants, fully named, Mohammad Ali 'Alawi Ba'Alawi Mohammad bin Ali bin 'Alawi Ba'Alawi, (Sahib Mirbat) settled in Mirbat and this is the explanation given for the origins of the *sada* in Dhofar. Other shrines in Dhofar of the *sada* are in the Ba 'Alawi cemetery in Salalah (Oman 1983:285; 1989: Fig. 4).

The *mashayikh* are noble families which have the right to the hereditary title of *sheikh*, denoting a class distinction and *not* indicating a tribal chief (Peterson 2004: 263; Serjeant 1957: 3). *Mashayikh* are not descendants of the Prophet but retain their prestige through religious associations (Boxberger 2002: 20; Carter 1982: 64). They serve as mediators and are often associated with a tomb of a *waliyy* from which the *mashayikh* family is descended. Peterson states that current *mashayikh* families in Dhofar are considered *da'if* (weak) (2004: 263; see also Carter 1982: 64 and 81). This distinction for the *mashayikh* as a class is suspect and it is likely that his informant was not objective in his description of the Dhofari *mashayikh*. It should be noted, however, that the role the *mashayikh* currently play in Dhofar has changed dramatically over the past generation due to modernization and nation building. For example, the *ziyara* is still very popular in Yemen (particularly the Hadramaut), but such visitation to shrines by Omanis in Dhofar has lessened as tribal mediation has not been necessary (see Peterson 2004: 263; Janzen 1986: 274). The *mashayikh* in Dhofar, however, often still serve as mediators in the mountains and care for some shrines and mosques (Peterson 2004: 263).

The final category is at present perhaps the least documented in Dhofar. Religious schools or centers for seekers of spiritual wisdom, *ribat* (Boxberger 2002: 155), were an important part of the Islamic experience in Dhofar, particularly throughout the medieval period. Boxberger (2002: 165) states that students often studied in centers known as *zawiyah* and that after learning from the teachers in the community, a seeker of knowledge traveled in search of the opportunity of learning from noble teachers. As a seeker of knowledge, this is perhaps why Ibn Battuta visited various shrines in Dhofar during his travels. He remarks on various *zawiyah* in Dhofar and it is possible that he visited many *madrasahs*, including one that was built in Zafar by a Rasulid daughter of the Sultan (Sadek 1989: 124), which was probably in the vicinity of modern al-Robat, just north of al-Baleed. Undoubtedly Muslims traveled here to study with various religious scholars. It is likely that many potential Hajjis passed through Zafar and studied or at least visited its *ribat*. Shiekh Mohammad (see below) is just one of many *'ulamā* revered in Dhofar. Refer to Tab. 1 for at list of shrines in Dhofar; see also Figs. 1 and 2 for their locations.

Landscape Archaeology: Shrines and al-Baleed

Enshrined al-Baleed

The site of al-Baleed, ancient Zafar, is a medieval Islamic period port. The site has evidence for trade and interaction with China, SE Asia and East Africa from at least the 10th century CE. Al- Baleed is a UNESCO World Heritage site and has been developed as an archaeological park. The park is fenced in and covers an area of more than 1500 x 800 m (Zarins 2007: 309). Even with such an immense size, the entirety of the site, which is at least twice this size, is not part of the park. The closest and most obvious extant remains lie just northwest and west of the site where mosques, two of which were excavated by a team from Sultan Qaboos University in 2004, and a well are located. Shifting north of the site, which is currently an agricultural area with coconut and banana groves, more archaeological evidence for the extension of al-Baleed can be found. Recent archaeological survey has revealed structural and additional archaeological remains that are contemporary with those found at al-Baleed.

Recent archaeological work is painting a vivid picture of trade, but very little is known about *local* history of medieval Zafar. One possible way to shed light on local history is to examine the numerous contemporaneous shrines located near the site. Within the immediate vicinity of al- Baleed are a total of five shrines: Ba Kindi, Sahib al Hadra, Samiri and Sheikh Mohammad.

'Afīf Shrine and Mosque

The shrine of this 'Afīf (see Tab. 1 for others) is in the cemetery of the 'Afīf Mosque which is located just to the west of the older ruins of mosques mentioned above. The 'Afīf Mosque is important for two reasons: 1) its associated cemetery has graves and gravestones similar to those found in the extensive cemetery at the western end of al-Baleed Archaeological Park (see Oman 1983 for examples) (Fig. 7). Therefore, it is contemporary with the site of Al Baleed. 2) There is a shrine of an 'Afīf in this cemetery (Fig. 6). This is an open-air shrine that has been plastered and painted white and has a small plastered wall surrounding it. It is likely that the 'Afīf buried here founded this mosque. It is possible that the modern mosque was built on top of an older one (perhaps an "al-Baleed type").

The 'Afīf are *mashayikh* and it is possible that this mosque in the past, with its shrine and *mashayikh* association, was a sacred enclave that provided protection during tribal disputes and was a place for locals to go to swear the truth when agreements were made or when one's honor was in doubt. Note that there are additional shrines of the 'Afīf in Taqah, Salalah and east of Mirbat (Tab. 1).

Sheikh 'Ali bin Mohammad Ba Kinda

The shrine of Sheikh 'Ali bin Mohammad Ba Kinda is located to the west of al-Baleed around the foundations of older mosques and south of 'Afīf (Fig. 7). The date of this mosque and its founding (and hence the shrine) is uncertain, but it is believed by many locals to be one of the oldest continually utilized mosques in the area. Information provided by the Sultan Qaboos Center for Islamic Studies states that this mosque collapsed and was rebuilt next to an older mosque in 850/1446. Therefore, this mosque was in use during the late occupation of al-Baleed. A modernized shrine, it currently has a cupola, but it is likely it was originally an open-air tomb. This mosque is socially active and offers many lectures, a tradition that may stem from its founder.

Figure 6. 'Afīf shrine near al-Baleed.

Figure 7. View of the shrine of Ba Kinda (cupola in the background). Note the "al-Baleed type" tombstones in the 'Afīf cemetery in the foreground (see Fig. 6).

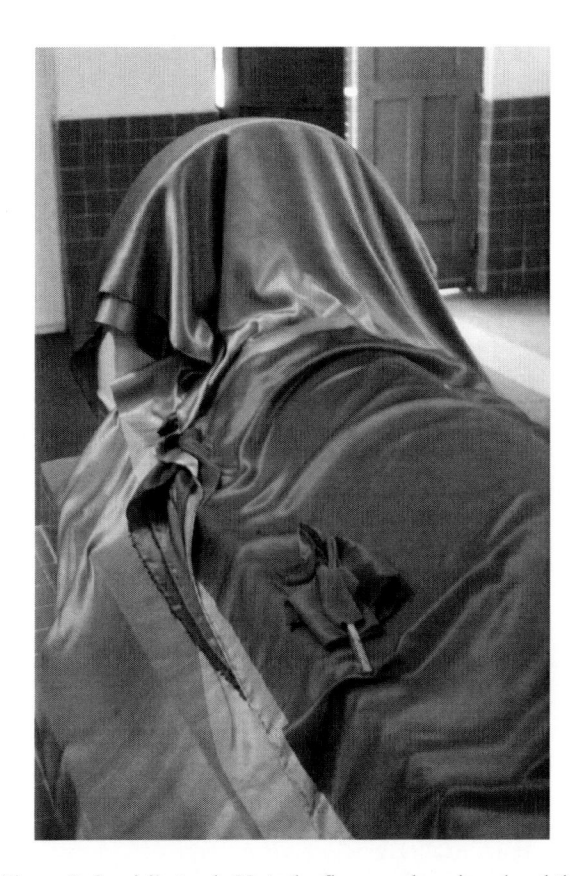

Figure 8. Samiri's tomb. Note the flag seen here is red and the cloths covering the tomb are green.

The Shrine of Samiri (Cheraman Perumal)

The shrine of Samiri has captured the curiosity of many in Dhofar and is perhaps the only shrine of a Muslim from South Asia in Dhofar (Fig. 8). This shrine is located in the groves to the north of the western arm of the al-Baleed lagoon. Miles visited this shrine in 1883 and wrote that this is the burial place of the former Hindu Raja of Cranganore (1919: 518). On a return visit to Dhofar in 1884 he visited this tomb again and notes that there is an inscription (which is no longer at the site) on a broken headstone. Miles interviewed the *qadi* of Dahariz, Sayyid Ahmed, who told him that "Samiri" was a converted *kaffir* and it was through his sanctity that Dhofar was first blessed with rain (Miles 1919: 552-553). Miles also offers a description of the site:

The tomb of Al Samiri lies about half a mile from the sea and is enclosed by an unroofed wall of mud and stones twenty-five feet by ten, the grave being eighteen by four, lying north and south, with a broken headstone of black basalt or limestone. The inscription is imperfect; the lower part, bearing the date, has disappeared, while at the foot of the tomb is a small cavity for holding oil, the lamp being kept lighted throughout the year by devotees. The roof of the building collapsed many years ago, but last year a slave named Saeed saw the saint in a dream and was warned that if the tomb was left exposed to the sun the whole district would be parched for want of rain; a subscription was therefore raised and some repairs were effected, but sufficient funds to renew the roof were not available (Miles 1919: 553).

Note that this is as a shrine of a foreigner and that it had a roof at one time as indicated above. Miles offers the date 216/831, but does not indicate where he obtained this information. This shrine has very wide appeal and it is particularly important to South Asian Muslims (Mappilas). The shrine has been modernized and now has a cupola and a mosque next door.

Cheraman Perumal

The last king or emperor of Malabar was Cheraman Perumal (Logan 1887: 192). While his conversion probably occurred much later in the 12th century (S. Prange, pers. comm.), he is incorrectly believed by many Mappilas to have converted to Islam as early as the 7th century and had an audience with the Prophet Mohammad. Logan, an English Malabar magistrate, wrote two descriptive volumes on the history and cultures of the region. He summarized the conversion of Cheraman Perumal and how he came to Zafar (al-Baleed) (Logan 1887: 192-194), a story that matches the descriptions of many of my South Asian Muslim informants currently working in Dhofar.

Cheraman's story begins with a dream where he saw the moon split into two halves. Through contact with Arab traders in Kodungallur (Cranganore) he learned that the Prophet Mohammad wrought a miracle on the same night as he sundered the moon before a crowd of observers (Sura 54: 1-5 *Shaq al Qamar*). This news inspired him to learn about Islam and he decided to travel to Mecca to learn more about the religion. He traveled with an entourage of Arab traders (who happily did so, as it would allow them to expand their trade along the western coast of India). One of the Arab traders is believed to be Malik ibn Dinar. Originally a Hindu king, as a Muslim convert that controlled the famous port and trading center of Kodungallur his conversion and subsequent endowments for the building of mosques in Malabar facilitated the spread of Islam in the region. Many versions of the story have Cheraman sailing to Al Shihr, a port town on the Mahra coast of Yemen (Logan 1887:192). He lived there for "considerable time" and then set sail for Zafar (al-Baleed) in 827 AD (Ibid: 196). Here he sent letters to his advisors back in Kadungallur before he left Mecca asking his advisors to follow his orders to help Malik bin Dinar and others build mosques in Kodungallur. Some versions mention that Cheraman Perumal married the sister of the King of Jeddah. He died in Zafar (al-Baleed) and was buried there.

Who is al Samiri?

If this is a shrine to a former Hindu Raja of Cranganore, Cheraman Perumal, then why is it locally attributed to someone known as Samiri? The Quran (Sura 20: 85-98) tells the story of how a person named Samiri deceived worshippers with a golden calf – thereby advocating a "false" religion. Melding this information with the personage of Cheraman Perumal, it is possible that during his travels to Mecca, as a former Hindu, he was given the nickname of "Samiri." From an Islamic perspective, the story of the golden calf could be relating to Samiri as an example of the rightness of Islam and the wrongness of false religions, such as those that revere cattle. From a literary perspective, the name Samiri may be used in the Quran as a double entendre: 1) Cheraman Perumal, "Samiri," formerly revered cattle (a literal golden calf in the sense that it represents a false idol) prior to his conversion to Islam (the true religion) and 2) perhaps the more general usage to exemplify that worshipping idols, such as the golden calf, is the active rejection of monotheism, of God. It is doubtful that an early convert from Hinduism would be explicitly named in the Quran as such, as he himself is not integral to the story of the golden calf, but the example it provides to promote the ideals set forth in the Quran. Miles (1919: 554) also mentions this idea: "Al Samiri signifies calf and is applied to the worshippers of the cow." In fact, as stated by Logan (1887:193), Cheraman Perumal took the Arabic Muslim name of Abdul Rahman Samiri, a name that may have been given to him in reference to his original Hindu beliefs (see also Miller 1976: 47). He apparently was last remembered in Zafar as Samiri and his shrine became known by this name.

Dating the Shrine of Samiri

At some point between the 9th and 12th centuries CE the last Chera ruler, Cheraman Perumal ended the line and was succeeded by a series of independent rulers (Miller 1976: 46-47). According to Zain al Din's dating, he died and was buried in Zafar in 822 (Miller 1976: 48). In a current study by S. Prange, however, the last Chera dynasty ended only in the early 12th century. Post-Chera polities subsequently competed to attract Muslim traders (Prange, pers. comm.). Nonetheless, the shrine known as Samiri was founded sometime during the occupation of al-Baleed, likely in the early 12th century, and was a place where Mappilas in Dhofar could visit a *waliyy* from their specific Islamic heritage.

Sahib al Hadhra

This shrine, called Sahib al Hadhra, is located just to the west of the current fenced off area of al-Baleed Archaeological Park. It is obvious from observing it, that this shrine was contemporary to greater al-Baleed (Fig. 9; see also Oman 1983: Fig. 4). The date of the founding of this shrine is not known, but given that the western part of al-Baleed contains a large cemetery, the shrine could be considered as an integral part of the city. Traditionally, this shrine is important to a family of the *sada*, the Ba Abood, as they visit this shrine each year on the 11th of Dhu al Hijja. Mawlids are performed here, as indicated in the shrine's name as it refers to "Lord of Incantation." At other times of the year festivals and various occasions are celebrated here. More recently it is also associated with Ahmed al-Kabir who was stabbed in the stomach with a *khanjar*, but did not die. This was deemed as a miracle

Figure 9. The shrine of Sahib al Hadhra. Al-Baleed Archaeological Park is immediately behind the coconut palms seen here (see also Shrine no. 9 in Fig. 1).

and people believed that he must be a good, holy person to have survived something that should have killed him.

It is interesting to note that Oman's study of the al-Baleed cemetery did not mention this grave (1983: 281, 283-284). A prominent grave, based upon architectural style, it would have been visible to him. He separates the burial ground at al-Baleed into two sections and section A is the area currently outside the fence that is now a farm where the Sahib al Hadhra shrine is located. Oman delineates this part of his map as "ruins." This area of "ruins" probably refers to the remains of an al-Baleed type mosque that is still visible here and the original grave of the Sahib al Hadhra, among others. The formal shrine as it is now, therefore, must have been constructed after he completed his study in the early 1980's. The only engraved gravestone dated in his study from al-Baleed has the year 1011/1602 (Oman 1983: 284, Pls 47, 48, 49, 50). This post-dates the peak of occupation at al-Baleed and is identified with a period of decline. Given the similar styles of the stones surrounding it, this part of the cemetery was probably in use from about 1500-1700. Following this argument, it is possible that the tomb of Sahib al Hadhra dates within this 200 year period.

Sheikh Mohammad

Ibn Battuta, who visited the tomb of Sheikh Mohammad in 1325 and again in 1340, describes it as a "hospice" (*zawiyah*) held in great veneration by them [Zafaris]; "they come out to it in the mornings and evenings and seek asylum in it and when the supplicant for asylum has entered it, the Sultan has no power over him" (Gibb 1929: 385). Sheikh Mohammad's tombstone is one of three finely carved examples most likely taken from his *zawiyah* at Al Robat (now held by the Victoria and Albert Museum in London). He died on 1 Dhu al Hijja 714/7 March 1315 (Lambourn 2004: 10). The stones were produced in Cambay in India as the high relief carving and the two split plantains are unique to Cambay and characterize the gravestones produced there during the first half of the $8^{th}/14^{th}$ century (Lambourn 2004: 14).

The headstone of Sheikh Mohammad provides a rare example of a grave memorial ordered for export during the lifetime of its patron and completed after his death (Lambourn 2004: 17), and which is directly associated with a known Dhofari *zawiyah*. It is only carved on one side (Porter 1988: 33) and there is some contention about the name (*nisbah*) on the stone. Guest suggests Damrini (1935: 409), Porter reads it is Damrani, while Lambourn (2004: 18) most recently has suggested Damirah, one of two small towns bearing the same name located near Samannud in the Nile Delta of Egypt. She contends that this would be possible as the contemporary Rasulids had close and regular contacts with Mamluk Egypt at this period. These connections may have encouraged the arrival of an Egyptian Sheikh in Dhofar. Miles (1919: 509) also mentions Sheikh Mohammad in another context in passing stating that "Said bin Ali al-Habd attacked Sheikh Mohammad bin Abu Bakr at Robat and destroyed his family" (800/1397).

Shrines and al-Baleed: A Landscape Perspective

Thus, there are at least five known shrines in the vicinity of al-Baleed. It is clear from survey work that the physical site of al-Baleed has a much greater range further to the north than that currently delineated for the formal fenced-in park. The latter most likely represents only the official administrative/governmental quarter of al-Baleed. The extension of the cemetery, particularly to the west and across the road (the 'Afīf mosque and cemetery, for example), and the presence of many al-Baleed type mosques to the north and west of the park demonstrate this (Fig. 2). The shrines located in the vicinity of al-Baleed, which date to at least the early 14th century CE (Sheikh Mohammad) if not earlier (Samiri), offer a unique opportunity to contemplate their roles in the human experience of the inhabitants, merchants and students who lived and/or worked in Zafar. Ibn Battuta mentions that Sheikh Mohammad's tomb was a hospice (*zawiyah*) (Gibb 2004: 386). The concept of a hospice is very similar to the term *hawtah* used in conjunction with many shrines in the Hadramaut, meaning "sacred enclave." The term used for such a place in Dhofar is currently not known, as *zawiyah* is the Maghrabi term used to describe them by Ibn Battuta. The tomb of Sheikh Mohammad was used in this manner as individuals would retreat there to be protected by the Sheikh's sons and descendents. Ibn Battuta also refers to the shrine of 'Aber bin Hūd as a *zawiyah*, so the example of Sheikh Mohammad is not an isolated case and probably indicates that many of the shrines in Dhofar served similar functions (see above).

The shrine of Samiri presents an interesting proposition as it may be as early as the 12th century. It is very close to the site of al-Baleed and was likely considered a shrine to visit when traveling to Zafar. This shrine appealed particularly to traveling Mappilas.

Overall, by viewing the shrines near al-Baleed in the context of the site, it is apparent that there were many places nearby that people would go to ask for help: be it spiritual or for protection from disputes with the Sultan or others. By considering these shrines with a landscape perspective, a window in to the spiritual and social lives of the rulers, residents, merchants and religious students is opened.

Acknowledgements

This survey was made possible by HE Abdul Aziz bin Mohammad Al Rowas, Advisor to HM the Sultan for Cultural Affairs in Oman. This fieldwork was funded in part by a Fulbright fellowship. I would like to acknowledge Hassan al Jabberi, Ghanim al Shanfari, Ahmed al Awaid, Hussein al Shanfari and Mohammad al Jahfali of the Office of the Advisor to HM the Sultan for Cultural Affairs for their support in the field and in the office. In addition, I am indebted to Ibrahim Nadhir Ashoor and Salem bin Mohammad Eid al Khaldi at the Sultan Qaboos Center for Islamic Culture in Salalah for their generosity, knowledge and enthusiasm for this project. I look forward to continuing this research together. And lastly, thanks to all who offered their suggestions and comments at the conference.

Prophets	**Saints**			
	Sada	*Mashayikh*	*'Ulamā*	Unidentified/Other
1. Hūd bin Aber 2. Aber bin Hūd (i) 3. Saleh bin Hūd (ii) 4. 'Amran 5. 'Ayyub (Job)	6. Sahib Mirbat (iii) 7. Ba 'Alawi 8. Hadad (Dahariz) 9. Sahib al-Hadhra	10. bin 'Afīf (Salalah) (iv) 11. bin Othman (al-Hawtah) (v) 13. Sheikh Ahmed bin 'Afīf (Mahalla) (vi) 14. 'Afīf (al-Baleed)	15. Sheikh Mohammad bin 'Ali al-Qalay (vii) 16. Sheikh 'Ali (viii) 17. Sheikh Mohammad 18. Ba Tahan 19. Sheikh 'Ali Said 20. Sheikh Salim ba Quayr 21. Sahib al-Sadra 22. Ba Qarhan 23. Ba Kinda 24. Sheikh Salim bin Arabiyya (ix)	25. Sheikh 'Isa (Taqa) 26. Sheikh Abdullah (Mohammad al-Saadi) (al-Dahariz) 27. Moqayyad al Jamal 28. Samiri 30. Goonayt 31. Zuhair (x) 32. Abdullah Ganeed 33. Fayrouz bin 'Ali 34. Umm Tabakh (xi) 35. al Jauhari (xii) 36. Sheikh Mubarak 37. Sheikh Faraj 38. Ba Alaaf 39. Sheikh Sa'ad ***Unknown Affiliation:*** 47. al-Hafa (xiii) 48-51. Salalah al-Wusta 52. al-Robat 53-54. al-Dahariz

(i) Mentioned by Ibn Battuta, this shrine is "a half day's journey from this city [Zafar] is al-Ahqaf where the people of 'Ad dwelt. There is a hospice (*zawiyah*) there and a mosque on the seacoast, with a village of fishermen surrounding it. In the hospice is a tomb over which is inscribed 'this is the tomb of Hūd bin Aber (but is actually Aber bin Hūd), upon whom the most copious blessings and peace" (Gibb 2004: 386). Ibn Battuta reasoned that this was the "true" tomb as Aber bin Hūd's country was al Ahqaf. Water is available here and this was a *zawiyah*, a safe haven, for travelers, such as Ibn Battuta.

(ii) Knysh (1997: 143) notes that *awliya* (sing. *waliyy*) is used to describe saints in the Hadramaut, but they can also be referred to as "*salih*" (i.e. literally "righteous" or "pious"). Therefore, instead of being the son of Hūd, it is likely a shrine that commemorates a pious eponymous ancestor. According to Carter, "a characteristic of Dhofar is the custom of swearing innocence at the tomb of a saint" and the shrine that is most important to the Mahra for this custom is Saleh bin Hūd (1982: 61). Medieval Islamic pottery was collected from the vicinity of this shrine. It is part of a larger cemetery with boat shaped (see Zarins, this volume) and traditionally Islamic graves.

(iii) Sayyid Ahmad b. 'Isa al-'Alawi is mentioned in the ancestral lineage of M. Ali al-'Alawi on one of his inscribed tombstones, date of death 556/1160-1161 (Oman 1982; Costa 2001:134). The Sahib Mirbat genealogy is discussed by Carter (1982: 164). The shrine is adjacent to a large archaeological site with Medieval and Late Islamic ceramics and stone foundations.

(iv) This shrine is an example of a sugar loaf dome (see Costa 2001: 135).

(v) This shrine is associated with a mosque attributed to Mohammad bin Othman bin Mohammad bin Mohammad bin Ahmed al-Jahfali who came to Dhofar from Aden in the 5th/11th century. The shrine is referred to as "bin Othman." A newly constructed road has recently allowed access to this previously secluded area on the coast west of Mughsay. The village and the shrine were likely accessed in the past by boat. There is an extensive archaeological site nearby where local redwares were collected. An old cemetery is associated with the mosque and there is a stone tower (*kūt*) on a rise closer to the foothills of the steep jebel here. A local story is that the "Minjuwi" had a cable attached to it from above and it is how they got supplies from on top of the jebel to the small village below (an archaeological assessment of this site is in preparation by the author).

(vi) This shrine is visited by the Mahra (Müller 1991: 83). Miles visited "the oldest and most revered shrine in Taqa, that of *waliyy* Afīf, who is regarded as a patriarch; the headstone bears the date 309/921" (Miles 1919: 554).

(vii) Al-Qalay is from Syria. He studied in Hadramaut and then traveled to Mirbat. He wrote many books, two of which are still extant. Apparently the "Minjuwis" asked him to stay in Mirbat instead of going on to teach in Baghdad. He died in 630 AH. Local redware punctate ceramics were collected near this shrine and an older mosque foundation.

(viii) This shrine is in South Awqad. It currently has no mosque associated with it, but there is a foundation of a much older one just to the east of the shrine. Al Baleed type artifacts, including pottery and a copper coin have been found on the surface.

(ix) The shrine of "bin 'Arabiya" is for Salim bin Ahmed bin Afīf or Sheikh Salem bin Ahmed bin 'Arabiyya, the son of Sheikh Afīf of Taqah. This shrine does not have a cupola, but is part of a larger cemetery (fitting the greater pattern seen in Dhofar). There is a sign currently posted with rules stating that dancing and drum playing are forbidden. Müller (1991: 83) mentions that this shrine is important to the Mahra.

(x) Local tradition says that Zuhair was the first Dhofari to visit the Prophet Mohammad. There is a local saying that the tomb is as old as Mirbat and a song that recounts that whoever is buried here gives Mirbat life. Another story adhered to by others says that it is the tomb of an Indian that arrived in a boat and died in Mirbat-perhaps mixing the story of Cheraman Perumal. Miles visited this tomb in 1883 and refers to it as "Seyyid Zubair bin Abdulla al-Hashima" and notes that it is rather dilapidated and the not date is visible (Miles 1919: 543).

(xi) Not on map. Mentioned by Thesiger (1984: 112) and Carter (1982: 61) states that it is one of the important shrines to the Mahra. The location of this shrine is still to be determined.

(xii) Not on map. Mentioned by Thesiger (1984: 112). The location of this shrine is still to be determined.

(xiii) This is an example of an open-air shrine. A modern wall with a gate has been built around it and the tomb and head and footstones have been recently plastered. The shrine sits on a small rise on top of an al-Baleed-type mosque foundation.

Table 1. Shrines in Dhofar.

Bibliography

Ali M.M. 2002. English translation and commentary. *The Holy Quran*. Ohio, USA: Ahmadiyya Anjuman Isaha'at Islam Lahore.

Boxberger L. 2002. *On the Edge of Empire: Hadhramawt, Emigration, and the Indian Ocean: 1880's-1930's*. Albany: State University of New York Press.

Branfoot C. 2006. Pilgrimage in South Asia. Pages 46-79 in R. Barnes and C. Branfoot (eds), *Pilgrimage: The Sacred Journey*. Oxford: Ashmolean Museum.

Bujra A.S. 1971. *The Politics of Stratification*. Oxford: Clarendon Press.

Carter J.R.L. 1982. *Tribes in Oman*. London: Peninsular Publishing.

Costa P. 2001. *Historic Mosques and Shrines of Oman*. BAR International Series 938. Oxford: Archaeopress.

Costa P. & Kite S. 1985. The architecture of Salalah and the Dhofar littoral. *Journal of Oman Studies* 7: 131-153.

Dresch P. 2000. *A History of Modern Yemen*. Cambridge: Cambridge University Press.

Ernst C. 1997. *Sufism*. Boston: Shambhala Publications.

Gibb H.A.R. 1929 [2004]. *The Travels of Ibn Battuta, AD 1325-1354*, Vol II. (C. Defrémery and B.R. Sanguinetti, eds). New Dehli: The Hakluyt Society.

Guest R. 1935. Zufar in the Middle Ages. *Islamic Culture* 7: 402-413.

Ho E. 2006. *The Graves of Tarim: Genealogy and Mobility Across the Indian Ocean*. Los Angeles: University of California Press.

Janzen J. 1986. *Nomads in the Sultanate of Oman.* Boulder: Westview Press.

Kennet D. 2004. *Sassanian and Islamic Pottery from Ras al-Khaimah.* BAR International Series 1248. Oxford: Tempvs Reparatvm.

Knysh A. 1993. Cult of saints in Hadramawt: an overview. Pages 137-152 in R.B. Serjeant, R.L. Bidwell & G. Rex Smith (eds), *New Arabian Studies, 1.* Exeter: University of Exeter Press.

Knysh A. 1997. The cult of saints and Islamic reformism in early 20th century Hadramawt. Pages 139-167 in G.R. Smith, J.R. Smart & B.R. Pridham (eds), *New Arabian Studies 4.* Exeter: University of Exeter Press.

Lambourn E. 2004. Carving and recarving: three Rasulid gravestones revisited. Pages 10-29 in G.R. Smith, J.R. Smart and B.R. Pridham (eds), *New Arabian Studies 6.* Exeter: University of Exeter Press.

Logan W. 1887. *Malabar, Vol. 1.* Madras: R.Hill.

Miles S.B. 1919. *The Countries and Tribes of the Persian Gulf.* London: Harrison and Sons.

Miller R.E. 1976. *Mappila Muslims in Kerala: A Study in Islamic Trends.* New Dehli: Orient Longman Ltd.

Müller W. 1993. Mahra. Pages 80-84 in C.E. Bosworth, E. Van Donzel, W.P. Heinrichs & Ch. Pellat (eds), *Encyclopedia of Islam, New Edition.* New York: E.J. Brill.

Museum of the Frankincense Land. 2007. *The Museum of the Frankincense Land: The History Hall.* Muscat, Sultanate of Oman: Office of the Advisor to HM the Sultan for Cultural Affairs.

Oman G. 1983. Preliminary epigraphic survey of Islamic material in Dhofar. *Journal of Oman Studies* 6/2: 277-289.

Oman G. 1989. Arabic-Islamic epigraphy in Dhofar in the Sultanate of Oman. Pages 193-100 in P. Costa & M. Tosi (eds), *Oman Studies: Papers on the Archaeology and History of Oman.* Rome: ISMEO.

Peterson J.E. 2004. Oman's diverse society: southern Oman. *Middle East Journal* 58/2: 254-269.

Prange S. 2008. Where the pepper grows. *Saudi Aramco World* 59/1: 10-17.

Rodionov M. 1997. Mawla Matar and other Awliya': on social functions of religious places in western Hadramawt. *Mare Erythraeum* I: 107-114.

Rodionov M. 2004. Mashhad 'Ali revisted: documents from Hadramawt. *Proceedings of the Seminar for Arabian Studies*, 34: 307-312.

al-Sabban, 'Abd al-Qadir Muhammad. 1998. *Visits and Customs: The Visit to the Tomb of the Prophet Hud.* L. Boxberger and A.A. Abu Hulayqa, translators. Ardmore: American Institute for Yemeni Studies.

al-Shahri A.A. 2000. *The Language of Aad.* Abu Dhabi: National Packaging and Printing.

Sadek N. 1989. Rasulid women: power and patronage. *Proceedings of the Seminar for Arabian Studies* 19: 121-136.

Serjeant R.B. 1949. The cemeteries of Tarim (Hadramawt). *Le Museon* LXII/1-2: 151-160.

Serjeant R.B. 1954. Hud and other pre-Islamic prophets of Hadramawt. *Le Museon* LXVII/1-2: 121-151.

Serjeant R.B. 1957. *The Saiyids of Hadramawt.* London: School of Oriental and African Studies.

Serjeant R.B. 1962. *Haram and Hawtah: The Sacred Enclave in Arabia.* 'Ab Al Rahman Badawi (ed.). Cairo: Ila Taha Husein.

Smith G.R. & Porter V. 1988. The Rasulids in Dhofar in the VIIth-VIIIth/XIII-XIVth centuries (Smith) and Three Rasulid tombstones from Zafar (Porter). *Journal of the Royal Asiatic Society*, n.v.: 26-44.

Thesiger W. 1984. *Arabian Sands.* Middlesex: Penguin.

Zarins J. 2007. Aspects of recent archaeological work at al Baled (Zafar), Sultanate of Oman. *Proceedings of the Seminar for Arabian Studies* 37: 309-324.

Author's Address
Lynne S. Newton
Office of the Advisor to HM the Sultan for Cultural Affairs
P.O. Box 1
Al-Hafa—al-Baleed
PC 216
Salalah, Sultanate of Oman
email: lynnesnewton@gmail.com

Wādī Ḥaḍramawt as a landscape of death and burial[1]

Mikhail Rodionov

Summary
Based on the author's long-term field work in the region as cultural anthropologist and folklorist, the paper gives general characteristics of the Ḥaḍramawt in South Arabia as a sacred landscape of death and burial. Mediaeval and modern vernacular poetry, oral and written traditions, local rites concerning pilgrimages and visitations of the graves provide ample resources to examine the configuration of a cultural space, with its levels of hierarchy, limits, routes, connections, centres-and-periphery, etc. Tombs of Islamic holy men stand by the cenotaphs of pre-Islamic prophets and ruins of ancient tribes destroyed by God. The well Barhūt, the utmost eastern extremity of the Wadi, is believed to be a gateway to the afterlife. Mutual characteristics of the examined ritual complexes help to map the spatial features of the Ḥaḍramī traditional culture.

Keywords: Ḥaḍramawt, cultural anthropology, oral and written traditions, tombs, pilgrimages

Denied by modern linguists, folk-etymology still explains the name of Ḥaḍramawt, a region in South Arabia, as "presence of death": *ḥaḍrah [al-] mawt*. Moreover, in vernacular poetry this toponym (in local pronunciation *Ḥaḍramūt*) is regularly rhymed with the Imperfect forms of the verb 'to die' (*yamūt*, etc.; see examples in Rodionov 1997a: 58-64; 2007: 190-191). This semantic play reflects local discourse which implicitly presents the region as a sacred landscape of death and burial. Indeed, the most picturesque features of its settlements are holy shrines with their usually whitewashed domes or flat roofs. These tombs and related constructions are built and used according to rather rigid hierarchy of cultural status and prestige (Rodionov 2001: 263-276).

The main route in this symbolic space can be defined in one sentence: a pilgrimage (*ziyārah*) to a sacred enclave (*ḥawṭah*) to the tomb (*qubbah*) of a holy man (*walīy*) being as a rule the patron (*mawlā*) of the area due to his, or sometimes her, vital force (*barakah*). Tombs of Islamic holy men stand by the cenotaphs of pre-Islamic prophets and ruins of ancient tribes destroyed by God. That is why the notion of death is so essential for a region with relatively favourable physical conditions for agriculture, trade and handicrafts. All of the sudden death comes not to the poor and hungry, but to the arrogant and rich who deny exhortation of the prophets and therefore are punished by God as a warning to human beings. Ancient ruins and sites scattered all over the region are traditionally regarded as a tangible proof of the vanities of this ephemeral world, the passed away pagans of ʿĀd and Thamūd (Rodionov 2007: 45-46).

The well Barhūt, the utmost eastern extremity of the Wadi, is believed to be a gateway to the afterlife, a gloomy cavity where, according to al-Qazvīnī and some other Muslim scholars, the souls of the hypocrites and infidels are confined (al-Ṣabbān 1998: 15-16 of Arabic pagination, 13; al-Shāṭirī 2001: 13-15). The tomb (*qabr*) of a pre-Islamic Prophet Hūd bordered by a perpetual stream of Wādī Masīlah, the only real river in the region, is placed nearby (see Fig. 1, Fig. 2). The most important cenotaph and *mazār*, or the place of visitation, in all Ḥaḍramawt (Newton 2009: 4-186), Qabr Hūd, preserves in its annual pilgrimage rites under the guidance of certain Sādah and Mashāyyikh families many archaic features. These include camel-races, folk-dances and chanting, and ritual teasing of villagers by the pilgrims on their way to Qabr Hūd and of first-time pilgrims (called *wuʿīlah*) who are usually likened to a she-camel while their companions imitate the behaviour of excited male camels (al-Ṣabbān 1998: 29-30, 36-37 of Arab pagination). The last custom reflects the story about the Prophet Hūd turning a she-camel into a rock near to his tomb. Noteworthy is the rite of bathing in the river and drinking its water but the most salient ethnographic phenomenon concerns clay figurines of camels, horses, donkeys and ibexes. Made in the town of Tarīm by the local potters of the al-Bānī clan, they are purchased by the pilgrims on their way back as a gift for their children. There is little doubt that the primitive function of these figurines was votive, and only in Islamic time have they been gradually transformed into a simple toy.

The symbolic topography of Ḥaḍramawt as a landscape of death and burial also comprises the town of ʿĪnāt with its seven tombs of the Sādah, the Prophet Muhammad's descendants, and the town of Tarīm, a renowned centre of Islamic scholarship and Sādah influence, famous for its numerous mosques, religious schools and – last but not least – three historical cemeteries where, as worded by local tradition, more than ten thousand Muslim martyrs and holy men lay (Serjeant 1949: 151-159; Ho 2006: 16-17).

The hub of the Wādī Ḥaḍramawt is marked with a two-level construction connected with a staircase, the tomb of ʿAlī b. ʿĪsā al-Muhājir, or the Migrant (died 345/956), the founding ancestor of the Ḥaḍramī Sādah line (see Fig. 1, Fig. 3). The plan of this construction drawn by Yuri Kozhin is given in Rodionov (2007: 276).

According to local tradition, the most northerly holy tomb in the region is that of Prophet Ṣāliḥ, a pre-Islamic messenger to the people of Thamūd. Located in Wādī Khawnab, the Western tributary of Wādī Sarr (Fig. 1), the tomb belongs to the long graves type, c. 10 x 2 m, and is comparable with the double grave (eastern part c. 21.5 m,

---

[1] This paper was supported by the 2007-2009 INTAS Yemeni Project 05-1000008-8067 "Elucidation of features of pre-Islamic religion in modern rites and beliefs of Yemen".

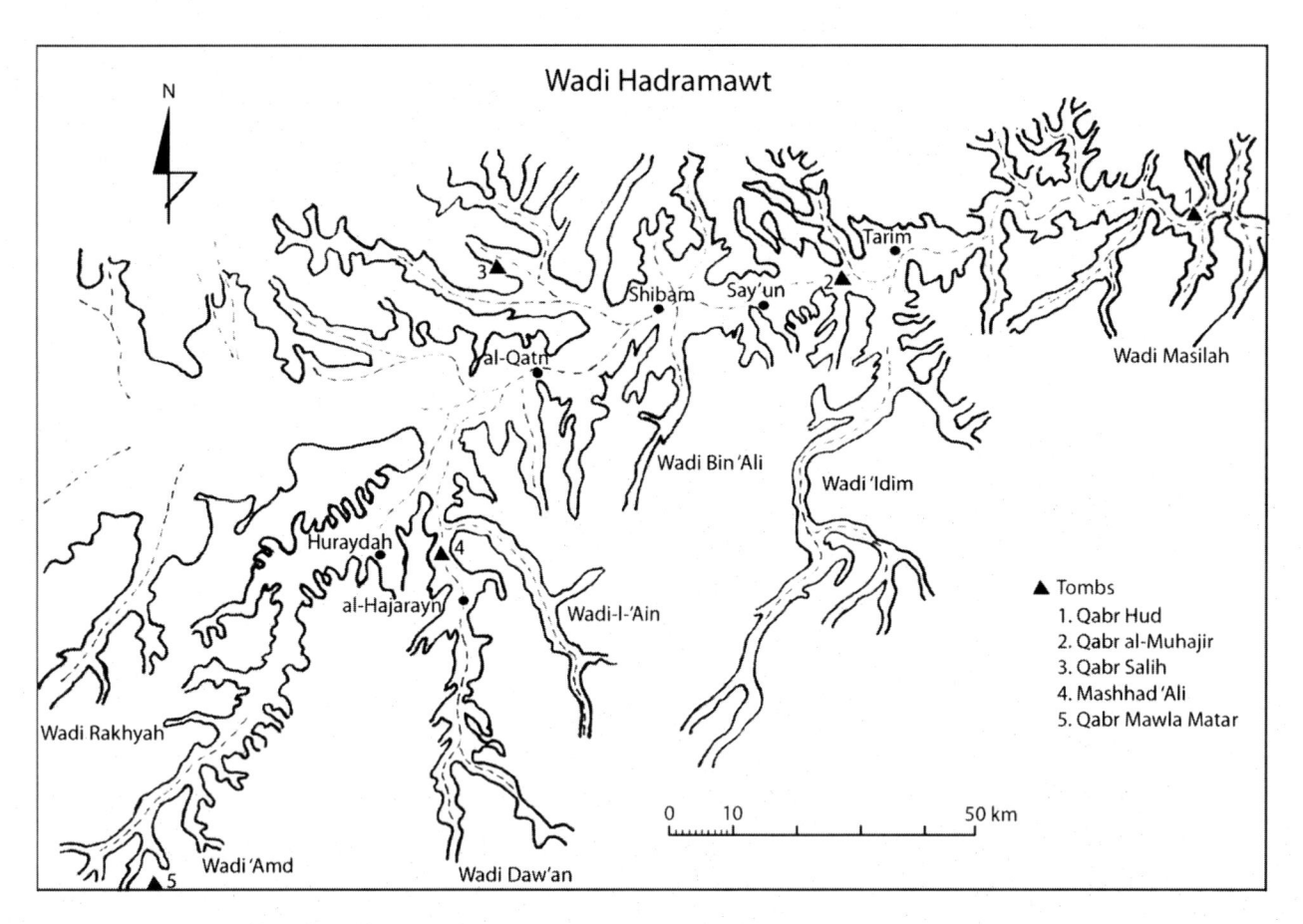

Fig. 1. Map of Wādī Ḥaḍramawt (M. Rodionov).

Fig. 2. Qabr Nabī Allah Hūd (photo M. Rodionov).

Fig. 3. Qabr Sayyid ᶜĪsā al-Muhājir, the Migrant (photo M. Rodionov).

western part c. 17 m) near the town of Būr ascribed to Ḥanẓalah, a minor pre-Islamic Prophet who, in contrast to Hūd and Ṣāliḥ, is not mentioned in the Qurʾān (Rodionov 1997b: 107-108, 111; 2001: 263, 270).

The southern outpost of our symbolic landscape is located in the area of the Saybān tribe on the Kawr Saybān plateau at its only pass to the coast. The local ritual complex of Mawlā Maṭar, or the Patron of Rain (Fig. 1), displays a set of pre-Islamic characteristics comprising construction and locality, rites of pilgrimage (in which the Sādah or another Islamic social stratum of Mashāyyikh play no role whatsoever), peculiarities of rain-prayer (istisqāʾ), and, in particular, the venerated Patron's origin who has nothing in common with standard heroes of Islamic hagiology (Rodionov 1997b: 108-112; 2001: 264-266, 271-272).

The ḥawṭah of Mashhad ᶜAlī, an important sacred enclave in Wādī Dawᶜan (Fig. 1, Fig. 4), deserves special attention due to abundant historical evidence connected with this site. We have the rare opportunity of tracing back a ḥawṭah formation process, step by step, narrated by its eponym Sayyid ᶜAlī b. Ḥasan b. ᶜAbdallah al-ᶜAṭṭās (1122/1710-1172/1758) in a noted manuscript known to Freya Stark, Robert Serjeant and Abdallah Bujra, Kitāb al-maqṣad fī shawāhid al-Mashhad, now in the Maktabat al-Aḥqāf Library, Tarīm; catalogue number 2179 (Rodionov 2007: 125-126, 170-177). Ascribed to Sayyid ᶜAlī b. Ḥasan al-ᶜAṭṭās, the manuscript is a pen-product of Sālim b. Muḥammad b. ᶜAbdallah b. Muḥsin al-ᶜAṭṭās, nick-named Hubhub or Hoopoe, dated 13 Rabīᶜ al-Awwal 1361/1 April 1942. The text consists of 477 pages and is rendered in the first person as if Sayyid ᶜAlī b. Ḥasan dictated his story to a scribe. The title specifies this by the words "dictated by the least of all men".

Sayyid ᶜAlī b. Ḥasan was not only a pious man and a member of a family of religious leaders, but also a distinguished poet and mystic. The manuscript includes passages of rhymed prose and various pieces of poetry. He is called the eponym of Mashhad 'Ali; however he started to build the ḥawṭah in honour of his great-great-grandfather ᶜUmar b. ᶜAbd al-Raḥmān b. ᶜAqīl al-ᶜAṭṭās, known as Quṭb al-Ghawth, the Pole of Salvation, buried

Fig. 4. Mashhad ᶜAlī, a water reservoir (photo M. Rodionov).

in Ḥuraydah, the biggest town in the north reach of Wādī ʿAmd. The area chosen for a new ḥawṭah occupies the northern part of Wādī Dawʿan (the Saybān and Bin Maḥfūḍ tribal area), at the crossroad between Wādī ʿAmd (the Jaʿda tribal area), Wādī al-ʿAyn (the ʿAwābithah tribal area) and Wādī al-Kasr (al-Ṣayʿar and Nahd tribal area, and towns of Haynin, Ḥawrah and al-Qaṭn) which connects a caravan-route from the coast with the main wadi of inner Ḥadramawt. At that time the place, a virgin land al-Jāhī, near the mountain al-Ghaywār, was deserted and nearly all communications have ceased since the tribes, mostly al-Ṣayʿar and Nahd, began cutting the roads and raiding the villages.

Sayyid ʿAlī b. Ḥasan took his decision to establish a ḥawṭah in 1160/1747, encouraged by a series of minor miracles (ishārāt, muqaddamāt, bishārāt, ʿalamāt). In the following year, in the ruins of the ancient site of Raybūn, excavated since the 1980s by Russian archaeologists, Sayyid ʿAlī b. Ḥasan found a great dry well; the finding strengthened his desire to dig a new one. He started his work to build the ḥawṭah in Rabīʿ al-Awwal 1160/April-May 1747, when he was 38, and finished it in mid-Rajab 1167/May 1754 when he was 45, four years before his death. From the very beginning he was called Shāhid al-Mashhad, the Witness for the Place of Martyrdom, and nobody doubted that the qubbah, or vaulted tomb, he built was intended not for his great-grandfather but for himself.

The new well started to give water with healing properties; during the period of al-Nathrah star (27.01-8.02) a rich rain-flood occurred; and mysterious silhouettes of Shaykh ʿUmar and al-Ḥiḍr blessed the place. As the ḥawṭah founder, Sayyid ʿAlī b. Ḥasan was supported by people of Ḥuraydah, al-Hajarayn, Khuraykhar, Naḥūlah and Qaydūn, the latter being the place of pilgrimage to Shaykh al-Saʿīd al-ʿAmūdī, and by the Mashāyyikh al-ʿAmudi in Buḍah, and al-Ribāṭ in the upper reaches of Wādī Dawʿan. As a sign of his new authority, Sayyid ʿAlī was handed a stick made of yew by a local Shaykh, a ceremony that seems to have had roots in pre-Islamic times.

The ḥawṭah's frontiers were defined from Ḥaṣat al-Luṣṣān, the Stone of Thieves, renamed as Ḥaṣat al-Zuwwār, the Stone of Pilgrims, in the north, to Wādī Mīkh and the village of the same name in the south-west. Pilgrimage to al-Mashhad begins on the 12th of Rabīʿal-Awwal, after the pilgrimage to Shaykh Saʿīd of Qaydūn, and lasts till the 15th. Twelve days before the pilgrimage special scoopers started filling the collector (al-jābiyyah) with potable water taking it from four wells – Biʾr al-ʿAṭiyyah, Biʾr al-Karāmah, Biʾr Shaykh Bā Wazīr, and Bīr al-Nūr.

The Manṣab (a Sayyid of the founder's stock responsible for the ḥawṭah) opens the pilgrimage, he unlocks the water and blesses it. During my first field-seasons in Wādī Dawʿan the office was held by ʿAlī b. ʿAbdallah al-ʿAttas (died 8.05.1986). The Manṣab reads the Yā Sīn (36) Sūrah of the Qurʾān and verses concerning the Prophet's descendants, especially ʿUmar b. ʿAbd al-Raḥmān b. ʿAqīl al-ʿAttās. On the 13th of the month every tribe and social stratum entered the place in the pre-set order. The first were the Sādah on thirteen horses with colourful banners of their own (sing. bayraq), for which the famous Bā Ṭarfī carpenters made special suspending rings at wooden mausoleums. Half a century ago up to two thousand camels would enter al-Mashhad at a time.

The pilgrims drank from siqāyahs (special water reservoirs); the largest are the Ḥawḍ al-Nabī to the west, for 52 people to drink simultaneously, and Siqāyah al-Dawlah to the east, for 73 people. They visited the qubbah with its seven graves, one of which is that of ʿAlī b. Ḥasan, the others, with one exception, belong to his descendants. The exception concerns Shaykh Bin ʿAfīf, one of the first supporters of the ḥawṭah project, who always desired to be buried near the Shāhid al-Mashhad, and his will was fulfilled by a miracle; a flood took his wooden mausoleum (tābūt) directly to the qubbah.

There were also warehouses; Dār al-ʿAwāliq, or a house of the ʿAwāliq tribe, for about fifteen guards to keep order during the pilgrimages; Dar al-Nūrah for the tribal nobility, and a special Ḥuṣn for the tribal hostages. Pilgrims could either pray or sing and dance according to the proverb, "Dancing has the same share as praying".

In his verse, ʿAlī b. Ḥasan maintained a question-and-answer dialogue with the ancient site of Raybūn. The Sayyid asked, why the place was destroyed and its population ceased to exist, and the site revealed the truth to him. The poet meditated melancholically that "the beauty of this life is unimportant for us as an abominable temptation, / that cannot be compared, taken in full, with a mosquito's wing. / Both its beauty and its shame – everyone suffocates in its cruelty" (Rodionov 2007: 170). And Raybū answered, "I will tell, oh Sayyid ʿAlī, the truth / about the people of ʿĀd who opposed God and never listened to persuaders: / they had no trust in His mercy, and He destroyed them with hurricanes and wind, / and sent on them winds of fire burning with heat. / For them, there came the [Day] of Resurrection, across the hollows [their remnants] were blown. / They died suddenly; none were [properly] buried in graves." (Rodionov 2007: 171).

Sayyid ʿAlī asked his questions again and again, and Raybū rephrased the answers, "Once there came a persuader, calling them to God, a shrewd one. / They renounced him, and expelled him, and did evil things to him. / God punished them with a devastating hurricane. / How many high fortresses collapsed above them and fell! / Defaced is the structure [once] filled with might, and it is curved. / How much had they toiled constructing these buildings! / And nothing but ruins was left, as prescribed by your Lord. / Anyone who sees it [= the ruins] in the night darkness escapes it. / How many instructive [things] are in this life, and how many amazing!" (Rodionov 2007: 173-174).

In commemoration of the pagans who disobeyed their Prophet Hūd and were perished by God's wrath, every ancient ruin in Hadramawt is up to now is called al-ʿĀdīyah, that of the ʿĀd origin. New *ḥawṭah*s are usually built near ancient ruins (in the case of Qabr Hūd one can name al-Maknūn, Thawbah and Ḥuṣn al-ʿUr) in order to keep the local tribes from temptation to violate the sacred status of tombs and *qubbah*s (Rodionov 2004: 307-312).

In fact, the examined ritual complexes of Ḥaḍramawt as a specific landscape of death and burial have some mutual characteristics. Most of these complexes are situated near archaeological sites and retain such pre-Islamic rites as dancing, chanting, performing poetry, sharing meals, and ibex-hunting (Rodionov 1994: 124-129); pious functions being connected with commerce and trade (markets and fairs). Practically all venerated tombs in the region are related to water, which can be explained by the pre-Islamic Arab belief in a correlation between water and vegetation at the graves as a path to revival (Vinnikov 1930: 367-377). The act of giving water either by rain and flood or by subsoil sources is locally called *al-raḥmah* or [God's] mercy, so al-Raḥmān can be regarded first of all as He who endows people with potable water and, thanks to His mercy, turns death into the new life. Some of the examined complexes, e.g. Qabr Hūd, retain such chthonic features.

Local rites of veneration of tombs have been ardently discussed in terms of the ʿAlawī - Irshādī conflict (Freitag 2003: 253-255; Rodionov 1996: 128; al-Shāṭirī 2001: 42-72) from 1920 up to the present day by both its partisans and opponents; the latter stigmatized their enemies as *qubūriyyūn* or tomb worshippers. Native and émigré poetry, press, documents and manuscripts are extremely important for mapping the spatial dimensions of the Ḥaḍramī traditional culture (e.g. Rodionov 2008: 277-282).

References

Freitag U. 2003. *Indian Ocean Migrants and State Formation in Hadhramaut: Reforming the Homeland*. Social, economic and political studies of the Middle East and Asia. Leiden: Brill.

Ho E. 2006. *The Graves of Tarim. Genealogy and Mobility across the Indian Ocean*. Berkeley: University of California Press. The California World History Library.

Newton L. 2009. *A Landscape of Pilgrimage and Trade in Wadi Masila, Yemen: al-Qisha and Qabr Hud in the Islamic period*. Archaeopress. BAR International Series 1899.

Rodionov M.A. 1994. The ibex hunt ceremony in Hadramawt today. *New Arabian Studies* 2: 124-129.

Rodionov M.A. 1996. Poetry and power in Hadramawt. *New Arabian Studies* 3: 118-133.

Rodionov M.A. 1997a. Death in the poetry of Hadramawt. *Sakral'noe v istorii kul'tury*. St. Petersburg: The State Museum of the history of religions: 58-64 (in Russian).

Rodionov M.A. 1997b. Mawlā Maṭar and other awliyāʾ: on social functions of religious places in western Hadramawt. Pages 107-114 in W. Daum et al. (eds), *MareErythraeum* I. Munchen: Staatliches Museum fur Volkerkunde, Munchen.

Rodionov M.A. 2001. Towards [a] typology of visited shrines in the Wadi Hadramawt (with special reference to Mawlā Maṭar). *Raydān* 7: 263-276.

Rodionov M.A. 2004. Mashhad ʿAlī revisited: documents from Ḥaḍramawt. *Proceedings of the Seminar for Arabian Studies* 34: 307-312.

Rodionov M.A. 2007. *The Western Ḥaḍramawt: Ethnographic Field Research, 1983-91*. Halle-Wittenberg: OWZ Orientwissenschaftliche Hefte 24.

Rodionov M.A. 2008. The jinn in Hadramawt society in the last century. *Proceedings of the Seminar for Arabian Studies* 38: 277-282.

al-Ṣabbān M.A. 1998. *Visits and Customs. The Visit to the Tomb of the Prophet Hūd*. [Arabic text and] translation by Linda Boxberger and Awad Abdelrahim Abu Hulayqa. Ardmore PA: American Institute for Yemeni Studies. Yemen Translation Series No. 2.

Serjeant R.B. 1949. The Cemeteries of Tarīm (Ḥaḍramawt) (with notes on sepulture). *Le Muséon* 62: 151-159.

al-Shāṭirī S. ʿA. 2001. *Nīl al-maqṣū fī mashrūʿiyyat ziyārat nabiy alla hūd*. Tarim: Dār al-imām al-Ghazālī, maktabat tarīm al-ḥadīthah.

Vinnikov I.N. 1930. Rain, water and vegetation at the grave of pre-Islamic Arabs. *Zapiski kollegii vostokovedov* V: 367-377 (in Russian).

Author's address
Mikhail Rodionov
Tul'skaya Street 8, app. 2
St.Petersburg 191124
Russia.
e-mail: mrodio@yandex.ru

Attitudes, themes and images: an introduction to death and burial as mirrored in early Arabic poetry

James E. Taylor

Summary

On the evidence of their poetry, which mainly limits the commemoration of death to the heroic deaths of rich and powerful men, the pre-Islamic Arabs adopted a fatalistic attitude to the certainty of their mortality, being more concerned with their posthumous reputations in this world than with their prospects of an afterlife. Nevertheless it was customary to spruce up the corpse before burying it and to lament the deceased in verse, which eventually evolved from the primitive rhymed prose known as *saj*ʿ into the poetic **genre** known as *rithāʾ*. Due to the prevalence of homicide and the rule of *lex talionis* great emphasis was laid on the pursuit of blood vengeance, which was conducted in accordance with accepted customs. One modern critic has attempted to interpret the pursuit of vengeance in the light of Van Gennep's concept of 'Rites of passage' but the argument is not wholly convincing. There is no suggestion in the poetry of the deliberate mutilation of the dead on the battlefield but despoiling them of their weapons and armour was apparently the norm. Although many must have been tempted by the severe famine and starvation revealed by the *ṣaʿālīk* (vagabond) poets there are no reported cases of cannibalism.

Keywords: pre-Islamic Arabic poetry, death and burial, blood vengeance, afterlife

Introduction[1]

One has to admit that early Arabic poetry is not to everyone's taste, especially when it is read in translation, where its nuance is lost, along with the elegant language, witty paronomasia and sonorous word music that an Arab poet uses to captivate his audience. Even among those with the linguistic skill and background knowledge to wring every drop of meaning from the Arabic texts, there are some who find its images and metaphors rough and far-fetched and its lengthy, detailed descriptions tiresome. But none can deny its unique value as a rich source of information on the lives, customs and beliefs of the pre-Islamic and early Islamic *Bedu*, on the natural features, flora and fauna of the harsh desert environment from which they scratched a precarious living, and on the domestic animals that were the *raison d'être* for their nomadic life style. Even if there were some truth in the now-discredited theories of Ṭaha Ḥussain (Ḥussain 1925 & 1927) and D. S. Margoliouth (Margoliouth 1925) that the entire corpus of pre-Islamic Arabic poetry was forged,[2] one suspects that it would still not detract from the reliability of its information because any forgery would have been executed at the time when the knowledge of Beduin life was still very much alive in the collective memory; and no forger worth his salt would have risked detection by failing to ensure that the circumstantial information was impeccable in its authenticity. And so, it is the purpose of this paper to present what a representative sample of their poetry reveals about the pagan Arabs' approach to the subject of death and burial: their manner of dealing with the corpse, of coping with the loss of the deceased, and of coping with the certainty of their own mortality.

One suspects it inevitable that scholars of all disciplines who investigate the death and burial practices of the past will find their discoveries slanted towards the rich and powerful, for these were the people that attracted the attention of historians and had the resources to build themselves monumental sepulchres that survived where the simple internments of the poor did not. Early Arabic poetry is no exception. There are two reasons for this. Firstly: many of the poets were clan or tribal chieftains or the close relatives of such, who boasted in verse about the achievements of themselves and their peers. Secondly: the professional poets were mainly panegyrists who made their living composing flattering verses about the rich and powerful in the hope of attracting patronage or at least a substantial gratuity.[3] But this is not all. There was also a strong bias toward violent death in battle or on the hunting field, for the ancient poets revelled in the martial prowess and heroic pursuits of their fellow tribesmen. The deaths of those who expired peacefully in their beds, and of servants, children and women were largely ignored.[4] Indeed, one can readily recall only one lament on the death of a woman and that one was probably inspired as much by mercenary motives as by genuine concern since it eulogized the mother of the poet's princely patron.[5] On the female infanticide roundly condemned in the Holy Qurʾān. (Qurʾān: 16:57-59 & 81:8-9) the poets are silent.

Dealing with the corpse

The usual method of disposing of a corpse was burial (Lyall 1918 & 1921 p. 8 v. 19) without a coffin. Ideally, the corpse was dressed in new clothes, perfumed and its

---

[1] References to poems are not given by page number but by poem number followed by verse number with the prefixes p and v respectively. In the special case of Lyall 1918 and 1921 the former gives the English translation and the latter gives the Arabic original. They share the same poem/verse numbering. Hence the reference Lyall 1918 & 1921: p. 67 vv. 24-28 applies equally to both Arabic and English versions.

[2] See Introduction to Lyall 1918 especially page xxi for a reasoned rebuttal of the claim.

[3] E.g. see Lyall 1918 Introduction to poem 11.
[4] An exception is Lyall 1918 & 1921 poem 126 in which the poet Abū Dhuʾaib laments the death of his five sons from plague.
[5] Al-Mutanabbī's *Elegy on the death of the mother of Saif al-Daula*. (Arberry 1967: 56-63).

hair combed. It was then wrapped in a white sheet and placed in the ground,[6] usually with a pillow of sorts beneath the head.[7] Earth was heaped over the grave to form a mound that was then covered with stone slabs,[8] presumably to deter hyenas from digging up the corpse and scavenging it.[9] The corpse was, and indeed still is, carried to the place of burial on a rough timber bier. A memorial of this sad perambulation is preserved in one of the Arabic names for the stars of the Great Bear, *Banātu Naʿshin* [The Bearers of the Bier], from their slow circulation of the Pole Star, which is likened in Lyall 1918 & 1921 p. 98 v.15 to the scarcely perceptible movement of a herd of oryx cropping the grass and moving on as they feed.

For the desert nomads burial was a very sensible use of resources, since there was plenty of space for graves but scarcely enough wood to satisfy domestic needs, let alone make coffins or provide kindling for the funeral pyres favoured by the Hindus. With the rise of Islam, burning was out of the question; for although there is nothing to say that a burnt body cannot be resurrected and enter Paradise there is nevertheless a ban on cremation.[10] Although the Zoroastrian practise of exposing the corpse to ravenous birds and the elements makes no demand on scarce resources it is doubtful whether it would have appealed to the Beduin. Those poems that describe the aftermath of battle with corpses scavenged by vultures and hyenas do so in a tone that suggests this to be a desecrated and ignoble end for a valiant warrior (Lyall 1918 & 1921: p. 60 vv. 3-6 and p. 113 v. 25). Moreover, the need to build and attend on 'towers of silence' as used by Zoroastrians to expose their dead; and to transport the body there would have proved an unattractive option for a people that were constantly on the move.

It appears that it was incumbent on a tribesman to see to the burial of his fellows. In a poem lamenting the killing of his elder brother Mālik, chief of the Banū Yarbūʿ, whilst a prisoner in the Riddah Wars, Mutammim b. Nuwayra al-Yarbūʿī praises one man for throwing his cloak over the dead Mālik and later attending to his burial then scornfully condemns another who failed to do so.[11]

The poem continues with the invocation "May God bring rain to land where Mālik's grave lies, heavy rain coming in abundance from the morning clouds, and may He make it verdant". The optative, *Saqā llāhu,* 'May God bring rain', used in this verse is quite common in pre-Islamic funeral poetry and not necessarily indicative of Islamic influence, although in this instance it is. To the Arabs in their thirsty land rain is so precious and desirable a thing that the wish for the area round a grave to be fresh and verdant may not be intended literally but rather as a form of blessing on the deceased.[12]

The ethnographer Arnold van Gennep (1873-1957), coined the general term 'Rites of passage' to define and explain the initiatory rituals through which people of some cultures are led when they move from one state of being to another; their purpose being to prepare the initiate for the new state of existence. According to van Gennep's theory, rites of passage have three phases: separation from the old, an intermediate state of limbo, which he calls liminality, followed by incorporation in the new (van Gennep 1977). He views lamentation as the ritual separation of the deceased from life and the ceremonies associated with the preparation and internment of the corpse as the ritual incorporation of the deceased into the afterworld.

On the evidence of their poetry, the pagan Arabs had no belief in an afterlife and so it is not surprising that we find no mention in their poetry of anything but the first phase, lamentation.[13] It was not until the advent of Islam and its concept of an afterlife that rites of incorporation appeared. These were prescribed in great detail and even included guidance to the Muslim, alone in the desert and feeling himself about to die, as to how he should prepare himself for death and inter himself (Lane 1989: 503-521)

One poem[14] alludes to the custom of blinding and hobbling the dead man's riding camel and leaving it to perish of starvation at his graveside. Sir Charles Lyall suggests the beast to be intended for the use of the dead in some 'world of shadows'. Were this true, one would expect the man's war mare[15] to suffer a similar fate and his weapons and armour to be interred with him, along with other personal possessions of use to him in this shadow world. I am more inclined to view the sacrifice of the animal in the context of separation rites, analogous to the *takhalluṣ* or separation phase of the traditional Arabic *qaṣīdah* or ode, in which the Bedouin shrugs off a spent love affair, an inhospitable place, or a tribe that has failed him in some way and rides off his frustration in an arduous camel journey.

In the domain of poetic imagery, the theme of unburied corpses lying on the battlefield ravaged by scavenging birds and beasts is often invoked to symbolize the lowest ebb of a man's fortunes; sometimes in the context of philosophical reflection (e.g. Lyall 1918 & 1921: p. 9 vv. 31-35) and sometimes in taunting a defeated enemy on its

---

[6] Lyall 1918 & 1921: p. 81 vv. 2-4 and p. 9 v. 45 (believed to have been written before the poet's tribe accepted Islam). The shroud is obligatory in Islam.
[7] See Lyall 1918: p. 107 v. 5 and note; also note to verse 47 in Lyall 1918: p. 67 v.19.
[8] *Muʿallaqa* of Ṭarafa b. al-ʿAbd (Arberry 1957: 87).
[9] The ancient poetry contains many allusions to hyenas hovering around dying warriors in anticipation of a feast. See Lyall 1918 & 1921: p. 9 vv. 31-34.
[10] See Hughes 1885: 47, under the entry 'Burning the dead'.
[11] Lyall 1918 & 1921: p. 67. This is reckoned to be one of the finest examples of the lamentation genre.

[12] See Lyall 1918 & 1921 p. 67 vv. 24-28 especially the first hemistich of v. 28 also Lyall 1918 p. 109 note to v. 6.
[13] Van Gennep's theory does not contemplate the possibility of a society with no belief in an afterlife sprucing up a corpse in preparation for internment and so those influenced by him might argue that the preparation of the corpse described above could indicate a primitive belief in an afterlife that is not reflected in poetry. There are counter arguments to this but here is not the place to air them.
[14] Lyall 1918: p. 109 v. 13 (second hemistich) and note.
[15] It was customary for the Beduin warrior to ride to the battlefield by camel but fight the battle on horseback.

losses (Lyall 1918 & 1921: p. 60 vv. 3-6 and p. 113 v 25 also Jones 1992: 242). In the poetry of the Islamic period, there is a particularly ingenious and rather sinister use of this image by Al-Mutanabbī in his ode celebrating the recapture of the frontier post of al-Ḥadath from the Byzantines by his patron Saif al-Daula, where he conceives the previous occupation of al-Ḥadath by the Byzantines as 'madness' and likens the corpses of the slain draped around the battlements to the amulets that were hung on mad persons to drive away their madness (Arberry 1965: p.13 v. 10 and note).

Although the old poetry frequently alludes to periods of extreme famine and starvation,[16] there is nowhere suggestion that this led to cannibalism. One occasionally encounters references to 'eating the flesh of men' but it is clear from the contexts in which they occur[17] that this is figurative expression for defaming them in their absence. Likewise, the expression 'to eat up' a people is an idiom for spoiling and destroying them (Lyall 1918 & 1921: p. 88 v. 7 and p. 87 v. 3). There is one poem hinting at the mutilation of the living (Lyall 1918 & 1921: p. 67 v. 49) but, whilst gloating over the scavenging of the enemy dead by wild beasts and birds (Lyall 1918 & 1921:.p. 83 v. 3, 4, 4a), the poets nowhere allude to the deliberate mutilation of the slain. However, the biographer Muḥammad b. Ishaq of Medina relates in his *Sirat Rasūlallāh* that after the Battle of Uḥud, at which the Muslims were put to flight by the Meccans under Abū Sufyān b. Harb, his wife Hind and her handmaidens cut off the ears of the Muslim dead and made necklaces of them. Then Hind cut out the liver of Muḥammad's uncle Hamza and gnawed on it, because she blamed him for the deaths of her father, her brother and her uncles at the earlier Battle of Badr.

Although mutilation of the dead may have been the exception, despoiling the dead of their weapons and armour appears to have been the norm.[18] Indeed, given the extreme poverty of the times, one suspects that the corpses of the slain would have been robbed of everything valuable. There is a hint of this in the Shī'ī passion plays lamenting the martyrdom of Al-Ḥussain at Karbala, in which he goes into battle wearing beneath his usual robe a ragged one that is too worthless to steal, so that his corpse will not be left naked on the battlefield (Pelly 1879 quoted in Hughes 1885: 414).

Coping with the loss of the deceased

The ancient poetry mentions only two aspects of coping with the loss of the deceased: lamentation and vengeance; and, due to the frequency of homicide among the pagan Arabs, the two were often linked.

Perhaps the best known and most spectacular display of public lamentation in the Muslim world is the one that occupies the first ten days of the month of Muḥarram, when those of the *Shī'a* persuasion still mourn the untimely death of the Prophet's grandson, Al-Ḥussain, at Karbala on the tenth of Muḥarram AH 61 [10th October 680 CE], the event that provided a focal point for smouldering *Shī'ī* grievances and set the seal on the *Sunni/Shī'ī* schism. Although Al-Ḥussain's martyrdom is movingly commemorated in drama (Pelly, 1879) it received scant attention from those Arab poets of the time whose work has survived. This is not hard to understand when we bear in mind that, in the period immediately after the death of Al-Ḥussain, the Muslim nation was ruled by the dynasty directly responsible for his death; and even after the subsequent, bloody regime change, the caliphate was still in the hands of a *Sunni* dynasty.

None that have witnessed the fervency and zeal with which the Daughters of Shem vocalise their grief at the death of a loved one are likely to quarrel with v 32 of al-Shanfarā's *Lāmiyyat al-ᶜArab* in which he likens the sound of wolves howling in the desert to that of bereaved women making lament on a high place. Elsewhere (Lyall 1918 & 1921: p. 8 v. 19) the poet Al-Ḥādirah likens those rolling on the ground, weeping round a corpse awaiting burial to drunken youths outstretched by the wine-booth, shedding maudlin tears.

From such noisy beginnings the poetic *Rithāʾ* or lamentation *genre*[19] is believed to have evolved. According to Alan Jones (1992:25):

"There is some evidence to show that the earliest *marāthī* were rhymed chants uttered at funerals by women mourners and that the *sajᶜ* [rhymed prose] used in them was of the same register as the utterances of the *kāhins* [soothsayers]. At some unknown period, presumably in the fifth century, there was a change to verse".

and according to Lyall:[20]

"The function of composing dirges on the dead was in ancient Arabia very largely exercised by women, and some of the finest elegies are of their composition. Indeed it may be said that the great bulk of the poems composed by women consists of lamentations for the dead. The official mourners at funerals were always women".

Poems bewailing the dead seldom conformed to the stereotyped form of the traditional *qaṣīdah* or ode, which admits of three movements: the amatory prelude (*nasīb*), the 'disengagement' cast in the form of an arduous camel

---

[16] Lyall 1918 and 1921: p. 71 v. 2; and ʿUrwa b. al-Ward *Man huwa l-Suᶜlūk* (Jones 1992: 127).
[17] E.g., Lyall 1918 & 1921: p. 77 v. 6; p. 40 v. 73, and Qurʾān: 49:12.
[18] E.g., Lyall 1918 & 1921: p. 83 v. 4a. Also Lyall 1918 p. 88 note to v. 5, which describes how a famous sword changed hands several times.

[19] "As Pellat points out in his article *marthiya* in Encyclopaedia of Islam (second edition), in theory *rithāʾ* refers to the genre, *marthiya* to a single lament and *marāthī* to a number of laments. However, the Arabs themselves ignored this distinction from early times, and single poems are known as *Rithāʾ Arbad* and so on" (Jones 1992: 25).
[20] Lyall 1918: Introduction to p. 69. Also see Lyall 1918 and 1921: p. 121 v. 11.

journey, known as *takhalluṣ*, and the final section, dealing with the real motive (*gharaḍ/qaṣad*) of the poem. The omission of the amatory prelude[21] is understandable. According to the ninth century critic ʿAbd Allāh ibn Muslim ibn Qutayba its function was to awaken the interest of the poet's listeners[22] and capture their attention, but one suspects that the mere announcement of a prominent man's death was sufficient in itself to make them prick up their ears, especially when uttered with the dramatic intensity of Taʾabbaṭa Sharrā in his *Qaṣīdah Lāmiyya* (Jones 1992: 231):

"A piece of news has come to us: terrible [news, so] serious that the most serious matter becomes dwarfed [by] it.
"There, in a ravine that is on this side of Salʿ, lies a dead man, whose blood is not [yet] avenged"

The pre-Islamic Arabs believed that when a slain man died unavenged, an owl emerged from his skull and haunted his grave, shrieking, *isqūnī, isqūnī*, 'Give me to drink! Give me to drink!' until the blood of vengeance was shed, when the owl's thirst was appeased and it ceased to cry. There are a number of oblique references to this belief in the old poetry,[23] which is thought to have arisen from a species of small owl (*hāmah*) that is said to frequent burial places (Lane 1997: 3046). A mildly amusing reference occurs in Lyall 1918 and 1921: p. 31 v. 3, where the poet, Ḥurthān of ʿAdwān (known as Dhu-l-Iṣbaʿ), exclaims:

"O ʿAmr, if thou leavest not abuse and detraction of me,
I will smite thee in that place where the owl cries 'Give me to drink!'"

In other words, 'If you don't shut up, I'll punch your head!'

There was no codified system of law prevailing throughout the lands of pagan Arabia. Relationships between independent tribes were regulated by a shifting pattern of alliances and agreements and, when these failed, war. But there appear to have been some generally accepted customs (*aʿrāf*), governing the pursuit of vengeance. Firstly: revenge for the slaying of a man was not necessarily pursued against his slayer but against a man of the slayer's tribe equal to the slain man in position and quality [his *bawāʾ*], and whose slaying would be a proper requital for the first killing.[24] Secondly: prior to the Qurʾānic recommendation to remit blood vengeance,[25] it was deemed dishonourable to accept blood-money for slain members of a tribe, instead of exacting blood for blood.[26] Thus the poet Jābir b. Ḥunayy reproaches his tribe for displaying a mercenary spirit that tarnished their renown as fighters (Lyall 1918 & 1921: p. 42 v. 15). On the other hand, we find the poet Ṣuraim b. Maʿshar bitterly railing against the men of Taghlib (Lyall 1918 & 1921: p. 66 vv. 1 – 9) who, in spite of their great wealth of camels, expelled him from the tribe rather than help pay blood-money for a man that he had killed. Thirdly: there are frequent allusions to vows of vengeance, and the forswearance of such luxuries as perfume, wine,[27] and trimming the hair, but it is unclear whether these are matters of custom or individual volition. Fourthly: as a condition of the peace settlements that ended the habitual spasms of inter-tribal warfare it was usual for the slain to be counted up, and if it was found that the number of the dead of one side exceeded that of the other, the blood-price of the excess number was paid by the side which had slain them (Lyall 1918: Introduction to p. 108).

In a thought-provoking paper, Stetkevych (1986) explores what she perceives to be ritual and sacrificial elements in the poetry of blood-vengeance and argues the act of vengeance as a rite of passage, basing her observations on two poems: one by Durayd ibn al-Ṣimmah and the other by Muhalhil ibn Rabīʿah. In statistical terms two poems selected for their concordance with the hypothesis being argued would be regarded as a biased sample, and too small to justify general application. But the allusions elsewhere to vows of vengeance and the forswearing of luxuries might well be interpreted as having ritual significance and cases of the cold blooded executions of unransomed prisoners and captives held culpable for the slaying of members of their captors' clans could equally be construed as sacrificial.[28] Unfortunately, the author undermines her own credibility by flights of fancy that owe more to a fertile imagination than to the words of the text, the most questionable when, with reference to the line "The hyenas drag off their limbs and get pregnant on them; They lie, even now, unburied" she says:

"The hyenas in this poem do not merely feast on the corpses of the dead but couple with them. This rather unfair advantage that the female hyenas take of the fallen warriors once rigor mortis has set in is

---

[21] Lyall 1918 and 1921: p. 54 is one of the few exceptions.
[22] The ancient poetry was delivered orally by professional reciters. It was not committed to writing until the late Ummayad and early ʿAbbāsid periods.
[23] E.g. ʿUrwa b. al-Ward *Man huwa l-Ṣuʿlūk* (Jones 1992:127), Lyall 1918 and 1921: p. 60 v. 3, Lyall 1918: p. 118 v. 12 and note, also p. 31 v. 3 and note.
[24] This strict literal interpretation of *lex talionis* could lead to some odd situations. Lyall 1918 and 1921: p. 12 tells of a war between the Banū Ṣirmah and the Banū Sahm that began when one of the Banū Ṣirmah killed a *dhimmi* [a person under protection of a tribe] of the Banū Sahm who killed a *dhimmi* of the Banū Ṣirmah in requital. Banū Ṣirmah retaliated and then in turn did Banū Sahm. This tit-for-tat killing eventually led to open conflict. There is a certain logic behind the killing of one *dhimmi* in requital for another because the killing of a person under the protection of a tribe impugns the honour of the tribe by challenging its ability to protect its clients, an insult that can only be requited by similar action against the killer's tribe.
[25] With the advent of Islam remission of retaliation as an act of charity was recommended. See Qurʾān: 5: 48. However, the practice was not explicitly condemned.
[26] This should not be confused with the ransoming of a prisoner against whom there was no demand for his blood. See Lyall 1918 and 1921: p. 94 v. 5.
[27] Jones 1992: 241 *Qaṣīda Lāmiyya* of Taʾabbaṭa Sharrā vv. 23 & 24, Lyall 1918: p. 109 vv. 6 and 11 and note to v 6.
[28] E.g., Lyall 1918 & 1921 p. 30. Also see poem 11 for a death in captivity of an unransomed prisoner. It is not known whether this was a deliberate act or merely neglect.

described in detail by al-Jāḥiẓ in *Kitāb al-Ḥayawān* and al-Nuwayrī in *Nihāyat al-ʿArab*."

Although claiming the support of distinguished sources, the act Stetkevych describes is physically impossible.[29] References to hyenas becoming pregnant on corpses have been discussed in the *Maqāmāt* of al-Ḥarīrī where the commentator gives the more credible explanation that this expression is used as a picturesque metaphor for the bellies of the animals distended by a surfeit of flesh.

It appears that not all our poets treated the matter of blood vengeance with quite the seriousness one associates with ritual, for Al-Marrār b. Munqidh jokes that, were he to die of love, his mistress would be guilty of his death, and the duty of retaliation, by slaying her, would be laid upon his brothers[30] while Murraqish the younger likens commencement of a blood feud to the start of a race (Lyall 1918 and 1921: p. 58 vv. 1 & 2) and others shirked their duty of retaliation (e.g. see Lyall 1918: p. 87 v. 4 and note).

Coping with the certainty of one's own mortality

The concept of an afterlife

Although there is ample evidence that the pagan Arabs accepted the existence of divine beings and supernatural creatures, one finds no reference in their poetry to the concept of an afterlife that brought comfort to other peoples and constrained their behaviour. It is highly probable they were exposed to the idea of life after death through their land and sea trade with foreign countries and through their contact both with the Christian and Jewish tribes living in parts of pre-Islamic Arabia, and with the Christian and Jewish merchants that monopolised the manufacture and distribution of the wine for which the *Bedu* had a considerable appetite. Apparently they were unconvinced by it, for Qurʾān: 50: 12 - 14 condemns the denial of the hereafter by specified communities of the Arab tradition, whilst a number of other verses[31] counter the stock argument of Muḥammad's detractors: "How can a heap of rotten bones rise up and be held accountable for the past deeds of their former owner?"

From the evidence of their poetry it seems that the pagan Arabs were more concerned with their posthumous reputations in this world than with their prospects in a future one.[32] Lacking the comforting prospect of an afterlife, they reconciled themselves to the ever-present menace of death, and, particularly, untimely death, by philosophical reflections on the vagaries of a rarely benevolent fortune and on death's inevitability.[33]

Euphemism

Euphemistic turns of phrase, similar to those used by other cultures to shrink from the mention of death, are quite common in *marāthī* and in many other poems dealing with death and fighting but it is difficult to say whether they are genuine euphemisms or just manifestations of the drive to create a memorable poetic image or an elegant simile. They occur even in satires or taunts directed against an enemy tribe, where one would hardly expect the poet to soften the impact of his words.[34] Moreover, there is a recognisable tendency among Arabs to refer to a person or thing by attribute or description instead of by name[35] and neither in Arabic literature nor in my dealings with Arabs have I encountered any reluctance to speak frankly of unpleasant things and on subjects that we regard as taboos. Consequently I am inclined to regard them as epithets or colourful metaphors rather than euphemisms.

L'envoi

I do not pretend this paper to be the last word on the subject but rather an appetizer; a taste of what might lie in store for those with more years at their disposal than I can reasonably anticipate for myself and with the skill, the diligence and the imagination to unlock the ethnological treasures buried in early Arabic poetry.

Acknowledgements

I cannot allow this opportunity to pass without acknowledging my debt to my former tutors Professor Kamal Abu Deeb, Dr Stephan Sperl, and Mr Muhammad Said whose enthusiasm for the old poetry eventually rubbed off on me. Nor yet can I overlook the combination of practical experience, sound common sense and academic brilliance in the late Sir Charles Lyall's work that has been a source of influence, inspiration and guidance to me. I have used his translations in the various quotations.

---

[29] Erection of the penis is due to the pressure of blood in the *corpora cavernosa* and blood pressure drops to zero as soon as the heart stops. With no blood pressure there can be no erection. Rigor mortis is due to chemical changes in the muscles, which have nothing to do with penile erection. Moreover, the unorthodox reproductive tract of the female hyena complicates copulation with its own kind. It would make copulation with a recumbent human being impossible. It has been suggested to me that a hyena might appear to be engaged in copulation whilst straddling a corpse to get at the highly desirable entrails, more so because of the hyena's crouching gait.

[30] Lyall 1918 and 1921: p. 16 v. 94 also see Lyall 1918 and 1921: Appendix poem 3 vv. 7 & 8.

[31] Qurʾān: 17: 49; 19: 66; 50: 3, and 79: 10-11.

[32] See The *Muʿallaqa* of Tarafa in Arberry 1957: 89 line 6 et seq, also Lyall 1918 and 1921: p. 30, and p. 67 v. 22.

[33] E.g., Lyall 1918 & 1921: p.1 v. 25; p. 9 vv. 38-45; p. 20 vv. 31 & 32; p. 54 vv. 9-17; p. 65 vv. 1-5; p. 74 vv. 10 & 12; p. 80 v. 1; and especially p. 126.

[34] E.g., see Lyall 1918 and 1921: p. 85 v. 7 'Verily the Sons of ʿIjl administered to you a morning draught that caused you to forget [all past things], delicious, hot!', where the 'morning draught' is sarcastic allusion to a sound drubbing.

[35] E.g., see Lyall 1918: p. 74: Introduction and vv 4-9. Also the 99 names of Allāh, which are all adjectives descriptive of His various attributes. Moreover, one frequently encounters picturesque epithetic expressions such as: *al-aḥmarān*, 'the two red ones' i.e., wine and meat; *al-aswad wa'l-aḥmar*, 'the black and the red' i.e., all humanity (Wehr 1980: 205).

References

Arberry A.J. 1957. *The Seven Odes: the first chapter in Arabic literature*. London: George Allen & Unwin.

Arberry A.J. 1965. *Arabic poetry: a primer for students*. Cambridge: CUP.

Arberry A.J. 1967. *Poems of al-Mutanabbī: a selection with introduction, translation and notes*. Cambridge: CUP.

Gennep A van. 1977. *Rites of Passage*, translated by M.B. Vizedom and L. Caffee. London: Routledge.

Hughes T.P. 1885. *A Dictionary of Islam: being a cyclopaedia of the doctrines, rites, ceremonies, and customs, together with the technical and theological terms, of the Muhammadan religion*. London: W.H. Allen.

Ḥusain Ṭ. 1925. *Fī 'sh-shiʿr al-jāhilī* (On Pre-Islamic Poetry), Cairo: Maṭbaʿat al-Iʿtimad.

Ḥusain Ṭ. 1927. *Fī l-adab al-jāhilī* (On Pre-Islamic literature) Cairo: Maṭbaʿat al Iʿtimad.

Jones A. 1992. *Early Arabic poetry. Vol. 1. Marāthī and Suʿluk poems*. Reading: Ithaca Press.

Lane E.W. 1997. *An Arabic–English Lexicon* (Facsimile of original 1863 edition). Beirut: Librairie du Liban.

Lane E.W. 1989. *Manners and Customs of the Modern Egyptians* (Reprint of the 1895 edition). London: East-West Publications [First published 1836].

Lyall C.J. 1918. *The Mufaḍḍaliyāt: an anthology of ancient Arabian odes*, Vol 2 Translations and notes. Oxford: Oxford University Press.

Lyall C.J. 1921. *The Mufaḍḍaliyāt: an anthology of ancient Arabian odes*, Vol 1 Arabic Texts. Oxford: Oxford University Press

Margoliouth D. S. 1925. The Origins of Arabic Poetry. *Journal of the Royal Asiatic Society* Part 3 (July): 417-449.

Pelly L. 1879. *The miracle play of Hasan and Hussain collected from oral tradition by Col. Lewis Pelly*, revised with explanatory notes by Arthur N Wollaston. London: W.H. Allen

Stetkevych S.P. 1986. Ritual and sacrificial elements in the poetry of blood-vengeance: two poems by Durayd ibn al-Ṣimmah and Muhalhil ibn Rabīʿah. *Journal of Near Eastern Studies* 45/1: 31-42.

Wehr H. 1980. *A dictionary of Modern Written Arabic*. Beirut. Librairie du Liban.

Author's address
James E. Taylor
52 North View Crescent
Epsom, Surrey KT18 5UR
United Kingdom.
Email: jasedta@ntlworld.com

Jewish burial customs in Yemen

Dina Dahbany-Miraglia

You cannot hold a good wo/man down.

Summary
Jewish Yemen was and remains one of the most conservative of Jewish cultures, denying women access to literacy and by extension access to the religious laws that control their lives. Yet individual women (and men) deliberately violated religious law and local custom, even under the onus of death and dying. The tale presented here illustrates some of the limitations of de jure control. Even when dying and possibly in fear of the next world, yet individuals will go their own way.

Keywords: Jewish Yemen, Jewish law, women's and men's rights, marital law, death and dying, de jure defiance, the supernatural

Introduction[1]

Jews have lived in Yemen, Aden and the Hadhramaut for more than 2500 years.[2] Data from Aden include gravestones inscribed in Hebrew beginning from the third century BCE to the mid-twentieth CE (Klein-Franke 2005). Then as now Muslim as well as Jewish cemeteries' locations must have been allocated by the local sheikhs who have controlled their tribal lands for thousands of years. Jewish gravesites were, for the most part, located near towns' and villages' Jewish quarters in the least fruitful soils, far from the Muslim cemeteries and far from Muslim residential neighborhoods. In Aden they often surrounded the local בתי כנסת/synagogues (Michal 1990: 19).

Jewish (and Islamic) law requires speedy burial. Exceptions include dying on the Sabbath and Yom Kippur/the Day of Atonement. Since earliest times and even with codifications, Jewish burial practices continue to vary considerably. For the most part the dead are buried naked, sometimes dressed in a pair of pants and a shirt, but most often in a shroud. A man must be buried wrapped in his tallith/טלית or prayer shawl. Men are referred to with respect to clothing; women's burial clothes are referred to as an afterthought. In-ground interments are preferred.[3] Tombs and elaborate clothing plus shrouds are discouraged (Babylonian Talmud Ketubboth 8b, Semahot 9) as are grave goods and grave robbing.[4]

With the codification of the Mishnah (oral Torah) in the Babylonian and Jerusalem Talmuds during the third to sixth centuries of the Christian era, and later, the further fixing of details in Joseph Caro's שולחן אורוך/Shulkhan Arukh and Maimonides' משנה תורה/Mishnah Torah, burial practices became highly prescriptive. From the moment of death and even throughout the lifetimes of the survivors, activities, such as bathing, shrouding and interment, assigning different cadres of individuals to carry out the sequences of tasks and mourning rituals, the kinds of prayers chanted at prescribed times, became fixed. *Din minhag wa minhag din* דין מנהג ומנהג דין 'Law is custom and custom law' frequently overrode religious prescriptions. The severe limitations imposed by the Talmudists on Jewish women meticulously detailed in the Babylonian's 7+ tractates of Seder Nashim, The Management of Women, were often ignored when personal goals were to be achieved—even when dying.

The story below illustrates how individual predilection successfully defies local custom time and again and even more significant, successfully superseded religious law (Dahbany-Miraglia 1999).[5]

The Tale

In small town in southern Yemen there lived a lazy but lucky Jew. An orphan, he acquired a well-to-do widow who was sickly, ill-tempered, childless, and almost ugly.[6]

---

[1] Special thanks to Ralph Romanelli and his terrific techies, and to Marcia Kovler, Maria Isabel Fernandes, Sandy Marcus and Connie Williams – all of Queensborough Community College's IT and library respectively, and to Brenda Gomez and Beth Posner of CUNY's Graduate Center library for their exceptional skills and unfailing kindnesses locating books and articles so quickly! More thanks go to the wonderful three of CUNY's MEMEAC for their constant support: Beth Baron, Anny Bakalian and Mehdi Bozorgmehr.
[2] According to Hart (1963: 145) Jews appeared in Yemen around ACE 70, just after the destruction of the Second Temple. If the biblical account of Bilkis, Queen of Sheba/Saba travelling to Solomon's kingdom in Judea is in any way accurate, it is likely that Jews were already in Yemen long before then, probably as traders. It is even more likely that when Bilkis returned to Marib in east-central Yemen a number accompanied her.
[3] For an excellent breakdown of the basic prescribed rituals associated with death and burial see http://en.wikipedia.org/wiki/Bereavement_in_Judaism. Key primary sources are, of course, the Babylonian Talmud's volume שמחות/Simahot/Rejoicing, Joseph Caro's Shulhan Arukh (1975, 3: 346-355) and Maimonides' Maqala fi Tihiyyat Ha-Metim (Finkel 1939). Also see Bender 1895, Gamlieli 2008, and Nahum 1962: 170-175. Not surprisingly Muslim funerary regulations and practices were very similar (c.f. Halevi 2004, Tritton 1938).

[4] In Yemen preferred burial sites were caves that could be sealed or tombs which were too expensive (cf. Klein-Frank 2005). Ancient burials in Jerusalem and elsewhere in the holy land were almost always swift, deeply dug in the ground or entombed, either in caves or free-standing buildings. Although Biblical accounts of interring individuals such as King David with an enormous number of items, since the 3rd century A.C.E. burying household objects, food, drink, flowers and jewelry with the dead has since been strongly discouraged (cf. Rahmani 1981a, 1981b, 1982). The Talmudist R. Gamliel observed that the custom of dressing the deceased in expensive clothing put such a terrible burden on the relatives of the deceased, that they would "abandon the body and run." No doubt they were also concerned about the predations of grave robbers (Babylonian Talmud Ketubboth 8b, Bender 1895: 263).
[5] This narrative is one of many told by Oldtimer women during their round robin visits every Saturday afternoon in the early 1980s.
[6] In Jewish law women are qinyan/قنىن/קנין moveable property. As such they are acquired. The "marriage" ceremony is an act of possession.

In spite of her faults the lazy man was glad to get her. She possessed one of the two most important requirements of an Esheth Hayil: wealth.[7] She was a gifted embroiderer who was much in demand. She brought with her a wealth of household goods: cast iron and ceramic pots, pans, plates and bowls, metal, wooden and straw utensils, all sorts of lamps as well as bedding and rugs, straw mats and tables, baskets with and without covers, and a variety of lidded clay storage jars. She also brought to her new home many items of jewelry, embroidered dresses, pants, headdresses and shawls.[8]

The woman's most beautiful and expensive outfit was a white, intricately detailed embroidered wedding dress. Gold and silver threads were stitched in tiny whorls, knots, waves and loops across its breast and halfway down the front. The front consisted of twisted gold- and silver-thread loops fastened with tiny exquisitely filigreed gold and silver balls. Attached to the sleeves were wide bands of cotton-backed silk similarly embroidered in tiny stitches. The matching pants' intricately embroidered cuffs reached up to just above the dress's hem. Her wedding outfit and her jewelry were in great demand. She earned a pretty penny renting them.

Initially her second owner/husband was delighted with the wealth she brought. He no longer had to scrounge for a living. He continued to make the small amounts of ננבד/יין/wine and نبيت/ערקי/'araqi (a brandy made from dried raisins) that gave him a small living. But he no longer had to beg or to work as an itinerant labourer to make up the slack. Instead he lay about most of the day chewing فات/גאת/qat, drinking 'araqi and smoking the shíshah/שישה/شيشة/mada'ah/מדעה/المدعة, the waterpipe.[9]

Although Jewish law permitted him to use and even sell her property without her permission, his "wife" refused to allow him access.[10] Her "stinginess" angered him. He

---

[7] The second is obedience to her owner's every wish. Esheth Hayil comprises the last 22 verses of Mishlei/משלי/Proverbs. An Alef to Tau acrostic or "Golden ABC (Toy 1977: 52)," it was most likely composed in its present form during the Achaemenid era, around 550–330 BCE, just in time to be added to the end of Proverbs in the Tanakh/תנך/Taj/תג/the Old Testament (Brenner 1993:11). Crawford H. Toy (1899: 542) comments. "[It] is often rhetorically bad, inducing unnatural diction in the order of couplets." Usually chanted during the Friday evening blessing over the wine in Hebrew, the language few women understood, Esheth Hayil lists in great detail the requirements a man demands in his woman. As Toy points out, "Nothing is said of [her] intellectual interests or pursuits (1899: 542)." See Dahbany-Miraglia 2009 for a discussion and analysis of Esheth Hayil.

[8] In most of Yemen the crafter Jews and the gabayil, the Muslim tribes who owned and farmed their lands, lived together in symbiotic relationships. With the exception of jewelry manufacture which were an almost entirely male-only occupation, the trades of weaving, tanning, embroidery, sewing, pottery, carpentry, construction, smithing and poem-singing (among Muslims as well) were family businesses. When one member exhibited unusual gifts and whose work was in great demand, woman or man, s/he usually claimed a larger share of the family's earnings. See Dahbany-Miraglia 1999 and Kofsky (1988: 332-3).

Most of the proscriptions and prescriptions pertaining to this ceremony can be found in the Babylonian Talmud's tractate Qiddushin/קדושין, Consecration. "the last tractate in the order Nashim in the Mishnah, Tosefta, and both Talmuds…[which] deals with acquisition of slaves and animals, of land and chattels, and with other extraneous matters including acquiring women by money, writ, and by intercourse, forced or consensual (Ehrman 2007:145-146). "A father is entitled to arrange the consecration or qiddushin [transference] of his daughter, whether she is a qetannah [pre-pubertal] or a na'arah [almost pubertal, 12 to 12 ½ years old] without her consent (Babylonian Talmud Qiddushin 44b and Shul£an Arukh EH 37:1 & 3). ..if a father effects קדושין/qiddushin, consecration, for his daughter by accepting kesef-qiddushin [money for transfer] for her, she is considered a married woman and cannot remarry until the death of her husband or her divorce from him (Babylonian Talmud Kiddushin 44b and Rashi; Tur and Beit Yosef, EH 37; Shul£an Aruch EH 37:1, 3)." A writ of "divorce" is actually a get, גט قت a writ of manumission. Only the owner/husband can free his "wife." The only change in 2000 years, monogamy replacing polygyny, was forced on Ashkenazim (Yiddish-speakers from Europe) by Christians about 1200 years ago, and finalized by the Rabbinical Synod of Worms in the 11th century (Mielziner 1884: 30). See Dahbany-Miraglia 2001 for a discussion. Also see the other Babylonian Talmud's tractates in the section Seder Nashim, the Management of Women, for more details "The wife was regarded as property (see Ex. xx. 17; comp. the Hebrew terms "ba'al" = "husband" and "be'ulah" = "wife"; literally, the "owner" or "master" and the "owned"). She was, however, valuable property (Singer et al 2003)." Some of the Talmudists deprecated acquiring a woman for her wealth (Qiddushin. 70a; "Seder Eliyahu Zuta," ch. iii., ed. Friedmann, 1902; Shulhan 'Arukh, Eben ha-'Ezer, 3, 1, Rothkoff 2007) but halfheartedly. See notes 10 and 11 below for further explication.

[9] Qat is *Catha edulis*, the leaves of a shrub that grows wild and in cultivation in Yemen and across the Red Sea in, for example, Somalia and Ethiopia. It is usually chewed and has mild narcotic properties, creating a sense of euphoria and staying hunger pangs. Some varieties are said to enhance sexual potency in men as well. The made-from-dried fruits brandy, 'araqi , is supposed to deepen qat's qualities. The waterpipe or shisheh/mada'ah, with or without tobacco, helps to hydrate.

[10] Until the late 19th and early 20th centuries, in common with most Jewish women, those in Yemen were illiterate in the religious languages of Hebrew and Aramaic. One result was minimal knowledge of the complex Talmudic prescriptions concerning their statuses and rights, particularly their property rights, throughout their life cycles (Dahbany-Miraglia 1999). Some, like the woman in the tale, ignored the laws designating females קנין/qinyan/moveable property when it suited them. Many were openly contemptuous of the favouring of men and what little they knew of their owner/husband's rights over the woman. One of the most offending was awarding a man's right to מלוג/ muluug, usufruct or free use of his "wife's" property and its fruit (Epstein 2005: 114, Zeitlin 1969: 97) without reciprocity. This principle of ownership, of the property of a man's property ("wife"), is called מלוג usufruct. The "use of fruit." "The Talmudists… operated on the assumption that a man contracting a marriage with a woman expected to benefit from the "usufruct" of all properties she owned, and that his decision to marry her was based, at least in part, on this expectation. If she were to sell or give away part of her wealth, the husband would be cheated. Once applied to wife-owned property, this principle led to further action aimed at assuring the husband income from all of his wife's property, regardless of when she acquired it, including even what she owned before contracting the marriage initially (Morrell 1982: 284)." In other words, Jewish men married for money and were encouraged to do so without compunction or shame. An owner can sell his usufruct right and can get away with selling her property with or without her permission (Epstein 2005: 103-119). Levine (1968: 281) states "If a woman died while married, her husband inherited all that she owned as of the moment of death…her children were not protected by arrangements guaranteeing them a portion of her dowry." In essence the Talmudists encourage a master to be, according to the ארוך שוחן/ Shulhan Arukh, a רשע/rosho'/evil man: "What is mine is mine and what is hers is mine." The Babylonian Talmud is quite clear "That which a woman has acquired her husband has acquired (Nazir 24a-24b.)." A woman's earnings after marriage belong to her owner when he is providing her maintainance. An acquired woman remains a ward unless widowed or divorced (Morrell 1982). The activist Ernestine Rose hit the nail on the head. "Father, guardian, husband-master still. One conveys her, like a piece of property, over to the other (Kofsky 1988:317)." Woman is a slave, from the cradle to the grave. See Frumkin 1930 for a brief and concise summary of Jewish women's legal disabilities and Koren (2005: 29-30) for further analyses regarding Jewish women as property.

wanted to use her wealth to buy a little girl who was young, pretty and healthy. Her family was poor. Her father was more than willing to sell her for two Maria Theresa thalers, a high price. Since his current "wife" could not have children Jewish law permitted, even adjured he acquire another.[11] Firmly holding onto the purse strings, she refused to even consider allowing him to acquire another "wife."

Frustrated by her lack of cooperation he became enraged, screaming and yelling at her, stopping just short of beating her. He was afraid of the neighbors and of her family who were protective of her. And he was terrified of her casting him with the Evil Eye (Garidi 1945, Ulmer 1994).

For more than a year the two lived together. She did not become pregnant. Instead her illness worsened. When she became bedridden he was forced to take care of her. As was customary in the Yemen community women—relatives, friends and neighbors—would visit when they could and help in her care. But the bulk of her care devolved onto him. Boiling with rage he was sorely tempted to kill her. A coward with a strong sense of self-preservation, he gritted his teeth and stayed his hand.

It soon became apparent that she was dying. Eager to take over her property he prayed fervently that she would die quickly. He would buy the other "wife" and live the rest of his life in comfort.

Well aware that her owner/husband was anxious to get his hands on her possessions, the dying woman violated Talmudic law. She distributed most of her wealth to her natal family, friends and neighbors. She bequeathed her owner/husband her remaining household possessions and only a few pieces of her cheapest jewelry. She then adjured her owner/husband and the rest of the community to bury her in her wedding gown and headdress, and to place in her grave her remaining property —the jewelry, headdresses, and dresses she had created and acquired. She demanded that in addition to a headstone her owner/husband cover her grave with a stone basalt. In that region only men of consequence had their graves covered with stone blocks. Threatening to haunt anyone who denied her last wish the dying woman made those around her—women and men—vow to obey her wishes.[12]

Her owner/husband was livid. How dare she deny him his inheritance! She was his property and her belongings were his![13] He refused to allow a stupid, illiterate woman to best him. In his fury he devised a plan.

When she died the men dug her grave in the hard soil of the small Jewish cemetery just outside the town's Jewish quarter. The women in her family washed her body with warm water, dressed her in her wedding gown and headdress before gently placing her remaining necklaces, bracelets and rings on her body. Finally they wrapped her in a large white cotton shroud.

Jews believe that the newly dead spirit is confused and angry. Reading Tehillim/Psalms helps the departed prepare for the next world (cf. Cohen 1999). Reading Tehillim/Psalms aloud is believed to placate the dead who may have been powerless in life, but in death become superhuman beings (Paton 1910: 80, c.f. Cohen 1999, Trachtenberg 1970).

Refusing to hire another man to do the honors, the widower insisted on reading Tehillim/Psalms over his "wife's" body the night before her burial. When certain he was alone with his dead "wife" the widower unwrapped the winding sheet, making sure he knew where each item of jewelry was located. He could not wait to put her in the ground. He was ready to acquire another wife to which, under Jewish law he was entitled, even during the seven-day mourning period.

The next morning his "wife" was interred. A procession of male family, friends, neighbors and two professional women mourners wailed their way to her grave (Gamliel 2008, Halevi 2004).[14] After rending the collar of his shirt

---

[11] Baskin (1989) citing Neusner concurs with the view that according women the status of property clearly illustrates the Talmudists' hostility towards them. A recalcitrant woman could forfeit her rights to maintainance, ransom and burial as documented in her כתובה/ketuboh/writ of ownership. A barren one should be replaced.

[12] Another blatant violation of religious law. Men can make vows at will, but "Judaism recognizes the sovereign authority of the father [and the owner/husband] over his daughter's ["wife's"] vows (Rosenblatt 1935-1936: 241)." See Numbers 30.6 and Bacher & Lauterbach (2003) for more details.

[13] "If a woman died while married, her husband inherited all that she owned as of the moment of death. In such situations, her children were not protected by arrangements guaranteeing them a portion of her dowry, but rather by the [כתובה/ketuboh/contract of acquisition] itself (Levine 1968 281)." Also see Babylonian Talmud (Mishnah Yebimot VII: 1: Mishnah, Ketuboth VIII: 1, IX: f., Bekoroth VIII: 10, Tosefta, Bekoroth VI: 9, 541. Baba' Batra' VIII: hal. 5. TB Baba' Batra' lllb). Like it or not a woman may not ordinarily alienate her property and thereby prejudice her husband's right to its inheritance (Babylonian Talmud Ketuboth 78a-78b). A Jewish woman's rights with respect to inheriting property from her parents varied considerably. When she died one might expect that her children or even natal family members would inherit from her. As Hiers (1993:129) states "In the story of Tobit, apparently contrary to the law of intestate succession set out in Numbers 27, when Tobias' mother-in-law and father-in-law died, their daughter, Sarah, evidently their only child, Numbers 29, did not inherit their property. Instead, Tobias, Sarah's husband, inherited it (Tobit 14:12-13)." In Yemen a man expected to inherit his wife's property. Also see Zeitlin (1969:97-99) regarding Jewish women's property rights and Schatzmiller (1995) for similarities between Jewish women's property rights and those of Andalusian Muslim women.

[14] In spite of Judaic and Islamic proscriptions professional women mourners have been practicing their craft for thousands of years (Gamlieli 2008, Halevy 2004). Jewish owners/ husbands were enjoined to lament their dead "wives" (Babylonian Talmud Ketuboth 15, Mo'ed Katan 46b, 8a, 24a, 27a-28b). Unless they were professional mourners Jewish women were forbidden the cemetery based on Joseph Caro's comment that men may become sexually excited by their presence during the funeral procession (Golinkin 2001:1). From the 1940s to the 1970s the American Yemenite Jewish חברה קדישה/Hebroh Qadishoh/cemetery association forbade women from attending the burials of their relatives. They could visit the cemetery when the community went en masse once a year before the High Holy days.

the widower read Kaddish, the prayer for the dead. Almost everyone returned with him to his house where he began "sitting Shiv'oh/שבעה" the mandatory seven-day mourning period.

Every morning and late afternoon a quorum of at least ten men congregated in his home for morning and afternoon: evening prayers in which he could not participate. Her family's women and her women friends took turns cooking, serving the widower and his guests, and keeping the house clean. Donating some but requiring her owner/husband to foot most of the bill, they prepared and served the ritual funerary and other foods, such as lentils, hard boiled/baked eggs, meat soup, hilbah and baked and fried breads of different kinds—saloof, galub, jihnun, mlowwah, lahooh, zalabiyeh, kubaneh and the like.

For most of the Shiv'oh/שבעה period the widower mulled over his situation. Selling the goods and jewelry his "wife" left him would not bring in much money. Begging was too embarrassing now. Itinerant labour could not support him. The only other job open to him was peddling. All that walking! Except for the few rings his "wife" gave him all his "wealth" was buried with her.

Most Yemeni Jews and Muslims believed that the human world was crowded with a plethora of unseen beings— spirits, ghosts, demons, and the angry spirits of the dead (Dahbany-Miraglia 1975, 2004, Encyclopedia Judaica 1971, Garidi 1945, Trachtenberg 1970, Ulmer 1994). His dead "wife's" threat to haunt him frightened and enraged her owner. The more outraged he became at his "wife's" perfidy the more he became accustomed to the horrific scheme of digging up her grave and taking the jewelry that rightly belonged to him. He could not wait until Shiv'oh/שבעה was over, until he was left alone.

At the end of the seven-day mourning period the widower and most of the men in the community visited his "wife's" grave to place a stone marker. He refused to pay for the stone slab she demanded to cover her grave. With a quorum of nine other men he chanted Kaddish, the prayer for the dead. Uneasy at his decision to open his "wife's" grave, yet he resolved to unearth it that very night. Returning home he could barely contain his impatience. He wished his guests to the Devil. Finally, after the evening meal, the last of them left.

It was the night of the new moon.[15] The sky was cloudless. The night was chilly, barely lit by the thousands of stars in the skies. He was impatient to get the deed over with. Around midnight the owner/husband filled a small clay lamp with oil, lighting the thick cotton wick from one of the תנאויר/تناویر/tanaawiir coals. Wrapping a short-handled shovel in a cloth, he tied it across his shoulders and onto his back. Covering the lamp with a large straw basket he sneaked out of his house, skirting the town the short distance to the cemetery.

The new grave's soil was still loose so the man had very little difficulty digging down to the shroud. Using the shovel he chopped through the shroud, slipping off several of the rings the dead woman wore on her right hand. Triumphant, the owner/husband covered up his "wife's" grave and crept back with his spoils to his house. He wrapped the rings in a small rag, tucked the packet into a small cracked clay pot and buried it under the ashes, far in the rear of the largest תנור/تَنّور/tannuur. Exhausted he fell immediately asleep and did not wake up until the next morning was well advanced, missing the morning prayers at the synagogue.

After breakfasting on leftovers the widower reviewed his options. How to turn his loot into Maria Theresa thalers and riyals, Yemeni money, so that he could buy staples, another woman, ערקי/عرقی/فات, 'araqi and other necessities. He could not sell the rings in town. The jewelers and most of the women would recognize them, including the girl he wanted to acquire. Besides, he could buy her for much less than the value of one of his dead "wife's" rings. Why pay more than he had to? The next day was a Friday. He decided to travel to a nearby town, a three-kilometre walk and sell one, maybe two of the rings at the Friday market.

As soon as morning prayers were over that Friday the widower returned home to eat breakfast. He chose two rings, slipping the remainder back in the hearth. Hoping he was the only one with business in the next town, he crept out of his township, avoiding the main streets. He found a Jewish jeweler in the next town's ghetto who gave him a good price for both rings. Returning home he smiled to himself. How easy! The next day was שבת, Shabboth, the Sabbath. He and the father of the girl he wanted met after morning prayers in the synagogue to arrange the acquiring ceremony. It was to take place the next day.[16]

Ignoring the men and their injunctions many of the women travelled to the cemetery, alone and in pairs, whenever they felt like it.

[15] Celebrating the advent of the ראש חודש/new moon was pre-Biblical (I Kings 18, 26). Although Mosaic law is silent regarding the new, full and declining moon, "Despite its heathen origin, the festival of the New Moon had necessarily to adapt itself in the course of time to the monotheistic faith and practice of Israel and become a festival in honor of the God of Israel (Rosen & Rosen 2000: 268)." The Old Testament and its commentaries adjure observance, even designating specific holy days—ראש השנה/New Year and חנוכה/Hanukkoh—to begin on the first evening. "The celebration is known as the 'sanctification of the moon', and is performed in the open air in the evening in the early days of the lunar month when the moon shines brightly in the clear sky...and with a prayer (Babylonian Talmud Sanhedrin 42a). "...the custom of abstention from work on the day of the New Moon has been sedulously preserved by religious Jewish women almost to our own day. This custom of the women is recorded with approval in the ancient Jerusalem Talmud (Jerusalem Talmud Ta'anith I, 6)." "Like the Sabbath the New Moon also was a festive day of joy which had its special additional sacrifices (Num. 28, II-I5, Segal 1963: 237)."

[16] Girl children can be married from the age of three (Wegner 1987). Schereschewsky & Elon (2007: 616-617) comment that although a few Talmudists opposed child transfers —"it is forbidden for a father to give his minor daughter in marriage until she has grown up and can say: 'I want so-and-so'" (Babylonian Talmud Qiddushin 41a), the prohibition was not accepted as halakhah (Tosefta, Qiddushin 42a, Shulhan Aruch EH 37:8). The reasoning? The vicissitudes of the Diaspora. The authors go on to say that transferring ownership of a minor girl from her father to her purchaser was seen as a mitzvah, an obligation (Maimonides, Ishut, 3:19; Shulh Aruch EH 37:8, Lebedinger 1916). The child is

Happy with his new docile acquisition and indulging in his penchant for spending, the owner/husband soon ran out of funds. Once again, on the night of the next new moon the widower returned to his dead "wife's" grave. Digging was harder as the ground had settled in a month. As he dug the stench from the decaying body was overwhelming. In his haste to finish the job he tore off his "dead "wife's" right hand. He shook loose the rest of the rings, jammed the rotting flesh-covered bones back into the ground, then quickly re-covered the grave.

The widower could not go home stinking of putrefaction. Detouring to a nearby stream he tore off his gown, scrubbed his hands nearly raw with the sand and pebbles, washing his face and body, hoping the stink would not rat him out. He returned home exhausted but he could not sleep. The stench of decay filled his nostrils. When his new "wife" woke he was already gone to the nearby town to sell the rest of the rings—and to buy a new جلبية/jalabiya, a new gown, throwing the soiled one in a garbage dump outside the town on his way home.

By the time he returned his "wife" had prepared a good dinner. The widower could not eat it. He could not sleep. He could not have sex. He was haunted by his dead "wife" day and night. She materialized in his dreams, gleefully saying that he would soon join her. He woke up screaming, drenched in sweat, ranting about his dead "wife's" ghost. His child "wife" was terrified. The next day she fled to her parents' home. Afraid he would have to return the money paid for her, her father threatened to throw his daughter out of his house if she continued to refuse returning to her owner/husband. He changed his mind when his daughter told him that her owner/husband was being haunted by his dead "wife."

The widower was a wreck. Praying did no good. In desperation he went to the מרי/mori, the teacher/rabbi for help. The מרי/mori was stunned when the widower confessed he twice dug up his dead "wife's" grave but then agreed to help him. Refusing to take any recompense he said, "Let me think about this. Come back tomorrow evening."

When the widower arrived the next evening the מרי/mori walked him outside the town. Everyone knew he was being haunted and they must have suspected it was his dead "wife," but not why. Once he was sure no one could overhear the מרי/mori told the widower to return all he had stolen. The widower was beside himself. How was he going to live? He had a new "wife" and maybe there will be children! He needed money! And his dead "wife's" property legally belongs to him anyway!

The מרי/mori adjured him to return every piece of jewelry, fast for three days and pray at her grave during that time. Maybe she will forgive him.

Filled with rage and dread the widower was torn. His greed overrode his terror. Day and night he chewed qat, drank 'araqi and smoked the waterpipe. He neither slept nor ate. The next month, at the new moon, he died of starvation. He was buried alongside his hated first "wife." The מרי/mori ruled that all his goods belong to his child bride.

References

Babylonian Talmud.

Bacher W. & Lauterbach J.Z. 2003. Vows and Nedarim. *The Jewish Encyclopedia.* C. Adler & I. Singer (eds). Varda Books, Centenial Electronic Edition.

Baskin J.R. 1989. Rabbinic reflections on the barren wife. *The Harvard Theological Review* 82/1: 101-114.

Bender A.P. 1895. Beliefs, rites, and customs of the Jews, connected with death, burial, and mourning (as illustrated by the Bible and later Jewish literature) V. *The Jewish Quarterly Review* 7/2: 259-269.

Berlin A.M. 2005. Jewish life before the revolt. Archaeological evidence. *Journal of the Study of Judaism: In the Persian, Hellenic & Roman Periods.* 36/4: 138-148.

Brenner A. 1993. Introduction. In A. Brenner, ed. *A Feminist Companion to Wisdom Literature.* Sheffield UK: 11.

Caro J. 1975. *Shulhan 'Arukh/שולחן ערוך*. III יורה דעה/Yorah Dei'ah. NY, M.P. Press: 346-355.

Cohen A. 1999. "Do the Dead Know?" The Representation of Death in the Bavli [Babylonian Talmud]. *AJS [Association for Jewish Studies] Review* 24/1: 45-71.

Dahbany-Miraglia D. 1975. Yemenite Verbal Protective Behavior. *Working Papers in Yiddish and East European Jewish Studies* 13, NY,YIVO, 13 pp.

Dahbany-Miraglia D. 1999. Getting away with murder: marital law in Jewish Yemen. *Women in Judaism*: 1-24.

Dahbany-Miraglia D. 2004. The languages of divination in Yemenite Jewish culture. *3rd Annual Hawaii International Conference on Social Sciences. June 16-19, 2004 Conference Proceedings*: 842-859.

Dahbany-Miraglia D. 2009. Was Judith an Esheth Hayil? *Fifteenth World Congress of Jewish Studies Jerusalem, August 2–6, 2009* 12pp.

Divination. 1971. *Encyclopedia Judaica*. VI. DI-FO. NY, The Macmillan Company: 111-122.

Ehrman A.Z. 2007. Qiddushin. *Encyclopaedia Judaica*. M. Berenbaum & F. Skolnik, (eds). XII, 2nd ed. Detroit: Macmillan Reference USA: 145-146.

---

contracted to the man from whom her parent has accepted money. Betrothals are considered equivalent to formal acquisition. In all too many cases girls were "married" off to older men without a ketuboh or contract explicating the man's responsibilities regarding maintainance, ransom and burial. All too often R. Meir's injunction "It is forbidden for a man to allow his wife to remain without a ketuboh even for one hour (Babylonian Talmud Ketuboth 57a, Baba' Qamma' 89b)" was ignored. See Rothkoff 2007. It was common for the קדושין/qiddushin, the "consecration" ceremony of acquisition to be carried out abruptly, frequently minus the required two male witnesses. After giving her father the price agreed upon, in many cases her owner-to-be tucks a few almonds and/or raisins in the girl's hand as he verbalizes the formula of ownership:

הרי את מקודשת לי בטבעת זו לדת משה וישראל/Harei at miqudesheth li be taba'at zu le dath moshe ve yisra'el/You are consecrated to me with this ring according to the laws of Moses and Israel (Mielziner 1884: 92-93).

Epstein L.M. 2005. *The Jewish Marriage Contract: A Study in the Status of the Woman in Jewish Law*. New York, Law Book Exchange Ltd.

Finkel J. 1938-1939. Maqala fi Tihiyyat Ha-Metim ظلمقلة /في تحية همتم מקלה פי תחית המתים. Maimonides' Treatise on Resurrection. The original Arabic and Samuel Ibn Tibbon's Hebrew translation and glossary. *The American Academy for Jewish Research*. 9: 57-142.

Friedmann M. 1902. Seder eliyahu rabah we-seder eliyahu zuta : tana_ debe eliyahu = Seder Eliahu rabba und Seder Eliahu zuta (Tanna d'be Eliahu). Wien: Achiasaf.

Frumkin J. 1930. Disabilities of Women under Jewish Law—Can They Be Remedied? *Journal of Comparative Legislation and International Law, Third Series*. 12 # 4 (1930): 269-277.

Gamliel T. 2008. Performance versus social invisibility: What can be learned from the wailing culture of old-age Yemenite-Jewish women? *Women's Studies International Forum* 31: 209-218.

Garidi S. 1945. Shedim v'ruhoth be?emunath yihudei Teiman (Yemenite Jewish beliefs in demons and ghosts). In Y. Yisha'yahu & A. Tsadoq, (eds). *Shivuth Teiman (Captured in Yemen)*. Tel-Aviv, Sifrei Publishers: 155-165.

Golinkin D. 2001. Ma'amad ha-ishah ba-Halakhah : she'elot u-teshuvot. Jerusalem, ha-Merkaz le-ḥeker ha-ishah ba-Halakhah shele-yad Mekhon Shekhṭer le-limude ha-Yahadut.

Halevi L. 2004. Wailing for the dead: the role of women in early Islamic funerals. *Past and Present*. 183, (May): 3-40.

Hart J.S. 1963. Supplement to the chronology: Basic chronology for a history of the Yemen. *Middle East Journal*. 17/1-2: 144-153.

Hiers R.H. 1993-4.Transfer of Property by Inheritance and Bequest in Biblical Law and Tradition. *Journal of Law and Religion*, 10/1: 121-155

Klein-Franke A. 2005. Tombstones bearing Hebrew inscriptions in Aden. *Arabian Archaelogy and Epigraphy* 16: 161-182.

Kofsky A.S. 1988. A comparative Analysis of women's property rights in Jewish law and Anglo-American law. *Journal of Law and Religion*. 6/2: 317-353.

Koren I. 2005. The bride's voice: religious women challenge the wedding ritual. *Nashim: A Journal of Jewish Women's Studies and Gender Issues* 10: 29-52.

Lebedinger I. 1916. The Minor in Jewish Law. *The Jewish Quarterly Review*, New Series 6/ 4: 459-493.

Levine B.A. 1968. Mulūgu/Melûg: The Origins of a Talmudic Legal Institution. *Journal of the American Oriental Society*, 88/2: 271-285.

Levine E. 1997-2001. Biblical Women's Marital Rights. *Proceedings of the American Academy for Jewish Research* 63: 87-135.

Michal A. 1990. *haKehilah haYihudit be Adan beyn haShanim 1900-1967 (The Jewish Community in Aden between 1900 -1967)*. Tel-Aviv, Published by the author.

Mielziner M. 1884. The Jewish law of marriage and divorce in ancient and modern times: and its relation to the law of the state. Cincinnati: Bloch Publishers & Printing Co.

Morrell, S. 1982. An equal or a ward: how independent is a married woman according to rabbinic law? *Jewish Social Studies*, 44/3-4: 189-210.

Murray M. 2007. Female in Graeco-Roman Rabbinic Literature. *Religion & Theology* 14: 284-309.

Nahum Y.L. 1962. *Mitsfunot Yehudei Teiman. (The Conscience/Shape of the Lives of the Jews of Yemen)*. Tel-Aviv-Yafo/Jaffa, Published by the author.

Palgi P. & Abramovitch H. 1984. Death: A Cross-Cultural Perspective. *Annual Review of Anthropology* 13: 385-417.

Paton L.B. 1910. The Hebrew idea of the future life. II. *The Biblical World* 35/2: 80-92.

Proverbs. Esheth Hayil 31: 10-31.

Rackman E. 1976-1977. A Jewish philosophy of property: rabbinic insights on intestate succession. *The Jewish Quarterly Review*, New Series. 67/2-3: 65-89.

Rahmani L.Y. 1981a. Ancient Jerusalem's Funerary Customs and Tombs: Part One. *The Biblical Archaeologist*, 44/3: 171-177.

Rahmani L.Y. 1981b. Ancient Jerusalem's Funerary Customs and Tombs: Part Two. *The Biblical Archaeologist*. 44/4: 229-235.

Rahmani L.Y. 1982. Ancient Jerusalem's Funerary Customs and Tombs: Part Three. *The Biblical Archaeologist*, 45/1 (Winter): 43-53.

Rosen D.M. & Rosen V.P. 2000. New myths and meanings in Jewish new moon rituals. *Ethnology*, 39/3: 263-277.

Rosenblatt S. 1935-1936. The relations between Jewish and Muslim laws concerning oaths and vows. *Proceedings of the American Academy for JewishResearch* 7: 229-243.

Rothkoff A. 2007. Puberty. *Encyclopaedia Judaica*. Berenbaum, M. & Skolnik, F. (eds). XVI, 2nd ed. Detroit: Macmillan Reference USA: 695-696.

Schatzmiller M. 1995. Women and property rights in al-Andalus and the Maghrib: social patterns and legal discourse. *Islamic Law and Society*. 2/3. Marriage, Divorce and Succession in the Muslim Family: 219-257.

Schereschewsky B.-Z. & Elon M. 2007. Child Marriage. *Encyclopaedia Judaica*. M. Berenbaum & F. Skolnik, (eds). IV. 2nd ed. Detroit: Macmillan Reference USA: 616-617.

Segal M.H. 1963. The Religion of Israel before Sinai. *The Jewish Quarterly Review*, New Series, 53/3: 226-256.

Singer I., McLaughlin J.F., Schechter S., Greenstone J.H. & Jacobs J. 2003. Marriage. *The Jewish Encyclopedia*. C. Adler & I. Singer, (eds). Varda Books, Centenial Electronic Edition.

Toy C.H. 1899. *A Critical and Exegetical Commentary on the Book of Proverbs*. NY, C. Scribner's Sons.

Trachtenberg J. 1970. *Jewish Magic and Superstition. A Study in Folk Religion*. NY: Atheneum.

Tritton A.S. 1938. Muslim funeral customs. *Bulletin of the School of Oriental Studies*. University of London. 9/3: 653-661.

Ulmer R. 1994. *The Evil Eye in the Bible and Rabbinic Literature*. Hoboken NJ, Ktav Publishing House, Inc.

Wegner J.R. 1987. Dependency, autonomy and sexuality: women as chattel and person in the Mishnah. J. Neusner, P. Borgen, E.F. Frerichs & R. Horsley, (eds). *New Perspectives on Ancient Judaism.* Lanham MD, University Press of America: 89-102.

Zeitlin S. 1969. Studies in Talmudic jurisprudence: I. possession, pignus and hypothec. *The Jewish Quarterly Review*, New Series, 60/2 (Oct.): 89-111.

Author's Address
Dina Dahbany-Miraglia
32-18 148th Street
Flushing New York 11354
U.S.A.
email: ddmqcc@att.net

In anima vili: Islamic constructions on life autopsies and cannibalism

José Mª Bellido-Morillas and Pablo García-Piñar

Summary

Dimitri Gutas reproduces the following testimony from the Syriac Christian physician and translator Yuḥannā ibn Māsawayh: "Had it not been for the meddling of the ruler and his interference in what does not concern him, I would have dissected alive this son of mine, just as Galen used to dissect men and monkeys. As a result of dissecting him, I would thus come to know the reasons for his stupidity, rid the world of his kind, and produce knowledge for people by means of what I would write in a book: the way in which his body is composed, and the course of his arteries, veins, and nerves. But the ruler prohibits this [Q 390-1]". The ethical problem of the vivisection of such reputed inferior forms of life (*animae viles*), like anthropoid monkeys and handicapped human beings, belongs, obviously, not only to the Medieval Islamic rulers or Islam, but to all ages and civilizations, from the Sumerians and their *umuls*. Our aim will be to study the Arabic and Islamic cultural constructions on the sense and uses of the death in relation with these *animae viles*, and its bonds with Islamic medicine, law, psychology and eschatology (including considerations on heretic positions such as metempsychosis).

Keywords: Bioethics, metempsychosis, vivisection, monkeys, nisnas

Bioethics is far from being a recent invention. In a Sumerian myth, human genetic disorders are attributed to gods, leaving an open door to deep and complex meditations. In it, after having drunk too many beers, Enki bets Ninmah that he will be able to rectify all the defects he burdens his human creatures with. Ninmah creates a weak-handed man, and Enki appoints him as an official; Ninmah creates a blind man (*a man with ever open eyes*) and Enki makes him a musician; Ninmah creates a cripple and Enki makes him a goldsmith (according to another version, he is not a cripple but a fool, and Enki appoints him as an official too). At the end Ninmah beats Enki (83-101). The first edition of the Oxford University's *Electronic Text Corpus of Sumerian Literature*, from which we have taken the Sumerian text, offers the following translation:

Enki devised a shape with head, [...] and mouth in its middle, and said to Ninmah: "Pour ejaculated semen into a woman's womb, and the woman will give birth to the semen of her womb". Ninmah stood by for the newborn [...] and the woman brought forth [...] in the midst [...]. In return (?), this was Umul: its head was afflicted, its place of [...] was afflicted, its eyes were afflicted, its neck was afflicted. It could hardly breathe, its ribs were shaky, its lungs were afflicted, its heart was afflicted, its bowels were afflicted. With its hand and its lolling head it could not put bread into its mouth; its spine and head were dislocated. The weak hips and the shaky feet could not carry (?) it on the field - Enki fashioned it in this way. Enki said to Ninmah: "For your creatures I have decreed a fate, I have given them their daily bread. Now, you should decree a fate for my creature, give him his daily bread too". Ninmah looked at Umul and turned to him. She went nearer to Umul asked him questions but he could not speak. She offered him bread to eat but he could not reach out for it. He could not lie on [...], he could not [...]. Standing up he could not sit down, could not lie down, he could not [...] a house, he could not eat bread. Ninmah answered Enki: "The man you have fashioned is neither alive nor dead. He cannot support himself (?)".

There is no doubt that the myth raises a question regarding mankind. Human beings have defects, but can a defect reach such a degree that it deprives man of his humanity? A man who cannot communicate, who cannot express his thoughts, could have his status lowered to a thing or a beast, like Kafka's Gregor Samsa, in a much worse situation that the one in Ausias March's verses "Lo viscaí qui es troba en Alemanya paralitic, que no pot senyalar"? Sumerians anticipated and dreaded this possibility, and as such it is captured in this myth, stuck in between the comical and the tragic (like in Kafka, like in March), in which drunk gods create imperfect creatures for pleasure.

There still remains a question that the gods do not know how to answer: what to do with these creatures? Although in the *Middle Assyrian Laws* induced abortion was punished with impalement and public exposition of the offender's corpse (Walls 2007: 20-21), in the forty Old Babylonian clay tablets called *Sakkiku* ('Symptoms'), it was prescribed to throw a newborn into a river as a remedy for what Scurlock and Andersen (quoted by Walls) identified as the Werdnig-Hoffman disease and the Prader-Willi syndrome. The point of this purifying ritual ('*namburbi*') is that the spirit ('*zaqīqu*') can attempt to come to life again in a better body than the current one, which is destroyed with a total lack of consideration. Walls (2007: 22) links this example to a similar treatment against the symptoms identified as Huntington's disease, and states: "These two texts thus prescribe treatment of the afflicted infants in accordance with the disposal of malformed (*izbū*) and developmentally normal (*kūbū*) stillborn infants, as though they were not fully human". Neo-Assyrian medical literature was even worse. In a text found at Sultan Tepe, for a similar disease, fire is prescribed, and in quantity. Burning the patient alive prevents him bringing misfortune to his home (Walls 2007: 20-21).

From India, with the run of centuries, a doctrine for which men were a little bit more esteemed in respectability terms than animals reached the Near East. This doctrine was supported on a system that considered these two conditions as exchangeable as a result of the reincarnation wheel. It was Buddhism. Reincarnation as inferior creatures, according to the Brahmanic system, is due to bad actions in a past life. But Buddhism prescribes compassion for all beings. That is why Ašoka worries about them (Wujastyk 2003: 10):

Everywhere in the dominions of King Priyadarśī [Ašoka], as well in the border territories of the Choḷas, the Pāṇḍiyas, the Satiyaputra, the Keralaputra, the Ceylonese, the Yōna king named Antiochos, and those kings who are neighbours of Antiochos –everywhere provision has been made for two kinds of medical treatment, for men and for animals. However, the Indian influences that can be tracked better arrive in "the 8th century A.D., when the physicians of India were invited to Jundishapur and Baghdad for consultation and were put in charge of the hospitals" (Sharma 1979: 71).

Islam is not completely strange to king Ašoka's goodwill: he respects fools and tries to be lenient with animals, for which, for example, it decrees a specific way of dying, not allowing excess. By the same way it grants rights and dignity to Abraham's and Noah's sons, it grants rights to all God's creatures.

Besides, there will be Islamic cults that postulate metempsychosis, whether they are of Indian influence or not (there is no need of searching for an Indian influence in the legends of Saint Andrew of Teixido's church, as an example of popular belief in metempsychosis within the most western cult among the varieties of Christianity). Actually, Manichaeism's influence has more strength, and, above all, Neoplatonicism.[1]

In India, mankind's vision as a microcosm starts in the myth from the dissection of a giant, but in the rite (that will originate a philosophical interpretation) is substituted by a horse. Animal dissection, therefore, is a prelude to human dissection:

"In the great sacrifices, a horse's corpse was ritually opened and torn to shreds, and the priest, according to the ritual formulas collected in the Yajurveda, offered the organs to the divinity, naming them according to the order of extraction: omentum, heart, tongue, etc. A certain methodical inspection of the human corpse – rather than a dissection – was later performed by physicians, rather than priests: it was submerged in water until the flesh was tender, then it was examined plane by plane, brushing the body with a brush made of hard roots, and at the end it was opened with a bamboo stick" (Laín Entralgo 1978: 30).

According to Claude Bernard, it seems that human dissection starts in Persia:

"It has been said that some Persian kings used to give those sentenced to death to physicians, so they could practice vivisections on them that could be useful to Medicine. As Galen narrates, Attalus III Philometor Euergetes, king of Pergamum, 137 years before Christ, experimented with poisons and antidotes in criminals sentenced to death" (Bernard 1994: 245).

But among Persians, vivisection had a rather recreational purpose: "la vivisection, l'arrachement de la langue, la crevaison des yeux furent de véritables marques de bienveillance" (Furon 1951: 51).

Celsus narrates how Herophilus and Erasistratus practiced vivisections on criminals (Celsus, *De medicina*, I, 23), and he definitely approves them, even though there still will be instances of those who think in the opposite way (Celsus, *De medicina*, I, 26).

John the Alexandrian (Joannes Alexandrinus, Dietz, *Scholia in Hippocr. et. Gal.*, 50, p. 216) accused Archigenes and Galen of practising vivisections. It has to be taken into account that Galen's treaty *De vivorum dissectione* deals with animals and that he had no choice but to dissect apes, according to his own account of the events. Pedro Laín Entralgo explains:

"Galen, who did not dissect human corpses, hominized the results of animal's corpses' results by analogy, and that was actually the origin of more than a few anatomic mistakes" (Laín Entralgo 1978: 76).

Vesalius, for instance, said: "novimus Galenum boum cerebri dissectione delusum, non hominis cerebrum uti neque ipsius vasa, sed boum recensuisse" (Scarborough 1976). Herophilus made these sorts of mistakes too, which seems to refute the actions that encyclopaedist Celsus attributes to him. José Alsina notices that mistakes come also from "the exclusive observation of human corpses – and not living beings – in which arteries have been drained" (Alsina 1982: 89).

But, as Husain Muzzafar says, "The Arabs did not accept the Greeks' interpretations of anatomy or Galen's *Book of Anatomy* irrationally" (Muzzafar 2004: 187), even though he is not exactly referring to an Arab but a Syriac Christian, Yuḥannā ibn Māsawayh, called *Mesue Senior* in Latin (who, by the way, must not be mistaken for *Janus Damascenus*, that is, *Serapion Senior*). Others wanted to make him representative of not only Arab, but Muslim science (Ahmed 2005: 78).

To present Yuḥannā ibn Māsawayh as an Islamic exponent is, as we are going to see, quite arguable. And, as we are also going to see, neither his figure nor the thought that is going to be subject to study in this paper are susceptible to recognition or appropriation by any sensible person.

Yuḥannā ibn Māsawayh profoundly despised the rest of mankind's intelligence. Ibn al-Nadīm relates in his *Fihrist* that, in the presence of the Caliph, he answered back to a courtier that if the ignorance that his brain was brimming with turned into understanding, and it was

---

[1] For a current example of this problem in Islam and a consideration on its origin see Blank (2001: 110).

shared out among one hundred beetles, every single one of them would become more intelligent that Aristotle (Browne 1921: 37). He rejected and publicly humiliated Ḥunayn ibn Isḥāq, who wanted to be his disciple, because he was from 'Hira, a village that was considered to produce only peddlers; Ḥunayn left his presence in tears, and he was only admitted as his disciple two years later, according to Ibn al-Qifṭī (Browne 1921: 24), when Yuḥannā ibn Māsawayh found him reciting Homer in Greek. Ibn al-Qifṭī also documents Ibn Māsawayh's words in relation to ʿAbdallāh al-Ṭayfūrī's daughter, who he considered beautiful but stupid. He had a son with her, who, according to his own testimony, possessed both his father and mother's worst attributes. Ibn Māsawayh decided then to perform a vivisection on him in order to find the origin of human stupidity and, simultaneously, to analyse how arteries, veins and nerves work (Gutas 1998: 119).

But the Caliph forbade him to do so. He brought Ibn Māsawayh a number of apes ready for vivisection to a special chamber located at the Tigris shore, and, in the year 836, he obtained from Nubia's sovereign an ape that was surprisingly similar to a human being. Even then, Ibn Māsawayh kept bitterly complaining on the Caliph's intolerable interference in his scientific activity:

"Had it not been for the meddling of the ruler and his interference in what does not concern him, I would have dissected alive this son of mine, just as Galen used to dissect men and monkeys. As a result of dissecting him, I would thus come to know the reasons for his stupidity, rid the world of his kind, and produce knowledge for people by means of what I would write in a book: the way in which his body is composed, and the course of his arteries, veins, and nerves. But the ruler prohibits this [Q 390-1]".[2]

For August Müller such a pretention clashes with his Christianity:

"Dieser Johanna war ein höcht gescheiter Zyniker, der von seinem Christentum einen sehr mässigen Gebrauch machte, aber auf eigene Hand allerlei Dinge trieb, auf die wir in diesen Zeiten kaum gefasst sind, z.B. Vivisection" (Müller 1885: 511).

For Toby E. Huff, it would instead be "a Christian and a free-thinking rationalist" (Huff 2003: 170). An allegoric interpretation can even be done:

"Ibn Māsawayh's story, reminiscent of Abraham's sacrifice, illustrates how the son was offered up as a sacrifice to scientific knowledge (a sacrifice prevented not by the intervention of the Divinity but of the ruler)" (Rahman 2008: 25).

From the anecdotes related by Ibn Abī Uṣaybiʿa, Selma Tibi suggests that:

He mocked both his own, Christian, faith and Islam: when his priest had unsuccessfully tried several remedies for a stomach complaint, Ibn angrily suggested that the priest should become a Muslim "because Islam is good for the stomach" (Tibi 2005: 30).

It is not surprising that, following that very same precept, he converted to Islam in order to be the Caliph's physician. Nevertheless, for some heretic Muslim cults that profess to believe in reincarnation, some animals would have more dignity than some human beings:

The sacred book of the Nusairi is the Kitab al-Majmu, a brief document consisting of sixteen short sections. From it, and from lesser sources, we learn that the Nusairi look upon rebirth as a terrible necessity, continued until the soul is purified. When initiating a new adept the Imam says to him, "If you unveil this mystery, the earth will not suffer you to be buried in it, and on your return you will not re-enter a human envelope: no, when you die, you will enter the envelope of a degrading transformation whence there will be no deliverance for you, for ever and ever". The soul of one who is observant passes through only seven lives, otherwise he is condemned to journey through eighty incarnations. As has been seen, it is even possible for a soul to be obliged to enter an animal. Such is the fate of those who do not pray to ʾAli ibn Abu Talib: they pass into camels, mules, donkeys, sheep. Nor are all human incarnations looked upon as equally fortunate: the worst fate is to be reborn into a Jew, a Sunnite, or a Christian. Finally, the purified soul takes its place among the stars (Besterman 1928).

Islam does not admit reincarnation, but it accepts that God can turn a man or a whole village into an animal (Cook 1999). Abū Ḥāmid narrates that:

In Ṣanʿā there is an Arab tribe whose members have been turned into half a man, in such a way that they have only half a head, half a body, a single hand and a single foot. [...] They lack intelligence, they live in the area of al-Ajām, in the country of al-Shiḥr, at the shores of the Indian sea. The Arabs call them *Nisnās* and they hunt them in order to eat them. The *Nisnās* speak in Arab and bear Arab names, they breed and declaim poems (Abū Ḥāmid 1990: 28; Viguera 1974).

Instead, in other wonderful tales, transformed men are recognised and respected as human beings because of their use of writing: it happens, for instance, in *The One Thousand and One Nights*.

In general, we can establish that for the Islamic world, an altered man – one who does not look like a man – does not have the same rights as the non-altered man and is, on top of that, edible. Neither has the transformed man's corpse, which does not look like a human corpse, the same rights as the others, which must be buried and respected. Egyptian mummies were disinterred and consumed by Muslims as a medical remedy.

---

[2] Gutas (1998: 119). There is a poor reference in Finger (1996: 447), cf. Campbell (2000: 137-64) and Sezgin (1970: 231-236).

References

Abū Ḥāmid al Garnati. 1990. *Tuḥfat al-albāb (El regalo de los espíritus)*. Ana Ramos (ed). Madrid: CSIC.

Ahmed M.B. 2005. Contributions of Muslim physicians and other scholars: 700-1600 AC. Pages 71-90 in M. B. Ahmed, S. Ahsani, and D. A. Siddiqi, (eds.), *Muslim Contributions to World Civilization*. Herdnon: International Institute of Islamic Thought/Association of Muslim Social Scientists.

Alsina J. 1982. *Los orígenes helénicos de la medicina occidental*. Barcelona: Labor, Guadarrama/Punto Omega.

Bernard C. 1994. *Introducción al estudio de la Medicina Experimental*. Ciudad de México.

Besterman T. 1928. The belief in rebirth of the Druses and other Syrian sects. *Folklore* 39, 2: 133-148.

Blank J. 2001. *Mullahs on the Mainframe: Islam and Modernity Among the Daudi Bohras*. Chicago: University of Chicago Press.

Browne E.G. 1921. *Arabian Medicine, Being the Fitzpatrick Lectures Delivered at the College of Physicians in November 1919 and November 1920*. Cambridge: Cambridge University Press.

Campbell D. 2000. *Arabian Medicine and Its Influence on the Middle Ages*, II. London: Routledge.

Cook M. 1999. Ibn Qutayba and the monkeys. *Studia Islamica* 89: 43-74.

Finger S. 1996. *Origins of Neuroscience: A History of Explorations Into Brain Function*, Oxford: Oxford University Press.

Furon R. 1951. *L'Iran: Perse et Afghanistan*. Paris: Payot.

Gutas D. (1998). *Greek Thought, Arabic Culture: The Graeco-Arabic translation movement in Baghdad and early 'Abbāsid society (2nd-4th / 8th centuries)*. London: Routledge.

Huff T. E. 2003. *The Rise of Early Modern Science: Islam, China, and the West*, Cambridge: Cambridge University Press.

Laín Entralgo P. 1978. *Historia de la medicina*. Barcelona: Salvat.

Müller A. 1885. *Der Islam im Morgen- und Abendland*. Berlin: Baumgärtel.

Muzzafar H. 2004. *Islam's Contribution to Science*. New Delhi: Anmol.

Rahman S., Street T., & Tahiri H. (eds.). 2008. *The Unity of Science in the Arabic Tradition: Science, Logic, Epistemology and their Interactions*. Heidelberg: Springer.

Scarborough J. 1976. Celsus on human vivisection at Ptolemaic Alexandria. *Clio Medica* 11, 1: 25-38.

Sezgin F. 1970. *Medizin-Pharmazie-Zoologie-Tierheilkunde bis ca 430 H., Geschichte des arabischen Schrifttums*, III. Leiden: E.J. Brill.

Sharma S. (1979). *Realms of Ayurveda: Scientific Excursions by Nineteen Scholars*. New Delhi: Arnold-Heinemann.

Tibi S. 2005. *The Medicinal Use of Opium in Ninth-Century Baghdad*. Leiden: Brill.

Viguera M.J. 1997. El *nasnās*, un motivo de ʿajāʾib. *Orientalia Hispanica sive Studia F. M. Pareja Octogenario Dicata* 1: 647-674.

Walls N. H. 2007. The origins of the disabled body: disability in ancient Mesopotamia. Pages 13-30 in H. Ávalos, S. J. Melcher, J. Schipper (eds.), *This Abled Body: Rethinking Disabilities in Biblical Studies*. Atlanta: Society of Biblical Literature.

Wujastyk D. 2003. *The Roots of Ayurveda*. London: Penguin Classics.

Authors' addresses

José María Bellido-Morillas (PhD. Eur.)
3 Studentski Trg
11000 Belgrade
Serbia
josemariabellido@gmail.com

Pablo García-Piñar (M.A.)
424 Morrill Hall
Cornell University
Ithaca, NY 14850
USA
pg254@cornell.edu

Instituting the Palestinian Dead Body

Suhad Daher-Nashif

Summary
The aim of this article is to describe the passage that Palestinian dead bodies undergo during the period between the determination of death and their final destination, prior to burial. The article, which is based on ethnographic fieldwork at the Palestinian Forensic Medicine Institute (FMI) through 2004-2007, discusses what happens to Palestinian dead bodies when they are found in doubtful circumstances, or what are called criminal circumstances. The article describes the lives of the dead bodies throughout their journey at the various institutions: Palestinian, Israeli, and in several cases, Jordanian. This multi-institutional passage is constructed by multi-bureaucratic logic. In this article I attempt to analyze the ways of instituting the dead body and show how at the same time this dead body institutes these institutions.

Keywords: corpse, institute, Palestine, forensic medicine, religion.

Introduction

One cold January day I drove to Abu-Dis to continue my ethnographic fieldwork at the Palestinian Forensic Medicine Institute, which is located in al-Quds University in Abu-Dis, south-east of Jerusalem. On arriving, I saw the ambulance parking near the entrance to the institute and said to myself (as usual), "Good, there is work today, I will have a fruitful ethnographic diary". Inside the institute I saw a black body bag on the ambulance bed, and, as expected, a dead body was in it. After greeting the staff members, I asked the ambulance driver about it. He was familiar with the work I did in the institute. He said, "It's the corpse of a young boy who was missing for forty five days, and the police found him in a field in the Ramallah area". From the material I have collected during my research I know that when a Palestinian corpse is found in doubtful circumstances, the policemen first arrive at the scene of the crime, and then, on the general prosecutor's instruction, the body is taken to the nearest hospital.[1] After this, in most cases the same general prosecutor issues an order to transfer the dead body to the Palestinian FMI in order to discover the immediate cause of death.

Methodology

The subject of this article is one of the issues that I am analyzing and discussing in my doctoral research on the social-political "enlivening" of the Palestinian dead body: the case of the Palestinian FMI. Most anthropological studies on the body relate to the living body, and the research on death addresses the ritual aspects of death. There are no studies describing and analyzing the socio-political processes that construct the Palestinian dead body and the practices performed on it. Therefore, the present study is based on the grounded theory approach. This is an inductive strategy which leads to the formation of a theory that emerges from the interrelationship of the researcher with the real, empirical world of the researched subject (Patton 1990: 153). Because the research focuses on the FMI, a qualitative ethnographic research methodology is appropriate. Researchers use ethnography to describe the various aspects of the researched culture (Byrne 2001: 82). The ethnographer bases his work on what people say, the way they behave and the objects they use. Hence I chose to use open in-depth interviews with the FMI staff, and with people who work with the Forensic Medicine System directly and indirectly. In addition, I conducted intensive observations (planned and non-planned participant observations). I performed a textual analysis of several formal and informal documents, media coverage, medico-legal documents, and so forth. I also analyzed the material culture of the FMI, including medical equipment, refrigerator for the dead bodies, and other materials. As revealed by the data collected, the Palestinian dead body passes through several bureaucratic logics: Palestinian, Israeli, and in several cases, Jordanian.

The dead body's journey

The ambulance driver said, "When I arrive at the crime scene, in most cases I find the policemen there with the general prosecutor. They describe what they see and write their notes; they check the corpse and try not to make any changes so that the doctor at the hospital can identify the cause of death. The general prosecutor orders me to take the corpse to the nearest hospital; I put the corpse in a body bag, and take it to the hospital". I asked, "Would you please describe what happens at the hospital?" He replied, "Sure. I go directly to the mortuary; the doctor who is on duty when I arrive comes in. The general prosecutor arrives and usually two policemen. Besides, members of the dead person's family are invited by the police in order to identify the corpse. The police identify the family through the ID card of the deceased. Usually, two family members come to the hospital. They confirm that the dead person is really their relative or not. The police call for the forensic physician to determine the immediate cause of death. In most cases this physician makes an external examination, and he always says that he cannot determine the immediate cause of death. He writes the results of his external examination and a description of the dead person. This document is signed by this forensic pathologist, the relatives, and the general prosecutor". I said, "OK, then what happens?" He

---

[1] The Palestinian territories are divided as separated areas, and in each area there is a main hospital to which the dead body is taken directly after it is discovered.

continued, "I take the corpse by ambulance to the FMI in Abu-Dis".

The presence of a dead body in any place agitates the people around it; it causes anxiety, disrupts the social order, and disturbs the social time-space. For this reason it is transferred far away to an institute, in order to re-order the environment, to restore the time-space of the living people. Throughout the cultural history of the human being the body has been used metaphorically to denote the stability or instability of society, the social order and social chaos. For some theoreticians, the body serves as a medium for maintaining social order and institutions (Schatzki & Natter 1996: 3). In her book on Abjection, Julia Kristeva (1982) analyzes the exclusion of the corpse as a result of its disturbing of the social order.

Through the ethnography I found that the dead body arrives at the FMI with several documents: the general prosecutor's order to transfer the corpse to the FMI (without this order the dead body is not moved or taken anywhere), the forensic physician's written report of the external examination he conducted in the hospital, the I.D card which is photocopied by the FMI. After the process that takes place in the FMI (which will be described later), the corpse is taken by the family or by the ambulance driver to the social-religious burial ceremony. If the dead body is not identified, the FMI keeps it for a period of time in the institution's refrigerator, until the police system finds the family. When the family is not sure that the dead body is theirs, the general prosecutor orders a DNA sample to be taken to Jordan for DNA analysis, because the Palestinians do not possess equipment for analyzing DNA. Hence that part of the dead body is interred in the Jordanian legal-medical bureaucratic systems.

Instituting the dead body within the Palestinian FMI

The Palestinian Forensic Medicine System (FMS) was established directly after the return of the PLO (Palestinian Liberation Organization) to the occupied territories as an autonomous authority after the Oslo Accords between the Palestinians and the Israelis in 1993. Yaser A'rafat who was the president of the Palestinian Authority, made several decisions for establishing future state institutes, one of the first being the Forensic Medicine System (FMS). The FMS is one of the state systems which aims to create social order and internal safety (Prior 1989: 67). In the Palestinian context, these systems functioned as the signs of the future nation state institutes (Shaine & Sussman 1998: 283). In 1994 the FMS began its work. In the years 1994-1996 the FMS functioned within hospital mortuaries, so that every dead body that was found in doubtful circumstances could be transferred to the main hospital of the area in which it was found. In 1996 the University of al-Quds in Abu-Dis, adopted all the functions of the FMI and allocated it a place in the university affiliated to the Faculty of Medicine. In 2000 a new building was constructed to house the institution with the help of donations from Australia and Denmark. Today this institution is one of the three FM institutions. The second was established in Gaza, also directly after the Oslo Accords; today it is located in Al-Shifa' hospital in Gaza, and "serves the population in the Gaza Strip". The third institution was established in 2006, in Al-Najah' University, Nablus, in order to "serve the population in the northern areas of Palestine". This institution was established as a result of the cutting of the Palestinian territories by separation walls and Israeli checkpoints, which made the arrival of a dead body at the FMI in Abu-Dis very difficult for the Palestinian systems and also for the families who wanted to be present at their relative's autopsy. The family's presence at the autopsy has to be approved in a written letter by the general prosecutor and sent to the FMI.

These data were revealed through archival data that I collected and analysed in the course of my ethnographic work in the FMI. From the observations and interviews I conducted I found that when a dead body arrives at the FMI it passes through several rooms, through several functions of the FMI and through several routine stages in the process of discovering the immediate cause of death. First, the dead body passes through the registration stage, and then it is taken to be weighed, afterwards to the X-ray room, and from there to the autopsy room. After the body is described externally and photographed,[2] it is opened. The director of the FMI and the pathologist who came with the body perform the autopsy, the nurses also take part in the autopsy, they check every part (outside and inside) of the dead body, they weigh the internal parts and take a small sample for the laboratory, they check the contents of the stomach and take a sample for the laboratory to check for poison, they examine the colour and smell of every part, and check to see if there was bleeding in any part. They deal with the body through its three spaces: the head, the chest and the abdomen, and they have to check each space. At the end of this autopsy the immediate cause of death is determined in most cases, but sometimes it takes longer and they have to wait for the laboratory results or the DNA analysis in order to reach a conclusive decision. The pathologists write the final forensic report and send it to the general prosecutor; he decides whom to send it to, and whether he wants to give the family the opportunity to read it. My informants stated that "this decision depends on the case". Case is the name given to the dead body in the FMI; it consists of a serial number for the year, for example 5/09. This number is relevant when they deal with the "case", even in the court. The dead body's death story, or the forensic report, is used in the courts as evidence.

The Palestinian FMI is related to several nation-state institutions:[3] it is affiliated to the Ministry of Justice, the

---

[2] During the first year and a half of my ethnographic work, the photographer was part of the staff involved in the autopsy; he photographed every single part of the body and every injury done on and to the dead body. After 18 months the photographer attended the autopsy only if there was a need for it, as decided by the general prosecutor, who also decided which part of the body should be photographed.
[3] One of the unique characteristics in the Palestinian context is that most of the modern state institutions are established in a reality of

Ministry of Health and administratively and academically to al-Quds University.[4] The affiliation to the ministries of health and justice derives from the definition of forensic medicine. Thus the law world derives from social perception and philosophical principles, and the medical world derives from scientific perceptions and statistical principles; both of these worlds meet in the forensic medicine world (De-Paz & Lifshetz 2003: 128). The affiliation to three Palestinian state institutes constructs the process that the dead body goes through, as it constructs the daily "lives" of the dead bodies.

Prior (1986: 153) claimed that the practices performed on the dead body are affected by social, political and religious norms. Most of the employees in the Palestinian FMI are Muslims, and I saw that they sometimes bring their own religious beliefs or ideologies into the autopsy. For example, the autopsy is completed as soon as possible because one of the religious beliefs is that part of respecting the dead is burying them. Sometimes I heard the ambulance driver and the technician reading Koranic verses while cleaning the dead body after the autopsy, constructing it and positioning it as required in Islam.[5] The FMI combines medicine and legal disciplines; the way of reading the bodily signs and dealing with the dead body are medico-legal approaches. By using the word social I mean the social reality, the social-political context and the social systems like the tribal one. These three systems exist through the daily "lives" of the Palestinian dead body/ies, and take part through instituting it.

The work of the FMI focuses on the body, the dead body. The dead body passes through a "medicalization" process, organizing death for the control of experiments and re-locating it from the family/public to the state institute. This means that death is instituted, and the dead body is instituted (Littlewood 1993: 5). The dead body is a tool for the justice system, for the state (in the Palestinian context, semi-state) for maintaining the sovereignty of the law, by the law, as stated by the director of the FMI: "The law requires an autopsy in order to determine the cause of death; if it is criminal, it is essential to reveal it for the sake of justice, so that the criminal cannot escape from punishment.... It's very important for the families, society and science".[6]

The relationship between the Israeli systems and the Palestinian dead body

The ambulance driver said: "I began my journey from the hospital to the forensic medicine institute. When I arrived at the Qalandya checkpoint, which is located between Ramallah and Jerusalem and is also the crossing point through the separation wall, I joined the line of cars waiting to pass through the checkpoint. When my turn came the Israeli soldiers asked me what I had in the ambulance. They know me, I'm so familiar on all the checkpoints of the West bank, because I pass through there very often, but every time they have to check what I have in the ambulance. So I said to myself, it's time for revenge. I got out of the ambulance and opened the back door. When they came very close I opened the body bag. They stepped back, holding their noses, expressing disgust, fear, and anger. I remember that one of them said, "Don't bring us such corpses", as if I could choose. I laughed to myself and said. "I'm sorry but I can't decide how a corpse should look". I closed the bag, shut the door, returned to my seat, and drove away from the checkpoint, where I could guffaw. Then I began my route through Jerusalem in order to reach Abu-Dis. Four kilometres before Abu Dis there was another checkpoint and a similar scene took place. Then I went to the Institute."

As revealed through the interviews, when a Palestinian person dies, the FMI issues the death certificate and permission for burial, then the family has to give these data, together with his ID card to the Palestinian Ministry of the Interior. This ministry, in turn, has to send the data to the Israeli side, so that the soldiers at checkpoints and officials in other relevant places know that this name, this body, no longer exists.

In the course of my ethnographic work I heard from families about their journey from home to the FMI, they have to pass through the checkpoints and the separation wall exactly like the dead, as one brother told me: "To reach the institute, we had to request permission from the Israeli military officials, because we have Palestinian ID and we need to enter Israeli territory in order to get from our village to the institute. It required so much work because we had to make the connection between the relevant Palestinian and Israeli officers".[7]

Conclusion

During the period between the determination of death and the last place, grave or refrigerator, the dead body exists within social-political conditions. It is the state of transition or transitional zone as Van Gannep calls it (1960: 153). Through this zone the binary discrimination between life and death is confused, so that this is a liminal stage, in which the body is betwixt and between, to use Turner's phrase (1969). What is special for the

---

occupation, in a reality of the absence of a state (Hlal 1998:7). This reality is reflected through the journey of both dead and alive bodies.

[4] Part of the relationship between the university and the FMI is that the medical and law students practice in the autopsy room of the institute, and study forensic medicine in the institute. In addition, the administrative employees of the FMI are affiliated to the university, al-Quds University.

[5] According to Islam, the dead body should be dealt with in specific way, including the way of washing it, of positioning the various body parts and shrouding it (Gatrad 1994: 522-523).

[6] As he stated through an interview published in *al-Hayat al-Jadidah*, a Palestinian newspaper, on 21.04.1999.

[7] Every Palestinian, dead or alive, has to receive official permission from the Israeli military officers, in order to move and transfer from one area to another, even into the Palestinian territories.

Palestinian dead body is that the social-political context is also liminal, hybrid and dynamic, a situation in which the boundaries between autonomy and occupation are not clear. There are multi-sovereign powers, Israeli and Palestinian, and the Palestinian situation is transforming and changing all the time. The double liminality is reflected through the existence of the dead, through its journey. The body is instituted through the various Palestinian and Israeli institutions, including the FMI, in which the body is a medium for maintaining institutions and social order (Weiss 2002: 58), but this dead body also institutes these institutions. If there were no dead body, these institutions would not function, would not perform their roles in maintaining the social order. The existence of the dead body is the beginning of the work of the police, the hospital, the FMI, and the Israeli military systems, so this dead body has a very dynamic role in maintaining the semi-state institutions and upholding the sovereignty of the law. So the dead body is a social-political actor; maybe it hasn't the characteristics of the living human actor, which are planning and intention, but this body causes change in the environment, it activates several systems, its story of death is revealed by its signs. Because of that I'm calling for giving the dead body an active social agency, it is instituted but also instituting at the same point of time-space.

References

Byrne M. 2001. Ethnography as a qualitative research method. *AORN Journal* 74/1: 82-84.

De-Paz M. & Lifshetz Y. 2003. Forensic-medicine autopsy: the need for keeping samples from body organs and tissues, accepted legal aspects in Israel and the world. *Medicine and Law* 28: 128-135.

Gatrad A.R. 1994. Muslim customs surrounding death, bereavement, post-mortem examination, and organ transplants. *British Medical Journal* 309/6953: 521-525.

Gennep A.V. 1960. *The Rites of Passage.* Translated by Monika B. Vizedom and Gabrielle L. Caffee. Chicago: The University of Chicago Press.

Hlal G. 1998. *The Palestinian Political System after Oslo.* Ramallah: Muatin.

Kristeva J. 1982. *Powers of Horror: Essays on Abjection.* Columbia and Princeton: University Presses of California.

Littlewood J. 1993. The Denial of Death and Rites of Passage in Contemporary Societies. Pages 69-85 in D. Clark (ed.), *The Sociology of Death: Theory, Culture, Practice.* Oxford: Blackwell Publishers.

Patton M.Q. 1990. *Qualitative Evaluation and Research Methods.* Second Edition. California University Press: Sage Publications.

Prior L. 1989. *The Social Organization of Death: Medical Discourse and Social Practices in Belfast.* New York: St. Martin's press.

Schatzki T.R. 1996. Practiced Bodies: Subjects, Genders, and Minds. Pages 49-77 in T.R. Schatzki and W. Natter (eds), *The Social and Political Body.* New York and London: The Guilford Press.

Shaine Y. & Sussman G. 1998. From Occupation to State-building; Palestinian Political society Meets Palestinian civil Society. *Government and Opposition Journal* 33/3: 275-306.

Turner V. 1969. *Ritual Processes: Structure and Anti-Structure.* Chicago: Aldine.

Weiss M. 2002. *The Chosen Body: The Politics of the Body in Israeli Society.* Stanford, California: Stanford University Press.

Author's address

Mrs. Suhad Daher-Nashif
Ph.D. Student in Sociology and Anthropology
Hebrew University of Israel, Jerusalem
Ovadyah St. 35
Haifa, P.C. 34563
Israel
Email: suhadh@hotmail.com

Papers read at the conference "Death, Burial, and the Transition to the Afterlife in Arabia and Adjacent Regions" held at the British Museum, London, on 27-29 November 2008.

Session 1. Introduction and Neolithic Arabia

Timothy Taylor
Materiality and the soul: challenges for the archaeology of death

Vincent Charpentier and Philippe Charlier
First evidence of necrophobia in Neolithic Arabia

Adelina Kutterer
Remarks on Neolithic burials in SE Arabia

Roland de Beauclair
Seashells in the desert: burial practices at the Neolithic graveyard of al-Buhais 18, UAE

Session 2. Bronze Age South-Eastern Arabia

Sophie Méry and Julio Bendezu Sarmiento
Results, limits and potential: burial practices and Neolithic and Early Bronze Age societies in the Oman Peninsula

Kath McSweeney, Sophie Méry and Walid Yasin al Tikriti
Life and death in an Early Bronze Age community from Hili, Abu Dhabi Emirate, UAE

Eugenio Bortolini and Maurizio Tosi
Prehistoric burial cairns and control of passage in Early Bronze Age Oman: The oasis of Zukayt (Ad Dakhiliyah, northern Oman)

Session 3. Bronze Age to Iron Age South-Eastern Arabia

Daniel Potts
The late Umm an-Nar period tomb at Tell Abraq, Sharjah Emirate, UAE

Debra Martin
Patterns of mortality and morbidity in the commingled tomb from Tell Abraq

Christian Velde
Wadi Suq period tombs in SE Arabia

Crystal Fritz
Ceramic remains from the Iron Age II burials in the Wadi al Qawr: investigating burial practices and status differentiation

Session 4. Bronze Age South-Western Arabia and Adjacent Regions

Edward Keall
A reverence for stone reflected in various Late Bronze Age interments at a Red Sea coastal site in Yemen

Jennie Bradbury
Mobility, territoriality and mortuary ritual: The role of cairn burials within the Levant and Arabia during the $4^{th}/3^{rd}$ millennium

Joy McCorriston, Prem Goel, Dorota Bzezinska, Michael Harrower, Tara Steimer-Herbet, Jacob Reidhead, Jihye Park, Matthew Senn, Eric Oches, and Kimberly Williams
Monuments, territories, ancestors, tribes: reconstructing social boundaries in ancient Hadramawt with remotely sensed imagery

Session 5. Dilmun

Moawiyah Ibrahim
Beliefs surrounding death in Dilmun

Steffen Laursen
The early Dilmun cemetery of Karzakkan – Bahrain

Eric Olijdam
Interpreting differences in early Dilmun burial practices: socio-cultural homogeneity examined

Christine Kepinski
The burial mounds of the Middle Euphrates (2100-1800 BC): the subtle dialectic between tribal and state practices

Session 6. South-Western Arabia in the 1st Millennium BC

Jérémie Schiettecatte
The funerary stelae: clues for cross-cultural contacts in South Arabia during the Iron Age?

Sabina Antonini and Alessio Agostini
Excavations of the Italian Archaeological Mission in Yemen: a Minaean necropolis at Barāqish (Wādī Jawf) and the Qatabanian necropolis of Hayb bin 'Aqil (Wādī Bayhan)

D'arne O'Neill
South Arabian miniature grave goods and the role of miniaturization in mortuary contexts

Stephen Buckley, Joann Fletcher, K. Al-Thour, M. Basalama and Don Brothwell
Cultural implications of new biomolecular findings on ancient Yemeni mummification

Session 7. Nabataea

Lucy Wadeson
Sepulchral space in the Nabataean funerary realm: a comparison of the façade tomb chambers in Petra and Mada'in Salih

Isabelle Sachet
Funerary meals in Nabataea

Nicolas Garnier
Biomolecular archaeology, burial and offerings: The case of Nabatean tombs from Petra

Session 8. North-Western Arabia and Adjacent Regions

Sebastiano Lora, Emmanuele Petiti, Mohammed al-Najem and Arnulf Hausleiter
Burial contexts at Tayma, NW Arabia – archaeological and anthropological data

Jill Baker
The Canaanite funeral kit: its genesis and extinction

Alexander Nagel and Hasan Rahsaz
Colouring the dead: new investigations on the history and polychromatic appearance of the tomb of Darius I at Naqsh-e-Rostam, Fars

Session 9. Late Pre-Islamic Arabia

Michel Mouton
The monolithic Djin Blocks at Petra: A funerary practice of pre-Islamic Arabia

Aurelie Daems and An De Waele
"Death is a black camel": Pre-Islamic animal burials in Arabia

Juris Zarins
Funerary monuments of southern Arabia: The Iron Age-Islamic traditions

Session 10. Islamic Arabia

Dick Nauta
Dry-stone built tombs in the western Red Sea littoral

James Edgar Taylor
Attitudes, themes and images: an introduction to death and burial as reflected in early Arabic poetry

Lynne Newton
Survey of saints' tombs in Dhofar

Session 11. Islamic History and Non-Islamic Traditions

Vered Madar
Ma m'a-al'adami 'ille ma kutib loh – "*A man has nothing but what the Heavens decreed*": on Jewish and Muslim lament traditions and mourning in Yemen

Matthew Suriano
Sheol and the tomb: locating the transition to the afterlife in the Hebrew bible

Jose Morillas and Pablo Piñar
In anima vili: Islamic constructions on life autopsies

Session 12. Death and Burial in the Muslim World and Closing Comments

Leor Halevi
Death and Burial in the Muslim World: The Role of Islam

Workshop 1. Death and Burial in the Islamic World: from Spain to Bangladesh

Corinne Fortier
The "living death" in Mauritania and in Maliki Islam

Suhad Daher Nashif
Instituting the dead body: the case of the Palestinian Forensic Medicine Institute

Sara Mondini
The commemoration of death and its representations: royal funerary complexes in the India of sultanates

Matt Yarrington
Assisting the recently deceased in Bangladesh

Workshop 2. Bronze Age Burial Traditions in SE and SW Arabia

Manfred Boehme
Hafit and Umm an-Nar period burials at Bat, Oman

Olivia Munoz
Around the graves: Funerary practices, social uses and rituals during the Umm an-Nar period

J. Giraud and S. Cleuziou
Early Bronze Age graves and graveyards in the in eastern Ja'alan (Sultanate of Oman): as assessment of the social rules working in the evolution of a funerary landscape

Juris Zarins
Bronze Age funerary monuments from the Mahra governorate, Yemen

Rémy Crassard, Holger Hitgen, Hervé Guy and Jérémie Schiettecatte
Reuse of tombs or cultural continuity? The case of Bronze Age tombs in Shabwa governorate, Yemen

Poster Presentations

Avriel Bar-Levav
Mourning rituals of Jews in Muslim countries

Anne Benoist
Inventory of finds from a second millennium grave in Dadna, Emirate of Fujairah, UAE

Ora Berger
The phenomenon of pilgrimage to Ta'izz to the grave of the Jewish Poet Shalom al-Shabazi from the point of view of Art History

Fabio Cavulli, Olivia Munoz and Simona Scaruffi
Burials in the middle Holocene fishermen settlement of KHB-1, Sultanate of Oman

Janet Cope, Debra Martin, David Miller and Daniel Potts
Discerning health, disease and activity patterns in a Bronze Age population from Tell Abraq, United Arab Emirates

Dina Dahbany-Miraglia
Jewish burial customs in Yemen

William and Fidelity Lancaster
Graves and graveyards of various locations in Ras al-Khaimah Emirate, UAE, and Musandam *wilayat*, Oman

Kirsi Lorentz
Hairy stories: Reconstructing life from human remains at 3rd millennium BC Shahr-e Sokhte (Sistan, Iran)

Olivia Munoz
The Graveyard of RH-5 heritage site (Sultanate of Oman): recent excavations

Diana Pickworth
Bintayn Methul – landscape of life, death, and burial

Marie-Jeanne Roche
Funerary Eye steles from Arabia: analysis and interpretation

Mikhail Rodionov
Wadi Hadramawt as landscape of death and burial

Waleed Al-Sadeqi
The Bahrain bead project: introduction and illustration

Anna Tozzi Di Marco
Cairo's City of the dead: the cohabitation between the living and the dead from an anthropological perspective